*Handbook of
Data Processing
for Libraries*

HANDBOOK OF DATA PROCESSING FOR LIBRARIES

SPONSORED BY THE COUNCIL ON LIBRARY RESOURCES

Robert M. Hayes

Director, Institute of Library Research
University of California, Los Angeles

Joseph Becker

President, Becker and Hayes, Inc.
Bethesda, Maryland.

A WILEY-BECKER-HAYES PUBLICATION

BECKER AND HAYES, INC

a subsidiary of John Wiley & Sons, Inc

New York · London · Sydney · Toronto · Bethesda

To our families

PREFACE

Data processing has become a subject of vital concern to librarians. Within the past decade, they have begun to realize that advances in technology and improvements in the techniques of information system design are certain to bring about changes in the character of conventional library operations. Scores of libraries are already using computers to reduce clerical burdens and accelerate service to readers. Others, including the Library of Congress, the National Library of Medicine, the National Agricultural Library, and a number of university libraries have started large-scale efforts aimed at establishing national library-based information networks that involve a high degree of mechanization.

Before the digital computer and associated new technology can be put to work constructively in libraries, their power and limitations must be understood by the professional librarian. Data processing clinics and data processing courses, which are beginning to appear in library schools throughout the United States, provide excellent opportunities for learning. But they have highlighted a demand for an integrated text appropriate to the needs of both the student and the practicing librarian.

The purpose of this book, therefore, is to assist libraries and librarians in resolving some of the problems faced in utilizing this new technology. The intent is to provide a concrete, factual guide to the principles and methods available for the application of modern data processing to library operations. For the operating librarian, it should be considered a handbook, a tool to guide him in decisions concerning the introduction of data processing techniques into his own library. For the student, it should be a textbook, educating him not only in methodology but also in the interrelationships between data processing and the library. For the system designer, it should be a summary of the state-of-the-art, serving as a bridge between library objectives and the technology. The book, throughout, lays special stress on the library and, particularly, on the significance of library values and policies for determining the choice of system. The book gives emphasis to the computer, but always in the context of applying this technology to the solution of operating problems, as an addition to resources for information service, as a tool of good management, and not as an end in itself. At most, therefore, the book aims to educate the profession in the use of these tools, and in the special problems of applying them to libraries. In this respect, much of the groundwork has already been done—the profession has been educating itself, has carried out analyses of library operations, has experimented with mechanization, and is developing better concepts of cost control. The book merely continues a process that is already underway.

But we would be concerned if this area continues to be a predominant focus of future interest by librarians. Recognition of the professional and social implications of the computer has led university after university to initiate an educational program in information science. These add to library education a responsibility for teaching the newer methods for analyzing and solving operational problems, for instructing in the methods of system analysis, for extending library control to include the newer educational media, for increasing the degree of specialization in library functions, for examining critical social problems in the use of information, and for understanding theoretical foundations. But existing library school curricula are not able, either in content or duration, to accept the added burden that the computer implies. It is clear that a completely new look must be taken. The issues relating to library education are considered to be so critically important that the subject is given special attention in this book.

The book is organized into five major sections, each covering a more or less well-defined segment of the problems in applying automation to libraries. Within a section, each chapter presents a principal topic of interest, and serves as an introduction to an annotated bibliography of primary references and additional recommended reading that follows.

R. M. HAYES
J. BECKER

Los Angeles, California
September 1970

ACKNOWLEDGMENTS

First and foremost, we acknowledge the financial and moral support of the Council on Library Resources. Their grant to the Institute of Library Research at UCLA made it possible to involve many more people, both directly and indirectly, in the creation of this *Handbook* than otherwise would have been possible. But it meant even more than that. The support of the Council lent prestige to the Institute and created for it a climate in which far more basic work in developing mechanization in libraries could move forward. The information and results obtained from the great many studies the Institute undertook, at both Los Angeles and Berkeley, gave a firm foundation to the content of the technical chapters of this book.

Second, we especially thank the members of the Advisory Committee, appointed by the Council on Library Resources to overview the development of the *Handbook.* They helped us immeasurably with their reviews and suggestions for improvements in early drafts:

David Weber, Stanford University
Ralph Shoffner, University of California, Berkeley
Ralph Blasingame, Rutgers University
Ted Hines, Columbia University

Third, several people have contributed directly to the preparation of this book. It is with deep appreciation that we acknowledge their assistance:

Mr. Fred Bellomy for his most important technical work, incorporated as the major part of Chapter 5.
Mrs. Ida Riordan, Mrs. Helen Meek, and Mrs. Diana Burkhardt for their technical work incorporated as parts of Chapters 15, 16, and 18.

x   Acknowledgments

Mrs. Nancy Brault for her many contributions, but especially for her work on Appendix 2.

Miss Cynthia Stolz, Miss Sue Hattori, and Mr. Stan Weiss for their work in compiling the tables in Chapters 10 to 13.

Sister Marie Ancille Kennedy for her contributions to innumerable chapters.

Finally, we are grateful to our secretaries who slaved over the most miserable handwriting and reworked drafts imaginable: Miss Carole Bailey and Mrs. Pat Honley.

R. M. H.
J. B.

CONTENTS

*Handbook of
Data Processing
for Libraries*

Part One   Introduction to Library Data Processing

Chapter 1

LIBRARY DATA PROCESSING SYSTEMS AND NETWORKS

Data processing technology, including computers and punched cards, has evolved into a multibillion dollar industry and has made its impact on almost every aspect of our society. Its practical beginning was in the late 1800's when Herman Hollerith of the Bureau of the Census cut a card to the exact dimensions of the American dollar bill, devised a method for representing numbers or letters by holes in the card, and used these cards to analyze statistics collected by the 1890 census.[1]

Herman Hollerith's biography in the *Dictionary of American Biography* reveals that the idea was suggested to him by a librarian.[2] Hollerith thus reports the incident in one of his letters: "One evening at Dr. B's tea table he said to me, 'There ought to be a machine for doing the purely mechanical work of tabulating population and similar statistics.' " The "Dr. B" to whom Hollerith refers was Dr. John Shaw Billings, who was then Librarian of the Army Surgeon General's Library and who became the first Director of the New York Public Library. To this chance remark, Hollerith attributes his inspiration for the development of the punched card. Since it was a librarian who started it all, is there any wonder that Dr. Billings' professional descendants should wish to emulate his foresight by considering the use of data processing in libraries?

Over the years, punched cards were gradually applied to diverse areas of business to perform functions associated with accounting. In 1930, Ralph Parker (then a librarian at the University of Texas) conceived the idea of using punched

---

[1] Heyel, Carl, *The Encyclopedia of Management.* New York: Reinhold, 1963, p. 589.
[2] *Dictionary of American Biography, Supplement 1.* New York: Scribners, 1944, p. 415.

card equipment for circulation work.[3] The Director of the University of Texas Library was Donald Coney, and Parker recalls, with good humor, how after many months of persuasion Coney finally gave him a $300 grant for experimentation—but only after cautioning him to spend the money wisely! Another milestone in the history of library use of punched cards was passed in the following decade when Margery Quigley, Librarian of the Montclair Public Library in New Jersey, acquired special-purpose equipment for controlling book transactions.[4] This system of circulation control was the first to adopt the method of joining a machine-readable book card and a machine-readable borrower's card as a single master record at borrowing time. This 25-year-old pilot punched card installation, which Miss Quigley fondly called "Punching Judy," was the forerunner of the IBM 357 Data Collection System used by some libraries today for computerized circulation work.

From these beginnings, the past 20 years have witnessed a rapidly increasing interest among librarians concerning the possibility of using punched card machines and, more recently, computers to carry out many library functions. The reasons are clear. First, the rate of publishing has climbed steadily, dramatically increasing the number of printed pieces to be acquired, processed, housed, and circulated by libraries. Second, a rapidly expanding and more literate population has generated demands for reader services that have far exceeded a library's ability to respond effectively with traditional methods and techniques. Third, the continuing improvement in the qualitative characteristics and economic efficiency of available technology has finally made feasible the mechanized solutions to these problems. Prospects for the future are even more staggering. Hence professional librarians, like other administrators, have been prompted to look for help to the new technology available in modern data processing equipment and systems.

The concern of the library profession with the ever-increasing costs of operating complex library systems is representative of comparable concern in all information activities throughout the United States. And it is natural to search for the answer to this concern in better solutions to operational problems and, particularly, to look for them in the techniques of methods analysis, mechanization, and cost control. External pressures have also come from administrators, engineers, and salesmen, all asking, "Why don't you automate?" This impact has been painfully evident at times, but it has resulted in many and varied projects in which machines are used to solve various types of library problems.

---

[3] Parker, Ralph, *Library Applications of Punched Cards.* Chicago: American Library Association, 1952.

[4] Quigley, Margery, "Ten Years of IBM," *Library Journal,* 77 (13), July 1952, 1152-1157.

LIBRARY DATA PROCESSING APPLICATIONS

Clerical Functions

Computer applications in individual libraries can be categorized into three classes. The first involves the use of computers for supporting the clerical functions found in technical processing and circulation work. Several libraries have had programs written which cause computers automatically to perform certain routine work, such as interfiling entries in a catalog, ordering books from publishers, writing requests to the Library of Congress for cards, preparing serial record lists, monitoring circulation operations, printing book catalogs, and analyzing service to readers. These applications, as in business, are designed to reduce the clerical burden, while at the same time increasing an organization's ability to perform more work. They will be discussed in detail in Chapters 14 through 18 of this book.

Information Storage and Retrieval

A second category of computer applications of obvious importance to the librarian is in the field of information storage and retrieval and the use of mechanization in reference work. At a most complex level, the objective is to develop new methods for automatically aiding various intellectual processes, such as extracting meaning from text and correlating facts or inferring subject relationships from the complete content of articles and books. Although there is much research in progress in these areas, a great deal more research will be required before such a capability will actually affect the duties of the reference librarian. However, at a simpler level, "reference retrieval of bibliographical information" has immediate significance to all library operations. In these cases, the text in question has been well formalized through years of library experience, and the problem is simplified because the elements of information are limited in size, fixed, and easily identifiable. These applications will be discussed in Chapters 19 and 20 of this book.

Operations Research

The third category includes operations research and systems analysis. These applications employ the computer as an aid in using the principles of scientific management in library administration. Until recently, librarians paid little attention to the application of mathematics and computers to the decision-making process in library management. Mathematical models and computer simulation, however, constitute a powerful tool for aiding library decision making. In the early 1900's, the founder of scientific management, F. W. Taylor, described scientific management as (1) an inquiring frame of mind, which refuses to accept past practices as necessarily correct; (2) the replacement of rules of thumb by more carefully thought out guides to action; and (3) the collection of data to support decisions rather than the reliance on casual judgments.[5] Operations research and systems analysis exemplify these principles and extend their power by engaging the computer's help. Mathematical models are used to characterize a process, object, or concept in precise mathematical terms. When these are incorporated into a computer program, it becomes possible to test variables and to see how the process, object, or concept will behave under different conditions. The use of these techniques will permit a director of a library to evaluate a course of action in advance of its actual implementation. These applications will be discussed in Chapters 3 through 8 of this book, with emphasis on computer system evaluation.

In summary, for the individual library, mechanization can be viewed as an aid toward more economical operation, as a tool to release the librarian from tedious nonintellectual activities, as a means for extending library services into new areas, and as an aid to better library administration. These applications are the primary concern of this book.

LIBRARY NETWORK APPLICATIONS

In addition, however, the use of modern data processing and modern communications technology offers a new dimension to cooperation among libraries. The significance it has for the creation of "library networks" is just beginning to be appreciated at the present time, but ultimately it will have great importance.

Centralized Processing

In part, the interest in library networks lies in the opportunity they provide for economical centralized services. A long-standing example of these services is the production of cataloging cards by the Library of Congress and commercial organizations and subsequent distribution of them to local libraries. The automation projects of the Library of Congress, of the National Library of Medicine, and of the National Agricultural Library are designed to support the

---

[5] Taylor, Frederick W., *Principles and Methods of Scientific Management*. New York: Harper, 1911.

library community in this way.[6-10] Therefore, they are vital to the development of a national library network. They are summarized in Chapter 2. Even on a local level, we see centralized processing centers in individual states and localities, serving community libraries; we see university cooperation in acquisition, cataloging, and use of materials.[11-16] In each case, the economic justification of mechanization becomes clearer as the number of libraries benefiting is increased and as the effects of "economics of scale" are felt.

Sharing of Resources

However, even more important than the role of centralized processing is the potential provided by library networks for sharing of resources. It has long been clear that some degree of cooperative allocation of resources among a set of libraries can produce not only a more efficient total operation but even a more responsive one. This historical recognition of the value of sharing rather than duplicating resources has resulted in the development of interlibrary loan systems and of cooperative arrangements such as the Farmington Plan,[17] the

[6] Markuson, Barbara Evans, "The Library of Congress Automation Program: a Progress Report to the Stockholders," *ALA Bulletin*, **61** (June 1967), 647-655.

[7] Cummings, Martin M., "The Role of the National Library of Medicine in the National BioMedical Library Network," *Annals of the New York Academy of Science*, **142** (March 31, 1967), 503-512.

[8] Mohrhardt, Foster E., and Blance L. Oliveri, "A National Network of Biological-Agricultural Libraries," *College and Research Libraries*, **28** (January 1967), 9-16.

[9] Lazerow, Samuel, "The U.S. National Libraries Task Force: an Instrument for National Library Cooperation," *Special Libraries*, **59** (November 1968), 698-703.

[10] Schactman, Bella E., James P. Riley, and Stephan R. Salmon, "U.S. National Libraries Task Force on Automation and Other Cooperative Services: Progress Report No. 1," *Library of Congress Information Bulletin*, **26** (November 30, 1967), 795-800.

[11] Leonard, Lawrence E., Joan M. Maier, and Richard M. Dougherty, *Colorado Academic Libraries Book Processing Center. Final Report Phase I and Phase II.* Boulder: University of Colorado Libraries, 1968.

[12] Agenbroad, James E., et al., *NELINET—New England Library Information Network.* Cambridge, Mass.: Inforonics, Inc., 1968.

[13] Holingren, Edwin S., "ANYLTS Reports Progress," *Bookmark,* **27** (February 1968), 193-197.

[14] Hayes, Phoebe F., "The PNBC of the Future," *PNLA Quarterly*, **32** (January 1968), 4-7.

[15] Merry, Susan A., "The Ontario New Universities Library Project—a Centralized Processing Experiment Completed," *College and Research Libraries*, **29** (March 1968), 104-108.

[16] Sherman, Don, and Ralph M. Shoffner, *California State Library: Processing Center Design and Specifications.* Berkeley: Institute of Library Research, University of California, April 1969.

[17] Williams, Edwin E., *Farmington Plan Handbook.* Bloomington, Indiana: Association of Research Libraries, 1953.

National Union Catalog,[18] and the Center for Research Libraries.[19] Thus, interlibrary cooperation is not a new concept, and the growth of library networks and systems, making larger library resources available to all readers, has been a continuing theme of modern librarianship. But the effects of the computer, of modern communications, and of data processing in general will vastly increase the scope and context in which we can see library cooperation. Recent progress in electrical transmission indicates that we have reached an important communications threshold.[20] The next step can remove the remaining barriers to direct communication between libraries. For the first time the technology will allow libraries, within economic limits, to transmit and receive all forms of messages virtually without spatial or temporal constraints. Communication links can consist of any combination of telephone lines, coaxial cables, microwave stations, or communication satellites. They can accommodate audio, digital, and video signals. Voice communication, the digital exchange of information between and among computers, remote inquiry of electronic files, and the video transmission of films and other graphic materials can therefore be carried by the same network.

Direct Access by Readers

Furthermore, instead of requiring patrons to come to them, libraries will soon be able to send printed and graphic materials directly to users in their homes, offices, or local libraries. The ability of libraries to engage in two-way, multimedia communication not only with other libraries but with their own users is likely to bring about a significant change in the library's role as a social institution.[21] By devising means for direct use of materials, the library community will have created an educational and research capability more versatile than anything previously developed.

General Network Structure

Let us present a picture of what the major elements in a library network are and of what role mechanization will play.[22]

---

[18] Haykin, David J., "Some Problems and Possibilities of Co-operative Cataloging," *ALA Bulletin*, **21** (10), October 1927, 355-358.

[19] Esterquest, Ralph T., "Midwest Inter-Library Center," *College and Research Libraries*, **XV** (1), January 1954, pp. 47-49, 89.

[20] Becker, Joseph, "Communications Networks for Libraries," *Wilson Library Bulletin*, **41** (4), December 1966, pp. 383-387.

[21] New York, N.Y. Mayor's Advisory Task Force on CATV and Telecommunications. *A Report on Cable Television and Cable Telecommunications in N.Y. City*. (Fred W. Friendly, Chmn.) City Hall, New York, September 1968.

[22] Becker, Joseph, and Robert M. Hayes, *A Proposed Library Network for Washington State*, September 1967.

Component Libraries. A "library network" is constructed from a variety of cooperative groups of individual libraries, through contractual agreements among the libraries to share their resources, and arrangements for certain services. Figure 1.1 defines terms that are usually used in describing a library network, and Figure 1.2 gives a. schematic of existing elements from which it is constructed.

As Figure 1.2 shows, the library network is based on the individual libraries as the primary building block. From them, a variety of cooperative groups are formed through contractual agreements that call for the following commitments from each library to the group.

1. A commitment to make its collection and services available to the constituency served by other libraries in the group on the same basis of service provided to its own constituency.

2. A commitment to maintain an agreed-upon level of service (such as book budget and reference staff).

3. A commitment to pay for a proportionate share of the costs of a union catalog of the holdings of the group, from consideration of both the size of the population served and the contribution of resources provided.

4. A commitment to contribute to the establishment or augmentation of a collection strong enough to serve as a reference center.

Geographical Groups. The most evident kinds of groups are those by geographic area. Geographical groups may be expected to include all types of libraries in the area, including public, school, special, and governmental libraries. In each group, it is expected that at least one "dominant" member will serve as a "group reference center." This may be the primary resource on which the other libraries in the group draw; it may be the administrative center for the group; or it may be simply the best reference collection. Figure 1.3 presents the schematic relationship of groups and group centers.

Specialty Groups. Another (less evident but equally important) kind of grouping is by specialty. Examples include medicine, law, technology, educational media, and the like. These groups may be formed as a result of requirements for service to specialized constituencies (such as the medical community)[23] or to perform special services (such as technical information retrieval).[24] Figure 1.4 presents a schematic of the creation of specialty groups and specialty centers.

For a specialty group, the group center can serve much the same purpose as the reference center serves for the area group—that is, as a primary resource, as an administrative center, and as a central reference service. However, for some

[23] Cummings, Martin M., *op. cit.*
[24] *State Technical Services Act of 1965,* Public Law 89-182.

Figure 1.1 Library network terminology.

Term	Definition
1. Area	One of several geographical areas, whose definition is based on population trends, economic data, political boundaries, and geography.
2. Geographical Group	A compact of cooperating libraries within an area formed by contract to share resources through a common book catalog. Group affiliation within an area offers several benefits to a participating library: (1) it makes a much wider range of resources available to any one library or to any individual in the region; (2) through a common book catalog, it relieves local cataloging burdens, thus releasing professional time for better and increased reader services; (3) economies can be achieved through centralized purchasing and processing; and (4) reduction in duplicate buying makes more money available for the purchase of a greater variety of new materials and other purposes.
3. Reference Center	A library formally designated as the principal focal point for a geographical group. A group center coordinates title selections for the participating libraries in its area for acquisition and processing.
4. Information Center	Group center for a specialty group, particularly one which incorporates a high degree of substantive (subject) competence in the specialty.
5. Major National Resources	Those national institutions (including the federal and research libraries, professional societies, indexing and abstracting services, commercial services) which are the primary source of cataloging and indexing data and repositories of original references.
6. Major State Resources	The large libraries of a state which, because of the excellence and size of their collections, serve as ultimate reference points.
7. Processing Center	A formal organization for (1) ordering books for groups of libraries; (2) producing and maintaining book catalogs for common use; (3) processing books for library shelving.
8. Reader Service Point	The point of initial contact in a library system for servicing individual reader requests (including branches, bookmobiles, etc.).
9. Specialty Group	A compact of cooperating libraries whose common subject interests draw them together for the contractual use of specialized resources.
10. Switching Center	A formal organization for referring requests that cannot be satisfied by group centers and information centers to larger state or national libraries.

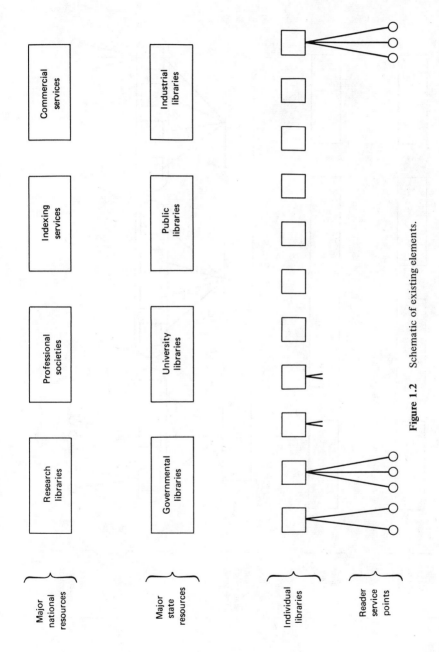

Figure 1.2 Schematic of existing elements.

11

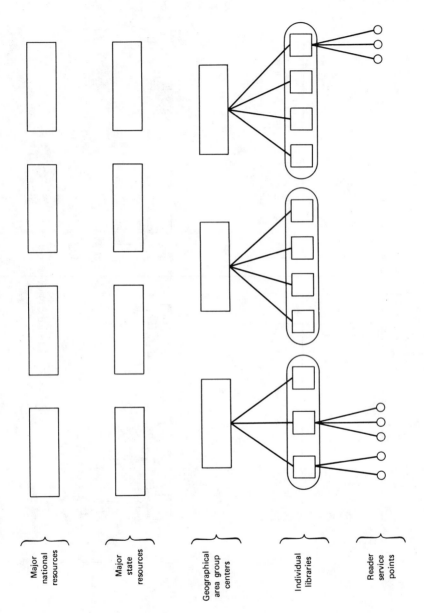

Major
national
resources

Major
state
resources

Geographical
area group
centers

Individual
libraries

Reader
service
points

Figure 1.3   Geographical area groups.

12

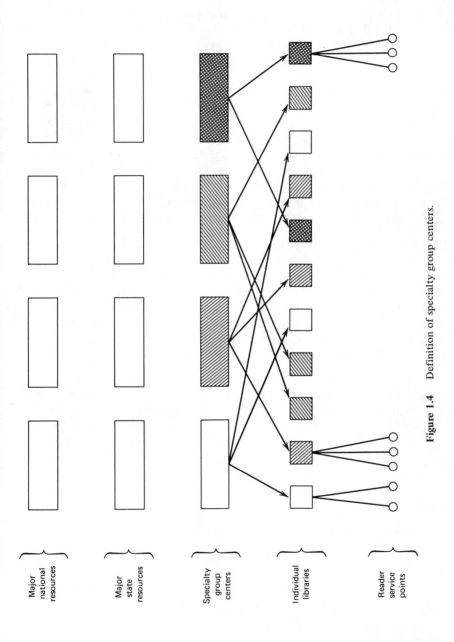

Major
national
resources

Major
state
resources

Specialty
group
centers

Individual
libraries

Reader
service
points

Figure 1.4 Definition of specialty group centers.

13

specialties, it may be even more. The concept of an "information center"—as a place of subject competence, of active research, and of analysis and synthesis of the literature—is becoming increasingly important.[25] The likelihood is great that many of the specialty group centers will be such "information centers" and will be associated with institutions of higher education in the state. In such cases, their catalogs probably will not be a "union catalog," but a catalog of the information center itself, produced by it as part of its research activity.

It is to be expected that many libraries will participate as members of both an area group and one or more specialty groups. Typically, for example, a school library will be a member of an area group (sharing resources with the public and special libraries in the area) as well as an educational media group (sharing films, slides, and the like, among the schools of the state) and perhaps even as part of an educational research group, drawing on the resources of educational research centers and laboratories.[26] Or, for instance, a hospital library might participate in an area group—usually drawing on the resources of the public library—as well as be a member of a medical specialty group.

Production of Union Catalogs. The production of a union catalog that can be widely distributed among the libraries of a group is an essential element in sharing of resources. The computer has a primary role to play in a "Catalog Production Service," which can utilize the nationally produced magnetic tapes containing catalog and index data now becoming available.[27,28] Figure 1.5 therefore presents, in schematic form, the acquisition of these nationally produced magnetic tapes and the production from them of catalogs that are distributed to the libraries and reader service points in each geographic area.

Major Resources. There are certain major resources that participate in a library network. Some of these resources (such as major industrial libraries) may be essentially outside the network and may be drawn on only through interlibrary loan cooperation. Others, particularly the universities, will be active participants in such a diversity of ways that they cannot be categorized. For example, for many of the specialty groups, universities will constitute the group reference center or information center. In addition, universities may provide the primary research collection of the state and, as such, the ultimate resource.

[25] Weinberg, Alvin J., *Science, Government, and Information,* President's Science Advisory Commission, January 10, 1963.

[26] Egerton, John, "The Acid Test of the Regional Laboratories," *Southern Education Report,* 4(6), January-February 1969, pp. 12-17.

[27] Hayes, Robert M., Ralph M. Shoffner, and David Weber, "The Economics of Book Catalog Production," *Library Resources and Technical Services,* 10 (Winter 1966), pp. 57-90.

[28] *Mechanized Information Services in the University Library.* Los Angeles: Institute of Library Research, University of California, 1967.

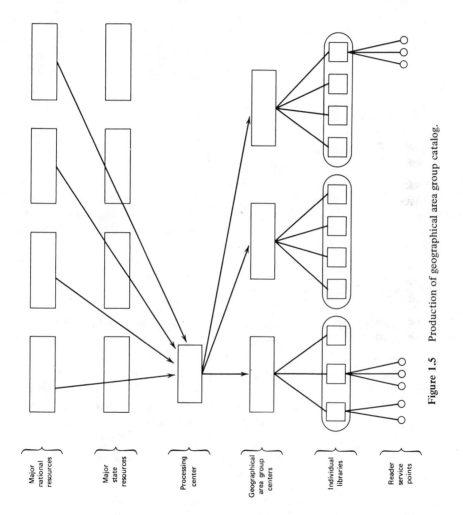

Figure 1.5 Production of geographical area group catalog.

Major
national
resources

Major
state
resources

Processing
center

Geographical
area group
centers

Individual
libraries

Reader
service
points

15

Switching Center. To provide access to these major resources and to the geographic and specialty groups, a switching center is established (Figure 1.6) with catalogs for the holdings of the major resources of the state, nation, and principal groups from which services are available on an interlibrary loan basis.[29,30] Figure 1.7 illustrates the operation of a switching center in transmitting a request from a reader at a local service point to state and national resources, followed by the transmission of relevant material back to him.[31] It also illustrates two of the key features of a library network as a system:

1.   The request and its answer can be transmitted over the paths most appropriate to each—the request through subject competence, the answer through the closest point of reception.

2.   Different communication equipment can be used at each level, commensurate with the kinds of utilization required.

Technical Services. In this kind of network, the individual library maintains its own identity and responsibility to its own constituency. In particular, each library remains responsible for selecting, ordering, and cataloging to meet its own special needs. However, the benefits gained from cooperative acquisition should impel most groups to establish guidelines for individual library responsibility in specialized areas of acquisition and for combined ordering of more common material.

INFORMATION NETWORK APPLICATIONS

The existence of a library network makes possible another kind of service, one of the most exciting developments that data processing has thus far offered the library profession. It is the use of libraries as the crucial administrative agent in national "information networks" that depend on the digital computer to search large files.[32,33] It promises a wholly new approach to the problem of gathering and retrieving essential information. If we, as professional librarians, are looking for an intellectual challenge, then this is it.

[29] Hayes, Phoebe F., "The PNBC of the Future," *PNLA Quarterly,* **32** (January 1968), 4-7.

[30] Esterquest, Ralph T., *op. cit.*

[31] Schieber, William D., and Ralph M. Shoffner, *Telefacsimile in Libraries: A Report of an Experiment in Facsimile Transmission and an Analysis of Implications for Interlibrary Loan Systems.* Berkeley: Institute of Library Research, University of California, 1967.

[32] Brown, George W., et al., *Edunet: Report on the Summer Study of Information Networks.* New York: Wiley, 1967.

[33] House Committee on Education and Labor (The Pucinski Committee), *National Information Center Hearings,* May, July, and September, 1963.

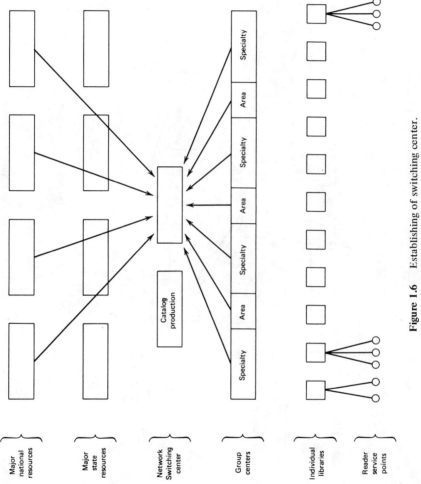

Figure 1.6 Establishing of switching center.

Major national resources

Major state resources

Network Switching center

Group centers

Individual libraries

Reader service points

Catalog production

Specialty | Area | Specialty | Area | Specialty | Area | Specialty

17

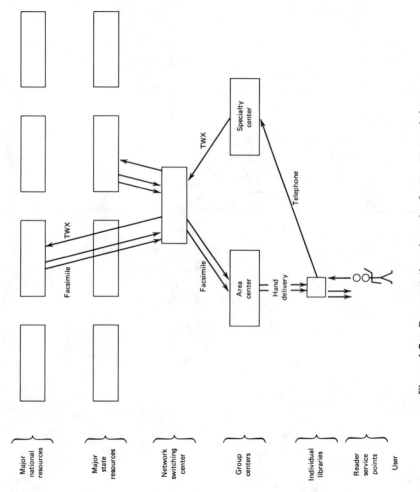

Major
national
resources

Major
state
resources

Network
switching
center

Group
centers

Individual
libraries

Reader
service
points

User

TWX

Facsimile

TWX

Facsimile

Specialty
center

Area
center

Hand
delivery

Telephone

Figure 1.7 Representative schematic of request transmission

In the University of Illinois' Windsor Lecture in 1951, the late Louis Ridenour referred to tomorrow's library as a "communications center of a specialized sort."[34] Ridenour, an engineer, based his prophecy on the research and development that he knew were under way in the field of electrical communications. He could foresee the ways in which the new technology would affect information transmission in libraries.

The major communications common carriers, such as the Bell System and the Western Union Telegraph Company, are currently upgrading their facilities in order to provide these new services. Standard telephone line facilities, for example, although originally designed for voice communications, are already being used for transferring the digital language of computers from one point to another. The American Telephone and Telegraph Company predicts that in the 1970's more than half of the traffic transmitted over its lines will be in the form of digital data rather than voice communications.[35]

However, although the technology needed to expand the library into an active transmitter of digitally recorded knowledge may be here, this technology alone is not enough. The basic responsibility for getting the job done creatively rests with the professional librarian and with those his new system is designed to serve.

As we shall discuss in detail in Chapter 2, information network operations are already under active study by several organizations, including EDUCOM (Interuniversity Communications Council), Project INTREX at MIT, and COSATI (The Federal Government's Committee on Scientific and Technical Information). EDUCOM represents the interests of more than 90 universities whose aim is to provide an interuniversity communications system linking the computing centers and libraries of the various campuses. At the same time, Project INTREX is attempting to apply the methods of information transfer engineering to a model development within the framework of the MIT library environment.[36] In 1966, the Federal Government through its Committee on Scientific and Technical Information (COSATI) Task Group on National Systems undertook a detailed study and examination of national document and information systems.[37] Its report emphasizes the role that the new technologies will play in modifying the existing decentralized structure of information-handling activities.

[34] Ridenour, Louis N., Ralph R. Shaw, and A. G. Hill, *Bibliography in an Age of Science*, University of Illinois Press, 1952.

[35] "For the Bell System, All Phones are Ringing," *Business Week,* 9 (January 1965), pp. 64-70 (especially p. 66).

[36] Overhage, Carl F. J., and R. Joyce Harman (eds.) *Intrex: The Report of a Planning Conference on Information Transfer Experiments.* Cambridge, Mass.: MIT Press 1965.

[37] Carter, Launor, et al., *National Information Systems for Scientific and Technical Information.* New York: Wiley, 1967.

All of these efforts envision a network serving objectives some of which are very speculative and others merely the mechanized counterpart of existing normal manual practices. Taken together, they represent a direction in current thinking with which the librarian should become familiar. To provide a context, the following is a hypothetical picture of the "Library Based Information System" as it might operate in 1980. It is conservative and represents an attempt to rationalize existing institutions with technology, the bounds of economics, and realistic rates of progress.

Information Services

In general terms, a library-based information system is viewed as a collection of storage media—books, serials, microforms, magnetic tapes and disks, and data cells—available at a number of physically separate libraries that represent both points of physical storage and points of access and service. The services include the functions of acquisition, cataloging, reference, information specialists in subject disciplines, mechanized information services, and current awareness services. By 1980 the library will be the point to which demands will be directed for computerized information services, utilizing existing data bases.[38] Such processing generally has been considered as including the following, as representative examples.[39]

(a)   Information retrieval based upon straightforward matching with index data.

(b)   Textual analysis and language data processing.

(c)   Question answering and similar deductive analyses of text data.

(d)   Statistical analyses of text, associations of terms together in indexes and text, and similar forms of reference.

(e)   Preparation of lists, including permutation indexes, subject authorities and thesauri, and citation indexes.

(f)   Analysis of word relations for derivation of classifications and other forms of structure for predicates of description.

(g)   Extraction of relevant numerical data fields from data bases (such as census tapes and socioeconomic data banks) and derivation of simple statistical relations.

The Role of the Library

Information services of all kinds will be regarded as a national resource, with libraries as major components in the national information system. The individual

[38] *Mechanized Information Services in the University Library, op. cit.*

[39] Salton, Gerard, *Automatic Information Organization and Retrieval.* New York: McGraw-Hill, 1968.

library will therefore be one of the principal nodes for entry into a variety of information networks. These will include a high level of mechanization in communication through which the library will handle requests for direct transfer of mechanized data bases, for facsimile transmission of printed material, and for real time transmission of video material (including video recording of it for later retransmission locally). To provide intellectual access to this material, the library will include a "union catalog" of mechanized data readily available through the network, including reference to its location, its form, and its means of access.[40] This will allow the library to service requests for data files stored elsewhere as well as its own.

Mechanized Catalogs and Indexes

The availability of mechanized catalogs and indexes will also simplify the handling of many library clerical tasks. Orders will be recorded, through typewriter terminals, directly into the computer data base and then printed out for mailing to the dealer. Existing catalog data will be used to facilitate the identification of desired material. Catalogs will be maintained, on both a centralized and a decentralized basis, in direct access stores for the recent material and most active data. Periodically, printed catalogs will be produced for the collection in specific areas. As needed, specialized catalogs will be printed for the needs of individual library patrons, information centers, and libraries. Circulation of printed material will be controlled by on-line recording at the time of check-out. This can be interrogated on-line at any subsequent time and requests for reserve or return of the material placed against the circulation record itself. Complete accounting data and statistics of operation will be maintained by a monitoring of all clerical activities (including ordering, cataloging, and circulation) and information services.

The Role of Information Centers

Many specialized areas of research will have the requirements and financial resources necessary to justify information centers. Usually these will provide information specialists, trained in librarianship and the technology of information service as well as in the specialized field being served.[41,42] They will provide indexing, abstracting, and dissemination services especially attuned to the needs of the specialized field. They will provide computer-based information

[40] Brown, George W., *Edunet, op. cit.*

[41] *Annual Progress Report of the NINDS Neurological Information Network*. Washington, D.C.: U.S. Department of H.E.W., Public Health Service, National Institutes of Health, January 1969.

[42] Burchinal, Lee G., *ERIC and the Need to Know*, GPO, Washington, D.C., 1967.

services, including information retrieval, question answering, text processing, and data analysis. A set of related information centers will be regarded as an information network, more or less closely interconnected and intercommunicating.

Major Resources

Certain of the major library resources of the United States will be regarded as primary stores of unique material, of material for general use but not used frequently enough to warrant duplication, and of material for fields not served directly by specialty libraries and information centers.[43] They will provide the primary equipment for computer-based services, both clerical and informational, particularly in support of the needs of specialty libraries and information centers. They will maintain a computer-based on-line catalog of recent accessions and other material of high frequency of use. They will provide a number of on-line consoles with direct access to the library's computer-based data files. They will store machine-based data (some in the form of magnetic tapes, but an increasing amount by 1980 in "read only" photographic stores[44]) acquired from national sources or produced by information centers, and will provide both scheduled and on-line access to those data. Particularly where material from the machine data bases has a frequency of use high enough to warrant it, that data will be available on-line in direct access stores. The specialty library will provide the services of a staff, trained in the utilization of machine-based data files, and will provide machine-based services to any qualified group or individual needing them. It will provide access to a union catalog of all machine-based data files that are available for use from anywhere in the network. It will serve as a major point of entry into the interlibrary communication network. Among the machine-based data that it maintains and catalogs will be programs, data recordings, and microforms in support of computer-aided instruction.

LIKELY PROGRESSION OF STAGES

To create such library networks and library-based information systems, the libraries of today must move through a progression of interim systems. Each of

[43] Weber, David C., *Index to the Minutes of Meetings of the Association of Research Libraries 1932-54*. Bloomington Indiana: ARL 1954. See, especially, under such leads as *Interlibrary Co-operation; Co-operative Acquisitions; Co-operative Cataloging; Farmington Plan; Interlibrary Loans; LC Library Co-operation Division*, etc.

[44] King, Gilbert, "Photographic Information Storage," *Control Engineering* (August 1955), 48-53.

them should be planned to be operationally viable, to be technologically and economically feasible, to be a reasonable extension from the preceding system, and to be a step toward the achievement of the desired system of the future. As a preliminary definition of such a progression, the following are projected systems likely to be operational at intervals of three to five years. In each case, activities will be estimated as either operational, developmental, experimental, or speculative.

The Present System

Operational Activities. All traditional library services are operational. A few local mechanized clerical systems are operational, but only on a limited basis and usually at major resource libraries. Printed book catalogs cover the holdings of only a limited number of local libraries and are available only at a limited number of points. Machine stored catalogs are virtually nonexistent. Access to the collections at other libraries by the users of one library is provided only by the "interlibrary loan" procedure and involves an average access time of much more than a week.

Development Activities. The creation of a variety of specialized information centers is a major developmental activity, primarily under funding from federal agencies. The mechanization of clerical processes is another major developmental activity at many libraries.

Experimental Activities. The mechanization of "information services" is an experimental activity in several specialized information centers. The use of more direct methods of circulation among libraries, including the use of facsimile transmission, is an experimental activity among several libraries.

Speculative Activities. Machine-based information services as a general part of the library, the connection of computers into a "network," the storage of large data bases in direct access memory, and the use of consoles for communication with large data bases are all still speculative.

The Second Stage System

Several activities, both national and local, should reach fruition within a three to five-year period and should bring many activities, which were either developmental or experimental, to an operational stage.

Operational Activities. Most of the clerical activities in the central library of many large systems should involve operational use of the computer in batch mode; a few will use consoles for on-line communication with a central computer.[45] A number of specialized information centers will be operational, and several of them will utilize mechanized data bases as an integral part of their services. The use of nationally produced magnetic tape catalogs and indexes as an aid to general internal library functions will be operational, in a batch mode.

Developmental Activities. The on-line use of the computer for clerical operations in circulation, acquisitions, and cataloging will be a continuing developmental activity. The use of nationally produced magnetic tape indexes and catalogs for service to users outside of the library will still be in development, but also nearly operational. Facsimile transmission of library materials will be in development.

Experimental Activities. Access to the entire collection of a network for qualified individuals, by direct call to any library in the network, with delivery by mail (or interlibrary bus for close libraries) will be an experimental activity. The storage of very large data bases in direct access and the use of consoles for direct access to library data bases will still be experimental. The use of a computer network for transmission of library data bases will be experimental. The use of microform "consoles," operating under computer control, will be experimental.

Speculative Activities. The use of the computer for storage and processing of a large amount of text material will still be speculative as will its use for "question answering" and similar sophisticated intellectual processing.

The Third Stage System

Operational Activities. Nearly all of the clerical activities in all libraries should be operational in a combination of on-line and batch modes (on-line for most of the input of circulation, acquisition, and cataloging data; batch for most of the processing and bulk output). Union book catalogs for the holdings of various groups of libraries will be computer produced. The use of nationally produced magnetic tape catalogs and indexes will be an integral part of library operations, including acquisition, cataloging, and reference. For recent material and highly active material, the use will be through on-line consoles. The use of nationally produced magnetic tape catalogs and indexes by the research community of the country will have been an operational service for some time. The transfer of mechanized data bases between libraries will be operational, or nearly so. Facsimile transmission between libraries will also be operational over interlibrary communication networks.

[45] Black, Donald V., "System Development Corporation's LISTS Project," *California School Libraries,* **40**(3), March 1969, 121-126.

Developmental Activities. Usage of consoles by the individual for access to data-base material from the library will be developmental. The use of microform consoles will be developmental,[46] as will the large-scale production of microforms by the library.

Experimental Activities. The storage of very large data bases in direct access stores will be an experimental activity insofar as the library is concerned.

Speculative Activities. The storage and processing of text material, including "question answering" and similar sophisticated intellectual processing, will still be speculative.

Suggested Readings

The following references are suggested as readings that will provide perspective on the subject matter of this chapter and the detailed references included in it.

Bush, Vannevar, "As We May Think," *Atlantic Monthly,* **176** (July 1945), 101-108.

The earliest, and perhaps the most important, single description of the potential uses of computers for information processing.

King, Gilbert W. (ed.). *Automation and the Library of Congress.* Washington, D.C., Library of Congress, 1963.

The report of the study that initiated the continuing work at developing mechanization at the Library of Congress, including its services to other libraries.

Knight, Douglas and E. Shepley Nourse, (eds.), *Libraries at Large.* New York: Bowker, 1969.

Based on the various reports contracted for by the National Advisory Commission on Libraries between September 1966 and October 1968, this book provides one of the most comprehensive pictures yet presented of the function of libraries in this country. Chapter VII is especially concerned with the effect of technology. Appendix F-3 presents detail about Library Technology.

Licklider, J. C. R., *Libraries of the Future.* Cambridge, Mass.: MIT Press, 1963.

Based on a study sponsored by the Council on Library Resources, this book presents the concept of the "on-line intellectual community," in which the computer becomes a switching center through which people communicate with each other and with large, mechanized data banks.

[46] Overhage, Carl F. J., *Intrex op. cit.*

Philipson, Morris, *Automation: Implications for the Future.* New York: Vintage, 1962.

A collection of essays that, together, provide a most valuable introduction to the effects of computers on our society.

Weinburg, Alvin, *Science, Government, and Information.* President's Science Advisory Committee, January 10, 1963.

A report recommending directions to be taken in development of a national program of information for science. It emphasized the need for information centers that would analyze the substantive content of the literature.

Chapter 2

REPRESENTATIVE
MECHANIZATION PROJECTS IN
LIBRARIES

As was indicated in Chapter 1, mechanization in libraries has been well under way and is now moving forward at an accelerating pace. To provide a perspective on its present status, it is useful to review a number of individual programs, each of which illustrates one or more of the driving forces behind mechanization in libraries. In doing so, our emphasis will be on activities in the United States, because they are the ones with which we are personally most familiar. It should therefore be noted, from the outset, that in many aspects other countries have been leaders as well. We think especially of Canada, England,[1] the Soviet Union,[2] and the Netherlands.

Some of these programs have been national efforts supporting and coordinating the development of mechanization—the Council on Library Resources, the Office of Science Information Service (NSF), the Committee on Scientific and Technical Information, the Office of Education, and the National Commission on Libraries.

Several are national programs, in both the federal goverment and the private sector, which are creating (as part of their own publication requirements) the mechanized data bases on which mechanization efforts in libraries can be

---

[1] *Program: News of Computers in British University Libraries.* Belfast, North Ireland: Queen's University School of Library Studies.

[2] Tareev, Boris M., "Methods of Disseminating Scientific Information, and Science Information Activities in the USSR," *American Documentation,* **13** (3) (July 1962), 340.

based—the Defense Documentation Center, the National Aeronautics and Space Administration, and the Atomic Energy Commission; the Clearinghouse for Federal Scientific and Technical Information; the Library of Congress, the National Library of Medicine, and the National Agricultural Library; Chemical Abstracts Service and other professional societies; and commercial organizations using mechanized publication.

Several programs represent efforts at the state and regional level, directed at the sharing of resources and processing services among libraries of all kinds. Many of these have been stimulated and supported by funds under the Library Services and Construction Act, with various "technical" processing centers being developed as part of state-wide programs. The programs in the states of California, New York, and Washington involve planning and experimentation for a significant degree of mechanization.

Several programs represent efforts, of varying degrees of success, to develop mechanized library systems in the academic community. Some have been focused within the single university research library—the University of Missouri, the Washington University School of Medicine, Florida Atlantic University, Harvard, the University of Chicago, Stanford, Columbia, and Massachusetts Institute of Technology. Others have been efforts to facilitate cooperation among academic libraries—Educom, the cooperative processing center for Colorado Colleges and Universities, the Ontario New Universities Library Project, and the University of California Task Force Project.

Finally, a great many programs have been simply on-going efforts, in libraries everywhere, to understand mechanization and to use it effectively.

NATIONAL EFFORTS TO SUPPORT AND COORDINATE LIBRARY MECHANIZATION

The development of mechanization in libraries has been a surprisingly difficult task. When data processing specialists first approach the task, they rightly wonder what the difficulty is, particularly if the problem is limited to clerical processing. But the fact is that, although mechanization of library clerical processing is probably not inherently difficult, it is inherently expensive, particularly in comparison with the usual library budget. The agencies that provide financial support and coordination, therefore, have occupied an especially important role.

The Council on Library Resources[3]

In 1955, two conferences were held in the Folger Shakespeare Library, Washington, D.C., under the auspices of a committee headed by Dr. Lewis B.

[3] Council on Library Resources, Inc., *Annual Reports* 1-9 (1956-1966) Washington, D.C. *Recent Developments* (Newsletters). The newsletters announce the initiation of projects; the annual reports describe their current status.

Wright, Director of the Folger Shakespeare Library; Dr. L. Quincy Mumford, Librarian of Congress; and Dr. Leonard Carmichael, Secretary of the Smithsonian Institution. These meetings brought together scientists, research scholars in the humanities, university administrators, and librarians to discuss proposals for the formation of a national library planning group to support research studies. As a result of their proposals, the Council on Library Resources, Inc., was established as an independent, nonprofit body incorporated in the District of Columbia, on September 18, 1956. The Ford Foundation made an initial grant of $5 million to support its activities during the first five-year period, under the direction of Verner W. Clapp who left his position as Chief Assistant Librarian of the Library of Congress to become first president and executive head of the organization.

Purposes. The Council's purpose, as first stated, was to assist in the solution of problems of research libraries by conducting or supporting research, demonstrating new techniques and methods, and disseminating the results. At the end of the first year of operation, the Council restated its views that the mere extension of present techniques would not serve future needs, and that the Council should seek new answers through support of: (1) *basic research* in the processes of distribution, organization, storage, and communication of knowledge; (2) *technological development* for the improvement of the physical and mechanical apparatus of library work, particularly the application of computers; and (3) *methodological development* through changed procedures and cooperative enterprises.

Early Grants. During the first five years of the Council's operation (1956-1961), many important studies were supported by its grants. A grant was made in the first year to Rutgers University School of Library Service for a study, "Targets for Research in Library Work," under the direction of Ralph R. Shaw; it resulted in the publication beginning in 1960 of the series *The State of the Library Art*, covering all areas of library work.[4] A grant to the National Library of Medicine made possible the conversion of *The Current List of Medical Literature* into *Index Medicus*, completed in 1961.[5] Its expanded coverage and improved arrangement were accomplished through mechanization of the production of printer's copy using a system of tape operated typewriters, machine-sorted punched cards, and a "sequential camera." (Subsequently, the project was expanded and led to the "Medlars" system discussed below.) The Council sponsored studies of photostorage and retrieval systems to solve problems of preservation, storage, and retrieval. A grant was given for a survey of the operations of the Library of Congress to see how computer data processing

---

[4] Shaw, Ralph R., *The State of the Library Art*. New Brunswick, N. J.: Rutgers State University, Graduate School of Library Service, 1960.

[5] Taine, Seymour, "The New Index Medicus," *Bulletin of the Medical Library Association,* 49 (1961) 43-63.

could be employed in the Library's operations. The resulting report, *Automation and the Library of Congress*, published in 1963, describes how automation at the Library of Congress could provide benefits for other libraries as well.[6] Since then, further grants to the Library of Congress have concerned conversion of the information on catalog cards to machine readable form for computer processing, and have led to the distribution of such data to other libraries.[7]

Subsequent Grants. To help determine the direction of future research, the Council contracted with the firm of Bolt, Beranek, and Newman, Inc., of Cambridge, Mass. for exploratory research on concepts and problems of libraries of the future (that is, in the year 2000). Directed by Dr. J. C. R. Licklider, formerly a professor of psychology and communication at M.I.T. and Harvard, it resulted in the report *Research on Concepts and Problems of Libraries of the Future,* published in 1963, and a book, *Libraries of the Future,* published in 1965.[8,9] Both works concentrate on the concepts and problems in man's interaction with the body of recorded knowledge and in the use of computers for information storage, organization, and retrieval.

Subsequent grants, made in 1966 and 1967, included support for the MARC (Machine Readable Catalog) pilot project of the Library of Congress;[10] a study of the costs of automation in the library;[11] an evaluation of the use of facsimile transmission between libraries;[12] studies of computerized book catalog production methods;[13] the design of regional cataloging and processing computer centers; and the study of new types of subject indexes. A grant was made in March 1967 to continue Project INTREX (Information Transfer Experiments) at M.I.T.[14] The experiments deal with means of document storage, selection,

---

[6] King, Gilbert. *Automation and the Library of Congress.* Washington, D.C.: Library of Congress 1963.

[7] See the descriptions of the MARC project, later in this Chapter and in Chapters 10 and 17.

[8] Bolt, Beranek, and Newman, Inc., *Research on Concepts and Problems of Libraries of the Future,* Cambridge, Mass., 1963.

[9] Licklider, J. C. R., *Libraries of the Future.* Cambridge, Mass: MIT Press, 1963.

[10] Markuson, Barbara E., "The Library of Congress Automation Program: a Progress Report to the Stockholders," *ALA Bulletin,* **61**(6) (June 1967), 647-655.

[11] See Chapters 14-18 of this book.

[12] Schieber, William D., and Ralph M. Shoffner, *Telefacsimile in Libraries: A Report of an Experiment in Facsimile Transmission and an Analysis of Implications for Interlibrary Loan systems,* Berkeley: Institute of Library Research, University of California, 1967.

[13] Hayes, Robert M., and Ralph M. Shoffner, *The Economics of Book Catalog Production.* Sherman Oaks, California: Advanced Information Systems Division, Hughes Dynamics, May 31, 1964.

[14] Overhage, Carl F. J., and R. Joyce Harmon (eds.), *INTREX: The Report of a Planning Conference on Information Transfer Experiments. September 3, 1965.* Cambridge, Mass.: MIT Press, 1965.

transmission, presentation, and reproduction as needed for a full text access system.

When the Council was established in 1956, it was the only agency exclusively concerned with assisting research in the solution of the problems of libraries. Since that time many others have been established, some supported in part by the Council: at the University of Illinois, a Library Research Center;[15] at the University of California, the Institute of Library Research;[16] at M.I.T., Project INTREX: at the American Library Association, the Library Technology Project.[17]

In summary, the Council on Library Resources has had a seminal role to play in bringing mechanization into libraries. At that initial, uncertain stage of development, when moral support is just as meaningful as financial, the Council provided both to projects that have since become the leaders.

The Office of Science Information Service, NSF

In 1958, the Office of Science Information Service was established as part of the National Science Foundation, under the leadership of Dr. Burton W. Adkinson. The three main functions of the office are:

1. Coordinating the scientific information activities of governmental agencies.

2. Supporting organizations performing research on advanced methods of indexing, abstracting, translating, and publishing scientific information.

3. Publishing reports on advances in the field of information retrieval.[18-20]

Science Information. Although the focus of OSIS interest is on information services to the sciences, the results of the studies and developments they have sponsored have had a real impact on mechanization in libraries.[21] Much of

[15] Garrison, Guy G., "Library Research Center, University of Illinois." *ALA Education Division Newsletter* No. 60. December 1966, p. 14.

[16] Hayes, Robert M., and M. E. Maron, *Institute of Library Research. Annual Reports* 1965-1969. Los Angeles and Berkeley: Institute of Library Research, University of California, 1966-1969.

[17] A.L.A. Library Technology Project. *Annual Reports* 1st–1959-60. Especially the *First Annual Report.*

[18] *Current Research and Development in Scientific Documentation,* 1958-National Science Foundation, Office of Science Information Service.

[19] *Non-Conventional Technical Information Systems in Current Use,* 1958, National Science Foundation, Office of Science Information Service.

[20] *Specialized Science Information Services in the United States,* National Science Foundation, Office of Science Information Service, November 1961.

[21] Tate, Fred A., "Progress Toward a Computer-based Chemical Information System", *Chemical and Engineering News,* XLV (Jan. 1967), 78-90.

the impact has been indirect, since it has come from a steady increase in the number of individuals and organizations concerned with mechanization of information handling.

Library Mechanization. Recently, however, OSIS has been directly concerned with mechanization in libraries as such, viewed as major components in national systems for information services to science. For example, starting in 1966, OSIS provided support to the University of Chicago for development of an integrated, on-line library clerical system.[22] A second project, at the Institute of Library Research of the University of California, was concerned with planning for the implementation of mechanized information services in a university library.[23] The premise of the latter is that as magnetic tape data becomes available, libraries will acquire it (just as they now acquire books, serials, and microforms), but they will be faced with vastly different and more complex problems in providing services from this form of data.

In summary, the work supported by the Office of Science Information Service has provided a new picture of the content of library services and particularly of the role that mechanization must play in them.

Committee on Scientific and Technical Information

A "Committee on Scientific Information" was established in 1962, which later became the "Committee on Scientific and Technical Information" (COSATI) in 1964. Its functions are to coordinate scientific and technical information services of government agencies; to examine interrelationships of existing information services, both within and outside of government; to identify gaps or unnecessary overlaps; and to develop government-wide standards for compatibility among systems. This group operates in the very shadow of the President of the United States. Therefore, although they are charged only to investigate areas of cooperation and to suggest paths of action, their recommendations have great significance.

Membership in COSATI. The following groups are represented on COSATI:

National Science Foundation	NSF
Atomic Energy Commission	AEC
Department of Defense	DOD
National Aeronautics and Space Administration	NASA

[22] "University of Chicago's Automation Program," *Library of Congress Information Bulletin,* **26**(4) (January 26, 1967), 72-73.

[23] *Mechanized Information Services in the University Library,* Institute of Library Research, University of California, December 15, 1967.

Office of Science and Technology (Office of the President)	OST
Department of Agriculture	DOA
Veterans Administration	VA
Department of Commerce	DOC
Department of Health, Education and Welfare	HEW
Department of State	DOS
Bureau of Budget	BOB

The Library of Congress is not in the Executive Department and therefore is not represented directly.

COSATI Publications. Among the accomplishments of COSATI are the following ones. Beginning in 1963, it has published a series of standards to aid information centers, documentation centers, and libraries in the use of scientific and technical reports.[24-27] In 1964 it published the *COSATI Subject Category List* and within a year, the Department of Defense *(DOD)-Modified List* was in use.[28,29] This list of 22 fields, with 178 subgroups and an index, is meant to assist in the subject arrangement of technical reports. COSATI surveys included a 1966 *Inventory of Information Science and Technology Activities* in which more than 1000 projects, supported by federal agencies, were reviewed.[30]

National Information Systems. COSATI has defined its major goal as the creation of a National System for Scientific and Technical Information. It feels that the federal government has the responsibility to ensure that there exists within the United States at least one accessible copy of each significant publication in the world-wide scientific and technical literature, and that this information must be announced and made available to qualified individuals and organizations in the United States.[31] It views information centers as a permanent part of any national system for scientific information, with document-handling systems tailored to serve different groups of users and

[24] COSATI *Standards for Descriptive Cataloging of Government Scientific and Technical Reports,* Washington, D.C. 1963 (Revised 1966).

[25] COSATI, *Guidelines to Format Standards for Scientific and Technical Reports Prepared by or for the Federal Government,* Washington, D.C., December 1968.

[26] COSATI, *Federal Microfiche Standards,* Washington, D.C., 1963 (Revised 1965).

[27] COSATI, *Guidelines for the Development of Information Retrieval Thesauri,* Washington, D.C., 1 September 1967.

[28] COSATI, *Subject Category List,* Washington, D.C., 1964 (Revised 1965).

[29] Department of Defense, *DOD-Modified List,* Washington, D.C., 1965.

[30] COSATI, *Inventory of Information Science and Technology Activities,* Washington, D.C., 1966.

[31] COSATI, *Recommendations for National Document Handling Systems in Science and Technology,* Washington, D.C., November 1965.

manual systems supplemented by "advanced technologies." It therefore has commissioned a number of studies of national information systems for science and technology.[32]

All of the studies made by COSATI have included the existing federal libraries as important resources. Thus it is easy to see that the actions in the name of COSATI can have far-reaching implications for practically every library in the federal government. Equally obvious are the effects on the many industrial, educational, and public libraries in this country and abroad.

Office of Education

The Office of Education has had a long history of support to libraries, best represented by the Library Services and Construction Act and recent federal legislation concerned with education that has consistently recognized the importance of library service.

Library Mechanization. In all this legislation, there has been an increasing emphasis on mechanization and "information science" as an expansion of library services into new areas.[33] This can be seen particularly in the Title III of the Library Services and Construction Act (which calls for the development of state-wide library networks),[34] in Title IIB of the Higher Education Act (which calls for support of research in "library and information science"), in Title III of the Public Broadcasting Act of 1967 (which calls for the study of the role of television in information service), and in the Title IX amendment to the Higher Education Act (which explicitly calls for mechanized information networks including libraries). Each of these is administered by the Office of Education.

ERIC. In addition to this context of direct support to mechanization in libraries, the Office of Education is itself embarked on a major development, which includes mechanization as an integral part. Mainly through government funding, so much educational research is carried on that it is necessary to control the reports and documents that result, so that their contents are accessible to educators, administrators, and teachers. Since 1956, when the Cooperative Research Act was passed, the research funds available through OE alone have increased from $2 million to $100 million annually. To make these research findings available and useful, the Educational Resources Information Center (ERIC) was created in May 1964.[35]

[32] Carter, Launor F., et al., *National Information Systems for Scientific and Technical Information.* New York: Wiley (Information Sciences Series), 1967.

[33] Nyren, K. E., "National Dimension: A Report on the Impact of Federal Aid to Libraries," *Library Journal,* 92 (January 1, 1967), 64-71.

[34] "Text of the President's Remarks re the Library Services and Construction Act of 1966," *Library of Congress Information Bulletin,* 25 (July 28, 1966), 449.

[35] Burchinal, Lee G., *ERIC and the Need to Know,* GPO, Washington, D.C., 1967.

ERIC, as a documentation and dissemination system, is decentralized. Clearinghouses, acting as national centers on specific topics, are established at universities and research institutions across the United States; their job is to collect and organize research results and related materials in their fields and to select, abstract, and index the most pertinent for inclusion in the national ERIC storage and retrieval system.

Documents and resumes are sent to a central computer center and converted to magnetic tape. Monthly, all input documents from the clearinghouses are merged into an author, subject, and sequential number index and published in a book catalog entitled, *Research in Education.* [36]

The National Commission on Libraries

The role of libraries today has become so important that a Presidential commission—the National Advisory Commission on Libraries—was appointed in 1966. The membership included Douglas M. Knight (Chairman), Estelle Brodman, Frederick H. Burkhardt, Launor F. Carter, Verner W. Clapp, Carl Elliott, Alvin C. Eurich, Mildred P. Frarey, Herman H. Fussler, Mrs. Marian G. Gallagher, Emerson Greenaway, Caryl P. Haskins, William N. Hubbard, Dan M. Lacy, Mrs. Merlin M. Moore, Carl F. J. Overhage, Harry N. Ransom, Wilbur L. Schramm, Mrs. George Romney Wallace, and Stephen J. Wright. They selected Melville J. Ruggles, of the Council on Library Resources, to serve as Executive Secretary.

With strong representation of computer oriented individuals on this commission, it was not surprising that the Commission contracted for studies which emphasized mechanization. For example, a report on *Technology in Libraries* was explicitly concerned with mechanization. [37] Another discussed the roles of industry as both a supplier of technology and a user of mechanized services. [38] As a result, although the effects of this advisory commission may not be really felt for several years, they are almost certain to include an increasing emphasis on mechanization in libraries.

The results of the work of the commission were reported to the President in October, 1968 and have since been published. [39] Among them was a recommendation that a permanent commission be established. This led to legislation proposed in 1969 and 1970 to do so. [40]

[36] *Research in Education,* U.S. Office of Education, Bureau of Research Monthly, November 1966—

[37] *Technology in Libraries.* Los Angeles: System Development Corporation, 1967.

[38] *Libraries and Industry: Background Study for Use by the National Advisory Commission on Libraries,* Programming Services, Inc., 1967.

[39] Knight, Douglas, and E. Shepley Nourse (eds.), *Libraries at Large.* New York: Bowker, 1969.

[40] HR-8839 and SB-1519.

NATIONAL EFFORTS TO PRODUCE
MECHANIZED LIBRARY RESOURCES

Much of the support for mechanization in libraries has come from efforts by the federal government to meet the demands for scientific and technical information generated from a variety of developmental projects. This kind of data has been very difficult for libraries to handle—highly technical reports, many of them of limited or dubious value, and that only for a short time. For most libraries, the costs of acquiring and cataloging this material far exceeded its value. It was therefore necessary to provide nationally produced indexes for adequate bibliographic control.

Defense Documentation Center

The Defense Documentation Center (DDC) had its beginnings after World War II when captured enemy documents were added to United States wartime research and development reports, and the Air Force and Navy jointly formed the Central Air Documents Office (CADO) to handle them. In 1951 the Armed Services Technical Information Agency (ASTIA) was established to serve all three military departments and their contractors, consolidating CADO and the Library of Congress Navy Research Section. ASTIA was the primary center for Department of Defense generated reports until March 1963 when it was reconstituted as the Defense Document Center for Scientific and Technical Information and transferred from Air Force operational control to the Defense Supply Agency.

Purposes. The basic purpose of DDC is the acquisition, storage, announcement, and dissemination of technical reports and documents generated by research, development, test, and evaluation (RDT&E) efforts sponsored by DOD. Announcement of new reports, acquired by DDC, is made through the Technical Abstract Bulletin (TAB), which is now prepared from computer tapes for publication by a photocomposition process. TAB is arranged by subject groups with subject and AD number indexes in each volume. There are also indexes for access by corporate author, monitoring agency, subject, personal author, and contract.

Mechanization. Experimentation with mechanization has been carried out at DDC since CADO first investigated various mechanized devices and then abandoned them as unfeasible at that time. With increasing demands for service and growing numbers of reports, however, ASTIA was convinced that electronic storage and retrieval of information was necessary for continued efficiency of operations. Various studies were made in the 1950's, including those by

Mortimer Taube of Documentation, Inc., which introduced the Uniterm System of Coordinate Indexing.[41-43]

Based on those studies, automatic data processing equipment was introduced in three stages. Stage one, operational in December 1959, provided punched card input and output, utilizing the Remington Rand Univac Solid State Computer (USS-90). Stage two added magnetic tape input and output. Stage three added random access capability and a large scale computer, delivered in December 1963.

Subject Control. As the machine retrieval system was being developed for ASTIA, one of the major problems was subject control of its literature. For years, ASTIA documents had been given subject headings and, beginning in 1953, the Uniterm system was also used. It was felt, however, that something different would have to be developed. The ASTIA Machine Retrieval System (Project MARS) was therefore given the task of developing an authoritative list of retrieval terms for the information contained in its collection and assigning the retrieval terms. A thesaurus of scientific terms, based primarily on the *ASTIA Subject Headings,* was compiled and published.[44]

This ASTIA thesaurus has been a tool in establishing a scientific vocabulary for automation. DDC was given responsibility for compiling the *Thesaurus of Engineering and Scientific Terms* (TEST), which is an interdisciplinary, interagency vocabulary of about 23,000 main terms. It is being prepared on computer tape, and DDC will be responsible for maintaining continued computer controls of the terminology.

National Aeronautics and Space Administration

The National Aeronautics and Space Administration (NASA) was established in 1958 as successor to the National Advisory Committee for Aeronautics. It was created to investigate and solve problems of flight within and outside the earth's atmosphere, and to develop, construct, test, and operate aeronautical and space vehicles for research and exploration. It is required to cooperate with the scientific community in using these vehicles for making observations and measurements and also to disseminate as widely as possible the information on space science and technology acquired in this program. Accordingly, the

[41] Taube, Mortimer, et al., *Studies in Co-ordinate Indexing,* Washington, D.C., Documentation Inc., 1953-1959. Especially volumes 1 and 2.

[42] Barden, William A., Lt. Col. William Hammond, and Heston J. Heald, *Automation of ASTIA: A Preliminary Report,* Arlington, Va., ASTIA, December 1959.

[43] Hammond, Lt. Col. William, *Evolution of the ASTIA Automated Search and Retrieval Systems,* Arlington, Va., ASTIA, January 1961.

[44] *ASTIA Subject Headings,* 4th edition. Arlington, Va., ASTIA, 1959.

agency's technical information program is designed to encourage the broadest, most effective dissemination of scientific and technical information generated by the agency, and also to further the distribution of similar information from other sources.

As its publications increased at a fast pace, NASA realized that traditional methods of information storage and retrieval would no longer suffice. They could not provide current aerospace information to their own scientists and engineers, to the scientific community, to industry, to the academic world, and to the interested public without an intolerable time lag.

Mechanization. In 1962, NASA established a Scientific and Technical Information Facility at Bethesda, Md. Managed by Documentation, Inc., under the policy direction of NASA's scientific and technical Information Division, it was the nation's first computer-based aerospace library-information center. Its task is to acquire the world literature, to report on aerospace science and technology, to maintain effective bibliographic control of this collection, and to disseminate information to contribute to the progress of the aerospace effort, in particular, and the national technological development, in general.

The Scientific Information System of NASA serves a complex of regional centers, NASA contractors, universities and, to a lesser extent, users and centers outside the aerospace industry. In addition to filling the role of an information center, the NASA facility has major functions in common with a conventional library. In keeping with the NASA practice of decentralization, the search system is available for local reference service.[45]

The bibliographic citations of reports follow the format recommended by COSATI.[46] In the citation of each item is the code indicating the subject category assigned to that document from the *COSATI Subject Category List.* These examples of standardized processing are instances of compatible arrangements which assist the exchange of information in readable form among government agencies.

Indexing and Abstracting Journals. The objective of providing rapid dissemination of research to users is met by the abstracting and indexing journals issued by NASA. They are the published catalog of aerospace literature and provide current awareness as well as retrospective search service. The semimonthly publication, *Scientific and Technical Aerospace Reports* (STAR),[47] was prepared by Documentation, Inc. (which subsequently became a division of

[45] *How to Use NASA's Scientific and Technical Information System,* Washington, D.C., GPO, 1966.
[46] COSATI, *Standards for Descriptive Cataloging of Government Scientific and Technical Reports.* Washington, D.C., 1963 (Revised 1966).
[47] *Scientific and Technical Aerospace Reports,* V.1–_____. Washington D.C., National Aeronautics and Space Administration, January 1963–_____.

Leasco, Inc.); *International Aerospace Abstracts* (IAA), prepared for NASA by the American Institute of Aeronautics, covers the published aerospace literature.[48] Copy for the abstract section of STAR is prepared by mechanized publishing methods using modified Photon equipment; the abstract section of IAA is prepared by offset printing. The computer is programmed to manipulate the data for each item on the tape to produce the indexes.

Air Force Materials Information Centers

The recent history of research and development in the Air Force particularly exemplifies the increasing volume of documentation. As a specific example, among many, the Aeronautical Systems Division is responsible for generating, collecting, collating, and disseminating "technical information related to the properties, characteristics, and application of materials." Information centers have been established to assist in accomplishing this mission. They include:

Thermophysical Properties Research Center
Purdue University
Lafayette, Indiana

Mechanical Properties Data Center
Balfour Engineering Company
Suttons Bay, Michigan

Electronic Properties Information Center
Hughes Aircraft Company
Culver City, California

Defense Metals Information Center
Batelle Memorial Institute
Columbus, Ohio

Each center has an information storage and retrieval system and provides research data, literature searches, and various publications. In addition, the Aeronautical Systems Division itself publishes the monthly Materials Briefs, Abstracts of Materials Central Internal Research Programs, and other bibliographic tools.[49]

The function of information centers is vital in such a vast program of research as the Air Force performs. Duplication of work is costly and unnecessary, and only through a well-coordinated network of specialized information centers such as this can scientific information be efficiently utilized by all concerned. This

---

[48] *International Aerospace Abstracts,* V.1 –_____. Philipsburg, N.J., Institute of the Aerospace Sciences, January 1969–_____.

[49] *Materials Briefs, Abstracts of Materials Central Internal Research Programs,* Aeronautic Systems Division, USAF.

has been illustrated in other information services and networks, and the method used to store and retrieve data has implications for effective library service of all kinds.

Clearinghouse for Federal, Scientific and Technical Information

Public Law 776, passed in 1950, called for the Secretary of Commerce to establish a clearinghouse to make the results of technological research and development more readily available to business, industry, and the general public. The Office of Technical Services (OTS) served as a clearinghouse for unclassified research reports from the Atomic Energy Commission, the Armed Services Technical Information Agency, and the National Aeronautics and Space Administration, and for technical translations. It provided various bibliographic and reference services in its endeavor to make the literature easily accessible, including major indexes, press releases, subject bibliographies, and a literature searching service. It was manually handling machine-produced materials from the contributory agencies.

However, lack of support for the program restricted OTS staff and procedures in the face of a rapidly expanding number of reports to be handled. Much discussion, from 1958 on, focused on the problem of truly creating a national center for scientific and technological information. The Crawford report (a task force study of government programs in science information),[50] the Weinberg report (the President's science advisory committee),[51] and other such studies recommended a federal center for collection and dissemination of scientific and technical information with centralized bibliographic and search services.[52,53] Finally, in February 1964, COSATI recommended the establishment of a Clearinghouse for Federal Scientific and Technical Information.[54]

The Clearinghouse that went into operation, as part of the Commerce Department in January 1965, helps to create a more effective network of agency information systems by centrally collecting, processing, and disseminating the documents. It is expected to handle 95 to 100 percent of the unpublished government technical report literature (as compared to the 70 percent by the

[50]Crawford, James H., Jr. (Chairman), *Scientific and Technological Communications in Government: Task Force Report to the President's Special Assistant for Science and Technology,* Office of Science and Technology, April 1962.

[51] Weinberg, Alvin, *Science, Government, and Information,* President's Science Advisory Committee, January 10, 1963.

[52] Orlans, H. (ed.), *Federal Departmental Libraries: A Summary Report of a Survey and a Conference,* by Luther H. Evans et al; The Brookings Institution, 1963 (see, especially, pp. 148-149).

[53] COSI, *Status Report on Scientific and Technical Information in the Federal Government,* Committee on Scientific Information, June 18, 1963.

[54] *Special Libraries* 56, January 1965, p. 59 (news item).

OTS).[55] It publishes a government-wide index to reports, in addition to the separate subject indexes such as Nuclear Science Abstracts.[56] It provides a source referral service and various reference services, including literature searching for selective bibliographies, information on unclassified projects currently underway, and technical translations.

Closely associated with the Clearinghouse is the *State Technical Services Program.*[57,58] This act is designed to facilitate the transfer of scientific and technical information to American business and industry. An Office of State Technical Services was formed to maintain a central reference service utilizing the Clearinghouse and other sources.

The National Library of Medicine

The manual production of an index to medical literature began in 1880. The tremendous increase in published medical literature since that date, and the recent need for a mechanized system to handle this literature, resulted in the Council on Library Resources awarding a two-year grant in 1961 for a study that led to the present MEDLARS system.[59-61]

The objectives of MEDLARS were to improve and enlarge the index, to increase indexing from about 2 to 10 headings per citation, to develop a system for special bibliographic requests, and to produce other publications similar to *Index Medicus.* All of them have been accomplished. In addition to *Index Medicus*, special recurring bibliographies can be requested by organizations having a special biomedical interest. These requests are run over MEDLARS tapes periodically, and have produced such publications as the *Index to Dental Literature* and *International Nursing Index*.

With the stimulus of the Medical Library Assistance Act, NLM greatly increased the scope of its service to the country[62] and of its work on

[55] Fry, Bernard M., "The Clearinghouse for Federal Scientific and Technical Information," in Newman, Simon M. (ed.), *Information Systems Compatibility*. Washington, D.C.: Spartan, 1965, pp. 35-43.

[56] *United States Government Research and Development Reports (USGRDR).* Washington, D.C.: Department of Commerce.

[57] State Technical Services Act of 1965, Public Law 89-182.

[58] *Fact Sheet,* U.S. Department of Commerce, Washington, D.C., November 1965.

[59] General Electric Co., Information Systems Operation, *Final Technical Report for MEDLARS Preliminary Design.* Washington, D.C.: General Electric Co., 1962.

[60] Austin, Charles J., "Data Processing Aspects of MEDLARS," *Bulletin of the Medical Library Association,* 52 (1964), pp. 159-193.

[61] Karel, L., Charles J. Austin, and Martin M. Cummings, "Computerized Services for Biomedicine," *Science* 148 (1965), pp. 766-772.

[62] Esterquest. Ralph T., et al, "Regional Plans for Medical Library Service," *Medical Library Association Bulletin,* 52 (July 1964), 497-523.

mechanized information systems. The "Lister Hill Memorial Center for Bio-Medical Communications" is now the focal point for creation of a national system for health service information.[63]

MARC (Machine Readable Catalog)

MARC started in 1966 as an experiment, to determine if it is feasible to produce a standardized machine-readable catalog record that can be manipulated and reformatted in local installations to serve local practices and needs. It was the second phase of the far-reaching Library of Congress Automation Program, initiated with the King Committee study on "Automation and the Library of Congress."

In response to a request from L. Quincy Mumford (the Librarian of Congress), the Council on Library Resources in 1961 supported a study. The resulting report, *Automation and the Library of Congress*, was published in 1963.[64,65] It covered the broad range of Library of Congress operations, and concluded that automation of many of the operations would be beneficial.

Since an important function of the Library of Congress is the provision of cataloging data to other libraries throughout the United States, many of which are large research libraries that have already begun to experiment with mechanization and computers in their own operations, the Library of Congress had to consider not only automation of its own internal functions but also how useful a distribution service of computerized bibliographical data might be to other libraries.[66,67]

Experimental Project. To experiment with the feasibility of such centralized production of machine readable data, 16 libraries were selected as participants in the MARC project. Selected on the basis of expressed interest, computer facility, and availability of staff and funds, the participating libraries included: Argonne National Laboratory, Argonne, Illinois; University of California, Los Angeles; University of Chicago; University of Florida, Gainesville; Georgia Institute of Technology, Atlanta; Harvard University; Indiana University, Bloomington;

---

[63] Davis, Ruth M., "Relationship of Regional Networks to the NLM Biomedical Communication Network," *Bookmark,* 28 (January 1969), 109-113.

[64] King, Gilbert (ed.), *Automation and the Library of Congress.* Library of Congress, 1963.

[65] Hayes, Robert M., Gilbert W. King, and Ralph H. Parker, "Automation and the Library of Congress: Three Views," *Library Quarterly* 34 (July 1964), pp. 229-239.

[66] Avram, Henriette D., and Barbara E. Markuson, "Library Automation and Project MARC," in *The Brasenose Conference on the Automation of Libraries.* London: Mansell, 1966.

[67] Markuson, Barbara E., "The Library of Congress Automation Program: A Progress Report to the Stockholders," *ALA Bulletin,* 61(6) (June 1967), pp. 647-655.

University of Missouri, Columbia; Montgomery County, Maryland, School System; Nassau County Library System, Hempstead, New York; National Agricultural Library, Washington, D.C.; U.S. Army Missile Command; Redstone Arsenal, Huntsville, Alabama; Rice University, Houston, Texas; University of Toronto; Washington State Library, Olympia; and Yale University.[68]

In the MARC project, the Library of Congress converted records for selected current catalog entries (English language monographs and some serials) into machine-readable form and transmitted them, via magnetic tape reels, to participating libraries.[69] The tapes included complete bibliographic information for each work, an abbreviated author title record, and subject and descriptive cross references. The participants used these records as input for local processing and experimentation to test this centrally prepared data for suitability in local use.

The MARC II Format. As a result of the experimentation, a revised format for machine readable cataloging data has been developed.[70] It is now accepted as the standard on which further development will be based, by both the American Standards Association and the American Library Association.

National Serials Data Project. A second, parallel effort was then started to develop a consolidated record of serials holdings of the three national libraries which could also be used by other libraries as the starting point for mechanization programs. By 1970, preliminary, "MARC-compatible," format had been developed and work was under way on implementation of a system as a joint effort of the Association of Research Libraries and the National Libraries Task Force on Automation.

National Agricultural Library

With the other great national libraries embarked on major mechanization efforts, it was natural for the National Agricultural Library to do so as well.[71] Fortunately, all three libraries have agreed to proceed in a cooperative development, with common standards.[72]

[68] *MARC Pilot Project, Final Report,* Washington, D.C., Library of Congress, 1968.

[69] Library of Congress, Information Systems Office, *MARC Manuals Used by the Library of Congress,* Chicago, ALA Information Science and Automation Division, 1969.

[70] Avram, Henriette D., et al., *The MARC II Format.* Washington, D.C.: Library of Congress, January 1968.

[71] Mohrhardt, Foster E., and Blanche L. Oliveri, "A National Network of Biological-Agricultural Libraries," *College and Research Libraries* 28 (January 1967), pp. 9-16.

[72] Schactman, Bella E., James P. Riley, and Stephan R. Salmon, "U.S. National Libraries Task Force on Automation and Other Cooperative Services: Progress Report No. 1," *Library of Congress Information Bulletin,* 26 (November 30, 1967), pp. 795-800.

In 1967, NAL initiated a two-year study of the requirements for a "NAL-Land Grant Institution Information Network." Within this general plan, mechanization occupies a central position, including an automated "Pesticides Information Center," mechanized production of the *Bibliography of Agriculture,*[73] and general mechanization of NAL clerical processes.

Chemical Abstracts Service

The Chemical Abstracts Service (CAS), with headquarters in Columbus, Ohio, is a self-supporting branch of the American Chemical Society (ACS), dedicated to the collection and dissemination of the world's chemical knowledge and is best known as producer of *Chemical Abstracts*, the English language "Key to the World's Chemical Literature." *CA* first was published in 1907 as virtually a one-man operation. By 1966, growing demand for *CA* related services coupled with an explosive increase in the world's chemical literature, resulted in the establishment of the Chemical Abstracts Service as a formal division of the American Chemical Society.[74]

The proliferation of new chemical knowledge is rapidly outpacing the capabilities of conventional information-handling and publishing techniques. Therefore, Chemical Abstracts Service, along with the entire ACS publication program, is converting from a publishing-abstracting-indexing operation to a computer-based information system from which publications will be derived as one form of output. The CAS part of this shift will be completed by mid 1970.

This change in the basic method of operation at CAS was by no means a sudden development. In 1959, CAS started research on applying modern data processing techniques to handle chemical information. Since its inception, this work has been partially supported by the National Science Foundation as part of a long term government effort to develop a unified chemical information program.[75] In its later stages, additional support came from the National Institutes of Health, the Department of Defense, the Food and Drug Administration, and the National Library of Medicine.

Chemical Titles. The earliest result of this research was the introduction of *Chemical Titles* (CT) in 1961. Another useful tool to emerge from the CAS research and development effort is the *Chemical Compound Registry*, under development at CAS since 1961 with substantial financial support from the National Science Foundation and other government agencies.[76] Techniques and

---

[73] *Bibliography of Agriculture,* U.S. Department of Agriculture, 1942–

[74] Baker, Dale B., "Chemical Literature Expands," *Chemical and Engineering News,* XLIV (June 1966), 65.

[75] Davenport, W. C and J. T. Dickham, "A Computer-based Composition at Chemical Abstracts Service," *Journal of Chemical Documentation,* VI (November 1966), 221-225.

[76] Park, M. K., "The Chemical Compound Registry," paper presented at a special conference on CAS Development Programs, Washington, D.C., February 1, 1967.

programs are complete for the registration of fully defined compounds. In 1965, CAS began its first abstract journal produced with the aid of the computer, *Chemical-Biological Activities* (CBAC). CBAC is a prototype of a family of specialized services to be introduced over the next several years. *Polymer Science and Technology* (POST), introduced in early 1967, extends this integrated search-awareness information-packaging concept to coverage of both papers and patents in the polymer field.

By the end of 1966, about 500,000 titles processed for CT since 1961 plus about 24,000 whole digests processed for CBAC were in the machine-manipulable data store. Computers are also helping to speed preparation of *CA* indexes and to maintain document acquisition records.

Magnetic Tape Distribution. By 1970, CAS hopes to provide a unified system that will produce both a full, printed record of chemical and chemical engineering knowledge and a variety of timely, specialized subject-alerting services, including a mechanized search-and-retrieval system that is sufficiently flexible to meet the varied needs of information users. Perhaps the most significant step in this direction was the decision to distribute magnetic tapes to various centers which could then provide the mechanized retrieval services directly to their own constituencies. Among the centers were one in England and one in Germany, as well as a number of universities in the United States.[77]

STATE AND REGIONAL LIBRARY NETWORK PROJECTS

Mechanization in libraries at the state and regional level has received a major stimulus from the Library Services and Construction Act and particularly from the new Title III. It provides for the establishment and maintenance of local, regional, state, or interstate cooperative networks of libraries. Interlibrary cooperation is defined as the establishment and operation of systems or networks of libraries including state, school, college and university, public, and special libraries, working together to provide maximum effective service to all library users. Such systems may be designed to serve a community, metropolitan area, region within a state, or a state-wide or multistate area.

The text of the President's remarks in signing the bill leaves no doubt as to the direction in which he felt we should be moving: "What part can libraries play in the Nation's rapidly developing communication and exchange networks? Computers and new information technology have brought us to the brink of dramatic changes in library techniques. As we face this information revolution, we want to be satisfied that our funds do not preserve library practices which are already obsolete."[78]

[77] *Association of Scientific Information Dissemination Centers,* University of Georgia.
[78] "Text of the President's Remarks re the Library Services and Construction Act of 1966," *Library of Congress Information Bulletin* 25 (July 28, 1966), 449.

State of California

The state of California has had a long history of interlibrary cooperation. A key element has been the state-wide union catalog. In 1965, the state library felt that the union catalog needed to be more widely distributed and that its own catalog, representing one of the primary interlibrary loan resources for the state, needed consolidation. This led to initiation of a study, by the Institute of Library Research of the University of California, of the implications of book-form publication of these two catalogs.[79]

The study concluded that a computer-based system for producing book catalogs would not only be economic, in itself, but would make possible multiple uses of the resulting machine language catalog data. In particular, with the availability of machine-readable data from the California Union Catalog as well as from national sources, it would be economically possible to produce subcatalogs of the holdings of any group of libraries in the state. It was therefore recommended that the services of the existing State Library Processing Center be expanded to include facilities for mechanized book catalog production, as a service to library systems of the state as well as to the state library itself.[80]

A related development arose as a response to the opportunity provided by the State Technical Services Act. With the view that the public library systems was an appropriate means to provide improved information services to business and industry, the state library initiated a pilot project to demonstrate what could be done through a cooperative network. In parallel with that, the Institute of Library Research developed a program for introducing mechanization as part of public library service.[81]

State of Washington

The state of Washington also has a long history of state-wide library cooperation. Futhermore, it has a great deal of experience with mechanized production of book catalogs as an aid to that cooperation. In particular, the Timberland Library Demonstration Project was begun in 1963 as a cooperative library system sponsored by the Washington State Library under the Library

[79] Shoffner, Ralph M., and Kelley Cartwright, *Catalogs in Book Form: A Research Study of their Implications for the California State Library and the California Union Catalog, with a Design for their Implementation.* Berkeley, California: Institute of Library Research, University of California, January 1967.

[80] Sherman, Don, and Ralph M. Shoffner, *California State Library: Processing Center Design and Specifications.* Berkeley: Institute of Library Research, University of California, April 1969.

[81] *Mechanized Information Services in California Public Libraries.* Los Angeles: Institute of Library Research, University of California, January 1968.

Services and Construction Act.[82] The first undertaking was the compiling of a union catalog. The objective was to list, in as complete bibliographical form as was financially possible, the total holdings of the existing collections of seven libraries (about 100,000 volumes). The book catalog was to be available in every outlet in the demonstration area, and was to be kept up to date by monthly cumulative supplements and an annual cumulated edition. Initially produced by using punched cards and a tabulator, it is now produced by a computer print-out from which a photo-reduced master is made for publication. The book catalog has proved economical and is particularly useful in a large system with many libraries, as a tool for interlibrary loan among them.

Washington State Library now has the facilities to provide book catalogs for other library systems in the state. Because of this, Washington State Library was one of the 16 participants in the Library of Congress MARC program, using the tapes in their catalog production system.[83]

The approach of using a mechanized processing center at the State Library, as an agency for production of catalogs for groups of libraries, has been incorporated within a general plan for a state-wide library network.[84] Other forms of mechanization are also included, with an automated directory-switching center providing facilities for rapid communication.

New York State

New York state has been pioneering in development of a state-wide library network, to provide improved service to all library users. In 1958, for example, the State Library installed teletype equipment to facilitate communication between it and other libraries throughout the state. As of 1964, 17 public library centers had the necessary machinery to take advantage of this operation.[85]

In 1960, the New York State Committee on Reference and Research Library Resources started to study reference service of an advanced nature across the state. Its report stressed that the library needs of research and higher education should be met by a single coordinated program that includes all types of libraries—academic, special, and public.

The resulting library program in New York became known as the "three R's"

---

[82] Cline, Catherine, "Procedures for Developing Timberland's Book Catalog," *PNLA Quarterly,* 28 (January 1964), 128-132, 136.

[83] *MARC Pilot Project, Final Report,* Washington, D.C., Library of Congress, 1968, pp 149-165.

[84] Becker, Joseph, and Robert M. Hayes, *A Proposed Library Network for Washington State,* September 1967.

[85] Hayes, O. R., "Improved TWX Strengthens New York's Interlibrary Loan Network," *Bookmark, 25,* November 1965, pp. 51-55.

(Reference and Research Resources).[86] Its purpose was "to provide improved access to advanced reference and research library materials to serious library users." Several studies were subsequently made including the Pilot Facsimile Transmission Project.[87] This 6-month program began in January 1967 and allowed 12 major library systems (public and university in addition to the state library) to draw upon each other's resources without the usual delays of interlibrary loan. Facsimile transmitters and/or receivers, connected by special telephone lines, were located in each of the 12 libraries. The idea was that a scholar at any library in the state could request material not available locally. Another part of the three R's program, of particular interest here, involved the "automation of the state library's serial holdings as the basis of a statewide union list of serials."

Another program in New York involved linking together of state medical libraries by computer.[88] Eventually it is hoped to include libraries of all the campuses of the State University of New York. The project includes the creation of a centralized catalog to be put in machine readable form, with periodic print-outs, subject searches, and selective dissemination of information.

ANYLTS. Several studies and recommendations for centralized processing led to the creation of a nonprofit corporation, ANYLTS, for providing such services.[89]

UNIVERSITY RESEARCH LIBRARY PROJECTS

University libraries have been at the forefront of the development of mechanization. The following projects are representative, not comprehensive, chosen because they were either very early efforts or especially forward looking.

Individual Universities

Washington University of St. Louis. Starting in 1963, Washington University School of Medicine Library experimented with computer-based serial control,[90]

---

[86] Stewart, Robert P., "Regional Reference Services. New York: The System Framework," *Library Journal,* 89 (8) (April 15, 1964).

[87] Nelson Associates. *The New York State Library's Pilot Program in the Facsimile Transmission of Library Materials,* New York, June 1968.

[88] Pizer, Irwin, "The State University of New York Computerized Biomedical Information System," in *The Brasenose Conference on the Automation of Libraries.* London: Mansell, 1967, pp. 151-162.

[89] Holingren, Edwin S. "ANYLTS Reports Progress," *Bookmark,* 27 (February 1968), 193-197.

[90] Pizer, Irwin H., Donald R. Franz, and Estelle Brodman, "Mechanization of Library Procedures in the Medium-Sized Medical Library: I. The Serial Record," *Bulletin of Medical Library Association,* 51 (July 1963), 334ff.

a punched-card circulation system,[91] and an acquisitions-cataloging system.[92] The machine methods are now operational and are routinely used in its library operations.

Ontario. The "Ontario New Universities Library Project" was established in 1963 to compile, by 1967, a catalog of the college library collections for five new Ontario universities.[93, 94] The first issues of the ONULP book catalog were produced in 1964. Computer-produced and computer-maintained catalog data are designed to provide author-title union catalogs for the five libraries, and individual shelf lists. The catalogs appear monthly, with quarterly, semiannual, and annual cumulations. The record is used to assist other library procedures, apart from catalog production: mechanization of acquisition procedures, systematic analysis of the collection, computation of required stack space, circulation control, and bibliographic information for retrieval.

University of Missouri. The University of Missouri Library, under the leadership of Ralph Parker, initiated an evolutionary approach to an integrated automated record system. Ralph Parker has pioneered in the study of machine applications to libraries since 1930.[95] At the University of Missouri Library, Mr Parker forecasts a gradual change from punched card to a computer system. "This conversion," said Parker, "will not be a radical change. . . . Punched cards will continue to be used since they are the primary form of data input for a computer system."[96]

Florida Atlantic University. Florida Atlantic University was a new library that attempted to use advanced data processing technology from its inception.[97] Work on the computer based system began in 1964. The intent was to use machines to facilitate library clerical functions in the areas of acquisition, cataloging, and circulation. The experience was not satisfactory, but it is an

---

[91] Pizer, Irwin H., Isabelle T. Anderson, and Estelle Brodman, "Mechanization of Library Procedures in the Medium-Sized Medical Library: II. Circulation Control," *Bulletin of Medical Library Association,* **52** (April 1964), 370ff.

[92] Brodman, Estelle, and Geraldine Cohen, "Change in Acquisitions—Cataloging Methods as WUSLML," *Bulletin of Medical Library Association,* **54** (July 1966), 259ff.

[93] Bregzis, Ritvars, "Ontario New Universities Library Project, An Automated Bibliographic Data Control System," *College and Research Libraries,* **28** (November 1965), 495-508.

[94] Merry, Susan A., "The Ontario New Universities Library Project—A Centralized Processing Experiment Completed," *College and Research Libraries,* **29** (March 1968), 104-108.

[95] Parker, Ralph, *Library Applications of Punched Cards,* ALA, 1952.

[96] Parker, Ralph, "Not a Shared System: an Account of a Computer Operation Designed Specifically and Solely for Use at the University of Missouri," *Library Journal,* **92** (November 1, 1967), 3967-3970.

[97] Heiliger, Fred, "Use of a Computer at Florida Atlantic University Library for Mechanized Catalog Production," *IBM Library Mechanization Symposium,* 1964, pp. 165-186.

instructive demonstration that an efficient library is an essential prerequisite to an effective use of mechanization.

Harvard. Widener Library, which is the main branch of the Harvard research libraries, is an old, very large (about 1.6 million titles) library, with catalog records in more or less conventional format. In 1964, it was evident that the shelflist was in the poorest condition of any of the library's major records. It had been compiled in large, loose-leaf form, with whole pages often requiring transcription in order to integrate new numbers. Conversion to machine language was therefore undertaken in 1964, under the direction of Richard De Gennaro, both to improve the existing situation and to make possible new approaches to the material.[98-100]

Yale. Yale University took a somewhat different approach to mechanization. Starting with the acquisition procedures at the Yale Medical Library, under the direction of Fred Kilgour, they experimented in 1963 with the use of machine-based cataloging data.[101] An experimental project was inaugurated, involving Yale, Harvard, and Columbia in a sharing of cataloging data. However, the project was in advance of the technological capabilities (and perhaps the willingness of people to cooperate) at the time.

Chicago. Another automation project, financed in part by the National Science Foundation, was started in 1966 at the Univeristy of Chicago Library, under the direction of Dr. Herman H. Fussler.[102, 103] The system developed there uses on-line storage of full bibliographical data available for many different library purposes, including catalog card printing, production of acquisition orders, maintenance of business records, maintenance of circulation records, and searching of catalog data. Later development of the system would permit

[98] De Gennaro, Richard, "A Computer Produced Shelf List," *College and Research Libraries,* **26** (July 1965), 311-315, 353.

[99] Palmer, Foster M., "Conversion of Existing Records in Large Libraries, with Special Reference to the Widener Library Shelflist," in *The Brasenose Conference on the Automation of Libraries.* London: Mansell, 1967, pp. 57-77.

[100] De Gennaro, Richard, "A Strategy for the Conversion of Research Library Catalogs to Machine Readable Form," *College and Research Libraries,* **28** (July 1967), 253-257.

[101] Kilgour, Fred G., "Basic Systems Assumptions of the Columbia-Harvard-Yale Medical Libraries Computerization Project," in *University of Minnesota Institute on Information Retrieval, 1965,* University of Minnesota, 1966, 145-154.

[102] Payne, Charles T., "An Integrated Computer-Based Bibliographic Data System for a Large University Library: Problems and Progress at the University of Chicago," in *Clinic on Library Applications of Data Processing, University of Illinois, 5th, 1967, Proceedings.* Urbana: University of Illinois, 1967.

[103] Fussler, Herman H., and Charles T. Payne, *Development of an Integrated, Computer-based Bibliographical Data System for a Large University Library, Annual Reports,* 1966-1968. Chicago: University of Chicago Library, 1967, 1968

simultaneous use of the computer by remote terminal equipment. The project started with identification of the basic data required by the library for its own operation and service to readers.

Similar projects were started at Stanford University and Columbia University in 1967. Under funding from the National Science Foundation and the Office of Education, the intent is also to create an integrated on-line library system.

INTREX

The university library of the late 20th century will be greatly influenced by the patient research being undertaken at Massachusetts Institute of Technology under Project INTREX. INTREX is an acronym for Information Transfer Experiments and represents a multimillion dollar research program aimed at developing new methods of information handling for university libraries.

Summer Study. A five-week program to outline a plan for this research was held on August 2 to September 3, 1965, at the Summer Studies' Center of the National Academy of Science at Woods Hole, Mass. Thirty-five full time and part-time participants and 41 visitors attended, including authorities from the fields of library science, engineering, computer technology, linguistics, publishing, education, government, and industry. Carl F. J. Overhage, professor of engineering at M.I.T. and director of Project INTREX, served as chairman of the conference. Preliminary working papers for consideration and debate by all the participants were prepared, principally by a small planning group composed of the M.I.T. INTREX staff, Herman H. Fussler of the University of Chicago, Herman H. Henkle of the John Crerar Library, Chicago, J. C. R. Licklider of IBM, Stephen A. McCarthy of Cornell University, and Foster E. Mohrhardt of the National Agricultural Library.[104,105]

Objectives of INTREX. The ideas behind INTREX reflect the earlier work of Vannevar Bush and later research of J. C. R. Licklider into future applications of advanced data processing technology to library systems design. The objective is "to provide a design for evolution of a large university library into a new information transfer system that could become operational in the decade beginning in 1970." Such a system could become a reality with the realization of three aims: "(1) The modernization of current library procedures through the application of technical advances in data processing, textual storage, and reproduction; (2) the growth, largely under federal sponsorship, of a national

[104] Overhage, Carl F. J., and R. Joyce Harmon (eds.), *INTREX: The Report of a Planning Conference on Information Transfer Experiments.* Cambridge, Mass.: MIT Press, 1965.
[105] Shera, Jesse H., "Librarian's Pugwash, or INTREX on the Cape," *Wilson Library Bulletin,* **40** (December 1965), 359-362.

network of libraries and other information centers; and (3) the extension of the rapidly developing technology of on-line, interactive computer communities in the domains of the library and other information centers."

Progress. Experimenting with real library users in actual working situations in M.I.T.'s Engineering Library, Project INTREX has made progress in the following promising technologies: "graphic storage of full text in microfilm or other reduced format, automatic selection through a time-shared computer utility, transmission of a scanned-image electrical signal over a communication network, and display and/or reproduction in full size or microform for temporary and/or permanent retention by the user; digital storage of encoded full-text in massive random-access storage, selection and transmission through a time-shared computer system, display and/or reproduction for user through remote computer terminals."[106]

Cooperative Processing Center for College and University Libraries in Colorado

The University of Colorado libraries received a grant in March 1967 from the National Science Foundation to initiate a study of the development of a cooperative book processing center to serve all publicly supported Colorado college and university libraries.[107] The objective of the study was to determine whether a centralized processing center for all Colorado academic libraries would improve the dissemination of materials to users throughout the state, and to determine the feasibility and desirability for such a center to store the data it acquires through processing so that the center would also be used as the hub of a state or regional bibliographical network. The information would also be made available to scientists and engineers in the area.

The study attempted to answer the following questions. Would a central agency be able to make materials available more rapidly and at a lower unit cost than under present processing procedures? Are the needs of the participating institutions compatible to a single system? Would the range of services requested by scientists and engineers be served best by a single system, or would they require additional subsystems? The project also investigated issues of compatibility among local and national systems in order to ensure that procedures and methods used would accommodate bibliographic data supplied by the Library of Congress and sources of scientific bibliographic data.

[106] *Project INTREX. Semi-Annual Activity Reports* (15 March and 15 September), 1966–____.

[107] Leonard, Lawrence E., Joan M. Maier, and Richard M. Dougherty, *Colorado Academic Libraries Book Processing Center, Final Report Phase I and Phase II.* Boulder: University of Colorado Libraries, June 15, 1968.

Ohio Cooperative College Program

A somewhat similar project was initiated in 1967 in the state of Ohio, when Fred Kilgour took over direction of the Ohio Cooperative College Program, to create a shared file of on-line cataloging data.[108]

University of California Task Force Project

In 1965 the Institute of Library Research of the University of California started its Task Force Project to attack the pressing operational problems of the libraries of the nine campuses of the University of California. Its work since then has encompassed a variety of mechanization issues.

One major emphasis has been on coordination of the efforts, on each of the nine campuses, toward development of mechanized systems.[109] Each campus was assigned responsibility for specification of one or another module in a total library system. The Task Force Project has served as a coordinating agency, to assure that the specifications met the needs of all campuses and that the modules would be mutually compatible.[110-112]

A second major emphasis has been on efforts which, by their nature, were multicampus efforts. For example, the University of California plans to produce a supplement to the existing book catalogs of the holdings on the Berkeley and Los Angeles campuses. The Task Force Project has had responsibility for evaluating the most effective means of doing so, including the use of computers. Another project has been an evaluation of facsimile transmission among campuses (including both Magnafax and Long Distance Xerography).[113] A third

[108] Kilgour, Frederick G., "Retrieval of Single Entries from a Computerized Library Catalog File," in *Information Transfer, American Society for Information Science.* New York: Greenwood, 1968, pp. 133-136.

[109] Hayes, Robert M., and Ralph M. Shoffner, *Mechanization in the Libraries of the University of California.* Los Angeles: Institute of Library Research, University of California, October 1969.

[110] Shoffner, Ralph M., *Technical Development Program: A Program Requirement for the Joint Design and Implementation of Library Systems.* Berkeley, California: Institute of Library Research, University of California, February 1967.

[111] Shoffner, Ralph M., *Report of Activities and Plan for Future Operations, Institute of Library Research Operations Task Force.* Berkeley, California: Institute of Library Research, University of California, March 1967.

[112] Shoffner, Ralph M., *Operations Task Force Project Status Report and Budget Request, Including a Preliminary Projection of Computer-Based Library Systems Development for the University.* Berkeley, California: Institute of Library Research, University of California, June 1967.

[113] Schieber, William D., and Ralph M. Shoffner, *Telefacsimile in Libraries: A Report of an Experiment in Facsimile Transmission and an Analysis*, Berkeley, Institute of Library Research, 1967.

project has been an evaluation of alternative methods for intercampus circulation of material.[114]

EDUCOM

Probably the most comprehensive project for mechanization among universities is EDUCOM, a consortium of more than 90 major colleges and universities throughout the United States. The major effort is to create an interuniversity communication network, which would provide facilities for transmission of data in a variety of forms, including facsimile and digital (from computer to computer).

As one step toward this aim, a Summer Study was held at Boulder, Colorado for four weeks, in July 1966. It clarified the present status of such networks, defined the information resources available, and outlined the applications to be served.[115]

EDUCOM has also considered specific types of information networks. In particular, it has had responsibility for study of the national medical information network for the National Library of Medicine and a comparable study for the National Agricultural Library.

INDIVIDUAL LIBRARY DEVELOPMENTS

A report, published in October 1966, on *The Use of Data Processing Equipment by Libraries and Information Centers* was over 160 pages long.[116] Of 1130 libraries included in the survey, over 50 percent reported using some form of data processing equipment and over 80 percent planned to do so in the future. Admittedly, the definition of "data processing equipment" was made so broad that it would be difficult for any library to avoid planning to use it. However, the results clearly demonstrate the extent to which mechanization is coming to libraries.

Information Science and Automation Division. The extent of involvement of librarians in mechanization may be even better represented by the formation of the Information Science and Automation Division of the American Library

[114] Shoffner, Ralph M., *Interim Report: Intercampus Circulation—Pilot Project: Phase I, Biology Library, University of California, Berkeley, August 15-October 31, 1966,* Berkeley, Institute of Library Research, University of California, February 1967.

[115] Brown, George W., et al., *Edunet: Report on the Summer Study on Information Networks.* New York: Wiley, 1967.

[116] *The Use of Data Processing Equipment by Libraries and Information Centers.* New York: Creative Research Services Inc., 1966.

Association. From its inception in 1965, it has had a phenomenal growth in membership. The journal it publishes is now one of the primary sources of information on library mechanization.[117]

GENERAL OBSERVATIONS

Reviewing all of the individual projects described above, there are some general observations that should be made. In a sense, they are a highly subjective evaluation, which we have arrived at after careful examination of the progress achieved to date in library mechanization projects.

1.   Almost universally, library mechanization projects have started out with overly ambitious aims. For example, instead of aiming for a step-by-step progression (from existing manual operations to relatively well-established punched card procedures to small-scale "batch" computer systems to the "integrated on-line" computer system), several projects have aimed at a complete conversion to a total, integrated, on-line library system. Such a revolutionary change, of course, can be accomplished. In fact, in another context, Gunnar Myrdal has claimed that "often it is not more difficult, but easier, to cause a big change rapidly than a small change gradually."[118] This view is consistent with the attitude, represented in many of the projects, that anything less than the ultimate system would not be a satisfactory answer to library needs. Our view, however, is quite the opposite. Not only are less ambitious systems likely to be adequate answers to library needs but they are absolutely necessary stages in the development of the more sophisticated ones.

2.   Almost universally, the development schedules of library mechanization projects have depended on overly optimistic rates of progress, rates that simply were not met. This results partly from the preconception, in the minds of data processing specialists, that libraries represent really quite trivial problems to which existing methods should provide ready solution. In part, it is a result of the real difficulties represented by the overly ambitious aims which, in many cases, have required development of new hardware (such as multifont printers) and new software (such as information retrieval packages). And in part, it is the result of the necessarily slow process of educating the personnel of the libraries themselves.

3.   Almost universally, library mechanization projects have reported overly inflated claims of success, not for the purpose of deluding others, but simply

---

[117] *Journal of Library Automation,* Chicago, ALA Information Science and Automation Division, 1968–

[118] Myrdal, Gunnar, *Asian Drama.* New York: Pantheon (Random House), 1968, V. 1, p. 115.

because plans are described as though they were already realized. The readers of those reports should therefore be very careful in their evaluation of what may be merely hopes or speculations and what may be reality.

4. Finally, a large number of these projects have depended on the availability of external funds, especially from various federal programs. Their economic viability therefore did not need to include consideration of the amortization of capital investment required for development. Of course, the result of this federal support is that a base of knowledge and experience has been created from which the library community in general will gain measurable benefit—provided that it builds upon the work done to date. Thus it is especially important that libraries contemplating the introduction of mechanization avoid duplicating the developmental work already done, by accepting the standards and packaged programs that it has produced.

This last point deserves emphasis: as a result of the developmental stages through which mechanization in libraries has been progressing, certain generally accepted standards have been produced—standards for catalog data, such as the MARC II format; standards for procedural organization; even standards for computer programs. These should represent the starting point for any library planning a mechanization project, and should be departed from only because of vitally important local considerations. The "not-invented-here" syndrome should be carefully avoided.

Suggested Readings

Among the references cited in this chapter are a few that are especially worth reading for background:

Brown, George W., et al., *Edunet: Report on the Summer Study of Information Networks.* New York: Wiley, 1967.

This reports the first major effort by Educom to define the requirements and development program for inter-university communication networks, linking computers, libraries, and university instruction together.

Carter, Launor F., et al, *National Information Systems for Scientific and Technical Information.* New York: Wiley, 1967.

This presents the substance of a study, undertaken by System Development Corporation for COSATI, the purpose of which was to evaluate alternative strategies by which the Federal Government could administer its large-scale programs for scientific and technical information.

Harrison, John, and Peter Laslett (eds.), *The Brasenose Conference on the Mechanization of Library Services.* London: Mansell, 1967.

This reports the set of papers presented at a conference held at Oxford, under the chairmanship of Sir Frank Francis and sponsored by the Old Dominion Foundation of New York, from June 30 to July 3, 1966.

King, Gilbert W., *Automation and the Library of Congress.* Washington, D.C.: Library of Congress, 1963.

Knight, Douglas, and E. Shepley Nourse (eds.), *Libraries at Large.* New York: Bowker, 1969.

Licklider, J. C. R., *Libraries of the Future.* Cambridge, Mass.: MIT Press, 1963.

Overhage, Carl F. J., and R. Joyce Harmon (eds.), *INTREX: The Report of a Planning Conference on Information Transfer Experiments.* Cambridge, Mass.: MIT Press, 1965.

This presents the starting point for the INTREX project at MIT, which has been carefully exploring many of the problems in mechanizing the information processes of the library.

Weinberg, Alvin, *Science, Government, and Information,* President's Science Advisory Committee, 1963.

Chapter 3

SCIENTIFIC MANAGEMENT OF LIBRARIES

Louis D. Brandeis was probably the first to make the phrase "scientific management" publicly known when, in October 1910, he used it to describe the application of scientific methods to management issues.[1] Since then, it has been a continuing theme of modern management, gaining acceptance in an increasing variety of management tasks.

"Scientific management" has been defined as an attitude of mind, a belief that the use of the scientific method—with its emphasis on definition of basic assumptions, measurement, experimentation, quantified evaluation, and repeated reexamination of assumptions and results—can produce better management than blind acceptance of existing practice or the choice of alternatives by intuition. It is debatable whether the underlying belief in the power of scientific method is valid. There are just too many issues in the management of large organizations, including libraries, which are not amenable to measurement or experimentation, at least in operational management. But there is little question about its value as an aid to management.

The time seems long overdue for scientific management to have become an integral part of library management, whether mechanization is an issue or not.[2-4] But it is especially important to any library that is considering the

[1] Brandeis, Louis, "Economies through Scientific Management," in *Evidence taken by the Interstate Commerce Commission in the Matter of Proposed Advances in Freight Rates by Carriers, August to December 1910,* Vol. 8, pp. 4756-4803.

[2] Coney, Donald, "Management in College and Research Libraries," *Library Trends,* 1 (July 1, 1952), 91.

58

development of mechanized systems. This chapter, therefore, reviews the historical background of scientific management and the present status of its applicability to various issues in libraries.[5-7]

HISTORICAL BACKGROUND

Scientific management developed at the beginning of this century, as the size of industrial organizations became so great that management was no longer able to maintain the day-to-day knowledge of operations necessary for direct, intuitive control. It became clear that objective, quantified standards of performance were needed.

Time and Motion Studies

Since the giant organizations of that era were manufacturing companies, it was natural that scientific management originated with the study of the production rates to be expected from manufacturing employees. The man generally regarded as the father of scientific management, Frederick W. Taylor, developed the early methods of "time and motion study" for measurement of industrial production. His book became the bible of the field.[8] Subsequently, other individuals (notably Frank and Lillian Gilbreth, with their definitions of "therbligs" as component "motions" in manufacturing operation) refined and extended Taylor's methods. Today, time and motion study is an integral part of the kit of tools of the "industrial engineer" in his solution of specific problems in industrial management.[9]

Project Management

But "time and motion studies" only measure the performance of the individual worker. Methods were also needed for measurement and control of

[3] *Library Trends*, **2** (January 1954). Articles by Everett W. McDiarmid, Herbert Goldhor, Lawrence J. Kipp, Richard H. Logsdon, Lucille M. Morsch, and John H. Ottenmiller et al.

[4] Biehl, W. J., "Libraries Need Good Management," *Library Quarterly,* December 20, 1962, pp. 317-319.

[5] Lamkin, B. E., "Decision-Making Tools for Improved Library Operations," *Special Libraries,* **56** (November 1965), 642-646.

[6] Laden, H. N., and T. R. Gildersleeve, *System Design for Computer Applications.* New York: Wiley, 1963.

[7] Joslin, Edward O., *Computer Selection.* Reading, Mass.: Addison-Wesley, 1968.

[8] Taylor, Frederick W., *Principles and Methods of Scientific Management.* New York: Harper, 1911.

[9] Barnes, Ralph M., *Motion and Time Study: Design and Measurement of Work*, 5th ed. New York: Wiley, 1963.

the management process itself—assignment of personnel, scheduling, and cost control, for instance—and they too were developed. Henry L. Gantt, during the period from 1911 to 1919, defined the precursors of almost every modern tool for "project management."[10] His charting techniques—called Gantt charts—provide the means of relating components, personnel, and machinery in an organization with the tasks assigned to them over time. Requirements, assignments, costs, and schedules are pictured in a form that is easy to visualize; management performance can be easily measured by comparison of actual production or expenditures with scheduled ones; problem areas can be readily pinpointed for management attention. Present-day refinements of Gantt's original concept include PERT (Program Evaluation and Review Technique), CPM (Critical Path Method), and LOB (Line of Balance) techniques.[11] They expand the capabilities of Gantt charts to show interrelationships among tasks (particularly, time dependencies), the ability to reflect uncertainties in schedules or costs, and the ability to predict problem areas.

Cost Accounting

These methods of management required the development of comparable methods for accounting and reporting, so that the actual status of progress and costs could be monitored. As a tool of scientific management, accounting is actually the most historic, dating from at least the renaissance. It was regarded so highly at the time that "double entry bookkeeping" was a trade secret of the Florentine merchants using it.[12] As modern scientific management grew, however, it was apparent that adequate control required far more detailed cost data than existing budgetary accounting provided. This led to the development (by about 1910) of "cost accounting systems," which related costs to work performed. These are now an essential part of modern industrial management.[13]

Systems and Procedures

As a result, whether "scientific management" was involved or not, there was a concomitant increase in the amount of paper work needed, to the point where it

[10] Rathe, Alex (ed.), *Gantt on Management,* American Management Association, 1961.

[11] Archibald, Russell, and R. L. Villoria, *Network-Based Management Systems (PERT/CPM).* New York: Wiley, 1967.

[12] Pacioli, Luca, "Ancient Double Entry Bookkeeping," in *The World of Business,* edited by E. C. Bursk et al. New York: Simon and Schuster, 1962; Vol. 1, pp. 89-115.

[13] Gillespie, G., *Accounting Systems: Procedures and Methods.* Englewood Cliffs, N. J.: Prentice-Hall, 1951.

became a management problem in itself. By the 1930's and 1940's the problem of paper work had become so great that a branch of scientific management— "systems and procedures"—was created to solve it.[14-19] The concern is with analysis of the process of information flow within an organization, with design of appropriate forms and procedures for facilitating the information flow, with management of the resulting reports and records, with measurement of the effectiveness of clerical work involved, and with design and evaluation of equipment systems for handling the clerical work. The growth in the number and variety of devices for "business data processing"—accounting machines, punched card equipment, computers—is a direct result of the need for systems and procedures to handle the "paper-work explosion." There has been a corresponding growth in the body of techniques available for systems and procedures work—flow charting, functional analysis, methods analysis, standards for forms design, and computer programming software.

Management Information Systems

Recently, the use of the computer has introduced a new approach to systems and procedures called "total management information systems." Specifically, the combination of modern communications with the computer allows the integration of administrative information to an extent previously impossible. As a result, data about an organization can easily be acquired, stored, processed, and used for management control. Even more important are the implications for scientific management. Whereas, before, it was at best difficult to acquire and process the data required for management decision making, the availability of integrated files that can be easily processed makes it easy to do so. The most complete exposition of the role of a total management information system in industrial organizations was expressed by Jay W. Forrester.[20] He used the phrase "industrial dynamics" to describe the application of modern engineering control techniques to the management of a company.

[14] Lazzaro, Victor (ed.), *Systems and Procedures: A Handbook for Business and Industry.* Englewood Cliffs, N. J.: Prentice-Hall, 1959.

[15] Neuner, J. J. W., *Office Management: Principles and Practices.* Cincinnati, Ohio: South-Western Publishing Company, 1959.

[16] Neuschel, Richard F., *Management by System,* 2nd ed. New York: McGraw-Hill, 1960.

[17] Optner, Stanford L., *Systems Analysis for Business Management.* Englewood Cliffs, N.J.: Prentice-Hall, 1960.

[18] Ross, H. John, *Techniques of Systems and Procedures.* Office Research Institute, 1949.

[19] *The Office: Magazine of Management, Equipment Methods.* Office Publications Incorporated, N.Y.

[20] Forrester, Jay W., *Industrial Dynamics.* Cambridge, Mass: MIT Press, 1961

Operations Research

Aiding management to make a choice among alternatives has therefore been an increasingly important theme of scientific management. A variety of techniques have been developed, usually grouped under the rubric of "operations research" (sometimes called "management science").[21-25] The need for them especially arose in the 1940's in managing large-scale military operations. Since then, of course, they have become an integral part of the management process in a large number of industrial concerns as well as in the military. In large part, operations research simply provides mathematical formalisms (or "models") by which to represent alternatives for the decision problem of concern. As such, they can serve as a quantitative basis for decision, since the data in the models can be processed according to the mathematics so as to "optimize" a measure of performance. The specific techniques most generally used include linear programming (or models based on linear inequalities), queuing and other models based on probability, game theory, and simulation.

Systems Analysis

Where the management decision-making problem is a large-scale one, the design and evaluation of alternatives requires a methodology, now generally called "systems analysis." It depends heavily on the kinds of mathematical models provided by operations research, but it is so much concerned with issues which are not amenable to quantification that other techniques have been required. In particular, systems analysis must be especially concerned with the definition of objectives that the "system" is to meet. Although some objectives can be measured, others are essentially qualitative, relating to policy, politics, or social values. As a result, systems analysis has had to be concerned with the balance between costs (usually measurable) and benefits (frequently unmeasurable). The concept of "cost/effectiveness" or "cost/benefits" evaluation have therefore been an integral part of systems analysis. Of course, from the earliest days of scientific management, it was recognized that an adequate criterion for evaluation required some balance between the cost and benefits derived. Harrington Emerson, around 1910, expounded the use of "cost/effectiveness,"

[21] Ackoff, Russell, Shiv K. Gupta, and J. Sayer Minas, *Scientific Method: Optimizing Applied Research and Decisions.* New York: Wiley, 1962.

[22] Baumol, William J., *Economic Theory and Operations Analysis.* Englewood Cliffs, N. J.: Prentice-Hall, 1961.

[23] Bierman, Harold, Jr., et al., *Quantitative Analysis for Business Decisions.* Homewood, Ill.; Richard D. Irwin, 1961.

[24] Bursk, Edward C., and John F. Chapman, *New Decision-Making Tools for Managers,* Harvard, 1962.

[25] Churchman, C. W., R. L. Ackoff, and E. L. Arrow, *Introduction to Operations Research.* New York: Wiley, 1957.

or efficiency, as the appropriate measure.[26] Since then, it has become the characterizing feature of systems analysis, perhaps best represented by the work of Charles Hitch. In 1960, Hitch defined the concepts and problems in a cost/effectiveness criterion when applied to the policy issues in national defense.[27] Since these techniques have been used with such success in the Department of Defense, they are being more generally applied throughout the federal government. Under the title "Program Planning and Budgeting System," each federal agency is required to relate its administrative budget to benefits to be derived, in terms of defined program objectives of the government.[28,29]

Summary

The history of the development of scientific management can be seen as a natural evolution of techniques. They were created to solve management problems that appeared in a succession of organizational contexts—manufacturing productivity, project management, paper-work control, decision making, and large-scale systems development—as each became large enough to require scientific management. In each case, the new techniques developed drew heavily on both the philosophy and the methodology of their predecessors.

Today, the magnitude of the management problem faced by libraries seems to be at a critical point. As libraries grow in size and services, as they participate in national networks, and as they introduce mechanization, they must develop tools for scientific management appropriate to the tasks they face. In doing this, they can draw on the tools that have been found to be of value in other organizations—time and motion study, project management, cost accounting, systems and procedures, management decision making, and systems analysis. But particularly in the last two areas, libraries must develop tools of their own, attuned to the particular characteristics of the library, its management problems, and its information system functions.

MANAGEMENT DECISION MAKING IN LIBRARIES

Library administrators are continually faced with situations in which they must make decisions and choose among alternatives. Some decisions relate to

[26] Emerson, Harrington, *The Twelve Principles of Efficiency*. New York, Engineering Magazine Co., 1912.

[27] Hitch, Charles, and Roland McKean, *Economics of Defense in a Nuclear Age*. Cambridge: Harvard University Press, 1960.

[28] "U.S. agencies get order: join McNamara's band: cost system imposed by the defense secretary on the Pentagon will be the model for all federal departments", *Business Week*, November 13, 1965, p. 182.

[29] Novick, David (ed.), "U.S. Bureau of the Budget. Program budgeting: program analysis and the federal budget." Washington D.C.: Superintendent of Documents, 1965.

strategic planning of the long-range objectives of the library, whether and how they should be changed, what policies are required to achieve them, and what effects they will have. Others relate to operational planning, where administrative decisions must be made about allocations of resources. Some simply relate to the management of specific tasks.

To date, most of these decisions are made by the librarian on the basis of experience and his resulting intuitive judgment. The generally high quality of library service, in the face of severe budgetary restraints, is attributable to the competence of the librarian. But are there any quantitative methods that the librarian can use to aid in making these decisions?

Projecting Library Growth

Perhaps the most fundamental issue faced by the librarian in his strategic planning is the issue of projecting the rate of growth of his collection. Budgets for acquisitions and operating personnel, capital investment for buildings, levels and kinds of service to be provided for—all ultimately tie back to this primary issue. How should the librarian predict such growth over a period of 20 to 30 years or more? Does he depend solely on his own experience, or the experience of his colleagues? Must he ask the community he serves to make predictions of what they will need? Or does he simply depend on a year-to-year balancing of immediate needs with apparently available funds?

This issue was recognized by librarians, at a very early time, as one susceptible to quantitative treatment. Fremont Rider applied a mathematical model to this issue in strategic planning when he fitted an exponential curve to the past data on research library collections.[30]

Exponential Growth Models. The model can be described very simply: "Library collections grow by a more or less fixed percentage each year, which results in a doubling in their size every 10 to 20 years (the period being different from one kind of library to another)." Such a growth model is a common one, particularly applicable to biological phenomena during their stages of early development. It is, in fact, the basis of projections of human population growth and Malthus' dire predictions that population would outpace the capabilities to produce sufficient food to maintain it.[31]

Since Rider first suggested this "exponential growth" model 25 years ago, the growth rates of libraries have equaled and even exceeded its predictions. In 1951, Louis Ridenour restated the same model in a now classic volume, *Bibliography in an Age of Science.*[32] Most recently, an extensive series of

[30] Rider, Fremont, *The Scholar and the Future of the Research Library.* New York: Hadham, 1944.

[31] Malthus, Thomas Robert, *Essay on the Principles of Population.* London, 1798.

[32] Ridenour, L., Ralph R. Shaw, and A. G. Hill, *Bibliography in an Age of Science.* Illinois, 1951.

calculations has been made, fitting exponential growth curves to the past histories of libraries in educational institutions of many sizes. The resulting curves, published in the report by Oliver Dunn and others, provide a statistical picture of the past and likely future of research libraries.[33]

Some efforts have been made to provide justifications for this apparent exponential growth on grounds other than simply fitting curves to historical data. In particular, the growth of libraries has been attributed to the more basic growth in publication rate (especially in the sciences and technology), mainly as the result of the increasing numbers of scientists and engineers publishing reports.[34]

Program Related Growth Models. A somewhat different and even more basic approach was taken by Verner Clapp and his associate Robert Jordan in their study of the library collections of the institutions of higher education in the state of Ohio.[35] Their premise was that library growth is not a result of a simple exponential growth formula. Instead, it is the result of the needs of the educational programs of the institutions themselves. Therefore, they adopted what is technically known as a "parameterized linear growth model"—a model that derives growth from a number of separate parameters (each characterizing some feature of the institution's academic programs), which are multiplied by corresponding coefficients for number of volumes and then summed. As Figure 3.1 shows, the characterizing parameters include "number of students," "number of faculty," "number of doctoral programs," and the like. Library growth is then predicted on the more fundamental growth pattern of increased numbers of students, faculty, doctoral programs, and so on. On the basis of this approach, the historical pattern of library growth could be interpreted as a result of the exponential growth in student population together with a continual fragmentation of areas of research.

Studies by the Insititute of Library Research (of the University of California), in applying both exponential models and parameterized linear models to a number of academic libraries, suggested that a more useful model was represented by a combination—that library growth resulted partly from the pressures of academic program and partly from the rate of increase in publication rates in already established academic program areas.[36] The resulting

[33] Dunn, Oliver C., W. F. Seibert, and Janice A. Scheuneman, *The Past and Likely Future of 58 Research Libraries, 1951-1980: A Statistical Study of Growth and Change.* Lafayette, Indiana: Indiana University Libraries, 1965.

[34] Trueswell, Richard W., *Determining the Optimal Number of Volumes for Library Holdings,* School of Engineering, University of Massachusetts, Amherst, Mass., October 1964.

[35] Clapp, Verner and Robert Jordan, *Quantitative Criteria for Adequacy of Academic Library Collections.* Washington, D. C.: Council on Library Resources, 1965.

[36] Hayes, Robert M., *Project Status: An Approach to Methodology (Criteria and Goals for the Libraries of the University of California).* Los Angeles: Institute of Library Research, January 31, 1966.

Figure 3.1   Formula for estimating the size for liminal adequacy of the collections of senior college and university libraries.

	Total Volumes
To a basic collection:	
1. Undergraduate library	50,750
Add for each of the following as indicated:	
2. Faculty member (full time equivalent)	100
3. Student (graduate or undergraduate in full time equivalents)	12
4. Undergraduate in honors or independent study programs	12
5. Field of undergraduate concentration— "major subject field"	335
6. Field of graduate concentration— Master's work or equivalent	3,050
7. Field of graduate concentration— doctoral work or equivalent	24,500

model (Figure 3.2), therefore, provides a set of coefficients somewhat different from the Clapp-Jordan formula, since some of the growth is represented by pure exponential increase. (It should also be noted that the rate of exponential growth is also smaller than is usually indicated, for the converse reason).

Now, the point is not that one model or another really describes the growth pattern for libraries. In fact, the likelihood is that libraries actually grow for a number of reasons that have little to do with quantitative models—a university chancellor is especially aware of the value of a research library, a donor provides funds for special acquisitions, an area of research becomes of world-wide renown

Figure 3.2   Summary of criteria (in volumes).

New campus	50,000
New college	15,000
Professional school	12,000
Master's field of concentration	3,000
Doctoral field of concentration	12,000
1000 Undergraduate students	2,000
1000 Graduate students	5,000
Faculty (for each member)	200
Research staff (for each member)	1,000
Years to achieve	5
Annual growth thereafter	2%

and attracts researchers and resources, the librarian is especially astute in his collecting policies, and there are existing interinstitutional cooperative arrangements. But it is also likely that, on the average, these effects balance out and that the librarian can use a rational model to lay out his long-range growth program. At least, a model lays bare the factors that must be considered in doing so—whether new program areas are involved, or increased publication rates, or other as yet unidentified aspects. Furthermore, a quantitative model may provide the justification necessary to support the librarian's long-range projections.

Storage Models

Rider, in applying his exponential growth model to library growth, was concerned with an operational planning problem: How were the resulting storage needs to be solved? The particular approach that he was interested in exploiting was micro-image storage (in the form of "Microcards"). Other approaches that have been suggested, since then, have included depository libraries, retirement policies, compact storage, sharing of resources through some form of network, and other forms of storage (such as digital).[37-40]

The management decision in this operational planning situation can be easily stated: How does the librarian choose among the alternative methods of storage, and how does he decide what material to allocate to each alternative? A number of models have been proposed as possible answers.

Frequency of Use Models. One of the most important models, called Zipf's law, was first applied to the description of the frequency of use of words.[41,42] In its simplest form, the model says that the number of books that will be used n times is (k/n) of the number that will be used just once (where k is a constant parameter, usually very close to 2). Figure 3.3 shows the resulting pattern of distribution of activity. Based on this model, books that are infrequently used can be allocated to remote or relatively inaccessible storage, without degrading the overall efficiency of operation and perhaps even improving it by making the

[37] Leimkuhler, Ferdinand F., and J. G. Cox, "Compact Book Storage in Libraries," *Operations Research,* May-June, 1964.

[38] Muller, R. H., "Economics of Compact Book Shelving," *Library Trends,* April 1965.

[39] Trueswell, Richard W., "A Quantitative Measure of User Circulation Requirements and its Possible Effect on Stack Thinning and Multiple Copy Determination," *American Documentation,* **16** (January 1965), 20-25.

[40] Orne, J., "Book Review of 'Optimum Storage of Library Material,'" *College and Research Libraries,* May 1965.

[41] Zipf, G. K., *Human Behavior and the Principle of Least Effort.* Cambridge, Mass.: Addison-Wesley, 1949.

[42] Simon, H. A., *Models of Man.* New York: Wiley, 1957.

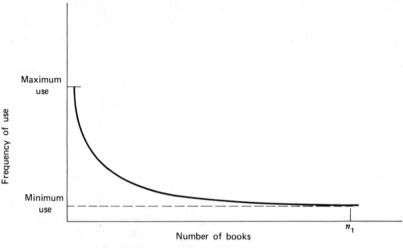

Figure 3.3   Zipf's law of frequency use.

frequently used material even more accessible.[43] Unfortunately, the nature of long-tailed "J-shaped" curves is that many items (n_1) in the long tail have effectively equal likelihood of being used. As a result, experience bears out the proverbial Murphy's law that "If it can go wrong, it will." Whatever material may be put in remote storage all too frequently turns out to be exactly the material that is next needed. Furthermore, the need for "browsibility" varies widely from one subject to another. Mere "frequency of use" can completely fail to account for such differences. Finally, the issue of what constitutes "efficiency in operation" must be specified. Usually, the system analyst would use a "cost/effectiveness" measure, comparing the cost of storage with the average response time (that is, time to locate and deliver needed material). If the access time to remote storage is significantly greater than that to local storage, it may be difficult to justify its use.

Frequency Related to Date. Total frequency of use data has been, at best, difficult to accumulate. Moreover, it is not at all clear that past frequency is a valid measure of future frequency. Therefore, in what is certainly a classic illustration of a quantitative model for library operational planning, Fussler and Simon studied "Patterns in The Use of Books in Large Research Libraries."[44] Their aim was to evaluate several factors as both independent and joint determiners of future activity. These included "years since publication," "years since accession," and "years since last use" as well as "frequency of use." The

    [43] Morse, Philip M., *Library Effectiveness: A Systems Approach.* Cambridge, Mass.: MIT Press, 1968.
    [44] Fussler, Herman H., and Julian L. Simon, *The Use of Books in Large Research Libraries.* Chicago, Ill.: University of Chicago, 1961.

data they used exhibited, with varying reliability, approximately the behavior one would have suspected.

Since Fussler's study, others have also related usage to publication date. For example, studies by Kilgour at Yale (on "Use of Books in the Yale Medical Library")[45,46] and by Advanced Information Systems (on "Activity Statistics for a Large Bio-Medical Library")[47] resulted in curves that were also "J-shaped" for publications in increasing order of age (see Figure 3.4).

The most recent models of this kind have been developed at Purdue. Professor Ferdinand Leimkuhler and a sequence of colleagues and students have been evaluating several quantitative models for allocating books to compact storage, with the thesis by W. C. Lister presenting the most complete summary of work to date.[48-51]

A discussion of the costs and benefits of various models of book storage was written by Ralph Ellsworth.[51a] It provides extremely valuable insight on these issues.

Network Models

The most far-reaching solution to the problems posed by library growth is the creation of cooperative library networks. By depending on the availability of material from other libraries and depository centers, the individual library can limit the size of its own growth and specialize in the materials that it considers to be of particular importance or high frequency of use. The design and evaluation of library networks is therefore a task of real strategic importance to individual libraries and to the group of libraries as a whole. It is in part a function of cost;

[45] Kilgour, Frederick G., "Recorded Use of Books In the Yale Medical Library," *American Documentation,* 12(4) (October 1961), 266-269.

[46] Kilgour, Frederick, "Use of Medical and Biological Journals in the Yale Medical Library," *Bulletin of the Medical Library Association,* 50 (3), July 1962.

[47] "Activity Statistics for a Large Biomedical Library," Part 2 of the Final Report on *The Organization of Large Files,* Sherman Oaks, California, Advanced Information Systems Division, Hughes Dynamics Inc., April 30, 1964.

[48] Leimkuhler, Ferdinand F., "Mathematical Models for Library Systems Analysis," *Drexel Library Quarterly,* 4 (July 1968), 18-196.

[49] Morelock, M., and F. F. Leimkuhler, "Library Operations Research and Systems Engineering Studies," *College and Research Libraries,* 25 (November 1964), 501-53.

[50] Baker, Norman R., and Richard E. Nance, *The Use of Simulation in Studying Information Storage and Retrieval Systems.* Lafayette, Indiana: Purdue University, November 22, 1967.

[51] Lister, Winston C., *Least Cost Decision Rules for the Selection of Library Materials for Compact Storage,* Ph.D. thesis, Purdue University, 1967. (*Dissertation Abstracts,* 28 (1), July-August 1967, p. 703-A).

[51a] Ellsworth, Ralph E., *The Economics of Book Storage in College and University Libraries.* Metuchen, N.J.: Scarecrow Press, 1969.

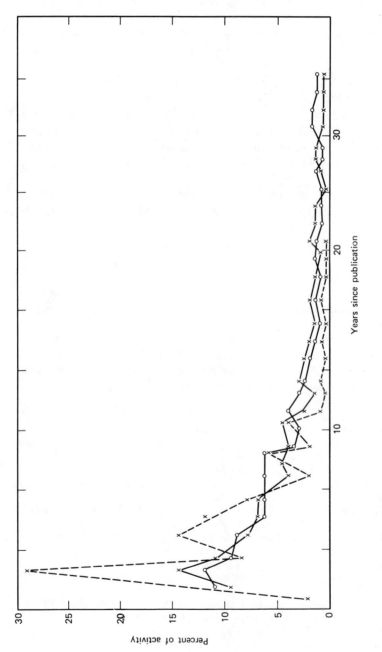

Figure 3.4 Circulation comparison: UCLA Bio-Medical Library and Yale Medical Library. Data are plotted by publication years prior to sample date. *Source.* Frederick G. Kilgour, "Recorded Use of Books in the Yale Library," *American Documentation* **12** (4) (October 1961), 266; "Activity Statistics for a Large Bio-Medical Library," Advanced Information Systems, April 30, 1964.] *Key:* O and solid line, Yale data; X and solid line, nonreserve monographs, Bio-Med; X and dotted line, reserve monographs, Bio Med.

in part, a function of the volume of traffic among libraries; and, in part, a function of the response time, both to be expected and to be actually achieved. Models have been developed that represent one or more of these considerations.

Cost Trade-Off Studies. The issue of cost is of paramount importance, since a major justification for a network is that there will be a cost saving if a group of system libraries can acquire and share a single copy of a book or journal rather than ten copies. Of course, the savings in cost of acquisition, cataloging, and storage of multiple copies must be balanced against the resulting increases in cost due to the need to use some interlibrary loan procedure (mechanized or otherwise). The Center for Research Libraries has been carrying out this kind of "trade-off analysis," accumulating data on the costs of both alternatives and determining the "break-even point"—the average number of uses at which one alternative is cheaper than the other.[52] Figure 3.5 summarizes the trade-off model used, with representative cost data.

Figure 3.5   Costs of serial usage.

The cost associated with a serial title is expressed as the discounted cost over the period of interest, that is the "present value." Thus

$$C = \sum_{t=0}^{T-1} C_t \left\{ \frac{1+j}{1+i} \right\}^t$$

where i is discount rate, j is inflation rate, and

$$C_t = I_o \, \delta(a_o - t) + A_t + S_t + W_t + U_t + B_t - R_t \, \delta(t - T)$$

Representative Value

\$60.60/title	I_o = cost of acquiring and cataloging a new serial title (incurred only when $t = a_o = 0$), if the serial is acquired.
	$\delta(x) = 1$ if $x = 0$.
	$\quad\quad = 0$ if $x = 0$.
19.18/year	A_t = cost of maintenance of title (check-in, claiming, binding, marking, subscription), if the serial is continued.
.134/vol	S_t = storage cost in year t, if the serial is stored.
.52	W_t = weeding cost in year t, if the serial is stored.
1.48/use	U_t = cost of using the title in year t (circulation, reshelving, etc.), if the serial is held.
6.49/request	B_t = cost of borrowing in year t, if the title is not held.
	R_t = salvage value, at end of period of interest (year T), if the serial is held.

[52] Bryand, Edward C., et al., *Library Cost Models: Owning versus Borrowing Serial Publications.* Chicago, Center for Research Libraries, August, 1968.

Communication Traffic Load. The volume of traffic among libraries is significant in part as it relates to the characteristics of the communication system required to handle it. This is a classic problem in the design of communication networks, with well established models for representing alternative configurations and choosing among them. One such model has been specifically applied to an interlibrary network for the State of Connecticut.[53] The crucial issues relate to the volume of traffic—the number of requests and amount of transmission of each. The model is best represented as a matrix (Figure 3.6) in which the numbers represent the traffic between each pair of

Figure 3.6 Matrix of intercampus borrowing, 1967-1968
(excluding photocopies in lieu of loan).

		B	D	I	LA	R	SD	SF	SB	SC	T
	B	①	2790	614	2149	884	595	210	1375	768	9385
	D	46	②	2	8	32	7	5	5	1	106
	I	2	0	③	6	1	0	0	0	0	9
Lending	LA	443	388	1190	④	1734	1399	39	2099	60	7352
campus	R	10	9	24	12	⑤	5	0	0	0	60
	SD	4	0	5	50	1	⑥	0	2	0	62
	SF	191	115	8	12	8	16	⑦	1	1	352
	SB	2	1	1	28	1	1	0	⑧	0	34
	SC	7	2	0	0	0	0	0	0	⑨	9
	T	705	3305	1844	2265	2661	2023	254	3482	830	17,369

Borrowing campus

"nodes" in the network. Various configurations of "switching centers" and hierarchical arrangements of transmission among libraries can then be generated by arithmetic processing of this matrix. They can be compared with each other for their relative costs and efficiencies.

Response Time. Perhaps the most significant operational issue in network planning is that of response time. Normally, one would expect that material which must be obtained from a remote location, through a network, would be less readily accessible than if it is available at the local library. To explore the significance of this issue, a number of simulation models have been developed. These models are traditional tools in operations research for exploring the

[53]Meise, Norman R., *Conceptual Design of an Automated National Library System.* Metuchen, N.J.: Scarecrow Press, 1969.

consequences of decisions in exceedingly complex situations. In them, different aspects of a situation are described by equations, which are interrelated with each other. The computer can then carry out the calculations to show the effects of different conditions on the situation or to show changes in the situation over time.

One such simulation was developed by HRB-Singer, Inc., to represent the response time from an information retrieval system.[54] The equations define the relations among different types of services, time schedules, work loads, and facilities. The simulation then generates requests for different types of services and shows what the effective response time of the system will be.

User Response. The Institute of Library Research has designed another simulation model, which includes consideration of the users' needs for response times from an operating network.[55] The model characterizes the users of a library network in terms of four factors: (1) their sources of information services (both within the library network and external to it); (2) their information requirements, in terms of services needed, subject areas of interest and, most important, the response time needed; (3) their expectations of quality and time of service from the library; and (4) the effects on them of both adequate and inadequate response time from the library. It is the last factor that represents the basic focus of the simulation. It assumes that if the user is disappointed, he will be less likely to use the library than he was before; if he is satisfied, he will be more likely to use it. The general structure of the model is presented in Figure 3.7.

The value of all these models is in their use as a means of exploring the alternative network designs in terms of their effects on cost, performance, or user satisfaction. As such, they do not serve as a substitute for judgment but as a support to it.

Models of Technical and Readers' Services

Probably the main burden of day-to-day library decision making is represented by the management of the tasks in technical service and readers' service.[56] The rules and priorities for selection of material and for scheduling of work loads in technical processing require the continued attention of library management. Yet, review of the library literature shows little, if any, attention

[54]Blunt, C. R., et al., *An Information Retrieval System Model.* State College, Pa.: HRB Singer, Inc., 1965.

[55]Hayes, Robert M., and Kevin D. Reilly, *The Effect of Response Time Upon the Utilization of an Information Retrieval System,* ORSA Annual Meeting, June 1, 1967.

[56] Dougherty, Richard M., and F. J. Heinritz, *Scientific Management of Library Operations.* New York: Scarecrow Press, 1966.

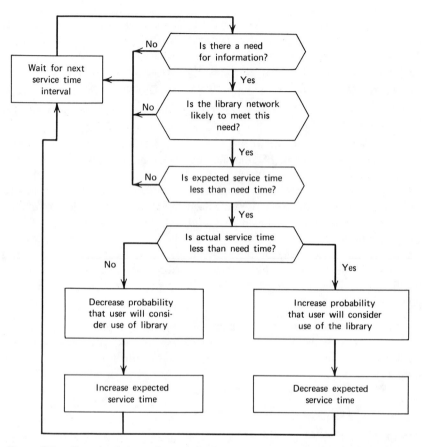

Figure 3.7 Gross level chart of user behavior subsystem model. The category of user (for example, subject area) is ascertained after each decision point in the model so that a complete breakdown of the number of needs, considerations, requests, and satisfied requests is obtained.

to the development of quantitative models to aid the librarian in the choices to be made. There are a few time and motion studies, a few costing studies, and several systems and procedures studies.[57-61] These help in the more or less procedural decisions, but not in the more substantive ones. One study, still under way, has explored quantitative criteria for selection.[62] The work at Chicago (under Swanson),[63] MIT (at Project INTREX),[64] and UC Berkeley (under Maron)[65] may eventually provide a quantitative basis for decision about cataloging data, entries, and filing sequence.

Similarly, although direct service to the reader constitutes at least the primary, if not the sole, purpose of most libraries, there has been little attention paid in library literature to quantitative criteria for choice among services, for assignment of priorities, or for scheduling of service operations. For example, what criteria would be meaningful in establishing a new branch library in a public library system? Or in instituting a new "current awareness" service? Or in establishing a "business reference center?"

These areas for scientific management in libraries, of course, represent the main focus of concern for this book. The methodology that is of particular importance is "library systems analysis."

LIBRARY SYSTEMS ANALYSIS

In subsequent chapters, we shall review the requirements for management of data processing development in libraries. In doing so, "library systems analysis" will be continually referred to as the technical methodology in aid of

[57] Pierce, W. O'D., *Work Measurement in Public Libraries,* Social Science Research Council, 1949.

[58] "Time and Cost Studies—a Bibliography," *Special Libraries,* (December 1964), 690-693.

[59] Voos, H., *Standard Times for Certain Clerical Activities in Technical Processing,* Ph.D. thesis, Rutgers University, 1965 (available through University Microfilms).

[60] Woodruff, Elaine, "Work Measurement Applied to Libraries," *Special Libraries,* **48** (April 1957), 139-144.

[61] *Manual for Time and Motion Studies,* Denver University Libraries, 1960.

[62] *Study of the Decision-Making Procedures for the Acquisition of Science Library Materials and the Relation of these Procedures to the Requirements of College and University Library Personnel,* ALA, 1968.

[63] Swanson, Donald R., "Dialogues with a Catalog." *Library Quarterly,* **34,** January 1964, 113-125.

[64] *Project INTREX. Semi-Annual Activity Reports* (March 15 and September 15) 1966-present.

[65] Maron, M. E., and Ralph M. Shoffner, *The Study of Context.* Berkeley: Institute of Library Research, University of California, January 1969.

management. Who is the systems analyst?[66],[67] What is his role in data processing development and implementation? What is his relationship to the library? What are the tools and techniques which he uses?

Overview

An image has been built around the concept of "systems analysis," which implies an unprecedented ability to resolve problems.[68],[69] Thus the "systems approach" is invoked as the answer to every major issue. The facts are, of course, that systems analysis is simply an approach to problems and a body of techniques to aid in their solution. As an approach, it follows the long history of scientific management theory; as a body of techniques, it draws on mathematics, operations research, and the use of the computer. As the most recent manifestation of scientific management, systems analysis reveals one thing, at least: each generation struggles with the task of discovering new principles that continually turn out to be the old ones. But the problems change and become more complex; consequently, even though the principles we rediscover may have been known, the difficulties in applying them require the use of even more powerful techniques. Systems analysis is merely the name we give, at the moment, to the most recent rediscovery of principles.

Library systems analysis is therefore neither new, revolutionary, nor a panacea. It is simply the latest version of the application of the scientific method to library problems. However, there are features of library systems analysis that particularly characterize it—its use of "cost-effectiveness" as the ultimate criterion for evaluation of library operation,[70] its view of the library in the context of the larger situation within which it occurs, and its attitude of question toward the very definition of the "library problem."

Steps of Systems Analysis.   The systems approach to library problems can be summarized in the following, simple set of steps.[71]

1. *Define* the library problem, including its scope, the environment within

[66] Minder, T. L., "Library Systems Analyst: A Job Description," *College and Research Libraries,* 27 (July 1966), 271-276.

[67] Simms, Daniel M., "What is a Systems Analyst?" *Special Libraries,* 59 (November 1968), 718-721.

[68] Bellomy, Fred L., "The Systems Approach Solves Library Problems," *ALA Bulletin,* 62 (October 1968), 1121-1125.

[69] Burkhalter, Barton R., *Case Studies in Systems Analysis in a University Library.* Metuchen, N.J.: Scarecrow Press, 1968.

[70] Meier, R. L., "Efficiency Criteria for the Operation of Large Libraries," *Library Quarterly,* 21, 215-234.

[71] Taylor, Robert, and Caroline E. Hieber, *Manual for the Analysis of Library Systems.* Bethlehem, Pa.: Lehigh University, 1965.

which it occurs, and the constraints on solutions to it. It is here that the attitude of questioning arises, since the library system analyst is continually asking whether the purposes defined for the library truly represent the requirements. Perhaps more than any other methodology of analysis, systems analysis adopts a teleological view. Even though the systems analyst may accept a definition of purpose as given, these is still an attitude of question. In part, this is a direct result of the recognition that any library exists as a component in a much larger system whose total purposes might be better met otherwise.

2. *Analyze* the library's operations and, in doing so, describe them in detail, showing the relationships among the parts. It is here that the body of technique is used. The systems study, the analysis of statistics and forms, and the drawing of flow charts, for example, provide the formalized tools to aid in this step.

3. *Synthesize* alternate solutions. This is the really creative part of "systems analysis" and perhaps the part around which the image has been built. Sometimes a solution is found by viewing the library as simply a part of a larger system, sometimes by a very simple change in the character of the operation. This is the creative side of the process, although we try to develop formalized tools to aid it.

4. *Evaluate* the alternatives according to defined criteria. It is here that the usage of "cost/effectiveness" has become characteristic of systems analysis in general. Although implicit in all cost-accounting systems, it has been made explicit only in the most recent applications of systems analysis. It is now the standard criterion in the Department of Defense, the Bureau of the Budget, and an increasing number of governmental agencies and industrial concerns. Even though issue may be taken with its applicability to essentially nonquantifiable tasks, it is likely to be the criterion in library system analysis as well.

5. *Iterate* these steps to increase the detail and to modify the results if they do not adequately solve the problem.

Definition of a System

For answers to the basic question—"What is a system?"—there are well-established definitions of both a structural and a functional nature. Perhaps the most general picture is portrayed by Figure 3.8. It shows the meaning that each of the typical system components has in the context of a library system.[72]

[72] Borko, Harold, "Design of Information Systems and Services," in *Annual Review of Information Science and Technology,* Vol. 2, edited by Carlos A. Cuadra. New York: Wiley, 1967, pp. 35-61.

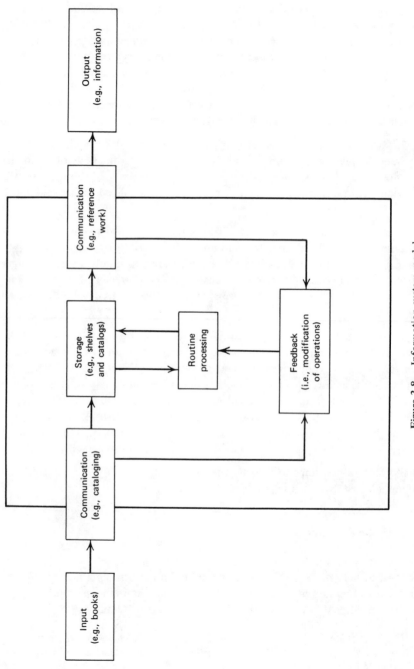

Figure 3.8 Information system model.

Types of Systems. Within this general framework, several types of systems can be distinguished, primarily in terms of the particular components that represent the problem in a given situation. For example, a communication system is a specialized instance of an information system in which the critical problems are involved with the communication components in the system— control of error in the presence of "noise," and maximization of the amount of data transmitted. Also a storage and retrieval system might be considered as a system in which the critical problems relate to the organization of a storage file for maximum effectiveness. A third special case is the servosystem—an information system whose problems are due to dynamic effects, particularly with respect to stability, which arise from the feedback time cycle compared with time cycles in the remainder of the system. Finally, although it is not usual to do so, one could define a class of "processing systems" in which the problems of principal concern relate to the routine logical processes in operation of the system; presumably, most systems for engineering computation and business data processing (such as inventory control, billing, and accounting) fall into this class.

Scope of System. In another (more important) sense, an information system, even a specialized one, involves all aspects. It epitomizes the concept of systems analysis. Specifically, the decomposition of a system into component parts (as exemplified in Figure 3.8) is the result of an analytical process. Each component can now similarly be treated as a system, with its own input and output as determined by the other components. As such, it can be analyzed into exactly the same kinds of components as the original system—communication, storage, processing, and feedback. Reversing this view, it is evident that any system can itself be considered as a component in a larger system. One of the significant problems in system design, and one of the difficulties in defining the concept of information systems itself, is therefore the determination of its scope. In fact, the psychological bent of the system designer is to increase that scope continually, to consider larger and larger contexts, and to reach for a "total system." It is also evident that valid system design requires a precise definition of the scope of the system and cannot tolerate grasping of ever-larger fields to conquer.

Defining the Scope of the Library System

Therefore, before a system can be studied, its scope must be defined. The way a person thinks of a system depends on the individual perspective from which he views his world. A circulation desk attendant might define a library system as the set of routines he uses for transporting library materials back and forth between library patrons and the stacks. The librarian will probably define the library system as including all of the things necessary for carrying out the policies established by his library's governing body. A library patron might include all of the communication channels through which he obtains information—both the library and machines for searching large data bases. In other words, every system has a place in the hierarchy of systems. What one man defines as a system may be a subsystem to another man.

What this means for library systems analysis is that all aspects of the library's operation must be considered, as well as some aspects of the operations of organizations outside the library which interface with it. The source of inputs and the destination of outputs from the library system must be traced far enough to determine their actual impact on the library operations.

Analyzing the Library's Operations

A library systems study then proceeds by assembling all available documentation covering the existing operations of the library. These include: samples of forms, reports, and publications; descriptions of files, equipment, physical plant; copies of written procedures, policy statements, organization charts, position descriptions, externally imposed regulations, and existing system descriptions.

These materials are then organized, and significant missing documentation is identified. It is almost always necessary to bring much of the existing documentation up to date, and it is usually desirable to prepare documentation covering these areas that previously have not been documented (for instance, position descriptions prepared years ago may be out of date). As documentation is assembled and organized, some omissions will become obvious. It is probable that a large number of undocumented policies will be in effect, and it is likely that many policies thought to be generally understood will be widely misinterpreted by personnel. Getting the generally understood policies into a written form will, in itself, contribute to a more smoothly running and effective library operation. Documenting the existing library service policies will permit the need for the various service activities to be assessed. With this documentation assembled, the detailed description of operations can be produced. Techniques of system description are discussed in Chapter 6.

However, the primary purpose of this phase of the systems analysis is the identification of inputs, constraints, and outputs for each component of the system, together with some measure of their actual importance. It therefore is clear that the analysis cannot be concerned exclusively with the existing system's operations. Forms and work flow are traced through the system as a means of determining the real requirements.

Designing Alternate Solutions

The results usually imply a need for a new design or for significant changes to the existing design. The justifications for initiating such changes involve improved effectiveness of the organization's performance and/or a reduction in costs, the primary objective of a systems program being the reduction of the cost/effectiveness ratio.

Evaluation

Early in the formulation of system specifications, a number of trade-off studies should be made. What are the advantages and disadvantages of on-line and batch-mode processing of data at various points in the system? What equipment is available, and what are the good and bad features of each? What are the different ways that data can be organized in machine files, and what are the strengths and weaknesses of each file structure? Where does a man best fit into the system, and where should machines be used?

Equipment vendors are always anxious to propose alternatives using their equipment. Recognizing that a vendor has a solution for which he is seeking a problem instead of the converse, they can provide valuable assistance. Where the dollar volume warrants it, equipment manufacturers will prepare detailed proposals for the application of their equipment in a library to solve a set of specified problems. However, their proposals should be treated with caution, preferably as input to the design work of the library's system staff.

Once the preliminary system specifications have been drafted, it will be possible to prepare an estimate of implementation and operating costs for the new system for comparison with the cost of the present system, as estimated during the study of it. If the costs of the new system (including amortization of the one-time-only implementation costs) are estimated to be less than those of the old system, the decision to proceed with the development of a new system is easily justified. However, usually, the cost of the new system exceeds that of the old system, and its development must be justified on the basis of a more effective operation, including the provision of new services not previously provided.

The information needs throughout the system and the required system outputs will have been determined during the systems analysis. Just how these needs are to be met will require a great deal of work. Certainly, it would be possible to design some portion of the system to meet a limited number of the needs and objectives, but the procedures developed probably would not be compatible with other procedures developed later on. Thus, it is really better to outline the entire system and to show, in a preliminary fashion, how the various parts fit together (for example, converting a file to a machine readable form could significantly alter the procedures of many secondary users of the file). In other words, the total system concept should be outlined before the detailed specification of a specific part of it is undertaken.

In the design of a total system, two significant external factors should be taken into consideration. First, the library receives many essential inputs from outside agencies—book publishers, patrons, national library systems, and library funding agencies. The library systems planner must take them into account to ensure compatibility of any new library systems with those of such external agencies. For example, the Library of Congress has begun to provide machine readable bibliographic data; this has profound implications for the new library system design. Second, library systems development is expensive, and yet certain problems are common to all libraries. Consideration should be given to the possibility of adapting systems developed by other libraries. When only a small number of compromises are required for the adaptation of a relatively complex system design, this approach can have enormous economic advantages.

Suggested Readings

Among the references in this chapter, there are several books and articles that are especially valuable, either historically or because of the quality of their content:

Brandeis, Louis D., "Economies through Scientific Management," *Evidence taken by the Interstate Commerce Commission in the Matter of Proposed Advances in Freight Rates by Carriers, August to December 1910,* V. 8, pp. 4756-4803.

This is a fascinating bit of history! Brandeis presented a "Brief on Behalf of the Traffic Committee of Commercial Organizations of the Atlantic Seaboard." He brought together all of the individuals—Taylor, Gantt, Gilbreth, etc.—who created the field of scientific management. Their testimony presents a clear and specific description of what could be done to improve efficiency of operation.

Bursk, Edward C., and John F. Chapman, *New Decision-Making Tools for Managers,* Harvard, 1962.

A reasonably nontechnical introduction to operations research and project management, with specific examples from business. It is a collection of articles published in *Harvard Business Review.*

Churchman, C. W., R. L. Ackoff, and E. L. Arnow, *Introduction to Operations Research.* New York: Wiley, 1957. Probably the best textbook and

Probably the best textbook and technical introduction to operations research.

Dougherty, Richard M., and Fred J. Heinritz, *Scientific Management of Library Operations.* New York: Scarecrow Press, 1966.

This is an excellent, even though mis-titled, handbook of methods and tools for methods analysis in the library, including management study, flow charting, forms design, sampling, and aids for computation. They are illustrated by a cost study of a circulation system.

Forrester, Jay W., *Industrial Dynamics.* Cambridge, Mass.: MIT Press.

A description of the use of mathematical models, which utilize data available from integrated management information systems, for planning and control in industrial corporations.

Fussler, Herman H., and Julian L. Simon, *The Use of Books in Large Research Libraries.* Chicago, Illinois: University of Chicago, 1961.

A model study of the application of techniques of scientific management to libraries, this report analyzes statistics of use in order to develop criteria for selection of books from a collection to be relocated from on-campus storage to remote storage.

Heyel, Carl, *The Encyclopedia of Management.* New York: Reinhold, 1963.

Of particular interest are the articles in Sections I (Basic Management Concepts), II (Pioneers in Management), VII (Decision-Making Processes and the New Management Sciences), X (Project Management), XII (Industrial Engineering), XVII (Accounting and Control), XIX (Systems and Procedures), and XX (Automatic Data Processing).

Hitch, Charles, and Roland McKean, *Economics of Defense in a Nuclear Age,* Harvard, 1960.

An extremely important description of the application of cost/benefit criteria to the handling of major policy issues. Although its special emphasis is on nuclear defense, the technique has since been extended to other policy areas.

Rider, Fremont, *The Scholar and the Future of the Research Library.* New York: Hadham, 1944.

One of the most important descriptions of the application of scientific management to a basic issue in both strategic and operational library planning—how to handle the exponential growth in library collections.

Ridenour, L., Ralph R. Shaw, and A. G. Hill, *Bibliography in an Age of Science,* Illinois, 1951.

Almost a companion work to Rider's, this discussed the same phenomenon, exponential growth in library collections, as exemplified in science and technology.

Taylor, Frederick W., *Principles and Methods of Scientific Management.* New York: Harper, 1911.

This book provides the first definitive description of the concepts and techniques used in scientific management. It also displays an intellectual arrogance, in its belief that workmen are incapable of functioning without the guidance of a scientifically trained elite, that has been a continuing subsurface attitude of enthusiasts for "scientific management."

von Neuman, John, and Oskar Morgenstern, *A Theory of Games and Economic Behavior,* Princeton, 1947.

Perhaps the most important and influential book in operations research. It provided the mathematical formalization of decision-making in a competitive environment, in terms of probabilistic strategies, based on "pay-offs" to be expected from each of a combination of alternatives. It requires a high degree of mathematical sophistication to understand it fully, but parts of it are quite readable even without knowledge of mathematics.

Chapter 4

COST ACCOUNTING IN LIBRARIES

Very few libraries have a sufficiently detailed picture of costs for their present operations to support scientific management. This lack of a cost picture has been long recognized in the historical and continuing discussion of the need for adequate cost accounting in library operations.[1-4] In fact, the need relates not so much to the issue of data processing as to the issue of good library management. Basically, good cost data is a prerequisite for the development and support of adequate budgets, and for the evaluation of alternative services and procedures, whether mechanized or not.

For these reasons it is essential to consider the introduction into the library of an adequate, detailed, cost accounting system. Although we are viewing the matter in the context of mechanization, it is important to reiterate that it has meaning to the library independent of this context.

DEFINITIONS

Before discussing the issues in cost accounting, let us make some important distinctions so that cost accounting is viewed in the proper perspective.

[1] Adams, Charles, J., "Statistical Chaos: Technical Services in Public Libraries," *Library Journal,* **91** (9) (May 1, 1966), 2278-2280.
[2] Parker, Ralph H., "Aspects of the Financial Administration of Libraries," *Library Trends,* April 1963.
[3] Rider, Fremont, "Library Cost Accounting," *Library Quarterly*, **6** (1936), 331-381.
[4] Brutcher, Constance, et al., "Cost Accounting for the Library," *Library Resources and Technical Services,* **8** (Fall 1964), 413-431.

1. *The distinction between cost accounting and methods analysis.* Many of the articles written about the measurement of costs in library operation have focused on detailed work measurement as part of a general methods analysis approach.[5,6] It is, therefore, important to recognize that a cost accounting system is basically different from methods analysis, although there is an important role for each. Specifically, in methods analysis (and work measurement), the intent is to evaluate quite detailed differences between ways of executing specific operations. In contrast, cost accounting is a management tool for control of an entire organization.[7] As a result, the level of detail required for work measurement is considerably finer than that involved in a cost accounting system.

2. *Cost accounting versus ad hoc cost studies.* Again, most of the articles written concerning library costs have reported one-time studies. In contrast to them, the value of the cost accounting system lies precisely in the continuing picture that it provides. We must emphasize that a cost accounting system is a tool for management of the library. It is valuable not only in providing a continuing picture of costs but also in the highlighting of *changes* in costs, in the single library, over time.

3. *Cost accounting versus library statistics.* Libraries have a tradition of maintaining various statistics—the number of books acquired, the number of titles cataloged, the number of volumes circulated, and the number of reference questions handled. But there is a great difference between statistics and cost accounting. In a sense, statistics provide only one side of the picture; they fail to describe what it costs to acquire a book, to catalog a title, to circulate a volume, or to answer reference questions.

4. *Cost accounting versus bookkeeping.* It might be argued that any library must maintain cost data in order to control its budget.[8,9] The problem, however, is that only rarely are the general bookkeeping accounts adequate for the evaluation of costs. Again, budget control presents only part of the picture, since it separates costs from the statistics of performance. However, it is clear

[5] Niteck, A., et al, "Cost Accounting Forms (Guides to aid librarians to determine the unit cost of technical services of a library)," *Michigan Librarian,* **29** (December 1963), 19-21.

[6] Pierce, Watson O'D, *Work Measurement in Public Libraries.* New York: Social Science Research Council, 1949.

[7] Horngren, Charles T., *Cost Accounting: A Managerial Emphasis.* Englewood Cliffs, N.J.: Prentice-Hall, 1962.

[8] Price, Paxton P., "Budgeting and Budget Control in Public Libraries," *Library trends,* XI (April 1963), 402-412.

[9] Price, Paxton P., "Financial Administration" *in Local Public Library Administration,* edited by Roberta Bowler, Chicago: International City Managers' Association, 1964, pp. 114-147.

that most libraries, in fact, now acquire almost all of the data—in statistics and in budget control—required for a cost accounting system. The cost accounting system, by tying together the statistics with costs, provides the total picture. The necessity is to do this in detail sufficient for the purposes of management control, but not in such detail as to impose an unbearable burden.

In summary, a cost accounting system is continuing rather than intermittent; it is concerned with the total library and not with some detailed aspect of it; and it ties together costs with effectiveness rather than being concerned with simply one or the other. Cost accounting is a management tool of primary value to the librarian in his day-to-day control of his own library. It is only of incidental value in comparisons of one library to another. The importance to good management is illustrated by the listing (Figure 4.1) of typical management reports that would be the continuing product of a good cost accounting system.

It must be recognized, however, that a cost accounting system for library operation does pose some significant problems. It is relatively easy to accumulate statistics or to control budgets; it requires a recording system to tie the two together. As a result, a cost accounting system represents a cost in itself. Its costs must be weighed against values received.

Figure 4.1   Management and Cost Accounting Reports

Management Reports

1. Direct cost total by account and by unit of work, for each account.
2. Overhead cost, by category, and as a percentage of both direct salary and total direct cost.
3. Total cost—direct and indirect, by administrative unit.
4. Each of these by time, by time period.
5. Time delays and backlogs, by department and by type of material.

Cost Accounting Reports

1. Weekly Transaction Listing
2. Weekly Labor Report
3. Weekly Inventory Usage Report
4. Weekly Cost Distribution Report
5. Cost Center Cost by Account Report
6. Cost Center Product Allocation Report
7. Fringe Calculation Report
8. Work-In-Progress Count Report
9. Work-In-Progress Calculation Report
10. Work-In-Progress Ledger Report
11. Work-In-Progress Summary Report
12. Cost Center Analytical Report
13. Cost Center Rate Report

Furthermore, the library represents a kind of organization for which accounting practice has developed few guidelines. First, the "product" of the library is a set of services, based on continuing investment in acquiring and cataloging a collection of information (the books and journals). There are still no standards for capitalizing such investment or for determining how overhead should be calculated. Second, most libraries are not "profit-making" institutions. Yet, most accounting practice is oriented to the need to determine the *profitability* of individual products of an organization. It is only recently that the value of cost-accounting data has been considered as part of the decision processes in *allocation of resources*. It is the latter, however, which is usually of importance in the library.

A fact that, in the past, has complicated the problem in introducing a cost accounting system in libraries has been the general lack of availability of the mechanized equipment for processing the comparatively large volume of recorded data involved. For many libraries this may still represent a significant barrier, but as the larger libraries gradually introduce mechanical procedures for various clerical operations, and as the smaller libraries combine into library systems, these difficulties should become relatively minor. In fact, the principle should be adopted that whenever a program for mechanization is initiated, a parallel system for cost accounting should be considered as well.

Perhaps the most significant barrier to the introduction of a cost accounting system in the library is the extent to which it will find acceptance by the library staff itself. Professionals rightly are very reluctant to have their performance, in any way, "measured." Actually, intellectual work is, by its nature, difficult (if not impossible) to measure and, where measurement is attempted, all too frequently it causes a misunderstanding of what was actually accomplished. Library work, in particular, involves such an intermixture of intellectual with clerical processes that measurement of them is almost certain to create many difficulties. Thus, even if we recognize the value of a cost accounting system to library administration, we must be aware of its effect on the professional staff. Basically, the only answer to this problem lies in the extent to which the system for recording, processing, and reporting is simple and includes a means for recognizing the intellectual content of library work. But it is useful to provide the staff with advance explanation of the value of a cost accounting system to both the organization and the individual, with emphasis on the fact that cost data is used to aid in making valid judgments not to replace them.

GENERAL PRINCIPLES OF COST ACCOUNTING

A cost accounting system is a procedure for recording operations, times, and costs for various parts of an organization, together with a procedure for processing, reporting on, and acting upon the resulting data. It must include provision for representing all sources of costs, including the salaries of staff and administrative personnel, capital investment, and all categories of expense. It must include provision for the measurement of work performed in terms of both quantity and, for library operations, quality and complexity. It must include provision for the recording of the time required to handle given operations.

In the recording of this data, a distinction is usually made between "process costing," where the data is related to a specific process, and "job costing" where the data is related to a specific item being processed. Let us explain the basis of the distinction. In the acquisition of a single book, we see a succession of processes—ordering, receiving, cataloging, mechanical preparation, and shelving.[10] If we are concerned only with the issue of costs for these individual processes, it would be sufficient to have a cost accounting system that simply recorded data about each of them. But if we wish to relate costs to different types, forms or kinds of material, we need the more detailed job costing system that ties costs to the specific item being processed as well. The point is that job costing involves the same processes that process costing would account for, but the detail will be much greater. Figure 4.2 is an approximate classification for operations in the library into those for which process costing seems appropriate and those for which job costing may be desired. It further summarizes some of the distinguishing characteristics of the two.

No matter what form of recording and amount of detail is utilized, there are always certain costs that cannot reasonably be assigned directly to a process or to a job. Administration, for example, is required for all operations in the library, and its costs cannot rationally be ascribed specifically, say, to the cataloging of a particular book. The distinction, therefore, is made between these costs that can be related to a specific process or job (called direct costs) and the costs that cannot be (called indirect costs or overhead). The importance of this distinction arises when we ask the question, for example, "What does it cost to catalog a book?" Clearly the costs of administering the library, of payroll accounting, of rent, and of utilities must, in some sense, be considered as part of the costs of cataloging a book. The issue is: How should these indirect costs be allocated to particular processes or jobs? The variety of possibilities for such allocation is great, but the usual basis is to allocate the indirect costs proportionally to the direct ones. However, some specific issues must be resolved: (1) Should the storage space for the collection be regarded as an overhead expense, or should it be included in the allocation to cataloging or to reader services for which the collection seems more directly related? (2) In the allocation of administrative expenses, should the costs of the book be regarded

----

[10] Franklin, Robert D., "Book Acquisition Costs," *Library Journal*, 90 (April 1, 1965), 1512-1513.

Figure 4.2   Examples of types of operations.

Examples

Process-Type Operation	Job-Type Operation
Selection	Unique orders
Ordering	Blanket orders
	Standing orders
	Approval orders
Receiving	
Fund accounting	
Catalog production	Monograph cataloging
	Serial cataloging
	Document cataloging
	Microform cataloging
	Magnetic tape cataloging
Circulation control	
Ready reference	
	Bibliographical work
	Catalog reference
	Information specialty service

CHARACTERISTICS

Process Costing	Job Costing
1. Less effort	1. More detailed
2. Periodic recording rather than continual	2. Specific costs continually available
3. Unit averages more easily obtained	3. Clarifies differences among materials or service groups
4. Responsibility for costs more clearly defined	
5. Overhead allocation is simpler	

as part of the direct costs of acquisition or should the allocation of administrative costs be based solely on the salaries of the personnel involved? We raise these issues, here, solely to illustrate some of the detailed problems that must be resolved in the introduction of a cost accounting system. The particular decision made as to the basis for allocation will reflect the management needs of the library.

A final problem, in the creation of a cost accounting system, concerns the distinction between capital costs, which must in some way be amortized over the useful life of the capital investment, and expense costs which are charged as costs as they are incurred. Let us comment on the significant points. If capital costs are not amortized, they distort the cost picture, since they unduly increase costs at one point in time and decrease them later. To illustrate, if equipment is acquired to aid in the circulation function of the library and if this major capital expense is allocated to the cost of circulation at the time of purchase, the expenses in this department will be unnaturally high; later, if it serves its function properly, the costs of service will be significantly lower. The cost accounting system would completely fail to provide precisely that kind of management information for which it is intended, that is, describing what the effect of this capital investment was on operational costs. If, alternatively, the purchase of this piece of equipment is regarded as a capital investment, with costs amortized over the useful life of equipment and allocated against operating costs on that basis, a truer picture is obtained and the cost accounting system indeed serves its purpose. But the question now is: What constitutes capital investment? Most particularly, it seems that the book collection itself should be treated as a capital investment. The U.S. government curricula A-21 (concerning acceptable overhead accounting practice for universities on government grants and contracts) requires that books be treated as current operating expense (because there is a continuing budget for it). However, there is a huge initial investment represented in the university library's collection, the value of which should be recognized and which should be amortized. Of course, there are significant issues that must be resolved concerning the basis for an amortization schedule and standard depreciation rates, but the principle should be clearly established that the book collection represents the major capital investment in the library.

ISSUES IN OPERATION

The normal operation of a cost accounting system can be conveniently divided into four aspects: (1) operations involved in the actual recording of direct cost data; (2) operations involved in the allocation of overhead to that data and in its distribution to cost accounts; (3) operations involved in the analysis, preparation, printing, and distribution of management reports; and (4) operations involved in revision of the system, particularly toward the end of introducing more specific detail. In the following sections we will discuss each of these categories.

Direct-Cost Recording Operations

The major element of cost and cause of difficulty in acceptance of a cost accounting system lies in the recording of data for operation and jobs.

Figure 4.3   Chart of cost-accounts–direct expenses.

	A	B	C	D	E
Account Code	1 2 3	4 5 6	7 8	9 10	

The following chart should be regarded as tentative and illustrative. Any final list will require a very careful examination of the actual needs for management reporting in the individual library.

A.	*Type of Process*	*Unit of Work*

100.	Acquisition	Title order
	110. Selection	
	120. Ordering	
	130. Fund accounting	
	140. Receiving	
200.	Preparation	Volume
	210. Labeling	
	220. Jacketing	
	230. Book cards and pockets	
	240. Distribution	
	250. Binding	
300.	Cataloging	Title
	310. Descriptive cataloging	
	320. Subject cataloging	
	330. Classification	
	340. Subject authority revision	
	350. Shelf-listing	
400.	Production of catalogs	Entry printed
	410. Key-punching	
	420. Sorting and merging	
	430. Creation of master	
	440. Printing	
500.	Circulation	Volume
600.	Reference	Request
	610. Formulation of request	
	620. Initial searching	
	630. Compilation of answer	
	640. Transmission to request	
700.	Administration and general	

B.	*Level of Complexity*

0.	Simple
5.	Averages
9.	Complex

C.   *Source of Cost*

---

    10.   Salary
        11.   Professional library
        12.   Professional technical
        13.   Clerical

    20.   Expenses

    30.   Capital investment (including book funds)

D.   *Type of Material*

---

    10.   Books
        11.   Fiction
        12.   Nonfiction
        13.   Juvenile

    20.   Serials

    30.   Phonograph records

    40.   Documents

    50.   Microform

    60.   Magnetic tape

E.   *Administrative Unit*

    10.
    20.   Departmental
    30.   or branch
    40.   Library organization

Therefore, it is vital that this recording be made as simple, as uncomplicated, and as easy to perform as possible.

The requisite data that must be recorded are the cost, time, and amount of work performed (in terms of some appropriate units for measurement of work). Usually, cost associated with a process is determined from the salary of the staff or equipment performing it; for most libraries, it is important to identify uniquely each person or piece of equipment, although for certain purposes (such as circulation charging) it is sufficient to identify the type of person. The data concerning time are relatively easy to define, the only real issue being the degree of precision with which it is recorded (usually, in library operations, we might reasonably record time to five minute intervals).

The real difficulty lies in the definition of the categories of processes and of suitable units for measurement of the work performed in each of them. In accounting terms, this is represented by a "chart of accounts." A representative chart for a typical library is shown in Figure 4.3. As this chart of accounts shows, the processes being measured can be identified at as many levels of detail as may be appropriate to management needs at the moment. Presumably, one would start a system at a relative gross level (even so gross as "ordering," "cataloging," "circulation," and "reference") and then refine the detail when necessary or desirable.

As should be evident from the chart of accounts (Figure 4.3), several considerations are relevent in the definition of process accounts. In addition to the process itself, the type of material being processed, the level of complexity, special features (such as language), the department, and required response times all become significant in the exact specifications of a process account.

Since qualitative judgment is so important in library work, the chart of accounts pays particular attention to the issue of complexity. Although we recognize that complexity is difficult (if not impossible) to define, it is essential to provide some mechanism for the recognition of it. The chart of accounts does so by providing a relative coarse measure, divided into three categories: simple, typical, and difficult. These could be determined by the type of material, the language, or other factors relating to the difficulty in the task. (Of course, they need not be applicable to all classes of operation.)

As mentioned previously, a distinction is usually made between "process-

Process-cost reporting form.

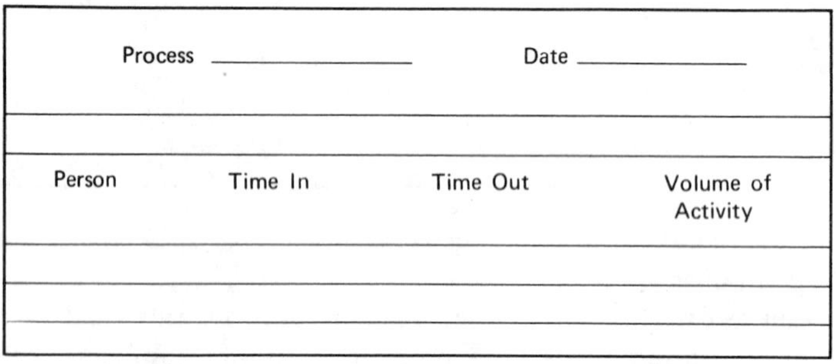

(a)

Process-cost punched card.

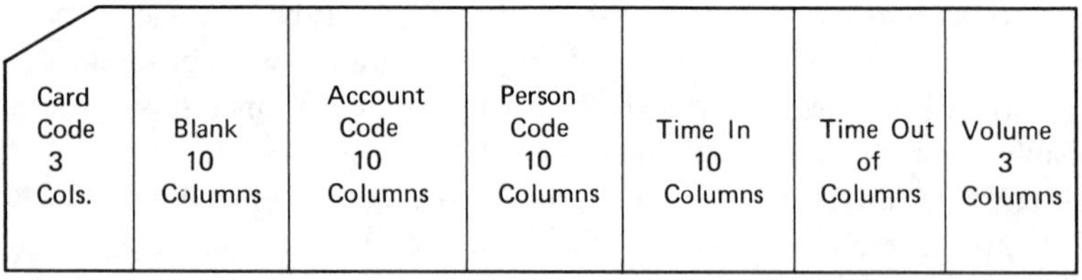

(b)

Figure 4.4   (a) Process-cost reporting form. (b) Process-cost punched card.

type" operations and "job-type" operations. Figure 4.4 shows a typical form for the recording of cost accounting data for a normal process-type operation. There would be a separate form for each such process, in which the recording on each line identifies the person (or machine) performing that operation, the starting time and ending time for each, and the volume of the activity handled at each of the three levels of complexity. Usually, such a form will be placed at a charge-out desk, and the clerk will then simply record his identity, starting and ending times, and tallies of the number of items charged out in the defined categories.

Acquisition Number		Vendor		Date of Ordering	
Author					
Title					
	Process Code	Complexity	Person	Time In	Time Out
1	Ordering				
2	Receiving				
3	Cataloging				

(a)

Card Code	Acquisition Number	Account Code	Person Code	Time In	Time Out
3	10	10	10	10	10
Cols.	Columns	Columns	Columns	Columns	Columns

(b)

Figure 4.5   (a) Job-cost reporting form (illustrated by ordering and cataloging) (b) Job-cost punched card.

The recording of data for job-type operations involves a somewhat different form (Figure 4.5). As shown, each line in this form would allow the recording of one in the succession of processes through which the job moves, together with the identification of the persons (or machines) performing the successive jobs and the time taken for the level of complexity of the particular process for the particular job. Generally, this form will be, in some sense, physically attached to the job and will move with it from one process to the next. For example, if a request for information services is received which, from its nature, warrants the establishment of a job for it, a job accounting sheet would be created and would follow the job through the successive steps of (1) definition of request, (2) catalog searching, (3) acquisition of material, (4) analysis of relevant data, and (5) development of report.

Such a form thus serves a variety of purposes:

1.   Issued by person responsible for initiation.
2.   Authorizes the work and provides for a chronological record of the time consumed.
3.   Describes the nature of the job and indicates what should be produced.
4.   Outlines the steps to be taken.
5.   Follows physical work through production.
6.   Controls the accumulation of cost data.
7.   Becomes the source record for cost accounting.
8.   Can provide a permanent record.

In both process and job costing, the form of recording would be manual, on preprinted forms with self-explanatory codes to facilitate both the recording and subsequent key-punching. This raises a basic assumption: if a cost accounting system is to have any real chance of success, the later stages of processing and reporting should be performed with data processing equipment. This implies that the data in the manual recording forms must be transferred to machine language by key-punch operations. Figures 4.4 and 4.5 include typical punched-card formats. For each line entry in the manual recording form, a single punched card will be created.

Allocation of Overhead

Certain categories of data, as we have indicated, cannot be directly attributed to particular processes or jobs. For example, these include administrative expenses, rent and utilities, and certain generally used supplies. Figure 4.6 lists some of the usual kinds of overhead costs. Although the costs from these sources cannot be determined from the forms of recording defined above, they must be included in the later processing. Normally, this is handled by assigning several costs on an a priori basis to specific overhead categories. The salaries of administrative personnel, for example, would be automatically accumulated as an overhead expense without the necessity of a recording operation. Where a staff member may, during some portion of time, be performing direct work, that time will be recorded as part of a process or a job, and the remainder of this salary will be automatically allocated to overhead. Similarly, expense items such as rent, utilities, and supplies will be automatically charged to overhead as they

Figure 4.6   Overhead cost accounts

---

100. Salary related
     110. Benefits
          111. Social Security
          112. Insurance
          113. Etc.
     120. Vacations, leaves, holidays
     130. Nondirect time
     140. Overtime Premium
200. Supervision
300. Rent, utilities, maintenance
400. Supplies
500. Travel
600. Depreciation of collection
700. Depreciation of equipment
800. Legal and other services

---

are incurred. For direct personnel, the time such as sick leave, vacations and holidays, and the like, which cannot be assigned directly to jobs or processes, will be determined by the difference between total salary and that charged directly to jobs or processes.

As a result, the total of all costs of operation—including both those recorded and those automatically allocated—must equal the actual costs of operation as accumulated in the General Account (Figure 4.7). The intent of allocating overhead is then to arrive at a figure for the total costs assignable to each process and/or job in the library. To arrive at these costs, the following sequence of steps are followed.

1. The costs directly associated with each line item recorded in a report form must be determined by multiplying the salary or machine costs by the amount of time spent.

2. These resulting costs are then accumulated to the level of detail appropriate to reporting needs.

3. The overhead costs must then be allocated, proportionate either to the direct salary costs, where this is appropriate, or to the total direct costs where other categories of expenses are significant.

The Effects of Rules for Overhead Allocation. The choice of a rule for the allocation of overhead has some unexpected effects of which the library must be aware—not only in the context of its own internal accounting but in the larger

Figure 4.7 Budget of accounts versus cost accounts.

General Accounts	Cost Accounts
Accounts payable	Direct material
Rent and utilities	Processes
Supplies	Jobs
Materials	Direct labor
Payroll	Processes
Prepaid expenses	Jobs
Insurance	Overhead allocations
Depreciation	Salary related
	Administration
	Indirect expenses
Total cost of service equals	Total cost of service

context of any organization of which it is a part. The usual rule is "allocate overhead in proportion to the amount of costs for direct *labor*." The word "labor" is italicized to emphasize the contrast with total costs. The effect of this rule is to provide positive encouragement to the replacement of labor by other kinds of direct cost and, especially, by mechanization. It also has the effect of penalizing the parts of an organization that do not attempt to use mechanization.

To highlight these effects, consider two departments as an organization: (1) the library, and (2) some other department—each with comparable manpower and costs.

	Department A	Department L	Total
Direct salaries	$30,000	$30,000	$60,000
Other costs	5,000	5,000	10,000
Overhead	30,000	30,000	60,000
Total	$65,000	$65,000	$130,000

Now, suppose that Department A decides to mechanize, replacing personnel with machinery. If the overhead is allocated proportional to direct salaries, the figures might change as follows.

	Department A	Department L	Total
Direct Salaries	$10,000	$30,000	$40,000
Other Costs	40,000	5,000	45,000
Overhead	15,000	45,000	60,000
Total	$65,000	$80,000	$145,000

It appears that the *library* is the cause of the increase in costs! Of course, to some extent, this is an extreme picture, since the overhead total will probably also be reduced, but not usually by a comparable proportion. The lesson is clear: accounting practice is almost designed to favor mechanization, and the library should be distinctly aware of its effects.

Input for Machine Processing

Purpose of the Machine Processable Input. An effective cost accounting system implies more than just recording data on cost forms. Although this might be the initial step in the process, the full system will include procedures for the processing of the data and the preparation of the resulting information generated in report form. In order to process the large volume of data that would be forthcoming from the library network operations, the use of electronic data processing equipment is inescapable. Thus, to provide input for this equipment, the data on the reporting forms must be transferred to machine readable form.

Development of the Input Format. Given the library's job control form, the next stage in the development of the cost accounting system is to provide a medium and format for the translation of data from that report form to machine readable input. In the choice of a medium, it would appear logical to treat each activity performed by the researcher and listed on the reporting form as a unit record, and thus to use punched cards to hold the data, with each punched card acting as a unit record.

Reporting Operations

A cost accounting system is of value only to the extent that reports useful to the library management can be produced from the resultant data. The principle of such management reporting is that it makes evident long-term trends in cost, it highlights exceptional situations, it clarifies effects of changes and unusual situations, it pinpoints problem areas, and generally it allows the library management to maintain control, not only over costs but over the quality of services produced. To these ends, reports of various kinds can be rapidly produced from basic recorded data.

1. "Reports by person," which allow for comparison of productivity, particularly in terms of the "level of complexity" of work done. Admittedly, this is a sensitive issue, but has great importance for good library management.

2. "Reports by process" so that the cost of various parts of library operation are clearly and explicitly known.

3. "Reports by job" or by type of job so that the costs of handling particular types of requests for references or for cataloging particular types of books can be clearly known.

4. "Reports by time period" so that explicit comparisons between time periods can be made and seasonal variations can be exhibited.

Cost or financial reports should be based on the following fundamental qualities and characteristics.

(a)   Reports must fit the organization chart; that is, the report should be addressed to the individual who is responsible for the items covered by it and who, in turn, will be able to control those costs which fall under his jurisdiction.

(b)   Reports must be prompt and timely. Reports issued long after the occurrence of events lose their control value. Prompt issuance of a report requires that cost records be organized so that information is available when needed. Delaying a report until all data is assembled can become a costly matter, since it prevents the executive from taking immediate remedial measures.

(c)   Reports must be issued with regularity. Executives regard the receipt of reports at a definite hour of the day or week as the best means of arranging their plans and operations.

(d)   Reports must give comparative figures, that is, a comparison of actual with budgeted figures or a comparison of predetermined standards with actual results and the isolation of variances. Other reports might compare this week's results with last week's or with the same week of the previous year. The reporting of differences or exceptions is important.

(e)   Reports must be analytical. Merely the development of figures cannot suffice in the complexity of present-day management. If variances indicate good or bad performance, the reasons for the conditions should be stated.

(f)   Reports should, if possible, be stated in physical units. To make cost reports more valuable and useful, an effort should be made to show physical units as well as dollar values.

COST ACCOUNTING AND PROGRAM BUDGETING

Increasingly, governmental and industrial organizations are turning to "program budgeting" as a means of financial planning.[11] The principles of

[11] Young, Helen A., "Performance and Program Budgeting: An Annotated Bibliography," *ALA Bulletin*, 61, pp. 63-67.

program budgeting are quite straightforward. The organization defines a set of "programs" representing the aims and objectives of its management. Usually, there will be some *a priori* estimate of what investment management is willing to make in achieving each of these programs. Each part of the organization must then justify its *administrative* budget by showing how it contributes to each program.

For example, in a university, the library serves students, faculty research, organized research projects, the administration, other libraries, and perhaps local industry. Each of these activities represents a program of service which the university regards as more or less important and to which the library contributes. If a university were to adopt program budgeting, the library would need to demonstrate the extent to which its administrative budget was allocable to each program—faculties, schools, institutes, research projects, and students, for instance. Comparable examples are evident in public libraries (service to children, to the disadvantaged, to industry, and to other libraries), school libraries, or special libraries.

As libraries of all kinds move toward greater service to a broader clientele, program budgeting will become a necessity for the library itself. When it does, an adequate cost accounting system is an absolute necessity. It is the only way to evaluate what each program will cost, in terms of the magnitude of service required. For example, suppose a university decided that service to local industry was a significant program (perhaps represented by a research center). If it is undertaken, the burden on the library represented by information requests from industry is likely to increase a hundredfold. Without cost data on which to project the effects on such an increased burden, the library is virtually helpless in justifying the increase in budget which will really be required.

ILLUSTRATIVE UNIT COSTS

As we have pointed out, it is extremely difficult to find useful cost data in the library literature. What data are available are based on different units of work, different methods of measuring production and costs, and different allocations of overhead. Therefore, to provide at least a starting point for anyone considering use of cost accounting in libraries, we provide, in Figure 4.8, a summary of illustrative unit costs. These have been derived from a careful review of the literature and have been compared with the actual costs in several libraries. We consider them to be realistic, but whether or not they are, at least they can be used to highlight the effects of different methods of measurement and different allocations of overhead. To do so, we have listed these illustrative unit costs in four categories: minimum, basic, standard, and burdened.

Figure 4.8   Illustrative unit costs.

Function	Unit of Work	Nominal Hourly Rate	Minimum	Basic	Standard	Burdened
General and Administrative						
Processing	/employee	$3	$1.50	$2.10	$3.00	$4.00
Acquisition						
Selection	/order	$5	1.20	1.70	2.40	3.30
Ordering	/order	$3	.70	1.00	1.40	1.90
Invoicing	/invoice	$3	.70	1.00	1.40	1.90
Cataloging						
Cataloging	/title	$5	1.80	2.50	3.50	5.00
Creation of master	/title	$3	.25	.35	.50	.70
Printing	/title/catalog	$3	.13	.18	.25	.36
Sorting and Filing	/title/catalog	$2	.13	.18	.26	.36
Reader Service						
Circulation	/volume	$2	.07	.10	.14	.19
Shelving	/volume	$2	.05	.07	.10	.14
Serials						
Receiving	/serial/month	$2	.10	.14	.20	.28
Recording	/serial/month	$2	.10	.14	.20	.28
Physical Handling						
Receiving	/volume	$2	.03	.04	.06	.08
Labeling, etc.	/volume	$2	.12	.18	.24	.32

Minimum Unit Costs

These represent the costs one would expect to find in a time and motion study (averaged over a number of units of work), based on the nominal hourly rate indicated for the salary or wages of personnel assigned to the function. They do not represent peak rates of work, but rather typical rates for actually handling a single unit. The figures given are representative of several reported in time and motion studies and are similar to those discussed in Chapters 14 through 18.

Basic Unit Costs

These represent the costs one would expect to find as the "direct costs" (per unit of work) reported by a cost accounting system. They are therefore the average cost per unit of work including nonproductive time (such as coffee breaks), inefficiencies, and variations in workload.

Standard Unit Costs

These represent the costs for the same rates of production as the basic unit costs but include recognition of all "salary-related benefits," such as vacations, holidays, sick leave, unallocated time, severance pay, overtime premium, insurance, and social security.

Burdened Unit Costs

These represent the actual costs of providing the services of the library, including supervision, operational expenses (space, utilities, maintenance), and amortization of capital investments.

Suggested Reading

There are very few discussions of cost accounting in the library literature which provide more than a superficial or incomplete picture. It is therefore suggested that one or another basic text in "managerial accounting" be read in order to establish a proper framework within which to view the comments in this chapter:

Horngren, Charles T., *Cost Accounting: A Managerial Emphasis.* Englewood Cliffs, N.J.: Prentice-Hall, 1962.

Part Two   Management of Library Data Processing

Chapter 5

MANAGEMENT PLANNING

A mechanization program in a library is a major undertaking, requiring a commitment of resources and management talent. Management of such a program has been evolving as much through trial and error as through design. This chapter outlines some of the management considerations that should be recognized and planned for. Subsequent chapters discuss specific issues in more detail.

The fundamental operations that constitute the management cycle are diagrammed in Figure 5.1. Although phrased variously by different writers, they usually include (1) determination of objectives, (2) preparation of plans for achieving the objectives, including the development of cost and time schedules, (3) authorization and control of the required work, (4) monitoring and evaluation of progress toward the objectives, (5) identification of alternate corrective action as problems develop, and (6) repetition.

1. Perhaps most important, in this framework, is the fact that library management has the responsibility to establish the objectives to be achieved by the mechanization program, including the definition of priorities. In doing this, the "systems analysis staff" may well provide a picture of present operations and future possibilities, but the ultimate decision among the alternatives must rest with management.

2. The costs involved in mechanization are so great that budgetary allocations for each stage of development and implementation must be carefully planned. Development, no matter how carefully controlled, is very likely to be delayed at a number of points. One cause, having little to do with technical problems, arises from unforeseen delays in funding. This imposes a real and important constraint on the planning process, since the development plan itself

107

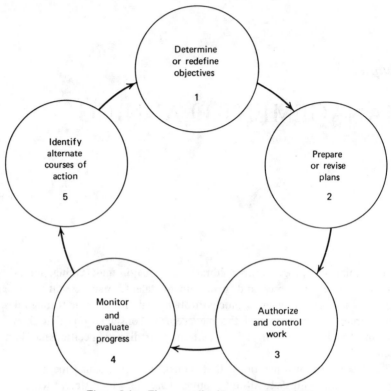

Figure 5.1   The generalized managment cycle.

must be designed to provide for intermediate systems whose operations can be continued even if later systems must be deferred for an indefinite time.

3.   The time schedule for development must be defined by library management. Again, the systems analysis staff can provide the technical support by defining likely series of events in time, but so many issues must be reconciled—many of them essentially non-technical in character—that the library management must ultimately determine when things are to be done.

4.   The management of the actual development and implementation itself rests with library administration. Unfortunately, it is a kind of management relatively unfamiliar to the librarian. The work is highly technical in character, and management of it requires a real appreciation of the technical issues involved. Furthermore, it is usually a one-time "project," rather than an on-going "operation" such as the library itself represents. As a result, the problems are very different from those normally encountered in library administration, and consequently the techniques outlined in this chapter may be relatively unfamiliar.

5. The development of a system requires many compromises among conflicting requirements and capabilities. Great care is required to avoid an overcommitment to the demands of one or another specialized interest—to those who regard the aim as "effective utilization of equipment," to those whose concern is with "cost/effectiveness," to those concerned with day-to-day operations, and to those with some ideal of perfection. Conflicts among these interests can be exemplified by the issue of filing rules. Do we use simple, alphabetical sorting, which makes for efficient machine utilization, or cataloging code that better fits the requirements of the staff and users? Where the conflicts cannot be resolved on technical grounds, library management must weigh the issues involved and arrive at a judicial decision.

6. A mechanized system will introduce significant changes in the relationships among the library, its staff, and its readers. The library management must therefore plan a program of education for the staff and public relations with the readers to ensure an understanding of the effects of mechanization and acceptance of them.

This chapter will introduce these issues of management planning—objectives, time schedule, and budget; project management; training and public relations.

Before doing this, however, it is important to establish the context within which management decisions will probably be made. Generally, it can be described in this way: automation of library clerical processes is not a trivial problem even though, superficially, they seem to be little more than analogues of business data processes that have now been computer-based for years. There are vitally significant differences that must be recognized in management planning.

Libraries are concerned with files of truly enormous magnitude. For example, whereas an inventory control file for a very large company might contain 10 million characters, the card catalog of a typical library will contain 10 times as much—100 million characters. The card catalog of a large research library will contain over 1 billion characters, and the National Union Catalog has been estimated at 100 billion characters! The conversion of such immense files into machine language is almost prohibitively expensive, but the storage and maintenance of them on a continuing basis is even more expensive—particularly since ready access to the catalog is essential.

Unfortunately, again in sharp contrast to business data processing, there is not a comparable degree of utilization by which to justify incurring such expenditures. For example, whereas a typical inventory control file will serve activity that utilizes an average of 10 percent of the file each day, less than 0.1 percent of a library's catalog will be used each day. There is thus a relatively small base of activity over which to spread costs. The investment in conversion, storage, and maintenance must therefore be justified by "increased benefits" to a much greater extent than in business data processing. And these intangibles provide an especially difficult basis for library management planning because of the limited discretionary resources usually available.

In fact, because libraries do operate on a very marginal economic basis, most library operations are remarkably "cost-efficient." As a result, there is little of the organizational "fat" that developers of mechanized systems usually depend on for demonstrating economies of operation.

Perhaps even more significant in management planning is the fact that library data processing involves the very substance of the library's functions. In this respect, the library's catalog, serial records, and even its circulation control files are comparable to the manufacturing plant of a company and not to its bookkeeping records. Changes in the basic records of the library, which are almost certain to occur with mechanization, therefore affect the character of the library services themselves and not simply that of peripheral accounting procedures. It may be for this reason that library data processing involves a degree of intellectual judgment far beyond that in normal business data processing. For example, catalog filing rules are, with good reason, much more complicated that simple alpha-numerical sorting. In fact, in this sense mechanizing library data processing is comparable in difficulty and complexity to the development of a "total management information system" for a company. It is therefore especially important that management planning make adequate provision for the effects on library service of the changes resulting from mechanization.

Finally, as was pointed out in the preceding two chapters, library operations and their costs are relatively ill-defined, at least in the form required for mechanization. Only recently have libraries added systems and procedures personnel to their staffs, and few libraries, even now, have detailed procedures manuals comparable to those in a business. There are still relatively few people available who combine knowledge of libraries with that of data processing. Management planning therefore must recognize the necessity for adequate systems work, including procedures analysis, and must accommodate the difficulties in finding or training personnel capable of doing this work.

OBJECTIVES, TIME SCHEDULES, AND BUDGETS

The first and most important step in the management of a mechanization program is the definition of objectives for it. Because program objectives must be compatible with library policies, the library administration must begin by reviewing existing library policies, both as documented and as generally "understood." In doing this, it probably will find it necessary to develop some new policies and to document many previously undocumented ones. Then, the situation that led to the decision to undertake a modernization program should be analyzed. Usually, these include demands for change coming from higher governing bodies; requirements for new services in response to changing conditions; increasing backlogs that result from inadequate budgets, staff, or space; and intolerable time delays in processing. In any case, program objectives must be established that reflect both library policies and current or anticipated needs.

The most ambitious general objective might be the orderly development of a "total system" that not only exploits as many of the new technologies as possible but does so with optimum balance of cost, effectiveness, and compatibility with other (state, local, or national) library systems. A more limited objective might be the documentation and analysis of existing library operations with the aim of limited improvement, through reorganization or simplification and through limited use of proven equipment techniques and technologies. Very limited and specific objectives could include faster processing of new book orders, better control over technical processing routines, availability of more comprehensive statistics, better management information, reduction in routines performed by clerical staff, availability of better bibliographic descriptions of the collection, more effective utilization of professional staff, improved reference services, better control over the physical collection, reduction of patron involvement in the charging transaction, and better circulation control. A typical list of library computer applications, representing quite specific objectives, is shown in Figure 5.2.[1]

In defining objectives, the librarian is confronted not only with the issues of cost and effectiveness of services as required now, but he should be even more concerned with the quality and quantity of services required in the future (in 5, 10, or 15 years). Will the library, with its present means, be capable of furnishing them? What must be done so that the expected services will be made available? What lead time is required to do so? What are the cost implications? As a result, the librarian must make predictions and projections about the future and must also clearly understand the present roles and purposes of his library. Admittedly, the dynamic development of our educational and cultural system, together with the revolutionary developments experienced by library science in the past few years, all tend to decrease considerably one's confidence in any prediction. Nevertheless, even poor projections are better than none, and they can be revised often (perhaps once every six months) in order to maintain a reasonable, though minimal, degree of credibility.

For this reason, it is particularly important to develop objectives in terms of a *planned progression of systems*, such as that illustrated in Figure 5.3, starting from the present ways of doing things and leading to some ultimate system.[2]

[1] Griffin, Hillis, Notes distributed in lecture at UCLA, 1968.
[2] New York State Library, Computer Applications Section, Division of Electronic Data Processing, *Plan for Automation of Library Services in New York State, 1967-1975*, November 20, 1967.

Figure 5.2 Typical library computer applications.

ACQUISITIONS

Books
    Selection lists–duplicate checking
    Purchase orders
    On order list (or in process list)
    Expedite
    Receiving
    Accounting records and check issuance
    Call down cataloging copy
    Catalog department expediting
    Desiderata list
    Financial status and forecast
    Historical file by:

1.	Vendor	2.	Date
3.	Account number	4.	Author

    Vendor performance analysis
    Citation performance analysis
    Cost increase analysis

Journals
    Renewal notices (letter or list)
    Renewal orders
    Current status
    Receiving reports–accounting records when appropriate
    Check in cards claiming
    Binding recall
    Binding list, slips and specifications
    Bid list
    Subscription summary by:

1.	Vendor	2.	Library
3.	Group	4.	User

    Routing
    Financial forecast
    History
    Cost increase analysis

Reports

Ordering	Assignment
Cards	Spine labels
Circulation records	Announcement bulletin
Printed report catalog	Shelf list
Weeding list	Fund balances

CATALOGING
    Input to cataloger (work sheet, precataloging information)
    Catalog card production:

1.	Sets	2.	Sorted sets

    Classification schedules

Subject authority file
Shelf list
Printed book catalog
Announcement bulletin
Book cards, pockets, spine labels
Serial list

CIRCULATION
    Overdue
    Inventory list
    Location of additional copies

    Reserves
    Activity (e.g., do we
        need to order more copies)

REFERENCE
    Bibliography preparation

SERIALS
    Union list of serials:
        1.   Alphabetical by title
        2.   Subject arrangement
    Union list by library

DISTRIBUTION
    Address labels

ADMINISTRATION
    Management information:
        Current costs and projected costs, effect
            of projected action
        Exception reporting (absence, overtime,
            high-dollar orders)
        Modeling techniques
        Personnel information

FILM LIBRARY
    Film scheduling
    Delivery scheduling
    Replacement prediction—also maintenance

CENTRALIZED CATALOGING INPUT
    Cataloger work sheets (proof sheets)
    Catalog cards (sets and sorted sets)
    Book selection lists (by subject, type,
        classification, etc.)
    Lists of monographic series (by subject,
        classification, etc.)
    Lists of serials
    Lists of foreign language translations (by subject,
        classification, type)
    Lists of reprints (by subject, classification, type)
    Book catalog input

Figure 5-3   (Typical) time schedule of functions for each stage.

Stage	Time	Functions Continued	Functions Changed	Functions Added
1	Present	All existing functions at existing levels of activity		
2	In 4 years	Present methods of selection cataloging and reference	Punched card system for circulation control Punched card system for ordering Substantial increase in interlibrary loan	Cooperative book catalog (as part of a library system) TWX for inter-library loan Cost accounting
3	In 6 years	Present methods of selection and reference TWX for inter-library loan Cost accounting	Batch computer system for serial record control circulation control, ordering, and catalog production	Facsimile trans-mission
4	In 10 years		On-line computer system for serial record control, circulation control, ordering, and catalog production	Batch mechanized reference services −including "selective dissemination," computer file search

The importance of this approach to library automation should not be underestimated. Libraries, as operational agencies, require that throughout development there must be some level of system at all times in regular, full-scale operation in the library. Even more significant is the necessity that they be capable of sustained, economic operation indefinitely. There is always uncertainty both with respect to the future and in the actual progress in development of new systems. For example, related programs elsewhere and the actual availability of technology are completely outside the control of the individual library and, yet, are essential to its planning. The progression of steps must be designed to articulate well with those programs as they actually develop.

Because of these considerations, such a progression should be planned around a logical succession of systems that perform essentially the same functions but at increasing levels of sophistication. Therefore, it may frequently be desirable that less sophisticated objectives be met first, as the basis on which later systems are built. Only in this way can the library avoid the pitfalls of overcommitment to some ultimate concept, on the one hand, and of a refusal to proceed ("because new machinery will soon appear"), on the other hand.

The management-planning task, assisted by the library systems analysis staff, is to delineate the functions that are to be served at each stage in the progression. Some of them will simply be continuations of existing functions, unchanged in any substantial way. Others will represent significant changes— such as a book catalog replacing a card catalog. Still others will represent totally new services—perhaps mechanized information retrieval or facsimile transmission. And some functions will represent the need to "interface" with other libraries.

The criteria used in this planning process include: (1) the economic value to be expected from including, changing, or even deleting functions; (2) the logical progression in conversion from an existing function to another, more sophisticated one (for example, in transition from a card catalog to a computer produced book catalog to an "on-line" computer catalog); (3) the need to relate with other efforts in other libraries; (4) the availability of budget and personnel; (5) the availability and reliability of the necessary hardware and software; (6) the flexibility and ease of change; and (7) the consistency with the ultimate objectives.

Especially important is the comparable planning for the methods for financing a project as complex as automation in a library. The methods need to be as carefully scheduled as the more technical aspects of hardware and software.[3] In particular, it would be short-sighted to expect that the methods for financing that would be appropriate to an ultimate, operational stage could be met in earlier, experimental, and developmental stages. It would be foolhardy to proceed as though the eventual requirements in these aspects would, in some way, naturally evolve from the experience during earlier stages.

We have already commented on the necessity to define a planned progression of stages. Each stage must satisfy a clearly delineated set of requirements, appropriate to the available technology and knowledge of how to do things; each stage must embody an equally well-defined set of administrative and operational controls; and each stage should be carefully planned so as to be consistent with the ultimate objectives. But each stage must also be based on equally well-defined financial considerations. The basis of financial support, therefore, should be as well planned as the technical implementation of hardware and

[3] Bierman, Harold, and Seymour Smidt, *The Capital Budgeting Decision*. New York: MacMillan, 1960.

software. This means that the planning should include considerations relevant to these financial issues just as it will for the technical ones.

In particular, cost/effectiveness measures of performance should be the primary basis for evaluation, and the decision of whether to automate mainly should be based on a comparison of costs of manual versus machine methods. Although cost/effectiveness is never a simple concept, it becomes particularly complex when it is applied to systems development that progresses through a number of stages, spread over a period of years. But this merely emphasizes the importance of a carefully planned progression of steps as an integral part of the development program.

PROJECT MANAGEMENT

The process of development and implementation of a mechanized library system is complicated and involves a large number of people. Therefore, the management of this effort must also be planned in advance; the tasks that are to be carried out must be assigned to a development staff; and time estimates must be established for each task with a target date for its start and finish.

Development Steps

The process of creating any mechanized processing system involves the performance of a series of activities called *steps* (or *phases*).[4-7] These steps, or similar ones, are commonly used in describing and planning computer work in both government and industry, and represent a "natural" sequence for development of mechanized library systems as well.[8]

1. Feasibility analysis.
2. Requirements specification.
3. Detailed design.
4. Computer programming and checkout.
5. Computer program functional test.
6. Installation and implementation.
7. Maintenance.

[4] Gregory, R. H., and R. L. van Horn, *Automatic Data Processing Systems: Principles and Procedures.* Belmont, California: Wadsworth, 1963. Especially Section VI.

[5] Brandon, Richard H., *Management Standards for Data Processing.* Princeton N.J.: van Nostrand, 1963. Chapter II.

[6] Martin, Edley W., *Electronic Data Processing: an Introduction.* Homewood, Ill.: Irwin, 1965. Chapters 14-17.

[7] Rosove, Perry E., *Developing Computer-Based Information Systems.* New York: Wiley, 1967, pp. 25-93.

[8] Veaner, Allen B., *Major Decision Points in Library Automation,* Talk given at ARL Meeting, Chicago, Ill., 17 Jan 1970.

Each of the seven steps encompasses a set of tasks that culminate in milestones or concluding events. The successive completion of the tasks becomes an objective measure of progress achieved.

Step 1. Feasibility Analysis. Based on a statement of the library's requirements, an estimate must be made of the resources required for the project, a summary project plan must be prepared, and a cost-versus-benefits comparison must be made. During this step, the level of analysis of the library's operating system is only the level absolutely necessary for cost estimation and preliminary planning purposes.

TASKS

Determine the general requirements to be met.

Determine the necessary development activities, including the number and identity of any subsidiary efforts.

Estimate the development costs for each step or task.

Check the reasonableness of estimates.

Prepare a summary budget plan for development.

Estimate the costs of both existing and proposed systems.

Prepare a cost-benefits evaluation of the proposed application.

Estimate the personnel requirements.

Step 2. Requirements Specification. This step consists of the detailed study of the existing library system and the formulation of the operational requirements for the proposed system.

TASKS

Determine the library's system requirements in detail.

Analyze the library's environment including projects with which it must be compatible.

Determine the needed computer program characteristics.

Compare with similar systems.

Prepare performance specifications.

Assure concurrence of library policy-makers with system performance specifications.

Step 3. Detailed Design. Based on the requirement specifications, this step proceeds to the definition of detailed design for both the computer system and the library personnel involved. It results in documents that detail the functions to be programmed as well as the operating procedures for personnel.

TASKS

Interpret the requirement specifications in terms of specific equipment, volume of activity, response times, and operating environment.

Produce a system flow diagram.

Define "interfaces" with other activities in the library or in other libraries.

Specify computations, logical manipulations, and transformations within each part of the library function to be done by the machine.

Design the formats and organization of all forms and files, including machine stored records.

Develop requirements for editing, formatting, storing, and updating of the machine stored data.

Produce documentation of the detailed design.

Define test requirements.

Indoctrinate programming personnel.

Step 4. Computer Programming. Based on the detailed design specifications, this step proceeds with all work necessary to produce, document, and test computer programs. Included are such activities as flowcharting, coding, integration of individual programs into a program system, preparation of the data base, detecting and correcting errors, compiling or assembling operating programs, and listing of code. It results in a completed computer program end product, tested for conformity with detailed specification.

TASKS

Flowchart each component computer program.

Specify all input and output forms.

Write programs from detailed flow charts or other program design documentation.

Compile and check the program code, and make necessary error corrections.

Test the performance of each individual program and of the total program system.

Step 5. Computer Program Functional Test. This step covers demonstration tests of the computer program system, for the library management, usually in a simulated environment at the library. Included are the conduct of the demonstration tests (based on test plans prepared as a part of Detailed Design) and an analysis of the test results. All necessary work to remedy design deficiencies revealed by these tests should be charged to the appropriate previous steps. The results should be a computer program that is proven to be in conformance with the detailed design specifications and accepted by library management.

TASKS

Conduct the test according to plan.

Analyze the test results.

Initiate any modifications needed for computer programs.

Document the test results.

Establish change procedures.

Step 6. Installation and Implementation. This step covers all work necessary to install the system at the library. It includes training as well as activities for conversion from the existing manual operation.

TASKS

Prepare documentation for the library staff.

Supervise the conversion of data required to make system operational.

Develop a training plan for the library staff.

Conduct a training program.

Step 7. Maintenance. System maintenance is required for improving, changing, and correcting operational computer programs. Revisions are needed because operational requirements are continually changing during both the development and operation of the system. Although operational needs are projected during requirements analysis, in most cases they can be neither totally defined nor totally implemented in the imposed time schedules. Also, corrections must usually be made to the computer programs because errors and operational deficiencies not detected in the routine testing of the programs are usually discovered when the system becomes operational. Much of the work of program maintenance personnel must be devoted to the handling of emergencies; the remainder must be devoted to modifications required to meet environmental changes.

TASKS

Develop a maintenance plan and an organization.

Provide continuing communications between the library operating staff and the computer programmers.

Process system changes.

Work Breakdown Structure

The formulation and documentation of such a comprehensive program requires the definition of a "work-breakdown structure" and an associated cost-accounting structure. The work-breakdown structure is a technique for showing the component tasks of a library development project in successively greater detail. Usually the tasks are related to the comparable detail in system description, as outlined in Chapter 6. As a basis for effective program planning, it ensures that no major program activity is overlooked. It provides graphic representation of the relationship of the various components of a complex program to each other and the achievement of stated program objectives. Finally, it provides a convenient means for monitoring progress toward achieving the objectives of a program.

The work-breakdown structure, presented in Figure 5.4, illustrates how a typical major development program at a large research library might be dissected into successively more detailed component parts. In this example, the total library system has been subdivided into three major subsystems and two major control activities, represented by the five blocks in the second level of the diagram. Each of these five subdivisions has then been further divided into more detailed elements, which represent work of a manageable size for program control. Each such "work package" must then be considered within the tasks of the seven steps in development. In summary, the work breakdown structure produces a classification of work as follows:

Library System

Component Subsystem

Step

Task

Figure 5.4. Library systems development program work breakdown structure, (and cost accounts structure).

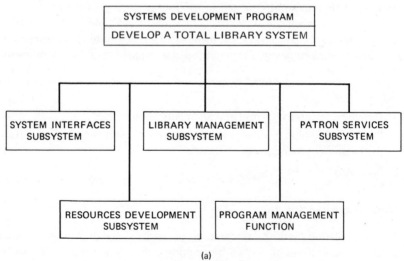

(a)

Figure 5.4a

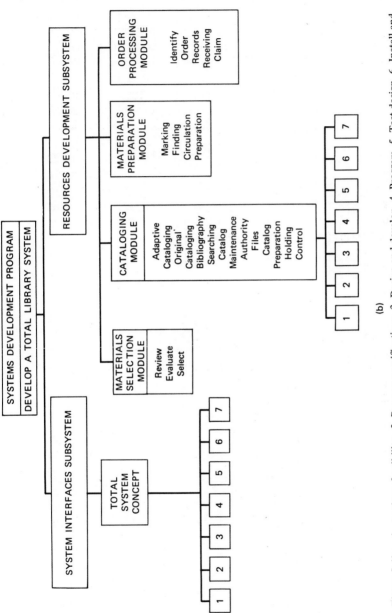
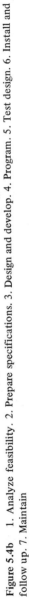

Figure 5.4b 1. Analyze feasibility. 2. Prepare specifications. 3. Design and develop. 4. Program. 5. Test design. 6. Install and follow up. 7. Maintain

121

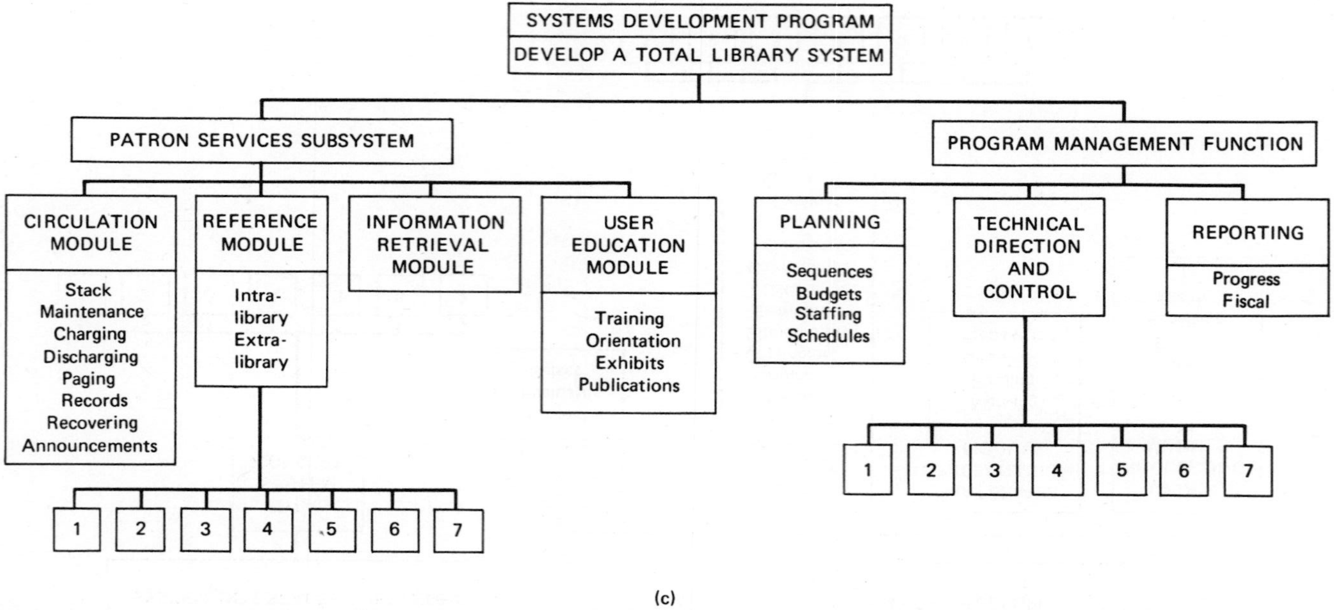

SYSTEMS DEVELOPMENT PROGRAM

DEVELOP A TOTAL LIBRARY SYSTEM

PATRON SERVICES SUBSYSTEM

PROGRAM MANAGEMENT FUNCTION

CIRCULATION MODULE

Stack
Maintenance
Charging
Discharging
Paging
Records
Recovering
Announcements

REFERENCE MODULE

Intra-
library
Extra-
library

INFORMATION RETRIEVAL MODULE

USER EDUCATION MODULE

Training
Orientation
Exhibits
Publications

PLANNING

Sequences
Budgets
Staffing
Schedules

TECHNICAL DIRECTION AND CONTROL

REPORTING

Progress
Fiscal

1 2 3 4 5 6 7

1 2 3 4 5 6 7

(c)

Figure 5.4c   1. Analyze feasibility. 2. Prepare specifications. 3. Design and develop. 4. Program. 5. Test design. 6. Install and follow up.
7. Maintain

122

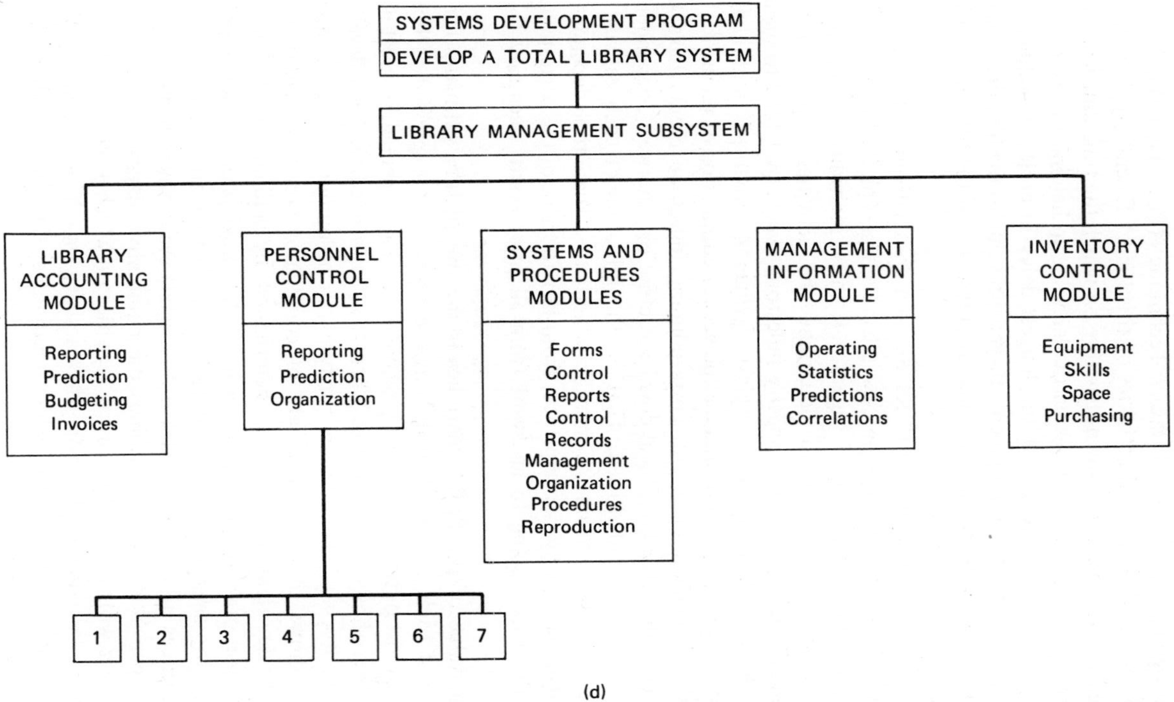

Figure 5.4d   1. Analyze feasibility. 2. Prepare specifications. 3. Design and develop. 4. Program. 5. Test design. 6. Install and follow up. 7. Maintain

(d)

Program Evaluation and Review Technique (PERT)

The "Program Evaluation and Review Technique" (PERT) is a well-developed analytical tool used to control activities of this kind.[9] Essentially, it is a "flow chart", tied to the work breakdown structure, in which the time dimension plays an especially important role. It has particular value in helping to determine the sequence of events that represent the longest delay in project schedule, called the "critical path" in the development. Its general value to the librarian is the aid that it will give him in making the most effective use of the time and resources available.

The mechanics of preparing a PERT diagram are relatively simple. Probably the best way for illustrating the process is to review a typical example based on the work-breakdown structure of Figure 5.4. In it, individual tasks have been identified. The next step is to determine the activities required for the completion of each task and to specify milestone events by which to measure progress. Figure 5.5 lists some typical "program activities," and includes representative estimates of time and manpower for completion of them.[10]

Once the individual tasks and corresponding milestone events have been identified (through the work-breakdown structure or otherwise), dependencies among them must be identified. That is, the initiation of each activity will require the completion of one or more prior activities. These time dependencies can be visually shown by the sequence, from left to right, of the corresponding events, with arrows going to an event from all prior events necessary for its initiation.

The real value of the PERT chart lies is the use of time estimates for the completion of each activity. Usually, these estimates are expressed as both a range (from most optimistic to most pessimistic) and an expected, or most likely value like that shown in Figure 5.6. When such estimates have been developed for each activity, an "elapsed-time" analysis can be produced. The example in Figure 5.6 shows the estimated date of completion for every event in the program. These elapsed times are determined by adding together all the estimated times for completion of each in the progression of activities and determining for each event the cumulated elapsed time to that point. Where several sequences of activities converge on a single event, the sequence requiring the longest period of time determines the cumulative elapsed time until that event. In other words, all sequences of activities on which a subsequent activity depends must be completed before that activity can be commenced. Those sequences leading up to an event, which require less time than the longest one,

[9] Archibald, Russell D., and R. L. Villoria, *Network-Based Management Systems (PERT/CPM)*. New York: Wiley, 1967.

[10] Bellomy, Fred, "Management Planning for Library Systems Development," *Journal of Library Automation,* **2** (4) (December 1969), pp. 187-217.

Figure 5.5   Activities and estimates

Number	Program Activities	Months Elapsed Time	Man-Hours by Category[a]				
			1	2	3	4	5
A	TOTAL SYSTEM CONCEPT	18	1800	1500	1600	–	–
1	Assemble documentation	5	200	200	100	–	–
2	Document organization	2	100	100	200	–	–
3	Document system	10	1000	1000	800	–	–
4	Policies and objectives	5	100	100	200	–	–
5	Define system requirements	1	200	–	100	–	–
6	Total system concept	1	100	50	100	–	–
7	Implementation plan	2	100	50	100	–	–
B	ORDER PROCESSING MODULE	26	1500	1600	2000	3000	800
1	Formulate objectives	3	100	10	10	–	–
2	Document operations	4	100	50	200	–	200
3	Analyze and summarize	3	100	50	200	–	100
4	Design concepts	1	50	50	100	100	–
5	Design specifications	1	50	10	90	100	–
6	Design and develop	12	600	200	600	1500	100
7	Assemble components	1	50	10	100	–	–
8	Test Design	1	50	–	90	150	–
9	Install module	2	100	1000	100	150	400
10	Follow-up evaluation	1	50	20	100	200	–
11	Refine design	1	50	50	100	300	–
12	Document design	3	200	150	300	500	–
C	SYSTEMS and PROCEDURE MODULE	18	4000	3000	700	200	500
D	MATERIAL PREPARATION MODULE	6	200	200	500	500	–
E	CIRCULATION MODULE	18	2000	2000	2000	3000	2000
F	LIBRARY ACCOUNTING MODULE	12	1000	500	1000	2000	–
G	USER EDUCATION MODULE	18	1000	400	500	2000	–
H	INVENTORY CONTROL MODULE	6	100	300	500	300	–
I	PERSONNEL CONTROL MODULE	12	1000	500	1000	700	–
J	CATALOGING MODULE	24	4000	1000	3000	4000	–
K	MATERIALS SELECTION MODULE	12	1000	200	1000	1000	–
L	MANAGEMENT INFORMATION MODULE	18	1000	300	2000	1000	–
M	REFERENCE MODULE	24	2000	2000	3000	3000	–
N	INFORMATION RETRIEVAL MODULE	36	4000	2000	4000	5000	–

[a]1, Librarian; 2, clerk-typist; 3, analyst; 4, programmer; and 5, general assistance.

will have slack time (waiting time) built into them. This can be used for adjusting schedules in order to concentrate effort on other tasks or to minimize peak manpower, equipment, or facilities loading.

When the elapsed time analysis is complete, it may be determined that the total elapsed time estimated for the program is incompatible with the required program completion date. If this happens, it will be necessary to reinspect the

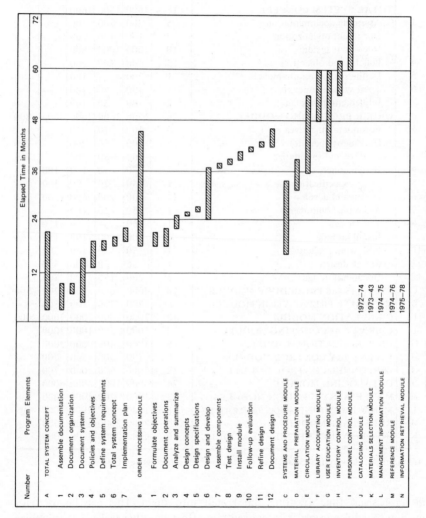

Figure 5.6 Systems development program schedule.

program logic in an effort to identify activities originally planned to occur in sequence which can, in fact, occur in parallel. Such a change in the plan, however, will almost always imply an increased risk of failure to perform as planned. Sometimes it will be possible to compensate for the increased risk by adding additional backup efforts or by assigning the same activity to two different groups for simultaneous, parallel performance. On closer scrutiny it may be found that some of the activities originally thought essential are, in fact, only desirable and can be eliminated from the plan entirely. Eventually, this strategy will force the planned program elapsed time to be compatible with the program completion date specified by the program manager.

Next, it is necessary to analyze each week of activity in the planned program to determine what level of manpower or special facilities will be required. This has been illustrated for the example and plotted in Figure 5.7 as a function of time. During the first weeks of the program it will be noted that there are heavy demands being made on various categories of manpower, and that later in the program there are periods when practically no demand is made for the same categories of manpower. It frequently is possible to minimize the peaks by shifting some of the activities to later times when fewer demands are being made.

Cost Accounting and Control

An integral part of the planning function involves the budgeting and control of available funds among the various program activities. A convenient structure for doing this is the work-breakdown structure itself. During later stages in the planning, all of the specific activities required to accomplish program objectives will be identified as parts of individual blocks in the work-breakdown structure. Each of the tasks (or portions of a task) may, in turn, be assigned a cost-account number for which funds may be budgeted. The six-position code shown in Figure 5.8 should prove satisfactory in most instances. One position is needed for step identification. Obviously, the number of positions for the other entries required by a library would be a function if its own particular approach to analysis of its operations. Also, if several libraries work on separate portions (systems, components, sub-systems, or even steps) of a total information-processing system, they should coordinate their numbering conventions and identify the individual libraries.

The cost-account structure is used in implementing cost-accounting routines. Each increment of cost (man hours or materials dollars) is posted periodically against each of the cost-account numbers. The individual elements are added together in such a way as to provide cumulative cost records at each one of the summary levels in the cost-account structure. At the highest level in the structure, the total cumulative cost for the entire program is summarized. This

128

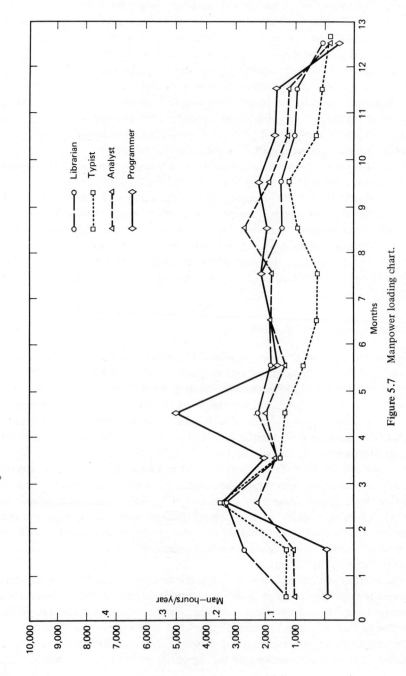

Figure 5.7 Manpower loading chart.

Figure 5.8   Typical work numbering for cost data collection.

Library system		Component Subsystem		Step		Task
(XX)	.	XXX	.	X	.	XX

number is plotted on a program status chart and monitored closely by program management. Any significant deviations of actual cost or performance from the planned cost/performance curve is the signal to program management to initiate appropriate corrective action.

EDUCATION

Among the most important activities that should be included in project planning is the education of both staff and users in the operation, implications, and effects of the system. It is necessary for several reasons.

1.   The staff are rightly concerned about the effects that automation will have on them personally. Unless they have a sense of involvement, this concern can develop into outright fear and antagonism. A well-planned program of education, scheduled to proceed in parallel with the development project, can help to overcome this concern.

2.   The staff will need to change many of the ways in which they have carried out their assigned tasks. Some of the tasks themselves may even change. In principle, the procedures manuals and task descriptions generated as part of the programming work during development are sufficient to show each staff member how the work should be performed. Actually, of course, intensive training is usually required, if only to show each person how his work relates to the system as a whole. In this respect, it must be recognized that while automation of clerical processes may not change the basic professional content of librarianship, it will change much of the detail. Even professionals, therefore, will need to see why these changes may be necessary and how they relate to the major objectives.

3.   Directly related to the second reason is the fact that, many times, only the staff is really in a position to recognize a serious flaw in an operating

procedure. Unless they have been given the opportunity to see what the purposes are, they can hardly begin to bring out what would otherwise be only intuitive feelings that "something's not right."

4.   Any change of system (even from one manual method to another one) is bound to produce temporary traumas. Failures, changes from the familiar, bruises to esthetics—all are bound to occur, if only because something is new. Therefore, particular care must be taken to prepare both staff and readers for these traumatic effects. This means that not only is a program of education needed, but "public relations" is needed as well.

For all of these reasons, education and public relations should be planned as an integral part of the development program. Because of the importance of an educational program, some of the considerations to be planned for are discussed in Chapter 8.

Suggested Readings

Of the references in this chapter, several are especially good summaries of issues and techniques in the management of data processing development:

Archibald, Russell D., and R. L. Villoria, *Network-Based Management Systems (PERT/CPM).* New York: Wiley, 1967.

This is probably the best available summary of the variety of presently available techniques for project management. It provides the reader with a step-by-step guide through the process of creating a management "network," of maintaining it, and of using it.

Gregory, R. H., and R. L. Van Horn, *Automatic Data Processing Systems.* Belmont, California: Wadsworth, 1963.

An excellent summary of all aspects of data processing system development and use.

Rosove, Perry E., *Developing Computer-Based Information Systems.* New York: Wiley, 1967.

Although the emphasis of the book is on military "command and control" systems, there are many analogies with libraries and information centers. It is based upon the wealth of experience created at System Development Corporation in virtually all aspects of this kind of work.

Chapter 6

METHODS OF SYSTEM DESCRIPTION

INTRODUCTION

The central process in library systems analysis and design is that of *description*. It is the means by which the library, with all the complexity inherent in any actual organization, is represented in a form that can be communicated, understood, and modified. This chapter discusses the methods for system description. First, however, there is a *caution*: the process of description is, by its nature, analytical. The library is represented in terms of its constituent parts and those parts in terms of their parts. As a result, many important relationships within the library may be lost or distorted. Furthermore, the very way in which the result is organized will impose its own bias on the picture that it presents. However, despite these limitations, description is essential, since without it the library can be viewed only through personal experience and intuition.

The task is to develop a picture of the administrative and operational structure of the library that will present the functions performed, showing the relationships among them and who does them. The results are especially useful if they are in a form that can be manipulated, since the system analyst wants to experiment (on paper, at least) with alternatives. He wants to see what the effects may be of eliminating functions, of combining and simplifying other functions, and of changing the assignment of them to parts of the library's administrative structure. He wants to see what changes may be necessary and appropriate for the introduction of a new, mechanized system. In carrying out analyses of this kind, the analyst uses the representation of the library as his

131

starting point and, from it, generates new representations that show how the alternatives would look.

The issues of concern in description can be grouped in terms of four "dimensions" and four sets of "parameters" (or quantitative characteristics).

The "Dimensions of Description"

The dimensions of description are the aspects of a library and its operation that constitute the principal means for developing and organizing the description of the library: (1) data files, (2) functions, (3) time, and (4) components.

Data Files. The representation of a library must show the "data files"—the collection of books, the catalogs, the vendor files, the circulation files, and the like. These form the basis for all of the library's services and are affected by all of the library's operations.

Functions. The work of a library is carried out by the performance of a highly interrelated set of functions upon these data files. At a gross level they include selection, acquisition, cataloging, filing, reference, and circulation. These must be defined in detail, including the functional relationships among them.

Time. Processes occur in sequences in time and, frequently, at prescribed points in time (like "once a month"). It is therefore essential that the representation show these relationships in time.

Components. The operations in the library are performed by people and equipment, organized into administrative units. These functional "components" must be described, together with their organizational relationships and the assignments of operations to them.

The Forms of Description

Representations take many forms. Some are essentially verbal—for example, policy and procedures manuals, job descriptions, and high-level computer language programs. Others are essentially graphical. Some are concerned with the structure of the library with respect to only a single one of the four dimensions—organization charts or file structures, for instance. Others are concerned with the relationships among several dimensions. The set of patterns for description is summarized in Figure 6.1 in terms of the way in which the four dimensions are represented. Each will be discussed in detail later in this chapter, but to provide an overview, we will outline them briefly:

Organization Charts. These graphically show the internal structure and the relationships among the organizational components of the library, usually in the form of an administrative hierarchy.

Figure 6.1 Forms of Description

Form of Description	Dimensions Represented
1. Organization Chart	C
2. Data Structure Matrix	D
3. File Management Matrix	D ⌐ (C,T) ⌐ F
4. Flow Chart	D ⌐ (F,C) ⌐ T
5. Gantt Chart	C ⌐ (F,D) ⌐ T
6. Responsibility Matrices	D ⌐ (F,T) F ⌐ (D,T) ⌐ C C

Key: D, data; F, function; T, time; and C, component.

Data Structure Matrix. This shows the relationships among files, forms, and data elements, frequently as a matrix (that is, as a rectangular array of numbers).

File Management Matrix. There are certain standard processes inherent in the operation of any data processing system. Data must be generated, they must be transmitted, they must be filed, they must be processed, and they may be deleted and discarded. File management matrices are used to describe, for each of these functions and for each file, who performs what.

Flow Chart. For each file, the functions occur in a sequence in time. The "flow chart" shows that sequence, including the relationship of operations affecting one file to operations on others.

Gantt Chart. Each component carries out functions assigned to it in a sequence in time. The Gantt charts show that time sequence, including the dependence of one component on the work done by others.

Responsibility Matrices. Each component is responsible for operations upon files, forms, or elements of data. The assignment of this responsibility is shown in a "data responsibility matrix."

These various patterns for description are clearly mutually dependent on each other and, in fact, simply represent different arrangements of the same basic data. However, each has its role in aiding the analyst in understanding, communicating, and experimenting with alternative arrangements of processes in the library.

The "Parameters of Description"

The parameters of description are the quantitative characteristics of the library that are needed to represent the magnitude of the processing task that it involves: (1) size, (2) activity, (3) processing time, and (4) cost.

Size. The data files are formed from various numbers of records (of various sizes) and are stored in various sequences. In order to describe them, these quantitative characteristics must be determined and specified.

Activity. The frequency with which the processes that the library carries out are performed must be characterized by an amount of activity (during some unit of time) for each. (For example, "books circulated each day," "titles cataloged each month," and so on.) These activity figures represent the work load placed on the library. Usually, they are subject to wide changes from hour to hour, month to month, and season to season. The determination of them must therefore recognize this statistical variation.

Processing Time. The execution of a process itself takes time, and therefore the description of the process must include a parameter of "processing time." Furthermore, since this is time spent by a person or a device, it becomes a commitment of time by the component of the library involved. (Incidentally, it is important to recognize the twofold role that "time" plays. In one respect, it is a dimension of description, to which the time-sequential relationships among processes are tied; in another respect, it is a quantitative characteristic of the individual process.)

Cost. Finally, the costs of the individual processes and components of the library must be determined—purchase costs for the collection, costs for personnel and equipment, costs for each process, and costs for buildings and capital equipment. Usually, it is the need for this kind of quantitative data, in order to provide adequate description of the library, that leads the system analyst to place so much emphasis on a "cost-accounting system."

The Steps in Description

In summary, the aim is to create a representation of the library that will be useful, that will properly relate files, processes, components, and times, and that will contain adequate and accurate quantitative characteristics. In order to do this, the following natural steps usually will be taken.

1. The administrative and physical organization of the library will be described. This involves creating organization charts, policy manuals, and personnel job descriptions. The result is the description of dimension four of the

library—the components with which it does its work and the organizational relationships among them.

2. The forms and files by which the results of library processes are recorded, communicated, stored, and controlled will be described. This involves accumulating samples of forms, analyzing the relationships among the data elements recorded on them, and determining sizes, numbers, and amounts of activity for them. The result is the description of dimension one of the library—the data it processes, and the relationships that each form of data bears to the others.

3. The operations will be described. This involves a detailed examination of the flow of work through the library and the creation of "flow charts," "Gantt charts," and the other graphical descriptions of processes and their interrelationships. The result is the representation of dimensions two and three of the library—its functions and their timing.

4. Finally, data will be accumulated on file sizes, amounts of activity, processing times, and costs—the parameters of the library.

DESCRIPTION OF LIBRARY ORGANIZATION

The first step is the description of the administrative and physical organization of the library. An organization chart is a graphic picture of the various administrative entities (for example, divisions, branches, and departments) that make up an organization, showing their hierarchical relationship. In surveying the library, the first step is to trace the organization chart at a very abstract level; then more detailed organization charts will be drawn. Of particular importance are the points in the organization where decisions of one kind or another are made.

There are at least five methods in use for organization of the administrative structure of libraries:

1. By function (cataloging, circulation, and reference).
2. By subject (biology library, arts library, and physics library).
3. By material (books, reports, microforms, periodicals, and maps).
4. By location (main library and branch libraries, for example).
5. By objectives (undergraduate library, research library, and the like).

Most libraries have found it necessary to employ a combination of several of these methods in developing their organizations, with one method being used as a basis for departmentalization at one level in the library and another being used to departmentalize the subunits.

The division by function, however, is a particularly useful one for description, even though it may not coincide with the actual administrative organization, since it leads directly to the subsequent step: description of files and processes.

Typical Library Functional Organization Chart

A library system structure might divide functions into "staff services" (associated directly with the Librarian), "processing services," "public services," and (in the context of a library using computer-based operations) "mechanized services" (Figure 6.2).

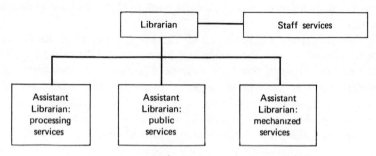

Figure 6.2   Typical library-system structure.

Processing Services. The processing services operations consist of all the activities necessary for acquiring and preparing library material for use by its patrons. All of the acquisitions, cataloging, and physical preparation of material acquired by the library are functions presently included in processing operations. The substructuring of the processing services operations is illustrated by Figure 6.3.

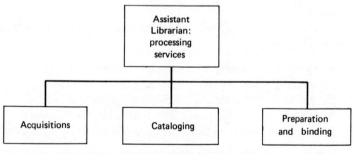

Figure 6.3   Processing services subsystem.

Public Services. The public services operations consist of all the activities necessary for providing library materials and services to library users. All of the reference, circulation, and various branch library service operations functions presently are included in public services operations. The substructuring of the public services operations is illustrated by Figure 6.4.

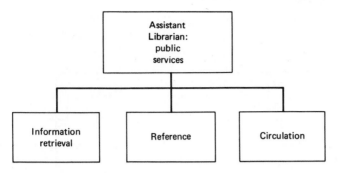

Figure 6.4   Public services subsystem.

Mechanized Services. The mechanized services operations could include the activities directly related to the development, operation, and use of data processing equipment and mechanized data bases (see Figure 6.5.)

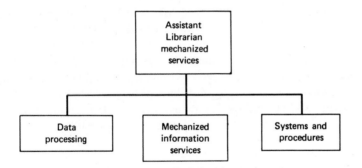

Figure 6.5   Mechanized services subsystem.

Staff Services. The staff services operations include all of the activities that are integral to the administration of the library system, but are not peculiar to any of the other three operations. Some of the functions within the staff services operations include services to all of the others; in this category fall such functions as budget control and personnel. Those primarily concerned with the overall operation include the remaining functions: public relations, editorial coordination, policy and planning, buildings (their planning and management). (See Figure 6.6.)

When the organization chart is ready, a list of the functions of each of the departments should be compiled (Figure 6.7) and, for each type of employee, job descriptions must be created.

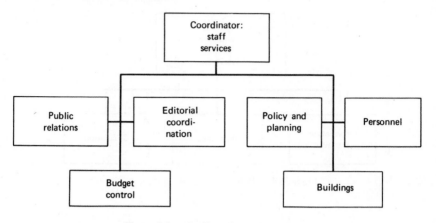

Figure 6.6   Staff services subsystem.

Administrative Changes in Organization

Any major change in the library system will be accompanied by implied changes in the organizational structure associated with that system. The functions of an organizational unit may change radically. Some significant operations previously handled manually (for instance, financial accounting) may be performed by machines in the new system, while entirely new functions (for example, key-punching and report distribution) may need to be undertaken; the types of materials handled by a unit may change. New reports generated by electronic data processing machines will require special handling, and procedures

Figure 6.7 Sample List of Functions: Acquisitions Department

1. Receive requests for purchasing items for the library.
2. Verify requestor's authority.
3. Verify availability of funds.
4. Approve or reject requests.
5. Check requests for accuracy and correct them.
6. Survey publishers, jobbers, or dealers for requested items.
7. Prepare and send orders.
8. Order LC cards.
9. Follow-up orders.
10. Receive items and check for concurrence with orders.
11. Prepare forms for routing received materials.
12. Route items received to cataloging department.
13. Maintain statistics.
14. Maintain records and accounts of vendors.
15. Pay bills.
16. Conduct and negotiate purchases of collections.

must be developed. The performance of library functions may be handled at new locations (for instance, remote input of recommendations for new purchases, and the like). Because of the availability of brand new capabilities, even the objectives of the organizational units themselves may change. The organization will therefore need to reflect the changes in processing requirements resulting from the changes in the unit's objectives.

An ideal organizational structure would presumably represent, as nearly as possible, a logical division of functions. However, capabilities of available personnel, when matched against the new requirements of the library, will imply that there are some jobs for which there is no obvious candidate, that there are some personnel that do not seem to fit into the organization anywhere, and that some of the "obvious" assignments would have disastrously demoralizing effects on the concerned individuals.

Will it be necessary to hire new people with the requisite skills not possessed by any of the personnel in the present organization? Should certain individuals be transferred to other parts of the library? Can any of the existing personnel acquire the new skills required through special training programs? Can temporary multiple assignments be made to some individuals until more compatible solutions can be worked out? Should the organizational structure be modified to accommodate particularly competent individuals in the organization? It is necessary to consider all such alternatives for organization of the library to create a compatible and relatively efficient structure. Unfortunately, few rules are available to the administrator faced with such a set of complex problems. The process of dealing with people is still more art than science.

DESCRIPTION OF FILES, FORMS, AND DATA

There is a kind of hierarchy in the data that a library processes. Files consist of records which, in turn, consist of data elements. Specifically, an "information file" is a collection of data having a common purpose and a common use, stored in an organized manner and processed by the library. A library will maintain many information files: the list of patrons, the catalog, records, bibliographical lists, vendor files, and the loan file are just a few examples.

Files are built up from records, frequently called "forms" (for instance, "order form"). The usual means of describing a file is to specify exactly what records it contains and what their sequence is. The specification of the type of record is the task of "forms design." It involves not only description of the data in each record type, but definition of their sequence and spacing in the record, the number of characters and the rules for recording them, the number of copies, and other issues relating to the physical form itself.

The variety of forms is as great as the methods for storing data—printed, punched, and magnetic—and as great as the tasks to be done—ordering, cataloging, accounting, and circulation. Therefore, records may be punched cards for circulation control records, magnetic tape records for document descriptions, typed order sheets, and punched tape copies of catalog cards.

The design of efficient, economical forms in itself requires evaluation and analysis. The objectives are to develop forms that are legible, simple to use, and efficient to prepare. To assist in meeting these objectives, there are general principles of good design, applicable to the forms of any system but particularly applicable in a mechanized one.[1]

1.   Every effort should be made to control and limit the number of different forms and copies of forms. It is perhaps obvious that superfluous forms are uneconomic, but the important reason is not simply the waste of paper; unfortunately, a form by its very existence creates processes—to record data on it, to carry it through subsequent operations, to file it, even to get rid of it—and a superfluous form creates superfluous operations.

2.   Every effort should be made to utilize common data as much as possible, so that a single recording of an item of data can be used to satisfy all later uses, either directly or through mechanical copying. To facilitate this, it is very desirable that a specific item of data appear in the same position in all forms to which it applies.

3.   All records should therefore be designed with as nearly the same sequence and positioning of data items as possible. In this way, transfers from one form to another, whether manually or by machine, can be made rapidly, consistently, and with a minimum of error.

4.   To the end of further reducing errors, forms should be designed to be self-explanatory and to facilitate detection of errors when they occur.

Figure 6.8 presents a typical sheet for description of types of records in a library system.[2] It shows the following information.

1.   RECORD TYPE NAME. This is a unique name for the record type.

2.   RECORD TYPE NO. This is the unique identifying number for the record type.

3.   OTHER NAMES USED. Frequently used alternate names and synonyms are listed.

4.   LAYOUT NO. Layout is the physical format of a form; each is identified by a layout number. The layout is independent of both the forms using the format and the data within the format. Several form types may use the

---

[1] Brandon, Richard H., *Management Standards for Data Processing.* Princeton, N. J.: Van Nostrand, 1963.

[2] *Reference Manual on Form and Card Design,* International Business Machines, 1961.

Figure 6.8 Record Type Description

Record Type Sheet.

Record Name ①		Record Type No. ②
Other Names Used ③		Layout No. ④
		Related Record Type Nos. ⑤
		No. of Copies ⑥

Media ⑦	How Prepared ⑧

Operations Involved In ⑨

Remarks ⑩

CONTENTS

No.	Data Name	Freq.	Characters			A/N	Origin
			Min.	95%	Max.		
⑪	⑫	⑬		⑭		⑮	⑯

Date   Analyst   Source   Page

Study

same layout number, with the fields differently interpreted on each. Layout numbers define physical locations of fields and field characteristics, permitting relatively flexible form design for a series of forms having the same layout number.

5.   RELATED RECORD TYPE NOS. These numbers identify related record types.

6.   NO. OF COPIES. This figure includes both the number of copies prepared with the original and the number of copies later reproduced.

7.   MEDIA. This entry displays the media employed in original and later reproduction.

8.   HOW PREPARED. This describes the means by which basic fields are entered on the original form (by hand, typewritten, card-punched, etc.).

9.   OPERATIONS INVOLVED IN. This is the identifying number of each operation using the form as input or output.

10.   REMARKS. Enter here all supplemental data on record type definition or handling (security, access, and so forth).

11.   NO. The identifying number of the data element can be any number from 01 to 99. The form number and this number uniquely identify the data element for later reference.

12.   DATA NAME. This is the title for the data element.

13.   FREQUENCY. Three types of entries appear here. If the data does not appear on every form carrying this record type number, the frequency of appearance is entered as a decimal fraction. If the data appears once on each form, the entry is 1; if more than once, the number of appearances, or the possible range and average, is entered. Whenever a range is entered, the average must also be noted.

14.   CHARACTERS. These fields show the minimum, the 95th percentile (that is, the number of characters which 95 percent of the records have fewer than), and the maximum number of characters in the data element.

15.   A/N. Enter A for alphabetic, N for numeric, and AN for alphameric (including special symbols).

16.   ORIGIN. Enter the operation number for the operation that either initially accepts the data element into the system, or originates the data. Operations that merely post the data to the form are not entered.

A picture of the degree to which data elements are common from one form to another can be provided by the use of a relatively simple technique—the "Data Structure Matrix." Copies are acquired of each of the forms used in the library, with actual data recorded on them. A chart or worksheet should be prepared, in the form of a *matrix*, similar to the following much-abbreviated illustration:

Data Items	Order Form	Catalog Form	Circulation Form
Call number		X	X
Author	X	X	
Title	X	X	
Borrower ID			X
Vendor ID	X		

As shown, types of records are listed across the top; the data items, along the side. (Care should be taken to include every record type, even intermediate worksheets, reports, sources, and the like and, similarly, to include every item of data found on any type of record.) By checking each item under every type of record to which it applies, one can readily see what data are common, what forms are similar and how they differ, and what data are superfluous because they are used only once, for instance.

As a further aid, the entries that must be generated by a manual typing can be circled in one color pencil and those that can be generated by mechanical copying with another color pencil. In this way, the points of initial entry of data are clearly exhibited.

In addition to these more or less qualitative principles, there are some quantitative factors that must be recognized. In particular, the number of characters required for each item of data—the size of the "field" in which it must be recorded—should be determined. For example:

Number of Characters

	Minimum	95th Percentile	Maximum
Call number	4	6	10
Author	10	20	50
Title	10	40	100
Borrower ID	6	6	6
Vendor ID	3	3	3

This is especially important in automated systems that must fit within limits—such as those of the 80 or 90 characters on a tabulating card, for example. But it is also necessary, in manual systems, to assure that adequate space is allowed in the record for such items as "name" or "address."

It is desirable, as a principle, to locate data for easy transfer from one form to another. As a specific issue in the design of forms, therefore, positions should be defined for the data so that the location and sequence of identical data will be consistent from one form to another.

Forms and records are stored in files, which must also be described. A "file sheet" for doing so is shown in Figure 6.9.[3] It provides the following information about each file:

1. FILE NAME. There is a unique name for each file.

2. FILE NO. There is also a unique number for the file.

3. LOCATION. The name or number is given for the organization housing the file (or portion of the file) and the physical location if pertinent.

4. STORAGE MEDIUM. This is the type of housing for the file, such as tub file, tape storage cabinet, and three-ring binder. This entry is indirectly related to the medium of the information itself.

5. ACCESS REQUIREMENTS. Several types of information appear here: who is or is not permitted access to the file, classified by job titles or by such entries as "military—Top Secret" or "Company Confidential"; the availability of the file, in terms of what hours and how long the file is open daily; and access characteristics, including how often and how quickly reference must be made.

6. SEQUENCED BY. File sequence keys are described in this field. File sequence is described by minor key *within* intermediate keys *within* major key. A file of open book orders might, for example, be sequenced by transaction date within book order number within branch library. Sequence keys are sometimes not contained in the forms themselves, yet must be described in this field. In the case of the book orders, transaction date might be missing from the forms; new transactions would be filed in back of existing transactions within the book order number and branch library sequences.

7. CONTENT QUALIFICATIONS. Details are displayed on file contents if file name is not sufficiently descriptive. A file named "Book Order File" might, for example, be qualified as book orders for vendors within 25 miles.

8. HOW CURRENT. This gives the age of transactions when entered in the file.

9. RETENTION CHARACTERISTICS. Removal rules for each type of form in the file are entered here.

10. LABELS. These identify the file, carrying a code or phrase such as "shelf-list roll" to uniquely establish the file identity. Other information, such as date, number of records, and so forth, is often carried as well. This entry is particularly used for magnetic-tape files.

11. REMARKS. Noted here are miscellaneous data and problems such as rapidly expanding size, excessive or inadequate retention cycles, or need for duplicate files differently sequenced.

12. SEQUENCE NO. This gives the relative sequence number for order of records within the sequence keys of the file (for files in which multiple records are filed together). If report A and report B are to be processed for a common

---

[3] *Reference Manual on Form and Card Design,* International Business Machines, 1961.

Figure 6.9 File description   File Sheet.

File Name ①		File No. ②
Location ③	Storage Medium ④	
Access Requirements ⑤		
Sequenced By ⑥		
Content Qualifications ⑦		
How Current ⑧		
Retention Characteristics ⑨		
Labels ⑩		
Remarks ⑪		

CONTENTS

Sequence No.	Record Name	Volume		Characters Per Record	Characters Per File	
		Avg.	Peak		Avg.	Peak
⑫	⑬	⑭	⑮	⑯	⑰	⑱

Date   Analyst   Source   Page

Study

master report C, and report A must be filed in front of report B, then it is given sequence number 1 and report B is given sequence number 2.

13.   RECORD NAME. This shows name and number of record appearing in the file. The name should correspond to the name on a related form sheet.

14.   (VOLUME) PEAK. The peak number of this type of form in the file is shown.

15.   (VOLUME) AVG. The average number of this type of form in the file is shown.

16.   CHARACTERS PER RECORD. This field displays the size of an average record. The number entered here is the total of each data element's character count multiplied by frequency; if a range and average appear, the average is used.

17.   (CHARACTERS PER FILE) AVG. The average file size for this record is given. Multiply the character count per record by the volume average to arrive at this figure.

18.   (CHARACTERS PER FILE) PEAK. The peak file size for this record is given. Multiply character count per record by volume peak to arrive at this figure.

DESCRIPTION OF OPERATIONS

The "description of operations" provides the means by which the organizational components of the library, the files and forms that constitute the basic data, and the operations are tied together in a coherent picture. To do this, data must be acquired about the operations and then organized in one of many ways.

Data Gathering

Basically, there are two methods for learning what the processes in the library are: (1) following forms through successive processes and (2) observing what individual machines or people do.

Processing of Forms. This is the simplest and probably the most effective means of learning what the library's processes are. As each form is acquired, a sample of it is followed and observed as it moves through the library. As the form progresses, things are done with it; it is originated, data is recorded on it, it is transferred from one location to another, it is filed, it is retrieved, data are copied from it, and it is destroyed. As each of these occurs with the sample, details are recorded about what happens. What was the process? When did it happen? Who or what did it? What other forms or files were affected? When was it finished?

It is useful to record each of these processing "events" by identifying the data

Figure 6.10 Process description   Process Description Sheet

Sub-System	Forms & Files			
Components				

DESCRIPTION

Form	Related Forms & Files	Process	Time	Component

Date   Analyst   Source   Page

Study

about the relevant "dimensions of description." Figure 6.10 provides a standard form for doing so. Its use can be illustrated as follows:

Form	Related Forms and Files	Process	Time	Component
No. 23	No. 17	Record	10:45	Order Clerk
No. 23	No. 35	File	11:15	Order Clerk
No. 23	—	Transfer	12:00	File Clerk

The result presents a step-by-step picture of the processes through which the form moves.

An especially effective feature of this method of learning about the processes in the library is that it automatically provides checks on their purposes and on the utility of them. Thus, the analyst will observe (or ask) the reason for a given process (for example, "why did you record that item of data on the form?") and then, at a subsequent time, observe (or ask) whether, in fact, the reason was valid (for example, "did you use that item of data?").

Observation of Components . A second means of learning what the processes in the library are is to observe individuals and machines, keeping track of what they do. It is actually the only means of doing so in the cases where a form is not implicit in the operation. Thus, an order clerk may be observed for several hours and, during that time, may execute a variety of different processes on a large number of different forms. For each of them, a record is maintained of exactly what was done, to what form (if one is involved), and at what time.

The same method of recording is useful here:

Form or File	Forms or Files Affected	Process	Time	Component
No. 17	No. 23	Copy	10:40	Order Clerk
No. 23		Record	10:45	Order Clerk
No. 23	No. 35	File	11:00	Order Clerk
No. 35		Sort	11:10	Order Clerk

Normally this method of observation will be used (rather than that of "following forms") when a more detailed description of operations is wanted. Typically, for example, it will be used in a "time and motion" study, when the time will be measured to the hundredth of a minute, and processes will be very simple motions. On the other hand, as a tool for a description at a more general level, it is less useful.

Procedural Analysis

The resulting data can then be analyzed, usually by arranging them in a variety of ways. For example, the observations can be grouped and sorted by categories of forms, or processes (for instance, all "record" processes brought together), or by category of personnel (for example, all "order clerk" operations brought together), or by time, or by forms affected. In this way, alternative assignments of processes or sequences of them can be visualized.

The method outlined above for recording observations makes it particularly easy to do this mechanically. Methods for such procedural analysis, even to the degree of "automatic flow charting," have been developed.[4-7]

The results can be then presented in a comparable variety of ways, each representing a means of showing the relationships among the four dimensions of description. For example, the flow chart is derived directly from the time sequence of operations upon forms. It graphically shows the two dimensions of "data" and "time"; the other two dimensions ("component" and "function") must be recorded symbolically rather than graphically. On the other hand, Gantt charts graphically show relations between "components" and "time" with the remaining two dimensions being recorded symbolically in each case. "File management matrices" and "responsibility matrices" provide a visual description of the assignment of functional responsibilities. In the following sections, we explain how this is done.

FILE MANAGEMENT MATRICES

There are certain standard data management functions that occur simply because they are inherent in the nature of data processing: files are created; records are added to them, are changed periodically, and are deleted; files are searched; files are processed to produce a variety of reports; and so on. Once the set of files, forms, and data elements have been determined, a "file management matrix" can be set up:

[4] Denver Research Institute, "Formalized Analysis Techniques—Aids to Computer Design and Computer Use," in *Fourth Annual Symposium on Computers and Data Processing*. Denver, Colorado: August 29, 1957.

[5] Gatto, O. T., *AUTOSATE: An Automated Data Systems Analysis Technique*. Los Angeles: Rand Corporation, May 1962 (Rand Memorandum RM-3118-PR).

[6] Ridgway, A. O., "An Automated Technique for Conducting a Total System Study," in *Engineers Joint Computer Conference*, 1961, pp. 306-322.

[7] Scott, A. E., "Automatic Preparation of Flow Chart Listing," *Journal of the Association for Computing Machinery*, 5(1), January 1958, 57-66.

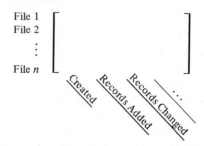

As the forms are traced through the library and as each of the standard data management functions occurs, entries can be made in this matrix which indicate who is responsible for a given function on a given file. In this way, gaps that arise because insufficient information was acquired in the examination of the library will be made evident.

Other arrangements of the same data are convenient for clearly showing the functions and files for which a given individual, piece of equipment, or organizational unit is responsible:

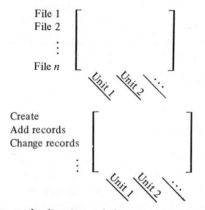

These clearly show a duplication of function across administrative lines and allow the analyst to visualize where reassignments of functional responsibility can, in principle, be made.

All three arrangements are useful for exhibition of faults in a proposed or existing organization of the library—overlapping responsibilities, unassigned responsibilities, authority incommensurate with responsibility and the like.

FLOW CHARTS

Although in principle the organization of the processes in the library can be described in a narrative manner, in practice it usually involves a technique of organized thinking known as a "flow chart," which utilizes a very limited number of symbolic conventions as a means for describing the flow of forms or data and the sequence of operations on them.[8-12]

Before describing the technique of flow charting in detail, let us discuss some principles. In certain respects, these principles are simply a result of the basic concepts of systems analysis—namely, that it is a process of successively dividing a complex problem into parts of progressively greater and greater detail. Actually, flow charting is more than a method of description; it is a concrete realization of the concepts of systems analysis.

Types of flow charts have been distinguished by different names. The names are not in themselves important, but the differences in level of detail that each type of flow chart provides are important. Specifically, at the level of least detail (and greatest generality), the term "system schematic" is used more or less to represent the level of *functional description,* where the concern is with major tasks and even requirements. In the context of library operation, a system schematic might involve the major elements, in the relatively gross organization, shown in Figure 6.11.

At this level of detail, the component functions are so interrelated and operate in such a parallel, or simultaneous, fashion that the description of a sequence of flow is relatively meaningless. Therefore, a system schematic usually represents merely a division of functions for purposes of discussion, for administrative organization, and as a first stage of analysis.

The next level of detail is called a "general flow chart." It represents the subdivision of each of the functional blocks in a system schematic into major stages in the movement of documents and data. The detail is sufficient to describe the purposes of each functional block and even to present the approach to handling of those purposes, but not sufficient to show the actual processes involved. Continuing our example of the library, the 5 blocks outlined above would be subdivided into a total of perhaps 40 to 50 major steps. For example, the block for circulation control might be as shown in Figure 6.12.

At this level of detail, the flow of information is reasonably well described, although the actual processing steps may not be evident. Therefore, a general

[8] Dougherty, Richard M., and Fred J. Heinritz, *Scientific Management of Library Operations.* New York: Scarecrow, 1966. Chapters II-V.

[9] Gregory, R. H., and R. L. Van Horn, *Automatic Data Processing Systems: Principles and Procedures*, Section III. Belmont, California: Wadsworth, 1963.

[10] Hall, D., *A Methodology for Systems Engineering.* Princeton, N. J.: Van Nostrand, 1962.

[11] Hare, Van Court, Jr., *Systems Analysis: A Diagnostic Approach.* New York: Harcourt, Brace, & World, 1967.

[12] Martin, Edley Wainwright, *Electronic Data Processing: An Introduction.* Homewood, Ill.: Irwin, 1965. Chapters 8 and 9.

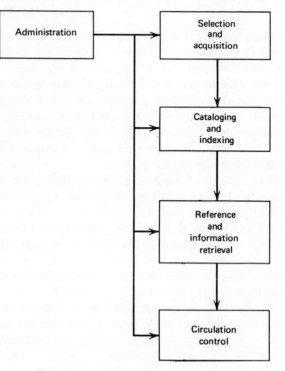

Figure 6.11 Library system schematic.

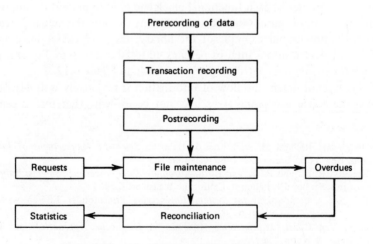

Figure 6.12 Circulation subsystem flow chart.

flow diagram usually represents a division of functional parts into major steps for the purposes of evaluation of alternative methods of processing. The amount of detail in a general flow chart is usually appropriate to the description for purposes of communication to top management, to the general public, and to outside users. Each of the library subsystems is described in later chapters by such a general flow chart, as a framework for the discussion of various methods for mechanizing each major step and as a prelude to the presentation of several specific systems.

When specific systems are described, the level of detail must be sufficient to permit a person familiar with data processing methods to understand the approach utilized and to evaluate the effectiveness of the processing steps. This amounts to a "detailed flow chart," which not only describes the flow of documents and data but presents the operations to be performed at each step in the flow. It is therefore very much dependent on the specific approach involved, the degree to which it is mechanized, and the methods of data handling employed. For example, in the "file maintenance" step in the circulation operation outlined above, a "transaction card" system, utilizing punched card equipment, might be the specific system. The detailed flow chart for that step might then be as shown in Figure 6.13.

The level of detail is about what one would derive by following forms through successive operations. It is sufficient to permit an estimate of the time required to perform each step, for the given sizes of files and volumes of activity. It is therefore the level at which the system design usually makes an evaluation of the relative efficiency ("cost-effectiveness") of potential methods. It is also usually the form in which the system is communicated to the programmer. Incidentally, if the fairly typical factor of 5 to 10 steps per block is continued, a detailed flow chart of an entire library might involve 250 to 500 steps.

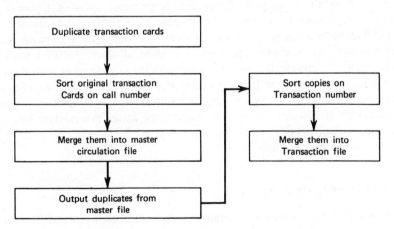

Figure 6.13   Circulation subsystem detailed flow chart.

Although the analysis by the system designer may be virtually completed at this level of detail, the analysis by the programmer is just beginning. Each step in a detailed flow chart must now be described in terms of specific process steps. This will take the form of what is usually called a "general block diagram". Actually, it is a flow chart in the sense that we have defined, at a level of even greater detail. However, there is one basic factor that reflects the difference in emphasis of the programmer. Whereas the flow chart is oriented more to the documents that flow through the system and the processes that occur on them, the block diagram is very definitely concerned with the *data* and operations performed on them. It is, therefore (for the programmer, particularly), both a method of description and an aid to analysis. Again, the factor of 5 to 10 steps per block might result in a general block diagram of, say, 2000 steps.

At this stage, the programmer is ready to construct a "detailed block diagram" or, more usually nowadays, a program in a high-order programming language. (In Chapter 10, we shall discuss a variety of such languages, including for example, COBOL, the common business oriented language, designed for the kinds of operations that occur in library data processing.) This is virtually in the form for direct machine operation, based on the instructions that it embodies. (In certain respects, the detailed block diagram may be considered as "machine-independent," since programs written in higher languages can be interpreted by many different machines. However, in fact, any program will usually be designed around the characteristics or "configuration" of a specific set of equipment so as to be efficient in operation. As a result, although the same program can be used on any of several machines, it would not necessarily be equally efficient on all of them.) Again, the factor of 5 to 10 steps per block means that the block diagram may involve about 10,000 individual steps in the higher-order language.

But we aren't done yet! Either the programmer or, if a higher-order programming language is involved, the machine must now translate the detailed block diagram into machine language—another factor of 5 to 10 steps per block and a result, for a library operation, estimated at about 100,000 machine language steps! Fortunately, the developments in the programming profession, as we shall discuss, have transferred much of this burden onto the computer and thus have made it faster, cheaper, and enormously more accurate than it would be otherwise. In Chapter 10, we shall illustrate the nature of a machine language program on a portion of the table look-up function.

For a summary, see Figure 6.14.

Flow Charting Techniques

How is anyone to pursue such a fantastically complicated process? How could anyone possibly visualize not only 10,000 to 100,000 individual steps but (even

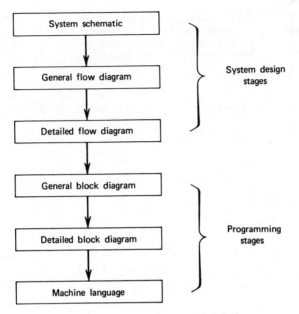

Figure 6.14   Levels of process description.

more complicated) all of the interrelationships among them as well! Of course, there is actually nothing miraculous about it, nor are system designers and programmers geniuses of some high order, able to look at a complex task and immediately analyze it into a myriad (literally) of individual steps. The answer is the method of organized thinking that systems analysis and the flow chart provide. (Incidentally, even with the aid of these tools, a good programmer might usually be able to develop about 20 to 50 individual steps, at a given level of flow chart, in a day. A detailed block diagram of, say, 2000 steps might, therefore, take 3 to 6 months.

This method of thinking is really so simple that it can be described in a small flow chart, which might lead one to wonder what all the excitement is about. To flowchart a complex task, go through the progression of steps shown in Figure 6.15. The simplicity of this process should not blind one to its power and particularly the power derived from the last two stages: (1) Is the detail sufficient? (2) If not, treat each step as a new task to be analyzed. It is these steps that produce the transition from system schematic—the grossest level of description—to machine language programs with hundreds of thousands of individual steps.

Flow charts are constructed from a relatively few, simple symbols: rectangular boxes, which contain statements about the process to be performed at that step; diamond shaped boxes, which describe decisions resulting in a

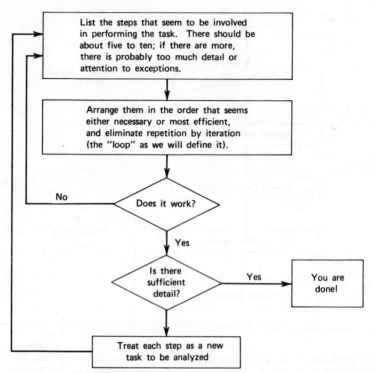

Figure 6.15   The process of flow charting.

choice among alternative sequences of operations; lines and arrows, which describe the direction of flow from one process to another (usually from top to bottom and from left to right, although this rule is violated so frequently that it represents, at most, an esthetic desire); and circles (called remote connectors), which contain symbols tying the flow from one box to another box located at a remote spot, such as on another page.

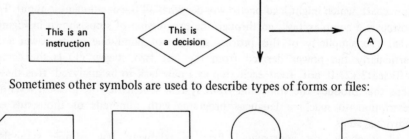

Sometimes other symbols are used to describe types of forms or files:

Punched Card   Report   Magnetic Tape   Punched Tape

Templates exist so that these boxes can be neatly and easily drawn. Thus, the mechanical combination of them in the description of a given task is quite straightforward, if certain simple principles are followed:

1. The flow chart may be drawn in horizontal or vertical sequence, depending on the situation, but the eye of the viewer should be generally carried from top to bottom and from left to right as he follows the flow. Whatever choice of presentation is made, all charts in a given study should be presented in consistent form.

2. The entire picture should be legible and as easily grasped in a totality as possible. This is the primary reason for limiting the number of steps presented at a time to the range of, say, five to ten. In addition, however, the picture should not be crowded and should be neat and pleasing in appearance—even symmetrical, if possible.

3. Each document or single piece of data should follow a single line of flow—vertical or horizontal—as it progresses through the steps that affect it. In this way, the eye can easily see what happens to it as a totality.

4. Every effort should be made to avoid the crossing of flow lines, and each line should have a single, well-defined, beginning and end.

Decision Tables

A critical portion of a flow chart is the set of steps that represent various decision points. For some tasks, the decisions to be made are so complex, depend on the status of so many different conditions, and involve so many alternative procedures that the flow would become almost unreadable if the decisions were to be completely described. Because of this, a technique known as a "decision table" has been utilized to summarize these complex decision problems.[13]

A decision table consists of four parts: a condition stub, a condition entry, an action stub, and an action entry, usually arranged in the following format:

Condition Stub	Condition Entry
Action Stub	Action Entry

The "condition stub" defines a set of *rows* in the decision table corresponding to the set of different factors entering into a decision. The "condition entry" defines a set of *columns* corresponding to the set of possible combinations of conditions. For each set of possible combinations of conditions, the decision table describes the set of actions to be taken. The alternative actions are

---

[13] Grad, Burton, "Tabular Form in Decision Logic," *Datamation,* 7 (July 1961), 22-26.

defined, by the action stub, as a set of rows and the particular actions to be taken for a given set of conditions are described in that condition entry column.

Since many of the tasks in a library operation require extremely complex combinations of many conditions, the decision table is a particularly appropriate tool. One thinks immediately of filing rules or of serials processing.

For example, consider the ALA cataloging rule number 39 concerning surnames with prefixes. It can be described by a decision table (Figure 6.16).[14] As Decision Table No. 1 shows, one set of conditions does not allow a choice of action and, thus, the action taken involves reference to a second decision table (Table 2, shown in Figure 6.17).

Because these tables summarize the decision blocks in a flow chart so well, they have become more than simply a technique. They are now regarded as a specialized programming language, and "compilers" have been developed to accept decision tables as input and to construct the necessary programs directly. An example is TABSOL, developed by General Electric for their computer systems.

The steps in the construction of a decision table are quite simple, but if they are carefully followed they not only aid in the process of description but also in the process of analysis.

Step 1.   Define the set of conditions that seem to characterize the decision problem, and record them as rows in the condition portion of the table. These can be expressed as questions that can be given a "yes" or "no" answer, or as quantitative characteristics that can be specified by a set of ranges of values.

Step 2.   Define the set of alternatives that seem to characterize the decision

Figure 6.16   ALA Cataloging Rule No. 39 (surnames with prefixes)

Decision Table No. 1 (of 2)	Rule Number			
	1	2	3	4
Usage has established a preferred form	Y	N	N	N
Name is written as one word		Y	N	N
Prefix is attributive; e.g., A', Ap, Fitz, M', Mac, Mc, O', Saint, San, etc.			Y	N
Enter established form	X			
Enter under prefix		X	X	
Make Cross-References from alternate(s)		X		
Go to Table 2				X

[14] Pratt, Allen D., *Syllabus for X413: Advanced Systems Analysis for Librarians.* Berkeley, California: University of California, March 1966.

Figure 6.17 ALA Cataloging Rule No. 39 (Surnames with prefixes)

Decision Table No. 2 (of 2)

CONDITIONS

	1	2	3	4	5	6	7	8	9	10	11	12	13	14	15	16	17	18	19	20	21
Author changed citizenship	Y																				
Name is Danish		Y	Y																		
Dutch				Y																	
English					Y																
Flemish						Y															
French							Y	Y	Y												
German										Y											
Italian											Y	Y	Y								
Norwegian														Y	Y						
Portugese																Y					
Scandinavian (af, av, von)																	Y				
Scandinavian (romance)																		Y			
Spanish																			Y		
Swedish																				Y	
Other																					Y
Prefix is an article	Y				Y		Y				Y										
contains an article		Y										Y									
is a preposition								Y													
contains a preposition									Y												
is a contracted pre & art.				Y																	
is an uncontracted pre & art.						Y															
Enter under prefix		X		X		X	X			X			X	X				X		X	
Enter under name, prefix following			X		X			X			X	X			X	ᵃX	X		ᵃX		X
Enter under article, with preposition following name									X												
Make cross-references from alternate(s)	X	X		X		X	X			X			X	X				X		X	X
Use rule for adopted country; return to Table 1	X																				

ᵃ Rare exceptions to this rule.

159

problem and record them as the set of columns for the condition entries and action entries.

Step 3.   Describe each of the alternatives by the appropriate answers or values for each of the conditions. In doing this, it may turn out that some of the alternatives are not adequately described by the defined set of conditions and that additional conditions will need to be included.

Step 4.   In order to check whether all possible alternatives have been included as condition entries, other combinations of conditions should be checked to see whether they represent valid situations. If so, they should then be included as further columns.

Step 5.   Define the set of alternative actions and record them as rows in the action stub.

Step 6.   For each of the columns for alternative situations, indicate the actions to be taken. It may become evident that, for some of the alternatives, the set of actions are not adequate. If so, additional action rows should be provided.

GANTT CHARTS

Up to this point, we have emphasized a particular method of system description—the flow chart—which is concerned with the sequence of operations upon data. There are other relationships that also are important and that must be described. One method for describing them is called the "Gantt chart," named after the man who first suggested its use.[15]

Specifically, since a system consists of components that perform the operations described by the flow chart, it is essential to indicate when each component performs an operation and on which data. The principles are relatively simple: a Gantt chart is a two-dimensional picture describing the relationships between components and time. As such, it is the precursor of all modern project planning and control techniques, including the PERT procedure illustrated in Chapter 5. It is equally useful in showing the flow of operations from one person, or machine, to the next in day-to-day operation of the library.

Schematically, the Gantt chart takes the form shown in Figure 6.18. The vertical axis lists the set of organizational components (usually in much greater detail than is shown), and the horizontal scale shows the sequence of events in time. The body of the chart then shows each function assigned to a component, including the transfer of responsibility from one component to the next.

A Gantt chart is similar to a flow chart to the extent that it shows the time sequence of operations. It differs to the extent that it *graphically* shows the

---

[15] Gantt, H. L., *Organizing for Work.* New York: Harcourt, Brace, & World, 1919.

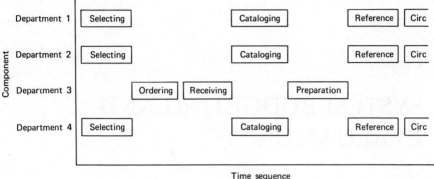

Figure 6.18   Gantt chart.

relationship to components rather than the relationship to data, which the flow chart exhibits.

The analyst uses the Gantt chart to evaluate the work load with which each organizational component is faced, over time. It exhibits the causes of fluctuation in work load due to variations in the time taken by other components of the organization in completing preceding operations. It allows the analyst to experiment with realignments of responsibility that might reduce the dependence of one component on the work of another, with consequent gain in independence and operational efficiency. It provides a management tool by which the librarian can evaluate the performance of individual departments and their dependence on the performance of other departments.

Suggested Reading

The techniques of system description are presented in almost any text on "methods analysis," "systems analysis," "systems and procedures," or other book on procedural analysis. Among them, however, the following seem to be especially well done or especially relevant:

Dougherty, Richard M., and Fred J. Heinritz, *Scientific Management of Library Operations.* New York: Scarecrow, 1966.
Gregory, R. H., and R. L. Van Horn, *Automatic Data Processing Systems: Principles and Procedures.* Belmont, California: Wadsworth, 1963.

Chapter 7

SYSTEM BUDGETING AND EVALUATION

As indicated in previous chapters, the process of library systems analysis and design involves the successive steps of analysis, synthesis, and evaluation. The techniques of system description discussed in Chapter 6 are aids to the first two steps. The techniques to aid system evaluation are the subject of this chapter.

CRITERIA OF EVALUATION

The use of "cost/effectiveness" as the criterion for evaluation of a system is an integral part of the basic philosophy of systems analysis. As a result, the library systems analyst will continually look for the best balance between cost and performance rather than, on the one hand, simply trying to reduce costs, or, on the other hand, striving for maximum performance. At times, this may mean reduced expenditures for roughly the same performance that a present system provides. More likely, however, is greatly improved performance for roughly the same cost. And frequently it means that the benefits from added services must be considered, since it is nearly always the case that new systems will actually cost more than existing ones.

In order to apply a cost/effectiveness criterion, the analyst must have a clear picture both of present costs and of the costs of alternative systems. He must also have adequate measures of performance. We shall examine these matters in detail in subsequent sections of this chapter but, first, let us summarize the significant considerations.

Evaluation of Cost

The "cost" of a new library system is made up of many parts.[1] The system must be developed; it must be installed; and it must function on a day-to-day basis. Each of these concerns will generate costs that, to one extent or another, must be considered in the cost/effectiveness evaluation.

Estimates of future operating costs are extremely difficult to ascertain. The effects of the interaction of new equipment, new procedures, new forms, and new bibliographic data cannot be determined with any precision. However, they are comparable, in nature at least, to present operating costs. What is really necessary is a cost-accounting system that will provide sufficiently accurate cost data with which to make comparison.

The costs of development and installation of a new system, on the other hand, raise many issues concerning accounting policy. Should the costs be charged to the new system or should they be regarded as necessary expenses of maintaining the efficiency of the organization? Are some of these costs covered by sources outside the usual budgetary support of the library (such as federal funds) or is the library proceeding essentially on its own? Are some of the funds regarded as capital costs (perhaps included as part of a building fund) or do they all come out of operating expenses? However, even recognizing that the situation varies from one context to another, it seems appropriate for the library system analyst to consider these costs in his evaluation, whatever their source may be, and to "amortize" them over some estimate of the life of the new system (usually, over a five-year period of operation). Unfortunately, since few nonprofit institutions amortize their capital investments, the system analyst will be dealing with only a hypothetical "amortization." However, only in this way can he maintain a true picture of overall efficiency in operation and avoid changes in system in a frivolous manner.

Evaluation of Performance

It is with the evaluation of the expected performance of a future system that the real problems arise. Whereas cost is generally easy to define, the benefits and functions on which performance would be judged are always difficult to define. And whereas cost is easy to measure, many of the most important characteristics of system performance are essentially qualitative.

For our purposes, it is valuable to distinguish between two kinds of performance factors in the evaluation of systems: (1) the quantitative factors, which relate primarily to the questions of "How many?" and "How fast?" and

[1] Fasana, Paul J., "Determining the Cost of Library Automation." *ALA Bulletin,* 61 (6) (June 1967), 656-661.

(2) the qualititive factors, which relate primarily to the question of "How good?" We shall raise these questions about each of the types of equipment presented in the next section, and then about each of the library subsystems presented in the chapters that follow.

Quantitative Factors. These are, of course, the easiest factors to define and to determine, precisely because they are quantified. However, they raise important questions and require a most exhaustive analysis of the system, They involve some very tricky issues of what constitutes a "unit of work." Furthermore, before even these issues can be resolved, the level of detail in the analysis must have been appropriately chosen and the analysis itself must have been completed so that the quantitative factors can be related to specific functions and components.[2]

Consider, for example, the quantitative factors encompassed by the question "How many?" For each of the functions defined by the flow chart, at a given level of detail, a unit of work must be defined, and the number of times that function must be performed (the "work load") is then expressed in terms of that unit of work. To illustrate this, consider the library system schematic outlined in Chapter 6 (Figure 6.11). We wish to provide a quantitative measure of the cataloging load, for instance. To do this, we must define an appropriate unit of work. And now the problem should be evident. Is the unit of work the "book," the "title," or the "catalog entry?" Shouldn't we really distinguish between types of books, perhaps? Aren't there different degrees of difficulty in the cataloging of different kinds of material, and shouldn't these be recognized by the unit of work? And so on.

Here we cannot reconcile these questions, but we can distinguish between types of them. Some of the questions (such as differences in type of book or degree of difficulty) arise because of the level of detail. For a given function, at a given level of detail, only a single unit of work can be defined; if, for one reason or another, this is insufficient, then the system must be analyzed to levels of greater detail (perhaps "cataloging" itself must be subdivided by type of material or type of catalog).

On the other hand, some of the questions (such as "the book," or "the title," or "the catalog entry") represent the fundamental issue—what is the appropriate unit of work? Unfortunately, any choice made—and one must be made—will be somewhat unsatisfactory. We live with the results of our choice, and we hope that they are the least of the evils we might have faced.

For the purposes of illustration, suppose we choose the "catalog entry" as our unit of work for cataloging. Then we are faced with a relatively simple task, all the really hard work has been done. We merely count the number of

---

[2] Pierce, W. O'D., *Work Measurement in Public Libraries.* New York: Social Science Research Council, 1949.

catalog entries that are required during some time period, such as a month. The quantitative factor of "How Many?" for cataloging is then the number

$$N_c = (\text{catalog entries}) \text{ per month}$$

Similar measures of the load on all other functions, at similar levels of detail, would need to be defined and counted in a similar manner.

The second set of quantitative factors relate to the question "How fast?" which must also be asked of each function. Fortunately, much of the difficult work has been done, since the unit of work—the catalog entry, for example—is the basis for answering these questions. In particular, we ask "How fast can a catalog entry be generated?" Notice, incidentally, that we try to determine the time required for the *individual* unit of work. We could, of course, answer the question in a very simple manner: for example, we produce 500 catalog entries each month: there are 10,000 minutes in a month; ergo, it takes 20 minutes to produce a catalog entry. However, this simple approach obscures many significant problems in efficiency of operation. It is therefore desirable to deal with the individual unit of work itself—the actual time to produce a *single* catalog entry—rather than the average over a large number of them. For this reason, the industrial engineers and methods analyst actually stand beside a worker with a stop watch and measure time to the hundredths of a minute! Only in this way can a true picture be obtained of "How fast?"

Now, one should legitimately raise a difficulty: the time to produce a catalog entry will vary from one time to the next, as a result of differences in the material, or the individual cataloger, or the time of day. Since we must limit this value to a single quantity, therefore, it must be taken as an average over a large number of catalog entries. However, it should be emphasized that this average will not be the same as that derived by simply dividing the total number of catalog entries by the number of minutes in a month; in fact, it is obviously less (since, otherwise, a backlog would build up) and usually it will be much less. It is this difference, in part, with which the system designer is concerned when he tries to produce an optimum system. It is this difference that is reflected in the columns labeled "minimum unit cost" and "basic unit cost" in Figure 4.8.

In summary, for each functional subdivision and component at a given level of analysis, quantities characterizing the volume of work, the amount of time, and the cost—all expressed in terms of an acceptable, useful unit of work—must be developed. This will inevitably involve compromise and frequently will require further analysis with a finer degree of detail.

Qualitative Factors: But none of those quantitative factors really resolve the more basic question, "How good?" In fact, there is little that does. By its very nature, dealing with the substance of human communication as it does, the library involves a high proportion of essentially judgmental issues. It acquires material whose value is unknown; it attempts to describe the material for the future uses that must be unknown; it must find material when the relevance of the content was, until then, unknown. It must do this for a great variety of material and users, and within a limited budget.

With so many significant factors essentially unknown, it is remarkable that libraries function well at all. That they do is certainly a reflection of the relative consistency of people and their needs for information. But still, how do we determine how well they do function? How do we measure the value of "information" or "service?"[3-8] What constitutes "good cataloging" or "good reference?" How do we measure typographic quality and readability? Indeed, what is the value of a library itself?

Obviously, these are questions so deeply imbedded in the very concept of library service that they can be answered only by the professional judgment of the librarian. At best, the system designer can clear out the underbrush of extraneous issues—those that can be quantified—so that the alternatives are presented free of them. But the choice among the alternatives must be made by the librarian in terms of these qualitative issues.

In later chapters of this book, we shall define specifically the essential qualitative factors—the ones that characterize the very purpose of the library— for each of the subsystems of the library. The intent is to separate clearly and to highlight the things that cannot and should not be handled by the technician.

Perhaps the most important factors are those that relate to *response time*: the recentness of the information provided by the system, the delay between a need for information and its availability to the user of it, and the time that the user must spend in analysis of data retrieved. Most of these appear to be readily quantifiable, if only because the parameter of time itself seems so clear, but actually their value and importance are highly qualitative issues. For example, one can speak of the "half-life" of the information in a file as reflecting the steady decrease in its value over time.[9,10] One can perhaps quantify a relation

[3] McDonough, Adrian M., *Information Economics and Management Systems*. New York: McGraw-Hill, 1963.

[4] Malmgren, H. B., "Information, Expectations, and the Firm," *J. of Economics*, 75 (3) (August 1961), 399-421.

[5] Marschak, Jacob, "Towards an Economic Theory of Organization and Information," in R. M. Thrall et al., *Decision Processes*. New York: Wiley, 1954.

[6] Marschak, Jacob, *Problems in Information Economics*. Los Angeles: University of California, November 25, 1962.

[7] Radner, Roy, *The Evaluation of Information in Organizations*. Berkeley, California: University of California, 1961.

[8] Stigler, G. J., "The Economics of Information," *Journal of Political Economy*, 69 (3) (June 1961), 213-225.

[9] Burton, R. E., and R. W. Kebler, "The 'Half-Life' of Some Scientific and Technical Literature", *American Documentation*, 11 (1) (January 1960), 18-22.

[10] Kilgour, Frederick G., "Recorded Use of Books in the Yale Medical Library," *American Documentation*, 12 (3) (October 1961), 266-269.

between the value of a decision based on information from a file and the time at which that decision is made—presumably that value will tend to decay over time. The operating time of the system will be directly reflected in the cost, yet it is the basis for the user's interest in the system and willingness to pay for it.

Also important are the factors related to the quality in selection and acquisition of information, in analysis and description of it, organization and processing of it, and retrieval of it. Certainly these are the most difficult factors, precisely because they deal with the very substance of an information system—the information itself: the total amount of it, the accuracy of it, the relevancy of it to a user or even to the entire set of users, the degree to which it can be analyzed and organized, and the problems in communication with it. Many of these questions can perhaps be handled at the level of "communication theory," which deals with the statistical properties of information. But the bulk of the really significant problems relate primarily to the relation between that information and the *specific* user, who is by no means governed by statistics—nor is his response to the information. This has represented the great gap in adequate theory for information science.

The value and relative importance of each of these criteria—time, quality, and information—can be determined only by a careful analysis of the user of the system. The methods for making such an analysis are few: standard interview and survey forms, statistics of utilization, examination of ideals, experimental "system tests", and simulations. As a result, there is little qualitative data (and less quantitative data) on which to base criteria and measures.[11-17]

However, as a step forward, the operation of an information system can be divided into a succession of stages: communication, file processes, and equipment operation. For each stage, criteria and measures can be defined. To be specific:

[11] The Study of Criteria and Procedures for Evaluating Scientific Information Retrieval Systems. Chicago, Ill.: Arthur Anderson, March 1962.

[12] Bare, Carole E., "Conducting User Requirements Studies in Special Libraries," *Special Libraries,* 57 (2), February 1966.

[13] Bourne, C. P., and G. C. Peterson et al., *Requirements, Criteria, and Measures of Performance of Information Storage and Retrieval Systems.* Menlo Park: California: Stanford Research Institute, December 1963.

[14] Davis, Richard Allen, and Catherine A. Bailey, *Bibliography of Use Studies.* Philadelphia, Pa.: Drexel School of Library Science, 1964.

[15] Gilman, Henry, "What the Scientist Expects of the Librarian," *College and Research Libraries,* 7 (3) (July 1947), 329-330.

[16] Herner, Saul, *The Relationship of Information Use Studies and the Design of Information Storage and Retrieval Systems.* Rome, N.Y.: Griffiss Air Force Base, 1959.

[17] Resnick, A., and C. B. Hensley, "The Use of Diary and Interview Techniques in Evaluating a System for Disseminating Technical Information," *American Documentation,* 14 (2) (April 1963), 109-116.

1. The degree to which a vocabulary has been standardized can be characterized by the extent to which inter-term relations have been made explicit (for example, by the size of the subject authority).

2. The process of communication—translation from one vocabulary to another—can be characterized by the required capacity of the communication channel.

3. The relevancy of the stored data to particular requests can be measured by a variety of measures of "similarity."

4. The adequacy of the file organization can be measured by the response time it provides.

These are the criteria that will be emphasized in the final section of this book.

Evaluation of Equipment

In addition to the functional criteria of performance outlined above, there are other issues in evaluation of a proposed new system that become especially important when mechanization is involved. In part, the performance of a set of equipment can be evaluated in terms of the the extent to which it meets the cost/effectiveness criteria—as expressed in the demands and desires that the library defines.[18-21] But there are also some intangibles that should be considered.

First, equipment will be acquired from a manufacturer or supplier. How reliable is he? What supporting services does he provide? Will he meet delivery schedules? What kinds of financial arrangements will he consider?

Second, characteristics of the equipment, in addition to its functional performance, should be considered: Is it readily available or does it require development work? How reliable is it? It is compatible with other equipment? Is it easily expandable to greater capacity?

The relative importance of these intangible considerations vary from one context to the next. However, many libraries that undertake mechanization programs underestimate their importance and, as a result, experience delays, costly changes from one set of equipment to another, and operational difficulties. Therefore, it is probably wise to place heavier emphasis on these intangibles than on cost/effectiveness *per se.*

[18] Becker, Joseph, and R. M. Hayes, *Information Storage and Retrieval: Tools, Elements, Theories.* New York: Wiley, 1963 (Chapter 15).

[19] Conway, B., J. Gibbons, and D. E. Watts, *Business Experience with Electronic Computers.* New York: Controllers Institute Research Foundation, Inc., 1959.

[20] Gregory, R. H., and R. L. Van Horn, *Automatic Data Processing Systems: Principles and Procedures.* Belmont, California: Wadsworth, 1963 (pp 191-200, 552-638).

[21] Peat, Marwick, Mitchell, and Company, *Appraising the Economics of Electronic Computers,* Controllership Foundation, 1956.

COST AND BUDGETARY FACTORS IN EVALUATION

The budgeting for costs must consider the following categories: capital budget (for equipment and buildings, for instance), developmental costs, installation costs, and operating costs.

Capital Budget

The capital budget should be set in the context of a detailed, long-range, capital-outlay program.[22,23] It should specify the cost of investing in building and equipment implied by the mechanization objectives. An important part of the capital budget is the source-of-funds statement, a comprehensive list of available funds including funds from state and/or municipal sources, funds from grants, gifts, bequests, and the like. However, it is quite reasonable to expect that funds apparently available for mechanization will fall considerably short of the actual amount needed, and the budget will indicate to the librarian the size of the deficit facing him. If the chances for filling the gap between required and available funds are remote, the librarian must set up a priority list, and he must modify his mechanization objectives accordingly. Subsequent revisions of the mechanization objectives should be immediately tested for their effects on the capital budget, and should be incorporated into it.

Developmental Costs

The costs in development of a system include: (1) system design, in which objectives are established, alternative systems designed and evaluated, and specifications set; (2) programming, in which operating computer programs are developed; and (3) testing, in which the system is "debugged."

System-design costs are primarily a function of the scope of the system to be considered. However, they are probably best budgeted as a continuing yearly commitment of library systems analysis personnel to these tasks.

Programming costs are totally a function of the scope of the system and can be roughly estimated in terms of the number of computer instructions to be written.[24,25] A typical estimate of production rates for programming is about

[22] Bierman, Harold, and Seymour Smidt, *The Capital Budgeting Decision*. New York: MacMillan, 1960.

[23] Dean, Joel, *Capital Budgeting*. New York: Columbia, 1951.

[24] Farr, Leonard, and Burt Nanus, *Cost Aspects of Computer Programming*. Santa Monica, California: System Development Corporation, January 1964.

[25] Gottlieb, C. C., "The Cost of Programming and Coding," *Computers and Automation*, 3 (September 1964), 14-15.

15 instructions per man-day. (For example, a library subsystem, such as circulation control, will probably require 5000 instructions and take 1 to 2 programmers 1 year to complete). Testing is likely to require one half of the time and manpower required for programming. In each case, provision also must be included for machine time required for testing and debugging. If the machine is readily accessible, with rapid "turn-around," both programming and testing can be done much more rapidly. If, on the other hand, the machine is inaccessible—operating under a "closed-shop," for example—with the results of testing available a day later, the rate of progress will be very slow.

It is to be expected that, as the library community gains experience with data processing, it will create a pool of common knowledge and standardized programs that may help to reduce some of these costs for libraries coming along at a later time. However, large differences are likely to continue among libraries and the computing facilities available to them. It is, best therefore, to be conservative in the estimates of these developmental costs and not to count heavily on the work done by others

Installation Costs

The installation of a new system will involve a number of significant costs: (1) the preparation of physical facilities, (2) the conversion of files, (3) parallel operation and changeover, and (4) training.

The costs for preparation of physical facilities vary so greatly in different situations that no generally applicable estimates can be made. They depend too much on the existing space, wiring, air conditioning, and on the particular equipment involved.

The costs of conversion of files are especially significant for libraries since, in a sense, they are set up to handle very large files.[26] They can be the largest single element of cost in converting from a manual system to a machine system. The existing files must be checked for their accuracy; they must be edited to ensure accurate, efficient conversion; and they must be converted to machine language. The cost of checking the accuracy and validity of existing records is likely to be very large. As much as $2 to $3 per record might be incurred in checking records of serial holdings, for example. The cost of editing will also be large. Based on the experience with the MARC II format, this cost is likely to be as much as 80c per catalog entry (including overhead).[27] The cost of actual conversion into machine language depends on the procedure and equipment

[26] Lipetz, Ben-Ami, "Labor Costs, Conversion Costs, and Compatibility in Document Systems," *American Documentation,* 14 (2) (April 1963), 117-122.

[27] The MARC Pilot Project, *Final Report,* Washington, D.C., Library of Congress, 1968. Chapter VIII.

involved. This cost, of all the costs in conversion, is the most likely to be reduced as time goes on. For example, optical character-reading equipment will become more widely used and will result in significant savings. Based on present-day experience with the use of punched card key-punchers or punched tape typewriters, production rates of 6000 to 10,000 key strokes per hour are standard. Based on the experience with MARC II format, the costs for keypunching can be estimated at about 30c to 40c per catalog entry (including overhead).[28]

The cost of parallel operation can be roughly estimated from expected operating costs under full-scale operation, but can be added to the costs of present operation for the time of changeover. At times, attempts have been made to avoid these costs, at least in this form, by setting up what was called a "turn-key" operation with effectively "instant" changeover. The experience seems to argue against this kind of approach.

Finally, significant costs are incurred in the training of personnel in their work with the new system. Time of systems staff, of administrative staff, and of the operating personnel themselves must be allocated for this purpose. Frequently, other costs are incurred in development of teaching materials, hiring of special instructors, and usage of machine time.

Operating Costs

These are the most clearly defined costs. Methods for estimating them are the principal concern in our subsequent discussions of library clerical systems (Section IV). They include costs for equipment, operating personnel for equipment, library personnel, and supplies.

METHODS FOR QUALITATIVE EVALUATION

The purpose of qualitative evaluation is to establish criteria for comparison of systems that recognize the relative importance of the functions they provide. To do this, the functions must be categorized by type and by qualitative characteristics. Then the user of the library must be studied in order to evaluate their relative importance.

It is surprising that there are really so few methods available for study of the user and his view of a library's services. About the only methods available are questionnaires and interviews, statistics on utilization, and idealized models and simulations.

[28] *Ibid.*

Questionnaires and Interviews

The appendix to this chapter shows a sample "Information System Value Interview Form" that emphasizes the "critical incident" approach.[29] It is fairly typical of such questionnaires, which force the person being interviewed to phrase his answers to questions in the context of *specific* incidents. The purpose is to avoid the natural tendency of someone to think in terms of atypical situations, remembered because of the extremes that they represent.

Statistics on Utilization

The statistics derived from past utilization of the library present a quantitative picture of the relative importance of various activities in the library. As such, of course, they reflect the nature of past services rather than of future services, and therefore may not be a complete answer to the question of user needs. For this reason, many researchers have emphasized the need for more basic studies, including simulated environments in which the response of the user to new services can be tested. On the other hand, for the individual library, faced with the need to move ahead, statistics on past utilization still represent the most reliable form of data on usage of the library.

The type of information to be sought includes the following.

Circulation Statistics. Annual circulation statistics can be analyzed into quarterly, monthly, weekly, daily, and hourly averages. For example, in process of preparation for automation. The University Research Library at UCLA saved all transaction cards of the Circulation Department for three years.[30] With the aid of a computer, they were sorted and analyzed for the frequency of circulation of individual books and categories of books. Data of this kind help to define user needs and can be used in determining the number of copies that should be purchased of any one title, the period for which a type of book should be loaned, and so on.

Demand Time Distribution. A study of average circulation volume during peak hours and peak days (for instance before examination time in a university library) can help in establishing queueing patterns for determining the number of points at which patrons can receive service. In most libraries the pattern of demand will vary, both during the year and during the day. Knowledge of these variations will help to determine the optimal number of checkout points and, in libraries that employ manual or partially manual systems, the size of the staff at the charging desk.

[29] Bourne, C. P., et al., *op. cit.*

[30] Cox, James R., *Automated Circulation Control in the University Research Library at UCLA,* Los Angeles: University of California, 1965.

Use of Reference Services. The frequency of use of the reference department provides statistics on the average number of reference requests made per month, week, day, and hour; the average amount of time needed for service; seasonal fluctuations in service (that is, the frequency of requests during various times: prior to examination time, in the middle of the quarter, and during vacations).

User Needs–Acquisitions. Satisfying user needs for items not available in the library is one of the prime functions of the acquisition department. To determine the extent to which this function is performed satisfactorily, the total number of requests for new (or additional) items (books, periodicals, and publications) can be compared with the number of such requests that were approved and executed. The resulting ratio should be one of the factors influencing the library's acquisitions policy.

Simulation

In Chapter 3, simulation was discussed as a technique applicable to library-management decision making. If the operation of a library can be described by such idealized models, the means are available to evaluate the comparative value of various systems. The simulation can provide illustrations of the effects that each of the alternatives will have on service to the user. Although the models may be idealized, they give the analyst a picture of how systems will function in practice that could not otherwise be obtained.[31]

METHODS OF QUANTITATIVE EVALUATION

The aim in "quantitative evaluation" is to provide a direct "cost/effectiveness" comparison between alternative systems. For example, the analyst will want to plot the alternatives on a modified "break-even" chart. In the hypothetical example shown in Figure 7.1, it appears that a manual system would give the lowest cost per 1000 books circulated as long as the annual circulation is less than 250,000 books. If 250,000 to 450,000 books are circulated annually, a mechanical system (for instance, punched-card system) appears to be the most efficient. At any greater circulation, the automated system appears to be the most efficient.

Similar relationships can be found and plotted for each of the separate functions in the library, matching costs against the respective units of work. A separate analysis of each of the objectives, in this way, can provide the librarian and the analyst with a rough indication of the relative merits of the alternatives.

---

[31] Chodrow, Mark, et al., *Information Service System Modeling: Analytical Tools for Management Evaluation,* Information Dynamics Corporation, December 1963.

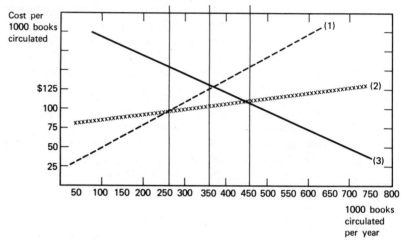

Figure 7.1   Illustrative "trade-off" chart. Cost per 1000 books circulated (manual system, mechanical system, and automatic system). (1) Manual system (----------). (2) Mechanical system (xxxxxxxxxx). (3) Automated system (————).

However, it must be recognized that the separate evaluation of individual functions in the library will not lead to an adequate evaluation of the efficiency of a total library system which combines all of the required functions. To do so requires a quantitative model for *system* evaluation.[32]

Approach to Analysis

In Chapters 14 to 18, we shall provide parameters, equations, and illustrative examples of the estimation of processing times and costs, as required for quantitative evaluation. In doing this, the approach to analysis will be as follows.

1.   To define the various forms and files involved.
2.   To outline the requirements they place on each of the basic file management functions (as discussed in Chapter 6).
3.   To specify the parameters involved in the estimation of processing times and costs, including representative values where feasible.
4.   To develop equations for such estimation, and to illustrate them on a hypothetical, fairly large library.

Forms and Files. Each of the library subsystems involves the maintenance and use of a number of data files. For example, a circulation system may require a

---

[32] Becker, Joseph, and R. M. Hayes, *Information Storage and Retrieval: Tools, Elements, Theories.* New York: Wiley, 1963. Chapter 15.

borrower registration file, a call-number file, or a scheduling file; an ordering subsystem may require a book fund file, a vendor file, or an "in-process" file. Files are numbered $F_1, F_2, \ldots$ for each subsystem. Thus, the book fund file might be F_1 for the ordering subsystem, the vendor file, F_2; and so on. In each case, the file becomes a focal point for the processing operations of the particular subsystems, because they arise from the requirements for file management functions associated with each file.

File Management Functions. In Chapter 6, we outlined the functions involved in the maintenance and use of a file: A file must be *created*. It must be *maintained*, so that the effects of all kinds of transactions—producing additions to the file, changes in existing records in the file, and deletion from the file—can be handled. It frequently must be *interrogated*, so that answers can be provided from it in response to needs for data as they arise. *Reports* must be produced from it, so as to "pre-answer" many standard, predictable needs for information. These functions are specified for each file, so that F_{11} might be "creation of book fund file", F_{23} might be "interrogation of vendor file"; and so on.

Processing Operations. For each file management function, there are certain standard operations—data must be converted, by *key-punching* or otherwise, to machine language; it must be *input* to the computer; frequently, it must be *sorted* into one or more sequences; the files must be *searched*; data must be *processed*; and results must be *output*. These become the ultimate means for estimating the processing times and costs. These are specified for each file management function for each file, so that F_{111} might be "key-punching in creation of the book fund file", F_{234} might be "processing requests for information from the vendor file", and so forth.

Work Loads. For each file management function—even, sometimes, for each processing operation—work loads must be defined. Generally, these can be related to some specific characteristic of the library itself; sometimes they are determined by the nature of the data processing system itself. These are specified as V_{jkl}, a "work load per month" on operation F_{jkl}.

Components. To arrive at adequate criteria for evaluation of times and costs, the set of equipment must be analyzed into components whose processing rates can be somewhat well specified for each of the processing operations. Generally, the division into *personnel* (*key-punching* and *operating*), *input* equipment, *terminal* equipment, the *computer* itself, *tape files, direct access files, communication* lines, and *output* equipment is an appropriate one.

Cost and Time Estimates. It is possible (in principle) to develop estimates of costs and processing times for each component on each processing operation. Generally, we will do this by estimating the following quantities: (1) the overall processing time for each unit of work on a process, (2) the percentage of that time during which a component is committed to the operation, and (3) the cost of the component. These will then be combined into a "measure of efficiency" of the component on the operation. This really is only a means of describing, for example, "the commitment of direct-access files during the processing of requests for information from the vendor file." For each file of each subsystem, we shall outline the parameters relevant to the evaluation of processing times for each processing operation. Where it is appropriate, representative values will be assigned to these parameters, not as "prescriptive" values but solely as a basis for illustration.

Overall System Evaluation. From the data as presented in this way, several results essential to system evaluation can be derived. In particular, if the respective efficiency measures (a_{ijkl}) are multiplied by the work loads (V_{jkl}), the results can be summed to provide a measure of the extent of utilization of each component.

$$\left\{ \sum_{j,\,k,\,l} a_{ijkm} V_{jkm} = U_i \right\}$$

Alternatively, they can be summed to provide a measure of the cost of each operation.

$$\left\{ \sum_i a_{ijkl} V_{jkl} = X_{jkl} \right\}$$

Summing both ways provides an estimate of the total commitment of the equipment to the processing subsystem.

Generally the extent of utilization of each component will be significantly less than its actual processing capacity, even when all subsystems are considered. To a degree, the excess capacity that this implies represents "overhead" that might be allocated to each subsystem, usually proportional to its use of the system as a whole. To an extent, however, it represents a necessary part of the system as a whole, to provide capacity for peak-load requirements, additional functions, and a margin of safety. As such, it should be charged to an overall system requirement and not to individual subsystems.

Equation. Figure 7.2 provides the format that we shall employ in Chapters 14 to 18 for exhibiting the equations used in evaluation of processing times and costs.

The key to Figure 7.2 is as follows.

1.   SUB-SYSTEM. This identifies the subsystem for which estimates are being made.
2.   FILE. This identifies the file or files included in the estimates.
3.   LEVEL OF ANALYSIS: COMPONENT. This describes the general level of detail at which the component equipment and personnel are being considered.

Figure 7.2   Processing time and cost estimation (estimation sheet)

Subsystem ①				File ②					
Level of Analysis: Component ③									
Level of Analysis: Function ④									
Basic Unit of Work ⑤									
Comp	Operation	Number	Size	Freq.	Rate	Time	Cost	Percent	Total
⑥	⑦	⑧	⑨	⑩	⑪	⑫	⑬	⑭	⑮
	Total ⑯					⑰			⑱
	Cost/Effectiveness = ⑲								

Date   Analyst   Page

Study

4.   LEVEL OF ANALYSIS: FUNCTION. This describes the general level of detail at which processing tasks are being considered.

5.   BASIC UNIT OF WORK. This identifies the basic unit of work by which the effectiveness of the operations being considered will be measured. For example: "titles cataloged," "title orders issued," and "volumes circulated."

6.   COMP (Component). This identifies the particular component or set of components involved in the estimates of the given line, consistent with the *Level of Analysis: Component,* identified in (entry 3).

7.   OPERATION. This identifies the particular operation or set of operations involved in the estimates of the given line, consistent with the *Level of Analysis: Function,* identified in (entry 4).

8.   NUMBER. This is the number of units of work processed by the component and operation, for purposes of the estimation.

9.   SIZE. This is a unit of "size," such as "number of characters," as needed to derive time estimates from standard processing rate figures.

10.   FREQUENCY. This is the frequency with which the specified number of units of work occurs in a time period (usually one month). If the basis for (entry 8) is daily, then (entry 10) might be 20 to 30; if it is weekly, then (entry 10) might be 4 1/3; if it is monthly, then (entry 10) would be 1.

11.   RATE. This specifies the rate at which the component performs the operation, in terms of time for (entry 9).

12.   TIME. This is simply (entry 8) x (entry 9) x (entry 10) divided by (entry 11). It provides the estimate of processing time during which the component is committed (during a month, for example) to the specified operation.

13.   COST. This is the cost of the component for the unit of time involved in the activity in (entry 10). For example, "dollars per month."

14.   PERCENT. This is the percentage of the cost of the component allocable to the specified operation. (Determined primarily by the extent to which the component can handle a number of jobs simultaneously.)

15.   TOTAL. This is simply (entry 12) x (entry 13) x (entry 14). It provides the estimate of costs allocable to the specified operation.

16.   (Number of Basic Units of Work). This is the total number of basic units of work, as specified in (entry 5) by which effectiveness will be measured.

17.   (Total Processing Time). This is the total processing time, as estimated from the individual times. (It may be less than or equal to the sum of them.)

18.   (Total Cost). This is the sum of (entry 15).

19.   COST/EFFECTIVENESS. This is the ratio, (entry 18)/(entry 16).

Problem Areas

In the model as defined, there are a number of problem areas. The first area relates to the difficulties involved in determining the efficiency values. The second area relates to the variability in the basic volume data. The model, as it has been used, assumes that the work-load figures are sufficiently representative of the character of the activity on each function for the purposes of system design. It must be recognized, however, that an average value of a variable distribution provides little insight on the effects of peak-load activity, such as queuing or system saturation. Therefore, the work load must be examined carefully and must be defined so as to reflect these effects.

The third area of difficulty, in the model as defined above, is in the definition and selection of the functions and components to be considered in the system design. Thus, the model assumes that the choice of operations and the assignment of performance of them to the component subsystems have been completely prespecified. This essentially begs certain questions: What should be the choice of operations for the performance of some desired task? What should be the component subsystems? What should be the assignment of tasks to the components? These are the crucial problems in system design.

Appendix

Sample Information System Value Interview Form (emphasis on "Specific Incident" approach) (see following pages). A survey technique, using personal interviews among a specific user population for determining user requirements, is outlined below. It consists of a preliminary interview guide, incorporating the so-called *specific-incident* approach. The interview guide is designed to obtain four kinds of information.[33]

1.   A list of critical requirements, using the specific incident technique.

2.   Measurements of selected requirements that are considered both important and susceptible to measurement.

3.   Rank order of the importance of factors that were believed to be important to users and were amenable to ranking.

4.   Background variables that might influence the user needs (age, type of field, type of information, and the like).

INFORMATION SYSTEM VALUE INTERVIEW FORM

We are conducting a study to evaluate the performance of an information system. To do this, we have to know the needs of users of it. Let me give you definitions for two terms I'll be using throughout this interview. (HAND RESPONDENT CARD AND LET HIM READ IT WITH YOU.)

> First, I am concerned with a specific type of information—that is, (explanation of the information system and its purpose). I am *not* concerned with other types of information—that is (eliminate similar purposes which might confuse the respondent).
>
> Second, is the term *service need.* This is when you, or someone else at your request, wants to obtain information from the system. A service need can be extensive and made through one or more means, or it can be very brief—such as looking through sources you keep in your own office. *Not* included are requests for specific information that you know deal with the subject. For example, you are not being serviced when you ask the system to (explain what is not included).

(TAKE BACK CARD A)

1.   Keeping this definition in mind, have you, or anyone requested by you, needed any service in the last year?

_____ Yes _____ No (IF NO, TERMINATE INTERVIEW)

(IF YES, ASK:)

[33] Adapted from Bourne et al, *Requirements, Criteria, and Measures of Information Storage and Retrieval Systems,* Stanford Research Institute, 1961.

2. Roughly, how many times?

3a. Here is a list of some activities men in your position work in (HAND RESPONDENT CARD B). In what *one* activity do you spend the most working time?

3b. Which activities account for the majority of your service needs? (IF RESPONDENT GIVES MORE THAN THREE, ASK FOR THREE THAT ACCOUNT FOR THE MOST SERVICE NEEDS.)

3c. Now I'd like to ask you about the most recent service need you had while engaged in one of the activities you named. Which of the activities you named required this service?

---

a. General project planning

b. Theoretical design of experiments

c. Design of equipment, systems, and procedures

d. Conduct of lab experiments or field tests

e. Correlation of experimental results with theory, or vice versa

f. Review and evaluation of a specific project or product (a critique)

g. Technical report writing

h. Technical proposal writing

i. Preparation of lectures or technical papers

j. Keeping current with technical advances

k. Search for novel technical ideas on which to base new projects or new research

l. Serving as a consultant

m. Other

(TAKE BACK CARD B)

4. Do you recall some of the details of this service need?

_____ Yes _____ No (IF NO, SKIP TO QUESTION 19)

5a. Do you recall anything happening during the service need that made for an easier or better response, or that made the response difficult? For example, what was the most difficult or irritating thing that happened? (PROBE)

5b. What was the easiest or most gratifying thing that happened? (PROBE)

5c. If a young engineer who had just joined the staff had this same service need today, what advice would you give him to make the response easier? (PROBE)

5d. What would you warn him about? (PROBE)

6. Who provides the service—you, a co-worker, a system operator, or someone else?

Self_____
Co-worker_____
System operator_____
Other_____
Computer_____

7. Do you recall the exact nature of your request—that is, did you just generally describe the subject, were certain terms used, or what?

8. Which of these statements most nearly describes how urgently you needed the results when you requested them? Ignore the importance of the results when you received them—we'll get to that next (HAND RESPONDENT CARD C)

> a. Very urgent; other work held up.
>
> b. Important; needed to help determine course of future work or to help fill in gaps in your knowledge.
>
> c. Not very important; completeness of results had little priority

(TAKE BACK CARD C)

9. Sometimes a response turns up significant information and sometimes it adds little to your knowledge. Which of these statements most nearly describes how important the results were? (HAND RESPONDENT CARD)

> a. Very important. E.g., changed the course of a project.
>
> b. Not very important. E.g., results were used as supplementary or back-up material.
>
> c. Unimportant. E.g., results had little or no effect on course of work.

(TAKE BACK CARD D)

10a. Approximately how long was it from the time you made your request until you had received the major group of relevant information?

10b. Was this adequate or did you really need the material sooner? (IF NEEDED SOONER, ASK HOW SOON)

10c. What was the maximum amount of time you could have waited for the major group of relevant information?

11a. How old was the most recent information provided? In other words, how recent was the material covered?

11b. Was this adequate or did you really need more recent material? (IF NEEDED MORE RECENT MATERIAL, ASK HOW RECENT)

11c. Could you have gotten by with data that were all   (START WITH TIME PERIOD AFTER "ADEQUATE" AND CONTINUE UNTIL RESPONDENT SAYS "NO")

12a. In what forms did the data come to you? (READ LIST OF DIFFERENT FORMS)

12b. Which of these do you generally prefer for this type of service?

12c. Which of the others are not preferred but generally adequate?

12d. Are there any that you consider inadequate for this type of service?

13a. Some irrelevant material is usually provided in response to a need. What proportion of the total time you spent would you guess was spent in culling out irrelevant or duplicate material?

13b. Was that about right or should you have had to spend less of your time culling out irrelevant or duplicate material? (IF LESS, ASK WHAT PROPORTION)

13c. Of the time you spend, what is the maximum proportion of your time you would have been willing to spend culling out irrelevant material?

14. (HAND RESPONDENT CARD E AND READ ALONG WITH HIM) I am going to show you 7 cards, each of which contains a statement about a performance measure by which information systems can be judged. It is important to realize that these measures are to a degree in conflict with one another. For example, if you want your requests satisfied as quickly as possible, you normally must expect that some relevant material will be overlooked. Similarly, if you want the system to produce all, or nearly all the relevant material, the you must expect a large number of irrelevant material in the results. (HAND RESPONDENT GROUP OF CARDS)

Please put these items in the order in which you would *least* want to compromise on the type of service we've been discussing. Put those you feel strongly you wouldn't want to compromise on your left, those you wouldn't mind compromising on your right, and the others in the middle. Now, put those in each group in order. If you feel two items are equal in importance, put them together.

Order

a.	Minimum time to get the major group of relevant material to you.
b.	Minimum of irrelevant material produced by the response.
c.	Minimum of relevant material overlooked by the response.
d.	Material comes to you in form you prefer.
e.	Minimum of effort on your part to communicate your request for service.
f.	Certainty that specified sources over certain period of time were analyzed.

(AFTER RECORDING, TAKE BACK CARD E AND GROUP OF CARDS)

15a. On the type of service we've been discussing, how long from the time you make your request can you generally wait for a response which covers 50% of the potential information?

15b. How long for a response covering 80%?

15c. How long for a response covering all or almost all potential information?

16a. Again on the type of service we've been discussing, how many of your own working days, weeks, or months would you be willing to spend on the work if you could be sure 50% of the relevant information were located?

16b. How much if 80% of the relevant information were located?

16c. And if almost all were located?

17a. Let's assume for a moment that you initiated a request for service of the type we've been discussing. Let's say that you personally have spent X amount of time and that the response covered data up through (a period of time) but nothing more recent. Proportionately how much more working time would you personally be willing to spend to see that sources up through (b period of time) were covered? (OBTAIN ANSWERS IN MULTIPLES OF "X"—"Half again as much time", "Twice as much", etc.)

17b. How much to see that sources up through (c period) were located?

17c. And sources up through (d period) ago?

18. And now a general question about your needs for coverage—that is, the number of sources and period of time covered—for *all the kinds of service* you have needed in the past few years. *How often could you have used these services* ignoring the fact that you may have been unable to get them with current tools? (HAND RESPONDENT CARD F)

19. Background information.

Suggested Readings

The problem of evaluation of mechanized library systems, important though it is, has been virtually untouched by the library literature. The comparable problem in business is sufficiently different that it's not clear that the literature there will be of great value. However, the following references seem to be useful:

Cuadra, Carlos, *Annual Review of Information Science and Technology,* Vols. 1 and 2, New York: Wiley, 1966, 1967; Vol. 3 and 4, Chicago: Encyclopedia Brittanica, 1968, 1969.

Each volume has had a chapter on system evaluation which will provide the reader not only with an up to date summary of the present state of knowledge but with a comprehensive coverage of the relevant literature as well.

Gregory, R. H., and R. L. Van Horn, *Automatic Data Processing Systems: Principles and Procedures.* Belmont, California: Wadsworth, 1963, pp. 191-200 and 552-638.

Lancaster, F. W., *Information Retrieval Systems: Characteristics, Testing, and Evaluation.* New York: Wiley, 1968.

This book is remarkably clear in its presentation of methods and concepts of system evaluation. It emphasizes both the operational aspects and the economic ones, and combines both into a true cost/effectiveness criterion.

Chapter 8

SYSTEM IMPLEMENTATION

Once the evaluation and final selection of a system has been made, the time has come to implement it.[1,2] The following aspects must be considered: (1) planning the implementation, (2) staffing and administrative organization, (3) hardware selection, (4) preparation of the physical site, (5) programming, (6) data conversion, (7) phase-over, and (8) orientation of library staff and users.

"Planning" has at least the same importance during implementation that it has in other phases of development. The issues here relate to schedules, budgetary control, and general management of the implementation. The management of data processing system design, development, and operations will require the addition of new staff. This means that a person must be selected and assigned the management responsibility as well as the appropriate authority and administrative organization to support his work.

"Hardware" is a term used in data processing to denote the actual equipment—the computer, tape units, disk drives, card readers, high-speed printers, consoles, and terminals. The tasks here consist of developing detailed specifications of the equipment to be purchased, obtaining bids, selecting suppliers, setting delivery schedules, and establishing the related time schedules for installation and testing until the equipment is completely ready for use.

The "physical site" is the space within which the hardware will be installed. Electronic components of a computer system require special electrical wiring, environmental control (such as air conditioning, dust and humidity control),

---

[1] Rosove, Perry E., *Developing Computer-Based Information Systems.* New York: Wiley, 1967.

[2] Wallace, E. L., *Management Influence on the Design of Data Processing Systems.* Boston, Mass.: Graduate School of Business Administration, Harvard, 1961.

and architectural specifications (such as floor loading factors and raised floors). The implementation plan must ensure that the physical site is ready in time for the installation of the hardware.

"Software" is the set of programs and procedures used in a data processing installation. Development of them is the most complicated phase of the implementation, and perhaps the most expensive. Since the amount of programming necessary for an installation such as a library is quite large, enough programmers must be available to ensure that programs will be operational within the time scheduled for implementation.

"Conversion of data" is the process of transferring existing manual records into machine-readable form (producing all the basic files that will be utilized by the computer), and loading the data into storage media for access by the computer.

A period of parallel running, where results obtained from a new system can be compared with those achieved by the prior system, is usually necessary as part of the switchover to a fully automated operation. Parallel run may be compared to a comprehensive test, where the new system is called upon to demonstrate its ability to perform the required functions. The success of this trial is directly related to the amount and quality of planning undertaken from the very beginning. A conscientious planning effort, at all levels, and strict controls at the time of implementation are essential if the conversion and ultimate switchover is to be a success.

Training and the orientation of staff and users are a vitally important part of implementation. They must be made aware of the implications that mechanization will have for them; they must be prepared for the temporary dislocations that always arise in conversion to a new system; and they must be trained in the specific details of their own operational work.

Some of these functions will be carried out, partly, in parallel. For example, programmers must commence writing programs even though the hardware necessary for testing may not yet be available in the library, and the programs must be tested on machine time borrowed elsewhere. The design of formats for the main master files must be completed at an early stage in the programming, but the actual conversion of existing files to the new formats will be done while the programs are being written.

PLANNING THE IMPLEMENTATION

Our previous comment on the planning of a systems study applies even more to the planning of the implementation phase of the program. Budget control will be especially important during this phase, because of the relatively larger sums of money involved. Therefore, a work breakdown structure must be developed to reflect new system specifications as well as the various activities peculiar to the implementation phase itself; goals must be established which reflect priorities; and a PERT planning diagram must be developed, which identifies the interrelationships among tasks required to achieve the implementation.[3]

The activities of other agencies (such as equipment vendors or contract programming and conversion personnel) that will participate in the implementation phase of the library development program must also be considered in the PERT diagram. In the estimation of the required elapsed times, manpower loading, and equipment and facility loading, special attention must be given to the uncertainties in the performance of these outside agencies, over which the library has little direct control. Contingency factors must therefore play a more significant role in scheduling activities involved in the implementation phase than in the study phase.

Because of the large number of organizations involved in the implementation phase, reports on the progress of the program schedule will have great significance. Outside organizational units may have infrequent access to information about the status of the library program beyond the most recent revision of the published program schedule. Thus, it is especially important, during this phase, to review the program with them periodically and update and publish the new program schedules that result from the review.

A list of activities necessary for installation of a new system in the library is shown in Figure 8.1. A typical "network schedule" for them is shown in Figure 8.2, including representative overall time estimates.

Figure 8.1   Events in the implementation of a library system

A.   Events prior to beginning implementation
1.   Initiate planning study
2.   Establish budgetary conditions
3.   Complete feasibility study
4.   Complete general design
5.   Complete review of budget
6.   Complete system evaluation

B.   Events related to staffing
1.   Hire Assistant Librarian for Mechanized Services
2.   Hire Systems Department staff
3.   Hire Data Processing Department staff

C.   Events related to procurement of hardware
1.   Complete preparation of Requests for Proposal (RFP's)
2.   Receive bids
3.   Complete review of budget
4.   Complete evaluation and selection of equipment

[3] Archibald, Russell, and R. L. Villoria, *Network-Based Management Systems.* (PERT/CPM). New York: Wiley, 1967.

Figure 8.1   *(continued)*

5. Contract for delivery of equipment
6. Begin to accept delivery of equipment
7. Complete installation of equipment

D. Events related to site preparation
1. Complete preparation of Requests for Bid
2. Receive bids
3. Complete review of budget
4. Complete evaluation of bids
5. Contract for preparation of site
6. Begin preparation of site
7. Complete preparation of site

E. Events related to system development
1. Establish implementation program plan
2. Establish general specifications for programs
3. Complete preparation of RFP's
4. Receive bids
5. Complete review of budget
6. Complete evaluation of bids
7. Contract for programming
8. Complete choice of programming language and operating system
9. Complete definition of formats
10. Complete detailed design of modules
11. Complete programs
12. Complete off-site debugging of system
13. Begin on-site debugging of system
14. Complete on-site debugging of system
15. Complete full-scale system test
16. Complete phase-over
17. Follow-up

F. Events related to conversion
1. Complete preparation of RFP's
2. Receive bids
3. Complete review of budget
4. Complete evaluation of bids
5. Contract for conversion
6. Complete conversion of test files
7. Complete preliminary quality tests
8. Complete conversion

G. Events related to training and orientation
1. Begin orientation of library staff
2. Begin orientation of library users
3. Begin training of conversion staff
4. Complete training of conversion staff
5. Begin training of operating staff
6. Complete training of operating staff
7. Complete orientation of library staff
8. Complete orientation of library users

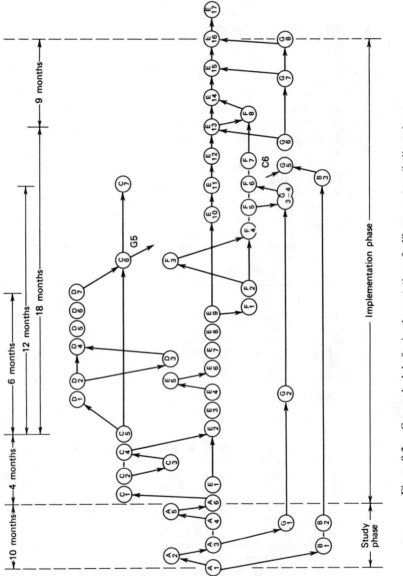

Figure 8.2 Gross schedule for implementation of a library system (indicated times are illustrative only)

ADMINISTRATIVE ORGANIZATION

Design and development of mechanized library systems may require the addition of as many as three major new groups to the library: (1) a library "Data Processing Department" for management of computer operations (if a library-based computer installation is involved); (2) a library "Systems Department" for development and maintenance of mechanized systems; and (3) a "Mechanized Information Services Department" to provide special expertise in mechanized information handling (if such services are added to the library's functions) and to serve as liaison with information service activities in other departments in the library.

Figure 8.3 is a schematic organization chart in which the role of each department is highlighted, under the conditions requiring such a major involvement of mechanization.

STAFFING

Mechanized operation will require the addition of new staff as well as special training for the existing staff of the library.[4] However, there are some particularly difficult staffing problems. The following paragraphs enumerate the kinds and numbers of personnel required and, in each case, estimate the salary level that the position calls for in terms of an existing library salary structure. Unfortunately, there are serious inconsistencies between those salaries and the competition for the limited number of people who combine knowledge of data processing and information retrieval with knowledge of libraries. The problems raised are particularly acute for the position of "Assistant Librarian for Mechanized Services" and those of the three department supervisors.

It is possible that in order to attract personnel with the required competence, it will be necessary to depart radically from existing salary scales. On the other hand, this departure would raise problems in the working relationship between people in library positions of equivalent responsibility but with disparate salaries. Because those problems ultimately could destroy the effectiveness of mechanized services, it has been assumed that salary scales consistent with others in the library will be used. This means that personnel may need to be found among those with less experience but real capability.

---

[4] Heiliger, Edward M., "Staffing a Computer Based Library," *Library Journal,* 89 (July 1964), 2738-2739.

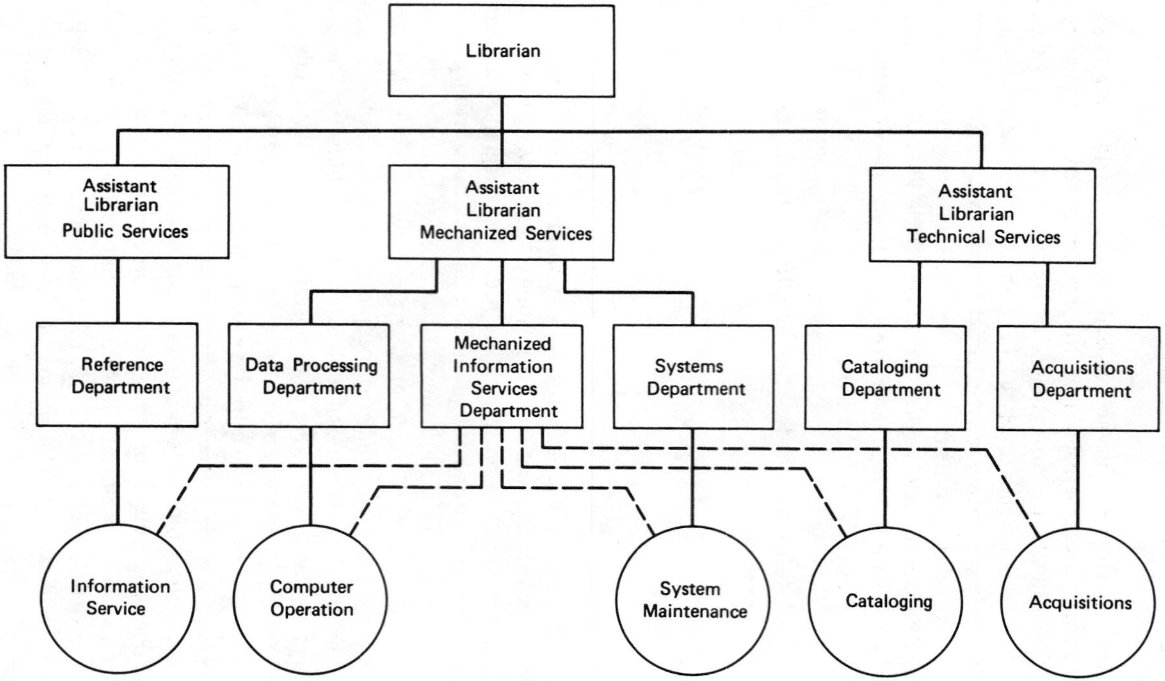

Figure 8.3 Organization chart.

Assistant Librarian for Mechanized Services

The key person is the "Assistant Librarian for Mechanized Services." Within the general guidelines established by the librarian, he will be responsible for the analysis and design of the library's information system and for administration of the professional staff required for such work. He analyzes prospective projects to ensure that all sources of data pertinent to the program have been identified. He evaluates existing services and those proposed for the future with regard to user needs, efficiency of equipment, and methods of operation. He applies detailed technical knowledge of both computer-based and manual library systems in such evaluation. He prepares specifications for such services, including relating them with various existing programs. He communicates results as necessary to carry out liaison with organizations, agencies, and individuals, in the library as well as outside it. A salary comparable to that of an Assistant Librarian for Technical Services should be planned on. In 1968, for example, this might have been from $16,000 to $18,000 in a large library.

Falling under the direction of the Assistant Librarian for Mechanized Services are the aspects of library operation that involve the mechanized equipment and its utilization. Specifically, he is responsible for the Mechanized Information Services Department, the Data Processing Department, and the Systems Department.

Mechanized Information Services Department

When mechanized information services are involved in a new system, a "Mechanized Information Services Department" (MIS) would provide the special expertise in information handling in support of the other departments of the library. Its primary staffing needs are for "information specialists," who will function under the direction of the Supervisor of the MIS Department (an "Associate Information Specialist"). A salary comparable to that of other library department heads should be planned on. In 1968, for example, this might have been in the range of $12,000 to $15,000. He plans, organizes, and coordinates the activities of the other departments of the library to assure successful operation of mechanized information services. He provides liaison with other libraries with respect to such services. He assigns information specialists, under his direction, to assist in determining requirements for magnetic tape acquisitions, in cataloging and describing acquisitions properly, in phrasing of requests for service, and in scheduling the processing of files. (This aspect of his responsibilities will be discussed in Chapter 19.)

His staff consists of two or more Assistant Information Specialists (with salaries in 1968 of about $10,000 to $12,000), who serve as the means for communication between librarians and mechanized data files and reference files.

They evaluate mechanized data to ensure complete accuracy in the description of material and in an appropriate depth of indexing for value in later retrieval. They assist in determing the needs for information in formulating requests for mechanized search and in analyzing retrieved information for presentation to the user. They ensure appropriate dissemination of incoming information to users. They have sufficient technical knowledge of information storage and retrieval systems to use them effectively.

Data Processing Department

If a library-based computer installation is required, a Data Processing Department is needed to manage its operation, with responsibility not only for the computer itself but for peripheral equipment elsewhere in the library.[5] The Supervisor of the Data Processing Department (with a salary in 1968 of $12,000 to $15,000) would plan, organize, and control the operation of the computer and peripheral data processing equipment to obtain maximum usage. He would assign personnel under his direction to various operations and instruct them where necessary so that they are trained to perform assigned duties in accordance with established methods and procedures. He would provide technical liaison with computer facilities outside the library in order to coordinate activities. He would review equipment logs and reports on equipment operating efficiency. He must be familiar at the working level with all phases of the operation, and should have a knowledge of computer programming sufficient to diagnose malfunctions that result from operation, equipment, or programming.

He would require the assistance of a Lead Computer Operator for each shift (with a salary in 1968 of about $10,000 to $12,000), who should have technical knowledge of computer operations comparable to a Senior Computer Operator (see below) and also supervisory capabilty for instructing, assigning, directing, and checking the work of the other computer operators, including the seniors. They assist in the scheduling of the operations and the assignment of personnel to the various items of equipment required for computer functions. They may act as shift supervisors in the absence of the Department Supervisor. The staff should include a Senior Computer Operator for each shift (with a salary in 1968 of about $8,000), who should be competent to work at all phases of computer operation with very little assistance. Other personnel—a total of perhaps ten for a two-shift operation—should include junior or trainee computer operators (three: two for a day shift and one for a second shift), a clerical staff to receive requests for computer use and to process the requests according to pre-

[5] Lawson, C. M., "A Survey of Computer Facility Management," *Datamation,* 8 (7) (July 1962), 29-32.

determined rules, and key-punchers. In 1968, their salaries would have been from $5000 to $7000 each.

Systems Department

Under the general direction of the Assistant Librarian for Mechanized Services, the Systems Department is responsible for the analysis and design of data processing and information handling systems for the library.[6] It functions under the direction of the Supervisor of the Systems Department, who is an Associate Information Systems Specialist (with a salary in 1968 of $12,000 to $15,000). He is responsible for direct supervision of analysts and programmers, and for outlining detailed procedures to be followed. He works closely with librarians and other library personnel in the definition of their specific requirements.

Under his direction is a staff of Information Systems Specialists (with salaries in 1968 of $9000 to $12,000) who are capable of one or more of the following tasks: analysis of information handling functions and the development of general system design, application of analytical techniques to the study and evaluation of both existing systems and procedures to assigned tasks, conversion of existing operations to new ones, and preparation of detailed manuals for operation. Also under his direction is a staff of Programmers (with salaries in 1968 from $9000 to $12,000), responsible for the actual work of programming the computer.[7]

In other library departments there may also be need for additional or different personnel. There is, however, a real need for orientation of the present staff to the particular problems of mechanized services and the methods for solution of them.

HARDWARE

The requirements for equipment to be used in the system must be specified in sufficient detail so that manufacturers, or other suppliers, can prepare proposals. These requirements are embodied in "Requests for Proposal" (RFP's) and are sent out to a selected list of bidders. An RFP usually specifies factors such as those listed in Figure 8.4, to which the bidders should respond.[8]

[6] Minder, Thomas, "Library Systems Analyst—A Job Description," *College and Research Libraries,* **27** (4) (July 1966), 271-276.

[7] Percy, D. K., *Computer Programmer Selection and Testing.* Santa Monica, California: System Development Corporation, March 21, 1962.

[8] Gregory, R. H., and R. L. Van Horn, *Automatic Data Processing Systems: Principles and Procedures.* Belmont, California: Wadsworth, 1963, pp 634-636.

Figure 8.4 Check list of data to be provided in a manufacturer's proposal

1. General description of proposed system
    (a) Equipment configuration
    (b) Software system
    (c) Procedural system

2. Details of equipment configuration
    (a) Description: make, model, and quantity of each unit of equipment
    (b) Form of data handled: numeric or alphanumeric, and fixed or variable field data structure
    (c) Storage capacities and methods: direct and sequential access
    (d) Adequacy of controls, method of checking, and average "mean error-free time"
    (e) Operating instructions for each major unit

3. Details of software and procedural issues
    (a) Form of input documents and data
    (b) Time estimates for each piece of equipment to handle each major job, and the total time available
    (c) Flow charts of jobs showing recommended techniques
    (d) Examples of detailed coding for representative applications
    (e) Operating supplies needed

4. Delivery schedules
    (a) Delivery date
    (b) Length of time to check equipment and get it into operating condition
    (c) Penalties for late delivery or failure to deliver equipment that is contracted for

5. Installation requirements, including both recommended and extreme conditions for manufacturer's guarantee
    (a) Size, weight, floor space, and height for each unit, including auxiliary equipment
    (b) Electric power—public utility or special equipment—and wiring requirements
    (c) Air conditioning: humidity, temperature, dust, and special protection
    (d) Space for files, supplies, maintenance parts, test operations, personnel, and visitors

6. Support to be provided by manufacturer
    (a) Availability of engineers or technicians for analysis, programming, and installation
    (b) Training courses for library's programmers and operators
    (c) Availability of equipment for use in program debugging
    (d) The manufacturer's software package for programming and assistance available by participating in the equipment users associations

7. Financial aspects
    (a) Rental rate, term of contract, renewal, and cancellation
    (b) Differential in rates for one, two, or three shifts operation or on a monthly basis and rate adjustment for excessive down time
    (c) Terms of payment, discount, and financing arrangements
    (d) Guarantees on equipment operation, availability of special supplies
    (e) Terms of any purchase option: initial deposit required, fraction of rental payments credited toward purchase, and expiration date

194

Figure 8.4   *(continued)*

---

8. Maintenance contracts
   (a) Maintenance contract cost, service personnel, scheduled maintenance period, availability of a similar machine during extended down time, and renewal conditions
   (b) Terms and rate of initial contract and renewal period
   (c) Provision for replacing parts, testing equipment, and maintenance
   (d) Cost of maintenance parts and supplies
9. Design changes
   (a) Replacement of unsatisfactory units
   (b) Arrangements for securing improvements or new models including trade-in value
10. Expandibility
    (a) Additional units that can be added: input, output, storage, processing, and interrogation
    (b) Other equipment that will accept media directly from this equipment
    (c) Equipment available for media conversion

The proposals received must then be evaluated for their relative merits, for the extent to which they indeed meet the library's needs, and for the effect that the proposed costs will have on the library's budgetary program. On the basis of this evaluation, contractors will be selected and equipment will be scheduled for delivery.

In the evaluation, a fundamental question is: Does the manufacturer's proposal provide sufficient detail and show that he understands the problems of the library and is in a position to submit appropriate equipment recommendations? This question can be answered by evaluating the equipment proposal against the criteria established during the applications study and stated in the bid invitation.

Frequently, this process of requesting and evaluating proposals is by-passed. For example, when the salesman for a supplier (say, a computer company) has been able to convince the librarian that a system designed around his company's equipment will provide the best answer to the library's needs, the library will usually sign a "letter of intent"—a statement of interest that is not binding on the library but that does ensure that equipment will be made available on the schedule desired. Then the formal contract for delivery is signed at a later time. However, if this approach is adopted, it should be remembered that manufacturers have interests different from those of the library. Although a manufacturer can readily specify the technical capabilities of his equipment, the library must be responsible for determining whether they will meet its particular requirements. This is true even though the manufacturer may assist in analyzing applications requirements. An exception may arise when a manufacturer guarantees satisfactory performance for an application. Usually, however, he will merely deliver equipment. It is the customer's responsibility to apply it efficiently.

A long period of time—the lead time—usually occurs between the contract with a manufacturer and the delivery of electronic equipment. For developmental equipment, this can be especially long and subject to change, because the manufacturer may take longer to design, construct, and test than he planned. This point is important because it is not uncommon for a new piece of equipment of potential value to libraries to be so widely discussed that many people are led to believe that it is operational, proven, and "off-the-shelf." However, it is not unusual for one or two years or more (depending on the complexity of the equipment) to elapse between the time people begin discussing the characteristics of a device and the time when it is actually available. Unfortunately, the pressure of competition has sometimes led vendors to promise unrealistically short delivery schedules for equipment despite the extraordinarily high risk of inadequate performance or slippage in delivery schedules for a newly developed piece of equipment.

Even so, libraries usually will find that they still will have insufficient time for analysis, programming, and debugging. Unfortunately, scheduling equipment delivery only when the end of programming and testing is in sight produces a lead time that is likely to be too long. The problem is much simpler when new equipment replaces similar equipment and if only minor changes are made in the operating system and processor programs.

Complex equipment is almost always installed and checked out by the manufacturers before being turned over to the user. The manufacturer has "diagnostic routines" specifically designed for testing various features, and newly developed equipment, in particular, requires more thorough testing of this kind than established equipment.

PHYSICAL SITE

At the architectural level, the use of computers means a new look at library layout, since the effects of automation can radically change organizational relationships in library technical services and the flow of information and material. At the engineering level, it means concern with environmental control, with needs for cabling, with structural planning for equipment, with lighting for consoles and microfilm reading, and with acoustics of input and output devices such as typewriters and printers.[9]

The location of space for equipment and personnel depends on many factors.

---

[9] *General Reference Manual: IBM 360 Physical Installation Planning.* Poughkeepsie, New York: IBM Systems Development Division, September 1968.

Cost is important and is a suitable criterion, if all costs—intangible as well as tangible—are counted. The impact of a remote location on communications between the data processing center and other parts of the library is just as important as the cost of installing an air-conditioning system. Other factors in selecting a suitable location and layout are:

1.   Adequate floor strength to support the weights involved.
2.   Head room sufficient for largest components.
3.   Isolation from machinery or other factors creating an unfavorable environment.
4.   Appropriate electric, water, and other utilities.
5.   Location of entrances and exits adequate for equipment and convenient for personnel and traffic flow.
6.   Adequate operating and maintenance space around each component.
7.   "Show-room" window for viewing by casual visitors.

The layout of space should be determined early, so as to fix the location of power lines, lighting, and air conditioning. Engineering and detailed planning of the area to be used or constructed for data processing equipment can be handled in the same way as other library building modifications. The manufacturer's representatives and the library's building staff are best able to convert equipment specifications into space layouts and facilities plans. The library building staff can then supervise the preparatory work (including writing the RFP's), the awarding of contracts, and actual installation. An alternative approach (probably best suited to special design equipment) is to contract with the manufacturer for a complete installation. In this case, a manufacturer's representative functions much like a building or plant engineer during the construction and installation phase.

Space

Provision must be made for the central processing facility itself. A representative space allocation might be as follows.

(a)   For the central processing facility itself—1000 square feet (see Figure 8.5).
(b)   For immediately adjacent service area for storage of spare parts and test equipment—100 square feet.
(c)   For storage of tapes, discs, and other forms of mechanized storage—300 square feet adjacent to the central processing facility (see Figure 8.6).
(d)   For storage of cards, forms, and other supplies—200 square feet (located away from central processing facility, but convenient to it).

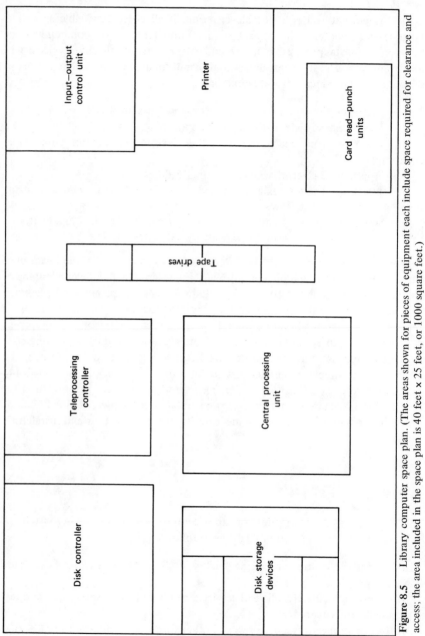

Figure 8.5 Library computer space plan. (The areas shown for pieces of equipment each include space required for clearance and access; the area included in the space plan is 40 feet × 25 feet, or 1000 square feet.)

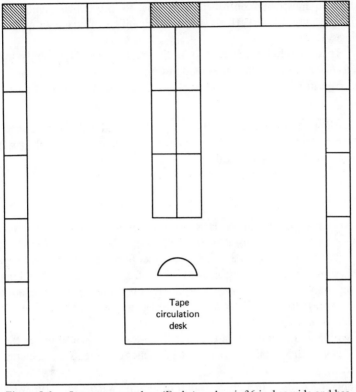

Figure 8.6   Storage space plan. (Each tape bay is 36 inches wide and has 6 shelves. The total capacity of a bay is 120 tapes or 30 disk packs. There are 20 bays shown. The area included in the space plan is 17 feet x 18 feet, or 306 square feet.)

(e)   For offices to house the manager, operating personnel, and programmers—400 square feet (convenient to the facility).

(f)   For key-punching personnel—100 square feet (convenient to the facility in an acoustically controlled room).

Environment

The central processing facility itself needs to be environmentally controlled:

(a)   Temperature must be held near $75°F$ (in the range of 60-90). (Since the heat load generated by a typical installation is about 52,000 btu, this implies roughly 4 1/2 tons.)

(b)   Humidity must be held near 50 percent relative (in the range of 40 to 60 percent). This has particular significance for the magnetic tapes, which tend to change their operating characteristics under excessively low or high humidity.

(c)   Dust must be controlled according to prescribed standards, again primarily because of its effects on the reliability of magnetic reading and recording systems.

(d)   There should be recorders for both temperature and humidity so that as variations occur they can be pinpointed in time.

(e)   A cut-off for the air-conditioning system should be provided within the facility.

The various mechanical units—such as printers, card readers and punches, and key-punches—tend to be noisy. Acoustical control is thus essential, particularly where card equipment is involved.

Power Supply

The required power supply is a function of the specific configuration of equipment. A typical load is 20 kVA at 175 amp. This can be either 208 or 230 and includes both three phase and single phase. Because a stable power source is essential, surges must be controlled to within 5 to 10 percent. This implies an "isolation transformer" a power cutoff in the facility, and a ground wire ("green" wire) to a well-defined "building ground." There should be a continuous recording of the voltage.

The wiring and cabling within the facility should be placed under the floor, which implies either a false floor raised 12 inches or a recess of 12 inches under the floor.

Peripheral units, including point-of-action recorders, typewriter-type terminals, and displays, will be located throughout the library building. They usually involve connection by cables to multiplexing units or buffers and then by telephone line to a teleprocessing terminal in the facility. In particular, a typical peripheral unit is an IBM 1030 Data Collection System, which accepts prepunched cards (such as book cards and borrower cards) and transmits information from them to a key-punch or to an on-line computer. A second type of unit is a typewriter terminal. These can have the necessary buffer equipment directly associated with each and thus require connection only to a telephone line. A third type of unit is the cathode ray tube display, which requires a higher transmission rate and uses a separate multiplexing unit.

PROGRAMMING

Workable and efficient processor routines must be prepared before the new system can become operational. The newcomer to the problem of programming might wonder why this work would not be done by the supplier of equipment.

Sometimes the supplier of equipment will even imply that it is a negligible task, completely solved by the packaged routines he provides. Unfortunately, it is not that simple, and the equipment supplier will usually be of assistance only if and when disaster looms.

In fact, the task of programming a library system of any significant magnitude is a major one, requiring a fairly large staff of programmers. Most libraries will not want to build up such a staff within their own administrative structure and will therefore turn to outside organizations. This implies (just as for hardware) the preparation of "Requests for Proposal" to be sent to a selected list of "software firms" (that is, companies providing programming services). A set of general specifications for these programs should have been prepared by the time the total system was designed and evaluated. These specifications could not, however, detail exactly how the performance requirements would be achieved on the equipment finally chosen to be used. They only indicate how the system might be subdivided into a number of program modules for implementation, with due consideration given to the kinds and amount of equipment which might be required. Now these generalized and preliminary ideas must be translated into concrete and detailed specifications for the operational computer program modules and embodied in the RFP.

Once the proposals have been received and evaluated, a software contractor will be chosen (or the decision will be made to do the job within the library itself). At this point, however, the greatest caution must be taken. Few software firms today have real knowledge of the character and complexity of the library's data processing tasks. They tend to view them as relatively trivial and, at most, simply analogous to standard data processing functions in business. Unfortunately, it is almost impossible to provide sufficient detail in an RFP to guarantee a full understanding and appreciation of the real requirements. The potential contractors will therefore regard the general specifications of the RFP in a familiar context and will quotes costs and times that are likely to be far too low. The results will be either a failure to meet the real needs of the library, a significant slippage in time, a significant increase in cost, or all three.

Unlike the acquisition of equipment, in which the only major interaction between library and contractor will relate to the actual installation, the acquisition of software requires continual interaction. Programming must relate to the library's work in conversion of files, in changing its own procedures, and in phasing-over from previous operations to new ones. It is therefore extremely important for the library to understand, to monitor, and even to control the work of the software group.

This work will proceed in at least five separate stages of special importance to the library: (1) selection of the programming language and operating system, (2) definition of the formats of files, forms, and reports, (3) detailed specification of program modules, (4) programming, and (5) debugging.

The selection of the "programming language" and "operating system" is the first step. Machine manufacturers ordinarily support their equipment with packages of "utility" programs for performing a wide range of basic data processing functions (like sorting, merging, file structuring, and file modification). These utility programs are usually available as parts of the equipment's "operating system." Thus, when a programmer finds a requirement to perform one of the functions for which a standard utility program exists, he need only call in that program for execution as one step in the program he is writing. It is not inconceivable that a library application program written for a very restricted phase of a library operation could be adapted the same way. However, in order to use the utility programs provided by the equipment manufacturers, application programs require adaptation of them to the library's requirements. Thus, a study of the characteristics of the programming languages themselves and the selection of an optimum language for library systems programming may be without meaning unless the computer's operating system is capable of handling the particular language selected.

Following the choice of programming language and operating system, each of the formats must be defined—internal, computer-based files; input forms; and output reports. This will have immediate significance to the library, since many existing files of data will need to be converted to the new formats (as will be discussed later). From this point, the programming group must be continually aware of the library's requirements as the programs become more and more specific until, finally, computer programs are debugged.

In contrast to mechanized systems, manual systems can continue to operate reasonably well, despite their very high rates of error, because people can tolerate a modest number of some kinds of mistakes and can still function efficiently. The number of mistakes and inconsistencies in files, uncovered during the conversion phase, usually indicate that manual systems have more faults than is generally realized. Equipment, on the other hand, when faced with a mistake, either stops operations or follows the mistake to what may be absurd and catastrophic conclusions. Since data processing programs, when first prepared, are almost certain to contain erroneous logic, elaborate procedures (called "debugging") are needed for screening out the mistakes in program preparation. Locating program mistakes is essentially a refined process of trial and error, and can take a lot of time, especially in the early stages of system development, before the programmers develop full knowledge of the routines. Accordingly, the programmers should write routines and substantially debug them before the equipment is installed.

Debugging time is sometimes furnished by the equipment manufacturer, although additional time is usually needed and must be obtained at a service center or at another user's installation. On the other hand, there are two cautions about "off-site" debugging. (1) Rarely is the machine time for debugging at other installations available on an optimal schedule. The "turn-around time"—from the submission of a program to be tested until the results are available for analysis—can be as much as 24 hours. This means that the time for debugging is likely to be far longer than was initially planned. (2) The off-site equipment is almost certain to be a different configuration from that which will be installed as the operating equipment. Therefore, it will still be necessary to check-out the programs at the "on-site" facility.

DATA CONVERSION

Existing files (manual or mechanized) must be converted to new formats and media. Catalogs, serial records, borrower registrations, circulation records, vendor files, book fund records, and personnel files must eventually be transferred from their present form.

Because of the sizes of the files that are the heart of a library's operation, this part of implementation is likely to involve the largest single capital investment. It is of such magnitude that, to some extent, the spread of mechanization in libraries has awaited the development of adequate, economic approaches to it. The most important steps are the ones taken by the Library of Congress in its MARC project and "national serials project," since these steps will provide both a set of national standards for data formats and a central source of mechanized library data.[10] Related efforts are those by libraries, throughout the country, trying to develop a cooperative program of data conversion, sharing common data bases in standard format with each other for a consequent reduction in conversion costs to the individual library. Despite these efforts, however, the individual library will always be faced with the conversion of its own files, and all that these national efforts may do is to make the conversion a little easier to accomplish.

Because of the size of manpower commitment for conversion, the library is unlikely to want to add the staff necessary for this one-time effort or to provide the day-to-day management that it requires. Again, Requests for Proposal must be prepared, which specify the magnitude of the task to be done, the required formats, and the time schedule. The tasks will involve one or more of the following (some of which may be done by the library and others by contract personnel): (a) planning the schedule with which files and portions of each file will be converted, (b) copying files so that the conversion will not interfere with existing operations, (c) verifying the accuracy of existing records and reconciling

[10] Avram, Henriette, et al., *The MARC II Format*. Washington D.C.: Library of Congress, 1968.

differences among them, (d) editing the records so that they will be complete and ready for the clerical operations of conversion, (e) key-boarding, (f) input to mechanized files, and (g) error detection and correction.

There are many methods for scheduling the conversion. Records in some files may be converted only when they become active. Other files may be converted in the order in which they are filed. Other files may be converted in inverse chronological order (the most recent items being converted first). Some files may be converted record by record, from verification to editing to key-boarding to input to correction. In other files, records may be batched—all being verified, then all being edited, and so on. The variety of scheduling possibilities is so great and so dependent on the specific situation in the individual library that no general rules can be formulated. But one point can be made: the conversion *must* be scheduled and very carefully so.

Copying the files may or may not be necessary. Normally the process of conversion would require delivery of the existing records to the location of the conversion staff and therefore would remove them from the present operation. When this would cause disruption of present operations, they should be copied. Furthermore, the subsequent steps of editing and key-boarding are likely to be facilitated if the staff has its own copy of the record to work with.

Verification of records also may or may not be necessary. Records of serial holdings, for example, are so likely to be erroneous that verification may be called for. Financial records usually must be verified simply because of their nature. On the other hand, the size of a catalog is so great that verification would seem to be out of the question.

Editing is needed because the content of existing records may differ from that of the corresponding mechanized records. Some data may need to be added (for instance, codes for identification of different fields), and other data may need to be deleted. Moreover, the efficiency of subsequent key-boarding will be vastly increased, at relatively minor cost during editing, if the beginning and end of each field of data are indicated on the source record.

Key-boarding and input are the processes by which manual records are actually converted to machine-readable form. In Chapter 11, many different ways of carrying out these steps are discussed.

Error prevention (through proper design of forms), detection, and correction is necessary because of the inaccuracies inherent in any manual operation. Some of it may be carried out by the computer itself, by comparing input data with defined criteria of consistency. Some of it may involve proofreading. One point, however, is important: it is certain that files of the size involved in the operation of a library will contain errors and, in fact, no amount of error detection and correction can eliminate all of them. The only issue is: What degree of error is acceptable, and what will it cost to achieve it?

PHASE-OVER

A phase-over plan must be developed so that the new system will assume operational responsibility with minimum degradation of the library's performance. This implies some period of time in which the manual system is gradually phased out and the replacement system is phased in.

Approaches to Phase-Over

There are four fundamental approaches to system phase-over: total, pilot, phased, and parallel. Each has its own particular advantages and disadvantages for each specific installation situation. Consequently, a single approach cannot be prescribed for all system installations.

The *total* (or all-at-once) approach to system installation is by far the most demanding of the four. With this approach, on a given date the old system is abandoned and the new system takes its place. It requires unusually careful planning and coordination: personnel must be well indoctrinated, trained, and prepared for handling a host of problems. The all-at-once approach to system installation, therefore, should not be selected when the new system involves a radically modified approach, major items of new equipment, widely separated elements in the operation, a significant degree of personnel resistance, or an enormous volume of work that must be handled.

When the library can be divided into many sub-units (such as branches), which are relatively self-contained, it may be possible to implement the system in one of the subunits without significantly affecting the operation of the other units. This kind of *pilot operation* has several advantages. (1) It permits the selection of the particular organizational unit in which the personnel are most ready to accept the new system. The successful operation of the system in one branch of the library can provide a strong motivating influence on hesitant personnel in other units. (2) It makes the operation of the new system more manageable during the initial shakedown period, since the smaller processing load minimizes the risk of operating people being overwhelmed by the problems that always accompany the installation of a new system. (3) The installation of a system module on a small scale can usually be accomplished more quickly. This could be significant where the system installation has been preceded by a long period of analysis and design, and management personnel are anxious to see some results of the effort. (4) This technique of system installation permits the phase-over to progress at a more relaxed pace; installation in other branches does not need to commence until everyone is satisfied that the pilot operation is running smoothly.

In the *phased* (or piecemeal) approach to system installation, the system itself is broken down into a number of modules or discrete procedures that are installed one at a time, in sequence, until the entire system has been implemented. All of the arguments against adopting the all-at-once approach to system installation become arguments for adopting the phased approach. Although the phased approach takes longer, there is more time to detect and correct problems resulting from deficiencies in system design. It is the cautious, careful, conservative approach to system phase-over. Unfortunately, not every system can be installed in this way, because it may not be possible to break the system down into significant and relatively independent procedures. Installation of only a portion of a system may introduce inefficiencies. While these will not be present when the entire system is finally implemented, some personnel may regard them as support for their contention that "the old way was better." By stretching out the installation period, one runs the risk that personnel will lose interest in the project, making installation of subsequent procedures more difficult.

The fourth basic approach to system installation—the *parallel* approach—is one in which both the old and the new system are operated side by side for a period of time. Only when the new system is performing satisfactorily is the old one dropped. This approach is indicated whenever the consequences of failing to produce the operational output by a specified time would be disastrous. Therefore, it is very likely to be the one adopted by the library. Naturally, this approach is the most costly of the four, because two systems must be operated simultaneously to perform the same functions. Discrepancies between the information provided by the two systems might be difficult to resolve. On the other hand, this approach does permit operating personnel to compare the efforts required and the results produced by each of the two systems and, thus, to arrive at their own conclusions about which of the two systems is better.

Stages of Phase-Over

Several distinct stages can be distinguished in phase-over from an existing system to a new one: system integration, parallel operation (if that approach is involved), final conversion, and follow-up.

System Integration. System integration is particularly essential as part of a phase-over plan, since many organizations and agencies will normally have been involved in development and installation of the system. During installation, the culmination of all the efforts of these diverse organizations is reached. For the first time, all the components of the system are brought together as a functioning entity in the library, and an environment is available for a critical series of full-scale tests—tests in which the system is put through its operational paces, involving operational personnel, operational computer programs, operational facilities, and operational equipment. In these tests, system performance is measured by the highest-level performance standards—the formally specified system requirements. Thus, these tests supercede all prior tests, which have evaluated only the components according to their respective subsystem standards. Even if all parts of the system may have passed these tests with flying colours, the total system may still fail when measured against *its* requirements.

This testing must be accomplished without a chaotic situation in which the representatives of the various organizations attempt to install and test different elements of the system at the same time in the same space: the computer manufacturer is concerned with checking out the computer itself and its utility programs; the software system developer wants to test out his operational computer programs on the computer; and the library's own operating staff will need to test the computer, both for hardware operation and for the operation of computer software. To prevent confusion, inadequate testing, and the waste of valuable computer time, it is essential that this period in utilization of the computer be carefully scheduled by the library in cooperation with its contractors.

The pressure to attain maximum use increases quickly after the equipment is accepted. This pressure will critically test the adequacy of all prior planning; hence, an established plan in imperative for guiding an orderly phase-over and for evaluating its progress.

Parallel Operation. Mistakes and errors can be detected without contaminating real data and disrupting actual operations by use of a period of operation in parallel with the existing system. The new system handles samples of transactions, in parallel with the old, for comparison of results; the old system continues to handle all transactions and remains the primary source of operating information.

Final Conversion. When system reliability is proved by such parallel operations, processing can be shifted to the new system. The old system may be operated a little longer in order to continue to verify the accuracy of results and to serve as a safeguard against system failure during final conversion but, usually, users of automatic equipment find that the output from a logically correct and debugged program is so accurate that such parallel operation is not required.

Follow-Up.   After test, parallel operation, and final conversion, it is necessary to follow-up and continually review the operation with all operating personnel who run the system and people in adjacent departments who receive information from the new system. Particular attention should be paid to the problems that they have experienced and to the corrective measures that they recommend. No system is perfect, and even a brand new one may be significantly improved.

One of the functions of follow-up, therefore, is to isolate the causes of system malfunctions. This is a surprisingly difficult task. Information systems involve complex interactions among men, computer programs, and equipment. Operating personnel will (at least, initially) blame the equipment or the computer programs for what are really human failures, or they will report as "errors" and "malfunctions" results which, on close examination, will turn out to be the originally stated requirements and design specifications. Experience has shown that operating personnel, gradually (as they become more familiar with the system), begin to observe that system malfunctions may be a result of their own mistakes. Tracking down the causes of system malfunctions therefore requires experienced development personnel who understand the characteristics of the system as well as the nature of the library's operations and organization.

Some preliminary measurements of operating costs for the new system should have been collected during earlier stages of the phase-over period. However, these measurements could have been unrealistic because the system was not yet operating in typical, routine fashion. How have production costs and system outputs varied since installation? Unrealistically low production costs could indicate that some essential processing step is being omitted; on the other hand, production costs that drastically exceed the predicted costs indicate a whole range of possible troubles. A well-designed system will produce a variety of management reports for control of its own operation, and these can prove invaluable aids in assessing the general health of the operation during the follow-up analysis.

Of all aspects of system work, follow-up probably receives the least emphasis. This is unfortunate because, without it, significant gains predicted during the earlier phases of analysis, design, and installation can be lost through inadequate attention to operational difficulties that develop only after the system has been in operation for a while. All systems, new and old, evolve and change as requirements, personnel, or constraints change in time. Periodically, every system must therefore be reviewed to ensure that it is effectively performing the functions for which it was designed and continues to accommodate to the various changes affecting its operation.

ORIENTATION AND TRAINING

The introduction of a new system, mechanized or not, creates real problems for both the staff of a library and the users of it, but these problems are especially formidable when mechanization is involved. Bruno Bettelheim once said that "man, who used to be haunted in his dreams by other men, is now haunted by the machine."[11] It seems to move in upon us inch by inch until we no longer are able to flex our own muscles and feel surrounded by an enemy. For librarians, coming from a humanist tradition, these feelings are particularly acute. Librarians are both overly fearful and overly hopeful about what automation can do. Some may be overawed by the complexity of the equipment and afraid that they won't be able to learn "all those new things." Others may resist the introduction of equipment because of sound intuitive judgment of the problems they see, but they may be unable to describe the problems because they lack the knowledge to do so.[12]

Yet, the success of any new system depends almost completely on the cooperation and active interest of the library's staff.[13] In another context (but just as applicable to the library), David Riesman quotes an industrial sociologist: "Workmen in an oil-cracking plant in Oklaholma . . . got angry because . . . management had referred to them as semi-skilled. They proceeded to carry out literally the instructions of the chemist—instructions which they had previously treated as a good chef will treat a recipe—soon bringing the plant to a halt. It turned out that they understood the idiosyncracies of the machines better than did the supervising staff."[14]

In *Advanced Data Processing in the University Library*, Louis A. Schultheiss and his co-authors comment: ". . . a more progressive attitude must be fostered in the thinking of librarians at all staff levels.[15] It is recognized that library administrators will be the ones who ultimately decide whether or not changes will be made in the existing system, but it should not be forgotten that it is the line staff who will either make or break the new system and their attitude toward it and their ability to work with it. A program of education of the staff members of any library making major system changes is a prime requirement."

It is therefore very important for the library administration to plan and carry out a careful program of orientation of the library staff. It must make the staff knowledgeable about what the equipment coming into the library will do and what their own part will be in the new system. Only then will they be willing and able to participate with personal interest in successful operation.

Fortunately, time is a great factor in adjusting to the encroachment of the machine. Automation does not take place from Friday night to Monday morning. The library administrator can take advantage of the few years that the development will require to get his staff actively involved. And this should not

[11] Perhaps best exemplified in his article, "Joey, A 'Mechanical Boy,' " *Scientific American,* **200** (March 1959), 116-20.

[12] Postley, John A., *Computers and People.* New York: McGraw-Hill, 1960.

[13] Pratt, Allan D., "Living with Computers," *California Librarian,* 29 (1) (January 1968), 57-61.

[14] Riesman, David, *Individualism Reconsidered.* Glencoe, Ill.: Free Press, 1954.

[15] Schultheiss, Louis, Don S. Culbertson, and Edward M. Heiliger, *Advanced Data Processing in the University Library.* New York: Scarecrow, 1962.

be a voluntary involvement, left to the discretion of "interested" personnel, which ignores the very person who most needs to be drawn into the activity.

Orientation of Library Staff

It is especially important to inform staff personnel (as soon as rumors start) of the plans for a change in system. The decision to introduce a new system is made only after extensive analysis of the impact that the new equipment and system will have on the library's interests. By the same token, the employee is just as anxious to learn what impact the new system is likely to have on his interests. But an important difference exists: management can independently obtain facts and make decisions, whereas employees are dependent on management for facts and decisions. Frank and open discussions by management are therefore necessary to reduce rumors that otherwise may give a distorted view of the situation.

A well-planned information policy throughout the organization has advantages even after a commitment is made to obtain equipment. If the introduction of a new system is tactfully presented, it can generate pride and satisfaction in the organization, but the program should not be oversold or potential difficulties minimized. The important point is the realization by management that all employees need complete and accurate facts.

Orientation is a planned program by which the staff and users of the library are introduced to a new system. The larger and more complex the computer-based library system is, the more essential it is that staff and users be provided with knowledge of it, both at a general level before the installation phase and then again at an intensive, detailed level during the installation phase. Experience has shown that library personnel must have an opportunity to comprehend the system intellectually and as a totality before they work with it in an operational environment.

Thus, an orientation program requires intensive and careful planning comparable to that carried on for the other aspects of the development and installation. The different requirements of various types of library staff and users for information about the system must be considered. Appropriate techniques must be developed for the dissemination of necessary types of information. The procedures for conducting the orientation must avoid interfering with on-going operations.

The extent to which a formal orientation program is needed, of course, depends on the experience and knowledge of the library staff. However, since most librarians are relatively uninformed about computers and programming and have had little prior experience with information-systems development, the content and scope of the orientation program must necessarily be detailed and cover the complete range of elements.[16] The first step should be to acquaint the staff with automated data processing in general. The indoctrination could begin with a tour of an existing computer facility, preferably one associated with a library. A special course in data processing, with emphasis on applications within the library itself, could be organized. Certain of the library staff should be sent to special training schools operated by the equipment suppliers.

Once the library personnel are somewhat familiar with data processing, and realize that it is within their ability to understand and deal intelligently with this subject, the professional staff should be involved in planning the introduction of automation to their respective departments.[17] In this manner, they will envision the project in terms of their own needs and will be motivated to plan and execute it well.

Schultheiss, Culbertson, and Heiliger continued, "The most important phase of staff orientation was a series of staff meetings held by the librarian with all the professional staff to discuss the problems and opportunities inherent in library automation. These continued all through the study to keep the staff fully informed of topics under consideration by the project staff and to stimulate staff thinking in relation to new proposals for the project."

A pilot operation in progress in the library provides a means by which the characteristics of the system can be even more easily studied by other operating personnel. Furthermore, if the response of the personnel directly involved with the pilot operation has been favorable (and such attitudes are typical), these people can be counted on to sell the system to other people who will be working with it. In some cases it may even be possible to provide some on-the-job training in the pilot operation prior to the full implementation of the new system. Descriptions presented on the spot while touring through the library can help individuals to visualize the characteristics of the new system. Other techniques can be used to maintain a high level of interest in the new system during the time just preceding the installation. Appropriate posters, demonstrations of new equipment or techniques, as well as lectures and directed reading can stimulate continued interest in the new system.

The installation phase is critical since, at that time, the majority of the library staff are exposed for the first time to the system as an operational entity. This is a period in which the basic attitudes of personnel who must operate and depend upon the system are solidified.[18] If negative attitudes are established, if the users do not acquire confidence in the system, if they are less than cooperative

[16] Parker, Ralph, "What Every Librarian Should Know About Automation", *Wilson Library Bulletin*, 38 (May 1964), 741-749.

[17] Covill, G. W., "Librarian + Systems Analyst = Teamwork? *Special Libraries,* 58 (February 1967), 99-101.

[18] Postley, John A., *Report on a Study of Behavoral Factors in Information Systems.* Los Angeles: Advanced Information Systems, Hughes Dynamics, 1964.

in ensuring that the system accomplishes its goals, and if they reject the system out of hand and refuse to use it, the result may be a disaster from the users', management's, and the developer's points of view. Such disasters can, and do, happen. They can be prevented if appropriate steps are taken as part of the development planning to ensure the psychological acceptance of the system by the users.

Orientation of Users

The usual experience with the introduction of a mechanized system is that the users of the library will be immediately affected and probably adversely so. There are always temporary dislocations that arise in the conversion to a new system, as the numerous accounts in magazines and newspapers amply demonstrate. A carefully planned program of "public relations," by which the users of the library are prepared for these changes, is therefore essential.

Of perhaps even greater importance is the need to make the users aware of the financial implications in the development of a mechanization program. Ultimately, it will probably be the users who will pay for it, and therefore, to that extent they must be involved in the planning from the beginning. In this respect, we emphasize that mechanization in libraries almost certainly will not result in reduced operating costs. It must be justified on the basis of improved service and the capacity to handle increased work loads in the future. The experience of several state-wide programs to inform the interested public has been that the public is not only willing but anxious to see programs proceed on that basis, but they must be informed about the program plans and their cost implications.

Training of Operating Staff

One of the first jobs that the Assistant Librarian for Mechanized Services will face is to staff his organization. Members of the applications study group are obvious candidates, since their experience is valuable for detailed planning and operations. But feasibility and applications study groups frequently are temporary, formed from people with a variety of backgrounds. Some, who willingly served on a temporary basis in the feasibility and applications groups, may want to return to their basic careers in librarianship or data processing. Others may not be suited by training or temperament for a career in library systems analysis and data processing. A person may not be appropriate for a continuing assignment because he is either underqualified or overqualified. Then, too a person who finds preparatory studies interesting because of their variety may not do well when work becomes routine.

Employees within other departments of the library are another source of personnel. Their knowledge of operating procedures is a valuable background to the specialized skills that can be acquired in operating assignments. In general, it is desirable to seek people from within the library rather than from outside, since the people already available are probably equally capable and are acclimated to the library.

People with specialized skills for programming are apt to be in short supply. Any people trained during the systems analysis and applications projects should be used, if possible. Despite all the arguments for obtaining staff within the organization, there is merit in having a balance of viewpoints and experience. People already skilled in the use of specific equipment are a desirable complement to people with library experience and systems know-how. They can speed up successful system implementation.

Adequate training is necessary, whatever the source of personnel.[19] An equipment manufacturer's training courses and on-the-job training give a practical working knowledge of equipment. Courses in programming and processor operations are offered regularly at customer-service locations by most manufacturers and, in addition, many provide resident instruction for specified periods. Large companies and government agencies often conduct their own courses in programming and operating principles at both elementary and advanced levels.[20] Key personnel should be educated as well as trained. University courses and professional association meetings are valuable for learning more than basic programming and operating principles; they also furnish background knowledge and permit the exchange of ideas about new equipment and applications. [21,22]

The classroom, it should be remembered, is not a substitute for experience on the job. Analysis and programming work should be started as soon as some people are trained to develop essential experience toward getting the work done. Formal training is most valuable when supplemented with on-the-job training since, in this way, advanced techniques can be absorbed and used as soon as the programmer is ready. A schedule for training and programming in conjunction with medium-scale equipment installation should include training sessions for programmers, management, and operators. The training period should be interspersed with periods spent designing the proposed system, flow charting the programming, and correcting programs. Training and programming should be

[19]Gull, C. D., "Personnel Requirements for Automation in Libraries," in John F. Harvey (ed.), *Data Processing in Public and University Libraries.* New York: Spartan, 1966.

[20] Holzbauer, Herbert, "Inhouse Automated Data Processing Training", *Special Libraries,* **58** (July 1967), 427-428.

[21] Bracken, Marilyn C., and Charles W. Shilling, *Survey of Practical Training in Information Science,* Biological Sciences Communication Project, April 1967.

[22] Goldwyn, A. J., "Advanced Automation: Its Implications for Library Education," *Library Journal,* **88** (July 1963), 2640-2643.

done, if possible, at the library's location. Also, training periods should be scheduled for working on equipment at the manufacturer's plant on several different occasions. Such test periods offer concrete operating experience with equipment and furnish an opportunity to reexamine the quality of programmer education and training.

Training of Conversion Staff

The task of conversion represents such an enormous investment for the library and is so dependent on the quality of the work done by one-time clerical staff that especial care must be taken to train the staff adequately. The forms and procedures for copying, editing, and key-punching must be clearly laid out in the planning for conversion. Training procedures must be carefully planned, with attention to the fact that the conversion staff will continually change and new personnel must be trained.

Training of Library Staff

Finally, the day-to-day operation of a mechanized library system will require that the entire library staff be trained in operating procedures. A procedures manual must be prepared as part of the programming effort. Each staff member must be trained in the proper execution of the procedures for which he is responsible.

Suggested Readings, Films and Filmstrips

Among the references cited in this chapter, the following are especially valuable as basic sources of information:

Gregory, Robert H., and R. L. Van Horn, *Automatic Data-Processing Systems: Principles and Procedures.* Belmont, California: Wadsworth, 1963.
Postley, John, *Computers and People.* New York: McGraw-Hill, 1960.

This book is a highly readable review of the use of computers in business which emphasizes the impact on the day-to-day activities of ordinary people as well as on people who are closely associated with the computers.

Schultheiss, Louis A., Don S. Culbertson, and Edward M. Heiliger, *Advanced Data Processing in the University Library.* New York: Scarecrow, 1962.

This book was the first formal description of the steps required to develop a mechanized library system. It is therefore of historical interest as well as being of value in itself.

There are some films and filmstrips available which could be especially useful as part of a library's orientation and training program.

FILMS

Information Retrieval. 18 Minutes. Color. I.B.M., loaned free.

Shows a theoretical large company solving communication problems by adopting modern information retrieval procedures, using conventional I.B.M. data processing systems. Deals with K.W.I.C. indexing, research project retrieval, S.D.I., document retrieval, skill indexing.

Methods Analysis. 9 Minutes. Black and white. University of Colorado, $3.25.

Methods analysis is used to reduce production costs by increasing administration. Shows a job analyst preparing a job specification that lists the skills and abilities required for the job, and analyzes several methods of job rating. The work of time study engineers is described.

More Than Words. 13 Minutes. Color. Purdue, $ 4.65.

Discusses the objectives of communication, choice of communications methods, barriers to communication, and methods of circumventing communications barriers of various kinds. Outlines factors to consider in determining the method of communication. Points out the use of feedback in modifying communications to maximize understanding.

Motion Study on the Job. 25 Minutes. Black and white. State University of Iowa, $4.

Desirability of maintaining orderly progression of events in work method improvement project. Analysis of the job, synthesis of possible improvements, selection and utilization of best possible improvements. Before and after versions of twelve jobs.

Overcoming Resistance to Change. 30 Minutes. Black and white. Penn State, $6.75.

Through dealing with emotional factors which breed resistance to change, supervisors can prevent or overcome the normal tendency of their people to oppose new ideas and procedures and help to avoid serious drops in efficiency and morale.

The Scientific Method. 12 Minutes. Black and white. University of Colorado, $4.50.

Demonstrates the method of problem solving as applied by scientists and stresses the value of scientific thinking in dealing with problems of everyday life.

What is E.D.P.? 13 Minutes. Color. I.B.M., loaned free.

Discussion of basic principles of electronic data processing, provisions for input, storage, processing, output of data; deals with punched cards, paper, magnetic tape, magnetic ink, magnetic drum, disk, tape storage.

Work Simplification in the Office. 25 Minutes. Black and white.

Explains the five tools used in work simplification: work distribution chart, flow processes chart, work count, motion economy analyses, layout studies. Illustrates specific examples of work simplification ideas that have been put into effect in various offices.

SLIDES AND SOUND FILMSTRIPS

Automation in Today's Modern Office. 35 mm filmstripp and script. Color. Friden, loaned free.

Shows the evolution of office automation in clear non-technical terms and illustrates modern equipment. The development of record keeping in a representative industry is traced from 1850 to the present.

The Magic Window: Principles of Punched Card Accounting. 35 mm filmstrip with tape. Color. 16 minutes. I.B.M., loaned free.

Principles of punched card accounting. Explaines the punched hole in the unit record, recording, verifying, classifying, reporting. Photographs of unit record equipment are used.

Systems Analysis. 35 mm sound-filmstrip. Black and white. Standard Register, Denver Office, loaned free.

Part Three   Data Processing Technology

Chapter 9

MACHINE LANGUAGE FOR DATA

Data processing systems (manual or mechanized) deal with recorded data. This implies a process of coding and, for machine systems, a machine language. However, it should also be recognized that codes are essential in any system; we are just so familiar with the codes we use every day, in the form of words and numbers, that we usually don't regard them as such. Since the essential unity of data processing operations (no matter how they may be performed) is the theme of this book, we approach the representation of data as a basic problem of coding.

These codes must be organized into "data structures" so that they can be processed. The structures are defined in terms of "fields" (for individual elements of data), "segments" (or groups of fields), "records" (or groups of segments), and "files."

CODING OF DATA

Codes involve two fundamental concepts: symbol and position. Examples of sets of symbols are easy to find, and we shall use several examples to illustrate the principles of coding: the alphabetic characters from which we form our words; the decimal digits from which we form our numbers; the two together, called the alpha-numeric characters; and the binary digits, used by virtually every mechanized system.

[To digress for a moment, there is one question raised by the preceding statement that should be answered: Why *do* machine systems use binary codes? The answer is relatively simple (if we avoid the morass of philosophical issues of

219

"simplicity"). Binary codes are more reliable because the machinery need recognize only 2 states (corresponding, as we shall discuss, to the two binary digits, or symbols) rather than 10 or 20, or 30. This means, for example, that the punched-card reader needs only to detect whether or not a hole has been punched, rather than how large the hole is. As a result, slight displacements in the position of a hole will not result in errors.]

The concept of position, although equally fundamental, is not nearly as obvious because we tend to notice the symbols, while the position in which they occur is usually only implicit. But it is evident that, as codes, the only difference between "dog" and "god" is the position in which the alphabetic characters occur. There are a number of means by which we define position: our convention of reading from left to right defines positions of letters in words in terms of the spaces that separate words; position in numbers is defined in terms of the decimal point and the "radix notation" that we shall define later; in telegraphy, sequence in time defines position; on punched cards, rows and columns define positions; and so on. The significant point is that meaning, or interpretation, of a symbol is determined by the combination of symbol and position.

In library operation, there are traditional code systems that are familiar: Dewey class numbers, LC class codes, and Cutter numbers. There are other code systems, also traditional, that may not be as obvious: accession numbers and subject headings, for example. These all represent convenient examples that we shall use to illustrate the principle of coding.

The basic issue in coding is the relationship between the number of possible codes, the number of symbols, and the number of positions in which the symbols can occur. This relationship is simple:

$$C = S^n,$$

where C is the number of possible codes, S is the number of symbols, and n is the number of positions. For example, the number of possible codes given by three decimal digits is obviously $C = 10^3 = 1000$ (from 000 to 999). The number of possible two-letter words is $C = 26^2 = 676$. The number of possible six-bit codes is $C = 2^6 = 64$. And so on.

Now it must be recognized that this describes the number of possible codes, not the number of codes actually used in a given situation. For example, there are 26 possible one-letter words, but we actually recognize only three of them (A, I, and possibly O) as valid words. The excess of possible codes over actually used ones is called redundancy. On the one hand, this represents a loss of efficiency, since the invalid codes are implicitly in the system whether used or not; but, on the other hand, it aids us in recognizing and even correcting errors. For example, the redundancy of printed English text is notorious, and yet it allows us to read material filled with misprints and even to fill in missing letters and words. The redundancy of spoken English allows us to communicate reliably in extremely noisy environments.

A particular code system, then, involves the assignment of codes, based on symbols from a specified set of symbols occurring at positions in a defined set of positions, to the items being coded. The assignment is given by a "code book," which allows for the transformation from item to code and vice versa; it may also indicate what should be done with invalid, unused or forbidden codes. For example, a portion of a three-place Cutter table is shown in Figure 9.1.[1]

Figure 9.1 Sample of Cutter table.

Bear	38	Charles
Beau	381	Charli
Beauf	382	Charm
Beauj	383	Charo
Beaun	384	Charpy
Beaut	385	Chart
Beaux	386	Chas
Bech	387	Chasi
Beck	388	Chast
Beckm	389	Chaste

A familiar example of a code book is a telephone directory, which assigns codes (in the form of seven position decimal codes for telephone numbers) to names and addresses (Figure 9.2).

Figure 9.2 Sample of Telephone Directory.

Becker John	1938SArgyl	589-4673
Becker John D	361RositaLnPas	756-1786
Becker John R	500NSierraBonita	538-1235
Becker Jos	1174NShadowlwnAv	663-5796
Becker Joseph	340MeadowValleyTer	668-5967
Becker Karl	725 EchoPkTer	534-4325
Becker Kay	5906Piedmt	465-7789
Becker Keith G	965StonrdgDr	343-5647

It is clear then that a variety of code systems can be used and that the choice of a particular code system must be based on some useful criteria. These include the following guidelines.

1. *Reliability.* We have already commented on this reason for the choice of

[1] Cutter, Charles Ammi, *Three-Figure Author Table*, (Chicopee Falls, Mass.) Distributed by the H. R. Huntting Co. (no date).

binary symbols and on the value of redundancy, represented by an excessive number of positions, in detecting and correcting errors.

2. *Efficiency.* In certain respects, this is in opposition to the interests of reliability, since efficient codes will usually minimize the number of symbols and positions.

3. *Ease of Use.* When communication (particularly with human beings) is a significant aspect of operation, it is important to employ code systems that are convenient to use, that are familiar, that are mnemonic, and that convey "meaning" in some sense. For example, we are familiar with decimal digits and alphabetic characters.

4. *Special properties.* Some code systems are designed to simplify certain machine operations or to fit the characteristics of particular problems. For example, the so-called "excess-three" binary code simplifies the mechanization of certain arithmetic operations on decimal numbers; the so-called "gray" code involves a change of only one bit position as transition is made from one decimal digit to the next.

5. *Statistical considerations.* These actually are the basis for all of coding theory, including the other factors listed above. All of communication theory (also known as information theory) is essentially concerned with the relationship between the statistical properties of the items being coded and the optimum choice of codes.[2]

Binary Codes

For the reasons briefly indicated above, and others as well, binary coding is the basis for most representations of data in machinery. It is an almost trivially simple concept, using only *two* symbols. These are usually represented as "0" and "1" and are called "zero" and "one," but care should be taken *not* to confuse them with the decimal digits that look the same and are called the same. (In a sense it is unfortunate—at least, in terms of the process of education—that the limited number of simple shapes forces us to use the same shape for different purposes. Thus we write "10," and the question is: What does it mean? In the decimal system, it is ten; in the binary system it is two, despite the mistake that many teachers of the "new math" make when they call it ten. The apparent similarity in shape confuses the real difference in meaning.)

However, although we may represent these two symbols by 1 and 0, the forms that they take are quite varied: the appearance of a punch at a given position on a punched card, or the lack of it; a notch on the edge of a card, or a hole at the same position; a magnetic polarization of one direction or another; the flow of electricity in one direction or another; the two states of a bi-stable

2 Reza, Fezlallah, *Introduction to Information Theory*. New York: McGraw-Hill, 1961.

device called a flip-flop—each is a means of representing the two symbols that we record on paper as 1 and 0.

Earlier we stated the formula relating the number of possible codes with the number of symbols and number of positions:

$$C = S^n$$

For binary coding, we are therefore concerned with the powers of 2:[3]

$$
\begin{aligned}
2^0 &= 1 & 2^5 &= 32 & 2^{10} &= 1024 \\
2^1 &= 2 & 2^6 &= 64 & 2^{20} &\doteq \text{one million} \\
2^2 &= 4 & 2^7 &= 128 & 2^{30} &\doteq \text{one billion} \\
2^3 &= 8 & 2^8 &= 256 & 2^{40} &\doteq \text{one trillion} \\
2^4 &= 16 & 2^9 &\ 512 & 2^{50} &\doteq \text{one quadrillion}
\end{aligned}
$$

The significance for code systems is best illustrated in terms of the familiar examples of decimal digits, alphabetic characters, and alpha-numeric characters. Consider, therefore, the decimal digits: there are ten of them (0, 1, 2, 3, 4, 5, 6, 7, 8, 9) and, according to the formula, we must have at least four positions, called bit positions, in order to have enough codes (since $2^3 = 8$ and $2^4 = 16$). As we have indicated, the choice of a particular code system is subject to many criteria, but some classical codes are shown in Figure 9.3. The first, as we shall show, has the value of being consistent with "binary arithmetic." It is the simplest, and is the one that we shall use in all future illustrations. It is abbreviated "BCD." The second has certain advantages in mechanization of

Figure 9.3   Standard codes for decimal digits.

	Binary Coded Decimal	Excess-3	Gray-Code	Alpha-Numeric
0	0000	0011	0000	000000
1	0001	0100	0010	000001
2	0010	0101	0110	000010
3	0011	0110	0111	000011
4	0100	0111	0011	000100
5	0101	1000	0001	000101
6	0110	1001	0101	000110
7	0111	1010	0100	000111
8	1000	1011	1100	001000
9	1001	1100	1000	001001

[3] The number of stories and fables concerning the behavior of powers of two is great and indicates an appreciation in the earliest civilisations of their rapid growth, despite the apparent simplicity of the operation of doubling up. See, especially, Edward Kasner and James Newman, *Mathematics and the Imagination*. New York: Simon and Schuster, 1943, pp. 165-173.

decimal arithmetic operations. The third has the property that in going from one decimal digit to the next, only a single bit position changes its value; it is of use in devices which sense the position of rotary equipment. The fourth is simply an extension of BCD to be consistent with a typical alpha-numeric code system; since it uses six bits where four would otherwise be sufficient, it is not as efficient as BCD alone.

Codes for alphabetic characters are used in any system that involves the handling of names, words, and textual material, including punched-tape typewriters, teletype, punched card billing systems, and computers. Since there are 26 alphabetic characters, not counting punctuation marks and the "space," alphabetic codes must involve at least five bit positions. Some classical code systems are included in Figure 9.4. The first would be used by a "decimal" computer, designed to handle only decimal codes; in order to represent an alphabetic character, therefore, we would need to establish a decimal representation for it; the example chooses the number of the letter in the alphabet (from 1 to 26). The second code system is a fairly typical five-channel punched tape code. Notice that since there are only 26 letters, five bit-positions are sufficient. Also notice that there is little "logic" in the assessment of codes, so that a conversion table is essential. The third is the code used in the Remington-Rand punched-card system which we shall discuss in detail later. The last is an alpha-numeric code, which is consistent with that used for decimal digits.

Codes for alpha-numeric characters are usually defined (as we have indicated above) in such a way as to be consistent with the codes for both decimal digits and alphabetic characters taken by themselves. Since the two together involve at least 36 characters, any alpha-numerical code must have at least 6 bit-positions. Examples are given in Figure 9.5. The first is designed in terms of the needs in teletype communication. The second is designed to produce an arrangement of combined alphabetic and numerical information into sorted order which would

Figure 9.4   Standard codes for alphabetic characters.

	BCD Coded	Five-Channel Teletype	Remington Rand P/C	Alpha-Numeric
A	0000 0001	00011	010101	010001
B	0000 0010	11001	010100	010010
C	0000 0011	01110	100010	010011
...	...	...	...	...
L	0001 0010	10010	100001	100011
M	0001 0011	11100	100100	100100
N	0001 0100	01100	100101	100101
...	...	...	...	...
X	0010 0100	11101	100011	110111
Y	0010 0101	10101	011001	111000
Z	0010 0110	10001	000111	111001

Figure 9.5   Standard codes for alpha-numeric characters.

	Six-Channel Teletype	Standard Alpha-Numeric	IBM Punched Card
0	010000	000000	0010000000000
1	000001	000001	0001000000000
2	000010	000010	0000100000000
...	...	...	...
7	000111	000111	0000000000100
8	000100	001000	0000000000010
9	001001	001001	0000000000001
A	110001	010001	1001000000000
B	110010	010001	1000100000000
...	...	...	...
L	100011	100011	0100010000000
M	100100	100100	0100001000000
...	...	...	...
Y	011000	111000	0010000000010
Z	011001	111001	0010000000001

always place numerical data first, based solely on simple binary comparisons. The third is the standard punched-card code: the first three bits define the "zone," and the others define the "field" for the alphabet.

There are so many different code systems that problems of intercommunication among systems have become almost insuperable. This has led to the definition of two "standards": the USA Standard Code for Information Interchange (ASCII) and the Extended Binary Coded Decimal Interchange Code (EBCDIC), the first of which is a seven-bit code (plus parity).[4] The complete code system for each is shown in Figure 9.6. EBCDIC is the principal code system used by IBM 360 computer systems; codes for individual characters are addressed as "bytes."

Incidentally, there are methods by which a five bit-code can be used, in effect, to represent more than 32 things. An example is a standard 5-channel teletype code in which certain codes represent either a number or a letter, the meaning in any particular case being determined by whether a "shift" code (or a "numbers" code or "letters" code) has been previously recorded. Actually, of course, this is a method that really uses ten bits to represent a character; but it is efficient if there tends to be a large sequence of characters of the same kind, since then the "shift" character is applied to each of them. This technique is frequently used whenever "multi-font" character systems are required.[5]

[4] *U.S.A. Standard Code for Information Interchange* (USA Standard X3.4-1967) New York, U.S.A. Standards Institute, 1967.
[5] Buckland, Lawrence F., *The Recording of Library of Congress Bibliographic Data in Machine Form.* Maynard, Mass.: Inforonics, February 1965.

Figure 9.6   Standard ASCII and EBCDIC codes.

	ASCII	EBCDIC		ASCII	EBCDIC		ASCII	EBCDIC
0	011,0000	1111,0000		100,1010	1101,0001	NULL	0000000	0000,0000
1	011,0001	1111,0001	J	100,1011	1101,0010			
2	011,0010	1111,0010	K	100,1011	1101,0010			
3	011,0011	1111,0011	L	100,1100	1101,0011	And other special		
4	011,0100	1111,0100	M	100,1101	1101,0100	characters and		
5	011,0101	1111,0101	N	100,1110	1101,0101	punctuation marks		
6	011,0110	1111,0110	O	100,1111	1101,0110			
7	011,0111	1111,0111	P	101,0000	1101,0111			
8	011,1000	1111,1000	Q	101,0001	1101,1000			
9	011,1001	1111,1001	R	101,0010	1101,1001			
A	100,0001	1100,0001						
B	100,0010	1100,0010	S	101,0011	1110,0010			
C	100,0011	1100,0011	T	101,0100	1110,0011			
D	100,0100	1100,0100	U	101,0101	1110,0100			
E	100,0101	1100,0101	V	101,0110	1110,0101			
F	100,0110	1100,0110	W	101,0111	1110,0110			
G	100,0111	1100,0111	X	101,1000	1110,0111			
H	100,1000	1100,1000	Y	101,1001	1110,1000			
I	100,1001	1100,1001	Z	101,1010	1110,1001			

In subsequent chapters, when we discuss methods of input, output, and data storage, we shall present the full code systems for each medium.

Binary Arithmetic

Returning to the codes for decimal digits, we mentioned that BCD is the simplest, and it is interesting to explore exactly why it is. The basis of BCD is "binary arithmetic," which utilizes the simplest addition and multiplication tables possible (Figure 9.7).

Figure 9.7   Binary arithmetic tables.

+	0	1		x	0	1
0	0	1	and	0	0	0
1	1	10		1	0	1

Thus, if the number zero is represented by the binary digit 0 and the number one is represented by the binary digit 1, according to binary arithmetic, the number two should be presented by 10. This is continued in Figure 9.8.

Figure 9.8   Example of binary addition.

0 represented by   0
1 represented by   1
2 represented by   1 + 1 = 10
3 represented by   10 + 1 = 11
4 represented by   11 + 1 =   ?

The principle of "carrying" applies in binary arithmetic just as it does in decimal arithmetic (Figure 9.9).

Figure 9.9   Binary carry.

Carry = 11
              11
        +   1
        ———
           100

The result is that any number can be represented in binary form, and binary forms can be derived by the successive addition of 1 according to the rules for binary arithmetic. The BCD codes for the decimal digits are exactly the binary codes that would result from this process.

If we were to derive the binary codes for larger numbers by such a cumbersome process of counting, they would have little value. However, there is a concept, which binary codes derived in this fashion embody, called "radix notation." It is familiar to us in our use of decimal numbers:

$$176 = 1 \times 10^2 + 7 \times 10^1 + 6 \times 1$$

Therefore, to convert a number from binary form to decimal form, we simply interpret it according to the radix notation, with radix 2. Conversely, to convert from decimal to binary, we simply divide the decimal number successively by two and use the successive remainders as the binary digits (Figure 9.10 illustrates derivation of 10110000 as the binary number for 176).

Because of the simplicity of binary arithmetic, it is the most convenient for computers to use. Early in the history of computers, when they were used primarily for computation, binary arithmetic was therefore the mode of operation. However, most people are unfamiliar with binary arithmetic and are unwilling to accept data coded in this form. As a result, those early computers were forced to convert decimal data into binary form at input and vice versa at output, so as to allow easy communication of data and results. This was acceptable as long as the amount of data was small. But as the computer began to be applied to so-called "business data processing" problems and, more recently, to "information handling problems," the amount of conversion became

Figure 9.10   Binary Codes.

2/<u>176</u>		
2/<u>88</u>	+	0
2/<u>44</u>	+	0
2/<u>22</u>	+	0
2/<u>11</u>	+	0
2/<u>5</u>	+	1
2/<u>2</u>	+	1
2/<u>1</u>	+	0
0	+	1

too great. Therefore, most computers are now either decimal machines or alpha-numeric ones and perform arithmetic operations just as we do. This means, however, that all data are represented internally as binary coded decimal numbers or binary coded alpha-numeric characters.

(The reason that the excess-3 code has had some appeal for the engineer is that the binary addition automatically creates a decimal "carry":

$$
\begin{array}{rl}
7 & 1010 \\
+6 & 1001 \\
\hline
& 1,0011
\end{array}
$$

which simplifies some of the arithmetic circuitry.)

Complex Codes

Codes are more than merely ways of representing numbers and letters. By direct coding with binary numbers or by the intermediary of coding with letters and numbers (which are themselves coded in binary form), extremely complex concepts can be stored and processed. To illustrate this, let us consider several separate coding systems, with different roles and applications.

Consider names, for example. The familiar code for names is the simple alphabetic spelling, but there are a variety of others, some of which are familiar, some obscure, and some quite remote.[6] See Figure 9.11. The first column, the Cutter numbers, provide a more or less alphabetical arrangement. They are based on the statistical distribution of names, in such a way that each number is assigned to approximately the same number of names. To determine the specific code for a given name, a code book must be used. The second column is based on an attempt to code names that sound the same with the same code number.

[6] Bourne, Charles P., *Methods of Information Handling.* New York: Wiley, 1963.

Figure 9.11   Complex codes for names.

Alphabetic Names	Cutter Numbers	Soundex Codes	Abbreviations
Hayden, Richard	H 415	H 350	HDNR
Hayes, Arnold	H 417	H 200	HSRN
Hayes, Robert	H 418	H 200	HSRB
Hayler,	H 421	H 460	HLR
Hays,	H 425	H 200	HS
Backer,	B 126	B 260	BCK
Baker, Joseph	B 167	B 260	BKR
Baker, Martin	B 168	B 260	BKR
Becker, Joseph	B 395	B 260	BCK
Becker, Martin	B 395	B 260	BCK

The rules are simple and can be applied without the use of a code book. They involve coding the letters in the names as follows.

1.   The initial symbol is the initial of the name.

2.   Double letters, or pairs of letters with similar sounds as described below, are treated as single letters.

3.   A-E-I-O-U-W-H-Y are ignored when they occur within the name.

4.   Letters with similar sounds are coded with the same code number:

BFPV	1
CGJKQSXZ	2
DT	3
L	4
MN	5
R	6

5.   If there are less than three such letters in the name, zeros are added to produce a three digit code after the initial letter. If there are more than three, only the first three are used.

The Soundex Code is valuable because it brings together names that sound alike and that might have been misunderstood or misspelled. In this way, search is simplified when communication might be a problem.

Abbreviations, such as those in column three, are valuable as a means for providing more or less unique codes for names, which are easily determined from the name itself and which occupy a small number of symbol positions.

In addition to these fairly standard codes for names, special codes are sometimes developed, usually for unsophisticated punched-card systems, to facilitate the alphabetical sorting of name and subject headings.[7] The need for such codes arises (1) because names are relatively long and vary in length, which complicates the problem of sorting column by column as is done with the punched-card sorter, and (2) because the alphabetical arrangement of names, subject headings, titles, and other forms of text does not necessarily follow the mechanical rules of sorting followed by the machine (for example, we usually ignore the articles, "the," "a," and "an," when they start a title; foreign names frequently should be sorted on other than the beginning letters; spaces and punctuation marks often should be ignored, but the machinery cannot do so).

For these reasons, code systems are developed that assign a sequence number to the names in the numerical order corresponding to the desired alphabetical order. Of course, if it is anticipated that additional names will be added, space must be provided in the numbering system to accommodate them.

These code systems are relatively effective and easy to use, provided that the set of items being coded is stable. But as the rate of addition or change goes up, the difficulties in maintaining the code lists rapidly increases, and the process becomes so cumbersome that other solutions must be found. When we consider various forms of catalogs (in Chapter 17), the alternative approaches will be discussed.

DATA STRUCTURE

In order to be processed by a computer, codes must be stored in such a way that their meaning can be determined. This implies the prior definition of a set of "data structures" or "data formats."

Levels of Data Structure

The basic building blocks for a data structure are "fields." A field is a location in which an element of data, of a given kind, is stored. Thus, a data structure for cataloging data related to books would usually include an "author field," a "title field," an "imprint field," and a "subject-heading field."

The set of fields related to a single thing of interest (for instance, a single book) would be organized into a "record format." A simplified format for a catalog record is shown in Figure 9.12.[8]

---

[7] MacQuarrie, Catherine, and Beryl L. Martin, "Book Catalog of the Los Angeles County Public Library: How it is being made," *Library Resources and Technical Services,* 4 (3), Summer 1960, 208-27.

[8] Cline, Catherine, "Procedures for Developing Timberland's Book Catalog", *Pacific Northwest Library Association Quarterly,* 28 (January 1964), 128-132, 136.

Figure 9.12   Punched-card catalog record.

Card 1.   Author Card

Column	1	Card type (Type 1)
	2	Number within type (for multiple authors)
	3-12	Call number
	13-56	Author's name
	57-64	Author sort code
	65-72	Title sort code
	73-80	Subject sort code

Card 2.   Title Card

Column	1	Card type (Type 2)
	2	Number within type (for long titles)
	3-12	Call number
	13-56	Title
	57-64	Author sort code
	65-72	Title sort code
	73-80	Subject sort code

Card 3.   Imprint Card

Column	1	Card type (Type 3)
	2	Number within type (for annotations)
	3-12	Call number
	13-56	Imprint and annotations
	57-64	Author sort code
	65-72	Title sort code
	73-80	Subject sort code

Card 4.   Subject Card

Column	1	Card type (Type 4)
	2	Number within type (for multiple subjects)
	3-12	Call number
	13-56	Subject
	57-64	Author sort code
	65-72	Title sort code
	73-80	Subject sort code

Frequently, it is useful to introduce a level of structure (called the "segment"), intermediate between the field and the record. A segment is simply a collection of fields that play a separately definable role within a record. The need for segments can be illustrated with respect to the catalog record by considering the "publisher field," "city of publication field," and "date of publication field." Together, they constitute the "imprint" for the book. Since it may frequently be desirable to treat them as a whole, it is useful to define an "imprint segment." The value of segments is that it allows the description of a record format to be highly generalized and yet easily handled in a specific situation. With use of segments, record formats are defined as follows.

1. Fields may be grouped into segments (some of which may consist of only a single field).
2. Segments may be grouped into larger segments.
3. Segments are grouped into records.

Finally, although the individual record represents the logical unit in a data structure, records are then sequenced in one order or another and constitute "files." The sequence for a given file is an especially important consideration in defining a data structure.

Variety of Formats

It is useful to categorize formats into two types—fixed formats and variable formats—and then, for each type, to categorize the fields within the format again into two types: fixed fields and variable fields.

Fixed format, fixed field records are the simplest and the ones with which the data processing field has the most experience. They are therefore likely to be equally applicable to library operations of a relatively simple, clerical nature (administrative record keeping and circulation control, for example). They are best exemplified by the typical punched-card circulation record shown in Figure 9.13. As shown, a fixed number of characters (columns of the card) has been set aside for each of a fixed number of items of data. The result is that "call number," for example, will always occur in exactly the same position in each record. The processing is thus simple, because the computer program has one (and only one) place to go in the record for the desired data.

Fixed format, variable field records are a little more complex. The use of magnetic tape, in contrast to punched cards, has made it feasible to use such

Figure 9.13 Punched-card circulation record.

Column	Field Description
1-3	Day of the year
4-5	Hour of the day
6	0 = AM, 1 = PM
7	Transmitting station
8	Transaction code for book card
9	Branch library code
10	Type of book loan code
11-34	Call number
35-64	Short author and title
65-75	Borrower badge number
76	Transmission check character

formats where they are appropriate. For example, authors' names, titles, text, and similar elements of data tend to be of widely varying lengths. The fixed field structure acts as a bed of Procrustes, requiring names that are too long to be cut off and names that are too short to be lengthened to fit the preassigned space. The use of variable fields, on the other hand, allows the format to fit the actual data. Such formats are therefore likely to be useful in relatively simple catalog production systems. They are somewhat more difficult to process than fixed field formats, since the beginning and end of a field may vary from one record to the next. An "end of field symbol" must be used to demarcate one field from the next, and the computer examines each character to find out where fields end.

Variable formats, whether *fixed field* or *variable field,* are the most complex. They are needed when data elements (and, therefore, the corresponding field) may or may not be present in a given record or, in general, when a given data element may appear a variable number of times (from zero on up). For example, books or journal articles have different numbers of authors, and the "author field" can therefore occur a comparably variable number of times. The same is true for subject headings, descriptors, and index terms. In such cases, not only must the beginning and end of each field be identified but the kind of field as well. This means that the record must contain "field identifiers," which the computer examines in order to know whether a given field occurs and, if so, where. This highly generalized and flexible data structure is the one used in the MARC II format (Figure 9.14).[9] As the figure illustrates, such formats are needed to handle the full scale of cataloging data used in reference retrieval systems.

Because of the great variety of possible formats, it is necessary for the computer program to know what the format is in order to handle the records with which it is presented. Most business data processing records are fixed format, fixed field (perhaps because of the important historical role of punched card equipment). In such cases, the format is integrally embodied in the processing programs which, in fact, are written around the formats that they process.

On the other hand, the formats used in libraries are so variable that another approach must be used. Modern "generalized file management programs" are designed to handle all possible formats, within very broad limits. They depend on "file definition tables," which describe the format of a particular record or set of records to be processed. This kind of approach is therefore especially applicable to library data processing.

[9] Avram, Henriette, et al., *The MARC II Format.* Washington, D.C.: Library of Congress, 1968.

Figure 9.14   MARC II format.

SUMMARY OUTLINE

Record Leader

Name of Leader Data Element	Number of Characters	Character Position in Record
Record Length	5	1- 5
Record Status	1	6
Legend		
(a) Legend Control	1	7
(b) Type of Record	1	8
(c) Bibliographic Level	3	9-11
Indicator Count	1	12

Record Directory

Name of Record Directory Data Element	Number of Characters	Character Position in Directory
Tag	3	1- 3
Field Length	4	4- 7
Starting Character Position	5	8-12

Variable Control Number

Name of Fixed Length Data Element	Number of Characters	Character Position in Field
Library of Congress Card Number	11	1-11
Library of Congress Card Number Check Digit	1	12
Supplement Number	1	13
Suffix	1 or more	14-n

Variable Fixed Fields

Name of Fixed Length Data Elements	Number of Characters	Character Position in Field
Number of Entries in Record Directory	3	1-3
Date Entered on File	6	4-9
Type of Publication Date Code	1	10
Date 1	4	11-14
Date 2	4	15-18
Country of Publication Code	3	19-21
Illustration Codes	4	22-25
Intellectual Level Code	1	26
Form of Reproduction Code	1	27
Form of Content Codes	4	28-31
Government Publication Indicator	1	32

Figure 9.14   *(continued)*

Variable Fixed Fields (continued)

Conference or Meeting Indicator	1	33
Festschrift Indicator	1	34
Index Indicator	1	35
Main Entry in Body of Entry Indicator	1	36
Fiction Indicator	1	37
Biography Indicator	1	38
Language	3	39-41

Variable Field

Tag	Variable Field Data Element	Tag	Variable Field Data Element
002	Legend Extension		Title Paragraph
003	Languages	240	Title
	Control Numbers	250	Edition Statement
010	LC Card Number		Imprint
011	National Bibliography Number	260	Place
012	Standard Book Number	261	Publisher
013	PL 48 Number	262	Date(s)
014	Search Code	300	Collation
019	Local System Number	350	Bibliographic Price
	Knowledge Numbers	360	Converted Price
020	BNB Classification Number		Series Notes
030	Dewey Decimal Classification	400	Personal Name (traced the same)
	Number	408	Title
050	LC Call Number	410	Corporate Name (traced the same)
051	Copy Statement	411	Conference (traced the same)
060	NLM Call Number	418	Title
070	NAL Call Number	440	Title (traced the same)
071	NAL Subject Category Number	490	Series Untraced or Traced Differently
080	UDC Number		Bibliographic Notes
090	Local Call Number	500	Bibliography Note
	Main Entry	510	Dissertation Note
100	Personal Name	520	Contents Note Formatted
108	Title	530	"Bound With" Note
110	Corporate Name	540	"Limited Use" Note
111	Conference or Meeting	550	General Notes (all others)
118	Title	560	Abstract
120	Corporate Name with Form Sub-		Subject Added Entry
	heading	600	Personal Name
128	Title	608	Title
130	Uniform Title Heading	610	Corporate name
138	Title	611	Conference or Meeting
	Supplied Titles	618	Title
200	Uniform Title	620	Corporate Name with Form Sub-
210	Romanized Title		heading
220	Translated Title	628	Title

Figure 9.14   *(continued)*

Subject Added Entry *(continued)*

Tag	Variable Field Data Element	Tag	Variable Field Data Element
630	Uniform Title Heading	710	Corporate Name
638[a]	Title	711	Conference or Meeting
650	Topical	718	Title
651	Geographic Names	720	Corporate Name with Form Sub-
652	Political Jurisdiction Alone or with		heading
	Subject Subdivisions	728	Title
653	Proper Names Not Capable of	730	Uniform Title Heading
	Authorship	738[a]	Title
655	General Subdivisions (other than	740	Title Traced Differently
	period and place)	753	People Names Not Capable of
656	Period Subdivision		Authorship
657	Place Subdivision		<u>Series Added Entries</u>
660	NLM Subject Headings (MESH)	800	Personal Name
670	NAL Agricultural/Biological Vocab-	808	Title
	ulary	810	Corporate Name
690	Local Subject Heading Systems	811	Conference or Meeting
	<u>Other Added Entries</u>	818	Title
700	Personal Name	840	Title
708	Title	900	Block of 100 Numbers for Local Use

[a]Rare but occasionally found in old cataloging.

File Definition Tables

File definition tables record descriptions of aspects of data structure related to files, to records (for example, the means of defining record type and length), and to fields (for instance, the symbols or names for the fields, their length, the relative location of each field in the record, the types of records in which each field occurs, and the list of possible codes in a coded field).

To make matters more concrete, consider the example of the MEDLARS file. An approach to desribing the MEDLARS record is shown in Figure 9.15. The record consists of two levels and three segments. Segment 1 consists of items or fields that appear once. Segments 2 and 3, however, may be repeated, when a cited article has several "tag words" or several authors. The "COUNT" fields in Segment 1 tell the number of times these repeating segments actually occur in a record.

All fields in this variable record format are fixed-length fields (although variable fields can be handled in an efficient manner, as will be discussed later). The capability for repeating segments requires that we allocate only as many author segments in the record as there are authors of the cited article; on the other hand, 20 characters are assigned to each author even though less may be required.

Figure 9.15 MEDLARS file format
(structure of the MEDLARS file as it might exist in hierarchical structure).

LEVEL	SEGMENT	Request Number B-Part	Request Number A-Part	Form Code	Citation Number	Year Published	Place Published	Journal Title Code	Entry Date Year	Entry Date Month	Entry Date Day	Language Code
1	1	Author Type	Title	JTA	PAG	PUB D	COUNT TAG-WDS	COUNT AUTHORS				
1	1 (cont.)		TAG WORD IM	TAG WORD SUB-HEAD	TAG WORD MAIN HDCD	TREE WORD CATEG.	TREE WORD LEVEL-1	TREE WORD LEVEL-2	TREE WORD LEVEL-3			
2	1		AUTHOR PR-WDS	AUTHOR SR-WDS								
2	2											

237

Usually, the tables for description of such formats are created by filling in a standard form. To illustrate, assume as a starting point the file organization of Figure 9.15 as the format for the MEDLARS record. (We do not intend to endorse it as "the" format for the MEDLARS record but wish merely to use it as an illustration). The form that needs to be filled out is shown, in part, in Figure 9.16.

Variable Length Fields

In the example, fields are of fixed length. However, an approach for handling variable length fields (such as the title field of the MEDLARS file) is to treat them as collections of segments: instead of allowing 600 characters for the title, we allow a number of, say, 20 character segments to be assigned to it. Consider a particular case of an article title:

VARIATION OF PRESSURE WITH CYCLE LENGTH AND DURATION OF SYSTOLE IN THE TWO-CHAMBERED CARDIOVASCULAR MODEL

Figure 9.16   File definition table for MEDLARS file.

Field Name	Segment	Level	Relative Field Location	Field Length	Field Type	Segment Key	Count
Request Number B-Part	1	1	1	6	N	✓	
Request Number A-Part	1	1	7	1	A		
Form-CD	1	1	8	1	C		
...	...	...	...	...	...		
Count Authors	1	1	328	2	N		✓
...	...	...	...	...	...		
TAG-WORD-IM	2	2	1	1	N		
...	...	...	...	...	...		

Representation (in part) of the file description phase for the file of Figure 9.15, "C," "N," and "A" in the "field type" column refer, respectively, to "coded," "numerical," and "alpha-numerical."

Figure 9.17   Segment approach to variable-length fields.

Level	Segment	Segment Entry
k^a	n^a	VARIATION OF PRESSURE
k	n plus 1	E WITH CYCLE LENGTH
k	n plus 2	AND DURATION OF SYST
k	n plus 3	OLE IN THE TWO-CHAMBERED
k	n plus 4	CARDIOVASCULAR
k	n plus 5	MODEL

[a]The symbols k and n represent unspecified level and segment numbers.

This title has 105 characters in it. Thus, six 20-character segments would be required to specify the entire title (Figure 9.17).

Each segment is a repeating entry but not in the same sense as the "author" segments. Thus, while we could meaningfully ask for the fifth author segment, to ask for the fifth segment in the collection of title segments would be to ask for nonsense.

Validation Criteria

Now we have completed the essential aspects of file definition. Closely associated with file definition are criteria for field editing or validation. Validation criteria are usually set up for field editing or validation at the same time files are established. Generally, they relate to the issues in file definition: the type of field (for instance, coded, alphabetic, numeric); the number of characters; the range of an allowable entry (for example, between age 16 and 65). Validation may even specify that a given field *must* be present in the record or the maximum number of times it may occur. Validation criteria are normally used as a check of input of new information.

Suggested Readings

For readers unfamiliar with the "modern mathematics" as now being taught in elementary and secondary schools, it might be useful to read elementary books such as the following:

Adler, Irving, *Thinking Machines: A Layman's Guide to Logic, Boolean Algebra, and Computing.* New York: Day, 1961.

Beyond this elementary level, the reader may find it valuable to read the following, more specialized books:

Avram, Henriette, et al., *The MARC II Format*. Washington, D. C.: Library of Congress, 1968.

This represents the culmination of the most important single step taken by the library profession in development of computer systems for libraries. It provides a standard for storage and communication of cataloging data.

Beadle, George and Muriel, *The Language of Life*. New York: Doubleday, 1966.

This book provides a very readable introduction to the "genetic code," the means by which "symbols" (in the form of amino acids) in "positions" (defined by their sequence) are used to convey "information" by which genetic structure is transmitted from generation to generation. It illustrates the extent to which coding pervades all of life as well as technology.

Kahn, David, *The Codebreakers: The Story of Secret Writing*. New York: MacMillan, 1967.

An encyclopedic but highly readable coverage of the field of cryptography and cryptanalysis. It is remarkable that so complete a description of what had been among the most closely guarded secrets could have been written and published.

Reza, Fezlalla, *Introduction to Information Theory*. New York: McGraw-Hill, 1961.

This is merely one representative example of several excellent texts on modern "communication theory".

Chapter 10

PROCESSING OF DATA

In this chapter, we shall deal with the heart of modern data processing systems—the stored-program digital computer. What is the computer? How did it come to be? How does it operate? What are its characteristics? We shall answer these questions, at least to the extent of removing some of the mystery surrounding the computer.

INTRODUCTION

Perhaps the best definition of the computer was given by Ned Chapin: "An automatic computer is a machine that manipulates symbols, in accordance with given rules, in a pre-determined and self-directed manner." [1] The most significant word in distinguishing the computer from other, related devices (such as desk calculators) is "self-directed." The computer has the ability to accept data, to process it, and to provide results, all without human intervention, although the rules by which it does this must originally have been prepared by human beings.

Characteristics of the Computer

What does Chapin's definition imply? Basically, the computer is characterized by five features:

1. It has a set of built-in capabilities sufficiently rich for it to perform

---

[1] Chapin, Ned, *An Introduction to Automatic Computers,* New York: Van Nostrand, 1957.

virtually any task that can be defined to it, including communication with peripheral devices and control of them.

2.   It is controlled by an internally stored "program" of instructions and thus can operate independent of human involvement.

3.   Its instructions define the location of data rather than the actual data itself and therefore can be executed in the same way on any data.

4.   The program can be easily modified, thus allowing the same computer to be used on many different jobs simply by changing the set of instructions that it will follow.

5.   But perhaps most important, the instructions can cause the computer to change its own program, thus allowing it automatically to change from one job to the next and even to change the way it does a given job (in effect, to learn).

These five qualitative characteristics add up to a highly flexible robot, capable of performing a variety of jobs, capable of controlling its own environment, and capable of adjusting to that environment. People in the computer professions have therefore been understandably excited and sometimes view the computer in anthropomorphic terms.

In addition, there are some quantitative characteristics that are certainly important: (1) its speed, which allows the computer to perform literally millions of operations each second; and (2) its storage capacity, which provides it with access to millions (even billions) of characters of data.

History

The development of computers, with these capabilities, has depended on the corresponding development of a technology from which they could be built. In fact, most of the characteristics of the modern-day computer (or "analytical engine," as Charles Babbage called it) had been visualized by Babbage in the 1820's:[2, 3]

> The Analytical Engine consists of two parts: 1st. The store in which all the variables to be operated upon, as well as all those quantities which have arisen from the result of other operations, are placed. 2nd. The mill into which the quantities about to be operated upon are always brought . . . .
>
> Every formula which the Analytical Engine can be required to compute consists of certain algebraical operations to be performed upon given letters, and of certain other modifications depending upon the numerical value assigned to those letters. . . . The Analytical Engine is therefore a

[2] Babbage, Charles, *Calculating Engines,* edited by Philip and Emily Morrison, New York: Dover, 1961.

[3] Bernstein, Jeremy, *The Analytical Engine: Computers, Past, Present, and Future,* New York: Random House, 1964.

machine of the most general nature. Whatever formula it is required to develop, the law of its development must be communicated to it by two sets of cards. When these have been placed, the engine is special for that particular formula. . . . Thus the Analytical Engine will possess a library of its own. Every set of cards once made will at any future time reproduce the calculations for which it was first arranged. . . . Two great principles are embodied (in the Analytical Engine):

1st. The entire control over . . . operations.

2nd. The entire control over combinations of algebraic symbols, however lengthened those processes may be required.

Babbage attempted to construct mechanical devices to carry out these aims, but the limitations of the technology of the time prevented him from doing so. He simply was not able to get parts machined to the tolerance required.

For more than 100 years, the technology steadily improved. Gradually, equipment that could perform complex arithmetical computations under manual control became commonplace—the adding machine, the cash register, and key-operated accounting machines. In parallel, equipment was developed that could read punched cards, handle them, and use them as a source of input to such calculators. Finally, between 1939 and 1944, Howard Aiken at Harvard built the Mark I.[4] This was a realization of the dream of Babbage. It replaced the mechanical gears and cams of the "analytical engine" by relays, comparable to those used in telephone switching systems.

However, the machine was still limited in many respects. (1) It was slow because the speed of the relays, as electromechanical devices, was only about 30 operations per second. (2) Its operation was controlled by instructions stored in control panels, cards, and paper tapes essentially external to the machine itself. (3) The capacity for storage of data was limited to at most a few hundred digits.

World War II, however, had made very clear the need for an increased pace in the rate of data processing. In aircraft design, in nuclear physics, in cryptography, and in ballistics, new and prodigious requirements were encountered for the analysis of huge masses of data. Government and university laboratories were called on to provide answers for the limitations in machines like the Harvard Mark I. The development of electronic circuitry, based on the "vacuum tube," provided an answer to the first of its limitations; the ideas of John von Neumann answered the second; and the development of magnetic recording techniques answered the third.

Electronic circuitry replaced relays with "flip-flops"—combinations of vacuum tubes that could be controlled to store binary digits (that is, either of two states) just as did relays. These were capable of operating in thousandths of a second rather than hundredths. The first computer designed in this way was the

---

[4] Bernstein, Jeremy, *op. cit.*, pp. 50-53.

Eniac, built at the University of Pennsylvania in 1946 by Eckert and Mauchly.[5] It weighed nearly 30 tons, occupied 15,000 square feet of floor space, and contained over 19,000 vacuum tubes. (Put that in your television set and smoke it!) The concept of storing the program internally was directly attributable to von Neumann.[6] It led to the construction—by the National Bureau of Standards, by Princeton, and by Rand—of a series of machines based on this revolutionary concept.[7] These machines were designed and built during the period from 1948 to 1952 and were the real "first generation" of modern-day digital computers. During the same time, techniques for recording digital data in magnetic form were developed. People began to use magnetic drums and tapes to supplement the very limited vacuum tube internal memory of these first generation machines. As a result, the complexity of task they could perform, the amount of data they could handle, and the rate at which they could process it were all vastly increased.

Commercial versions of these machines began to appear, in a wide range of speeds and capacities—the Univac I (of Remington Rand), the IBM 701, the 1100 of Engineering Research Associates (later to become a division of Remington Rand), the IBM 650, and so on.[8]

But there were practical limits to the speed, size, and capacity of machines using vacuum tubes. Vacuum tubes are bulky; they demand large amounts of power and generate comparable amounts of heat. Gradually, they began to be replaced by semiconductors—diodes and transistors—for the logical circuitry and by magnetic cores for the internal memory. By the end of the 1950's, this changeover had been accomplished, and what has been called the "second generation" of computers became commonplace.

The use of such "solid-state" circuit elements—diodes, transistors, and magnetic cores—reduced the size, power consumption, and heat dissipation of computers by orders of magnitude. It allowed them to have greater capacity. But, most important, it allowed them to be faster.

During the past ten years, the technology of solid-state circuitry has continued to advance, primarily in the direction of miniaturization. Components are now so small that they are used not individually but only as part of complete logical packages, called "integrated circuits." Again, the effect has been to vastly decrease size, power consumption, and heat dissipation. At the same time, capacity and operating rates could be comparably increased. The result has been a quantitative change so great that the computer profession thinks of today's computers as the "third generation."

[5] *Ibid.*, pp. 53-57.
[6] *Ibid.*, pp. 57-63.
[7] *Ibid.*, pp. 63-64.
[8] Weik, Martin H., *Surver of Domestic Electonic Digital Computing Systems,* Ballistic Research Labs, 1955, 1957, 1961.

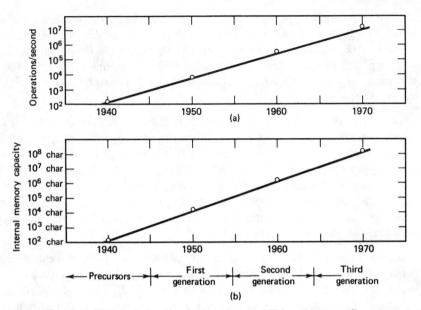

Figure 10.1 (a) Historical growth of computer capabilities. (b) Internal memory capacity.

Figure 10.1 presents a graphical picture of these changes in speed and capacity.[9] Everything indicates that the trends exhibited by this historical growth in capabilities will continue into the next decade and beyond.

Applications of the Computer

During the 25 to 30 years covered by this sequence of generations, computers have been successively applied to more and more complex tasks, until today they are used throughout our society.

Computing Tasks. Initially, of course, they were viewed as "computing" devices, intended for use in numerical analysis in the physical sciences.[10] For example, the development of atomic energy has depended to a great extent on the solution of equations that could only have been done with computers. Even today, research in atomic physics probably requires larger and faster computers than any other application. Later, comparable applications were seen in engineering, the biological sciences, and medicine. In engineering especially, the use of the computer in solution of equations and automation of design has

[9] Knight, Kenneth E., "Evolving Computer Performance, 1963-1967." *Datamation,* 14 (1), January 1968, 31-35.

[10] Gruenberger, Fred, *Computing Manual,* University of Wisconsin, 1953.

become increasingly important. Most recently, the social and behavioral sciences have begun to depend on the processing and statistical analysis of large volumes of data.[11] Of couse, this is no surprise. The Bureau of the Census historically was the place where punched-card data processing first became a reality.[12] When the computer was developed, it was natural for the Census to become one of the earliest users of it.[13]

Data Processsing Tasks. A completely different kind of "computing" is that involved in clerical data processing. It doesn't involve any of the mathematical sophistication of scientific computation, but it does involve large numbers of repetitive operations. From the early 1950's it has therefore become one of the most important applications.[14-16] Many industrial and commercial companies, as well as government agencies like the Department of Defense, have also experimented with the computer as an aid to management decision making using techniques of operations research.[17]

Symbol Manipulation Tasks. To regard the computer solely as a calculating device, however, would be to lose sight of its real potential. Basically, it is a logical device, with arithmetic operations only a limited part of its capabilities. As such, it is capable of processing any symbolic system, including natural language, provided that the programs can be written for it to do so. "Language data processing" has therefore become one of the most important and exciting areas for research in application of the computer.[18] In one sense, library operations require such capabilities—production of catalogs, automatic indexing and abstracting, reference retrieval, text collation, and preparation of con- cordances.[19] Most of the intellectual problems in these tasks have been so well solved that libraries can effectively use the computer for them. On the other hand, some forms of language data processing are still so speculative that some researchers have even claimed that they are impossible to program—language translation, conceptual analysis, and automatic "question-answering."[20]

[11] Borko, Harold, ed., *Computer Applications in the Behavioral Sciences,* Englewood Cliffs, N.J.: Prentice-Hall, 1962.

[12] *Dictionary of American Biography,* 1944. Supplement 1. s.v. Hollerith, Herman.

[13] Burck, Gilbert, et al., *The Computer Age,* New York: Harper, 1965, p. 8.

[14] Awad, Elias M., *Automatic Data Processing: Principles and Procedures,* Englewood Cliffs, N.J.: Prentice-Hall, 1966.

[15] Gregory, Robert H., and R. L. Van Horn, *Business Data Processing and Programming,* Belmont, California: Wadsworth, 1963.

[16] *Introduction to Data Processing,* New York: Haskins and Sells, 1957.

[17] Churchman, C. W., R. L. Ackoff, and E. L. Arnoff, *Introduction to Operations Research,* New York: Wiley, 1957. Especially pp. 376 ff, 467 ff.

[18] Borko, Harold, ed., *Automated Language Processing,* New York: Wiley, 1967.

[19] Becker, Joseph, and R. M. Hayes, *Information Storage and Retrieval: Tools, Elements, Theories,* New York: Wiley, 1963.

[20] Hayes, Robert M., Review of *Data Retrieval by Computer: A Critical Survey, Kasher, Asa.* In American Documentation, **18** (3), July 1967, 187-189.

Heuristic Tasks. The capability of the computer to change a stored program raises the possibility that it can "learn" or at least modify its behavior to fit its environment better.[21-23] Applications of this kind are called "heuristic," since the process of learning is not well understood, and the exercise of writing effective "learning programs" helps the investigation of it. At the simplest level, games such as chess, checkers, or "go" represent ideal heuristic applications, since the rules for legal play are well defined, and the results of "good play" are evident.[24] The aim is to devise programs by which the computer can develop its own rules for good play, hopefully well enough to beat the programmer. More complex applications include the composition of music or poetry.[25]

Control Tasks. Potentially the most controversial applications of computers are those called "control." Of course, there are non controversial, well-established examples—oil refineries, machine tools, production lines, and warehouses.[26] But there are also some that have raised real concern. The SAGE system is a highly computerized means of detecting enemy aircraft and missiles and relaying warnings to military command posts. In principle, it would be relatively simple to have the warnings trigger automatic computer control of defensive responses—with deceptively rational reasons to do so. But perhaps that represents too extreme an example. Seemingly more innocuous is "computer-aided instruction," based on the concepts of programmed teaching through conditioned response as expounded by B. F. Skinner.[27-28] Although not exactly "control," the relationship between computer and student is at least a kind of symbiosis. All the evidence indicates that this is indeed a most effective means of instruction for that type of material which requires knowledge of the "right" answer, but one wonders whether it is equally applicable to the real purposes of education. Learning is more than simply conditioned response. Furthermore, to what is the student being conditioned? To the material being learned, or to this process of learning?

[21] Berkeley, Edmund C., *Giant Brains: Machines that Think,* New York: Wiley, 1949.

[22] Bush, Vannevar, "As We May Think," *Atlantic Monthly,* 176 (July 1945), 101-108.

[23] Pfeiffer, John, *The Thinking Machine,* New York: Lippincott, 1962.

[24] Samuel, A.L., "Some Studies in Machine Learning, Using the Game of Checkers," *IBM Journal of Research and Development,* 3 1959, 210-230.

[25] Von Foerster, H., and James W. Beauchamp, eds., *Music by Computers,* New York: Wiley, 1969.

[26] Savas, Emanuel S., *Computer Control of Industrial Processes,* New York: McGraw-Hill, 1965. ("Forecasts indicate that by 1970 there will be over 3,500 computer control systems in operation."—Preface.)

[27] Suppes, Patrick, and Richard C. Atkinson, *Stanford Program in Computer Assisted Instruction,* Progress Reports 6 and 7 (1967). Palo Alto, California, Institute for Mathematical Studies, 1967.

[28] Skinner, B. F., "Why Teachers Fail," *Saturday Review,* 48 (October 16, 1965), 80-81.

Magnitude of Computer Usage. In summary, the computer is far more than a mere calculating device. It is finding application in every part of our society and will play an increasingly important role in it. Figure 10.2 shows the extent of growth of computer usage over the past 20 years.[29]

COMPUTER HARDWARE

The "hardware" of a computer system consists of the physical computer itself, its circuitry, its wiring, and its peripheral equipment. Figure 10.3 presents a typical block diagram for the configuration of equipment. As shown, a computer system involves an "arithmetic and control unit" (frequently called the "main frame"), an internal memory, and peripheral units including files, input-output units, and remote devices.

The arithmetic and control unit provides the capability of executing any one

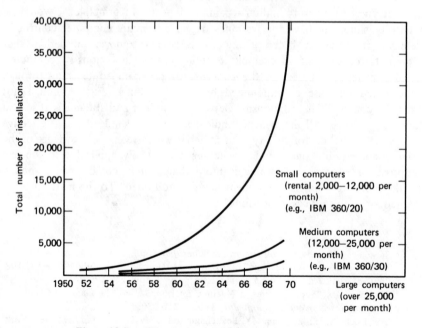

Figure 10.2   Historical growth in computer installations.

[29] Simplified from data in Ned Chapin, *Introduction to Automatic Computers* (New York: Van Nostrand, 1957), *Automatic Data Processing Newsletter* (March 3, 1958; January 12, 1959; January 11, 1960; January 23, 1961; January 22, 1962); *Computers and Automation* (January 1963, 1964, 1965, and 1966); *Datamation* (May 1963); and *Computer World* (1969).

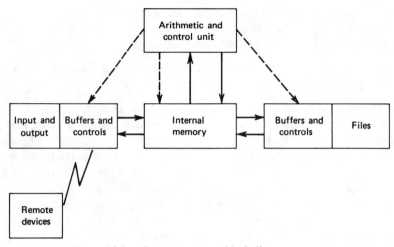

Figure 10.3   Computer system block diagram.

of several built-in elementary operations. It does this on the basis of interpreting a "command," which essentially describes the operation to be performed and the location of the data upon which it is to be performed. In carrying out these functions, the arithmetic and control unit must interpret each command, control the memory unit for the purpose of obtaining the data involved, execute the operation on that data, control other affected elements such as the files and the input-output equipment, and determine where to find the next command in the memory unit. The internal memory element thus serves as the location from which data are drawn to be operated upon and from which commands are obtained in succession by the arithmetic and control unit. The files provide for mass storage of data, available at high speed to the computer. The input-output elements, under the control of the arithmetic and control unit, provide the capability for communication to and from the world external to the computer.

In subsequent chapters, we shall discuss equipment for the peripheral components of a computer system—input, display, and output; files for storage of data; and means for communication. In this chapter, we shall deal with the computer itself—the arithmetic and control unit and the internal memory.

Criteria for Evaluation

Before examining the technical details of this internal hardware, let us place them in perspective by summarizing criteria for the evaluation of computers. Basically, there are four major issues.

(1).   How sophisticated and flexible is the set of built-in capabilities?

(2).   How fast is the operation of the computer?

(3).   How large is the internal memory?

(4).   How expensive is the main frame?

Figure 10.4 presents a summary of these issues for a number of representative past and present computers.[30]

Richness of Capabilities. As indicated previously, one of the characterizing properties of the general purpose digital computer is the existence of a set of built-in capabilities sufficiently rich for the machine to perform the kinds of tasks to which it will be applied. These capabilities are represented by the set of instructions that the computer can recognize and execute. This general characterization, however, is deceptive. The facts are that the set of built-in capabilities can be almost unbelievably simple, and the machine can still, in principle, perform exactly the same operations that an apparently far more complex device can perform. In 1937, an English logician, Alan Turing, defined such an extremely simple set of built-in capabilities (basically, being able to read and write a set of symbols on a tape, being able to move the tape forward and backward, and being able to change from one state to another based on a symbol read from the tape) capable of executing any computing task.[31]

The problem, however, is that the simpler the built-in capabilities, the more difficult is the work of programming (that is, instructing the machine how to carry out defined tasks). It is therefore important to have some means of comparison and evaluation.

Unfortunately, there is no simple answer to the question, "How complex is a given machine?" The number of instructions that can be recognized, the number of registers in which logical and arithmetic operations can be performed, the number of memory locations from which an instruction can obtain data—all of these, and more, can be considered. At best, therefore, this evaluation must be qualitative and must be made in the context of a given task or set of tasks.

However given no other criteria, the number of bits (or characters) in a typical instruction (expressed in Figure 10.4, column 4, *word size*) can be used to provide a rough scale of complexity since, in principle, the larger the instruction the more it can specify.

[30] In this chapter and subsequent chapters of this section, we will provide tables listing the characteristics of representative equipment. In doing so, we recognize that the data is likely to be out of date even when it is printed, since it represents available information in 1968 and 1969. However, there is value in having data of this kind immediately at hand, even if slightly in error, since it makes things specific which otherwise would not be. In each case, more up-to-date data can be found in several periodic publications. In particular, computer data like that in Figure 10.7 is published in: *Computer Characteristics Quarterly,* Charles Adams Associates, Cambridge, Mass.

[31] Turing, Alan M., "Can a Machine Think?" *In The World of Mathematics,* Newman, J. R. ed, New York, Simon & Schuster, 1956, V. 4, pp. 2099-2123.

Speed of Operation. The fantastic speed of internal operation of modern-day computers has been one of their most evident characteristics. In general, it is fairly easy to define and to measure—at least, for individual instructions. Thus, one can refer to an "add time" of "2 microseconds," or a "memory access time" of "1 microsecond," and so on. These do provide a kind of rough scale for comparison among computers and have therefore been included in Figure 10.4. Unfortunately, differences in performance on large tasks cannot be so easily described, since they involve execution of combinations of instructions in widely different ways from one computer to another. Thus, it has been traditional to define a "representative task" of one kind or another, which involves such a combination of instructions, and to use the execution time for it as a means of comparison.

Size of Memory. Perhaps the most significant single issue in the evaluation of a computer main frame is the size of the internal memory, expressed in terms of numbers of words or characters or bits. It determines, in a very real sense, the size and complexity of task that can actually be executed, since the program as well as the data to be operated upon must be stored there. Of course, programs can be much larger than the internal memory can hold and are written so that the computer will bring successive sections of them into the memory from files, as they are needed. But if there is much disparity between the size of memory and the size of cohesive program modules, the computer can lose all of its effectiveness. Fortunately, of all the criteria for evaluation, size of memory not only is the most significant but is the easiest to define and measure. It has been included in Figure 10.4, as a representative figure for each computer.

It should be noted that, within limits, one should look toward the goal of as large an internal memory as is economically possible—even at the sacrifice of other features.

Cost. The cost of a computer is an obvious issue in evaluation, and one that superficially appears easy to identify and measure. Nevertheless it is a very complex one.

First, and perhaps most important, we have continually emphasized the importance of "cost/effectiveness" as the central criterion for evaluation in systems analysis. Now, however, we must mention a vital caution. The cost/effectiveness ratio for computers has been characterized by what is know as "Grosch's law" (after Dr. Herbert R. J. Grosch, who first propounded it).[32] Basically, Grosch's law states that "the computing capacity is directly related to the square of the cost." Thus, if one computer rents for $1000 per month and another for $10,000 per month, the second will have 100 times the computing capacity of the first. Although first formulated in the 1940's, the law has been

[32] See in Orr, William D., *Conversational Computers,* New York: Wiley, 1968, p. 152.

Figure 10.4 Characteristic Parameters for Computer Systems

Manufacturer & Model Number	1(C) Minimum System Cost (in K/month)	2(T₁) Add Time (in Micro seconds)	3(T₂) Memory Access Time (in Microseconds)	4(N₁) Average Instruction Word Size (in Bits)[a]	5(N₂) Memory Capacity (in Bits)[a]	6 $\sigma_1 = \dfrac{\text{col 4}}{(\text{col 2})(\text{col 1})}$ $= N_1/CT_1$	7 $\sigma_2 = \dfrac{\text{col 5}}{(\text{col 3})(\text{col 1})}$ $= N_2/CT_2$
Burroughs							
B6500	25	.4	.6	52	16Kx52	5.2	54.1
B3500	4.8	32	1	32	10Kx 8	.208	16.7
B2500	4.2	64	2	32	10Kx 8	.119	9.5
B160	1.9	690	10	72	5Kx 6	.055	1.50
B170	1.9	690	10	72	5Kx 6	.055	1.50
B180	1.9	690	10	72	5Kx 6	.055	1.50
Control Data							
6800	65	.1	.25	60	131Kx60	9.23	48.4
6400	25	1.1	1	60	32Kx60	2.18	76.8
3400	20	3	1.5	48	16Kx48	.8	25.6
3300	12	1.5	.8	24	8Kx24	1.33	20
350	6	1.3	.8	24	8Kx24	3.08	40
General Electric							
415	4.8	27.6	9.2	24	32Kx24	.181	17.4
205	1.7	72	36	20	4Kx20	.164	1.31
Honeywell							
4200	17	7.5	.75	18	32Kx 6	.141	15.1
1200	4	33	1.5	18	8Kx 6	.136	8.0

Figure 10.4 (*continued*)

Manufacturer & Model Number	1(C) Minimum System Cost (in K/month)	2(T₁) Add Time (in Microseconds)	3(T₂) Memory Access Time (in Microseconds)	4(N₁) Average Instruction Word Size (in Bits)ᵃ	5(N₂) Memory Capacity (in Bits)ᵃ	6 $\sigma_1 = \dfrac{\text{col 4}}{(\text{col 2})(\text{col 1})} = N_1/CT_1$	7 $\sigma_2 = \dfrac{\text{col 5}}{(\text{col 3})(\text{col 1})} = N_2/CT_2$
IBM							
360/65	35	1.3	.75	32	128K x 8	.700	34.4
/50	14	4	2	32	64K x 8	.572	18.3
/44	5	1.75	1.75	32	32K x 8	3.660	29.1
/40	5	11.88	5.0	32	16K x 8	.536	5.2
/30	2.7	39	6.0	32	8K x 8	.304	3.9
/20	1.2	200	29.0	32	4K x 8	.133	.9
1130	.6	8	2.2	16	8K x 16	.003	97.0
RCA Spectra							
70/55	13.9	7.4	.84	32	65K x 8	.295	44.2
/45	8.5	22.02	1.44	32	65K x 8	.172	42.5
/35	6.9	47.6	1.44	32	16K x 8	.097	12.9
/25	5.8	33	1.5	32	16K x 8	.167	14.7
/15	2.7	56,000	2000	32	4K x 8	.0002	.006
Univac							
100 II	1.6	208	6.5	42	2K x 6	.126	1.15
I	1.4	256	8	42	2K x 6	.117	1.07
9300	1.7	52	.6	32	8K x 8	.362	62.8
9200	1	104		32	8K x 8	.308	53.3
1050	2.4	117		30	4K x 6	.107	2.22

ᵃK means "1000"; x means "times".

repeatedly (though roughly) confirmed by empirical results since then. A direct application of cost/effectiveness would, without question, lead to the decision to use the largest computer available, burying the library's task in a host of uses of a remarkably efficient machine. The difficulty, of course, is that issues of cost/effectiveness beyond the mere efficiency of the computer itself, with proper recognition of reliability, convenience, safety, and the like, must be considered.

Second, costs tend to be quoted in such a variety of ways that direct comparison is unrealistic, if not impossible—for instance, rental versus purchase; a complex of equipment versus a single component; and maintenance costs included versus maintenance costs not included.

However despite the difficulties and possible misinterpretations, Figure 10.4 includes an estimate of the cost of these typical computer systems.

Figure of Merit. With such a formidable array of parameters as needed to describe computers, it is useful to have some kind of "figures of merit" by which to rank them.[33] At the risk of over simplification, two have been included in Figure 10.4. Each is of the form N/CT:

(1) $\sigma_1 = N_1/CT_1$, where N_1 is the size of a word; T_1 is an add time; and C is the cost per month of the main frame.

(2) $\sigma_2 = \bar{n}\,N_2/CT_2$, where N_2 is the size of the memory; T_2 is a memory access time; and C is the cost per month of the main frame.

Arithmetic and Control Unit

The operation of the computer is controlled by the "Arithmetic and Control Unit," according to a sequence of instructions or "commands." Each command must specify three things: the operation to be performed, the location (in the memory) of the data that is to be operated upon, and the location (in the memory) of the next command. A typical form for a computer instruction is shown in Figure 10.5.

Built-In operations. The built-in operations that the computer is capable of carrying out can be of a great variety. A set of typical commands is shown in Figure 10.6. Some of these operations are arithmetic or pseudo arithmetic in nature. Commands calling for them will allow numbers from specified locations in the memory to be added, multiplied, subtracted, and so on. The power of these commands has led some people to view the computer simply in terms of the arithmetic operations and, thus, as a glorified calculating device.

This view ignores the fantastically greater power for complex manipulation of

---

[33] Matthews, M. V., "Choosing a Scientific Computer for Service," *Science,* **161** (3836) (July 5, 1968), 23-27.

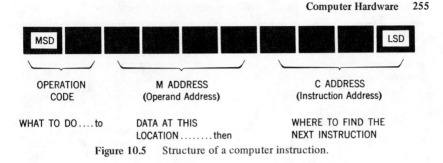

OPERATION	M ADDRESS	C ADDRESS
CODE	(Operand Address)	(Instruction Address)
WHAT TO DO....to	DATA AT THIS	WHERE TO FIND THE
	LOCATION........then	NEXT INSTRUCTION

Figure 10.5   Structure of a computer instruction.

data afforded by the other types of built-in operations. Probably the most significant of these operations are the "decision operations," which allow comparisons to be made between blocks of data, essentially independent of any arithmetical considerations. In this way, data coded in any form can be compared or matched against basic criteria and alternative paths of processing chosen. Other related operations provide the capability for extracting portions of data groups (such as a single alphabetic character), which can then be handled independently and examined by other operations. Thus, complex codes (including alphabetic) can be readily handled and deciphered.

Other operations, which can be provided as built-in hardware capabilities, will allow for the handling of groups of words, for a mass transfer of data, for the automatic rearrangement of blocks of data into prescribed order, for the automatic table look-up of one block of data against another, and the like.

A fourth class of commands—the input-output commands—provide for the control of peripheral devices and, thus, allow the computer to communicate externally under its own control. In this way, data can be input to the computer, processed, and organized for output without any manual intervention.

In summary, the tremendous variety of built-in capabilities of the computer makes it an extremely versatile tool for the manipulation of data.

Logical Design. The arithmetic and control unit accomplishes all of its functions by means of an array of "circuit elements," which represent combinations of the basic logical operations *and, or,* and *not.* They are therefore concrete realizations of what is known as "Boolean algebra," named after George Boole, the English logician who first formalized it at about 1850.[34] (Another English logician, Augustus de Morgan, a major contributor to the development of Boolean algebra, was also a major contributor to librarianship, serving as a witness at the Hearings of the Royal Commission on the British Museum and supporting Panizzi in his efforts to produce a rational catalog.)[35]

[34] Boole, George, *An Investigation of the Laws of Thought* . . . London: Walton and Maberly, 1854. (Reprinted by Dover Publications.)

[35] Gt. Britain, Commissioners Appointed to Inquire into the Constitution and Government of the British Museum, *Report,* London, HMSO, 1850. ("The Panizzi Report.")

Figure 10.6 Table of typical computer operations

Type of Operation	Operation Code	Operand Address	Instruction Address	
Arithmetic				
	70	m	c	$(R_1) + (m) \rightarrow (R_1)^a$
	75	m	c	$(R_1) - (m) \rightarrow (R_1)$
	80	m	c	$(R_2) \times (m) \rightarrow (R_1)$ Most significant digits, (R_3) Least significant digits
	85	m	c	$(m) \div (R_2) \rightarrow (R_1)$ Quotient, (R_3) Remainder
Transfer				
	21	m	c	$(m) \rightarrow (R_1)$
	61	m	c	$(R_1) \rightarrow (m)$
	22	m	c	$(m) \rightarrow (R_3)$
	66	m	c	$(R_3) \rightarrow (m)$
	23	m	c	$(m) \rightarrow (R_2)$
	63	m	c	$(R_2) \rightarrow (m)$
	25	–	c	$(R_1) \rightarrow (R_2)$
Compare				
	82	C_1	C_2	Go to C_1 if $R_1 = R_2$; go to C_2 if $R_1 \neq R_2$
	87	C_1	C_2	Go to C_1 if $R_1 > R_2$; go to C_2 if $R_1 \leq R_2$
Logical				
	31	m	c	Superimpose (m) on $(R_1) \rightarrow (R_1)$
	32	m	c	Erase (m) from $(R_1) \rightarrow (R_1)$
	35	n	c	Shift right n places $(R_1) \rightarrow (R_1)$
	36	n	c	Shift left n places $(R_1) \rightarrow (R_1)$
	90	–	c	Stop, ready to go next to C
Input Output				
	41	C_1	C_2	Printer free? Go to C_1 if yes, C_2 if no
	42	C_1	C_2	Printer free? Go to C_1 if yes, C_2 if no
	43	C_1	C_2	Tape unit free? Go to C_1 if yes, C_2 if no
	44	C_1	C_2	Disk unit free? Go to C_1 if yes, C_2 if no
	53	m	c	Read tape block, starting at m
	73	m	c	Write tape block, starting at m
	etc			

$^a R_1, R_2$, and R_3 are arithmetic registers in which the defined operations are executed.

Figure 10.7 defines some typical Boolean functions ($C = A \cdot B$, $C = A + B$, and the like) and illustrates them in terms of "Venn diagrams" (which provide a graphical presentation), "truth tables," and schematics for electronic components.[36,37]

The means of representing Boolean operations by truth tables emphasizes the importance that binary representation has in Boolean algebra, since membership in a class, or the truth of a statement concerning membership in a class, can be represented by 1 or 0.

It is possible to consider operations involving 3, 4, . . ., n classes according to the same rules of operation. Two of these, for $n = 3$ and $n = 4$, are shown in Figure 10.8.

Simple though these operations are, it is remarkable that from them flow all of the wealth of logical relations implicit in the logical design of the general purpose digital computer.[38] Figure 10.7 has included symbolic representations of electronic circuitry for their realization. To illustrate the usage of these circuits, consider the problem of adding two sequences of binary digits representing numbers (for instance, $A = 0101$ and $B = 1011$). At each step, the operation must consider the particular binary digits from each of the two sequences as well as the "carry" from the addition of the preceding pair. Thus, addition of binary numbers (not counting the carry digit resulting) at each stage is a function of three binary variables A_i, B_i, and C_{i-1}. The successive carry digits C_i are a similar function of the same variables. The truth tables for these functions are easily generated from the rules for binary addition; they are illustrated in Figure 10.9.

Internal Memory

There is a very close association between the memory and the arithmetic and control unit. Instructions involve the definition of the location of data in terms of fixed memory locations each of which holds a set of data (such as six alpha-numeric characters). The size of the set is usually fixed and called a "word," and the location of a word is called its "address." For example, if a given word consists of a set of alphabetic characters representing a name and it is desired that an operation should compare it with another set representing another name, the command would need to specify the operation of "compare" and the addresses of the particular words to be compared.

[36] Symbolic Logic, Boolean Algebra, and the Design of Digital Systems, *Framingham, Mass.: Computer Control Company, Inc., 1959.*

[37] Gardner, Martin, *Logic Machines and Diagrams,* New York: McGraw-Hill, 1958.

[38] Phister, Montogomery, Jr., *Logical Design of Digital Computers,* New York: Wiley, 1958.

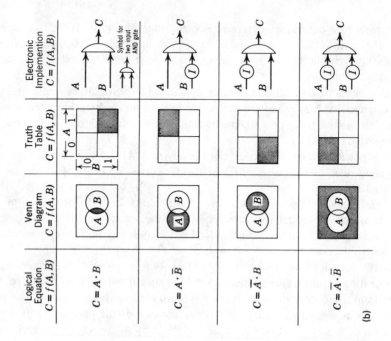

(b)

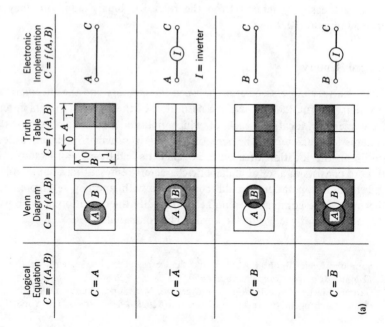

(a)

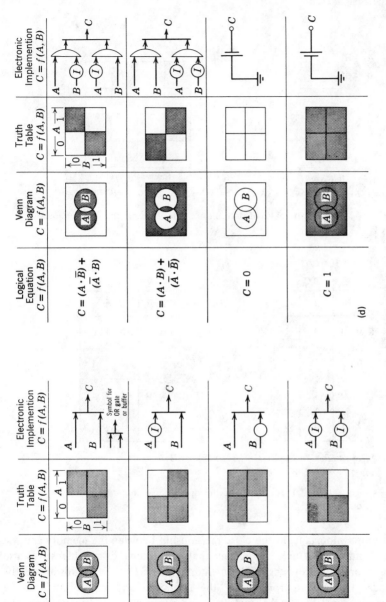

Figure 10.7 Illustrations of all Boolean functions of two variables.

259

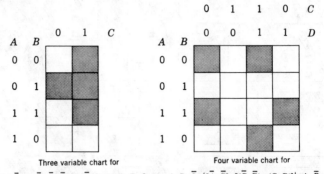

Three variable chart for   Four variable chart for

$$f = \bar{A} \cdot B \cdot \bar{C} \vee \bar{A} \cdot \bar{B} \cdot C \vee \bar{A} \cdot B \cdot C \vee A \cdot B \cdot C \quad f = A \cdot B \cdot \bar{C} \vee \{[\bar{A} \cdot \bar{B}] \cdot [(\bar{C} \cdot \bar{D}) \vee (C \cdot D)]\} \vee A \cdot \bar{B} \cdot C \cdot D$$

Figure 10.8   Truth tables of Boolean functions of three and four variables.

$$f_1 = (A_i + B_i + C_{i-1})$$

$A_i B_i$	C_{i-1} 0	1
0 0	0	1
0 1	1	0
1 0	1	0
1 1	0	1

$$f_2 = C_i$$

$A_i B_i$	C_{i-1} 0	1
0 0	0	0
0 1	0	1
1 0	0	1
1 1	1	1

$$f_1 = (\bar{A} \cdot \bar{B} \cdot \bar{C}) + (A \cdot \bar{B}) \cdot \bar{C} + (\bar{A} \cdot B) \cdot \bar{C} + A \cdot B \cdot C$$
$$f_2 = (A + B) \cdot C + A \cdot B \cdot \bar{C}$$

Figure 10.9   Truth tables of the operation of binary addition.

Even more important, in the close relationship between the memory and the operation and control unit, is the fact that the commands are themselves also stored as words in addresses of the memory. In the first place, this allows the commands that are interpreted by the operation and control unit to be automatically available to the computer and successively picked up from the memory. In addition, however, since commands are stored in the same form as data, they can be operated upon and changed as the result of other operations. This last feature—the ability to modify the stored commands—gives the general purpose computer its greatest power and has led the persons involved with computers to consider them as self-regulating devices.

Magnetic Cores. Most present-day computers use magnetic cores as the basic medium for storage in the internal memory.[39] A magnetic core is a tiny ring of ferromagnetic material, a few hundredths of an inch in diameter. A single magnetic core can hold one binary digit—zero or one—by being magnetized to one of two magnetic states represented by the points ZERO and ONE on the hysteresis loop of Figure 10.10a. If the core is in the ZERO state, the application of full current, H_t, drives it to the ONE state; negative full current, $-H_t$, drives it back to the ZERO state. The "squareness" of the loop makes it possible to apply somewhat over half of H_t without materially changing the magnetic state. This permits a "coincident-current" type of operation, requiring the coincidence of two partial currents for switching a core, with $H_t/2$ appled to each of the X and Y lines shown in Figure 10.10b. When a core is in the ONE state, the coincidence of two negative half currents will switch it back to the ZERO state producing a flux change which induces a signal voltage into the sense winding as shown in Figure 10.10c as a ONE signal. When a core is in the ZERO state, the same negative drive currents will move it slightly further into saturation, causing only a very small "disturb" voltage as shown in Figure 10.10c as a ZERO signal.

The cores are mounted in a rectangular array (Figure 10.10d and e). Each core is linked by a horizontal X line, a vertical Y line, and a sense winding. A core is selected by the application of half currents to an X and to a Y line (corresponding to an address in the memory). Only the core situated at the intersection of the two selected lines receives the full current necessary to turn it from one state to the other. (Incidentally, notice that the operation of reading a core automatically puts it in the ZERO state and therefore destroys the data. Hence, if the data is to be saved, it must be rerecorded again).

Sets of core planes are "stacked" to produce a memory module. For example, with 100 X lines and 100 Y lines per plane, 32 planes would store 10,000 addresses each containing 32 bits. To read or store data in one of the 10,000 addresses (say, address 1234), the same X line (say, line 12) and the same Y line (say, line 34) would be selected on each of the 32 planes.

COMPUTER SOFTWARE

Computer "hardware" provides the capability for executing a variety of tasks, but computer "software" is what actually causes the computer to do what is wanted of it.

---

[39] Richards, R. K., *Digital Computer Components and Circuits,* New York: Van Nostrand, 1957 (Chapter 8, "Magnetic Core Storage").

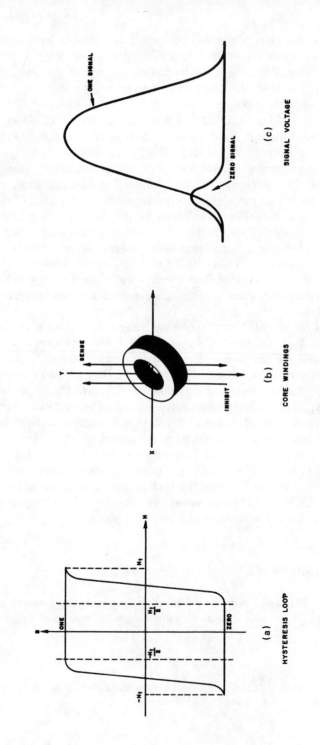

(a) HYSTERESIS LOOP

(b) CORE WINDINGS

(c) SIGNAL VOLTAGE

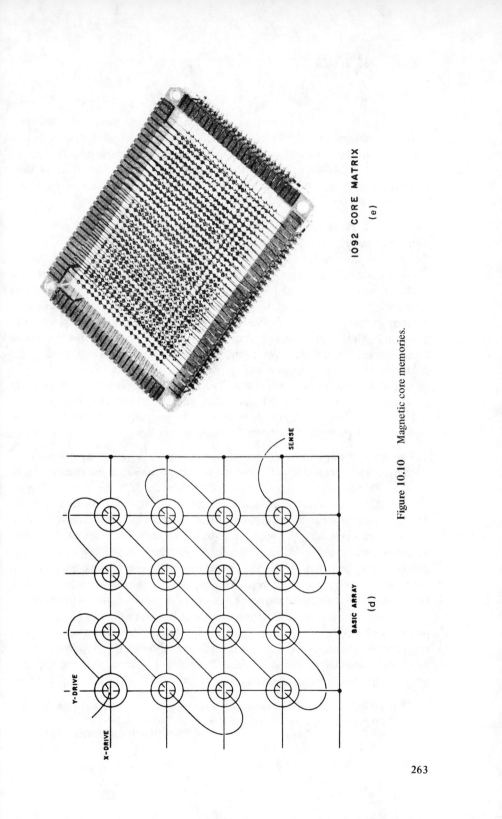

1092 CORE MATRIX

(e)

SENSE

Y-DRIVE

X-DRIVE

BASIC ARRAY

(d)

Figure 10.10   Magnetic core memories.

263

Basic Programming

A computer performs a complex operation as a sequence of the elementary built-in operations available to it. The task of analyzing a complex problem into a sequence of the elementary steps that the computer is capable of performing is the work of a professional group known as programmers. The result of their efforts—the sequence of commands that the computer will obey—is called a program.[40-42]

Parts of a Program. Within a program, there are certain critical portions to which particular attention must be paid by the programmer. The first of these is the portion that establishes the starting conditions. This will define certain constants such as the number of words in a message or the maximum size of a word of text. It will make certain preliminary checks for consistency and accuracy of the data and of the program itself. A second critical portion of a program is known as the "bookkeeping" portion, which allows the program to maintain control of its own operation. This will include counting the number of times certain operations have been performed; it may include timing the functions of external devices; and it will include facility for handling error situations or other unusual situations. The third critical portion of the program are the decision points at which alternative paths or sequences of program steps will be chosen. The fourth critical portion of the program is the actual operation that is to be performed—the "heart" of the program.

The Role of Flow Charting. Programming requires a very clear definition of the nature, purpose, and logical structure of the job for which the computer is to be used. This generally takes the form of a "flow chart," (discussed in Chapter 6), consisting of a number of boxes connected by arrows and other symbols. This technique of analyzing a total problem by means of flow charts is standard not only for developing the program but for explaining its function. Each box describes some major portion of the total job which, depending on the detail provided, may be at the level of the elementary operations of the computer or at the level of much more gross steps. The sequence of the boxes, as indicated by the arrows, then defines the sequence of steps in the solution of the problem.

The ability to choose from alternative paths has led to the usage in computer programs of iterations or "loops," which involve the repeated execution of a sequence of commands. At the end of each execution of the loop, the program will decide whether to repeat it again. The number of times that the sequence will be repeated is controlled by the program itself on the basis of several

[40] McCracken, D. D., *Digital Computer Programming,* New York: Wiley, 1959.

[41] McCormick, E. M., *Digital Computer Primer,* New York: McGraw-Hill, 1959.

[42] Wrubel, M. H., *Primer of Programming for Digital Computers,* New York: McGraw-Hill, 1959.

possible criteria. For example, the number of times that a loop will be repeated may be determined by preset constants or it may be determined as a result of the particular nature of the data being operated upon. In any event, this technique of iteration allows a relatively few commands to perform the work not only a very large number but even of an indeterminate number of commands, since the number of iterations actually performed may vary widely from one run to the next.

Figure 10.11 illustrates the process of programming and the use of loops, and shows a program (using the instruction set of Figure 10.6) for the operation of "table look-up"—a fundamental one.

Subroutines

If each problem for which a computer were to be used needed to be programmed from scratch, it is unlikely that the computer would have achieved its present success. Fortunately, there exists a technique not only for utilizing past experience in order to reduce the programming task but (as we shall show) for doing this in such a way as to effectively extend the range of built-in operations that the computer can recognize. The basis of this technique is the concept of a "subroutine"—a sequence of commands developed as a program for handling a general class of problems. A subroutine is designed in such a way that it can be drawn upon whenever a particular problem involves any situation from this general class. It is utilized by being appropriately integrated into a larger program and even combined with other subroutines. For example, the "table look-up" program from Figure 10.11 would probably be formalized as such a subroutine.

Programs, called "assemblers," have been written by which the programmers can easily establish subroutines and combine them, without concern for essentially clerical tasks such as where the program or data may be stored.

Compilers.

The concept of the subroutine alone, however, would not result in a real extension of the built-in capabilities of the computer, since the determination of the subroutines to be used and the recording of them as part of the sequence of instructions for a given problem would still be the job of the programmer. Thus, although the subroutine can perform a job that is more complex than those of any elementary built-in operations, in order for it to directly represent an extension of the computer capabilities there would need to exist a means by which the programmer could call for the subroutine in the same way in which he would call for an elementary operation. A "compiler" is a program that will interpret commands calling for subroutines of a far more general nature than those that the computer itself interprets.

The development and use of a compiler requires three things: (1) a set of subroutines; (2) a formal language by which the programmer can define the subroutines that interest him and their relationship to each other; and (3) the compiler itself, which interprets this language and then brings together the subroutines required to perform the operations called for by the programmer. When the compiler is in the computer, the computer has become effectively a new device capable of recognizing a totally new, "higher-level" language.[43] It can assemble and execute sequences of instructions expressed in that language, or construct "compiled" programs for subsequent use. In this way, the burden of bringing together the appropriate subroutines for solution of a complex problem, in a form of such a nature that they fit with each other, has been removed from the programmer and placed on the compiler. In a very real sense, this new machine (consisting of the old computer with the compiler) communicates with the programmer at a much higher level of complexity and abstraction and much closer to natural language. The present aim in the

[43] Galler, Bernard, *The Language of Computers*, New York: McGraw-Hill, 1962.

Figure 10.11a   Illustrative program: table look-up.

"Table look-up" is a fundamental task in the handling of complex data by a computer. For example, it is frequently used for conversion of codes; it is part of the process of merging (or "interfiling"); it can be used to choose among a set of alternatives; it is an integral part of any procedure for searching a file. It therefore represents an illustration with more than academic interest.

A "table" is regarded as a sequence of items, each consisting of an identifier (such as a name) together with associated codes or related data (such as a code for the name and an address). An example of a table is the three-place cutter table in which an entry defines a range of names and the associated code is the corresponding three place "cutter number":

Becke to Becker	B 394
Becker to Becker, P.	B 395
Becker, P. to Bechi	B 396

Table look-up is then the process of comparing the indentifier of an item with, in turn, each of the identifiers in the Table until the relevant entry (item) in the Table is found. Then the corresponding codes or related data can be assigned from the table to the original item. For example, if we wish to find the cutter number for "Becker, Joseph," table look-up would compare that name with each of the names in the table to see whether it is alphabetically "less than" the name in the Table. Therefore:

(1) Is "Becker, Joseph" less than "Becke?"
No (2) Is "Becker, Joseph" less than "Becker?"
No (3) Is "Becker, Joseph" less than "Becker, P.?"
Yes (4) Assign B 395 to "Becker, Joseph."

To see how the computer might be programmed to carry out such a task, let's first construct a flow chart. [Figure 10.11 (*b*)].

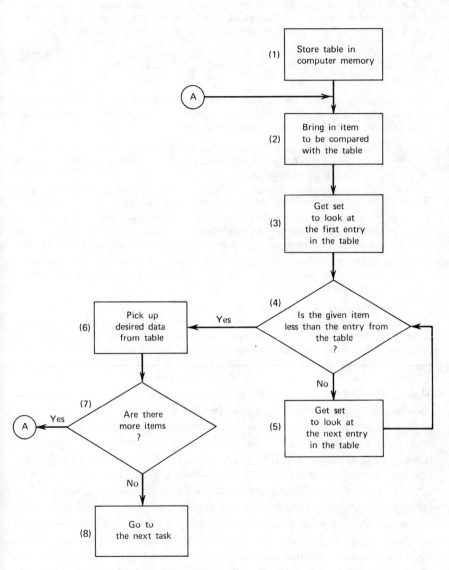

Figure 10.11b Flow chart.

Figure 10.11c   Data storage allocations

Figure 10.11(d) is a program that executes Steps 4, 5, and 6 of this flow chart. It assumes, solely for the sake of illustration, that the table contains 999 entries, previously stored (for example, by Step 1) in successive addresses of the memory as follows:

	1st entry	2nd entry	–	999th entry
Identifiers in addresses:	0001	0003	–	1997
Related codes in addresses:	0002	0004	–	1998

It also assumes, again solely for the sake of illustration, that the item of interest has been stored in address 2000, and that the first instruction in the program is to be stored in address 5000. There are some things to pay especial attention to:

(1)   The instruction in 5001 is twice used as a number (in instruction 5004 and 5008) so as to change the program so it will successively step through the table and then get the related code.

(2)   If this program is to be used again, the instruction in address 5001 will need to be reset to contain the starting instruction (25 0001 5002).

(3)   Although we specified addresses 0001 and 2000, they could be changed to any other appropriate addresses and, in fact, previous steps in the program could have done so by recording different instructions in addresses 5000 and 5001.

(4)   The length of each item in the Table could be changed simply by changing the number in address 5005, and the location of the code relative to its identifier could be changed simply by changing the number in address 5009.

The program, as written, fails to handle a possible source of error, which leads to a catastrophe: If the given item is greater than every identifier in the table, what would happen? What can be done to the program to avoid such a catastrophe if errors of this kind can occur? Alternatively, what can be done to the table?

programming field is to bring this level of abstraction ever closer to the normal communication process of the programmer himself.

The historical development of compilers roughly parallels the historical development of applications. Thus, compilers and a corresponding specialized language have existed in the field of numerical computation since an early time. One such language is called FORTRAN (FORmula TRANslator), and compilers to interpret FORTRAN have been developed for most major computers.[44] The development of subroutines for business-data handling came considerably later; the development of a language was correspondingly delayed. Finally, as a result primarily of pressure from the federal government, the language COBOL (COmmon Business Oriented Language) was established, and compilers have been prepared to interpret COBOL for several different computers.[45] The language PL/1 (Programming Language I) promises to become the most widely used

[44] McCracken, D. D., *A Guide to FORTRAN Programming*, New York: Wiley, 1961.
[45] McCracken, Daniel D., *A Guide to COBOL Programming*, New York: Wiley, 1963.

Figure 10.11d Program

Instruction Address	Code	Operand Address	Next Instruction Address	Explanation
5000	23	2000	5001	Item of interest copied into R_2
5001	(21	0001	5002)	Entry from Table copied into R_1
5002	87	5007	5003	If $R_1 \leq R_2$ we must get next entry
5003	21	5001	5004	Pick up the "table look-up" instruction (that is, the one in Address 5001)
5004	70	5005	5006	Increase the table address by 2
5005	00	0002	0000	The constant for adding
5006	61	5001	5001	Stores "table look-up" and then goes to it
5007	21	5001	5008	Pick up "table look-up"
5008	70	5009	5010	Changes it to pick up code associated with entry found
5009	00	0001	0010	The constant for adding
5010	61	5011	5011	Stores code look-up and then goes to it
5011	(		)	The word set aside for code look-up
5012	Next instruction			

today.[46] It combines many of the best features of FORTRAN, COBOL, and a number of other programming languages.

It is expected that as the application of the computer to library problems develops, including information retrieval and language data processing in general, standard subroutines will be established. A special language may be required, and compilers will be prepared for each of the major computers. When this occurs, the user of a library computer will very probably phrase his request in a form close to natural language and have it completely interpreted by the compiler. The appropriate subroutines will then be automatically brought together for

[46] Weinberg, Gerald M., *PL/1 Programming Primer,* New York: McGraw-Hill, 1966.

execution of the request. This is no dream; it is very much a part of the growth in understanding and increasing capabilities of computer usage.

Figure 10.12 presents a list of representative programming languages.

Figure 10.12   Representative higher-level programming languages.

Language	Implementation	Developer	Date	Characteristics
ADAM	IBM 7030	Mitre Corp.	1965	Aid in design and evaluation of data management systems
ALGOL	No standard version implemented	International committee from different organizations	1958 1960 1960[a]	Algorithmic
APL/360	IBM System 360 (used internally by IBM)	IBM	1967	On-line subset of Iverson language
BASIC	GE 225	Dartmouth College	1965	Training language prepatory to learning FORTRAN or ALGOL
COBOL	Most computers	Committee of computer manufacturers and military and government agencies	1960 1961 1961[b] 1965	Business oriented
COMIT	IBM 7040/44 IBM 7090/94	Massachusetts Institute of Technology	1961	String handling
DATA TEXT	IBM 7090/94	Harvard University Department of Social Relations	1967	Numerical computations for Social Scientists
FACT	Honeywell 800	Computer Sciences Corporation for Minneapolis-Honeywell	1959	Business oriented
FORTRAN	Most computers	IBM	1957 1958 1962	Solution of numerical problems
GPSS	IBM System/360 Univac 1107	IBM	1965	Simulation
IPL-V	IBM 709/90, 650 CDC 1604 Bendix G20 Philco 2000 Univac 1105 AN/FSQ-32 Probably others	Carnegic Institute of Technology	1961	List processing

Figure 10.12   (*continued*)

Language	Implementation	Developer	Date	Characteristics
JOVIAL	IBM 7090 CDC 1604 Philco 2000 AN/FSQ-7 AN/FSQ-31, 32 CDC 3600 IBM 9020	Systems Development Corporation Santa Monica, California	1959 : : : 1966	Algorithmic
LISP 1.5	IBM 709/90, 1620 AN/FSQ-32 PDP-1, 6 AFRCL M460 SDS 930/40 B 5500 Probably others	Stanford Research Institute Menlo Park, California	1962	List and tree processing
LISP 2	AN/FSQ-32V IBM 360–65 PDP-6	Systems Development Corporation Santa Monica, California	1966	Arbitrary mix of list processing and arithmetic computation
PL/1	IBM Systems 360	IBM– SHARE Committee	1965	General purpose
QUIKTRAN	IBM 7040–44	IBM	1964	On-line version of FORTRAN with debugging facilities
SIMSCRIPT	IBM System 360 IBM 7090 Many other computers	RAND Corporation Santa Monica, California	1963	Simulation
SNOBOL	IBM Systems 360 IBM 7040/44 IBM 7090/94 RCA 601/604 SDS 930/940 CDC 3100	Bell Telephone Laboratories	1964	Arbitrary string transformation

[a]Revised.
[b]Extended.

Generalized Programs

Many tasks for which the computer will be used are so similar that "packaged programs" can, in principle, be developed, which satisfy the requirements of an entire set of applications. An early example was the task of preparing reports, which led to generalized "Report Generators." Within the past five to ten years, other tasks in file management have become sufficiently well identified so that generalized "file management programs" could be produced (Figure 10.13).[47-53]

Generally, these task-oriented file management programs provide capability for executing a variety of basic operations on a file of any format, within very broad limits. Specifically, they can be used in the following ways.

1. To establish files, including definition of file formats.
2. To maintain files, including adding, changing, and deleting individual records as a result of transactions.
3. To search files, for purposes of retrieving specified records or fields of data according to request criteria phrased in Boolean form.
4. To prepare reports and other forms of output from files, including sorting data, arranging output formats, and controlling the printing.

From the standpoint of library application, these task-oriented programs represent the most important single step to be taken in solution of the software problem.

Operating Systems

Compilers are the means by which the task of the programmer can be simplified, but the subsequent operation of the computer itself requires other kinds of programs, called "operating systems."[54] Many aspects of the computer's operation are common to all programs. Although it is possible to include them in each individual program, it is more efficient to centralize the subroutines that perform them. They include the following operations.

1. Controlling the compilation of each program.

[47] Hayes, R. M., "Generalized Programming Systems," *Proceedings, ASPO Conference,* Chicago, 1965.

[48] *Report on Generalized File Management Programs,* Washington, D. C.: CODASYL Committee, 1969.

[49] Brown, Robert R., and Peter Nordyke, Jr., *ICS: An Information Control System,* Downey, California: North American Aviation, 1967.

[50] Bryant, J. H., and Parlan Semple, Jr., "GIS and File Management," *Proceedings of the ACM National Meeting,* 1966.

[51] Introducing the MARK IV Management System, *Sherman Oaks, California: Informatics, Inc., 1967.*

[52] *Generalized Information System: Application and Description,* New York: IBM, 1965 (E20-0179-0).

[53] Postley, John A., and T. Dwight Buetell, "Generalized Information Retrieval and Listing System," *Datamation,* 8 (12) (December 1962) 22-25.

[54] Chapin, Ned, *360 Programming in Assembly Language,* New York: McGraw-Hill, 1968, pp. 192 ff.

Figure 10.13   File management systems.

Developer	Name	Computer Number	Cost	Availability
Auerbach	DM/1			Not yet available
Control data	Infol	CDC 3600	NA	Available only for CDC equipment
Informatics	Mark IV	IBM 360/30	NA	Available on contract
IBM	FFS GIS	IBM 7090 IBM 360/40	NA NA	No longer available Not yet available
SBC	CFSS	IBM 360/30	NA	Available on contract
SDC	TDMS		$1 490/mo.	Available on contract
North American	ICS	IBM 360/50	NA	Available on contract
Computer Science Group	COGENT II	IBM 360	500/mo.[a]	Available on contract

[a]Monthly price obtained by dividing given purchase price by 50.

    2.   Scheduling the time sequence of execution of a series of individual programs.

    3.   Controlling the execution of each program.

    4.   Controlling the input and output operations.

    5.   Testing programs and helping to debug them.

    6.   Monitoring the utilization, and accounting for operating times.

    7.   Protecting files and programs.

The most advanced operating systems—multiprogramming systems—can control these operations at the same time on several different individual programs.[55] In this way, several programs can be debugged, compiled, and executed in parallel, thus using the computer to full capacity and providing individual users with their results sooner than if they had to wait in line.

A related kind of operating system—a teleprocessing system—is specifically

[55] Head, Robert V., *Real-Time Business Systems,* New York: Holt, Rinehart, and Winston, 1964, pp. 238 ff.

concerned with the tasks in control of peripheral input-output equipment.[56] It has special value in "interactive" multiprocessing systems.

Among the functions performed by operating systems, perhaps the most important is the protection of files and programs—particularly where many different users are being served. First, data stored in the files of the system must be protected from undesired change, whether deliberate or inadvertent. Second, while programs are being executed, they must be protected from the effects of execution of other programs.

The first function is accomplished by establishing "security codes" for the individuals who have access to a given file for various levels of usage:

1.   Those who can use data from a file, but only under the control of specified programs (for example, a file of answers associated with a program for computer-aided instruction, to which students have access but only through the CAI program).

2.   Those who can copy data from a file (for instance, a file of summary census data used by a number of researchers).

3.   Those who can add data to a file (for example, a file of circulation records to which new charges can be added through any one of several terminals).

4.   Those who can change data already in the file.

The operating system will require that someone trying to use a file identify himself with his code which is then checked against a table to determine the level of use he can make of it.

The second function—protection of programs from the effects of other programs—requires that the operating system allocate memory locations, registers, input-output equipment, and the like, to each program. It must then check programs to guarantee that each refers only to those parts of the equipment allocated to it. In a multiprocessing and on-line environment, this becomes so extremely difficult and time consuming that the "overhead" in the operating system itself can consume a large percentage of the machine's capacity.

COMPUTER OPERATION

The operation of a computing facility involves many management decisions. Will it be a dedicated, shared, or time-shared facility? A batch, remote batch, on-line, or interactive facility? An ad hoc or production facility? These issues are of utmost significance to the library because of the special problems that library data processing involves. Unfortunately, the library is usually faced with a choice

[56] Parkhill, D. F., *The Challenge of the Computer Utility*, Reading, Mass.: Addison-Wesley, 1966.

of Scylla or Charybdis—the difficulties of managing its own facility, with all the problems involved, or the use of some external facility, usually not oriented towards the needs of libraries.

Dedicated, Shared, or Time-Shared

Perhaps the most fundamental choice is this one: Does the library establish and manage its own facility or does it share one with some other organization? In Chapter 8 we outlined, to some extent, the staffing and facilities that an installation dedicated to library needs implies. The disadvantages of this choice are obvious—the magnitude of investment, the difficulties in acquiring satisfactory personnel, the necessarily limited capacity of the facility. On the other hand, the advantages are also obvious. The facility will schedule its operations to satisfy the library's needs; the programs and services provided will be designed to serve those needs; and the facility will be near to the library and readily accessible.

The choice of a shared facility has many appealing features. Frequently, the library is a component of a larger organization—a university, an industrial company, a community, a school—which already has a computer facility or plans to acquire one. It is natural to expect the library to use the large organization's computer facility and even to justify some of the costs on that basis. The advantages for the library are the easy availability of computing capacities far beyond the needs of the library, and usually at very economic levels of cost. On the other hand, it must be recognized that even these larger, shared facilities face severe management problems. The number of people with the combination of technical and managerial expertise required is very limited. In fact, many university computing facilities during the past several years have had great difficulty in simultaneously serving the needs of research, instruction, and administration. If the problems represented by the library are added, they are very likely to be given short shrift or low priority, inappropriate to the operating needs of the library.

A third choice—a time-shared facility—has great appeal.[57-58] Whether it takes the form of a time-shared computer in a company or a commercial service, it is probably designed to serve all users on a relatively equal basis. Figure 10.14 lists some commercially available time-sharing systems. Unfortunately, despite the inherent capacity of the hardware represented by these systems, the software is very restricted and inappropriate to the requirements of library data processing (except in limited areas that are simply analogues of business data processing).

[57] "Time-Sharing: A Computer for Everyone," *Electronic Design,* **16** (9) (April 25, 1968), Cl-C74.

[58] *Time-Sharing System Scorecard,* Los Angeles: Computer Research Corporation, Fall 1968.

Figure 10.14   On-line sofware systems.

Manufacturer	Name	Model Number	Languages	Character-istics	Commercial Services	Price in Dollars (Minimum per Month)
Computer Corp. of America		103		Uses 2260 CRT display		
Control Data		CDC–3300	BASIC (EXT) FORTRAN II and IV, EDIT DEBUG		Computer Time Sharing Corp.	
	Time-Sharing System	CDC–6600		Extended core memories		
Data Corp.	Data Control		COBOL, FORTRAN, JOVIAL, ALGOL, PL/1	Uses 1050 console dataphone		
Digital Equipment Corp.		PDP–6	FORTRAN IV, AID DDT, SNOBOL, COBOL		Applied Logic Inc.	
		PDP–10			Bolt, Beranek & Newman	
		PDP–10/50				
Burroughs		B5500		Computer Network Corp. REALTIME		500.00
General Electric		GE–265	BASIC, ALGOL FORTRAN		Call-a-Computer	108.50
					CEIR Inc.	250.00
					GE Information Systems	350.00

Figure 10.14 (Continued)

Manufacturer	Name	Model Number	Languages	Characteristics	Commercial Services	Price in Dollars (Minimum per Month)
General Electric (continued)		GE–420	FORTRAN IV, BASIC (ADV)	Uses GE 415 computer & Datanet 30	Rapidata Inc.	100.00
					McDonnell	100.00
		GE–635			GE Information Systems	350.00
IBM		360/50	PL/1		ITT Data Services	150.00
					Allen-Babcock	100.00
	Time-Sharing System	360/67				
	Quicktran	7040/7044		Uses 1050 Terminals		
Lockheed	Dialog			Uses 2260 CRT		
Programmatics	TORQUE					
Systems Development Corp.	TDMS					
	LUCID-QUUP					
Scientific Data Systems	Time-Sharing	SDS–940	BASIC, CAL, DDT TEXT, EDITOR, FORTRAN II, and IV		Com-Share, Inc	100.00
					Computer Sharing Inc.	
					Data Network Corp.	100.00
					Dial-Data	100.00
					Tymshare Inc.	390.00

Batch, Remote Batch, On-Line, or Interactive

The choice between a batch operation and an interactive one is a major technical decision concerning the kind of computer system, the kind of service, and the kind of relationship to the user.

Batch operation has been historically the most widespread and is the best understood. It is the most efficient in use of the equipment and a natural step in the progression from manual systems to more automated ones. However, many people concerned with the development of library data processing believe that batch processing is a cul-de-sac, uneconomic, and inappropriate in the context of library operations as a totality.

Remote batch operation represents an interim step, with batch processing but on-line acquisition of the data to be processed. As such, it combines the efficiency of the former with the ease of communication of the latter. Many "on-line" circulation systems are better described as "remote batch." Most commercial services for libraries will operate in remote-batch mode.

On-line operation has been the goal of most people developing large-scale computer systems today. It combines on-line data acquisition with the use of direct-access files—usually magnetic disks—so that as transactions are received by computers the relevant data can be retrieved from the files, processed, and the results transmitted to the user.

Interactive operation represents the present ultimate in man-computer relationship. Superficially, it differs from less extreme on-line operation only in the speed of response, but this is a world of difference. The effect of interactive computer operation is to produce a symbiosis, in which the results of the computer's operation have an immediate impact on the man's own thought processes.

Ad Hoc or Production

The dichotomy represented by this choice highlights the problem faced by the library. Most university research computing facilities are designed to serve ad hoc computing needs, in which jobs submitted bear little if any relationship to each other. For such facilities, the contrast between open shop (in which programming is done by the individual himself) and closed shop (in which it is done by the facility) is a most important one. In sharp contrast is the situation in most industrial corporations in which the work of the computing facility is almost completely production oriented, utilizing standardized programs.

Unfortunately, the library falls into a kind of limbo. In its internal ("technical") operations, it requires a production-oriented faciltiy; in its external, service operations, it requires an ad hoc facility.

The Combination of Facilities

In the confusion of all of these choices, it is hard to determine exactly what the library should do. However, perhaps it is not a question of "either/or" but of "both"—dedicated and shared, both batch and on-line, both ad hoc and production. To be specific, libraries seriously considering mechanization should design the system around a combination of a small-scale, library-based, batch processing computer to satisfy the production requirements with a large-scale shared facility, operating on-line and providing ad-hoc services to both the library and its patrons. Such a combined system underlies most of the evaluations of library subsystems persented in Parts IV and V of this book.

The use of a combination of facilities has many obvious advantages. The library is able to maintain control over its own records and schedule operations on its own facility to its own convenience. And yet, when a large-scale computing capacity is needed, the library can call on much larger resources.

On the other hand, a combination of facilities raises some very significant problems in the compatibility of the separate facilities. Strangely, they are not usually problems of physical compatibility (such as the ability of the tape handler in the larger installation to read tapes produced by the smaller one) so much as a problem of software compatibility. For example, a major difficulty of the moment are the apparent incompatibilities among OS (for "Operating System," used in the very large IBM computers), DOS (for "Disk Operating System," used in smaller IBM computers), and RPG (for "Report Program Generator," the programming system used on very small IBM computers). This becomes evident, in an especially exasperating manner, in the area of "tape labeling," with one computer's software being incapable of understanding the most basic forms of data produced by another computer's software—that is, the data that describe the organization of the files themselves.

Any library considering the use of several facilities must therefore be very conscious of the problems in compatibility and consider them carefully before commiting resources in what may become a cul-de-sac.

Suggested Reading

The literature of computing today is so rich and diversified that it is difficult to encompass its scope in a limited reading list. Some is highly popular and speculative; some, highly technical and abstruse. Some is concerned with hardware; some, with software; some, with applications. At best, therefore, we can suggest a set of representative works which will lead the reader into this vast literature:

Babbage, Charles, *Calculating Engines,* edited by Philip and Emily Morrison. New York: Dover, 1961.

This is of more than passing historical interest. It is, in addition to being of valid technical content, a commentary on the problems faced by the technologist in his attempts to achieve the results he visualizes, some of which arise from his relationships to private and public sources of financial support.

Bernstein, Jeremy, *Analytical Engine: Computers, Past, Present, and Future,* New York: Random House, 1964.

Based on a series of articles in the *New Yorker,* this is a highly readable description of the computer in all of its aspects.

Huskey, H. D., and G. A. Korn, *Computer Handbook,* New York: McGraw-Hill 1962.

This is an encyclopedic work, covering various aspects of computer hardware and software, including analog computers. It heavily emphasizes "computing" at the expense of other applications.

Chapter 11

INPUT, DISPLAY, AND OUTPUT

Although machines process data recorded in machine language, the staff and users of the library require data that they can read. For data to be communicated between people and the computer, a means must be provided for the conversion of it from printed form to machine language (input) and from machine language to printed form (display and output). This chapter describes the operating characteristics of the available equipment for input, display, and output.[1-2]

The requirements for communication of data vary somewhat from library to library and between types of libraries (public school, college and research, industrial, and so on), but there are four characteristics of printed data that are especially relevant to all library operations.

1.   *It's voluminous.* There's a lot of it and its rate of growth is astronomical.

2.   *It's alphabetical.* Letters and other symbols are involved, with numbers playing primarily a symbolic role, not a computational one.

3.   *It's of differing type fonts.* Original copy and output may appear in any type 'font, including italics, upper and lower case, and the alphabet of any language.

4.   *It's prepared in a variety of ways.* Standardization of printing and format is not always possible or even desirable.

[1] Gregory, R. H., and R. L. Van Horn, *Automatic Data Processing Systems: Principles and Procedures,* Belmont, California: Wadsworth, 1963 (Chapter 4, "Input-Output Equipment").

[2] *Survey of Computer Peripheral Equipment* (Report to the Office of Naval Research), Auerbach Corporation, August 1962.

REQUIREMENTS FOR DATA

To show the relative significance of these characteristics, library data can be classified into a number of major categories: management data, circulation data, cataloging/indexing data, selection/acquisition data, and texual data.

Management Data

Management data usually has no special requirements in terms of fonts or print quality, and it therefore raises few difficult format problems on either input or output. Almost any standard equipment may be utilized for management data in libraries of any kind.

Circulation Data

Input for library circulation control depends on the methods for borrower registration and book charging. Information concerning borrower registration is straightforward and does not require any special characters or specialized data collection equipment. Book charging, while not requiring special characters, must be accomplished at a charging desk and therefore places significant requirements on the form of data about the borrower, the book, and the conditions of loan.

Cataloging/Indexing Data

The requirements for cataloging and indexing data are subject to especially wide variance among libraries. Universities and other major research libraries catalog materials in great depth of detail, in many languages, and frequently require character sets for non-Roman alphabets. Very specialized input equipment or complex coding techniques are needed to meet the input needs of such libraries. On the other hand, public libraries without major research collections and school libraries deal with few multilingual materials, and usually catalog in less depth. Their catalogs can often be restricted in their fonts. For even a moderate-sized library, the amount of data in a catalog represents a major problem for both input and output.

Selection/Acquisition Data

There are two general kinds of data in selection/acquisition: bibliographic and accounting. The former can pose problems equivalent to those encountered in cataloging/indexing. The latter usually poses no special requirement, since it is comparable in nature to management data.

Textual Data

As libraries begin to consider storage of textual material (books, articles, and abstracts) in mechanized form, the problems of input and output become almost insurmountable. The volume and variety of data are so great that only a major national program of acquistion of data at its source can really make mechanization feasible. Even at the relatively simple level of conversion to microforms, most studies have indicated that the cost for conversion of a major collection would be prohibitively expensive.

CONVERSION TO MACHINE LANGUAGE

To convert printed data to machine language, one can capture the data as a by-product of the key depressions made on a keyboard; one can use "reentry" documents, produced as output from a machine system, with the same data recorded in both printed and machine-readable form; or one can attempt to scan or "read" printed information automatically.[3] The devices for doing this include the following ones.

1. Punched-card equipment.
2. Punched-tape (and "strip-punched" card) equipment.
3. Magnetic-tape recording equipment.
4. On-line terminals.
5. Optical character readers.
6. Displays.

At the present time, key depression is the most widely used for conversion to machine-readable form. It is especially effective as a by-product of the creation of the original printed data. This means, however, that the data must be acquired at its source. Since this is seldom possible when publishing is uncontrolled, it is usually necessary to *rekey* or *retype* original material in order to obtain machine-readable data. Punched-card keypunching is the oldest and most proven method of capturing data. Punched paper tape is frequently obtained as a secondary output from a typewriter, a cash register, an adding machine, or similar devices and is then fed into a computer to be reformated, edited, and output onto magnetic tape or punched cards. Magnetic tape writers are keyboard devices that write information directly on magnetic tape. On-line terminals are used for keying information directly into a computer or peripheral processing system. As data is keyed, it frequently is simultaneously displayed on a cathode

---

[3] Hayes, R. M., "Forms of Input," in *Electronic Information Handling,* Kent, A., and O. E. Taulbee, eds. Washington, D.C.: Spartan Books, 1965, pp. 21-34.

ray tube (like a television screen) with on-line verification and correction procedures possible.

Inasmuch as typing is tedious, slow, and error prone, ways and means have been developed for the automatic "reading" of some forms of printed data. "Character recognition" involves the use of devices with sufficient discriminatory power to scan letters and produce unique electrical signals for each that can serve as input to a machine. The primary problem faced by all character recognition methods is to obtain clean-cut, discrete signals for each letter, number or special symbol scanned.

Criteria for Evaluation

In order to evaluate the relative merits of these devices, the nature of library requirements must be considered. The relevant issues are as follows.

1.   Likely rates for key-punching or typing and for input to the computer are important because of the sheer volume of data.

2.   Methods for error detection and correction are important because of the high rates of human error in typing and the still significant rates of erroneous conversion with optical character reading equipment.

3.   Flexibility of format is important because of the high proportion of variable formats and variable fields in library work.

4.   The character set and method for coding it are important because of the alphabetical nature of library material and the variety of fonts (including non-Roman alphabets) which it involves.

Typing Rate. This depends heavily on the quality and format of the source material. If it is messy, illegible, or badly arranged, production rates can drop to one half or less of what would be normal. Of equal importance is the extent to which the typist (or key-punch operator) is required to make decisions or choices among alternatives. For this reason, most large-scale input conversion projects introduce an "editor" to made all necessary decisions and put the material into a form for easy typing.

Aside from these considerations relating to the source material itself, typing (or key-punching) rates are controlled by the characteristics of the equipment. The machinery for card transport in a key-punch, for example, results in rates roughly one half that achieveable on a typewriter. With on-line typewriters and displays, rates are dependent on the nature of the software system and the number of terminals simultaneously operating.

Input-Rate. This depends entirely on the nature of the machine-readable medium serving as the means of conversion. Since punched recordings (both punched-card and punched-tape) and printed recordings are low-density media, input rates are inherently limited by the rate of transport of the medium, usually to a maximum of 2000 characters per second. In principle, magnetic recording can permit extremely high rates of input, but the cost of buffer storage necessary to achieve them has limited the input to rates of about 1000 characters per second. With on-line terminals and typewriters, the input rate is limited primarily by the capacity (band-width) of the communication channel. With normal telephone lines, only 250 to 300 characters per second can be transmitted.

Error Detection. The rates of error in most manual clerical operations are extremely high. Typical estimates on errors in typing range are from 1 error per 5000 characters (for purely numerical data) to 1 error per 1000 characters (for library type material). The kinds of errors include substitution (of one character for another), omission, insertion, transposition, and combinations of these. Because of the magnitude of these errors, it is usually necessary to include some means of error detection as a control over the quality of data input.

Another source of error arises if optical character-reading equipment is used. Errors from misinterpretations of characters arise at rates that seem to be comparable to manual rates (roughly 1 error in every 5000 characters is claimed by one manufacturer, for alpha-numeric data).

The most obvious method of error detection is proofreading—the visual comparison of the source data with a printed copy of the input data. Unfortunately, it is slow and not especially effective. There are some kinds of errors that the mind seems to accept without question, and other kinds of errors (such as the insertion of superfluous spaces) that the eye finds it difficult to see.

In punched-card installations, it is the common practice to punch all data (at least, that for which accuracy is important) twice and then to compare the two sets of data. Usually, this involves the use of a "verifier" that makes the comparison as part of the second punching operation. The problem is that this level of accuracy is not warranted by much of library data (since it effectively doubles the cost of input).

Some kinds of input data can be tested for consistency and validity by the computer. For example, data exceeding the size of a fixed field or outside the range of values known to be acceptable can easily be detected by the computer and flagged as a potential error.

Unfortunately, however, the nature of library data probably makes any of these techniques relatively expensive and even ineffective. As a result, the library must search for some other means of error control—one that recognizes the realities and is willing to tolerate a moderate level of error. This implies some statistical approach to quality control, in which samples are taken of input data and tested for an acceptable or unacceptable level of error. If the level of error in the sample is below a prescribed value, the batch from which it was selected is accepted. Otherwise, the batch is keyed a second time and then matched with the first data. A typical rule might be as follows:

If the library requires that less than 1 percent of the records be in error, 80 records will be chosen at random out of each batch of 1000 and inspected for errors. If two or more entries in that set of 80 contain errors, the entire set of 1000 will be repunched; if at most one contains an error, the set of 1000 will be accepted.

Error Correction. This can be done as part of the input conversion operation itself, with correction of the erroneous data as it is recorded. This might be used with on-line equipment and programmed validity checks, and it is the method frequently used with simple errors on punched cards and punched tape. The preferred approach, however, is to identify lines of data at the time of original input and then, subsequently, to provide the computer with "correction lines" with the same identification. The computer then makes the indicated corrections by replacing the erroneous lines with the new ones.

Format. As indicated in Chapter 9, library data tend to involve variable formats. Some means of input—punched cards, in particular—therefore introduce artificial limitations that must be weighed against other apparent advantages.

Character Set. Most input equipment provides only a limited range of fonts—far more limited than most library data involves. As a result, the library must either accept those typographic limitations or adopt complex and cumbersome methods of encoding multiple font "shifts." [In its study of input requirements of the Library of Congress, Inforonics outlined a method for such coding, using an "alphabet shift key" (■) followed by a "font code" and then by a normal font character corresponding to the desired character.][4]

Figures 11.1*a* to 11.1*e* summarize the characteristics of each of the five types of input devices with respect to these criteria.

Punched Card Equipment

Punched card key-punching is usually regarded as part of a complete punched card data processing operation,[5-8] but it may also serve as means of input to a computer which will subsequently perform operations on the data.

[4] Buckland, Lawrence F., *The Recording of Library of Congress Bibliographical Data in Machine Form.* Washington, D.C.: Council on Library Resources, 1965, p. 11.

[5] Casey, Robert., and James W. Perry, *Punched Cards: Their Applications in Science and Industry.* New York: Reinhold, 1951.

[6] Friedman, Burton D., *Punched Card Primer.* Chicago: Public Administration Service, 1955.

[7] *An Introduction to IBM Punched Card Data Processing.* New York: IBM (F20-0074).

[8] Parker, Ralph, *Library Applications of Punched Cards.* Chicago: American Library Association, 1952.

Figure 11.1a   Summary of characteristics of input devices

Equipment	General Evaluation	Trends
(1) Punched Cards	Fair. Error correction simple, but separate verification equipment considered undesirable; relatively expensive; typing rate low; format usually limited.	Many agencies are considering conversion to other forms of input equipment.
(2) Punched Tape (and strip-punched cards)	Fair. Error correction cumbersome; inexpensive for many applications (even when a secondary conversion to 80-column cards must be made); typing rate high; format very flexible	Many agencies are considering conversion to other forms of input equipment.
(3) Magnetic Tape Encoders	Good. Error correction simple; format reasonably flexible; most feasibility studies indicate distinct speed advantages, however when cost is considered, throughput advantage does not defray increased cost.	Many high-volume punched card and punched tape operations involving secondary translation to tape are being converted to magnetic encoders.
(4) On-line Typewriters	Good. Error correction excellent; relatively expensive; moderate speed of typing; great flexibility possible in formats.	Growth indicated by trend to on-line, time-shared systems.
(5) Optical Readers	Unknown but probably excellent; (optical character readers still being tested for large scale input of library data). Error rates depend upon material; error correction can be difficult; large capital investment, but most economic input of all; typing rate can be maximum, and input rate is high; formats may be restricted but are generally flexible.	Greatest potential for growth; trend to development of hand-printing reader and readers capable of automatically sensing font and size changes.
(6) Alphanumeric Displays	Good (but of marginal economy, and still being tested for library usage). Error correction excellent; relatively expensive; typing rate can be limited but is likely to be near maximum; formats may be limited.	Growth indicated by trend to on-line, time-shared systems.

Figure 11.1b

Equipment	Typing Rates	Input rates
(1) Punched Cards	Dependent upon quality and format of source, but typically 6000 characters per hour.	Up to 2000 characters per second.
(2) Punched Tape (and strip-punched cards)	Dependent upon quality of source, but typically 12,000 characters per hour.	Up to 2000 characters per second.
(3) Magnetic Tape Encoders	Dependent upon quality of source, but typically 10,000 characters per hour.	Up to 1000 characters per second.
(4) On-line Typewriters	Dependent upon software system, but varying from 6000 characters per hour to 18,000 characters per hour.	Limited by bandwidth of communication channel and size of buffer, normally to about 300 characters per second.
(5) Optical Readers	Up to maximum (18,000 characters per hour).	Varies from 350 to 2000 characters per second.
(6) Alphanumeric Displays	Dependent upon software system but varying from 6000 characters per hour to 18,000 characters per hour.	Limited by bandwidth of communication channel and size of buffer, normally to about 300 characters per second.

The basic medium used by punched card equipment is the punched card itself, a card produced out of a good quality paper that can withstand a remarkable amount of rough treatment. It is 7 3/8 inches in length, 3 1/4 inches in width, and .007 inch in thickness. Exactness in meeting these specifications on size and quality in the card stock is of the utmost necessity if the machines are to process the cards accurately and if the card is to be used for any length of time.

In an IBM (Hollerith-code) card (Figure 11.2), there are 12 horizontal rows across the card, corresponding to 12 bit positions. Each card has 80 vertical columns, numbered from left to right, so that it is possible to record 80 letters, or numbers, or special characters, or any combination of them. Numerical digits (0 to 9) are represented by a single punch in the corresponding row of the column in which they are recorded. Alphabetic letters are formed by the

Figure 11.1c

Equipment	Error Detection	Error Correction
(1) Punched Cards	"Verifier" involves rekeying entire set of data. Proofreading involves printing contents of cards and then visually reading hardcopy produced by typing.	Rekeying of entire card.
(2) Punched Tape (and strip-punched cards)	Proofreading of hardcopy produced by typing (although double punching and validity checks are possible).	Cumbersome rekeying (usually of entire line, sometimes of a single field or character).
(3) Magnetic Tape Encoders	Proofreading of hardcopy, usually of a printout from the tape. Validity checks are likely to be used before printout.	Relatively simple rekeying (usually of entire line, sometimes of single field or single character).
(4) On-line Typewriters	Proofreading of hardcopy, produced by typing. On-line computer checks of validity and consistency.	Relatively simple rekeying, usually of entire line.
(5) Optical	Double reading and internal comparison will significantly reduce error rates due to the reader. Errors in original typing detected by proofreading	Rekeying, usually of an entire line.
(6) Alphanumeric Displays	Proofreading of displayed data. On-line computer checks of validity and consistency.	Simple rekeying.

combination of a punch in the "zones" (rows 11, 12, 0) and a punch in one of the rows 1 through 9. For example,

A—12 zone punch and digit 1 punch
N—11 zone punch and digit 5 punch
Z— 0 zone punch and digit 9 punch

Figure 11.3 presents a comparable picture of the format and coding for the punched card used in the Univac systems of Sperry-Rand. It shows that the card uses "round holes" instead of rectangular ones (because of differences in the methods for card reading), and therefore can record only 45 columns per card.

Figure 11.1d

Equipment	Format	Keyboard Layout and Functional Controls
(1) Punched Cards	Keypunch has generally required rigid card format which dictates careful design.	A standard keyboard layout is universal except for special symbols.
(2) Punched Tape (and strip-punched cards)	Proper form design demands that forms, output tape, and program tape be considered as a single system.	General typewriter format, with variations in placement of special symbols and functions.
(3) Magnetic Tape Encoders	More format free than keypunches, but buffer limits line to 80 or 90 characters. Special progam potential should be taken advantage of in forms design.	Basic keypunch arrangement, with option of other layouts. Has more functional controls than keypunch
(4) On-line Typewriters	Except for standard "good design procedures" few restrictions. Since most controls are manual, number of carriage returns, etc., should be minimal.	General typewriter format, with variations in placement of special symbols and functions.
(5) Optical Readers	Forms must be designed with OCR in mind, with respect to form size, font, ink, etc.	Current manual entry keyboards under study. Not critical to system.
(6) Alphanumeric Displays	Form design must be related to limits of CRT Display.	Multiplicity of keyboards available in both basic keypunch and typewriter formats. Wide variation in number and position of functional controls.

However by using a more efficient coding system, with only 6 bit positions for each alpha-numeric character, two characters can be recorded in each column for a total of 90 characters per card.

Card Punch. The card punch is basic to all punched card data processing equipment.[9] It is the means by which to transcribe data into the form of punched holes in cards.

Figure 11.1e

Equipment	Code	Character Set and Fonts
(1) Punched Cards	Hollerith code used with most card equipment.	Two basic sets in use: 48 and 64 characters. Many uses for special character representations.
(2) Punched Tape (and strip-punched cards)	Eight-channel code is now standard.	Some deviation between different manufacturers. Upward compatibility in single manufacturer's line.
(3) Magnetic Tape Encoders	All six-level BCD-NRZ1 codes possible. On new equipment EBCDIC will be used. "ASCII-S" being considered.	Both 48 and 64 character sets available. Key-punch oriented.
(4) On-line Typewriters	Baudot and USASCII both in use.	Only minor deviations.
(5) Optical Readers	No output code restriction.	Font style critical. Multifont readers are considerably more expensive and less reliable.
(6) Alphanumeric Displays	Most output in USASCII, but some output in 6-level BCD code.	A wide variety of special symbols.

A most important feature of the card punch is the capability that it provides for automatic control of the fields to be recorded on cards—skipping fields when they are not needed, duplicating fields from one card to the next when desired, or automatically shifting from numeric to alphabetic fields without necessitating keyboard operations. A "program card" mounted on a rotating drum is the basic means for such control. It acts as a complex version of the "tab" on a typewriter. A card is prepared for each different field structure or punching application and can then be used repeatedly. Punches in various columns in the program card control the automatic operation for the corresponding columns of the cards being punched, with each row in the program card controlling a specific function.

[9] *Reference Manual, 026 Key Punch.* White Plains, New York: IBM Data Processing Publications.

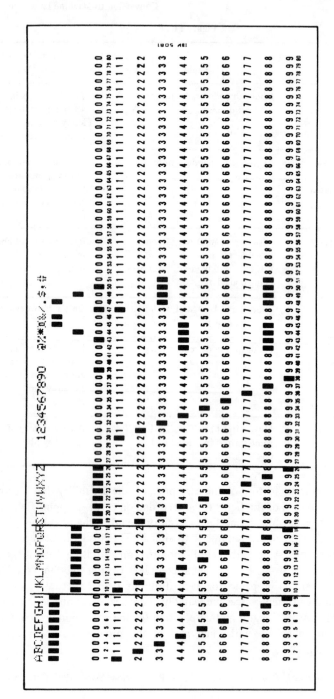

Figure 11.2   IBM punched card (80 characters).

292

Figure 11.3 UNIVAC punched card (90 characters).

Operating speeds of the key-punch are variable, since they depend on the operator and the nature of the material to be punched—its readability, organization, and sequence. However, an approximate rule of thumb is a production rate of 6000 key-strokes (characters) per hour for typical material, including allowance for nonproductive time of the operator.

Key-punching was, at one time, the only major means available for data input, tracing its origins to punched card applications in use long before the computer. As a result, every format, regardless of how arbitrary, had to be forced to fit within the constraints of the 80-column punched card—a real "bed of Procrustes." The actual source of data therefore usually does not correspond with the form required for key-punching. The usual procedure is to have certain categories of information on the form assigned to a given card record (for example, a "title" card or an "author" card). This often requires that either the operator skip around the source of data to bring order to the card record, or that many operators encode different categories of information separately.

To eliminate some of these format problems, certain types of format-free encoding have been developed. In the government, experimentation with coded identification of fields rather than rigid fixed formats has resulted in considerable time savings.

In general, however, because of the problems involved in key-punching, highly organized pre-encoding procedures are usually used. Before the document is presented to the key-punch operator for punching, edit-coders prepare the document for punching—converting codes, defining fields, making illegible entries legible, and referring items carrying non-standard data to a professional librarian. Figure 11.4 lists typical card-punching devices.

Card Readers. From the standpoint of modern-day digital computer systems, punched cards serve primarily as a means of input of data to the computer. Figure 11.5 lists typical card-reading equipment.

Card-Handling Equipment. In smaller data processing installations, punched-card handling equipment is used to perform those operations that the computer would do internally. These include duplicating, verifying, sorting, selecting, merging, and printing.[10-12] Figure 11.6 lists typical card-handling equipment.

"Duplicating" is automatic punching of repetitive information from a "master card" into a group of succeeding "detail cards," normally as part of card-punching. Instead of depressing keys repetitively for common information

[10] *Reference Manual, 083 Sorter.* White Plains, New York: IBM Data Processing Publications.

[11] *Reference Manual, 087 Collator.* White Plains, New York: IBM Data Processing Publications.

[12] *Reference Manual, 407 Tabulator.* White Plains, New York: IBM Data Processing Publications.

Figure 11.4   Card-punching equipment.

Manufacturer	Name	Model	Rate	Price per Month (Dollars)	Characteristics
IBM	Key Punch	024	10 cps[a]	40	Alpha-numeric
	Key Punch	026	10 cps	60	Alpha-numeric
	Key Punch	029	10 cps	60-89	Alpha-numeric
	Tape-to-Card	046	20 cps	140	Converts from paper tape to card
	Tape-to-Card	047	20 cps	160	Card punch and print
	Transceiver	065	16 cps	90	Connects telephone lines to 026
	Card Punch	534	10 cps	50-70	Similar to 024 but programs
	Print Card Punch	536	10 cps	75	Programmed card punch and print
	Typewriter Punch	824	20 cps	95-125	Typewriter to 024
	Typewriter Punch	826	18 cps	115-145	Typewriter to 026
	Cardatype	858	10 cps	195	Accounting machine with cards
	Key Punch	1057		75	Part of 1050 system
Sperry-Rand	Tape-to-Card	308 -58	7 cps		Reads 8 channel tape

[a]cps means characters per second.

(such as "date of charge-out," which is to be punched as the same date in every circulation record for a given day), the operator punches the common information once in the first card of each group, and it is automatically punched into all remaining cards for the group (under control of the program card). This reduces the work per card, ensures consistency of common data, and increases productivity of the operator.

"Card verifying" is simply a means of checking the accuracy of the original key-punching. A second operator key-punches (using a verifier) while reading from the same source of data used by the first one. The machine compares the key depressed with the hole already punched in the card. A difference causes the machine to stop, indicating a discrepancy between the two operations.

Figure 11.5   Card reading equipment.

Manufacturer	Name	Model	Rate	Price per Month (Dollars)	Characteristics
Burroughs	Serial Card Reader	BC 122	200 cpm[a]	220	Used with B 100 and B 500 series
	Card Reader	B 123	475 cpm	NA	Used with B 100 and B 500 series
	Card Reader	B 124	800 cpm	400	Used with B 100 and B 500 series
Computer Industries Inc.	Cope	.32	200 cpm	NA	Part of on-line system
	Cope	.36	200 cpm	NA	Part of on-line system
	Cope	.38	600 cpm	NA	Part of on-line system
	Cope	.45	1200 cpm	NA	Part of on-line system
General Electric	Card Reader	200	400-1000 cpm	NA	Part of 200 series
	Card Reader	CRZ-100	300 cpm	NA	
	Card Reader	CRZ-120	600 cpm	NA	
		CRZ-201	900 cpm	NA	Used with GE-400 systems
General Precision Corp.	Card Reader	9460	400 cpm	400	Used with RRC 9000
Honeywell			800 cpm	NA	Used with Honeywell 200, 800-III, and 1800

[a]cpm means cards per minute.

"Sorting" is the process of grouping cards in numerical or alphabetical sequence according to any data punched in them (such as call number, for instance). The "sorter" provides this capability for rapidly arranging cards for the preparation of various reports—all originating from the same cards, but each requiring a different sequence or grouping of information.

Figure 11.5   (*continued*)

Manufacturer	Name	Model	Rate	Price per Month (Dollars)	Characteristics
IBM	Card Input	711	250 cpm	NA	Used with 7094-II
		7502	60 cpm	NA	Used with 7080
		1056		70	Part of 1050 system
		1402	800 cpm	NA	Used with 1401 and 360
		1442	400 cpm	NA	Used with 1420 bank system
		2501-B1	600 cpm	268	Used with 360/30
Mohawk Data Sciences	MDS	3011	75 cpm	NA	Card to magnetic tape
NCR	High Speed Card Reader	380-3	2000 cpm	750	Used with 315
	Low Speed Card Reader	472-2	400 cpm	450	Used with 315
Philco		158	600 cpm	610	
		258	2000 cpm	800	Part of 260 card system
RCA		323	600 cpm	NA	Used with RCA-301
	Card Transcriber	527	400 cpm	NA	Card to magnetic tape
	Card Reader	70/237	1435 cpm	NA	Part of Spectra 70
Sylvania	Read-Punch	9481	100 cpm	850	Part of 9400 series

[a] cpm means cards per minute.

"Selecting" is the function of pulling from a sequence of cards those that require special attention. Selection of individual cards is accomplished automatically by either the sorter or another device called a "collator." Typical criteria for selection are as follows,

Catalog cards punched with specific call numbers.

Circulation control cards with a specific due date.

Order cards containing a specific vendor number.

Author cards from each group of punched cards storing catalog data.

Title cards from each group of punched cards storing catalog data.

Cards out of filing sequence.

"Merging" is the process of combining two sets of punched cards into one set of given sequence. Both files of cards must be in the same sequence before they are merged. This function makes possible automatic filing of new cards into an existing file of cards. It can also be used to check for agreement between two sets of cards. Unmatched cards or groups of cards in either file may be selected or separated from the files. This function is therefore frequently performed in conjunction with selecting.

"Printing" is the printing of information from each card as the card passes through the "tabulator." The function is used to prepare reports that show complete detail about the contents of each card. During this listing operation the machine can add, subtract, and print many combinations of totals. "Group printing" summarizes groups of cards and prints many combinations of totals.

Re-Entry Records. One of the most effective answers to the problems of input is the use of "re-entry records"—punched cards produced as output from a mechanized system and containing data in both printed form and machine-readable form. These records can communicate data to people and then, subsequently, re-enter the same data into the mechanized system without the need to key-punch it. They are perhaps most familiar in their use as utility bills, mailed to the customer with the request "Please return this part" imprinted on the re-entry portion. In libraries, they are especially useful in circulation control systems, in the form of prepunched book cards, transaction cards, and borrower cards.[13]

Transaction Recorders. One of the principal values of punched cards in modern data processing is the ease with which individual events—transactions—can be recorded on them. The data involved in a specific transaction is recorded in machine language, preferably as a direct result of the action itself. For example, through a hook-up with a central data processing unit, information gathered at remote locations may be fed into the central unit and used to construct transaction records there. In circulation control, units at check-out

[13] *General Information Manual, Teleprocessing in Circulation Control at Public Libraries.* White Plains, New York: IBM, 1959, 1960 (E20-8040 and E20-0077).

Figure 11.6   Punch card handling equipment.

Manufacturer	Name	Model	Rate	Price per Month (Dollars)	Characteristics
IBM	Sorter	083	1000 cpm[a]	110	Automatic reject and pre-edit
	Collator	087	240- 480 cpm	215-270	Alphabetical
	Statistical Sorter	101-1	450 cpm	500	
	Tabulator	407	150 cpm	1035	Calculates and prints output
	Reproducing Punch	514	100 cpm	70-140	Reproduces or gang punches
	Card Reproducer and Gang Punch	528	100 cpm	360-440	
	Alphabetic Interpreter	557	100 cpm	130-305	
Sperry-Rand	Multi-Control Reprod-Punch	310	100 cpm	NA	Compares two files and punches the second
	Reproducing Punch	314	125 cpm	55	Reproducing can be modified
	Collating Reproducer	315-1	100 cpm	170	Simultaneous Punch and merge
	Duplicate Card Detector	325	130 cpm	45	Control for individual columns
	Numeric Collator	319-2	240 cpm	125	
	Electronic Sorter	420-1	800 cpm	85	Automatic stop control

[a]cpm means cards per minute.

points would receive prepunched re-entry cards for the book (giving call number, author, and title,) and for the borrower. The information thus collected would be used to create a record of each transaction, to be processed subsequently by the computer.[14-16] Figure 11.7 lists some typical transaction recording equipment, each of which uses punched cards as re-entry documents.

Figure 11.7   Transaction recording equipment.

Manufacturer	Name	Model	Transfer Rate	Price/ Month (Dollars)	Characteristics
Communitype		100SR	200 cps[a]	232	Punched card or Magnetic tape input
Control Data	Data Collector	180	16 cps	115[b]	Accepts cards, paper tape, and variable information
	Data Collection system	8010	54 cps	50	Requires central equipment
	Transactor		60 cps	85	Input station for punched cards and compiler
	Message Data Switching System	8050	10 cps	NA	
Dasa Corporation	Message Compiler	TX100	10 cps	19[b]	
Datel Corporation		Thirty-21	15 cps	66[b]	Transmits to computer and other terminals
Demex Inc.		CRU-DS5-S	75 cps	160	Punched card input
Friden	Collecta-data	30	30 cps	70	Requires central equipment, $2500/mo
General Electric	Datanet	21	6800 cps	200	Single-line controller
	Datanet	70	6800 cps	200	Multiline controller
	Datanet	3101	110 cps	70[b]	Requires central equipment, $4000/mo.

[14] Eldredge, K. R., et al., "Automatic Input for Business Data Processing Systems," *Proceedings Eastern Joint Computer Conference.* New York, T-92, December 10-12, 1956, pp. 69-72.
[15] *General Information Manual, Teleprocessing in Circulation Control at Public Libraries.* White Plains, New York: IBM, 1959, 1960 (E20-8040 and E20-0077).
[16] Perlman, Justin A., "Data Collection for Business Information Processing," *Datamation,* 9 (2) (February 1963), 54-58.

Figure 11.7   (*continued*)

Manufacturer	Name	Model	Transfer Rate	Price/ Month (Dollars)	Characteristics
IBM	Data Collector	357	20 cps	70[b]	Requires central equipment
	Data Trans- Mission System	1001	12 cps	30[b]	Requires central equipment
	Data Collector	1030	60 cps	140[b]	Requires central equipment
NCR	Transactor	473-1	60 cps	80[b]	Requires central equipment, $20,000/mo.
Philco	High Speed Communi- cations Processor	PCPI50	50-400 cps	NA	
RCA	Edge	6201	28 cps	104[b]	Requires central equipment, $35,000/mo.
Standard Register	Data Ray	401	12 cps	20[b]	Requires central equipment, $3000/mo.
SDC	Transactor	2020	60 cps	70	Requires central equipment, $18,000/mo.

[a] cps means characters per second.
[b] Monthly price obtained by dividing given purchase price by 50.

Punched Tape Equipment

There are a large number of devices that punch "paper tape."[17] They have the following advantages.

1.   They tend to be less expensive than other devices for data conversion and input.

2.   They can be used to create machine language as a "by-product" of some other operation.

[17] "All About Paper Tape," *Datamation,* May/June and July/August, 1959.

3.   They are relatively easy to use.

4.   There is such a wide variety of devices that can accept paper tape as input that it serves as a "common language" for communication among them.

5.   They are not limited by the restrictions on format imposed by the 80 (or 90) character capacities of a punched card. As a result, the variable formats typical of library operation can be more easily recorded.

They have the primary disadvantage that the correction of errors is cumbersome. There are four approaches that can be taken to error correction:

1.   The tape can be reproduced until the erroneous data is reached, and then correct data can be inserted.

2.   Individual characters can be "deleted" (by being over-punched with a "code-delete" character) and then followed by the correct data.

3.   Delete codes can be inserted that will subsequently be interpreted by the computer as requiring that preceding characters, words, lines, or other sets of characters are to be deleted and replaced by what will follow.

4.   As data is punched, lines can be identified by number; subsequently, if a line contains an error, a "correction line" will be punched with the same line number.

This last approach has special importance to librarians, since it has value for other purposes as well. Line codes can be used to identify fields and data elements within records. They therefore can be used to provide the computer with the data it needs for control of the subsequent processing of records.

Although the use of punched tape does not have the same limitations as the keypunch imposes, certain of its characteristics directly affect design of the input system.[18] The system can be designed to capture source data at the same time a source document is being created (typed), to capture source data as it is being transcribed to a new document from a prior source document, or to use earlier captured data on tape in conjunction with new source data to produce a new transcribed output.

In all cases, the source document, the output card or tape, and the input card or tape must be considered together and must all be designed with the entire system in mind. The format of the hard copy produced at the time of typing may dictate special functions, which must appear on the tape. For computer input, the tape must clearly delineate fields.

Punched-Tape Typewriters.   Punched-tape typewriters convert data to machine language, the medium usually being paper tape (although cards can also be punched in a strip along their edge). They can read, punch, or copy punched tape, and can type hard copy by manual or automatic means. The tapes can be

[18] Koriagin, Gretchen W., "Experience in Man and Machine Relationships in Library Mechanization," *American Documentation,* 15 (3) (July 1964), 227-229.

used for repetitive clerical tasks, such as typing letters or maintaining invoice records, or as input to the computer.

The basic tape operations involve a reader, a writing unit, and a punch (see Figure 11.8). The reader senses a hole-or-no-hole code and generates electrical impulses from it at a rate of about 10 characters per second. Another unit is responsible for converting these impulses into a mechanical operation which causes a key of the writing unit keyboard to be depressed, thus typing a hard copy. When the keys are depressed, either by an electric impulse or manually by a typist, another set of electric impulses is generated. These impulses can activate a punch that creates a punched paper tape, thus completing the cycle.

The keyboards (a sample is shown in Figure 11.9) come with the usual array of alphabetical letters, numbers, and a great number of special characters. The "lower case" and "upper-case" shift keys allow the typewriter to produce two fonts; the same character code punched on tape can therefore be interpreted as representing two different characters depending on the most recent shift

Figure 11.8   Punched tape typewriter.

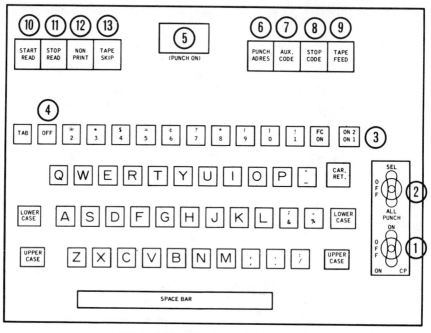

Figure 11.9   Representative keyboard

character punched. If more than two fonts are needed, more elaborate coding schemes are necessary. In addition, there are, as on a typewriter, a "carriage return," a "tab" and "tab stop" lever, and a "back spacer." All of these can be operated either automatically (by the tape or strip-punched card) or manually.

The punched area (on tape or cards) is 1 inch wide and records an 8 bit code. A typical code system (Figure 11.10) uses 4 channels for the standard BCD code for the numbers 0 through 9; channels 6 and 7 are used as "zone" bits for alphabetic characters; channel 8 is for carriage return; and channel 5 is used for parity checking (that is, a hole is punched or not in channel 5 so that there will always be an odd number of punches; if the machine senses an even number of punches, something is wrong and the operations stop).[19] There are also "sprocket holes," which assure proper placement of the code for each character.

The uses of punched tape are many. For example, in the original input system for MEDLARS all of the records for citations (consisting of the journal title, date, authors, article title, paging, and indexing terms) were typed by a typist using a Flexowriter.[20] The manual typing generated a paper tape, which was fed

[19] "Considerations in Choosing a Character Code for Computers and Punched Tapes," *The Computer Journal* (British), 1961, pp. 202-210.

[20] Austin, C. J., "Data Processing Aspects of MEDLARS," *Bulletin of the Medical Library Association,* **52** (January 1964), pp. 159-63.

into the computer. Other users of paper tape involve transmission of codes over teletype, duplication of catalog cards,[21-24] mass production of "personally typed" letters, and even control of machine tools. Figure 11.11 lists some typical punched-tape typewriters.

Accounting Machines with Paper Tape Attachments. Several of the accounting machine manufacturers have added a paper tape attachment to accounting machines, cash registers, window posting machines, and the like. This allows them to produce integrated accounting systems that combine the usefulness of manual records, created by their key-operated accounting machines, with the processing power of the computer. Figure 11.12 lists some typical devices.

Typographic Composition Machines. Several machines that compose and cast type utilize perforated tape. (See Figure 11.13) For example, the "Monotype" consists of two main components: a keyboard and a caster. When each key is struck, two perforations are made in a paper tape. The perforated tape passes to the casting machine where compressed air, passing through the perforations, controls the action of the casting apparatus. The matrix case is moved in the proper direction (backward, forward, or sideways) by levers so that it is over the mold. Molten metal is forced against the mold to cast each letter, character, or space. The cast characters are then assembled line by line.

The Photon also provides photocomposition through use of a punched paper tape. When the data is typed, control codes are interspersed which specify the style and size of print, the spacing, and details of the format. The photographic images of any set of 1440 characters are contained in 8 concentric annuli on a disc which is in continuous rotation between a flashing light and a sheet of film (at a speed of approximately 1800 revolutions per minute). During each rotation of the disc, a light beam may be projected through one of the annuli on the disc. The image of any character on the disc thus can be reproduced for a very short interval during each rotation.

The Linofilm is a phototypesetting system composed of four or five different machines. The keyboard unit is a console with a keyboard, much like the standard typewriter, and a perforator which punches a 15 channel paper tape, recording all the keyed information. The Linofilm photographic unit reads and decodes the punched tape and selects one of up to 18 fonts. When the correct font is in place, a light source exposes an entire 88 character grid. A shutter

[21] Electronic Tape-Activated Typewriter Used for Automatic Catalog Card Processing," *Law Library Journal,* November 1960, p. 508.

[22] Johnson, Noel W., "Automated Catalog Card Reproduction," *Library Journal,* **85** (4) (February 15, 1960), pp. 725-726.

[23] Luckett, George R., "Partial Library Automation with the Flexowriter Writing Machine," *Library Resources and Technical Services,* **1** (4) (Fall 1957), pp. 207-210.

[24] Witty, Francis J., "Flexowriter and Catalog Card Reproduction: Perfect Solutions for Short Runs?" *District of Columbia Libraries,* **28** (3) (July 1957), pp. 2-4.

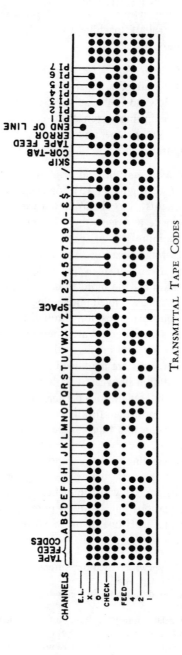

Figure 11.10   Punched tape code systems.

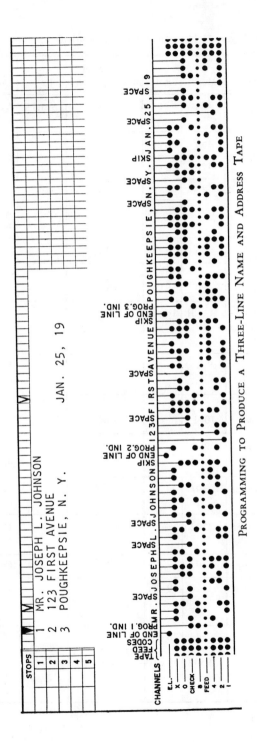

PROGRAMMING TO PRODUCE A THREE-LINE NAME AND ADDRESS TAPE

Figure 11.10 *(continued)*

307

Figure 11.11   Punched tape typewriters.

Manufacturer	Name	Model	Rate	Price per Month (Dollars)	Code	Characteristics
Burroughs		454		NA	6 and 7	Verifies and duplicates
		466	60 cps[a]	NA		
		470	60 cps	NA	7	
Creed	Reperforator	25	33 cps	NA	5,6,7	
		54	10 cps	NA		Keyboard and page receiver
		85	10 cps	NA		
	Tape Verifier	90	16 cps	NA		
Dura	Automatic Typewrite System	MACH 10	16 cps	70[b]		Replaceable "golf-ball" unit for added fonts
	Word Processor	941		NA		Used for text editing
	Word Processor	1041		127[b]		Uses typewriter keyboard
Epsco	Edityper	200		NA		Single punch and dual reader
Friden	Flexowriter	2201	20 cps	86[b]		Most generally used
	Flexowriter	2302		76[b]		Can upgrade to 2201
	Flexowriter	2303		56[b]		Cannot upgrade
	Justowriter		10 cps	180		Automatic justification of hard copy
General Precision Corp.		342	20 cps	NA		
	Tape Type Writer System	9500	30 cps	150	7	Inquiry on off-line system

Figure 11.11 (*continued*)

Manufacturer	Name	Model	Rate	Price per Month (Dollars)	Code	Characteristics
IBM	Card Controlled	63	10 cps	110	5	
	Tape Punch	961	16 cps	25-50	8	Can be connected to 858 accounting machine
	Tape Punch	962	20 cps.	50	5	Connected to 024 or 026 card punch
Invac	Tapemaker		20 cps	NA	5-8	Typewriter with tape auxiliary
Kleinschmidt		122	20 cps	NA	5	
		195	6-8 cps	NA		
NCR		351	10 cps	NA	7	
		370	60 cps	NA	5,6,7	
RCA		523	10 cps	NA		Keyboard
	Type-writer		10 cps	160	7	Uses RCA Daspan Code
Robotyper	Robotyper			100		
	Tape Perforator			35		
SCM	Typetronic	2816				
Sperry-Rand	Synchio-Tape		20 cps.	150	5-8	
	Card to Tape Converter	318	15 cps.	110	5	Input 90 column cards
Tally		420			5-8	
	Tape Preparation System	MARK 45	16 cps	235	5-8	IBM Selectric
Teletype	Teletype-writer	19		NA	5	Punches from telegraphic signals

Figure 11.11   (*continued*)

Manufacturer	Name	Model	Rate	Price per Month (Dollars)	Code	Characteristics
Teletype	Reperforator	28RT	6-20 cps	NA	5	Punches from telegraphic signals
	ASR	37	15 cps	NA		Automatic send-receive
Underwood	Codewriter			NA		
Western Union	Automatic send-receive	19	10 cps	78	5	
		28	10 cps	52	5	
		28LPR	10 cps	39	5	

^acps means characters per second.
^bMonthly price obtained by dividing given purchase price by 50.

system composed of eight shutters operates to cover all the characters except the one being photographed. A multiprojection lens system then projects each character to the film plane.

Punched Tape Readers. Most punched tape devices (such as punched tape typewriters) provide the capability for reading the tapes as well as punching them. Unfortunately, however, the reading process they use is essentially mechanical and therefore limited to rates of 10 to 30 characters per second. For higher speed input, photoelectric readers are commonly used. They provide rates as high as 2000 characters per second. Figure 11.14 lists some typical readers.

Magnetic Tape Devices

Since magnetic tape represents one of the principal media for data storage in a computer system, it is surprising that only recently have devices become generally available which provided sufficiently reliable input directly onto magnetic tape, which can be input directly into the computer.[25] Furthermore, in contrast to paper tape, the correction of data on a magnetic tape is relatively easy. On the other hand, magnetic tape typewriters are also relatively more

[25] Hirst, Robert I., "Adapting the IBM MT/ST for library Applications—A Manual for Planning" *Special Libraries,* **59** (8) (October 1968).

Figure 11.12   Punched tape accounting machines.

Manufacturer	Name	Model	Price per Month (Dollars)	Characteristics
Burroughs	Sensimatic	F1500PA	185	Operates with A524 tape punching unit at $48 per month
	Sensimatic	E3000PA	250-350	Electronic system with internal programming and memory
	Sensimatic	E4000PA	350-600	Electronic system with internal programming and memory
	Sensimatic	E6000PA	600-	Electronic system with internal programming and memory
Clary	Programatic		NA	Add-print tape punch using 5-8 channel codes
Friden	Computyper	C5023	400	Billing machine with typewriter keyboard. Paper tape read and punch
	Accounting Accumulator	4501	NA	Ten-key attachment to flexowriter with arithmetic capability
NCR	Accounting Machine	33	125-260	
	Accounting Machine	35W	120	Wired for paper tape; 3 memory units
	Accounting Machine	36W	180	Wired for paper tape; 6 memory units
		395	450	Electronic computing capabilities
	Paper Tape Recorder	461	40	Operates at 15 cps; can be attached to tabulate for paper tape production
Olivetti	Audit	722, No. 26	NA	Accounting machine with simultaneous posting and calculating
		930, No. 27	NA	Special typewriter

Figure 11.12 (*continued*)

Manufacturer	Name	Model	Price per Month (Dollars)	Characteristics
Clary	Print-Punch Adding Maching		75	Operates at 20 cps Operates at 20 cps
IBM	Electronic Typing Calculator	632	175-395	IBM electric typewriter connected to calculator
Monroe	Synchro-Monroe		145-235	Operates at 20 cps 5-8 channel tape

Figure 11.13   Punched tape composition equipment.

Manufacturer	Name	Model	Price per Month (Dollars)	Rate	Font Range	Comments
Addressograph Multigraph		AM725	NA	12 cps[a]	336 c[b]	
Fairchild	Photo-Text Setter	2000	NA	20 cps	216 c	Six level tape
	Photo-Text Setter	8000		30-60 cps	576 c 576 c	
Mergenthaler	Linofilm		370[c]	18.5cps	1584 c	Fifteen level tape
	Linofilm	COL-28	NA	10.5cps	2464 c	Fifteen or sixteen level tape
	Linofilm	Quick	NA	10.5cps	736 c	Six level tape
Monotype	Monophoto	Mark III and IV	NA	4 cps	272 c	Thirty-one level tape used for science & math work

[a] cps means characters per second.
[b] c means characters.
[c] Monthly price obtained by dividing given purchase price by 50.

Figure 11.13   (*continued*)

Manufacturer	Name	Model	Price per Month (Dollars)	Rate	Font Range	Comments
Photon	Display-Master	513	NA	10 cps	1440 c	Six level tape computer controlled
	Display-master	560	NA	10 cps	1440 c	Eight level tape computer controlled
	Tapemaster	201	NA	7 cps	1440 c	
Filmotype	Alphatype		NA	8 cps	168 c	6 level tape
ATF	Photocomp	20	NA	10 cps	360 c	6 level tape
Berthold	Diatronic		NA	10 cps	1008 c	
Intertype	Fototronic		NA	10 cps	2400 c	
Photon	Textmaster	713-5	NA	10 cps	384 c	
Photon		713-10	NA	25 cps	768 c	
Fairchild	Photext-Setter	2000	NA	20 cps	216 c	

expensive. Figure 11.15 lists some typical magnetic tape typewriters and input devices.

Optical Character Recognition

Since so much of the data of interest to libraries already exists in printed form, it is natural to look to the use of equipment that could convert it to machine language directly. Robert A. Wilson comments, "The most obvious and most immediate function of optical reading machines is to provide a new and very fast way of converting printed pages into computer language, freeing us from the constraints imposed by present key-stroking methods. . . . But there is much more to the story than this. Disciplines whose literature has heretofore been considered too bulky to be processed by computer because of the expense of keypunching the source documents will be able for the first time to utilize the machines to their benefit, opening up entire new areas of historical, literary, and

Figure 11.14 Punched tape readers.

Manufacturers	Name	Model	Rate	Price per Month (Dollars)	Code	Characteristics
Bendix		PR-2	400 cps	NA	5-8	Used with GE 115
Burroughs	Photoreader	440	1000 cps	NA	7	Part of B2200
Control Data	Photo electric		250 cps	NA		Tape to drum
		350	350 cps	NA	7	Part of 1604
	Photo electric	8074	350 cps	NA	5-8	Used with 8090
	Photo electric	8075	120 cps	NA	5-8	Used with 8090
		PR-2	400 cps	NA	5,6,7	
	Paper-Tape Station	PT-10	500 cps	NA	8	
Creed		92	20 cps	NA	5	
Digital Equipment	Paper Tape Reader	PDP-3	300 cps	NA		
Epsco	Oykor	PTR826	600 cps	NA	8	
Ferranti		TR3	440 cps	NA	7	
		TR5	330 cps	NA	5,7,8	
		196	270 cps	NA		
Friden	SFD		10 cps	NA	8	Tape to card
	Selecta-Data			20		
	Collecta-Data	2	13 cps	NA		Reads and transmits
		4201		NA		Paper to magnetic tape
General Electric	PTR	200	500 cps	NA	5,7,8	
	PTR	100	500 cps	NA	5,7,8	

Figure 11.14 (*continued*)

Manufacturers	Name	Model	Rate	Price per Month (Dollars)	Code	Characteristics
General Precision Corp.	Reader	341	200 cps	NA	5-8	Photoelectric
	Read-Punch	342	200 cps	NA		
	High Speed	9410	500 cps	300	7	Used with RPC9400
	Tape System	9500	60 cps	150	7	Off-line
IBM		382	20 cps	NA		
		1054		30	6,7	Part of 1050
		1011	500 cps	NA	5-8	Use with 1401
		1017	120 cps	NA	5-8	Use with 360
Kleinschmidt		144	25 cps	NA	5	
NCR		351	10 cps	NA	7	
		360	1800 cps	NA	5-8	
		472-1	1000 cps	450		Used with 315
Olivetti	CBS	24	800 cps	NA		Tape to card
Omnidata	PTR	60	150 cps	50	5-8	
Philco		245	1000 cps	2200 (sys. price)	5,7	Part of 240 system
Potter		3277	150 cps	NA		
		909	1000 cps	NA		
RCA	Reader-Punch	321	160 cps	NA		
Sperry-Rand	Paper-Tape Reader	920	300 cps	NA	5-8	Part of subsystem
Sylvania		9460	1000 cps	NA	5-8	Part of 9400
Tally		424	60 cps	NA	5-8	
		500	1000 cps	NA		Part of series
		R-30	30 cps	NA	5-8	

315

Figure 11.15   Magnetic tape typewriters.

Manufacturer	Name	Model	Price per Month (Dollars)	Characteristics
Vanguard Data Systems	Data-scribe	MDS	150	Verification and searching 64 characters, standard codes
Control Data	Magnetic Tape Compiler	2025	NA	Collects, edits, verifies, reformats from several remote stations
IBM	MT/ST	2	185	One tape station
	MT/ST	4	243	Two tape station
	MT/ST	5	NA	Graphic-keyboard for setting type, used with MT/SC
	MT/SC		365	Magnetic tape selectric composer
	Tape Cartridge Reader	2495	350	Transfers data from tape cartridge to computer memory; operates at 400 characters per second
	Magnetic Data Inscriber	50	NA	
Mowhawk Data Sciences	Data Recorder	MDS	150	Controller $176/month
NCR	Magnetic Tape Encoder	735	150	
Sperry-Rand	Unityper II		90	
Mohawk Data Sciences	Data Recorder	1160	NA	Reads cards and accepts variable data from keyboard
Viatron	Micro Processor	System 21	40	System includes keyboard cartridge, printer, and display unit

linguistic research. The diffuse materials of economics, political science, sociology, psychology, and the other social sciences can be more effectively brought to bear on the solving of modern problems. The literature of medicine, the law, engineering, and science can be made more amenable to research than ever before."[26]

The purpose of "optical character recognition" (OCR) is to convert alpha-numeric characters or symbols directly into machine-readable code, the output being in the form of punched cards, punched paper tape, magnetic tape, or signals representing digitalized data for on-line input to a computer. The basic problem that the engineers had to solve in developing equipment for OCR was, of course, the multiplicity of fonts in which printed data occurs. As the number of characters that must be discriminated increases, different characters will be sufficiently similar to be confused, and the equipment will produce an increasingly high error rate (that is, percentage of erroneous conversions). One approach to solution of the problem represented by multiple fonts is to restrict the characters to a set that can easily be discriminated. Figure 11.16 shows several standard fonts designed specifically for reading by OCR equipment.

Optical character readers consist of three basic functional units: (1) document transport, (2) scanner, and (3) recognition unit. Feidelman offers the following block diagram of a character reader (Figure 11.17).[27]

The function of the *document transport* is to move each document to the reading station, position it properly, and move it into an "out" hopper. Transport mechanisms can be divided into two basic types, one for handling individual documents (paper sheets or cards) and the other for handling continuous rolls (cash register or adding machine tapes).

The function of the *scanner* is to convert the alpha-numeric characters, symbols, codes, or marks on a document into analog or digital electronic signals that can be analyzed by the recognition unit. Scanning techniques include mechanical disc scanners (as employed in the pioneer Farrington machines) or flying spot scanners, image dissectors, and TV pickup tubes. Optical scanning involves projecting an image of the character by reflected light to a lens system. The optical system sharpens the image and transmits it on through two intersecting slits to a photomultiplier (a tube capable of converting light patterns into electrical signals). Since the white parts of the image reflect more light than the black portions of the image, the photomultiplier essentially receives a continuous stream of "spots of light." Theoretically, if the combination of spots of light for the image of each character is different, the converted electrical signals will be different. These differences are the basis of the ability to discriminate between characters.

The *character recognition* unit accepts the signals from the scanner and compares them with a "signal library." This is a reference store and set of rules

---

[26] Wilson, Robert A., *Optical Page Reading Devices.* New York: Reinhold, 1966.

[27] Feidelman, Lawrence A., "A Survey of the Character Recognition Field," Datamation, **12** (1) (February 1966), pp 45-50, 52.

(a)

(b)

Figure 11.16 Fonts for optical character recognition. (a) ASA standard character set for optical character recognition. (b) NCR optical type font. (c) Farrington 7B type font. (d) Farrington 12L type font.

(c)

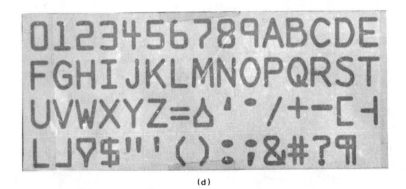

(d)

providing well-defined recognition criteria by which to decide which letter or character a given signal represents. Three methods are presently used for making this comparison:

1. *Exact Match*—requiring an absolute match with all or part of the character in the store.

2. *Best Fit*—a unique identification of the character but not necessarily absolute.

3. *Threshold*—which allows for an acceptable degree of match between the character and the store.

As might be expected, the Exact Match method is very accurate but will reject many characters as unidentifiable. The Threshold method is least accurate and may produce a high rate of ambiguous identification.

Probably the most comprehensive and recent research on optical character recognition in its application to libraries is *An Optical Character Recognition Research and Demonstration Project* (1968), undertaken by the Los Angeles County Public Library System under the sponsorship of the Council on Library

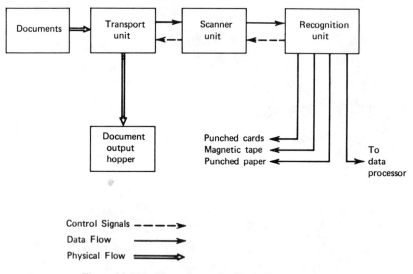

Figure 11.17   Character reader block diagram.

Resources, Inc.[28] The Los Angeles County Public Library, a leader in the development of automated book catalogs, is currently designing and implementing a computerized book catalog production system with optical character recognition as the input method.

A "Character Reader Comparison Chart" drawn up by Feidelman in 1966, summarizes the significant characteristics of representative optical and magnetic character readers in terms of the type of document feed and transport unit, document size, document speed (documents/minute), types of scanners and recognition units, type font, character set, and potential reading speed (the actual speed is dependent on the size and number of documents being read)[29] Figure 11.18 presents some of the relevant data, from his summary, augmented from other sources.[30]

On-Line Input

The ability of the computer to communicate directly with a variety of peripheral devices has led to an increasing use of "on-line" typewriters, terminals, consoles, transaction recorders, and other means of direct input to the

---

[28] *An Optical Character Recognition Research and Demonstration Project.* Los Angeles County Public Library System, June 1, 1968.

[29] Feidelman, *op. cit.*

[30] Dyer, Ralph, et al., *Optical Scanning for the Business Man.* New York: Hobbs, Dorman, and Company, 1966.

Figure 11.18 Optical character readers.

Manufacturer	Name	Model	Rate	Price per Month (Dollars)	Characteristics
Addressograph Multigraph Corporation	Optical Code Reader	9500	240 cps[a]	850-1800	Card, paper tape or magnetic tape output
		9600	10 cps	NA	Card to paper tape
		9620		NA	Card or paper tape output
Burroughs	Typed Page Reader		75 cps	NA	
Control Data		915		NA	Reads USASCSOCR
	OCR Document Reader	935		NA	Scans 3 lines from typewriter/printer
Farrington	Document Readers	ID Series	440 cps	2700-3400	Reads self check, IBM 403, 1428
	Page Readers	IP Series	280 cps	3200-4000	Reads ASA, self check, IBM 1428
	Series III	3010	440 cps	NA	Reads ASA, IBM 1428
	Series III	3020	550 cps	NA	Reads IBM 1428 E
	Series III	3030	440 cps	NA	Reads ASA, self check
	Journal Tape Reader	3040		NA	Cash register to magnetic tape
	Self punch	9SP	180 cps	NA	Reads self check numerals
General Electric	Banfont Reader	COC-5	1200 cps	NA	Reads COC-5 numeric
	DRD	200	1200 cps	NA	Reads paper
IBM	Optical Page Reader	1231	2000/hr.	430-505	Reads data sheets for 360/30
		1282	200 cps	1550	Reads 1428 numeric

Figure 11.18 (*continued*)

Manufacturer	Name	Model	Rate	Price per Month (Dollars)	Characteristics
IBM	Page Reader	1288	750 cps	5000[b]	Reads USASCSOCR
		1418	420 cps	2700-3175	Reads IBM 407
		1428	400 cps	3100-3475	Reads IBM 1428
NCR	Optical Character Reader	420-2	1664 cps	1900-	Reads into computer and off-line
Optical Scanning Corporation	Optical Scanner	25	400 doc/minute	NA	Reads check size documents
	Digitek	70		NA	Reads alphanumeric
	Digitek	100	2400 sheets/hr	NA	Scanner part of system
		288	600 cps	NA	Reads ASA
Philco	Print Reader	5820	360 cps	NA	Reads multiple fonts
	Print Reader		2000 cps	NA	Reads multiple fonts
Rabinow	RUR	3200-1	400 cps	NA	Reads numeric
	Document Reader	4500			Reads 3 alphabetic fonts
RCA		5820	1800 cps	NA	Reads RCAN-2 numeric
	Videoscan	70/251	2400 cps	NA	Reads RCAN-2
Recognition Equipment	Page Reader		2400 cps	NA	Reads multiple fonts
Sperry-Rand	Optical Scan Punch	5340	200 cps	NA	

[a]cps means characters per second.
[b]Price per month obtained by dividing purchase price by 50

computer. In this manner of operation, the peripheral equipment provides a means for both input to the computer and output from it, so that a kind of "dialogue" or "man-machine" communication can be carried on.

The significant advantages of on-line operation are: (1) the speed of response of the computer system to the input data, (2) the processing which the computer can do to aid the communication process (for example, by presenting the operator with preestablished formats to be filled in or with questions to be answered), and (3) the processing that the computer can do to check the data as it is input for consistency, accuracy, and reliability.[31]

On the other hand, on-line operation has some drawbacks. First, the equipment (including the terminals themselves, the associated buffers and controls, the communication lines, and the dedicated commitment of on-line computer time) tends to be significantly more expensive than typewriters and key-punches, and the saving in the time of the personnel is unlikely to compensate for the added costs. Second, if for some reason communication with the computer is lost, the process of input is likely to be lost as well. (This second consideration is so significant that most on-line systems must provide a facility for alternative use—a "back-up" computer, a separate manual procedure, or some other means for continuing data acquisition.) Third, on-line operation requires a computer large enough and fast enough to monitor and control the number of terminal devices which may be operative at any one time. Such a facility actually may be larger than is warranted by the processing tasks themselves. Fourth, the complexity of the input operation and related computer processing is controlled, on the one hand, by the "software" with which the computer is provided and, on the other hand, by the number of peripheral devices that must be handled at the same time. This means that, although in principal on-line operation can provide very sophisticated means of man-machine communication, it is likely to be limited to the most simple processes of data input. (Figure 10.14 listed some typical software systems for on-line input.)

The kinds of terminal equipment that can be used in an on-line system vary from typewriters to "cathode ray tube" consoles (discussed in detail in the next section). Among them are the devices listed in Figure 11.7, designed for transaction recording. Others, listed in Figure 11.19, operate like normal electric typewriters.

DISPLAYS

"Cathode ray tube" (CRT) displays are visual communication terminals designed for those applications that require direct interaction between a

[31] Damerau, Fred J., "A Technique for Computer Detection and Correction of Spelling Errors," *Communications of the ACM,* **7** (3) (March 1964), pp. 171-176.

Figure 11.19 On-line terminals

Manufacturer	Name	Model	Rate	Price per Month (Dollars)	Characteristics
Control Data		161		NA	On-line I/O typewriter
Digitronics	Photoelectric Keyboard	P K 200		NA	
	Invac Unicorn System		80 or 266 cps[a]	110[b]	Accepts paper tape or keyboard entry
Dura	Conversational Terminal	1041/1015	15 cps	NA	Accepts paper tape
Friden	Conversational Terminal	7100	20 cps	90	
IBM	Inquiry Station	838		175	Interrupts central processor; used with 650
	Inquiry Station	1407		NA	Attaches Model 3 console to obtain data
	Communications Terminal	2740	25 cps	82	Links to other 2740 terminals on 360
	Communications Terminal	2741		NA	
		2980		NA	Banking terminal used with 360/25
Mohawk Data Sciences	Data Recorder	1103 LDC	200 cps	225	
NCR	Data Communicator	735-801	200 cps		Links to computer or other 735 terminals
Tally	Send/Receive Terminal	311	200 cps.	285	Accepts punched card and paper tape
	Data Terminal	1021	200 cps.	226	Accepts cards, punched tape and magnetic tape

Figure 11.19   (*continued*)

Manufacturer	Name	Model	Rate	Price per Month (Dollars)	Characteristics
Teletype		33	10 cps	100	
		35	10 cps	100	
		37	10 cps	100	Upper and lower case
Western Union	Telex				Sends typed message after station is dialed
Mathetronics	PKB Keyboard		NA	60.00	

[a] cps means characters per second.
[b] Monthly price obtained by dividing given purchase price by 50.

computer and a person.[32-33] Information generated by the person is displayed prior to transmission to the computer so that he can make any changes that may be needed. Data transmitted from the computer is displayed to the operator immediately.

There are two major categories of CRT displays: alpha-numeric and graphic. Alpha-numeric displays show only a preestablished set of characters, usually limited to a single font and usually on predetermined lines. They are therefore comparable to upper-case typewriters, differing mainly in the speed of communication with a computer. The characters are generated on the face of the CRT by transmission of a stream of electrons (Figure 11.20). Inside the tube, in front of the electron gun, is a small circular metallic mask. The mask has tiny holes in it shaped as the letters, numbers, and symbols to be displayed. The matrix on the mask acts like a stencil and allows only a tiny beam of electrons to pass through in the form of the character desired. Any of these characters can be projected to any one of a set of positions on the phosphor screen at the front of the tube. (For example, a usual display will provide positions for 64 lines with up to 132 characters per line.) The information from the computer tells the tube to which letter the beam should be directed on the matrix and then where the formed beam should go on the screen. This beam striking the phosphor screen causes an area of the same shape to glow making that letter visible from the

[32] Luxenberg, Harold R., ed., *Display Systems.* New York: McGraw Hill, 1968.
[33] Davis, Samuel, *Computer Data Displays.* Englewood Cliffs, New Jersey: Prentice-Hall, 1969.

CHARACTRON®SHAPED BEAM TUBE

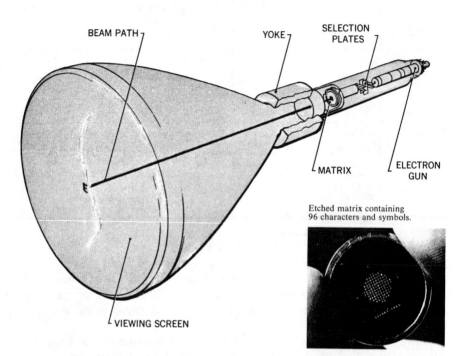

Figure 11.20   Cathode ray tube character generation.

front of the tube. The number of different characters is limited in part by the size of the matrix, with a total of about 200 separate symbols being maximum at this time.

Graphic displays, on the other hand, can present line drawings, curves, and other graphic information as well as alpha-numeric information. Desired data is generated in the CRT by tracing its outline with a stream of electrons. In this way, virtually any shape and form can be generated, including multiple fonts of alphanumeric characters (Figure 11.21). Initially, such graphic displays were developed for use in military command and control. Now, mainly because of the work of Dr. Ivan Sutherland on "Sketchpad" in the early 1960's, their use is growing rapidly. They are being used in engineering design, in simulation, in computer-aided instruction, and in graphic arts composition. Research is under way on their use in medical research, in pattern recognition, and in computer produced motion pictures.

For library applications, CRT displays have roles both as communication devices and as printing devices. Figure 11.22 gives a list of typical display units.

Invitation   COMMUNICATION   *Publication*

ECONOMY   *VERSATILITY*   Quality

ARTOGRAPHY   Standardization   TYPOGRAPHY

Γραμμα   Συμβολον   Αριϑμος

Графика   СЛОЖНОСТЬ   Фонетика

EXTENSION

   CONDENSATION   ROTATION

Inclination   ΛΕΞΙΚΟΝ   *INCLINATION*

Art   書道   Music

Meteorology   Wiffenfchaft   Astronomy

CHEMISTRY   *Electronics*   MATHEMATICS

Figure 11.21   Characters generated by the Stromberg Data Graphic SC 4060.

Direct input of data to the computer can be accomplished more easily, more rapidly, and probably more accurately with a CRT display than with any other input device. The speed of input is limited only by that of the operator and not by any mechanical equipment. The computer can check data for consistency, validity, and accuracy and can indicate immediately if there are any discrepencies.

Figure 11.23 is a schematic of the structure of an average display system. As it shows, the display unit includes a keyboard (for data entry by the operator), a memory or buffer in which the data to be displayed is held (whether input by the operator or transmitted by the computer), and the display itself.

Figure 11.22 CRT display equipment.

Manufacturer	Name	Model	Terminals per Controller	Screen Capacity	Price per Month (Dollars)
Bunker-Ramo		204		768 c	70
	BR	700		960 c	50[a]
	Data Display	2204		960 c	190
Burroughs	Input and Display System	9351		2000 c	295
Computer Communications		CC-30		800 c	122[a]
Control Data	Visual Display	210	63	1000 c	850
	Data Display	212	1	1000 c	380
	Data Display	250	6	8192 c	3330
	Digigraphics	270	3	1500 c	4950
	Digigraphics	274	1	1100 c	2225
	Data Display	280	3	8192 c	4800
A. B. Dick Company	Display	990			142[a]
	Control		16	512 c	
Digital Equipment Corp.	Programmed Buffered Display	338 339 340	1 8 8	2000	720[a] 940[a] 700[a]
General Electric	Data Net	760	32	1196	620
General Precision	Character and Vector Generator	GPL-TV	10	3000	500-900[a]
Geo Space Systems, Inc.	SAND		100+	500	1600[a]
Honeywell Computer Group	VIP	304		768	
		312		384	

Figure 11.22 (*continued*)

Manufacturer	Name	Model	Terminals per Controller	Screen Capacity	Price per Month (Dollars)
Information Display Inc.	IDIIOM		8	8192	1360[a]
	CM	10009	8	8192	1900[a]
IBM	Visual Display	1015		1200 c	NA
	Visual Display	2250		3848 c	1100
	Visual Display	2260		480 c	460
	Visual Display	2265	1		350
Philco	Color Display	D-20	1	768 c	144[a]
	Alphanumeric	D-21		1536 c	184[a]
Raytheon	DIDS	400	64	520-1040 c	157
RCA	Video Data Terminal	70/750		1080 c	190
		70/751			NA
		70/752		1080 c	190
Sanders Associates		720	12	2080 c	NA
Scientific Data Systems		7550/ 7555		2752 c	250
		7580	1	2752 c	1300
		9185	1	400 c	475
SEFAC	Mark II			400 c	460
	RANG			525 c	200
Sperry Rand	Uniscope	300		1024 c	NA
Stromberg Datagraphics	Charactron	SD 1110	24	1030 c	100[a]
Tasker Industries	Modular Display	9000	5	2000 c	900[a]
		9100	6	2000 c	NA
		9210	6		NA

[a] Derived from dividing purchase price by 50.

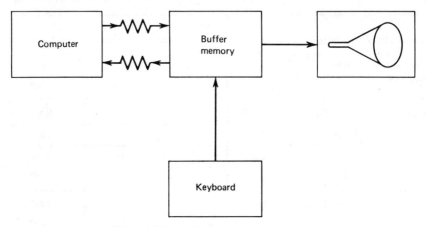

Figure 11.23   Display systems schematic.

OUTPUT

Ultimately, the results of computer operation must be printed. Historically, the printing was in small quantities of relatively small reports. Early computer printers therefore could be slow in speed and frequently were simply stripped-down versions of punched card tabulators which operated at rates of about 100 printed lines per minute (that is, 200 characters per second).

However, as the pace of computing increased, the need for higher printing rates comparably increased, until today mechanical printers in computer installations print at rates anywhere from 500 lines per minute to 2000 lines per minute (that is, about 1000 characters per second to 4000 characters per second). The result is that huge quantities of printed matter can be rapidly produced.

A great variety of such printers are available on the market, most of them as part of the complement of equipment provided by data processing manufacturers. Figure 11.24 lists a number of typical output printers.

Some of these printers operate by a direct mechanical impression. Generally, such machines print a line at a time, varying in length up to 100 to 150 characters. They normally operate at rates up to 1000 lines per minute. Most of them have the capability of producing multiple copies (up to perhaps five) through the use of carbon paper. Where more copies are required, a master can be produced that is then used in some other printing process.

Other types of output printers use styli to create individual characters from combinations of dots, lines, and other forms. These printers are primarily used in the high-speed printing of labels and other information where quality is not of primary significance.

Figure 11.24   Output printers.

Manufacturer	Name	Model	Rate	Price per Month (Dollars)	Characteristics
Anderson Nichols	Anelex	56120	900 1pm[a]	NA	120 characters per line
	Anelex	Series 5	1250 1pm.	NA	120 characters per line
Burroughs		G	900 1pm	NA	Card input 48 characters per line
	High Speed	272	1225 1pm	NA	Used with B220 series
	Line Printer	321	700 1pm	1200	120 characters per line
Computer Industries	Cope	.32	300-360 1pm	1545[b]	Part of on-line system
		.36	400-480 1pm	1750	Part of on-line system
		.38	400-480 1pm	1885	Part of on-line system
		.45	700 1pm	3380	Part of on-line system
Control Data	High Speed	501	1000 1pm	NA	136 characters per line
	Line Printer	505	500 1pm	NA	136 characters per line
		512	1200 1pm	NA	Used with CDC 6000
		1612	1000 1pm	NA	120 characters per line
IBM		716	150 1pm	NA	Used with 7094-II
		719	1000 1pm	NA	60 characters per line
		720	500 1pm	NA	120 characters per line
		1053		50	
		1403	600 1pm	900	Used with 1401

Figure 11.24 (*continued*)

Manufacturer	Name	Model	Rate	Price per Month (Dollars)	Characteristics
IBM		1404	1100 lpm		Card and paper output
		1443	240 lpm		
		2203	600 lpm		
Mohawk Data Sciences	Bufferd Line Printer	1320	300 lpm	NA	
NCR		340	600 lpm	NA	120 characters per line
		340-3	680 lpm	1425	Alpha-numeric
		344			Multiple list
Philco		151-1	900 lpm	1425	120 characters per line
		153-1	300 lpm	210	
		256	900 lpm	2340	Part of 250 system Price includes controls
RCA		70-242-1	625 lpm		132 characters per line
		70-243-2	1250 lpm		160 characters per line
	Bell Feed	70-249	600 lpm		
		333	1000 lpm		120 characters per line
Shephard Laboratories		190	900 lpm		120 characters per line
Sylvania	Printer Buffer	9441	900 lpm	3200	132 characters per line; part of 9400 system

[a] lpm means lines per minute.
[b] System prices are given for all Computer Industries, Inc. printers.

Unfortunately, the typographic quality of the output from computer printers is unsatisfactory for any large scale distribution such as a book catalog would imply. The computer field has therefore continually searched for output printing equipment with graphic arts quality. The cathode-ray tube display has provided a more than adequate answer, and today there are a number of devices for computer-controlled photocomposition that will print in multiple fonts (although photocomposition, as the general process of placing type images on photographic film or paper, dates from the 1950's when experimentation began with photocomposing machines unaided by computers).[34]

The following elements are common to CRT photocomposing machines:

1.   A matrix of characters in negative form (the template in the CRT).

2.   A light source (the beam of electrons).

3.   A lens or optical system.

4.   A magazine or other container for photographic film or paper.

5.   A method for identifying the character to be exposed (the coded data stored in the computer or on magnetic tape).

6.   A method for moving the film or paper after each line has been exposed.

7.   A method for positioning the character horizontally and vertically (the control being provided by codes from the computer or on magnetic tape).

It has been estimated that there are today over 400 installations of computer-controlled photocomposition equipment in the United States.[35] As a result, this method is now becoming increasingly important in publication of books, newspapers, and journals.[36-42] But it also has significance to mechanization in libraries.[43]

[34] Atkinson, Frank, "Cold Composition on Film or Paper," *Australian Lithographer*, February 1968.

[35] Kuney, Joseph, "Publication and Distribution of Information", Carlos A. Cuadra (ed.). in *Annual Review of Information Science and Technology*, 3, Chicago: Encyclopaedia Britannica, Inc. 1968, pp. 31-59.

[36] Duncan, John, "Advanced Computer Printing System," *Penrose Annual*, 59 (1966), pp. 258-261.

[37] Gardner, Arthur E., "Economics of Automated Printing," in Lowell H. Hattery and George P. Bush (eds.), *Automation and Electronics in Publishing*. Washington, D.C.: Spartan, 1965, pp. 123-127.

[38] Hattery, Lowell H., "Computers, Typesetting, Printing, and Publishing," in *Computer Yearbook and Directory*. Detroit, Michigan: American Data Processing, Inc., 1966, pp. 196-206.

[39] Kuney, J. H., et al, "Computer-Aided Typesetting for the Journal of Chemical Documentation," *Journal of Chemical Documentation*, 6 (February 1966), pp. 1-2.

[40] Markus, John, "State of the Art of Computers in Commercial Publishing," *American Documentation*, 17 (April 1966), pp. 76-88.

[41] "Newspaper Production: A New Approach," *Data Processing*, 7 (November/ December 1965), pp 325-330.

"Libraries and information centers are studying computer-aided typesetting", writes Barbara Markuson.[44] She points to the Deutsche Bibliothek, the National Library of Medicine, and the NASA Documentation, Inc. facility, all of which use computer-controlled photocomposition devices. For example, the prototype version of the Photon 900 AIP, called GRACE (Graphic Arts Composing Equipment), was purchased from Photon by the National Library of Medicine when MEDLARS (Medical Literature Analysis and Retrieval System) went into operation in early 1965.[45]

There have also been a number of projects to use computer controlled photocomposition equipment for printing of even more complex forms of data than multifont text. For example, both mathematical equations and chemical formulae involve nearly pictorial images; the American Mathematical Society and the Chemical Abstracts Service have each had active development programs underway for several years.[46-48]

Figure 11.25 lists some typical photocomposition equipment for computer output printing.

ANALYSIS OF COSTS

Determining the cost of converting library source data to machine-readable form by alternative methods is a laborious task. It is futile to discuss the merits and costs of alternative data collection methods without relating them to the specific areas of application (that is, cataloging, ordering, and the like), the specific requirements (for instance, character set, size of record, and organization of records), the actual range of alternatives that may be considered, and the

---

[42] Stern, Michael M., "A Look at Typesetting Computers," *The DI/AN Font Magazine,* 1 (June 1952), p. 2.

[43] Berul, Lawrence H., et al., "Output Printing for Library Mechanization," in Barbara E. Markuson (ed.) *Libraries and Automation,* Library of Congress, 1964, pp. 155-200.

[44] Markuson, Barbara, "Automation in Libraries and Information Centers," in Carlos A. Cuadra (ed.), *Annual Review of Information Science and Technology,* Vol. 2. New York: Wiley, 1967, p. 278.

[45] "Medical Library Acquires GRACE," *Library Journal,* 89 (September 1, 1964), p. 3722.

[46] *Development of Computer Aids for Tape Control of Photocomposing Machines* (Final Report on NSF Grant GN-533). Providence, Rhode Island: American Mathematical Society, January 1969.

[47] Davenport, William C., and John T. Dickman, "Computer-Based Composition at Chemical Abstracts Service," *Journal of Chemical Documentation,* 6 (November 1966), pp. 221-225.

[48] Feldman, A., "A Proposed Improvement in the Printing of Chemical Structures which Results in their Complete Computer Codes," *American Documentation,* 15 (3) (July 1964), pp. 205-209.

Figure 11.25 Card or computer controlled Photocomposition

Manufacturer	Name	Model	Character Set	Rate	Price per Month (Dollars)	Characteristics
Computer Industries	Microfilm Printer/ Plotter	CI-120			2400[c]	Magnetic tape to microfilm
California Computer Products		835			1200[c]	
Friden	Compos-O-Line			160 cps[b]	625	Card actuated camera, film output
Harris-Intertype	Fototronic			400 cps	1000	
	Fototronic	CRT	4000 c[a]	1100 cps	NA	
IBM	CRT Printer	2680			NA	Text projected on CRT device and moving roll of film
Kodak	KOM	90	NA	90000 cps	NA	Magnetic tape to microfilm
Lithoid	Compos-O-List			160 cps	625	Card actuated camera
Mergen-thaler	Linotron	505	960 c	70 cps	1000	
	Linotron	1010	264 c	10Kcps	NA	
Photon	Textmaster	713			1000[c]	
	Grace	900	226 c	300 cps	NA	16 or 35 mm film output
	Zip	901			NA	Magnetic tape input
	Textmaster	900			4000[c]	
RCA	Video-comp	70-830		6Kcps	8000	
Stromberg-Datagraphics	Output Recorder	SC4020	200 c	100Kcps	4200[c]	16 or 35 mm film output
	Output Recorder	SC4060	200 c	100Kcps	8000	16 or 35 mm film

Figure 11.25   (*continued*)

Manufacturer	Name	Model	Character Set	Rate	Price per Month (Dollars)	Characteristics
	Micromation Printer	4360			1928	Magnetic tape to microfilm output
	Document Records	SC4400	64 c	62Kcps	NA	16 or 35 mm film output
	Document Records	SC4400	64 c	90Kcps	3200	
Varityper	Fotolist	90		160 cps	370[c]	Card actuated camera
	Fotolist	270			700	

[a] c means characters.
[b] cps means characters per second.
[c] Monthly price obtained by dividing given purchase price by 50.

quantity of data to be converted. Therefore, rather than present general conclusions concerning the costs of various data-conversion methods, the following hypothetical case study illustrates an approach that might be taken. (It was adapted from the study made by the Los Angeles County Public Library.)[49]

Case Study

Consider a large public library system which desires to convert its present catalog to a computer produced book catalog. A major cost would be the huge one-time data conversion. Alternative methods must be considered.

Suppose that the size of the data file to be converted is 300,000 title records (averaging 450 characters each but with some as large as 2500 characters). They contain 20 possible types of field, many of variable length. Some fields, such as subject, may be repeated. The input character set to be used by the library consists of upper- and lower-case alpha-numeric and 18 symbols (such as punctuation). Although the library includes foreign material, diacritical marks can be removed and only the Roman alphabet is to be used.

Five basic alternatives for data conversion might be considered:

1.   Key-punching (punched cards), prooflisting (by a service bureau),

[49] *An Optical Character Recognition Research and Demonstration Project,* Los Angeles County Public Library System, June 1, 1968.

proofreading the lists, repunching corrections, and converting of cards to magnetic tape (by a service bureau).

2. Perforating punched tape, proofreading the typed sheets, perforating punched tapes for corrections, and converting the paper tape to magnetic tape (by a service bureau).

3. Typing onto magnetic tape, prooflisting (by a service bureau), proofreading the lists, typing corrections onto magnetic tape, and converting to computer processible magnetic tape (by a service bureau).

4. Typing at on-line typewriter terminals, prooflisting (by the service bureau), proofreading the lists, and retyping corrections at terminals.

5. Typing on electric typewriters with fonts specially designed for OCR, manually proofreading the typewritten sheets, retyping corrections, and optical scanning of sheets (by a service bureau) onto magnetic tape.

Figure 11.26 represents a worksheet that summarizes costs of the five alternatives, based on the equations and nominal values given in Figure 11.27. (This analysis by Los Angeles County led them to choose optical character reading of specially typed sheets, that is, alternative 5, as their means of conversion.)

Figure 11.26 Representative cost analysis (dollars).

Item	Key-punch	Paper Tape	Magnetic Tape	On-Line	OCR
Personnel					
Keying	6,000	5,575	5,575	6,000	4,620
Proofing	1,590	1,590	1,590	1,590	1,590
Equipment					
Keying	1,050	975	1,170	16,100	300
Service					
Computer listing	1,050	1,050	1,050	1,050	
Media conversation	250	725	725		2,887
Space, utilities and office furniture	372	351	351	372	331
Forms and Supplies	450	197	467	138	136
Monthy cost	10,762	10,463	10,928	25,250	9,864
Cost of conversion of 300,000 entries	258,288	251,112	262,272	606,000	236,736

[a]This assumes that all methods could utilize the same original source data (3 x 5 card). In practice, an input worksheet might be necessary for all except the OCR method. This could amount to a sizeable cost. Also it is possible that key-punch operators are not as readily available as typists.

Figure 11.27 Equations and nominal values for cost estimation.

PERSONNEL COSTS

Keying
1. (Entries/month x characters/entry + 5% (errors rekeyed)) = characters/month keyed
2. (Characters/month keyed) ÷ (keying speed x work hours x work days) = keying personnel + ½ person (supervisor) required
3. (Keying personnel x cost/month) + differential for supervisor = keying cost/month

Proofing
4. (Entries x characters/entry) + 5% (errors reproofed) = characters/month proofed
5. Characters/month proofed ÷ (proofing speed x work hours x work days) = proofing personnel + ½ person (supervisor) required
6. (Proofing personnel x cost/month) + difference for supervisor = proofing cost/month

Equipment
7. Number of keying personnel x cost/machine = equipment keying cost/month

Service
8. Records/month x 1.05 = records listed
9. Records listed x cost/record = listing cost
10. Entries/month x media conversion cost/entry = media conversion cost/month

Space etc.
11. Persons x space cost/person = space cost/month

Forms and Supplies
12. $\dfrac{\text{(Forms/entry x entries/month)}}{1000}$ + (15% x cost/month) = forms cost/month
13. Persons x supply cost/person = supply cost/month

FORMULAS FOR WORKSHEET COMPUTATIONS

Item	*Average Cost/Month*
Personnel	
Key-punch or machine operator	$425.00
Key-punch or machine operator supervisor	485.00
Typist clerk	385.00
Typist clerk supervisor	435.00
Equipment (Including Maintenance)	
Key-punch	75.00
Paper tape typewriter	75.00
Magnetic tape writer	90.00
Electric pinfeed typewriters	25.00
On-line keyboard + computer time, line costs, etc.	1,150.00

Service	
Computer listing—200 lpm upper/lower case printer	.08/entry

338

Figure 11.27   (*continued*)

Service *(continued)*

Media conversion—700 cpm to tape	.02/entry
Media conversion—magnetic tape writer to computer tape	.05/entry
Media conversion—paper tape to magnetic tape	.05/entry
OCR to magnetic tape	.22/entry

Space, Utilities

Office furniture	20.50/month/person

Forms and Supplies

Tabulator cards	2.00/m
Typewriter sheets (8½ x 11 pinfeed)	8.00/m
Perforated typewriter sheets + tape	12.00/m
Magnetic tape	30.00/m entries
Miscellaneous supplies	1.00/month/person

Other Factors

Typing speed (library data)	4,250 chars./hr.
Keypunching speed (library data)	3,600 chars./hr.
Tape writing or perforating	3,850 chars./hr.
On-line typing	3,600 chars./hr.
Proof Reading	13,500 chars./hr.
Average work hours/person/day	6
Average work days/month/person	20
Entries to be prepared/month	12,500
Rekeying—typing, etc. of errors found in proofing	5% of original number keystrokes
Characters/entry (average)	450
Supervisor time spent in data preparation	50%

Notes:

1. Personnel cost does not include fringe benefits.
2. Typewriter rental of $25.00/month is for IBM pin-feed Selectrics.
3. Computer listing and card to tape conversion assumes an IBM 360/30 configuration with 1403N1 printer are average and setup is assumed in speeds indicated.
4. Space utilities and office furniture cost/person/month was calculated as follows:

60 sq ft/person @ .25/ft =	$15.00
Utilities/person =	2.00
Office furniture (cost of chair, desk, or file cabinet, etc., amortized over five years)	3.50
	——
	$20.50

5. Miscellaneous supplies/person includes ribbons, writing tools, correction materials, etc.

Suggested Reading

Among the references in the chapter, there are two that provide especially good coverage of the major issues:

Cuadra, Carlos A., *Annual Review of Information Science and Technology*, Vol. 1 and Vol. 2, New York: Wiley, 1966 and 1967; Vol. 3, Vol. 4, and Vol. 5, Chicago: Encyclopedia Brittanica, 1968, 1969, and 1970.
Luxenberg, Harold R. (ed.), *Display Systems. New York: McGraw Hill, 1968.*

Chapter 12

STORAGE OF DATA

Data must be stored in a form that is easily and rapidly accessible to the data-processing equipment that will operate on it. In manual systems, data are stored as typed or printed information on cards and pages. But, although these printed forms of data storage may be very suitable for manual systems, they are space consuming and generally unsuitable for mechanized handling.

A crucial contribution to the entire effort to mechanize library operations has, therefore, been the development of new storage media and new methods for recording digital data and document images. Some of these developments have been among the most spectacular technological advances in modern engineering. Some have been prosaic improvements in existing methods. The results, in any event, have provided a great variety of methods for storing all forms of data at high density and with rapid mechanical accessibility. In particular, the great mass of data that the computer must analyze can be readily available for processing or for display and output.

In this chapter, we describe the developments in data storage in order to provide a picture of the many available methods and to illustrate the criteria significant in the evaluation of them. In each case, the method involves a storage medium, a means' of recording coded or image information on it, and an associated set of equipment. The equipment to be considered has been grouped as follows:

1. *Equipment for Manual Storage*

> Printed pages
> Edge notched cards
> Punched cards

2. *Equipment for Magnetic Storage*

         Magnetic tapes
         Magnetic drums
         Magnetic disks
         Magnetic strips

3. *Equipment for Photographic Storage*

         Microfilm and cartridge film
         Microfiche and other photographic cards
         Photographic strips

CRITERIA FOR EVALUATION

Before considering these individual means of data storage in detail, however, it is important to discuss in general terms the criteria significant in evaluation of them. Basically, there are five relevant issues: (1) the physical nature of the storage medium and its handling and filing equipment; (2) qualitative characteristics of the means for recording (ease of change of stored data, capability for storage of images, and the like); (3) quantitative characteristics (data capacities, access times, and data transfer rates); (4) methods for file organization; and (5) costs.

Physical Nature of Storage Medium

Storage media come in a variety of shapes and sizes; they use a variety of methods of recording; they differ in their inherent capacity for data storage; and they react differently to environment and use. When the physical nature of the storage medium is important in its evaluation, we shall discuss the effects.

Qualitative Nature

Some storage media are essentially "read only," providing little or no capability to change data once it has been recorded; other media are easily changeable. Some media record images; others, only digital data. Some media provide capability only for sequential access to the data recorded on them; others allow for direct access, without scanning over unwanted data. Each of these qualitative differences affects the ways in which storage media will be used, and we shall therefore consider their influence on the usage of each medium discussed.

Quantitative Characteristics

The quantitative characteristics of storage media are both the easiest to define and the most useful for comparative evaluation.

Data capacity is simply the number of images (for image storage) or characters (for digital storage) that can be recorded on the medium. Basically, it is determined by the size of the medium and the density of recording, but it is greatly affected by the methods used for file organization. For this reason, as discussed below, we shall pay especial attention to the effects of file organization on data capacity.

Access time is simply the time required by the handling equipment to get to the position to read specific data desired, wherever it may be located. It is usually expressed as an average, under the assumption that desired data is located randomly in the file; if requests are batched and sequenced in file order, of course, the access time will usually be much less. This means that the effects of file organization are again important.

Data transfer rate is simply the maximum rate at which data can be transferred from the storage medium to the computer. It is usually expressed in terms of the "number of characters per second." It must be recognized, however, that this maximum rate can be a deceptive figure, since the effective reading rate will also be greatly affected by the file organization.

To provide a basis for rough comparison of these quantitative characteristics across the variety of storage media, it is useful to choose a standard file as a unit of measure. A four-drawer file cabinet will usually store about 10,000 type-written 8½ x 11 inch pieces of paper in a space of 10 cubic feet. This is a file of about 15 million characters, and it will be used as the standard file of comparison.

Methods of File Organization

Because of the great effect of file organization on the quantitative characteristics of storage media, it is useful to review some of the considerations relevant to it.

File Sequencing A file of records may be placed in random sequence. It must then be searched sequentially each time a record is needed. As the quantity of material increases, therefore, one is forced either to establish some kind of preferred filing sequence or to develop indexes that describe where desired items are to be found, and usually one does both. Typically, for example, one field of each record will be regarded as the sort field—the "identifier" for purposes of file sequencing. Alternatively, the file could be sequenced in order of activity, with frequently used items located so as to be more accessible. In discussing each of the storage media, the methods for sorting into file sequence will be considered, and estimates will be made of the time required for each method.

Indexing. Several storage media provide capability for addressed, direct access to individual physical records. To take advantage of this capability, indexes must be established and used to determine the address at which a desired record is stored. The structure of these indexes constitutes a separate problem in file organization. The effects of different kinds of indexes vary so widely that no general principles can be defined. However, although no specific comments can be made about the relation between indexing and "direct access times," it probably represents the most important problem in file organization.

Record Blocking. Rarely are "logical records" of the same size as physical records. Sometimes they are larger and must be stored in several physical records. (For example, catalog records are usually much longer than a punched card and must be stored in several of them.) In other cases, they are shorter than the physical record, and several logical records must be stored in a "block," which will be recorded and read as a complete group. Where record blocking has a significant effect on quantitative characteristics, it will be discussed.

Costs

The costs associated with data storage can be categorized into four groups: (1) costs to store the file (that is, the cost of the storage medium itself and of the processing required to record the data in the file), (2) costs to maintain the file (the cost of sorting transactions and processing them against the file), (3) costs to have the file available for direct access, and (4) the costs to process a request against the file (the cost of processing and search time allocable to a search request). For each kind of storage medium, estimates will be provided for each of these costs.

Figure of Merit

It is frequently convenient to establish a "figure of merit" by which to obtain a gross evaluation of the combined effects of the quantitative criteria. One figure of merit that is appropriate to storage media is N/CT—where N is the capacity (in bits) of the storage unit, C is its cost (in dollars per month), and T is the average access time (under a given file organization and processing system).[1]

Summary

Figures 12.1 to 12.3 provide a summary of these general characteristics for each kind of storage medium. Subsequent sections will discuss each of them.

---

[1] Becker, Joseph, and R. M. Hayes, *Information Storage and Retrieval: Tools, Elements, Theories.* New York: John Wiley, 1963, Chapter 15.

Figure 12.1 Summary of general characteristics of files.

Medium	General Evaluation and Trends	Physical Nature
Printed pages	Books and other printed forms will be with us for many decades (despite McLuhan's claims).	Typically 8½ x 11 inch pages. Of varying life and stability.
Edge-notched cards	Useful up to 10,000 cards, especially for personal files.	Typically 4 x 6 inch cards with notches around edges. Of varying life and stability.
Punched cards	Primary use for transaction recording. Useful up to 50,000 cards for transaction files, tub files.	3 ¼ x 7 ⅜ inch card with either rectangular or round holes. Able to stand hard use for long life.
Magnetic tape	Primary file medium for computer. Being replaced by disks for direct access processing.	Usually ½ inch wide by 2400 ft long. Subject to wear and environment effects (such as dust).
Magnetic drums	Generally limited to small files. Being replaced by disks in most uses.	Typically 1 ft in diameter by 3 ft long. Requires close control of environment.
Magnetic disks	Increasingly important as primary storage medium for direct access processes.	Typically 2 ft in diameter. Requires close control of environment.
Magnetic strips and cards	Will become increasingly important for very large digital file storage.	Typically 3 inches wide by 14 inches long. Requires close control of environment.
Microfilm	Very valuable for large volume, compact storage. Cartridge film is becoming widely used.	Typically 16 mm by 100 ft. Sensitive to temperature changes and physical damage.
Microfiche and other cards	Increasing use in publication.	Typically 4 x 6 inches transparency on heavy film stock.
Photographic strips	Extremely useful for "read only," very large master files. Will be a primary medium for distribution of digital data bases.	Still under development.

Figure 12.1   (*continued*)

Medium	Easily Changeable	Image	File Organization	Capacity
Printed pages	No	Yes	Indexed, sequential.	1500 Characters on 8 ½ x 11 inch page.
Edge-notched cards	No	Yes	Indexed, random.	40 characters (digital) on 4 x 6 inch card.
Punched cards	No	Yes	Indexed, sequential (to card of 80 characters).	80 characters on 3 x 7 inch card.
Magnetic tape	Yes	Yes	Sequential (in blocks of typically 2000 characters).	20×10^6 characters on 2400 ft reel
Magnetic drums	Yes	No	Indexed (to words of about 10 characters).	10^6 characters on typical small drum
Magnetic discs	Yes	Yes	Indexed (to sectors of 100-200 characters).	5×10^6 characters on small Disk-Pack up to 20×10^6.
Magnetic strips and cards	Yes	No	Indexed (to segments of about 2000 characters).	4×10^8 characters on Data Cell.
Microfilm	No	Yes	Sequential.	3000 frames on 100 ft cartridge.
Microfiche and other cards	No	Yes	Indexed, sequential.	60 (or 72) frames 4 x 6 inch (COSATI Standard)
Photographic strips	No	Yes	Indexed.	10^6 bits per square inch.

EQUIPMENT FOR MANUAL FILES

Although nominally outside the scope of this book, manual files provide a useful bench mark for comparison with mechanized files. Furthermore, many mechanized systems depend on the use of manual files for some part of their

Figure 12.2   Example of 10,000 pages.

Medium	Access Time to 1 of 10,000 Pages	Space for 10,000 Pages	Reading Rate
Printed pages	60 sec (in file cabinet)	10 cu ft (in file cabinet)	100 characters/second (by person)
Edge-notched cards	30 sec (by needling)		
Punched cards	10 sec (in tub file)	30 cu ft (in tub file)	1000 characters/second
Magnetic tape	100 sec	1 cu ft (one reel)	100,000 characters/second
Magnetic drums	.015 sec		10,000 characters/second
Magnetic disks	.03 sec	3 cu ft (one disk pack)	30,000 characters/second
Magnetic strips and cards	.25 sec	1 cu ft	100,000 characters/second
Microfilm	3 sec	.03 cu ft	100 characters/second
Microfiche and other cards	.5 sec	.03 cu ft	100 characters/second
Photographic strips	.25 sec	?	?

operation. (For example, a standard system for serial record control uses a punched-card "tub-file" for storage of cards describing serial issues that are expected to arrive. They must be interfiled and later found when issues arrive.) For these reasons, we first consider essentially manual files—printed pages, edge-notched cards, and punched (EAM) cards.

Printed Pages

The physical nature or qualitative characteristics of printed pages, are familiar to everyone.

Figure 12.3   Representative costs (dollars).

Medium	Cost of Medium	Cost to Store 10,000 Pages	Cost to Have 10,000 Pages Available	Cost/Access to 1 Page in 10,000	Cost to Read 1 Page
Printed pages		$40-50		.05-.10/ Access (person)	.02- .05 (person)
Edge-notched cards	5-15/ 1000 cards			.02-.05/ Access (person)	
Punched cards	1- 2/ 1000 cards	200-400	50/mo. (tub file)	.01-.02/ Access (person)	
Magnetic tape	40-60 per reel	50-60	1000/mo. per handler	.40/ Access (computer)	.003 (computer)
Magnetic drums	Included in cost of availability			.003/ Access (computer)	.003 (computer)
Magnetic disks	500-700/ disk pack	1000	2000/mo. per handler	.003/ Access (computer)	.003 (computer)
Magnetic strips and cards	NA		2000/mo. per handler	.003/ Access (computer)	.003 (computer)
Microfilm	6/ 100 ft cartridge	24	4/mo. (viewer)	.01-.02/ Access (person)	.02- .05 (person)
Microfiche and other cards	.10/fiche	20	4/mo.	.005-.010/ Access (person)	.02- .05 (person)
Photographic strips	NA	NA	NA	NA	NA

Quantitative Characteristics. These are probably also familiar to everyone, but it is useful to record some representative data. For example, a double-spaced 8½ x 11 inch typewritten page will normally contain about 1500 characters (counting spaces between words and punctuation marks); a typical 6 x 9 inch printed page will contain about twice that, or 3000 characters; a 3 x 5 inch catalog card can contain up to 500 characters. Direct access (by a person) to a random page within a file of 10,000 typewritten pages (15,000,000 characters), will normally take about 1 minute. He can then read such a record at a rate of, at most, 100 characters per second.

File cabinets for typewritten pages are about 15 to 18 inches wide, 30 inches deep, and 60 inches high. To provide room for drawers to be extended, they require 7 square feet of floor space. They can contain up to 15,000 8½ x 11 inch sheets of paper or 30,000 3 x 5 inch cards (allowing space for work and expansion in drawers).

A number of manufacturers have developed mechanical devices to speed up the access to individual printed records. For comparison, these have been listed in Figure 12.4. Typically, they provide capacity for 15 million characters

Figure 12.4　Equipment for storage of manual files
(including punched cards)

Manufacturer	Name	Model	Cost (Dollars)	Capacity	Access Time
	Card cabinets			30,000 cards	
	File cabinets	4 drawer		15,000 sheets	
Bell & Howell	Microfilm cabinets	1220A		408 reels 35 mm film/ 600 reels 16 mm film	
		1222A		612 reels 35 mm film/ 900 reels 16 mm film	
Diebold	Power shelf	12 shelf	1580		3 sec to a shelf
	Power shelf	16 shelf	2990		3 sec to a shelf
		SD500		6×10^6 microfiche	8 sec
Mosler		Various			

Figure 12.4   (*continued*)

Manufacturer	Name	Model	Cost (Dollars)	Capacity	Access Time
Sperry Rand	Kardex	Various			
	Lek-triever	I		160,000 sheets	6 sec
	Lek-triever	III		460,000 6 x 4 cards	6 sec
	Kard-Veyer			16,000 8 x 5 cards	3 sec
	Check-veyer			.5 x 10^6 checks	3 sec
	Select-A-Matic			18,000 references	3.5 sec
	Aristocrat Kardex			5 x 1 ¾ to 11 x 9, 305-2530 pockets	
	Robot Kardex	Visible Record Cabinet		4000 records	4 sec
	Kolect-A-Matic trays				
Wright Line	Gold Star File			12,000 cards	

(usually stored on cards), with mechanical access time of 3 seconds (to which must be added the time taken by the operator to scan cards in a tray). However, some units will store over 2.5 billion characters, with mechanical access time of 6 seconds.[2]

File Organization. Methods for organization of manual files are also very familiar. They are almost always organized in a prescribed sequence (alphabetically by name, for example). Frequently, "logical records" will be recorded on many physical records (as in a dossier file) and stored in file folders. Visual guides or tabs are used to assist in finding desired groups of physical records. A

[2] Meeks, Bertha M., *Filing and Records Management.* New York: Ronald Press, 1964.

normal rule of thumb is "one guide card for every 40 to 50 data cards."[3,4] Cross indexes are very frequent. (The card catalog in the library, for example, represents a cross index to the collection of books, with the call number serving as the address for direct access.)

Costs. The cost of paper as a storage medium is not as low as most people think. Ten thousand sheets of 8½ x 11 inch paper, capable of storing 15 million characters, will cost about $40 to $50. As we shall see later, this is comparable to the cost of other storage media. The costs to maintain a manual file are basically the costs of personnel time to sort transactions and merge them into the file. Estimates of these times are remarkably hard to find. Figure 12.5 provides a chart of some representative times as a function of the number of transactions to be sorted and the size of the file into which they are to be merged.

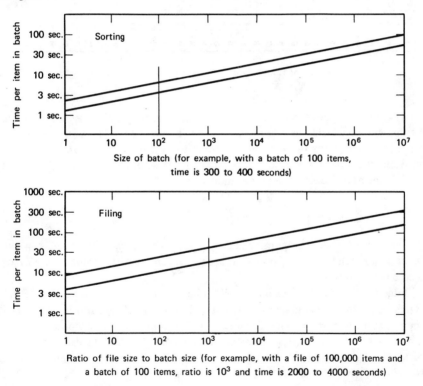

Figure 12.5   Manual sorting and filing rates (3 x 5 catalog cards).

[3] Odell, M. K., and E. P. Strong, *Records Management and Filing Operations.* New York: McGraw-Hill, 1947.

[4] *How to Measure Filing Costs and Efficiency,* Remington Rand.

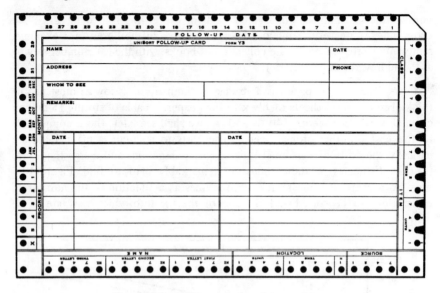

Figure 12.6   Edge-notched card (example).

The costs to have the file available for access are simply the costs of the filing equipment in which the records are stored (Figure 12.3). The costs to consult the file are those for the time of personnel to obtain a record from the file. To provide an approximate means of comparison, this has been estimated in Figure 12.3 in terms of a clerk at $400 per month.

Edge-Notched Cards

On edge-notched cards, information is represented by binary codes in the form of a notch (or lack of notch) at each of specific positions along the edge of a card (see Figure 12.6).

Edge-notched cards were the subject of an intensive review prepared by Felix Reichman.[5] In it he enumerated the many different kinds of cards in use, traced their historical development, discussed several applications, and described the advantages and disadvantages of each. Appended to his text is a list of suppliers of marginal punched cards throughout the world, which constitutes an excellent roundup of what is available in the field (see Figure 12.7).

Qualitative Characteristics. As Figure 12.6 shows, edge-notched cards can

[5] Reichman, Felix, "Notched Cards," in Ralph R. Shaw, ed., *State of the Library Art.* New Brunswick, New Jersey: Graduate School of Library Service, Rutgers University, 1961. Volume 4, Part 1, pp. 9-54.

Figure 12.7   Edge-notched card systems.

Manufacturer	Card Name	Cost (Dollars)	Comments
E-Z Sort Systems	E-Z Sort	NA	366 position
Royal McBee Co.	Keysort	20-40/ 1000 cards	250 cards are handled without disturbing the file order.
Zator Co.	Zatocard	15/1000 cards	Pilot holes, use printed marks.
Todd Co. Division Burroughs	Unisort System	NA	
Superior Business Machines, Inc.	Flexisort System	NA	
Arizona Tool & Dye Co.	Needlesort System	NA	
Practa Data-Card System	Practa Data-Card	36-50/ 1000	Folded paper with 21 notches in the centerfold. Plastic tab. 34 coding positions for the loops. Cards may be recorded by removing and repositioning the tags
Acme Visible Records, Inc.	Electrofile	60-68/ 1000	

Source. Based primarily on C. Bourne, *Methods of Information Handling.* New York: Wiley, 1963.

easily accommodate both image data (printed on the body of the cards) and binary coded digital data in the form of notches. Neither form of data, however, can be changed easily. (Gummed tabs can be used to cover up previously notched codes, but the process is cumbersome and hardly represents "erasability.")

Quantitative Characteristics. Notches can be recorded at a density of four or five per inch. The digital capacity of a card is therefore determined by the card's circumference. A representative figure, using a four or five bit code, might be 20 to 30 characters of binary coded data. This technique of recording is therefore inherently of low density, and the amount of data that can be recorded on an individual card in this way is relatively small. Problems of efficient coding of the

index data required for access have therefore been important. Several manufacturers have developed coding systems to use the limited space for index storage
efficiently—for instance, the McBee Key-Sort system, the E-Z Sort system, and
the Zator system of Calvin Mooers.

The method for access to individual cards involves inserting needles through
the prepunched holes at notch positions defining characters of interest; the cards
that have been notched at those positions will not be held on the needle. As a
result an entire file of cards can be simultaneously interrogated, and the
notched codes on each card compared with search criteria. In addition, and of
even more fundamental importance, the technique of interrogation not only
locates the desired card but allows for its physical extraction. In a very real
sense, therefore, the technique of edge notching represents a most powerful one;
devices have appeared that to a significant extent have mechanized the concepts
of edge notching (see the Diebold "Selectriever" and the NCR CRAM).

On the other hand, the manual operation of threading needles through decks
of cards is tedious and, as the size of the file gets large, very time-consuming. It
has been said by several authors that a realistic upper limit for files of
edge-notched cards is approximately 10,000.[6] Up to that limit, however, there
are some significant advantages in the ease with which these files can be
handled.[7]

File Organization. Because the notches on the cards provide the means for
indexing and direct access, these files can be arranged in random order. Usually,
however, some item of data recorded on the face of the card will be used for file
sequencing. For example, where edge-notched cards are used in a circulation
system, they will be filed in "call-number" sequence, for easy interrogation as to
the location of a desired book. The notches will be used to record "due date,"
for subsequent retrieval of overdue books.

Costs. Figure 12.7 includes data on the cost of cards and systems provided by
the various manufacturers. Other costs are primarily determined from clerical
time of personnel.

Electronic Accounting Machine (EAM) Punched Cards

Mechanized electronic accounting machine systems use punched cards as their
basic means of data storage. The punched card has therefore been most useful in
business data processing and as a preliminary stage in the development of
computer-based library systems. However, it appears to be unsuitable for any

---

[6] Schultz, Claire K., "Limits of Mechanization for Small Applications," ADI Conference, Lehigh University, Bethlehem, Pa., October 22-24, 1959.

[7] McGaw, Howard F., *Marginal Punched Cards.* New York: Scarecrow, 1952.

large scale storage of library data. Fundamentally, its density of storage is too low; it is not erasable, so that information can be changed only by replacing cards; and its information transfer rate is too slow. Even in business data processing, the punched card is being increasingly replaced by magnetic tape as the storage medium for files. However, punched cards will continue to find application in the field of transaction recording, where unit records are of predominant importance.

Physical Form. The physical form and general characteristics of punched (EAM) cards have been described in Chapter 11.

Qualitative Characteristics. Punched cards are usually regarded as media for storage of digital data, but they can be used to record image data—on the face of the card or, as described later in this chapter, as microimages placed in apertures. Neither form is easily changed, and the entire card must be replaced if it is to be updated. The fact that the card is a "unit record" has probably been its most significant qualitative characteristic. It means that cards can be easily sorted, interfiled, removed, and directly accessed without looking at other cards. As a result, punched cards have significant advantages for use in systems that combine machine operations with manual ones.

Quantitative Characteristics. However, as we have pointed out, the quantitative characteristics of punched cards—low storage capacity, low data transfer rate, and slow mechanical access—preclude their use as file media in large scale computer systems.

File Organization. Most punched card files will be stored in a defined sequence, according to a particular field of the card. To put cards in this sequence, they will be sorted into order and then merged with the existing file. The rates for the usual method of doing so are dependent on the number of cards to be sorted and merged and on the number of columns in the field for sequencing (Figure 12.8).

Costs. Punched cards are relatively expensive media for recording digital data. For example, to provide some perspective, consider the standard file of 10,000 typewritten pages (that is, 15 million characters). Recording this much data would probably require at least 200,000 punched cards, at a cost of about $300 (in contrast to the cost of $40 to $50 for the typewritten pages themselves).

The costs for maintaining a file of punched cards depend on whether mechanical or manual card handling is used. Figure 12.8 provides the basis for estimating the cost of mechanical methods; Figure 12.5 provides the basis for estimating the cost of manual methods. The storage of that many punched cards, available for access, would require a unit like those listed in Figure 12.4. The cost for direct access to a desired record is largely the time of clerical personnel, and is comparable to that for other manual files.

Figure 12.8   Punched card sorting estimates.

Parameters
n = number of cards to be sorted
d = number of digits in sort field
t = time for transport of a single card

Equation
$T = ndt$

For example
n = 10,000
d = 10 decimal digits
t = .060 sec

$T = 10^4 \times 10 \times .06 = 6000$ sec

MAGNETIC RECORDING

The need for a high-density storage medium that would provide a high information transfer rate has been a driving force in the data processing business. Magnetic recording was recognized at a very early date as the most likely to provide an effective answer. The recording of information in magnetic form has therefore been a key part of the entire development of electronic data processing equipment.[8-11]

Method of Recording

Magnetic recording is based on the fundamental relations between magnetism and electricity (Figure 12.9).[12] Thus, if an electrical current is passed through a wire wrapped around a small "u" shaped bar (called a "record head"), a magnetic field will be created at the "gap" in the writing head, which can be used to fix the magnetic state in a magnetizable surface. On the other hand, if a magnetized medium is passed by a similar "u" shaped bar (now called a "reproduce head"), an electrical current will be generated in the wire. On this basic relationship, the entire field of magnetic recording has developed, including that of audio signals, analog data, digital information, and video pictures.

[8] Gregory, R. H., and R. L. Van Horn, *Automatic Data Processing Systems: Principles and Procedures.* Belmont, California: Wadsworth, 1963. Chapter 5 and Chapter 7.

[9] Huskey, H. D., and G. A. Korn, *Computer Handbook.* New York: McGraw-Hill, 1962, Section 18.

[10] Richards, R. K., *Digital Computer Components and Circuits.* New York: Van Nostrand, 1957. Chapter 7.

[11] Pear, Charles B., *Magnetic Recording in Science and Industry.* New York: Reinhold, 1967.

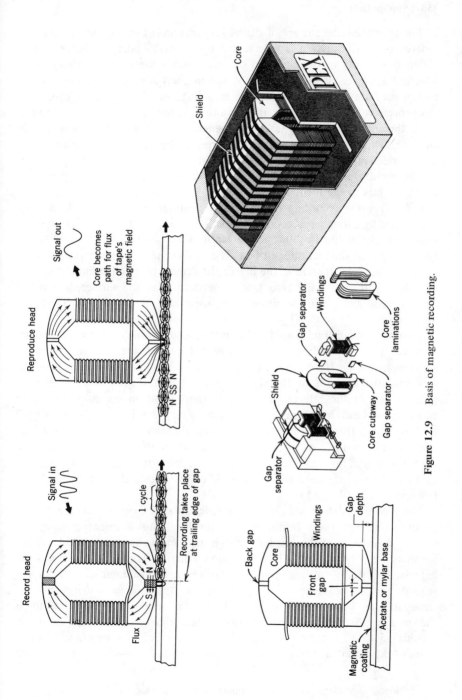

Reproduce head

Signal out

Core becomes path for flux of tape's magnetic field

Record head

Signal in

1 cycle

Recording takes place at trailing edge of gap

Flux

N SS N

S N

Shield

Core

Gap separator

Windings

Core laminations

Core cutaway

Gap separator

Gap separator

Back gap

Windings

Core

Gap depth

Front gap

Magnetic coating

Acetate or mylar base

Figure 12.9 Basis of magnetic recording.

357

For generating the storage of digital information in this way, the appropriate binary coded information is represented by a corresponding sequence of two different currents in the electrical current through the wire. The result is an identical sequence of magnetic fields, and magnetically polarized spots on the storage medium as it moves under the recording head. In the reading operation, the process is reversed and, as the recording medium passes under the reading head, the succession of magnetic spots generates a corresponding succession of currents in the wire. These are then interpreted by the logical circuitry as the binary coded representation of the stored data.

The density at which the binary coded data can be stored is described in terms of "bits to the inch," in the direction of recording, and "channels to the inch," across the recording medium. The densities possible in each case are determined by a number of considerations. The most fundamental of these is the basic geometry defined by the size of gap in the reading head and the distance from the gap to the recording surface. The smaller these two distances, the finer the resolution and, therefore, the higher the density possible; in fact, "contact" recording, with essentially zero spacing between head and surface, is standard for magnetic tape, and densities of perhaps 800 bits to the inch are not uncommon.

Another fundamental consideration is the speed at which the storage medium is moved past the reading head; the higher the speed, the stronger the signal generated, and therefore the better the resolution possible. This results from the fact that the strength of the signal generated in a reading head is directly proportional to the rate at which the magnetic field on the storage medium passes by the head. In general, the signal level is on the order of perhaps 20/1000 of 1 volt, and therefore the signal is at best difficult to distinguish from the background "noise" in the electrical circuit itself. At low speeds and correspondingly low voltages, dust particles, imperfections in the magnetic medium, and other sources of error could easily obscure the signal completely (Figures 12.10 and 12.11).

For recording data other than digital (such as audio, video, and other analog information), the same techniques are involved, but different measures of storage density must be used (although fundamentally even digital storage densities must be considered in the same light).[12] These considerations are expressed in terms of the available "bandwidth" measured in "cycles per second," which combine in a single measure the storage density and the transport rate. Typical audio magnetic tape recording provides a band width on the order of 20,000 cycles per second; present video magnetic tape recording provides 5 to 10 million cycles per second. Measured in somewhat the same framework, digital magnetic tape recording presently provides up to 150,000

[12] Videofile—A Micro Records Tool, Ampex Corporation, August 20, 1964.

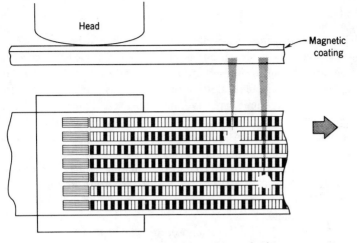

Figure 12.10   Effects of dust and imperfections.

bits per second from each channel, which can be considered as the equivalent of perhaps 500,000 cycles per second.

In the following pages, a number of forms of magnetic storage media will be discussed: tapes, drums, disks, cards, and strips.[13] They differ from each other significantly in their quantitative characteristics of capacity, access time, and reading rate. Perhaps the most significant issue in their use is that of file organization.

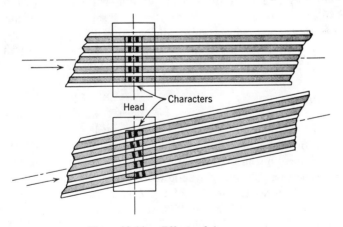

Figure 12.11   Effects of skew.

[13] Looney, Duncan H., "Magnetic Devices for Digital Computers," *Datamation,* 7 (8) (August 1961), 51-55.

The Issue of File Organization

Each of the magnetic storage systems described below represents a compromise between the problems and advantages, on the one hand, of scanning (or sequential access) and, on the other, of indexing (or direct access). In this sense, they represent various points along a spectrum. Thus, tapes are at one end of the spectrum, with a large unit capacity, and a long scan time (perhaps 25,000,000 characters requiring an average access time, by scan, of 100 seconds). The strip (for example, Data Cell, RACE, and CRAM) systems substitute some degree of direct access and provide capability for scanning a smaller, but still large, block of data (on the order of 100,000 characters requiring perhaps ½ second of access time and scanning time). At the far end of the spectrum are the disks and drum memories, which provide quite rapid direct access to small blocks of data (perhaps 100 characters).

However, although all of these approaches can be regarded as different points in a spectrum, to do so hides some significant qualitative differences in the way they are used. This is particularly confirmed by consideration of "activity" organized files. The particular range of parameters involved with strips has made evident the time and cost advantages in fitting the file organization to the statistical character of usage. That is, in these approaches the time for getting to a block of data and scanning it is small enough (unlike magnetic tape) that random access methods can be reasonably considered, but large enough (unlike magnetic disks) so that the time in doing so cannot be ignored.

Activity organization therefore attempts to reduce the average scan time in an indexed block by taking advantage of the existing patterns of record reference. Where a small percentage of records represents a large percentage of the activity, the average access time will be substantially reduced by placing those records where they will be readily accessible. This approach provides significant insight into the entire theoretical foundation of file organization.

Magnetic Tape

Physical Form. Magnetic tape represents a very large capacity file storage medium. Information is stored on magnetic tape in channels, much the same as with punched tape, but in magnetic form so that it can be erased and stored at much higher densities. Present magnetic tapes generally have 9 channels across a ½ inch tape and store at a density of 500 bits or more to the inch, utilizing contact recording. A typical reel of 2400 ft of magnetic tape can, in principle, contain over 200 or 300 million bits of information, the equivalent of 20 to 30 million alphabetic characters. Figure 12.12 summarizes the characteristics of typical magnetic tape units.[14]

[14] "Directory of Magnetic Tapes," *Systems, The Magazine of Management Methods,* September/October 1963.

Figure 12.12 Magnetic tapes.

Manufacturer	Name	Model	Price per Month (Dollars)	Capacity[a]	Read[b] Rate
Ampex	Videotape		4,000	5.4×10^6 pages	
Burroughs		9381	720	5.7×10^6c	9 kcps
		9382	880	5.7×10^6c	9 kcps
		B421	560	5.7×10^6c	18 kcps
		B422	640	5.7×10^6c	24 kcps
		B423	396	5.7×10^6c	24 kcps
		B425	680	5.7×10^6c	18 kcps
Control Data		601	240	5.7×10^6c	7.5 kcps
		604	504	5.7×10^6c	15 kcps
		607	736	5.7×10^6c	30 kcps
		626	920	23×10^6c	240 kcps
GE		200	244	5.7×10^6c	7.5 kcps
		300	336	5.7×10^6c	7.5 kcps
		402	404	5.7×10^6c	20 kcps
		492	624	5.7×10^6c	40 kcps
		680	680	5.7×10^6c	15 kcps
		690	824	5.7×10^6c	15 kcps
Datamec		2020	NA	5.7×10^6c	9 kcps
		3030	NA	5.7×10^6c	15 kcps
Honeywell		4130	300	5.7×10^6c	7.2 kcps
		4140	464	5.7×10^6c	16 kcps
IBM		2401-16	1080-1400	23×10^6c	30 kcps
		2415-16	620-1660	23×10^6c	15 kcps
		2402	840	46×10^6c	320 kcps
		7370	380	5.7×10^6c	7.2 kcps
		7335	560	16×10^6c	20 kcps
		7330	380	5.7×10^6c	15 kcps

Figure 12.12 (*continued*)

Manufacturer	Name	Model	Price per Month (Dollars)	Capacity [a]	Read[b] Rate
Midwestern		4000	480	$5.7 \times 10^6 c$	15 kcps
		4700.	320-608	$5;7 \times 10^6 c$	15 kcps
		4800	320-640	$5.7 \times 10^6 c$	15 kcps
NCR		332-204	560	$5.7 \times 10^6 c$	24 kcps
		333-101, 102	780, 660	$5.7 \times 10^6 c$	83 kcps 30 kcps
		334-103, 104	240 180	$5.7 \times 10^6 c$	12 kcps
		334-131, 132	320 240	$5.7 \times 10^6 c$	12 kcps
Potter		906 Mark II	NA	$5.7 \times 10^6 c$	24 kcps
		MT	NA	$5.7 \times 10^6 c$	15 kcps
		SC	NA	$5.7 \times 10^6 c$	30 kcps
RCA		581	435	$9.6 \times 10^6 c$	33.3 kcps
		582	692	$9.6 \times 10^6 c$	33.3 kcps
		681	NA	$16 \times 10^6 c$	120 kcps
Scientific Data		7321	520	$23 \times 10^6 c$	60 kcps
		7323	760	$23 \times 10^6 c$	120 kcps
		7361	440	$16 \times 10^6 c$	20 kcps
		7371	520	$23 \times 10^6 c$	60 kcps
		9546	520	$5.7 \times 10^6 c$	15 kcps
Univac		IIA	380	$3.6 \times 10^6 c$	12.5 kcps
		IIIA	632	$28.8 \times 10^6 c$	100 kcps
		IIIC	624	$5.7 \times 10^6 c$	22.5 kcps

Figure 12.12   (*continued*)

Manufacturer	Name	Model	Price per Month (Dollars)	Capacity[a]	Read[b] Rate
		VIC	412	5.7×10^6 c	8 kcps
		VIIIC	329	5.7×10^6 c	24 kcps
		12	448	46×10^6 c	68 kcps
		16	672	46×10^6 c	192 kcps

[a] c means characters.
[b] kcps means thousands of characters per second.

One important issue concerning this method of recording is its "permanence." What is the life of magnetic tape and how permanent is the recorded data? In one sense, this has not been a significant issue. Methods for processing magnetic tape are usually designed to recopy files as they are updated. As a result, yesterday's tapes can provide the data needed if something happens to today's tapes. However, if libraries begin to store large amounts of essentially static, unchanging data in magnetic form, permanence will become a very significant issue. At this time, there is little data on which to base a general evaluation, but there are clear problems. "Read-through," for example, produces changes in magnetic tape data as a result of the effects of the magnetic state in adjacent layers of the reel. To counteract those effects, even tapes that are not undergoing change should periodically be rewritten.

Qualitative Characteristics. As we have indicated, magnetic tapes can be used for recording almost any form of data—digital, video, audio, or analog. In most computer systems, of course, the emphasis is on digital data. However, some "videofile" systems have been developed that combine digital with video data for a complete file system.

Data on magnetic tape can be erased easily. All that is needed is to rewrite new data over it. To change data, however, usually involves copying the entire tape, incorporating changes as they occur. The result is a set of two tapes: the original and the updated copy. Frequently, as we have indicated, the original is saved for a time to protect the file, while the updated copy is used in later processing.

By its nature, magnetic tape is used for sequential processing; only under extreme conditions would data be searched for at random. This means that the use of magnetic tape imposes severe limitations on the kinds of processing system in which it will be used—batch processing, with scheduled production operation.

Quantitative Characteristics. Figure 12.12 includes representative data on the capacity and reading rate available from magnetic tape. Returning to our example of 10,000 typewritten pages, the 15 million characters they contain would easily fit on a single reel of magnetic tape. Access to a random record would average about 1 minute (although this would rarely be done), and the entire file could be read within about 3 minutes.

However, quantities (such as those in Figure 12.12) for "maximum capacity" of magnetic tape must be used with caution. Data is recorded on tape in "blocks," separated by "interblock gaps," which are blank. Basically the gaps arise from the need to accelerate the tape to full speed before reading or writing and then, afterward, to decelerate the tape. In this way, a single "Read" operation will transfer only the contents of a single block to the computer, rather than the contents of the full reel (which would be far more than the internal memory could handle).

Typically, for example, the best utilization of the internal memory might call for blocks of perhaps 2000 characters (using about 4 inches of tape at a density of 500 bits per inch). Interblock gaps are usually about ¾ inch and would therefore waste almost 20 percent of the tape's capacity for data. If blocks were only 750 characters, one-third of the capacity would be lost to interblock gaps. Figure 12.13 illustrates a typical organization of files on magnetic tape. As it shows, several logical records (catalog entries, for example) may be stored in a single tape record, bounded by inter-record gaps (IRG). Groups of tape records may be treated as an identifiable subfile, with a "segment marker" (SM) identifying the group. Several segments can then occur on a single tape. The records involved in a single file or related set of files can require several reels of tape.

The tape handling devices transport the tape at high speed (200 to 300 inches per second) past the reading and recording head. The information transfer rate is therefore fantastically high—in some cases, over 100,000 characters per second. An entire reel of 20 million alphabetic characters can, in principle, be completely scanned in little more than 3 minutes. Again, however, care must be taken to consider the effects of interblock gaps. The time to accelerate and decelerate— usually about 5 to 10 msec—must be added to the reading time for each block. With blocks of about 2000 characters, the tape transport time would be nearly twice the actual data transfer time.

File Organization. Even at the storage densities and data transfer rates provided by magnetic tape storage, the access time to a randomly located item of data averages 1 minute or more—an intolerable length of time. It is therefore standard practice to use magnetic tape files only in a batch mode of operation—accumulating transactions, sorting them into file sequence, match-merging them with the file, processing affected records in sequence as they

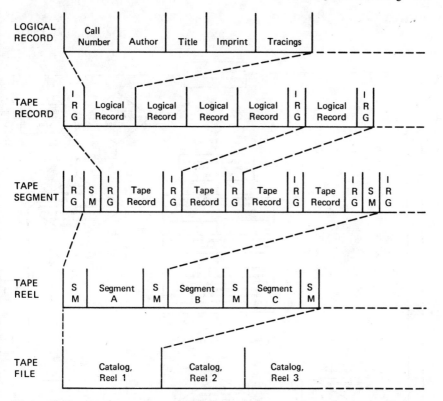

LOGICAL RECORD

| Call Number | Author | Title | Imprint | Tracings |

TAPE RECORD

TAPE SEGMENT

TAPE REEL

TAPE FILE

Figure 12.13   Magnetic tape file format. IRG, inter-record gap; SM, segment marker.

come, and storing the updated file on a new tape. But this implies that magnetic tape files must be stored in a sequence according to a defined field in each record, that transactions must contain that field of data, and that they must be sorted on it.

Magnetic tape sorting is a complex operation, involving comparisons and rearrangements of data within the internal memory during a succession of several passes of data from magnetic tape into the memory and out again. The process of tape sorting is schematically represented by the flow chart in Figure 12.14.[15] Typical equations for estimation of sorting times are given in Figure 12.15.

Costs. Figure 12.12 includes data on the costs of both the handling equipment and the magnetic tape itself. To put these in perspective, 10,000 typewritten pages (15 million characters) would require about a reel of tape—a cost of $50 to $60, not very much more than the cost of the paper would be.

[15] *705 Generalized Sort Program.* White Plains, New York: IBM Data Processing Publication.

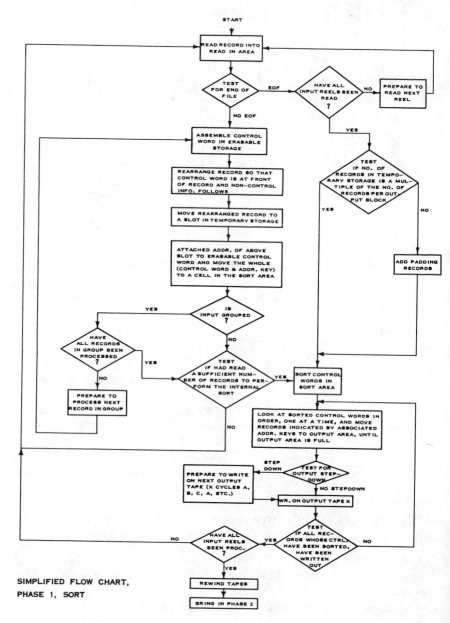

START

READ RECORD INTO
READ IN AREA

TEST
FOR END OF
FILE

EOF

HAVE ALL
INPUT REELS BEEN
READ
?

NO

PREPARE TO
READ NEXT
REEL

NO EOF

YES

ASSEMBLE CONTROL
WORD IN ERASABLE
STORAGE

REARRANGE RECORD SO THAT
CONTROL WORD IS AT FRONT
OF RECORD AND NON—CONTROL
INFO. FOLLOWS

MOVE REARRANGED RECORD TO
A SLOT IN TEMPORARY STORAGE

ATTACHED ADDR. OF ABOVE
SLOT TO ERASABLE CONTROL
WORD AND MOVE THE WHOLE
(CONTROL WORD & ADDR. KEY)
TO A CELL IN THE SORT AREA

TEST
IF NO. OF
RECORDS IN TEMPO-
RARY STORAGE IS A MUL-
TIPLE OF THE NO. OF
RECORDS PER OUT
PUT BLOCK

YES

NO

ADD PADDING
RECORDS

YES

IS
INPUT GROUPED
?

HAVE
ALL RECORDS
IN GROUP BEEN
PROCESSED
?

NO

YES

NO

TEST
IF HAD READ
A SUFFICIENT NUM-
BER OF RECORDS TO PER-
FORM THE INTERNAL
SORT

YES

SORT CONTROL
WORDS IN
SORT AREA

PREPARE TO
PROCESS NEXT
RECORD IN GROUP

NO

LOOK AT SORTED CONTROL WORDS IN
ORDER, ONE AT A TIME, AND MOVE
RECORDS INDICATED BY ASSOCIATED
ADDR. KEYS TO OUTPUT AREA, UNTIL
OUTPUT AREA IS FULL

STEP
DOWN

TEST FOR
OUTPUT STEP-
DOWN

PREPARE TO WRITE
ON NEXT OUTPUT
TAPE (X CYCLES A,
B, C, A, ETC.)

NO STEPDOWN

WR. ON OUTPUT TAPE X

HAVE ALL
INPUT REELS
BEEN PROC.
?

NO

YES

TEST
IF ALL REC-
ORDS WHOSE CTRL
HAVE BEEN SORTED,
HAVE BEEN
WRITTEN
OUT

NO

YES

REWIND TAPES

BRING IN PHASE 2

SIMPLIFIED FLOW CHART,
PHASE 1, SORT

Figure 12.14a   Simplified flow chart, Phase 1, sort.

366

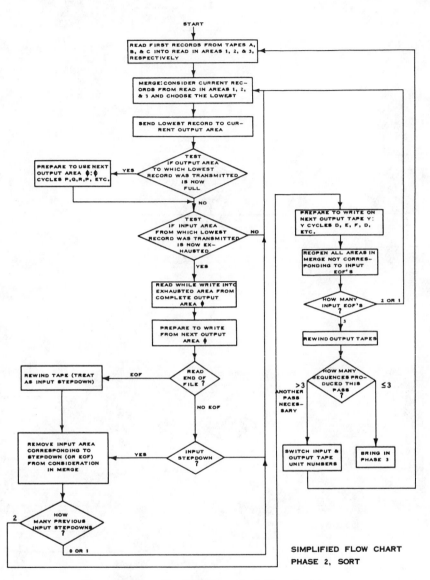

START

READ FIRST RECORDS FROM TAPES A, B, & C INTO READ IN AREAS 1, 2, & 3, RESPECTIVELY

MERGE: CONSIDER CURRENT RECORDS FROM READ IN AREAS 1, 2, & 3 AND CHOOSE THE LOWEST

SEND LOWEST RECORD TO CURRENT OUTPUT AREA

TEST IF OUTPUT AREA TO WHICH LOWEST RECORD WAS TRANSMITTED IS NOW FULL

YES

PREPARE TO USE NEXT OUTPUT AREA φ:φ CYCLES P,Q,R,P, ETC.

NO

TEST IF INPUT AREA FROM WHICH LOWEST RECORD WAS TRANSMITTED IS NOW EXHAUSTED

NO

YES

READ WHILE WRITE INTO EXHAUSTED AREA FROM COMPLETE OUTPUT AREA φ

PREPARE TO WRITE FROM NEXT OUTPUT AREA φ

READ END OF FILE ?

EOF

REWIND TAPE (TREAT AS INPUT STEPDOWN)

NO EOF

REMOVE INPUT AREA CORRESPONDING TO STEPDOWN (OR EOF) FROM CONSIDERATION IN MERGE

YES

INPUT STEPDOWN ?

HOW MANY PREVIOUS INPUT STEPDOWNS ?

2

0 OR 1

PREPARE TO WRITE ON NEXT OUTPUT TAPE Y: Y CYCLES D, E, F, D, ETC.

REOPEN ALL AREAS IN MERGE NOT CORRESPONDING TO INPUT EOF'S

HOW MANY INPUT EOF'S ?

2 OR 1

3

REWIND OUTPUT TAPES

HOW MANY SEQUENCES PRODUCED THIS PASS ?

>3 ANOTHER PASS NECESSARY

≤3

SWITCH INPUT & OUTPUT TAPE UNIT NUMBERS

BRING IN PHASE 3

SIMPLIFIED FLOW CHART
PHASE 2, SORT

Figure 12.14b   Simplified flow chart, Phase 2, sort.

367

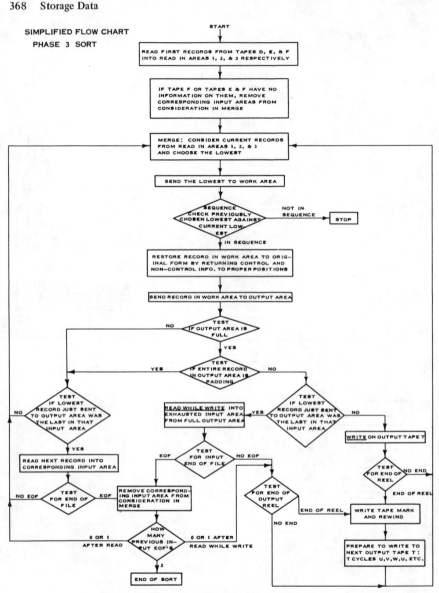

Figure 12.14c   Simplified flow chart, Phase 3, sort.

The cost of maintaining such a file can be derived from the equations of Figure 12.15. The cost of having a magnetic tape file available for use and access is exactly that of the tape handlers, buffer, and control which must be dedicated to it. For the file of 15 million characters, this would mean at least the cost of

Figure 12.15 Estimates for magnetic tape sorting times.

Parameters

n = number of records
r = record size (in characters)
b = block size (in characters)
s = size of first pass sort group (that is, number of records)
t = time for reading and writing a block of b characters
c = internal comparison time

Equations

$$T = cn \log_2 s + t\, nr \left(2 + \log_2 \frac{n}{s}\right)$$

For example

$N = 10{,}000$	$s = 50$
$r = 100$	$t = .1$ sec
$b = 2{,}000$	$c = 2.0 \times 10^{-4}$ sec

$$T = 2 \times 10^{-4} \times 10^4 \times 6 + .1 \times \frac{10^6}{2 \times 10^3}(2 + 8) = 512 \text{ sec}$$

the handler (normally about $1000 per month). The cost of interrogation of the file is the commitment of computer time involved in the formulation of the request, search of the file, and preparation of response.

Magnetic Drums

A magnetic drum is a cylinder coated with a material that will retain magnetic polarity. It is rotated at extremely high speeds so that the size of the signal and access rates will be correspondingly large. The reading and recording heads are placed in fixed positions close to the surface of the drum as it rotates under them. Each recording head will generate a "channel" of information. Most drum systems are limited by physical boundary conditions to a drum diameter of between 3 and 24 inches and to perhaps 100 channels (Figure 12.16). As we have indicated, the density at which information can be recorded is a function of the distance between the reading head and the drum surface; the smaller this distance, the higher the density. Most drum systems utilize a 2 mil (thousandth of an inch) spacing to provide typical densities on the order of 100 to 200 bits per inch.

Qualitative Characteristics. Drums are almost completely limited to storage of digital data (although there has been some use of them in "audio-response" systems, in which prerecorded audio messages are stored on them). Data on them is easily changed and updated. They are intended for use as "direct-access," addressed files, and are usually not effective for sequential processing

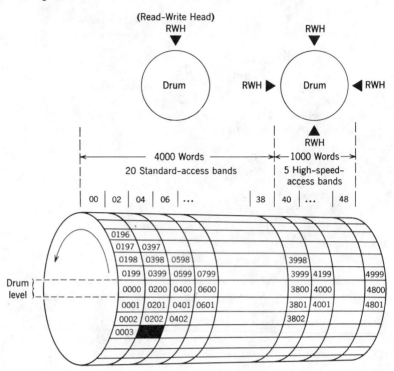

Figure 12.16   Magnetic drum.

because of the delay (about 15 msec on the average) from one read command to the next.

Quantitative Characteristics. Except for the very large capacity drums of Sperry-Rand (Univac), drums are relatively unsuitable for large capacity storage. They are generally limited to less than 1 million characters and are therefore usually not useful for the storage of large files. Figure 12.17 lists the characteristics of representative magnetic drum systems.

File Organization. Files are almost always organized in a direct access, addressed manner, using indexes stored in the internal memory (although they will be transferred to memory from other files, even the drum itself).

Costs. Most drum systems are completely self-contained and designed for making the data accessible at all times. Their costs therefore include all related circuitry and not just the storage medium itself.

Figure 12.17 Magnetic Drums.

Manufacturer	Name	Model	Price per Month (Dollars)	Capacity[a]	Access[b] Time	Read[c] Rate
Bryant		10000	NA	1.96×10^6c	16.7	117 kcps
		75000	NA	$.72 \times 10^6$c	8.3	159 kcps
		185000	NA	7.6×10^6c	25	145 kcps
		A101024	NA	4.72×10^6c	8.3	275 kcps
		PhD	NA	42.5×10^6c	16.7	235 kcps
Datanet	Magnetic Drum	MD30		12×10^6c	8.5	370 kcps
IBM		7320	NA	1.2×10^6c	8.6	202 kcps
	Drum Storage	2301	3,720	4×10^6c	8.6	1200 kcps
		2303	2,800	3.9×10^6c	8.6	312 kcps
Philco	High Density	Drum System	NA	67×10^6c	17	24 kcps
RCA	Drum Memory Unit	70/565-12	NA	0.8×10^6c	8.6	210 kcps
		70/565-13	NA	1.6×10^6c	8.6	210 kcps
		70/567-8	2,885	4.12×10^6c	8.6	333 kcps
		70/567-16	5,770	8.25×10^6c	8.6	333 kcps
Scientific Data		7202	520	0.75×10^6c	17	188 kcps
		7204	8,060	3×10^6c	17	188 kcps
		7212	1.224	5.37×10^6c	17	3000 kcps
Vermont	Ten-Inch Drum		NA	7.7×10^6c	8.5	1300 kcps
	Fifteen-Inch Drum		NA	11.5×10^6c	8.5	3000 kcps
	Twenty-Inch Drum		NA	15.4×10^6c	17	2000 kcps

Figure 12.17   (*continued*)

Manufacturer	Name	Model	Price Per Month (Dollars)	Capacity[a]	Access[b] Time	Read[c] Rate
Univac		FH330	1,660	$.78 \times 10^6$ c	34	75 kcps
		FH432	2,572	1.5×10^6 c	8.5	1440 kcps
	Drum Storage System	FH880	2,960	4.7×10^6 c	17	368 kcps
		FH1782	4,068	12×10^6 c	17	1440 kcps
	Fastrand	1A	3,200	66×10^6 c	126	150 kcps
	Fastrand	II	4,264	132×10^6 c	92	156 kcps

[a] c means characters.
[b] in milliseconds
[c] kcps means thousands of characters per second.

Magnetic Disks

Indexed or "direct access" magnetic disk storage units now are a feature of almost every electronic data processing system.[16,17] Such files are like drums, in the sense that every unit record is stored in its own addressable location. Thus the file need not be scanned and examined in order to find particular data. All that is required is an index storing the addresses which locate desired records. Figure 12.18 lists the characteristics of representative disk systems.

Physical Form. These memories store information on the surface of disks (like phonograph records) coated with magnetic material and rotating at extremely high speeds. Typically, the disks will be from 2 to 4 ft in diameter and will store binary coded information in perhaps 100 concentric channels across the surface of the disk. In most cases, several disks are stacked parallel to each other (as in "juke box" record players), but are physically separated so that the magnetic reading and recording head can be moved from one recording channel to another, and sometimes even from one disk to another. The movement of the head is controlled by an addressing mechanism that determines, from the disk and channel identification supplied to it, the physical position to which the head must be moved (Figure 12.19)

Qualitative Characteristics. Most disk systems are presently used for recording digital data, although there are some devices that record video images. They are

[16] Hobbs, L. C., "Review and Survey of Mass Memories,"
[17] "New Disc Files," Datamation, 9 (6) (June 1963), 48-49.

Figure 12.18 Magnetic disks.

Manufacturer	Name	Model	Price per Month (Dollars)	Capacity[a]	Access Time (Milliseconds)	Read[b] Rate
Bryant		4000	NA	629×10^6c	130	168 kcps
Burroughs	Disk File	B475	1,700	9.6×10^6c	20	100 kcps
	On-Line Disk System	B472	5,000	48×10^6c	20	100 kcps
	Disk File	9372	680	10×10^6c	20	200 kcps
CDC		852	314	2×10^6c	105	77 kcps
		813	2,760	100×10^6c	25-110 25.5	196 kcps
		814	4,400	200×10^6c	25-110 25.5	196 kcps
		6603	4,720	74.7×10^6c	201-268 33.5	143 kcps
		6638	7,520	$131\text{-}167 \times 10^6$	25-110 25.5	1680 kcps
		9420	660	4×10^6c	25-300 12.5	200 kcps
Data Disc		M6-B	NA	1.62×10^6c	125-358 25	124 kcps
Data Products		5022	3,784	27.5×10^6c	55-250 26	700 kcps
		5025	5,424	27.5×10^6c	55-250 26	1400 kcps
		5026	4,364	27.5×10^6c	55-250 26	700 kcps
		5045 II	5,720	54.5×10^6c	50-250 26	2400 kcps
		5045 III	6,284	109×10^6c	50-250 26	2400 kcps

Figure 12.18 (*continued*)

Manufacturer	Name	Model	Price per Month (Dollars)	Capacity[a]	Access Time (Milliseconds)	Read[b] Rate
GE		160	904	7.68×10^6 c	36-165 26	208 kcps
		204	936	4.7×10^6 c	95-305 26	62.5 kcps
		388	3,084	341×10^6 c	145-170 30	80 kcps
		4548-1	1,096	1×10^6 c	30-155 12.5	52 kcps
		4548-2	1,260	2×10^6 c	30-155 12.5	52 kcps
	Datanet	DS-15	4,320	7.8×10^6 c	70	260 kcps
	Datanet	DS-25	45,000	400×10^6 c	60	300 kcps
	Datanet	DS-25	65,000	800×10^6 c	60	300 kcps
Honeywell		258	728	4.6×10^6 c	30-125 12.5	208 kcps
		259	848	9.2×10^6 c	30-150 12.5	208 kcps
		261	3,440	135×10^6 c	15-120 26	190 kcps
		262	5,520	270×10^6 c	15-120 26	190 kcps
		4600	569	3.6×10^6 c	30-140 12.5	156 kcps
IBM	Disk Storage	1301-1	3,000	28×10^6 c	177	90 kcps
	Disk Storage	1302-2	5,000	58×10^6 c	50-180 17	156 kcps
System no longer marketed	Disk Storage Drive	1311	930	2×10^6 c	270	77 kcps
	Disk Storage	1405	1,200	20×10^6 c	625	22 kcps
		2301-1	5,040	113×10^6 c	182	
		2302-2	7,100	226×10^6 c	182	

Figure 12.18   (*continued*)

Manufacturer	Name	Model	Price per Month (Dollars)	Capacity [a]	Access Time (Milliseconds)	Rate
IBM	Disk Drive	2302-3	5,040	150×10^6c	182	156 kcps
		2302-4	7,110	300×10^6c	182	
	Disk Storage Drive	2311-1	575	7.25×10^6c	87.5	156 kcps
	Storage Facility	2314	5,000	29.2×10^6c	87.5	312 kcps
		2310A-1	300	1.8×10^6c	358	36 kcps
		2310A-2	480	3.7×10^6c	520	
		2310A-3	700	5.5×19^6c	520	
Philco	Disk File System	NA	NA	167×10^6c	33	000 kcps
RCA	Disk Storage Unit	70-564	460	7.25×10^6c	87.5	156 kcps
Univac	Disk File	8140	560	12.8×10^6c	135	

[a] c means characters.
[b] kcps means thousand characters per second

designed to make it easy to get to desired data and to change it. They are intended for use as direct access, addressed devices. If used for sequential processing, the delay from one read commmand to the next will be about 15 msec.

Quantitative Characteristics. Present-day disk systems usually use a replace-able "disk-pack" which, like a reel of tape, can be stored separate from its handler. Where this is the case, the quantity for "capacity" in Figure 12.18 is that for a disk-pack.

File Organization. Addressed access has a great deal of appeal, and certainly where usage is well defined it provides an extremely powerful approach to replacement of scanning by indexing. However, the problems in providing the item address so essential to the functioning of the unit must be recognized. Ultimately, they all are a result of the fact that utilization depends on an index.

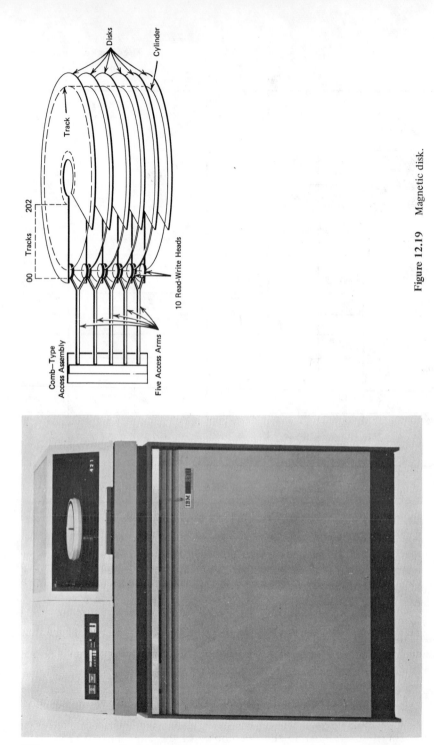

Figure 12.19   Magnetic disk.

376

Two methods are standard for handling this problem: the "indexed sequential" method and the "cross-indexed" method, with a number of variations of each. With an indexed sequential file, records are stored sequentially, according to an identifier (a field of the record). An index, arranged in the same sequence, indicates the range of identifiers to be found in a range of addresses. The computer looks up the identifier of a desired record in this index, determines the range of addresses within which it is supposed to be stored, and then reads them. To accommodate the addition of new records within the sequence, space is usually set aside at various points in the file to minimize the amount of rearrangement of stored data. Sometimes, when additions exceed the allotted space, they are addressed by "links" added to the contents of stored records.

Cross-indexed files are simple indexes that have an entry for all values, from every field of every record, on which access will later be desired. An "index record" for a given value will then list all the addresses in which a record containing that value is stored.

Costs. As Figure 12.3 shows, the costs for a disk-pack are roughly $500. Thus, the cost for storage of our file of 10,000 typewritten pages would be about $1000 (compared with $40 to $50 for paper and $50 to $60 for magnetic tape).

The costs for maintaining a file are simply the result of the time required for the computer to find the proper address for a record to be added, updated, or deleted plus the time to update the index tables.

The costs of having a file available for access are those of the disk handlers, buffers, and controllers required. For our representative example, this would be about $2000 per month.

Magnetic Strips

As we have indicated, magnetic tape must be searched sequentially in order to locate a particular record or to compare combinations of data. Furthermore, computer processing of continuous tape is comparatively slow when called upon to perform routine data processing operations such as sorting, merging, matching, and filing. It was natural, then, for companies to consider using magnetic strips as physically discrete media for storing information. Figure 12.20 lists the characteristics of some available devices of this kind.

Physical Form. A development of the National Cash Register Company, called CRAM (Card Random Access Mechanism), uses unitized tape for the storage medium.[18] Each strip is 14 inches long by 3¼ inches wide. Data is

[18] Angel, A. M., "The NCR Magnetic Card Random Access Memory," in *Large Capacity Memory Techniques for Computing Systems*, Office of Naval Research, May 1961.

Figure 12.20   Magnetic strips.

Manufacturer	Name	Model	Price per Month (Dollars)	Capacity[a]	Access Time (in Milliseconds)	Read [b] Rate	Comments
GE		MS-40	3,780	532×10^6c	NA	73 kcps	
IBM	Data Cell	2321	NA	40×10^6c per cell up to 10 cells 400×10^6c	375	55 kcps	2¼ x 13 inch strip
NCR	CRAM	353-1	760	5.5×10^6c	258	100 kcps	3 ¼ x 14 inch strip
	CRAM	353-2	580	8×10^6c	258	38 kcps	3 ¼ x 14 inch strip
	CRAM	353-3	640	16×10^6c	258	38 kcps	3 ¼ x 14 inch strip
	CRAM	353-5	1,080	83×10^6c	131	38 kcps	3 ¼ x 14 inch strip
Potter	RAM		240	8×10^6c	150	NA	
RCA	RACE	70-568	2,540	561×10^6c	136-235 30	70 kcps	

[a]c means characters.
[b]kcps means thousand characters per second

recorded on the magnetic strip in 56 parallel channels divided into 7 sets of 8 channels, each set being treated as the counterpart of a magnetic tape, with the bits for each individual character recorded in parallel. Successive characters are recorded sequentially at a density of 250 bits to the inch. The strips are stored in a replaceable cartridge that contains 256 cards, suspended on 8 binary coded rods which pass through notches at the end of each strip. Using the principles of edge-notched selection, by automatically setting the rods to a binary coded value from 000 through 255, any desired strip from the set can be chosen for reading or recording. Strips can be successively selected, read, and returned to the file at the rate of approximately five per second. RCA has a similar set of equipment, called RACE, and so does IBM represented by the "Data Cell." In the Data Cell, for example, data is recorded on strips 13 inches long and 2¼ inches wide. Sets of 10 of these strips are stored in cartridges, and a set of 20 cartridges is a Data Cell. Up to 10 interchangeable data cells can be stored in a single drive.

Qualitative Characteristics. These are all essentially devices for direct, addressed access to digital data. (Although WALNUT, an earlier IBM development similar in structure to a Data Cell, was a photographic store capable of both digital and image storage.) Data can be updated or changed relatively easily.

Quantitative Characteristics. As Figure 12.20 shows, these devices have truly enormous capacities. Our representative example of 10,000 typewritten pages would require only a small portion of any one of them. Access times are, on the other hand, somewhat longer than with smaller direct access devices, such as magnetic disks. This does raise some very significant prolems in the use of them for storing multiple files for many users in an on-line system. Specifically, as each user calls for data (from a Data Cell, for example), he will interfere in several ways with the use of the file unit by other users. Not only does he tie up the unit itself, but he causes it to move away from the location of someone else's file, thus making later access time longer.

File Organization. All the issues of file organization that are applicable to magnetic disk files are equally applicable to these larger file systems.

Costs. The costs listed in Figure 12.20 are self-explanatory.

EQUIPMENT FOR PHOTOGRAPHIC FILES

Microphotography is a general technique covering the use of any opaque or transparent carrier of a miniaturized image, including microfilm, microfiche, film strips, film inserts, and many others.[19-21] The possibility for producing miniature images is the result of developments in photographic emulsions with almost unbelievably high resolution. The most spectacular of these are some of the silver halides, possessing resolving power greater than 2000 lines per millimeter and with information storage capacity potentially over 3 billion bits per square inch.

In addition, new dry processes have been developed to overcome the disadvantages of wet chemical development normally associated with silver halide film processing. Diazo, for example, is a film that is exposed by ultraviolet light and developed by gaseous ammonia. Kalvar is exposed by ultraviolet light and

[19] Born, L. K., "The Literature of Microreproduction," *American Documentation* (July 7, 1956), pp. 167-187.

[20] Bagg, Thomas C., and Mary E. Stevens, *Information Selection Systems Retrieving Replica Copies: A State of the Art Report* (NBS Technical Note 1957). Washington, D. C.: Government Printing Office, December 31, 1967.

[21] Alexander, Samuel N., *The Current Status of Graphic Storage Techniques: Their Potential Application to Library Mechanization,*

developed by heat at a temperature equivalent to that of a warm iron. The latest dry process is "photochromics," claimed to have data-compression ratios up to 400:1 with practically no loss of resolution.[22,23] Photochromic film is exposed by ultraviolet light and can be erased by white light if required. In 1966, the Minnesota Mining and Manufacturing Company announced a new dry method for recording information on silver-halide film.

With the fantastic storage capability provided by microphotography, permanent messages can be greatly compressed. Actually, the ultimate practical limits become more a matter of the nature of optical systems, of the wavelength of light, and of the techniques for developing the image than of the storage medium itself. As a result, high ratios for reduction in size from document to recorded image are becoming a standard part of the art. For example, whereas ratios of 10:1 or 20:1 have been traditional in microphotography, Eastman Kodak used a reduction ratio of 60:1 in its Minicard system.[24] Others have experimented with ratios up to 1000:1, although it has been estimated that the practical limit is from 500 to 600:1, based on optical limitations in both recording and later reading.

A further consideration, which becomes particularly significant at the higher reduction ratios, is the physical size of the image carrier itself. This must remain on the order of several centimeters, no matter how many images may be stored on it, so that it can be handled by machines or human beings. In view of this, if the high reduction ratio is to have any real meaning in terms of storage efficiency, very many images must be stored on a single carrier, and the resulting problems in locating the desired image become very significant.

Another important issue is the quality of the microimage. Inasmuch as there is a loss of resolution from one generation of an image to the next, a microfilm system requires exacting quality controls at all stages of processing—in the optics at the time of filming, in the storage medium, and in the reproduction processes employed to enlarge the image back to its original dimensions.

In evaluating microforms for storage, it is important to consider the gradually declining cost of making copies from them—both hard copy and microform copy. Many companies are already engaged in commercial duplication of various microforms; in fact, some are even reproducing entire copies of out-of-print books from microfilm at reasonable cost and in bound book form. If this continues, then it is possible that in time readers will be willing to forego seeing

[22] Carlson, C. O., et al., "The Photochromic Micro Image Memory," in *Large Capacity Memory Techniques for Computing Systems,* Office of Naval Research, May 1961.

[23] Myers, W. C., and A. S. Tauber, *Photochromic Micro-Images—A Key to Practical Micro-Document Storage and Dissemination, "American Documentation,* 13 (4) (October 1962), pp. 403-409.

[24] Kuipers, J. W., et al., "A Minicard System for Documentary Information," *American Documentation,* 8 (4) (October 1957), 246-268.

the original material "on loan" from their library, in favor of getting a duplicate, expendable copy of the microform for desk viewing. L. B. Heilprin distinguished between a D (duplicating)-Library and a C (circulating)-Library.[25,26] He maintained that through increased microform usage and advances in communications, we can expect to see the D-Library achieving considerable popularity and prominence in the future. "Thus many problems of storing multiple copies: of loss through wear, mutilation, and stealing; of cost and effort of charging out and charging in; of binding and rebinding; can be simplified or eliminated in a D-Library. The D-Library can combine photoreduction of scale—i.e., compact storage—high mobility through optical and electronic transmission of images, and great economy of operation. The D principle of dissemination by reproduction of expendable or vendable copies will almost certainly alleviate many present physical problems."

The great variety of machine research in this area has exploited the techniques of microphotography, with its almost fantastic capabilities, and has attempted to find the most efficient shapes, sizes, and reduction ratios for microforms. Roll film, flat film strips, cards, inserts—all have been utilized in an effort to meet desired objectives most effectively.

Microfilm

Certainly the most familiar of these various forms is the now standard microfilm, which stores document images at reduction ratios usually around 15:1 to 20:1 on reels of film. Printed pages are recorded continuously on spools of film using special purpose microfilm cameras, commonly 16 mm and 35 mm. Along with the camera, other equipment has been evolved for viewing the film.[27-29] Desired images can be located by visual scanning of the set of stored images, assisted perhaps by an index of linear positions, in inches, along the film. The "Lodestar" microfilm viewer, manufactured by the Recordak Corporation, is typical of commercially available viewers of this type. It uses film reels stored in cartridges to simplify film loading and unloading. More recently, several developments have appeared which mechanize the process of searching frames to determine the location of desired ones on the reel. Figure 12.21 lists the characteristics of various microfilm equipment.

[25] Heilprin, L. B., "Communication Engineering Approach to Microforms," *American Documentation,* **12** (3) (July 1961), 217.

[26] Heilprin, L. B., "On the Information Problem Ahead," *American Documentation,* **12** (1) (January 1961), 6-14.

[27] Ballou, Hubbard W., *Guide to Microreproduction Equipment.* Annapolis, Maryland: National Microfilm Association, 1959.

[28] Hawkin, W. R., *Photocopying from Bound Volumes: A Study of Machines, Methods, and Materials.* Chicago: ALA, 1962.

[29] Verry, H. R., *Microcopying Methods.* New York: Focal Press, 1963.

Figure 12.21 Microfilm equipment.

Manufacturer	Name	Model	Price per Month (Dollars)	Operating Rate	Comments
Bell & Howell	Reader and Reader-Printer	Autoload I and II	22.8 55.5	144 frames per hour	Accepts 16 mm RF (Roll Film) C (Cards). Variable illumination, built in B & H metered index.
	Reader-Printer	510C	28.5		
	Reader-Printer	530D	19	144 frames per hour	16, 35 mm RF, AC (Aperture Card) J (Jacket) M (Microfiche). Manual; has scanning ability; metered index
	Reader-Printer	BH-206	6		16, 35 mm RF. Manual; has scanning ability.
	Camera	205F	42		
	Camera	205G	32		
	Camera Tabtronic		79.9	70 ft/min	16 mm x 100 ft. Index meter. Designed for continuous fan-folded forms, roll stock or individual documents.
	Camera Micro-Recorder		55.9	400 check-size doc/min	16 mm x 10 ft. Reduction 24x, 30x, 44x. Manual
Dibold	Reader	92-02	5.9		
	Reader	92-04	NA		
	Flo-Film Camera	750	16.5		
Itek	Reader-Printer	18-24	85	4 copies per minute	35 mm RF, AC. Produces opaque or translucent prints. Magnification 14.5x
	Reader	12-12	NA		16 mm RF. Manual

Figure 12.21 *(continued)*

Manufacturer	Name	Model	Price per Month (Dollars)	Operating Rate	Comments
IBM	Micro-Viewer Printer		63	2 copies per minute	16, 35 mm RF, AC, J, M. Produces translucent or opaque copies. Magnification 14.7x
	Micro-Viewer		4.5		16, 35 mm RF, AC. M. Optional reel carriers for 16, 35 mm RF. Magnification 6.5x, 15x.
	Micro-Camera	9951, 9956	143.8 147.8		35 mm x 100 ft. Automatic. Detachable film cutoff mechanism.
3 M	Reader-Printer	Filmac 100	18	6 copies per minute	16, 35 mm RF, AC, J, M. Magnification 7x to 26x. Manual, auto.
	Reader-Printer	Filmac 200	50	3 copies per minute	16, 35 mm RF, AC, J, M. Magnification 14.5x. Manual.
	Reader-Printer	Filmac 300	72	6 copies per minute	16, 35 mm RF, AC, J, M. Magnification 7x to 20x. Manual.
	Reader-Printer	Filmac 400	59.9	12 copies per minute	16 mm RF contained in self-threading cartridge. Magnification 10.6x to 29x. Motor driven.
	Camera Processor	1000D	67.9		35 mm. Exposes, automatically processes, and delivers film mounted in aperture cards. Reduction 16x. Manual. Process within 54 sec.
	Camera Processor	2000	135.1		35 mm. Reduction 16x24x. Manual.
	Filmsort Camera		over 60		35 mm. Processes within 45 sec; mounted in aperture card. Reduction 16x.

Figure 12.21   (*continued*)

Manufacturer	Name	Model	Price per Month (Dollars)	Operating Rate	Comments
Recordak	Lodestar Reader-Printer	PES-1	58	2 copies per minute	16 mm RF, C. Automatic film threading, motorized film drive. Image controlled keyboard.
	Starmatic Reader	PVM	13.9		16 mm RF
	Camera Reliant	400, RO-1	46.3	400 check-size item/ min	16 mm. Exposes 2 rolls of film simultaneously. Reduction 20x or 32x. Manual.
	Reliant	600K, RW	82	615 check-size item/ min	Reduction 24x, 32x, 40x, 45x. Automatic.
	Microfile	MRG-1	159		35 mm x 100 ft. Pushbuttor reduction selection; interchangeable film unit. Reduction 12x to 36x. Manual, auto.
	Reliant Microfilmer	500	30	Up to 30,000 exposure per hour	16 mm. Reduction 24x, 32x, 40x. Kodamatic indexing.
Sperry Rand	Reader-Printer	Film-A-Record F468	19	3 copies pcr minute	16, 35 mm RF, J, M, AC. Magnification 16x to 42x. Manual.
	Unitized Reader	F450	6.5		M, AC, J.
	Reader	F478	over 7		16, 35 mm, RF, J, AC. Has scanning ability. Manual.
	Camera	Film-A-Record F444AEC	19.9	80 ft/min	16 mm x100 ft. Reduction 25x. Automatic.
	Camera	Film-A-Record 555	over 30	125 linear feet per min	16 mm. Reduction 25x, 35x, 42x.

Figure 12.21   (*continued*)

Manufacturer	Name	Model	Price per Month (Dollars)	Operating Rate	Comments
Sperry Rand (*continued*)	Camera	F-35 CR	under 30		35 mm. Reduction 16x exposure counter and light meter available.
	Camera	F-1100	under 30		16, 35 mm. Reduction 16x, 20x; designed for microfilming of X-rays.
Stromberg-Carlson	Reader-Printer	S-C1700	NA		16 RF. Magnification 19x, 22x. Interchangeable modular display heads with different screen sizes.
	Reader-Printer	S-C1325	NA	1 in 10 sec	M, J, AC. Magnification 24x 40x. Print via S- 3500 printer.
Stromberg-Datagraphic	Inquiry Station	SD-1700	42		Accepts all 16 mm F loaded in SD micromation cartridge. Magnification 24x to 40x. Self-threading. Holds 200 ft of film.

Qualitatitive Characteristics. Microfilm is basically a means for recording images but, as discussed below, it can be used to record binary coded digital data for purposes of indexing and mechanized retrieval. Except for some of the more recent, mostly experimental photographic techniques (such as photochromics), microfilm is nonerasable, and therefore data is difficult to change. Finally, as we shall discuss in detail, microfilm is a continuous strip medium with all the problems in file organization and access to data which that implies.

Quantitative Characteristics. Images are recorded on microfilm at reduction ratios of 15:1 to 20:1. This means that a 100 foot cartridge will hold up to 3000 frames. Our example of 10,000 typewritten pages would therefore require about 4 cartridges. Certainly the most spectacular result of storage on microfilm is the reduction in space by factors of 300 and more—for the example, from over 10 cubic feet to less than 1/30 of a cubic foot!

Most viewers for microfilm transport the film at a rate up to 600 feet per minute. The access time to a desired frame, in a 100 foot cartridge, using one of the frame counting attachments like that in Figure 12.22, will average 5 to 10 seconds. The images can be read at normal human reading rates, or reproduced (with a viewer-printer) within 15 to 30 seconds.

In general, therefore, microfilm represents a high capacity, high density storage system with reasonably rapid access.

Figure 12.22   Frame counting.

File Organization. However, although microfilm satisfies the basic requirements for achieving more compact storage of printed information, its access time is still too slow for data processing needs, even when the difficulty of locating a specific image on the spool is overcome by organizing the original material in a logical manner before filming and using automatic frame counting. These technical considerations of access time and display may not be too important in routine operations (such as using microfilmed sets of material like newspapers and periodicals). But when continuous film is used as the primary recording medium for storing a heterogeneous collection of documents keyed to a subject or named object index, the questions of rapid access and display become very serious.

The basic principles of an electric microfilm searching system were advanced by Dr. Vannevar Bush of the Massachusetts Institute of Technology in the early 1940's as a means for overcoming these deficiencies. Government funds were provided for its development, and a prototype model called the Rapid Selector was designed and built by Engineering Research Associates of St. Paul, Minnesota. Dr. Ralph R. Shaw, Librarian of the Department of Agriculture, supervised the development of the work and performed most of the bibliographical experimentation. [30-32] The machine handled microfilm with associated binary code patterns which described the contents of documents. Code and document images were on large, 2000 foot reels of 35 mm. microfilm containing 72,000 image frames each, which went through the machine at five feet per second (2400 pages per minute).

The code was in the form of black and clear "dots," which identified each document by number, name, author, or contents. As the film passed through the selector, the coded area was projected on a photocell and compared with specified search criteria. Copies of documents selected by code recognition were copied "on the fly" photographically.

Since then, commercial versions of the same concept have become available. The FMA File Search system stores binary codes with each image frame, as shown in Figure 12.23, allowing as many as 56 alpha-numeric characters to be used for indexing each frame. [33] The File Search film is moved past the reading station at 200 feet per minute, corresponding to a rate of 6400 pages per minute. The Retrieval Unit searches the reel and selects those documents or other material, which have coding that matches that in a request. As the desired frames are found by the machine, the film is automatically stopped and the image is projected onto the viewing screen.

The Eastman Kodak "Miracode" system is similar, but stores the binary coded data between image frames (Figure 12.24) instead of beside them. [34] Figure 12.25 lists the characteristics of these devices.

The Rapid Selector, the Eastman Kodak Miracode, and the FMA File Search Machine all utilize microfilm with binary coded data stored for automatic searching. They thus each provide a means for mechanized image retrieval.

---

[30] Shaw, Ralph R., "The Rapid Selector," *Journal of Documentation,* No. 5, 1949, pp. 164-171.

[31] Shaw, Ralph R., *Machines and the Bibliographical Problem of the 20th Century,* U.S. Department of Agriculture, March 15, 1951.

[32] McMurray, James P., "The Bureau of Ships Rapid Selector System," *American Documentation,* **13** (1) (January 1962), 66-68.

[33] Condon, Richard A., *The FMA File Search System,* Talk presented to the Los Angeles Chapter of ADI, September 29, 1961.

[34] *The Miracode System of Automated Information Retrieval,* Recordak (Eastman Kodak), 1964.

Figure 12.23   File search, film image, and code.

However, none of them provides an answer to the basic operational disadvantages of continuous film files: it is awkward to interfile new material in an orderly sequence, and the search mechanism must examine the entire file to satisfy every search request.

Costs. The costs of microfilm as a medium vary greatly, depending on the size (16 mm or 35 mm), the length, and how it is packaged. However, to provide a

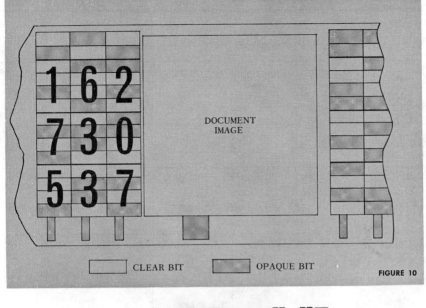

DOCUMENT
IMAGE

CLEAR BIT   OPAQUE BIT

FIGURE 10

Figure 12.24   Miracode film image and code.

rough basis for comparison: a reel of 100 ft of 16 mm microfilm, developed and
in a cartridge, will cost about $6. To record the 10,000 typewritten
pages—requiring 4 cartridges—would thus cost between $20 and $25.

The cost of file maintenance is controlled, to an extent, by the nonerasable,
continuous strip nature of microfilm. Basically, one merely adds new reels of
film and does not try to update the existing microfilm.

The cost of having a file accessible is merely the cost of viewers (or
viewer-printers), and the cost of access is determined by the time of clerical
personnel or, in the case of mechanized searching devices, the electronic
equipment.

Microimage Cards and Strips

Unitized film files are able to overcome many of these disadvantages. In fact,
virtually every consideration that led the data processing industry to consider
magnetic disks, cards, and strips as replacement for magnetic tape applies with
equal force to microphotographic storage. With a discrete medium, the need for
sequential handling disappears, and processing and finding operations can

Figure 12.25   Microfilm-code equipment

Manufacturer	Name	Cost per Month (Dollars)	Search Speeds	Comments
Eastman Kodak	Minicard	Estimated at over 20,000	1800 cards/m	16 x 32 mm filmchip; reduction ratio 60:1; high photograhic reduction, unitized cards, high transport rate, complex logical processing, high densities of coded data.
FMA	File Search	2860-3150	6400 pages/m	Recording unit, and retrieval unit. Reduction ratio 25:1; 35 mm film with binary code data.
Magnovox	Media	700-800	600 cards/m	Reduction ratio 30:1; 16 x 32 mm filmchip; code is stored along the edge Retrieval is based on document number.
National Bureau of Standards	Rapid Selector	NA	6000 pages/m	Reduction ratio: 8:1; 35 mm film with binary coded data.
Recordak	Miracode	500	600 pages/m	Reduction ratio 30:1; 16 x 32 mm filmchip offers automatic clerical help in a surprisingly small package. Search time 8 sec.
IBM	Walnut	Estimated at 10,000-20,000		Access time 5 sec.; reduction 1000:1. Refers to file storage mechanism only. Filmstrip technique. Capacity for over 999,000 pages.

become more flexible and random. Several methods now exist for placing microreductions of documents onto cards.

Physical Forms and Qualitative Characteristics. The *microcard* is an extension of conventional microfilming to allow for storage on cards.[35,36] Documents are filmed in a normal manner, then developed, cut into strips, and contact printed

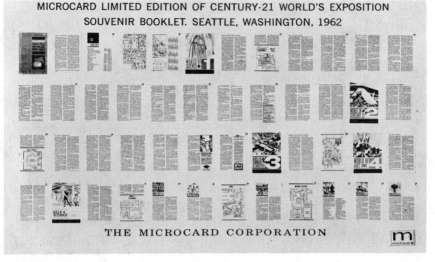

Figure 12.26   Microcard.

as opaque positive images on the face of a card. The extent of the photo-reduction determines how many document pages may be contained on one card. The standard Microcard (Figure 12.26) is 3 x 5 inches and, at typical reductions, may contain as many as 80 pages. The reverse face of the card may be used to record clear-text identification or index data. Special photographic equipment is required to process the cards and prepare them for use, and special viewers are needed to assist the user in reading the card. Futhermore, the opaque nature of a microcard makes it inconvenient to duplicate and enlarge.

The *microfiche* is intended to answer the problems involved in viewing and copying opaque microcards. The microfiche is a transparent film card of varying size, recording image frames in a rectangular array. Present standards for microfiche are shown in Figure 12.27. The "COSATI" Standard has become the form in which a majority of federal government reports (science, technology, and education, for instance) are now being distributed.[37]

Another widely used method is the *Aperture Card* (Figure 12.28), which utilizes small windows in an other wise solid card to store pieces of film.[38] The

[35] Rider, Fremont, *The Scholar and the Future of the Research Library.* New York: Hadham, 1944.

[36] Rider, Fremont, "The Challenge of Microphotography," in Louis Shores, ed., *Challenges to Librarianship.* New York: William C. Brown, 1953.

[37] COSATI, *Federal Microfiche Standards,* Second Edition, December 1965.

[38] Committee on Government Operations, U.S. Senate 86th Congress, 2nd Session, *Documentation, Indexing, and Retrieval of Scientific Information.* Washington, D.C.: Government Printing Office, 1961, pp. 63-64.

MICROFICHE AND HR-FICHE STANDARDS GUIDE

THE 4'' x 6'' MICROFILM CARD (105MM x 148.75MM) IS ONE SIZE COMMON TO ALL FICHE STANDARDS. ALL STANDARD FICHE HAVE A HUMAN READABLE TITLE AREA.

NUMBER OF ROWS (X-AXIS) AND NUMBER OF COLUMNS (Y-AXIS)	STANDARDS	MAXIMUM** REDUCTION RATIOS	TOTAL NUMBER OF MICRO-IMAGES, PAGES OR FRAMES
1 Column / 1 Row	**105MM STANDARD** FOR ENGINEERING DRAWINGS AND GRAPHIC ARTS	12:1	1 SIZE OF DOCUMENT: (ENGINEERING DRAWING)
12 Columns / 5 Rows	**COSATI** (COMMITTEE ON SCIENTIFIC AND TECHNICAL INFORMATION) **MICROFICHE**	20:1	60 SIZE OF DOCUMENTS: (8½'' x 11'')
14 Columns / 7 Rows	**NMA** (THE NATIONAL MICROFILM ASSOCIATION) **MICROFICHE**	24:1	98 SIZE OF DOCUMENTS: (8½''x 11'')

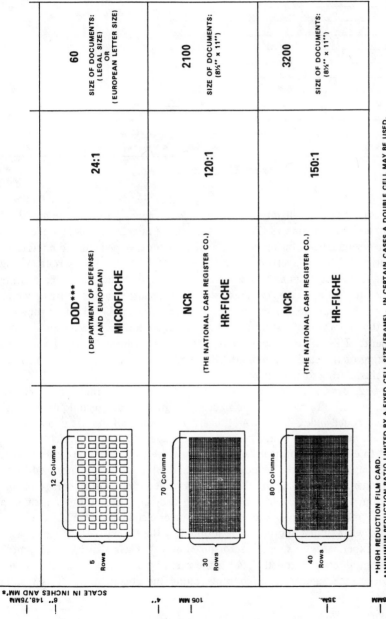

Figure 12.27 Microfiche and HR-Fiche standards guide (the 4 in. × 6 in. microfilm card (105 mm × 148.75 mm) is one size common to all Fiche standards; all standard Fiche have a human readable title area).

393

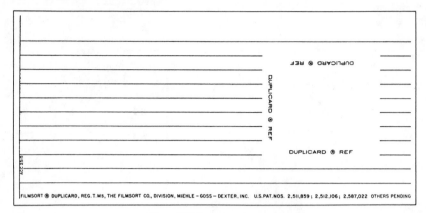

Figure 12.28   Aperture card.

number of apertures can vary, depending on the amount of space required for the stored document images. To place the images in aperture cards, documents are filmed sequentially on microfilm, which is later chopped and mounted to fit neatly into the precut apertures. The FILMSORT Division of Minnesota Mining and Manufacturing Company produces a mounter that cuts the frame of film, inserts it into the aperture, and presses it firmly against an adhesive frame which surrounds the aperture. Sometimes the apertures are combined into a punched card so that a portion of the card can be used for an index and selection by EAM equipment. This is not completely satisfactory, since it requires special engineering of the card-handling device to ensure that cards will not be mangled or scratched during sorting operations.

Minicard, developed by Eastman Kodak Company for the Department of Defense, was an effort to combine microphotographic card techniques for both image and coded index data.[39] A Minicard was about half the size of a standard postage stamp: 16 x 32 mm. The card was divided into 7 fields, which could be devoted to either code or image storage. Images were stored at the ratio of 60:1. In the code portion of the Minicard, black and white dots were arranged in 42 parallel channels and sets of 10 columns called fields. Depending on the application, a Minicard could contain a large code area and no image area, or a maximum of 12 images plus about 60 alphanumeric code characters.

A somewhat similar approach was adopted by the Magnavox Company, based on their experiences as subcontractor on Minicard. Their MEDIA development similarly produces the coded data on the cards by a process of photographing the code at the same time as photographing the documents.[40] This system

[39] Kuipers, J. W., et al., *op. cit.*
[40] *MEDIA*, A brochure of the Magnavox Company, Fort Wayne, Indiana.

utilizes a card of the same dimensions as the Minicard but with the code stored along the edge and consisting of less than 80 bits. The MEDIA system utilizes manual filing of the cards in small cartridges, each containing up to 200 cards. A selector matches the 15 to 20 decimal digits on the code with a single document number, retrieving on the basis of document number and not on the basis of content.

An entirely different approach to unitized microphotographic storage is that taken by IBM in their development of a film strip technique. Although this development is not yet commercially available, it is important to recognize that the use of strips in highly mechanized systems is as possible with microphotographic storage as it is with magnetic tape storage. The development was first begun in 1958 and was described in July 1961 along the following lines:[41]

WALNUT (as it is called) consists of a specially designed machine which stores photographic images on strips. Documents entering the system travel through a two-stage reduction in size. They are microfilmed on 35 mm film and placed in a converter which then optically reduces the image further and transfers it to the strip. Each strip contains as many as 99 images of an 8″ x 14″ page size, which represents a reduction of about 1/1,000th the original size. The strips are stored in a plastic cell with 50 strips to the cell and 200 cells to the machine. The machine can therefore store a total of 990,000 images.

Any one of the images can be found in a maximum access time of 5 seconds. Once the document number is addressed, a pickup mechanism locates the appropriate cell, withdraws the pertinent strip, and the image of the document is photographically transferred to an IBM aperture card. The selected images can then be viewed on a screen by the user or enlarged for hard-copy reproduction.

But the technique of high density photographic recording is likely to have great importance for libraries in perhaps an unexpected way. In the study, "Automation and the Library of Congress," there were hints of this in the discussion of "read-only" stores of bibliographical data.[42] Since such data is, by its nature, relatively static, it can be recorded on strips, as in the IBM Data Cell, but photographically at much higher densities.[43] Densities of 1 to 3 million bits to the inch are feasible. The result is that immense quantities of digital data can be distributed very compactly and inexpensively.

Figure 12.29 lists the characteristics of representative microimage card media.

[41] Bradshaw, P. D., "The Walnut System: A Large Capacity Document Storage and Retrieval System," *American Documentation,* **13** (3) (July 1962), 270-275.

[42] King, Gilbert W., ed., *Automation and the Library of Congress.* Washington, D.C.: Library of Congress, 1963.

[43] King, Gilbert W., "Photographic Information Storage," *Control Engineering,* August 1955, pp. 48-53.

Figure 12.29   Microimage card equipment.

Manufacturer	Name	Model	Price (Dollars)	Capacity	Acess Time and Comments
Microcard	Microcard		0.50 per card	24-48 pages	Reduction 17x, 23x. 3 x 5 inch micro-opaques. Reproduction is slow and costly. Used for the miniaturization of bulky, expensive technical periodicals, such as chemical abstracts and patent gazette.
3M	Aperture Card		0.10 per card	1-6 images	Documents are filmed sequentially in microfilm form, and later chopped and mounted to fit neatly in cards with precut apertures.
	Microfiche		0.25 per card	60-100 images	Reduction 18x, 24x. Related group of images are arranged on a card-shaped transparent sheet of film. Storage medium common to the scientist and librarian. Quick and economical means of preparing and distributing multipaged reports.
Magnavox	Media		NA	2 images	Utilize filmchip for automatic or semiautomatic storage and retrieval. Particular sizes of filmchips have little application apart from the system and equipment for which they are designed.
Sperry Rand	Aperture Cards		NA	1-6 images	

Qualitative Characteristics. Capacities of microimage cards vary widely (Figure 12.29). However, to provide a basis for comparison, storage of the 10,000 typewritten pages of our example will probably take 200 microfiche (COSATI standard). Access times (about 1 minute) and reading rates are comparable to other manual methods. (However, the Houston-Fearless CARD Reader provides access in 4 seconds.)

Figure 12.29   (*continued*)

Manufacturer	Name	Model	Price (Dollars)	Capacity	Access Time and Comments
Eastman Kodak	Minicard		NA	12 images	Reduction 60x. 16 x 32 mm film chips. Used primarily for a few special government file problems, because of its cost. Utilizes photographic technique for both image and coded index data.
IBM	Aperture Cards		NA	1-6 images	

[a]For the price of the equipment, see Figure 12.21.

Costs. Typically, microimage cards (such as microfiche) cost about 25c each. Thus, storage of the 10,000 pages of our example would cost about $50. The costs to maintain a file, to have it available, and to find specific frames are comparable to other forms of manual storage.

Suggested Reading

Hawkin, William R., *Copying Methods Manual*. Chicago: American Library Association, 1966.

A comprehensive coverage of microphotography, as well as other means of copying printed records.

Pear, Charles B., *Magnetic Recording in Science and Technology*. New York: Reinhold, 1967.

This provides a thorough technical discussion of the methods for recording and reading data magnetically.

Chapter 13

COMMUNICATION OF DATA

INTRODUCTION

"Data communication" is a process, a system, and a set of equipment by which data—in any of its forms—is transmitted from one geographical location to another. It is familiar to all of us in our use of the telephone for transmission of "voice data" and of television for transmission of image data. But it is playing an increasingly important role in modern data processing technology. What do we mean by the phrase "digital communications system?" What do we mean by "facsimile?" How do they work? And where can they be applied in libraries?

Digital Communication

In Chapter 10 we discussed the concept of an "on-line system"—the dream of every data processing specialist for the effective use of his equipment. And in Chapter 11 we discussed various kinds of on-line terminal equipment. The most important feature of on-line systems is the rapidity with which communication can take place between the computer and the remote terminal devices—usually so fast that the person is able to operate at his own rate of speed, without delays caused by the computer or the process of communication. The operation of such a system therefore depends on a communication system that can economically provide the means for transmission of digital data at the necessary speeds.

In a digital communication system, data is first encoded, usually in binary form. The codes can be generated from keyboard operations, such as from a punched-tape typewriter, or directly from existing binary coded data. For transmission over telephone lines, these codes are then converted into "tones"

398

(as in a "touch-tone" telephone) and sent as normal audio (voice) sounds; when received at the other end of the line, they are then reconverted to the original binary codes. The crucial issue in the design of a digital communication system is the "capacity" of the transmission line in terms of the amount of digital data that can be transmitted in a given length of time, expressed as the "bandwidth" of the channel. The capacity is significantly affected by the "noise" in the transmission channel, which causes errors to occur in the digital data. The task in encoding data for transmission is to provide codes that will allow such errors to be detected and corrected. (The entire field of "information theory" has arisen from studies of these problems in digital communication.)

Facsimile Communication

Ever since RCA conducted a demonstration of Ultrafax at the Library of Congress in the early 1950's, the library profession has been actively interested in the possibility of using facsimile transmission as a medium for conveying *printed* information from one library to another.[1] The progress in facsimile transmission has important implications for libraries and information centers. It offers the promise of making remote library materials speedily available to interested users, In essence, it would provide a visual data transmission technique to supplement audio communication by telephone.

Facsimile transmission is not a new technique. It has been known for many years, and long used by newspapers, wire services, magazines, the U.S. Weather Bureau, and other government agencies. However, because of the high costs of both the communications facilities and terminal equipment required, it has been too expensive for most libraries. Recently, however, charges have plunged, even for low-volume users, because of the introduction of inexpensive, "idiot-proof" facsimile systems that can send and receive documents over ordinary, or voice-grade, telephone lines.

Role of Communication in Library Data Processing

In the library situation the use of these forms of communication has seemed particularly appropriate. To put the discussion in a library context, let us visualize a future library network, with centers in each state serving as central nodes for the distribution of information to local libraries. For example, national centers might maintain central stores of machine-readable indexing and cataloging data. It could then be possible for any local library to obtain access to this electronic catalog by "dialing up" through the switching center and

---

[1] Adams, Scott, "Facsimile for Federal Libraries," *Special Libraries*, **44** (5) (May/June 1953), 1969–172.

transmitting a remote inquiry from its own terminal. The same machine could then later receive a response concerning the desired catalog data and type it out automatically.

Based on the data received, the library could then request transmission, by facsimile, of the documentary pages themselves from the library in the network from which they are available.

Of course, teletype (TWX) has been used for interlibrary digital communication for many years. However, it is not clear that it really serves a useful purpose, nor has the value of facsimile transmission been proven. Therefore, since neither form of communication is yet an integral part of library operation, several experiments have been carried out to determine how feasible such operations would be. The state of New York set up a network of 16 libraries and provided facilities for facsimile transmission among them.[2] This experiment, called FACTS, lasted six months. The results indicated that facsimile transmission is not yet an economic operation. This conclusion was generally confirmed by the experience of the University of California's Institute of Library Research with another series of experiments. These results indicated that the problems arise both with the equipment, its costs, and the procedures for using them.[3]

Despite the implications of these experiments, it should be recognized that they are relevant only in the context of today's technology and library procedures. It seems almost certain that, within the coming five to ten years, this context will have changed significantly, and that facsimile transmission will be a vital part of library operations.

The Functions in Data Communication

Such a system requires equipment, aside from the data processing equipment itself, to carry out the functions necessary to data communication. It is useful to divide this equipment into four kinds (Figure 13.1): *terminal* equipment at each end for sending and receiving; *controllers* near the terminals to convert their sending signals into communications language, to buffer them into the communications line, and later to reconvert them into human readable form at the receiving terminal; a *communications channel* needed to link together the controllers and the terminals; and, finally, a *switching network*.

A *terminal* can be a keyboard printer (such as an electric typewriter or teletypewriter), a key-punch, or a paper-tape typewriter. Terminals, however, are

[2] Nelson Associates, *The New York State Library's Pilot Program in the Facsimile Transmission of Library Materials.* New York: June 1968.

[3] Schieber, William D., and Ralph M. Schoffner, *Telefacsimile in Libraries: A Report of an Experiment in Facsimile Transmission and an Analysis of Implications for Interlibrary Loan Systems.* Berkeley, California: Institute of Library Research, University of California, February 1968.

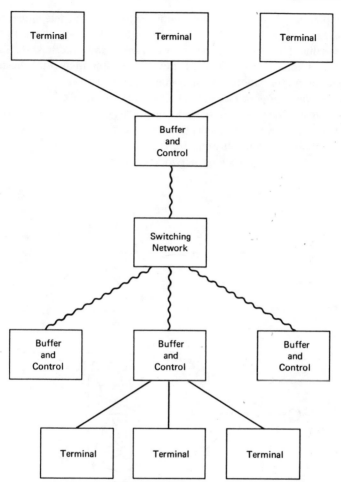

Figure 13.1   Schematic of communication flow.

not restricted to printing devices. They can also include visual display equipment, such as a TV screen, a graphical plotter, a magnetic recording station, or a telefacsimile. They can even include computers.

A *controller* is a device that converts the language of the terminal into signals compatible with the means of communication. It serves as buffer between the terminal and the communications channel to keep them synchronized. Automatic error detection and correction circuits built into the controller guarantee the accurate receipt and decoding of signals as sent. A controller may also provide a means for dialing connection with other specific terminals.

A *communications channel* is an electrical path of transmission between two or more points. The channel most familiar to us is the telephone line; new transmission techniques permit both voice and digital data to be transmitted over the same telephone channel. The capacity and transmission speeds of standard telephone lines are limited, however, and consequently the trend has been to develop alternate means of communication.

A *switching network* is needed because, as the telephone company recognized many years ago, it was neither practical nor economical to connect every telephone to every other telephone by direct wire. It is equally impractical to think that we can connect every library to every other library by direct line. Instead, some kind of switching network is needed. Figure 13.2 pictures the

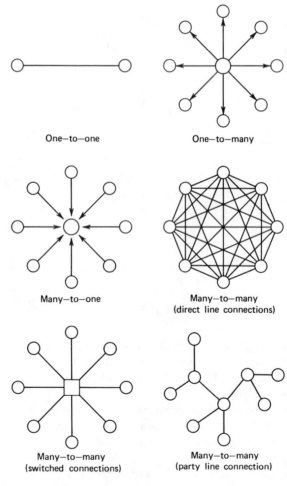

Figure 13.2   Basic network patterns.

variety of means of interconnecting a network of points—one-to-one, many-to-one, many-to-many, and so on. In general, the "many-to-many (switched connections)" network is the pattern of most modern communication systems.

In such switched networks, the central node can play many crucial roles. (1) It serves as the switching point, retransmitting messages from sending stations to the desired receiving stations. (2) It can provide directories and other aids to the switching function. (3) It can store messages and accumulate them for later transmission in a high-speed "burst." (4) It can serve as a focal point for management of an interlibrary communication network, including accounting for service costs. The design of a proper communications network depends on a clear definition of the traffic load that it must carry. In part, this depends on the number of messages that must be transmitted, the size or length of each, and their distribution in time and in space. Therefore, data on volume of activity (traffic load) must be gathered—point-to-point volumes, peak loads at various hours of the day and days of the year, and the like.

TRANSMISSION CAPABILITIES

Figure 13.3 lists the characteristics of a number of methods for transmission, including telephone lines of varying capacities as well as channels with broader bandwidth. AT & T has recently removed its restrictions against attaching devices to the regular telephone network.[4,5] This unprecedented change in policy will clear the way for makers of an array of message and picture transmission devices and remote computer terminals. Devices such as computers and their input and output equipment will simply plug into new units.

However, the "capacity" of telephone lines for the transfer of data is quite limited. The capacity of a communication channel itself is measured by its "bandwidth" (basically, the number of bits per second that can be transmitted over it without an intolerable error). Input and output devices, with speed characteristics of their own, may also impose limits on the useful bandwidth attainable by a channel to which they are directly connected (see Figure 13.4). Most of the research in the field of communication has been directed at providing means for greater bandwidth transmission methods.

"Microwave," for example, is the term that describes a "line of sight" communications transmission, by radio, capable of providing multichannel capacities. Microwave is in wide use today, and the common carriers depend heavily on it for their major routes. "Coaxial cable" is another high-capacity method, used in transmission of television signals (as in CATV). But no

---

[4] "AT&T opens the door," *Newsweek*, September 9, 1968, p. 72.
[5] "AT&T's new plug for phone lines," *Business Week*, September 7, 1968, p. 60 ff.

Figure 13.3 (a) Available communications services.

Service	Bandwidth	Bit Rate	Equivalent Voice Channels	Time (Seconds) to Transmit a Typed Page (Digital)	Cost
Low speed digital (Teletype)		75 bits/sec to 150 bits/sec (15 char/sec)	1/12	80	NA
Voice grade	4 kc	Up to 2000 bits/sec on usual dial network	1	6	NA
Telpak A	48 kc	Up to 40.8 kbits/sec with model 301 data set	12	.5	NA
Telpak B (withdrawn)	96 kc	Up to 80 kbits/sec	24	.25	NA
Telpak C	240 kc	Approximately 100 kbits/sec	60	.1	NA
Telpak D	1 mc	Approximately 500 kbits/sec	240	.03	NA
"Half video"	2 mc	Approximately 1 mbits/sec	480	.015	NA
Video	4–5 mc	Approximately 2 mbits/sec	1000	.007	NA
Microwave	8 mc	Approximately 4 mbits/sec	2000	.003	NA
Coaxial cable	8 mc	Approximately 4 mbits/sec	2000	.003	NA
Satellite	8 mc	Approximately 4 mbits/sec	2000	.003	NA
T–2 carrier		6 mbits/sec	3000	.002	NA
T–4 carrier		220 mbits/sec— sometime in the future	100,000	–	NA

Figure 13.3 (b)   Representative times for
telpak A transmission.

Typed page	0.5 sec (digital)
Low resolution black-white facsimile (100 lines/inch)	18 sec (digital) 12 sec (analog)
Low resolution half-tone facsimile (100 lines/inch)	1.3 min (digital) 12 sec (analog)
High resolution photo (1000 lines/inch)	2.2 hr (digital) 1/3 hr (analog)

discussion of the technologies pertinent to library communication would be complete without consideration of the role of long-range, global communications. Large-scale use of national libraries, regional reference centers, and specialized information centers by remote subscribers implies a continual and heavy flow of communication traffic. The newest and most promising high-capacity communications channel is the stationary communications satellite. The Communications Satellite Corporation's *Early Bird* satellite is located in a circular equatorial orbit 22,300 miles above the earth's surface. At this distance its speed keeps it in a stationary position relative to the earth. Consequently, it can be used as a communications channel between any two points within its reach. A signal beamed to the satellite from one point on the ground is amplified by the satellite and then rebroadcast to its destination. By 1967, COMSAT had placed two new communications satellites into orbit—one positioned over the Atlantic and the other over the Pacific. It is estimated that three communications satellites can reach every corner of the globe except for the North and South Poles. Satellite communications systems with many more channels will probably be in operation in a relatively few years. Their effect on world-wide communications will be tremendous and, in time, libraries undoubtedly will put them to use for both national and international bibliographical purposes.

Farther into the future is the use of "Lasers" for extremely wide-band transmission of as many as three billion (!) bits per second.

FACSIMILE

In facsimile transmission, images are transmitted by breaking them up into thousands—even millions—of tiny dots that are transmitted as electrical signals. A phototube scans each microscopic area of the document, registering its relative blackness. These signals are converted, either inside the facsimile equipment itself or in a Bell System Dataphone, to a form that can be transmitted over

Figure 13.4   Appropriate levels of service.

	Network			
	Narrow Band (150–300 cps)	Voice Band (4kc)	Broad Band (48kc–1mc)	Video (to 6mc)
(A) Alphanumeric data: Teletypewriters send and receive	X	X		
High speed printers		X	X	
Punched cards	X	X		
Punched tape	X	X	X	
Magnetic tape			X	
Cathode ray display tubes		X		X
Facsimile		X	X	
(B) "Static" graphic data: Electrowriters		X		
Cathode ray display tubes		X		X
Facsimile		X	X	
(C) "Telemetry" data: Sense/control devices	X	X	X	X
(D) Dynamic graphic data: EKG, other analog devices	X	X		
Television				X
(E) Voice: Telephone		X		

telephone lines, radio, or microwave. The picture is reassembled in the receiver, where the electrical signals recreate the original document, dot by dot. In some systems, the document is duplicated with the help of an electrostatic device similar to that in office copiers.

Copy Quality

Copy quality, of course, depends on how many dots are sent from transmitter to receiver. In a high resolution system, such as that used to send proofs of newspaper pages that can go right on a press, up to 1.5 million bits are sent per second. Only microwave or a special telephone line can handle this much traffic. For an office system, 1800 to 4000 bits are sent per second, which is about as much as the ordinary (or voice-grade) telephone line can handle. For example, LDX equipment comes with 135 or 190 LPI (lines per inch) resolution. The 190-line-per-inch machine provides better copy, but at the expense of speed. The 135 LPI resolution is normally adequate and does not present a problem unless one attempts transmission of pages where type fonts are smaller than six point.

Speed of Transmission

The use of facimile systems to provide rapid transfer of information has great appeal. For example, under current manual procedures, the service time for an interlibrary loan transaction usually takes over a week. By reorganizing the manual procedures leading to delivery via surface transport, it might be possible to reduce average service time to one or two days. By contrast, the use of telefascimile equipment, to replace surface transport, has the potential of providing an average service time of less than four hours. Such rapid interlibrary loan service would facilitate new modes of cooperative sharing and distribution of library resources.

Telefacsimile equipment alone, however, is not sufficient to provide this service. The equipment must be incorporated into a system whose manual procedures are efficient enough to take advantage of the rapid transmission speeds which the electronic equipment makes possible.

Processing Procedures and their Effects upon Speed

An assumption underlying the use of facsimile is a presumed ability to provide *rapid* response to requests. Its use can therefore be justified only if the delivery speed achieved is considered sufficiently important to justify the higher costs involved. A prime consideration in using facsimile as a means of transmitting library materials is therefore how fast the material can be placed in the hands of the user (the average service time).

Four major processing stages are distinguishable in the handling of a request: (1) manual procedures that involve accepting the request, getting the requested item from library shelves, and delivering it to the transmitting room; (2) waiting for transmission; (3) actual transmission of the request; and (4) manual procedures following transmission, which are concerned mainly with notifying the requestor that his material is ready to be picked up. The sum of the time required to accomplish these four stages is the service time.

Figure 13.5 shows the relationship of these characteristics in terms of service time and processing effort, as found in one facsimile experiment (at the University of California).[6] It shows total service time in terms of its two components: processing intervals and waiting intervals. The processing intervals represent the man-machine effort—that is, the time for the staff and equipment to perform some process on the transaction. During waiting intervals, no such processing is performed. From the chart it is apparent that by far the major portion of time is spent in waiting. (It is very significant that the elapsed time between notification and pickup accounted for 45 percent of the total service time from request receipt to pickup.)

The waiting time for transmission results from the fact that facsimile equipment operates at a fixed maximum rate. If the demand during a given period of time is less than this maximum rate, the excess capacity in the equipment cannot be used for other purposes and is lost. On the other hand, excess demand beyond the capacity of the equipment causes the accumulation of a backlog—a queue—of material waiting for processing. Much of it will, of course, be transmitted in periods of low service demand. To reduce the waiting time will necessitate providing excess machine capacity (at additional cost). Unfortunately, in all libraries variation in hourly demand is typical. During the University of California experiment, this variation caused as much as four hours of delay from the time the requested material arrived at the facsimile room until it was transmitted, even though the total request volume during the experiment amounted to only one-third of the total transmission capacity of the equipment.

Delays in the manual processing parts of the operation are caused by the same interplay of demand and capacity. Capacity, however, is not so fixed. The personnel use skills that are similar to those applied to other portions of library operations. As a result, it may be possible to utilize these personnel for other activities as well as for the telefacsimile system when the request rate requires it. In this kind of situation the additional cost of staff to take care of a high level of demand with little delay does not create as much lost productive capacity in periods of low demand as would be the case if the personnel were dedicated solely to the telefacsimile operation. But this sharing of personnel must be carefully planned and executed.

Costs

There are two major costs in responding to requests using facsimile equipment. The first is the fixed monthly cost regardless of the amount of

---

[6] Schieber, William D., and Ralph M. Shoffner, *op. cit.*

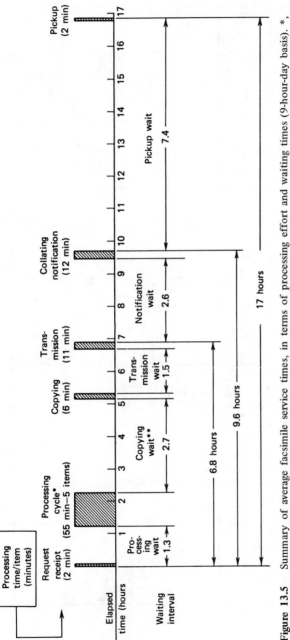

Figure 13.5 Summary of average facsimile service times, in terms of processing effort and waiting times (9-hour-day basis). *, Processing time/item = minutes; and **, copying wait is actually part of the transmission wait, since the copying equipment was faster and could readily keep ahead of the transmission equipment. (Thus the addition of copy equipment would not reduce the wait time.)

409

Figure 13.6 Summary of facsimile costs (UC Experiment).

Monthly Trans-action Volume	Average Number of Pages per Transaction	Total Pages per Month	Cost per Month (Dollars)				Cost per Page (Dollars)	Cost per Trans-action (Dollars)	Staff Cost as Percent of Total Cost
			Equipment and Supplies	Line	Staff[a]	Total (Dollars)			
50	10	500	1,287	2,321	89	3,697	7.394	73.94	2.4
	15	750	1,301	2,321	114	3,735	4.980	74.70	3.0
	20	1,000	1,324	2,321	139	3,773	3.773	75.46	3.7
100	10	1,000	1,314	2,321	178	3,812	3.812	38.12	4.7
	15	1,500	1,340	2,321	228	3,889	2.592	38.89	5.9
	20	2,000	1,367	2,321	278	3,965	1.982	39.64	7.0
250	10	2,500	1,393	2,321	444	4,158	1.663	16.63	10.7
	15	3,750	1,522	2,321	569	4,412	1.176	17.64	12.9
	20	5,000	1,651	2,321	694	4,665	0.933	18.66	14.9
500	10	5,000	1,651	2,321	888	4,859	0.972	9.72	18.3
	15	7,500	1,909	2,321	1,138	5,367	0.716	10.74	21.2
	20	10,000	2,166	2,321	1,388	5,874	0.587	11.74	23.6
1000	10	10,000	2,166	2,321	1,775	6,262	0.626	6.26	28.3
	15	15,000	2,556	2,321	2,275	7,652	0.510	7.65	30.0
	20	20,000	3,021	2,321	2,775	8,117	0.406	8.12	34.2

[a]Staff costs are computed on the assumption that transactions (service requests) represent 80 percent of the total request volume.

Figure 13.7   Facsimile equipment.

Manufacturer	Name	Cost (Dollars/Month)	Rate (Minute/Page)	Comments
A. B. Dick	Videograph	1170	.1	Telpak
Alden	Docufax	250	3–6	Rate depends on resolution
Dictaphone	Datafax	107	6	Telephone lines
Electronic Image Systems	Telikon	NA	1	Telephone lines
Graphic Sciences	Transceiver	100	6	Telephone lines
Litton	Litcom	170	3.5	
	Litcom	100	6	
Magnavox	Magnafax	65	6	Telephone lines
Muirhead	Mufax	230	6	
Stewart–Warner	Datafax	150	4.5	Telephone lines
Telautograph	Facsimile	210	6	
Xerox	Telecopier	65 and use charge	6	Adapted from Magnafax
	LDX Scanner	550	1	Requires Co-Ax or Microwave
	LDX Printer	650	1	Xerox output
	Document Feeder	40		Necessary for effective use
Victor Comptometer	Electrowriter	50	NA	Handwritten
Western Union	Datafax	100		Telephone lines

activity, and the second is the variable cost required to handle each of the requests in the system.

Figure 13.6 presents a summary of costs, based on the experiment at the University of California, under several assumptions: (1) that all installation charges would be amortized over a three-year period; (2) that the transmission line would be priced at the commercial rate, derived from interstate broad-band rates for a 48kc channel; and (3) that each scanner communicates with only one printer. Information is shown for varying monthly request volumes at each of three average request sizes. Thus, it is useful to show both the cost per page and the cost per transaction. (The cost of nonserviced requests is allocated to the serviced requests. In the experiment the ratio of serviced to nonserviced requests was 4:1.)

Equipment Costs. Figure 13.7 gives a summary of representative facsimile transmission equipment, and Figure 13.8 furnishes the equation for calculation of costs.

Transmission Costs. Any prediction of total cost of a facsimile system is complicated by the fact that transmission costs vary so widely, depending on local factors. Like equipment costs, there are two types of charges: recurring charges (usually expressed in terms of dollars per month) and one-time installation charges (which are amortized over a given period). The transmission line charges shown in Figure 13.7 use the commercial interstate rates for a 48kc

Figure 13.8   Telefacsimile equipment cost (excluding transmission link)

Total monthly equipment cost =

$$C_{equip} =$$

$$(C_{scan} \times Q_{scan} + C_{prnt} \times Q_{prnt} + C_{adf} \times Q_{adf})$$
$$+ (I_{scan} \times Q_{scan} + I_{prnt} \times Q_{prnt})/R$$
$$+ (C_{page} + C_{suppl}) \times V_{tr} \times A$$
$$+ (V_{xtra} \times C_{xtra})$$

Parameter		Experimental Value
C_{scan}	= monthly charge, each scanner	550
Q_{scan}	= number of scanners	1
C_{prnt}	= monthly charge, each printer	650
Q_{prnt}	= number of printers (where $Q_{scan} = Q_{prnt}$)	1
C_{adf}	= monthly charge, each ADF	40
Q_{adf}	= number of automatic document feeders	1
I_{scan}	= installation charge, each scanner	300
I_{prnt}	= installation charge, each printer	450
R	= amortization period, number of months	36
C_{page}	= unit cost/914 page	.05
V_{tr}	= number of transactions/month	Variable
A	= average number of pages/transaction	Variable
C_{suppl}	= monthly supply cost/page	.003
V_{xtra}	= number of pages in excess of 2500 x Q_{scan}	Variable

channel (Series 8000 service, formerly TELPAK "A"). The rates for this service are as follows:

Mileage	Cost per mile per month
0 – 250	$15.00
251 – 500	10.50
501 and up	7.50

To be able to transmit facsimile information, an interface unit (called a "data set" or "modem") is required at each station. The cost of each unit is approximately $450 per month. Installation costs are extremely variable; for this reason we have not attempted to estimate them.

Staff. Staff costs fluctuate considerably, depending on the method used to provide service. If requested items are to be obtained immediately from the shelves, are to be Xeroxed, and transmitted promptly, the elapsed time for the completion of transactions will be minimized; but staffing costs will be greater than with a slower, but more economical, method in which requests are batched.

Suggested Reading

Communication is such a technically complex field that it is difficult to find relatively readable surveys. The following, however, seems to provide a start:

Gentle, Edgar C., Jr. (ed.), *Data Communications in Business.* New York: American Telephone and Telegraph Company, 1965.

Part Four   Library Clerical Processes

Chapter 14

ADMINISTRATIVE DATA PROCESSING

INTRODUCTION

Previously, we have considered a variety of background issues related to data processing in the library—the general context, in terms of principles of good management and existing developments throughout the country; the specific context of data processing management within the individual library; and the nature of the technology involved. Now we examine the central issues in library data processing—the evaluation of specific library subsystems. In this chapter (and in Chapters 15 to 18), we shall discuss each of the major areas of application of data processing to library clerical operations. Then, in the final two chapters (Chapters 19 and 20) we shall similarly consider applications to the more intellectual aspects of library operation.

Library System Schematic

Before proceeding, however, let us fit each of these subsystems into the framework of a total library system schematic, so that the interrelationships among subsystems can be kept in mind as we consider each in turn. As shown in Figure 14.1, the library system schematic consists of six major functional subsystems (administrative, ordering, cataloging, circulation, serials, and information services) considered at four levels of processing (administrative, financial, mechanical, and intellectual).

	Chapter 14 Administrative Subsystem	Chapter 16 Ordering Subsystem	Chapter 17 Cataloging Subsystem	Chapter 15 Circulation Subsystem	Chapter 18 Serials Subsystem	Chapter 19 Information Services Subsystem
Administrative Processing	Personnel and Payroll; Cost Accounting; Statistics; Budgeting	In Process	In Process			
Financial Processing	Book-keeping; Purchasing; Accounts Payable	Fund Accounts; Ordering; Vendor Files		Overdues	Renewal; Claiming	

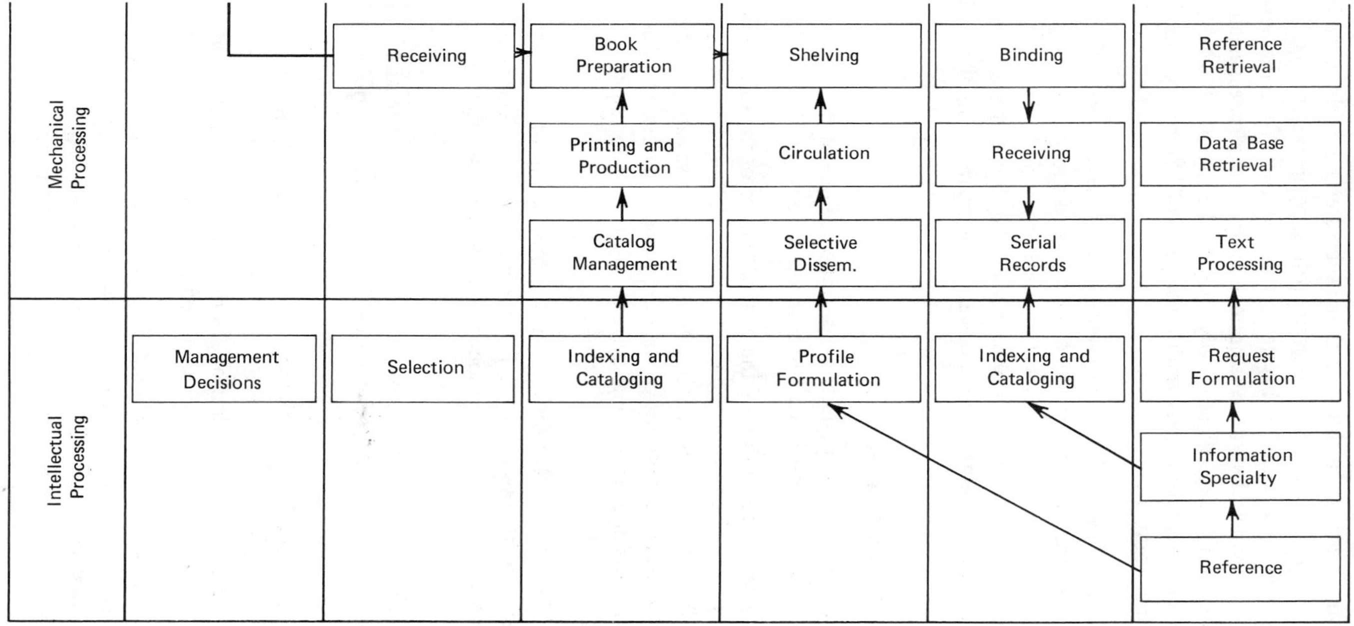

Figure 14.1 Library system schematic.

Functional Division. The division into functional subsystems is fairly obvious and consistent with the usual pattern of looking at library operations, except perhaps for the "information services" subsystem. This one arises from the new opportunities for service which data processing technology provides, especially through the increasing availability of nationally produced magnetic tape data files. The others are simply more or less traditional parts of library "technical services" and library management.

Levels of Processing. The division into levels of processing provides a relatively simple way of distinguishing between the kinds of processing that are somewhat comparable to processes in business (administrative and financial), the kinds of processing that are specialized to library operation but still are purely clerical or mechanical, and the kinds that involve a high degree of intellectual content.

Format for System Description

Each of the chapters in Part IV presents a description of one of these library subsystems. In doing this, the format described below is followed.

Background. This gives a description of the general nature of the subsystem, with emphasis on its role in the library and on the functional requirements that it must satisfy. Specific criteria (both quantitative and qualitative) are presented for the evaluation of alternative methods of meeting those requirements. Some of the relevant experiments and operational systems in libraries throughout the country are reviewed.

Forms and Files. Then the various forms and files involved in the subsystem are described (in the formats presented in Figures 6.8 and 6.9). The general character of file management functions associated with their maintenance are discussed.

Processing Schematic. For the subsystem, as a whole and where feasible for individual file management functions, schematics are presented describing the operation.

Parameters for Estimation. For each subsystem, parameters relevant to estimation of processing times and costs are presented. Where it is possible, representative values are provided. In addition, as discussed later, an illustrative example is used and the values implied by it are listed as well.

Equations for Estimation. For each subsystem, equations for cost estimation are presented. These are all examples of the basic model outlined in Chapter 7. An example is given, showing the application of these equations to the evaluation of alternative systems in a moderately large library, using the format of Figure 7.3.

It must be recognized that all of these descriptions and estimates are only illustrative. Although we feel they are realistic, they cannot be used to provide accurate estimates for any particular library. At best, they can serve as a starting point for the analyst in the description of his own library and in evaluation of alternatives.

Alternative Configurations of Equipment

To provide a picture of the nature of the alternatives for each subsystem, we consider three levels and kinds of installation: (1) a small library-based, batch processing computer system; (2) a larger batch processing system; and (3) a very large on-line system. Each of the latter two is representative of what might be available from a parent organization or a commercial service bureau.

Small-Scale Library-Based Facility. Figure 14.2 lists a typical small-scale facility, suitable for consideration by a library large enough to justify its own equipment. The internal memory limits the complexity of process that can be handled, and computers of this general size can perform only about 10,000 operations per second (for instance 100 microseconds add time). The operation must therefore be oriented around batch processing, with extensive card handling. The external file equipment that can be used with such computers

Figure 14.2   Small-scale batch processing computer.

Equipment Components	Monthly Costs (Dollars)
Computer (with 16,000 characters of internal memory)	1,800
Card input, output, and handling	500
Terminal equipment	1,000[a]
Printer (500 lines per minute)	500
Magnetic tape handlers	2,000
Magnetic disk unit	1,000
Communication lines	
Key-punch units	200[a]
	7,000

Personnel	Monthly Salaries
Operating	3,900
Supervisory	1,200
	5,100

[a] In a small-scale facility, terminal equipment and communication line charges will arise only from the circulation control sub-system and will function off-line.

tends to be limited both in capacity and in data-transfer rates. The magnetic tape they use, for example, will store about 10 million characters, and the tape handlers will transfer data at only 15,000 to 20,000 characters per second; magnetic discs will store about 5 million characters with random access time of about .1 second. However, the other peripheral equipment—printers, card devices, and the like—are comparable to those that larger computers will use.

Large-Scale Batch Processing Facility. Figure 14.3 lists a normal large-scale facility, suitable for use in a fairly large organization. Only the very largest libraries can justify a dedicated facility of this size, but many libraries will have such facilities available to them from their parent organizations or commercial service bureaus. The internal memory is large enough to handle even very complex tasks. The operating speed (usually about 20 microsecond add time) is fast enough for a limited degree of "on-line processing," but for efficiency such systems are primarily used for large-scale batch operations. External files can be maximum performance units with large capacities and high data transfer rates—up to 150,000 characters per second.

Large-Scale On-Line Processing System. Figure 14.4 lists a very large-scale very high-speed system, representing the kind of equipment on which most of the speculation about the future role of computing is based. The system would be found in very large companies, in large universities, and in a computer "utility." Particularly as the latter becomes a reality, libraries of all sizes may find themselves using such facilities. The size of memory is large enough to handle "multiprocessing" of several tasks at the same time, many of them on-line and even interactive, and many of them batch. The speed of operation (with add times of 1 or 2 microseconds!) is fast enough to meet all the needs of on-line processing of several simultaneous users. The peripheral equipment, magnetic tapes, and magnetic disks will have the highest possible performance. A complete installation will even include one or more subsidiary computers operating under the control of the master computer.

Summary of Capacities. These three facilities differ significantly in their efficiency (cost/effectiveness) as well as in their inherent capacity for processing and file storage. Since, in this chapter and the succeeding ones, we shall make rough comparisons of their relative performance on library subsystems, it is useful to summarize some representative data concerning these differences in capacity. These data, necessarily, will be simplified and therefore should be regarded only as illustrative. However, care has been taken to assure that they are at least reasonably close to reality.

One primary issue in evaluating processing capacity is the time for sorting. In Chapter 12, equations for estimating sorting time were presented. Here they have been simplified and specialized to the three alternative configurations of

Figure 14.3   Large-scale batch processing computer.

Equipment Components	Monthly Costs (Dollars)
Computer (with 128,000 characters of internal memory)	5,000
Card input, output, handling	1,500
Terminal equipment	2,000[a]
Printer (1000 lines per minute)	800
Magnetic tape handlers	4,000
Magnetic disk units	4,000
Communication controls	1,500
Key-punch units	1,000
	19,800

Personnel	Monthly Salaries
Operating	12,000
Supervisory	4,000
	16,000

[a] Terminal equipment is limited to circulation transactors and a few on-line typewriters.

Figure 14.4   Large-scale on-line computer.

Equipment Components	Monthly Costs (Dollars)
Computer (with 1 million characters of internal memory	50,000
Peripheral input-output (card equipment, printers, etc.)	10,000
Terminal equipment	10,000
Magnetic tape handlers	10,000
Magnetic disk units	20,000
Communication line	[a]
Communication controls	10,000
Subsidiary, slave computers	30,000
	140,000

Personnel	Monthly Salaries
Operating	37,000
Systems programming	20,000
Supervisory	13,000
	70,000

[a] Communication line charges depend on the volume of traffic and the geographic distances. (See Chapter 13 for a discussion of the typical costs.)

the equipment. Figure 14.5 presents them graphically by the ranges of times for sorting batches of various sizes (expressed in terms of "number of characters in batch").[1]

Fortunately for the computer user, manufacturers provide the user with various software packages that include the sort generator routines necessary to meet sorting requirements; manufacturers also provide sort-timing tables, graphs, and formulas like those in Figure 14.5.[2] The most important single factor in such timing estimates for library application is the rate of transfer from magnetic tape into memory, and out to tape after processing. Computer manufacturers estimate the character (or digit) per second transfer rate to magnetic tape units, calculated on the basis of the tape running continuously, from the very beginning of a reel to end, without any stops occurring until the entire tape has been read. The actual transfer rate is determined by this basic data-transfer rate, the size of blocks, and the degree to which reading from an input tape can be overlapped with writing the output tape. Figure 14.6 provides estimates of these, for the various sizes of files and for each level of equipment.

Another primary issue is the time for processing a simple "record up-date." In general, a transaction will affect several totals recorded in the stored records involved. The time to carry out the simple computations is therefore dependent on the basic add time of the computer and the number of totals affected. A typical "record up-date operation" is diagrammed in Figure 14.7. Included are estimates of the time for executing such an operation.

Normally, the easiest to estimate of all computer-system running times are the timings that occur as a result of input or output. The estimate is calculated as an elementary division problem as described below.[3]

(a)   For a card read operation estimate:

$$\frac{\text{Volume of cards to be read}}{\text{Card reader rated speed (cpm)}} = \text{minutes of processing}$$

(b)   For a card punch operation estimate:

$$\frac{\text{Volume of cards to be punched}}{\text{Card punch rated speed (cpm)}} = \text{minutes of processing}$$

(c)   For a print operation estimate:

$$\frac{\text{Number of lines to be printed}}{\text{Printer rated speed (1pm)}} = \text{minutes of processing}$$

---

[1] *Sorting Techniques.* White Plains, New York: IBM (C20-1639).

[2] *System 360 Operating System Sort (Merge).* White Plains, New York, IBM No. S360-33 (C 28-6543-3).

[3] Kudlinski, James R., "Estimating Computer System Running Time," in *Data Processing Systems Encyclopedia.* Detroit: American Data Processing, Inc., September 1965, pp. 21-31.

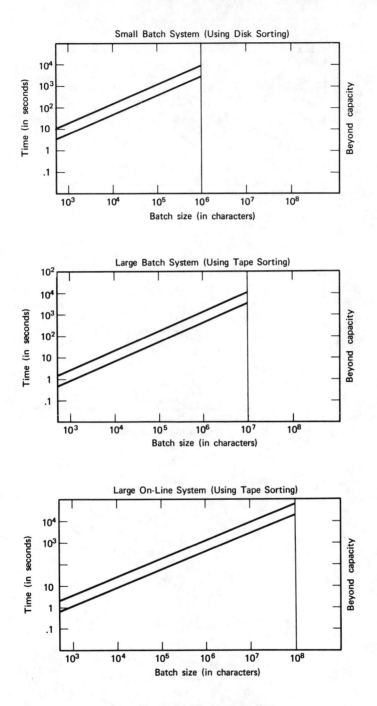

Figure 14.5 Estimates of sorting time.

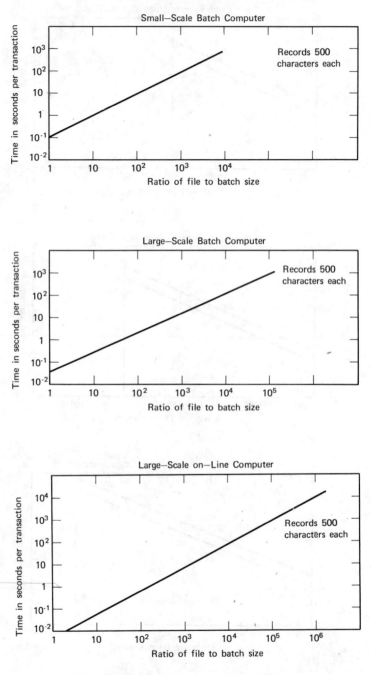

Figure 14.6 Sequential access times.

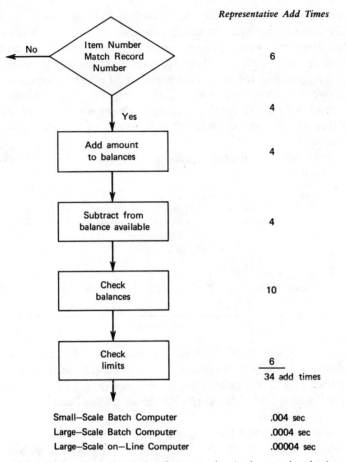

Figure 14.7   Typical record-update operation (and processing time).

These estimates also can be expressed in terms of characters.

Another issue affecting processing capacity is the degree of independence among components—that is, to what extent each component is "tied-up" or committed during the execution times required by other components. For example, during the time required for card input, the card reader is of course completely committed, but the computer may be committed for only a percentage of the same time. The size of that percentage depends partly on the relative speed of operation of different devices, partly on the availability of independent buffers, controls, and communication lines, and partly on the number of independent tasks that can be processed at the same time. Generally, of course, the larger the computer, the greater is the degree of independence in operation. Basically, the small-scale batch computer allows a bare minimum of independent operation, especially in the context of library tasks, which involve primarily input-output and file handling operations with only limited processing. The large-scale batch computer may have capacity for as many as 10 simultaneous tasks—with the library perhaps only one of the users—and can provide a high degree of independent operation of peripheral equipment; on the average, because of variation in work load, it might be expected that five tasks will be processed simultaneously. The large-scale, on-line computer has capacity for perhaps 50 simultaneous tasks although, again on the average, only 25 might be processed at a time.

The three facilities might compare with one another in approximately the ratios shown in Figure 14.8.

Figure 14.8   Comparison of computer systems.

	Cost	Computing Capacity	File Capacity	Input-Output Capacity
Small-Scale Batch	1	1	1	1
Large-Scale Batch	3	10	10	5
Large-Scale On-Line	20	400	100	25

Figure 14.9 summarizes the typical characteristics for the three levels of equipment, including estimates of the degrees of independence and resulting basis for charging for computer time. We shall use these in subsequent estimates for the processing times and costs of the three levels of computer facilities on each library subsystem.

For purposes of testing the approach to estimation and for comparison with the computer based methods, the comparable characteristics of a manual system and a punched card system are given in Figure 14.10.

Illustrative Example.

In this chapter and subsequent ones, the use of parameters and equations for estimation of processing times and costs are illustrated by an example of a fairly large library. Its characteristics are shown in Figure 14.11. The data-processing load that such a library creates is summarized in Figure 14.12, in terms of each of the three alternative computer configurations and the comparative manual and punched card system.

As we pointed out earlier, this comparison is intended only as illustrative. In particular, it considers only *direct* costs and only those for which comparison is possible. As a result, the total salaries for the manual system ($19,197/mo.) are at most 20% of the total salary budget for 200 full-time staff.

Figure 14.9 Equipment and personnel parameters.

Costs	Representative Values		
	Small-Scale Batch	Large-Scale Batch	Large-Scale On-line
C_P = Cost of input-output processing and file access	$30/hour	$225/hour x 20%	$625/hour x 4%
C_F = Cost of file availability (per 1 million characters)		$.20/hour	$.10/hour
C_K = Cost of key-boarding	$ 3/hour	$ 3/hour	$ 3/hour
C_T = Cost of terminals	$.30/hour	$.30/hour	$.50/hour
Processing Rates			
R_{IO} = Input-output rate	600 char/sec	2000 char/sec	2000 char/sec
R_{MT} = Magnetic tape read rate	15,000 char/sec	50,000 char/sec	100,000 char/sec
R_{PR} = Processing rate (representative operations)	250/sec	2500/sec	25,000/sec
R_{SO} = Sorting rate (average)	1000 char/sec	2000 char/sec	3000 char/sec
R_{KB} = Key-boarding rate	6000/hour	6000/hour	6000/hour
R_{FI} = File interrogation rate	5/sec	50/sec	100/sec
R_{CO} = File collation rate	7500 char/sec	25,000 char/sec	50,000 char/sec

Figure 14.10 Manual and punched card parameters.

Costs	Manual	P/C
C_P = Cost of input-output processing and file access	$3/hour	$6/hour
C_F = Cost of File Availability (per 1 million characters)	$.005/hour	$.005/hour
C_K = Cost of key-boarding	$3/hour	$3/hour
Processing Rates		
R_{IO} = Input-output rate		200 char/sec
R_{ME} = File update rate	10 char/sec	100 char/sec
R_{PR} = Processing rate (for a representative operation)	.01/sec	1/sec
R_{SO} = Sorting rate (typical batch of 500 character records)	10 rec/min	30 rec/min
R_{KB} = Key-boarding rate	10,000/hour	6000/hour
R_{FI} = File interrogation rate	.03/sec	.03/sec
R_{CO} = File collation rate	100 char/sec	200 char/sec

Allocation of Excess Capacity. As Figure 14.12 shows, the work load on even the small-scale batch-processing system does not completely cover the operating costs of the facility itself (Figure 14.2). There is thus an excess of capacity, and the problems discussed in Chapter 7, concerning how the uncovered cost should be allocated, become very important. If this cost is allocated proportionally to the directly attributable costs, the cost/effectiveness values presented in subsequent chapters must be correspondingly increased.

Figure 14.11   Illustrative library.

Size of collection	1,500,000 volumes
Size of staff	200 people
Circulation	100,000/month
Acquisitions	5,000/month
Size of catalog	4,000,000 entries
Number of serials	25,000 serials
Yearly Budget	$2,500,000

These issues also arise in the operation of larger-scale facilities. As Figure 14.12 shows, even a large library would use only a very small percentage of their capacities. Such facilities therefore can serve a large number of users, although the likelihood is that they will still have excess capacities uncovered by the total charges for direct time of all users. It is likely that such "overhead" will be allocated in proportion to total usage, but frequently small users will bear a heavier proportional load.

Cost of On-Line Availability. A second issue arises with respect to the costs displayed in Figure 14.12. Since they reflect only the charges for the time of actual utilization of the computer, they do not include any allocation for the costs of on-line availability. Of course, this issue is not relevant with respect to the small-scale system, which operates only in a batch mode. For the other two systems, however, it is especially important, and an understanding of these costs will provide significant insight into the problems involved in on-line operation.

First, on-line operation requires an operating system appreciably more sophisticated than does batch operation. This results in an increase, even to double, in the amount of internal memory devoted to the operating system— from 50,000 characters without on-line operation to 100,000 characters with it, for example. The result is a reduction in the amount of memory available for production programs.

Second, the dedication of any portion of this available memory to one user makes it unavailable to other users. The most reasonable and likely basis for estimating the cost of on-line availability is therefore to derive it from the proportion of available memory which is consumed. If 100 percent of the

Figure 14.12   Summary of monthly processing load, illustrative library

Hours (Equipment and Operating Personnel)	Administrative Hours	Circulation Hours	Order Hours	Catalog Hours	Serial Hours	Total
Manual						
Punched-card	52	220	158	243		673
Small-scale	11	65	47	95	12	230
Large-scale	2	10	12	59	2	85
On-line	1	7	11	25	2	46

Hours (Clerical Personnel)	Administrative Hours	Circulation Hours	Order Hours	Catalog Hours	Serial Hours	Total
Manual	109	3734	2223	518	785	7369
Punched-card	60	2758	876	581	785	5060
Small-scale	60	1720	642	125	300	2847
Large-scale	60	1720	642	125	300	2847
On-line	60	1720	642	125	300	2847

Total cost	Administrative	Circulation	Order	Catalog	Serial	Total
Manual	$326	$7544	$6669	$2303[a]	$2355	$19,197
Punched-card	492	6951	3573	3203	2355	16,574
Small-scale	413	6513	2724	3237[b]	1308	14,195[b]
Large-scale	274	5023	2445	1621	977	10,340
On-line	212	4819	2196	1000	936	9163[c]

[a] Card catalog maintenance (2 card catalogs).
[b] Normally, the production of catalogs will involve joint use of the small-scale computer and a large-scale computer for high-volume printing. These costs would be comparably reduced to about $1600 and $12,600, respectively.
[c] If full costs of on-line availability are also charged, this total will be about $20,000.

available memory is required, then 100 percent of the costs must be charged, even if no actual use is made of it.[4]

For example, in the large-scale batch system (Figure 14.3) with only 125,000 characters of memory, the available memory would be reduced from 75,000 characters to only 25,000. This remaining memory is therefore a very precious commodity. If the library requires on-line availability of the computer, a major

[4] A representative formula for charging was installed at UCLA (Campus Computing Network, *BITS,* Vol III, No. 10, March 5, 1969):

$$\text{Charge} = \$.04(T + .020\,I)\,(1 + .004\,R)$$

Where T = CPU dedicated time in seconds, I = number of input/output requests, and R = size of memory dedicated to task, expressed in thousands of bytes.

portion of its operating programs must be stored in the internal memory and the rest must be readily accessibly in direct access files. Everything indicates that this would mean devoting all 25,000 characters to the library—in effect, a dedication of the entire computer to the library, even though it may really use only 10 percent of its capacity. It is for this reason that such a facility has been regarded solely as a batch-processing one, even though its basic operating speeds would allow it to handle on-line interrogations.

For the large-scale on-line facility, with 1 million characters of memory, the situation is quite different. The on-line operating system, using 100,000 characters, would leave 900,000 characters for production programs. However, it must be recognized that internal memory is still a precious commodity. If the library's programs consume 25,000 to 50,000 characters, this will mean charging the library about 3 to 5 percent of the total costs of the facility, over and above its direct charges for actual utilization.

If this method of costing is applied, the cost of on-line operation would be increased by about $8000 per month. Of course, this cost might be distributed across a large number of libraries that were all customers of the single installation. However, these effects must be recognized.

Assignment of Responsibilities

The issue of excess capacity (or even, in some cases, deficiencies in capacity) implicitly raises a most important consideration, relevant to each of the subsystems being considered: Who does what? Libraries rarely exist independent of other institutions. Usually they are part of some larger organization, with its own data processing requirements and frequently even its own installation of data processing equipment. A most significant decision, then, is which functions (if any) are to be handled on the library's own "dedicated" equipment, which functions are to be handled on the equipment of the parent organization, and which functions may be contracted to commercial service bureaus.

This issue is most evident with respect to the subsystem to be considered in this chapter—the administrative subsystem. Frequently, if not usually, there will not even be a decision problem: the parent organization traditionally assumes responsibility for all administrative, financial, and managerial accounting. In fact, since this is so frequently the case, it might be considered that the administrative subsystem is irrelevant to library data processing. However, the issue of system evaluation is still relevant, wherever the processing will be done. Furthermore, the library has its own needs for administrative data and must be clearly aware of the nature of the data processing requirements they represent, even if they may be satisfied elsewhere. For the other subsystems, on the other hand, the decision problem is highly relevant.

ADMINISTRATIVE DATA PROCESSING SUBSYSTEM

It is useful to start out discussions of library subsystems with administrative data processing because, of all of them, it is the most nearly comparable to those that one finds in a typical small business. Thus there is a considerable amount of existing expertise, procedures, experience, and basis for evaluation on which to draw. On the other hand, there is a remarkable lack of descriptive information concerning library administrative data processing recorded in the library literature.[5-8] It is almost as if it were regarded as beneath the librarian's position to be concerned with such mundane issues as personnel records, payroll, purchasing, and accounting. Yet, the facts are that whether or not the librarian himself is responsible for the actual data processing work in these areas, the ways in which they are done have a direct and immediate impact on the library and its professional responsibilities.

General Nature of Administrative Data Processing

The files and functions in administrative data processing can be conveniently grouped into three categories: (1) those concerned with financial issues, (2) those concerned with personnel, and (3) those concerned with management.

Financial Issues. The librarian is responsible for management of and accounting for a number of kinds of funds: book funds, expenses, and capital investment, for example. He must prepare a budget to cover the library's requirements for funds; he must control the way in which that budget is spent; he must pay for what is received; and he must be accountable for the results. Accounts must be kept which record all sources of income and disbursements of funds; books and supplies must be purchased, and the vendors must be paid; reports must be prepared to describe and to justify how money was used; and the data from past experience must be used to determine what the future requirements will be. All of this requires the maintenance and use of files of data.

---

[5] Wheeler, Joseph L., and Herbert Goldhor, *Practical Administration of Public Libraries.* New York: Harper and Row, 1962.

[6] Wilson, Louis Round, and Maurice F. Tauber, *The University Library,* 2nd Ed. New York: Columbia University Press, 1956, pp. 101-105.

[7] Wright, E. A., *Public Library Finance and Accounting,* American Library Association, 1943.

[8] Yarboff, Arthur, *A Survey of the Business Records and Procedures of the Racine Public Library.* Racine, Wisconsin: Public Library, 1951.

Personnel Issues. The library is staffed with professional librarians, technical personnel, clerks, and hourly employees. They must be hired, assigned to work, and paid; their costs must be allocated to one or another financial account. Reports must be made to the government and to library management. This also requires the maintenance and use of files of data.

Management Issues. The management of a library requires reports that can only be obtained from the processing of large quantities of data—inventory control, cost accounting, assignment of work loads and planning for production, and maintenance of statistics for measurement of performance. Again, as we shall discuss, this requires the maintenance and use of files of data.

Qualitative Character of the Library

In reviewing these aspects of administrative data processing, there are the following special characteristics about the library that must be kept in mind.

Nonprofit. Most libraries (and especially public, school, and academic research libraries) are nonprofit organizations. Therefore, some of the practices appropriate to profit-making corporations are simply not applicable. This has been most evident in the historic differences in handling direct and indirect costs, with nonprofit corporations tending to put a far higher percentage of expenditures into direct costs. It is also evident in the infrequent use of "depreciation" in library accounting, presumably because, in contrast to a business, there is no reason for concern with the tax advantages that depreciation offers. (To an extent, it is a pity that nonprofit and particularly public institutions do not handle their accounting as do private institutions. The lack of any real indication of the sizable capital investment they represent makes them appear to be "tax sinks" rather than the productive elements of society that they are.)

Service. Libraries are service institutions and, actually, provide a most intangible kind of service: information. Consequently, there are significant differences from the accounting practices in manufacturing organizations. To an extent, there are now appearing on the scene commercial organizations with comparable accounting needs—the computer service bureaus, the "information industry" and the like.

Nonindependence. Few libraries exist as independent entities. Most libraries are a part of a university, a governmental agency, a school, or a company. The accounting practices that they must follow are almost certain to be those of the parent institution. In fact, as we have pointed out, they usually will be carried out by the parent institution itself.

Figure 14.13   Relative sizes of libraries and companies.

Employees	Libraries in California	Percentage	Manufacturing Establishments in California	Percentage
1-4	340	47.5	10,004	41
5-9	150	20.9	4,141	17
10-19	95	13.3	3,717	15.5
20-49	80	11.1	3,543	14
50-99	31	4.3	1,498	6
100-249	15	2.1	1,009	4
250-499	3	.5	359	1.5
500-2500	2	.3	210	.9
2500-up	0	0	28	.1
Total	716	100.0	24,509	100.0

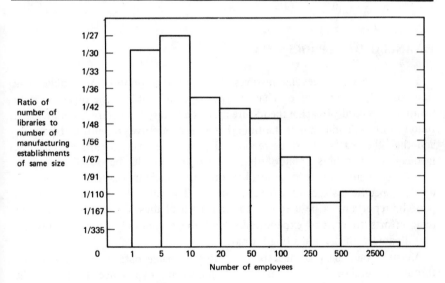

Quantitative Character of the Library

Some perspective on the sizes of libraries is provided by the comparison (Figure 14.13) of libraries in general with manufacturing companies.[9-10] As the

[9] Brault, Nancy W., "Statistics on the Libraries of the State of California," in *Mechanized Information Services in California Public Libraries.* Los Angeles: Institute of Library Research, University of California, January 31, 1968.

[10] *Census of Manufacturers. California:* U.S. Department of Commerce, Bureau of the Census, 1960.

figure shows, libraries are really quite small in size; a large library has a staff of 500 to 1000 (and a budget of only $5 million to $10 million). As a result, if only the standard accounting functions were being considered, at most a small level of computing capacity would be required. This becomes very clear as we consider the work load represented by, for example, the library's payroll.

On the other hand, as we shall observe in subsequent chapters, the services of the library involve a high work load of data processing, especially in terms of the sizes of files. For example, the catalog of a library can be as large as 10^9 to 10^{10} characters—a size that stretches the capacity of present technology. Even operations such as serial records maintenance, which is somewhat analogous to inventory control, are much larger processing tasks than their counterparts in manufacturing companies of comparable size. As a result, data processing is certain to be considerably more expensive for a library than for an industrial concern. In a sense, it becomes comparable to mechanizing the manufacturing process and not just the paper work.

FINANCIAL DATA PROCESSING

Financial data processing involves the normal accounting or bookkeeping functions, the control of purchasing, the payment of bills. The objective is to maintain a record of each expenditure against a library budgetary account. Each fund must be encumbered at the time that even a tentative commitment is made, and then the records must be reconciled with the actual amounts paid against invoices or vouchers. Major library accounts should be subdivided into allocations small enough for control by organizational units assigned responsibility for specific categories of expenditures. To make this effective, regular, periodic reports must be prepared to assist each of these organizational units in their efforts to control expenditures, and the accounting structure must be coordinated with the budgeting format.

Means should be provided for projecting probable patterns of expenditure through the end of the fiscal year, based on historical experience. To do this, the accounting module should provide a variety of special statistical summaries as required during the year.

The operation of the library's accounting subsystem is dependent on at least two other modules: the personnel-processing module (also discussed in this chapter) and the order-processing module (discussed in Chapter 16).

Forms and Files

Figure 14.14 lists some of the forms and files required in a library accounting subsystem. The files are presented in detail in Figures 14.14(a) to (c). One is

Figure 14.14 Forms and files in accounting modules.

F_1: Balance Sheet Accounts File   Purchase Order Form
F_2: Purchase Order File   Voucher Form
F_3: Accounts Payable File

File Name BALANCE SHEET ACCOUNTS FILE				File No. F1		
Location ✳			Storage Medium ✳			
Access Requirements LIBRARY ADMINISTRATION, ACCOUNTING DEPT.						
Sequenced By ACCOUNT NUMBER WITHIN DEPARTMENT NUMBER						
Content Qualifications CONTAINS DATA ON COMMITTED FUNDS AS WELL AS VOUCHERED FUNDS. ALSO LAST YR TO DATE INFO.						
How Current WEEKLY						
Retention Characteristics MONTHLY TO HISTORY TAPE FOR GENERATION OF LAST YR TO DATE INFO IN NEXT FISCAL YEAR						
Labels (SUBJECT TO PROCESSING SYSTEM)						
Remarks						

CONTENTS

Sequence No.	Form Name	Volume		Characters Per Record	Characters Per File	
		Avg.	Peak		Avg.	Peak
1	BOOKKEEPING ACCOUNT	1125		145	164,125	

1968	QBR	Figure 14.14a	1
Date	Analyst	Source	Page

Representative
Study

✳ Determined uniquely by each library.

Figure 14.14a Forms and files in accounting modules.

File Name	PURCHASE ORDER FILE		File No.	F2

Location	★	Storage Medium	★

Access Requirements LIBRARY ADMINISTRATION, PURCHASING
DEPARTMENT

Sequenced By PURCHASE ORDER NUMBER

Content Qualifications PURCHASE ORDERS FOR OTHER
THAN BOOKS OR JOURNALS

How Current WEEKLY

Retention Characteristics WHEN ALL LINE ITEMS ON P.O. RECORD
REC'D OR REORDERED, MOVE RECORD TO HISTORY FILE.

Labels (SUBJECT TO PROCESSING SYSTEM)

Remarks

CONTENTS

Sequence No.	Form Name	Volume		Characters Per Record	Characters Per File	
		Avg.	Peak		Avg..	Peak
1	PURCHASE ORDER JOURNAL	1000		328	328,000	

1968	JBR	Fig 14.14b	1
Date	Analyst	Source	Page

Representative
Study

★ Determined uniquely by each library

Figure 14.14b

438

File Name	ACCOUNTS PAYABLE FILE		File No. F3		

Location *   **Storage Medium** ↙

Access Requirements LIBRARY ADMINISTRATION, ACCOUNTING DEPT.

Sequenced By VENDOR NUMBER

Content Qualifications VENDOR NAME AND ADDRESS FILE, PURCHASE ORDER AND RECEIVING DATA.

How Current WEEKLY

Retention Characteristics FOR FISCAL YEAR THEN NEW FILE CREATED WITH ALL VENDORS AND ONLY OUTSTANDING ENTRIES.

Labels (SUBJECT TO PROCESSING SYSTEM)

Remarks

CONTENTS

Sequence No.	Form Name	Volume		Characters Per Record	Characters Per File	
		Avg.	Peak		Avg.	Peak
1	VENDOR RECORD	1000		907	907,000	

1968	BR	Fig 14.14c	1
Date	Analyst	Source	Page

Representative
Study

* Determined uniquely by each library.

Figure 14.14c

central—the "Balance Sheet Accounts File." It is the ultimate means by which the library controls the distribution of funds. The results of all financial transactions must be recorded in this file, and the data stored in it becomes the basis for all estimations of budget. The other forms and files control the commitment and payment of funds to agencies outside the library.

Bookkeeping. The Balance Sheet Accounts File stores financial data in considerable detail, for the library as a whole as well as for separate library subdivisions and departments, by budgetary classes. Figure 14.15 lists typical budgetary classes (bookkeeping accounts), and Figure 14.16 shows the kind of data in a representative record in the file of accounts. A chart of accounts might include as many as 40 or 50 separate records for each of 20 or 30 library subdivisions and departments (a file totaling about 164,000 characters). If separate book fund accounts are included here in addition to being part of the "Book Ordering Subsystem," they could add another 100 or 200 records. These records are used to provide accounting of expenditures in comparison with the budget by time period. For purposes of budgetary control and estimation of future budgets, a variety of reports (such as shown in Figure 14.17) are produced, giving variances from the budget in comparison with previous time periods and planned expenditure rates.

Figure 14.15   Representative bookeeping accounts.

Salary Related Accounts
   Salaries
   Payroll taxes
   Pension fund
   Insurance
   Social Security

Supplies Accounts
   Office supplies
   Book preparation supplies
   Automotive supplies
   Building maintenance supplies

Printing and Reproduction Accounts
   Office copying equipment
   Printed forms
   Reports

Office Expense Accounts
   Postage
   Telephone and communication
   Office services
   Office equipment, purchase
   Office equipment, rental

Facility Accounts
   Rent
   Utilities
   Construction materials
   Motor vehicles

Book Accounts

Financial Accounts
   Cash
   Accounts payable
   Accounts receivable
   Depreciation

Form Name *BOOKKEEPING ACCOUNT*						Form No. *R1*	
Other Names Used						Layout No.	
						Related Form Nos.	
						No. of Copies	
Media *MAGNETIC TAPE ∿ DISK*			How Prepared *KEYBOARDING*				
Operations Involved In *RECORDS STORED IN 'BALANCE SHEET ACCOUNTS FILE'*							
Remarks							

		CONTENTS					
No.	Data Name	Freq.	Min.	Characters 95%	Max.	A/N	Origin
01	DEPARTMENT NUMBER				3	N	
02	ACCOUNT NUMBER				5	N	
	TITLE OF ACCT				15	A	
	APPROP – THIS YR				10	N	
	APPROP – LAST YR				10	N	
	APPROP – NEXT YR				10	N	
	VOUCH TO COMPTROLLER						
	THIS YR TO DATE				10	N	
	LAST YR TO DATE				10	N	
	ORDER VOUCH TO A/C REC						
	THIS YR TO DATE				8	N	
	LAST YR TO DATE				8	N	
	BALANCE						
	THIS YR TO DATE				10	N	
	LAST YR TO DATE				10	N	

1968	*JBK*	*Figure 14.16*	*1 of 2*
Date	Analyst	Source	Page

Representative Study

Figure 14.16a   Account record.

One crucial concept in modern systems for providing such information to management is the use of "exception reporting."[1] The aim is to place much of the burden of pinpointing problem areas on the computer. Thus, if expenditure rates in a given budgetary account are within reasonable limits of the planned rates, there is little reason to do more than report that fact. But where they differ significantly from planned rates, management should be alerted. This is

[1] Bittel, Lester R., *Management by Exception.* New York: McGraw-Hill, 1964.

Form Name *BOOKKEEPING ACCOUNT*					Form No. *R1*	
Other Names Used					Layout No.	
					Related Form Nos.	
					No. of Copies	
Media			How Prepared			
Operations Involved In						
Remarks						

CONTENTS

No.	Data Name	Freq.	Characters Min.	95%	Max.	A/N	Origin
	COMMITTED TO YR END						
	THIS YR				*10*	*N*	
	LAST YR				*10*	*N*	
	FREE FR MGMT TO YR END						
	THIS YR				*8*	*N*	
	LAST YR				*8*	*N*	

1968   *BK*   *Figure 14.16*   *2 of 2*

Date   Analyst   Source   Page

Representative

Study

Figure 14.16b

Figure 14.17   Bookkeeping reports.

1. Trend reports, comparing activity over a period of time
2. Analytical reports, analyzing changes
3. Comparison reports among departments
4. Percentage expenditure analysis

best done by a report that includes only the exceptions, the departures from expectation, the problem areas.

A schematic of the processing for bookkeeping is shown in Figure 14.18. The sources of data include budgets for each department, records of appropriations of funds, purchase orders and other commitments, vouchers or invoices and other records of actual payments, and records of prior history. The computer processing itself is relatively uncomplicated, involving simply double-entry posting of changes to accounts with additions to and subtraction from existing amounts.

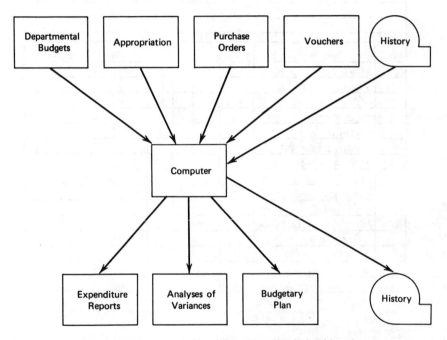

Figure 14.18   Schematic of data processing in bookkeeping.

Purchasing. The function of the "purchasing module" is to control the extent of commitments against library funds for other than acquisitions (the "ordering subsystem" covering the commitments against book funds). It includes checking requisitions and orders, securing quotations where necessary, issuing purchase orders, scheduling deliveries, checking receipts and verifying invoices, and corresponding with vendors. The basic file is the "Purchase Order File" described in Figure 14.14(*b*); a record in this file is as shown in Figure 14.19. Each record represents an outstanding purchase order, against which receipts are to be matched. As ordered items are received, they must be checked against the

Form Name *PURCHASE ORDER RECORD*					Form No. *P2*	
Other Names Used					Layout No.	
					Related Form Nos.	
					No. of Copies	
Media *MAGNETIC TAPE OR DISK*			How Prepared *KEYBOARDING*			
Operations Involved In *RECORDS STORED IN PURCHASE*						
ORDER FILE'						
Remarks						

			CONTENTS			
			Characters			
No.	Data Name	Freq.	Min.	95%	Max.	A/N	Origin
04	PCHS ORDER NO				6	A/N	
05	PCHS ORDER DATE				6	N	
06	PCHS ORDER AMT				8	N	
	DUE DATE				6	N	
	VENDOR NO				4	N	
	REQUESTED BY				6	A	
01	DEPARTMENT NO				3	N	
	DESCR EA LINE ITEM	5	20	30	85	A/N	
	QUANT EA LINE ITEM	5			4	N	
	UNIT PRICE EA LN ITEM	5			6	N	
02	ACCT CHGD EA LN ITEM	5			5	N	
10	INVOICE NO	2			6	A/N	
11	INVOICE DATE	2			6	N	
07	VOUCHER NO EA INV	2			6	N	
08	VOUCHER DATE EA INV	2			6	N	

1968	JBR	Fig. 14·19	10/2
Date	Analyst	Source	Page

Representative
Study

Figure 14.19a   Purchase order journal record.

purchase order for both quantity and quality; the prices, terms, and discounts on the invoice must be verified; and the purchase order journal record must be updated.

The size of the purchase order file will, of course, depend on the number of outstanding orders at any one time, the number of line items on each order, and the number of invoices. Representative figures might be: 1000 outstanding invoices, 5 line items each, and 2 shipments each. Under these conditions, the file would contain about 328,000 characters.

Form Name PURCHASE ORDER JOURWAL	Form No. K2
Other Names Used	Layout No.
	Related Form Nos.
	No. of Copies
Media	How Prepared
Operations Involved In	

Remarks

CONTENTS

No.	Data Name	Freq.	Characters Min.	95%	Max.	A/N	Origin
09	VOUCHER AMT EA INV	2			8	N	

Date   Analyst   Fig 14.17   2 of 2

Source   Page

Study

Figure 14.19b

Accounts Payable. The function of the "accounts payable module" is to handle the actual payments to vendors and to maintain records for the cummulative status of vendor accounts. The basic file is the set of vendor records (Figure 14.20). A schematic of the processing for accounts payable is shown in Figure 14.21. The sources of data include purchase orders, vouchers (forms that substantiate financial liability and confirm receipt of material), cash disbursement and "credit received" records, past cumulative records, and other history.

Form Name VENDOR RECORD							Form No. R3	
Other Names Used							Layout No.	
							Related Form Nos.	
							No. of Copies	
Media				How Prepared KEYBOARDING *				
Operations Involved In RECORDS STORED IN ACCOUNTS								
PAYABLE FILE.								
Remarks								

CONTENTS

No.	Data Name	Freq.	Characters			A/N	Origin
			Min.	95%	Max.		
03	VENDOR NO				4	N	
	VENDOR NAME		4	30	40	A	
	VENDOR ADDRESS		30	50	60	A/N	
	TERMS (STD CODE)				3	N	
04	ORDER NO EA ORDER	10			6	A/N	
05	ORDER DATE "	10			6	N	
06	ORDER AMT "	10			8	N	
10	INVOICE NUMBER	20			6	A/N	
11	INVOICE DATE	20			6	N	
04	PURCHASE ORDER CHGD	20			6	A/N	
	INVOICE AMOUNT	20			8	N	
07	VOUCHER NO	5			6	A/N	
08	VOUCHER DATE	5			6	N	
09	VOUCHER AMOUNT	5			8	N	

1968	JBE	Figure 14.20	
Date	Analyst	Source	Page

Representative
Study

* Vendor data is keyboarded. Purchase order and
invoice data are posted during processing.

Figure 14.20   Vendor record.

Reports can be produced showing the status of each vendor's account. Again, "exception criteria" can be used to highlight vendors representing one or another kind of problem (such as large outstanding balances and long delays in delivery). Reports on cash disbursements and cash requirements can be produced to aid management in financial planning.

The size of the accounts payable file depends on the number of vendors, the

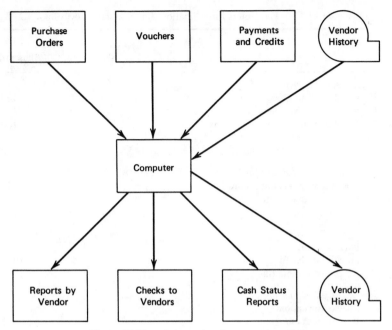

Figure 14.21   Schematic of accounts payable.

number of orders and invoices, and the number of payments. With 1000 vendors (each with an average for a year's historical record of 10 orders, 20 invoices, and 5 payments), the file would contain 900,000 characters.

Parameters for Estimation

Each of the three basic financial files that we have discussed is relatively small. (The Bookkeeping File might be as large as 165,000 characters; the Purchase Order File, 330,000 characters; and the accounts payable file, 900,000 characters.) File creation (conversion), therefore, represents a minor considera-tion in evaluating the work load. "File Interrogation" is primarily handled through the use of printed reports. "Maintenance" and "Reporting" are therefore the primary considerations in evaluating the work load. For each of these two file management functions, processing time estimates must be developed. Figure 12.22 summarizes the relevant parameters. The processing load is primarily determined by the number of financial transactions and file record reports each month and the processing time required for each. For illustrative purposes, these have been summed across the three files, to provide the estimates shown in Figure 14.23. In developing these, some assumptions were made; of course, for accurate estimation, these data would need to be examined in detail, in the context of the specific library.

Figure 14.22   Parameters for estimation (financial data processing).

	Representative Values	Illustration
1. Amounts of Activity (per Month)		
V_1 Number of purchase orders		400
V_2 Number of invoice vouchers		200
V_3 Number of financial transactions		400
V_4 Number of batch runs		4
V_5 Number of interrogations		0
2. Size of Records into Files (in Characters)		
R_1 Bookkeeping account record	145	145
R_2 Purchase order record	328	328
R_3 Vendor record	927	927
3. Number of Records		
N_1 Balance sheet accounts file		1000
N_2 Purchase order file		1000
N_3 Accounts payable file		1000
4. Size of Output (Lines per Form)		
O_1 Checks to vendors	5	5
O_2 Reports (per entry)	1	1
O_3 Purchase orders	11	11

Estimates of Key-Punching Time and Input. The data for financial processing comes primarily from data required for other operations, and therefore it is assumed that the key-punching and input will have been done as part of them (that is, the library is treated as an integrated system).

Estimates of Sorting Time. Since the nature of financial accounting does not require high-speed on-line access, batch processing once a week should be completely adequate. To do this efficiently with large-scale computers, it is necessary to sort transactions into order by the identification of file records affected (budgetary account, purchase order number, and vendor number); frequently, a given transaction affecting several files will be sorted two or three times. For the small-scale computer system, the sorting times are usually so great that direct-access processing may be more efficient.

The time required to sort transactions is determined by the size of the batch to be sorted, the size (number of characters) of each transaction, and the method of sorting. Representative sort times for each of the three levels of equipment have been shown in Figure 14.5.

Sorting is also required as part of the preparation of reports. The time to do this is determined by the number of file records to be included in each sort. For purposes of estimation, it has been assumed that every file record will appear in at least one weekly report.

Sub-System Administrative			File Financial Files							
Level of Analysis: Component Personnel and Equipment										
Level of Analysis: Function Sub-system Schematic										
Basic Unit of Work Orders										
Comp.	Operation	Number X	Size X	Freq. X	Rate =	Time X	Cost X	% =	Total
Cler. Pers.	Keyboarding of new orders	100	325 chars	4	10,000 chars/hr	13.0	$3/hr	100	$ 39
	Keyboarding transactions	50	80 chars	4	10,000 chars/hr	1.6	3/hr	100	5
	Sorting	150		12	10 rec/min	3.0	3/hr	100	9
	File Processing	150	1 Stand. Proc	12	.01 proc/sec	50.0	3/hr	100	150
	Output (Reports)	1000 (Bal. Sheet) only	100 chars	1	10,000 chars/hr	10.0	3/hr	100	30
	Totals					77.6 hours			$233
	TOTAL								
	COST/EFFECTIVENESS =								

Date _____   Analyst _____   Page _____

Study _____

Figure 14.23a   Illustrative library. Manual system.

Sub-System Administrative					File Financial Files						
Level of Analysis: Component Personnel and Equipment											
Level of Analysis: Function Sub-System Schematic											
Basic Unit of Work Orders											
Comp.	Operation	Number	X Size	X Freq.	Rate	= Time	X Cost	X %	= Total
Cler. Pers.	Keyboarding of new orders	100	325 chars	4	6000 chars/hr	21.7	$3/hr	100	$ 65
	Keyboarding transactions	50	80 chars	4	6000 chars/hr	2.7	3/hr	100	8
	Subtotals					24.4			$ 73
Equip. &	Set-up Time			4	.05 hr/batch	.2	6/hr	100	1
Oper. Pers.	Sorting	150x3	240 chars avg.	4	69 rec/min		6/hr	100	3
	File Access	1000x3	325 chars	4	200 chars/hr	5.4	6/hr	100	32
	File Update	150x3	1 Stand. Proc	4	1 /sec	.5	6/hr	100	3
	Output	3000	80 chars	4	200 chars/sec	1.3	6/hr	100	8
	Subtotals					7.9 hours			$ 47
	Totals								$120
	TOTAL								
	COST/EFFECTIVENESS =								

Date   Analyst   Page

Study

Figure 14.23b   Punched card system.

Sub-System						File				
Administrative						Financial Files				

Level of Analysis: Component
Personnel and Equipment

Level of Analysis: Function
Sub-System Schematic

Basic Unit of Work
Orders

Comp.	Operation	Number	X	Size	X	Freq.	Rate	=	Time	X	Cost	X	%	=	Total
Cler. Pers.	Keyboarding of new orders	100		325 chars		4	6000 chars/hr		21.7		$ 3/hr		100		$ 65
	Keyboarding transactions	50		80 chars		4	6000 chars/hr		2.7		3/hr		100		8
	Subtotals								24.4						73
Equip. &	Set-up Time						.02 hr/batch		.1		30/hr		100		3
Oper. Pers.	Input	150		240 chars avg.		4	600 chars/hr		.1		30/hr		100		3
	Sorting			No Sorting Proposed												
	File Access	150		2 access	12		5 /sec		.2		30/hr		100		6
	File Update	150		1 Stand. Proc	12		250 /sec				30/hr		100		
	Output	5000		80 chars		4	600 chars/hr		.7		30/hr		100		21
	Subtotals								1.1 hours						$ 33
	TOTAL														$106
	COST/EFFECTIVENESS =														

Figure 14.23c   Small-scale batch computer.

Sub-System					File					
Administrative					Financial Files					

Level of Analysis: Component
Personnel and Equipment

Level of Analysis: Function
Sub-System Schematic

Basic Unit of Work
Orders

Comp.	Operation	Number	X	Size	X	Freq.	/	Rate	=	Time	X	Cost	X	%	=	Total
Cler. Pers.	Keyboarding of new orders	100		325 chars		4		6000 chars/hr		21.7		$ 3/hr		100		$ 65
	Keyboarding transactions	50		80 chars		4		6000 chars/hr		2.7		3/hr		100		8
	Subtotals									24.4						73
Equip. &	Set-up Time					4		.01 hr/batch		.04		225/hr		20		1.8
Oper. Pers.	Input	150		240 chars avg.		4		2000 chars/sec		.02		225/hr		20		.9
	Sorting	150		240 chars avg.		12		2000 chars/sec		.06		225/hr		20		2.7
	File Access	150		2 access		12		50 /sec		.02		225/hr		20		.9
	File Update	150		1 Stand. Proc		12		2500 /sec				225/hr		20		
	Output	5000		80 chars		4		2000 chars/sec		.22		225/hr		20		9.9
	Subtotals									.36 hours						$ 16.2
	TOTAL															$ 89.2
	COST/EFFECTIVENESS =															

Date _____   Analyst _____   Page _____

Study _____

Figure 14.23d   Large-scale batch computer.

Sub-System				File						
Administrative				Financial Files						

Level of Analysis: Component
Personnel and Equipment

Level of Analysis: Function
Sub-System Schematic

Basic Unit of Work
Orders

Comp.	Operation	Number X	Size X	Freq. /	Rate =	Time X	Cost X	% =	Total
Cler. Pers.	Keyboarding of new orders (at console)	100	325 chars	4	6000 chars/hr	21.7	$ 3/hr	100	$ 65
	Keyboarding transactions (at console)	50	80 chars	4	6000 chars/hr	2.7	3/hr	100	8
	Subtotals					24.4			73
Equip. & Oper. Pers.	Set-up Time			4	.01 hr/batch	.04	625/hr	4	1
	Input	150	240 chars avg.	4	2000 chars/sec	.02	625/hr	4	.50
	Sorting	150	240 chars avg.	12	3000 chars/sec	.04	625/hr	4	1
	File Access	150	2 access	12	100 /sec	.01	625/hr	4	.25
	File Update	150	1 Stand. Proc	12	25,000 /sec		625/hr	4	
	Output	5000	80 chars	4	2000 chars/sec	.05	625/hr	4	1.25
	Subtotals					.16 hours			$ 4.00
	TOTAL								$ 77
	COST/EFFECTIVENESS =								

Date _____ Analyst _____ Page _____

Study _____

Figure 14.23e Large-scale on-line computer.

Estimates of File Access. Given the sizes of the three basic financial files, the only remaining issue in estimating file access is the frequency of file update (which has been assumed as weekly), since this determines the batch size in file searching.

Estimates of Computing. In general, a given transaction will affect at least one record in each of the three financial files. It has therefore been estimated in Figure 14.23 that about three file update operations, comparable to that shown in Figure 14.7, will be required per transaction. During reporting, each file record will affect several subtotals. Thus it has been estimated in Figure 14.23 that about two operations (comparable to that shown in Figure 14.7) will be required per file record.

Estimates of Output. Transactions that affect file records usually result in some form of output—for instance, a check, an error report, or an instruction to staff personnel. In Figure 14.23, this has been estimated at one line of printed output per transaction. For file reporting, the estimate is two lines of printed output per file record, each reporting period.

Estimates of Component Costs. For each of the three systems of equipment, it has been assumed that the costs would cover a two-shift operation, averaging 400 hours per month of productive working time.

Estimates of Traffic Load. The crucial issues are the number of financial transactions, V_T, to be handled each month and the number of file records, V_R, to be reported on. If each file record is reported on each week, then V_R would be four times the number of actual file records. To illustrate: with $V_T = 1000$ and $V_R = 12,000$, the three systems would compare as shown in Figure 14.23 (direct costs only).

PERSONNEL DATA PROCESSING

Regulations, procedures, records, and other aspects of data processing are as necessary in personnel management as in other parts of library management. All libraries must have personnel information centralized, confidential, and adequate for efficient operation. The administrative forms include, for example:

1. Employment applications, including personal history records.
2. References and interview reports.
3. Changes of status, vacations, and leaves of absence.
4. Service reports.
5. Performance evaluations.

The payroll forms include, for example:

1. Payroll records.
2. Checks.
3. Payroll reports.

Of course, administrative records are usually stored in personnel dossiers in their original form. However, a good deal of the information recorded on them could be effectively utilized if stored on magnetic tape files: listings of personnel can be prepared for a great variety of purposes; identification of those with specialized skills can be aided through computer processing; statistical analyses of the characteristics of different categories of personnel can be easily produced; and necessary personnel actions can be automatically generated.

The personnel data processing subsystem, therefore, should include all of the functions necessary for maintaining personnel records, displaying available resources, predicting future personnel needs, and reporting as required both by library management and by administrative departments within the parent institution. It should provide all of the necessary time-keeping functions for all categories of library employees. The system should provide, on demand or in regular periodic reports, information necessary for making a variety of personnel decisions. It should provide statistical summaries of data, describing in meaningful ways the character of the library work force and its distribution within the library.

Most of the functions can be designed to occur at regular periodic intervals. However, it is anticipated that there will be occasional needs for special summary reports prepared from the up-to-date files.

Forms and Files

Figure 14.24 lists some of the forms and files required in a library personnel subsystem. Figures 14.24(a) and (b) present details on the files.

Figure 14.24   Personnel forms and files.

F_4: Personnel File
      Application forms
      Interviews and references
      Appointments, transfers, promotions
      Performance ratings

F_5: Payroll Records File
      Time records
      Checks issued to employees
      Payroll change records

File Name *PERSONNEL FILE*			File No. *F4*	
Location *		Storage Medium *		
Access Requirements *LIBRARY ADMINISTRATION, PERSONNEL*				
Sequenced By *EMPLOYEE NUMBER*				
Content Qualifications *CONTAINS DATA FROM APPLICATION FORM,*				
REFERENCES AND INTERVIEWS, POSITIONS IN LIBRARY, AND				
How Current *BIMONTHLY* *PERFORMANCE RATINGS.*				
Retention Characteristics *WHEN EMPLOYEE TERMINATES DATA*				
TRANSFERRED TO A HISTORY TAPE				
Labels *(SUBJECT TO PROCESSING SYSTEM)*				
Remarks *MAY BE ACCESSED BY AUTHORIZED PERSONS ONLY*				

CONTENTS

Sequence No.	Form Name	Volume		Characters Per Record	Characters Per File	
		Avg.	Peak		Avg..	Peak
1	*PERSONNEL*	*200*		*3200*	*640,000*	
	RECORD					

1968	*JBR*	*Figure 14.24a*	*1*
Date	Analyst	Source	Page

Representative
Study

* *Determined uniquely by each library*

Figure 14.24a   Personnel file.

Personnel Records. Figure 14.25 lists the kind of data to be found in a personnel record. Initially, the data will come from an application form; it will then be updated from interviews, references, changes in status, and the like.

Form Name PERSONNEL RECORD					Form No. R4		
Other Names Used					Layout No.		
					Related Form Nos.		
					No. of Copies		
Media MAGNETIC TAPE OR DISK			How Prepared KEYBOARDING				
Operations Involved In							
Remarks AUTHORIZATION REQUIRED FOR USE							
CONTENTS							
No.	Data Name	Freq.	Characters			A/N	Origin
			Min.	95%	Max.		
12	EMPLOYEE NO.		2	4	6	N	
13	SOCIAL SECURITY NO				9	N	
14	NAME		7	20	25	A	
15	PRESENT ADDRESS		30	50	60	A/N	
	PRESENT TELEPHONE				7	N	
	PERMANENT ADDRESS		30	50	60	A/N	
	PERMANENT TELEPHONE				7	N	
	MARITAL STATUS				1	N	
	SPOUSE'S NAME		7	20	25	A	
	" COMPANY NAME		4	30	40	A	
	" BUSINESS ADDRESS		30	50	60	A/N	
	" BUSINESS TELEPHONE		7	7	14	A/N	
	" OCCUPATION		4	8	12	A	
16	NO OF DEPENDENTS		1	1	2	N	
	NO OF CHILDREN		1	1	2	N	

1968	JBR	Figure 14.24	1 of 4
Date	Analyst	Source	Page

Representative
Study

* Determined uniquely by each library

Figure 14.24b   Payroll records file.

Payroll. Figure 14.26 lists typical fields of a payroll record. Figure 14.27 shows a normal payroll change record, and Figure 14.28 shows typical reports to be produced from them. Figure 14.29 presents a schematic of the processing.

File Name PAYROLL RECORDS FILE				File No. F5		
Location ✱			Storage Medium ✱			
Access Requirements LIBRARY ADMINISTRATION, PERSONNEL,						
PAYROLL DEPARTMENT.						
Sequenced By EMPLOYEE NUMBER						
Content Qualifications RECORDS FOR ACTIVE EMPLOYEES						
FOR CURRENT CALENDAR YEAR ONLY.						
How Current BIMONTHLY						
Retention Characteristics WHEN EMPLOYEE TERMINATES						
RECORD MOVED TO HISTORY TAPE.						
Labels (SUBJECT TO PROCESSING SYSTEM)						
Remarks MAY BE ACCESSED BY AUTHORIZED PERSONS ONLY						

		CONTENTS				
Sequence No.	Form Name	Volume		Characters Per Record	Characters Per File	
		Avg.	Peak		Avg.	Peak
1	PAYROLL RECORD	200		1100	229,000	
2	PAYROLL CHANGE RECORD	10		80	800	

1968	BR	Figure 14.24b	1
Date	Analyst	Source	Page

Representative
Study

✱ Determined uniquely by each library

Figure 14.25 Personnel record.

Form Name PERSONNEL RECORD	Form No. R4
Other Names Used	Layout No.
	Related Form Nos.
	No. of Copies
Media	How Prepared

Operations Involved In

Remarks

CONTENTS

No.	Data Name	Freq.	Characters Min.	Characters 95%	Characters Max.	A/N	Origin
	CITIZENSHIP		3	7	15	A	
	BIRTHDATE				6	N	
	BIRTHPLACE		8	20	30	A	
	EDUCATION: SCHOOL	3	10	22	30	A	
	FROM	3	3	3	4	N	
	TO	3	3	3	4	N	
	MAJOR	3	5	15	22	A	
	DEGREE	3	2	3	7	A	
	SKILL OR PROFICIENCY	2	4	10	20	A	
	LANGUAGE	2	5	10	15	A	
	LEVEL OF COMPETENCE	2			1	N	
	PROFESSIONAL SOCIETY	2	3	25	40	A	
	OTHER SOCIETY	3	3	25	40	A	
	EXPERIENCE: COMPANY	4	4	30	40	A	
	COMPANY ADDRESS	4	30	50	60	A/N	

1968 Date — JBR Analyst — Figure 14.24 Source — 2 of 4 Page

Representative Study

Figure 14.25 *(Continued)*

Form Name PERSONNEL RECORD						Form No. R+
Other Names Used						Layout No.
						Related Form Nos.
						No. of Copies
Media				How Prepared		
Operations Involved In						

Remarks

CONTENTS

No.	Data Name	Freq.	Characters			A/N	Origin
			Min.	95%	Max.		
	FROM	4	3	4	4	N	
	TO	4	3	4	4	N	
	POSITION	4	5	16	25	A	
	STARTING WKLY SALARY	4	4	5	5	N	
	ENDING WKLY SALARY	4	4	5	5	N	
	SUPERVISOR	4	7	20	25	A	
	DUTIES	4	40	150	200	A/N	
	REFERENCES, INTERVIEWS						
	NAME	5	7	20	25	A	
	ADDRESS	5	10	50	60	A/N	
	RELATION	5	20	45	55	A	
	EVALUATION	5	2	50	100	A/N	
	POSITIONS IN LIBRARY						
01	DEPARTMENT NO	9	3	4	4	N	
	FROM	9	3	4	4	N	

1968	JBR	Figure 14.24	3 of 4
Date	Analyst	Source	Page

Representative
Study

Figure 14.25   *(Continued)*

Form Name PERSONNEL RECORD						Form No. R4
Other Names Used						Layout No.
						Related Form Nos.
						No. of Copies
Media		How Prepared				
Operations Involved In						

Remarks

CONTENTS

No.	Data Name	Freq.	Characters Min.	95%	Max.	A/N	Origin
	TO	3	3	4	4	N	
17	POSITION	3	5	16	25	A	
	STARTING WKLY SALARY	3	4	5	5	N	
	ENDING WKLY SALARY	3	4	5	5	N	
	SUPERVISOR	3	7	20	25	A	
	PERFORMANCE RATED						
	DATE	6			6	N	
	BY	6	7	20	25	A	
	EVALUATION	6	10	50	100	A/N	

1968   *JBR*   Figure 14.24   4 of 4
Date   Analyst   Source   Page

Representative
Study

Figure 14.25   *(Continued)*

Form Name *PAYROLL MASTER FILE RECORD*					Form No. *R5*	
Other Names Used					Layout No.	
					Related Form Nos.	
					No. of Copies	
Media *MAGNETIC TAPE OR DISK*		How Prepared *KEYBOARDING*				
Operations Involved In						
Remarks *AUTHORIZATION REQUIRED FOR ACCESS.*						

CONTENTS

No.	Data Name	Freq.	Min.	95%	Max.	A/N	Origin
12	EMPLOYEE NO				6	N	
01	DEPARTMENT NO				4	N	
14	EMPLOYEE NAME		7	20	25	A	
15	ADDRESS		30	50	60	A/N	
13	SOCIAL SECURITY NO				9	N	
16	NO OF EXEMPTIONS		1	1	2	N	
17	POSITION TITLE		5	16	25	A	
	PAY RATE - HRLY - NORMAL		3	3	4	N	
	PAY RATE - HRLY - PREMIUM		3	3	4	N	
	PAY PERIOD NUMBER	24	1	2	2	N	
	CHECK NUMBER	24			6	N	
	HOURS WORKED - NORMAL	24	2	2	3	N	
	HOURS WORKED - PREMIUM	24	1	2	3	N	
	GROSS SALARY	24	4	5	5	N	
	DEDUCTION - F.I.T.	24	3	4	5	N	

1968 *RBK* *Figure 14.26* *172*
Date   Analyst   Source   Page

Representative
Study

Figure 14.26   Payroll record.

Form Name PAYROLL MASTER FILE RECORD					Form No.	R5
Other Names Used					Layout No.	
					Related Form Nos.	
					No. of Copies	
Media		How Prepared				
Operations Involved In						
Remarks						

CONTENTS

No.	Data Name	Freq.	Characters Min.	95%	Max.	A/N	Origin
	DEDUCTION						
	FICA OR RET. CODE	24			2	N	
	AMOUNT	24	0	4	5	N	
	DEDUCTION (OTHER)						
	CODE	48			2	N	
	AMOUNT	48	3	4	4	N	
	YTD GROSS SALARY		6	6	7	N	
	YTD F.I.T.		4	5	6	N	
	YTD FICA OR RETIREMENT		5	6	6	N	
	YTD DEDUCTIONS (FOR EACH)						
	CODE	2			2	N	
	AMOUNT	2	4	5	5	N	

1968
Date

JBR
Analyst

Figure 14.26
Source

2 of 2
Page

Representative
Study

Figure 14.26   *(Continued)*

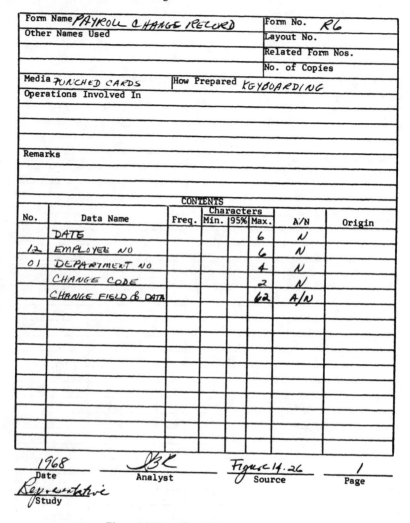

Form Name *PAYROLL CHANGE RECORD*					Form No. *R6*	
Other Names Used					Layout No.	
					Related Form Nos.	
					No. of Copies	
Media *PUNCHED CARDS*			How Prepared *KEYBOARDING*			
Operations Involved In						
Remarks						

CONTENTS

No.	Data Name	Freq.	Characters			A/N	Origin
			Min.	95%	Max.		
	DATE				6	N	
12	*EMPLOYEE NO*				6	N	
01	*DEPARTMENT NO*				4	N	
	CHANGE CODE				2	N	
	CHANGE FIELD & DATA				62	A/N	

1968 _____ *BL* _____ *Figure 14.26* ___ *1*
Date   Analyst   Source   Page
Representative
Study

Figure 14.27   Payroll change record.

Parameters for Estimation

The size of the task for personnel data processing is, of course, primarily determined by the size of the library staff. Figure 14.30 summarizes the relevant parameters, and Figure 14.31 gives some representative estimates of cost (considering all personnel data files).

Estimates of Key-Punching and Input. Change transactions represent

Figure 14.28   Payroll reports.

Management Reports (number of employees, average hours worked, average earnings, turnover rates, absentee rates . . . .)

Government Reports (FICA, witholding taxes)

Other Outside Reports (pension, insurance . . . .)

Cost Accounting (distribution)

---

additions to staff, special situations (such as vacation), and changes in status. Generally, these will affect as many as 10 percent of the records per month. A typical change transaction is estimated at 80 characters. Other input is the set of time reports, which for hourly employees can be provided by prepunched time cards.

Estimates of Sorting Time. Personnel data processing does not require high-speed on-line processing. Usually, personnel records will be updated twice a month (or perhaps biweekly). The volume of transactions is small enough so that sorting is either unnecessary or of negligible cost in time.

Estimates of File Access. The estimations of file access time are determined by the frequency of file update. For the estimates in Figure 14.30, this has been assumed to be a twice a month. A typical personnel record can involve as much

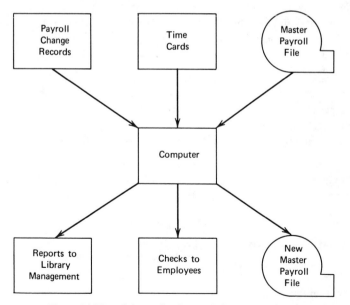

Figure 14.29   Schematic of payroll data processing.

Figure 14.30   Parameters for estimation personnel data processing.

		Representative Value	Illustration
1.	*Amounts of Activity (per Month)*		
	V_1 Number of payroll runs	2	2
	V_2 Number of changes		20
	V_3 Number of interrogations		
2.	*Size of Records into Files*		
	R_4 Personnel record	3194	3200
	R_5 Payroll record	1079	1100
	R_6 Payroll change record	80	80
3.	*Number of Records*		
	N_1 Number of employees		200
4.	*Size of Output (Lines per Form)*		
	O_1 Checks to employees		5
	O_2 Reports		400

as 3200 characters; a payroll record can involve 1100 characters per payroll period. With 200 employees, these files might contain, respectively, 640,000 characters and 220,000 characters.

Estimates of Computing. The primary computational load is imposed by payroll calculations. For the estimates in Figure 14.31, this has been assumed to be five file update operations, comparable to that shown in Figure 14.7, for each payroll record.

Estimates of Output. The printing of payroll checks is the major output requirement. In Figure 14.31 this has been assumed to involve five lines of printing per check. In addition, there are periodic reports (FICA, witholding tax, and the like), but these add up to less of a printing load by an order of magnitude. Finally, if prepunched time cards are used, they must also be output.

Estimates of Computing.   Each line entry of time data will involve two or three totals for each of four or five kinds of accounts, representing perhaps one file update operation comparable to that shown in Figure 14.7.

MANAGEMENT DATA PROCESSING

In Chapter 3, we discussed scientific management. The kinds of models discussed there are only effective if there is accurate, up-to-date, and sufficient data available about the library and its operations. In Chapter 4, we discussed

Sub-System				File						
Administrative				Personnel Files						

Level of Analysis: Component
Personnel and Equipment

Level of Analysis: Function
Sub-System Schematic

Basic Unit of Work
Number of Staff

Comp.	Operation	Number	X	Size	X	Freq.	/	Rate	=	Time	X	Cost	X	%	=	Total
Cler. Pers.	Keyboarding of new hires	2		3200 chars		2		10,000 chars/hr		1.3		$ 3/hr		100		$ 3.9
	Keyboarding of changes	10		80 chars		2		10,000 chars/hr		.2		3/hr		100		.6
	Keyboarding of exception time keeping	100		8 chars		2		10,000 chars/hr		.2		3/hr		100		.6
	Sorting	110				2		10 rec/min		.5		3/hr		100		1.5
	File Processing	200		1 Stand. Proc.		2		.01 proc./sec		11.1		3/hr		100		33.3
	Output (Checks)	200		5 lines= 400 chars		2		10,000 chars/hr		16.0		3/hr		100		48.0
	Output (Reports)	200		1 line = 80 chars		1		10,000 chars/hr		1.6		3/hr		100		4.8
	TOTAL									30.9 hours						$92.7
	COST/EFFECTIVENESS =															

Date	Analyst	Page

Study

Figure 14.31a   Illustrative library. Manual System.

Sub-System					File					
Administrative					Personnel Files					

Level of Analysis: Component
Personnel and Equipment

Level of Analysis: Function
Sub-System Schematic

Basic Unit of Work
Number of Staff

Comp.	Operation	Number	X	Size	X Freq.	/ Rate	= Time	X Cost	X %	= Total
Cler. Pers.	Keyboarding of new hires	2		3200 chars	2	6000 chars/hr	2.1	$ 3/hr	100	$ 6
	Keyboarding of changes	10		80 chars	2	6000 chars/hr	.3	3/hr	100	1
	Keyboarding of exception time keeping	100		8 chars	2	6000 chars/hr	.3	3/hr	100	1
	Subtotals						2.7			8
Equip. &	Set-up Time				2	.05 hr/batch	.1	6/hr	100	.6
Oper. Pers.	Sorting	110		80 chars	2	100 rec/min	.05	6/hr	100	3.6
	File Access (Payroll)	220		1100 chars	2	200 chars/sec	.60	6/hr	100	3.6
	File Access (Changes)	12		2100 chars avg.	4	200 chars/sec	.14	6/hr	100	.8
	File Update (Payroll)	200		1 Stand. Proc.	2	1 /sec	.11	6/hr	100	.7
	File Update (Changes)	12		2 Stand. Proc.	2	1 /sec	.22	6/hr	100	1.3
	Output (Checks)	200		5 lines= 400 chars	2	200 chars/sec	.22	6/hr	100	1.3
	Output (Reports)	200		2 lines= 160 chars	2	200 chars/sec	.08	6/hr	100	.5
	Subtotals						1.52 hours			$ 9.1
	TOTAL									$17.1
	COST/EFFECTIVENESS =									

Date _____ Analyst _____ Page _____

Study _____

Figure 14.31b   Punched-card system.

468

Sub-System					File					
Administrative					Personnel Files					

Level of Analysis: Component
Personnel and Equipment

Level of Analysis: Function
Sub-System Schematic

Basic Unit of Work
Number of Staff

Comp.	Operation	Number	X Size	X Freq.	Rate	= Time	X Cost	X %	= Total
Cler. Pers.	Keyboarding of new hires	2	3200 chars	2	6000 chars/hr	2.1	$ 3/hr	100	$ 6
	Keyboarding of changes	10	80 chars	2	6000 chars/hr	.3	3/hr	100	1
	Keyboarding of exception time keeping	100	8 chars	2	6000 chars/hr	.3	3/hr	100	1
	Subtotals					2.7			$ 8
Equip & Oper. Pers.	Set-up Time			2	.02 hr/batch	.04	30/hr	100	1.2
	Input	110	15 chars avg.	2	600 chars/sec		30/hr	100	
	Sorting				No Sorting Proposed				
	File Access (Payroll)	200	2 access	2	5 /sec	.05	30/hr	100	1.5
	File Access (Changes)	12	4 access	2	5 /sec	.01	30/hr	100	.3
	File Update (Payroll)	200	1 Stand. Proc.	2	250 /sec		30/hr	100	
	File Update (Changes)	12	2 Stand. Proc.	2	250 /sec		30/hr	100	
	Output (Checks)	200	5 lines= 400 chars	2	600 chars/sec	.07	30/hr	100	2.1
	Output (Reports)	200	2 lines= 160 chars	2	600 chars/sec	.03	30/hr	100	.9
	Subtotals					.20 hours			$ 6.0
	TOTAL								$14.0
	COST/EFFECTIVENESS =								

Date _____ Analyst _____ Page _____

Study _____

Figure 14.31c Small-scale batch computer.

Sub-System Administrative				File Personnel Files					

Level of Analysis: Component
Personnel and Equipment

Level of Analysis: Function
Sub-System Schematic

Basic Unit of Work
Number of Staff

Comp.	Operation	Number	X	Size	X Freq.	/ Rate	= Time	X Cost	X %=	Total
Cler. Pers.	Keyboarding of new hires	2		3200 chars	2	6000 chars/hr	2.1	$ 3/hr	100	$ 6
	Keyboarding of changes	10		80 chars	2	6000 chars/hr	.3	3/hr	100	1
	Keyboarding of exception time keeping	100		8	2	6000	.3	3/hr	100	1
	Subtotals						2.7			$ 8
Equip. &	Set-up Time				2	.01 hr/batch	.02	225/hr	20	.9
Oper. Pers.	Input	110		15 chars avg.	2	2000 chars/sec	.0005	225/hr	20	.02
	Sorting	110		15 chars avg.	2	2000 chars/sec	.0005	225/hr	20	.02
	File Access (Payroll)	200		2 access	2	50 /sec	.0044	225/hr	20	.99
	File Access (Changes)	12		4 access	2	50 /sec	.0005	225/hr	20	.02
	File Update (Payroll)	200		1 Stand. Proc.	2	2500 /sec		225/hr	20	
	File Update (Changes)	12		2 Stand. Proc.	2	2500 /sec		225/hr	20	
	Output (Checks)	200		5 lines= 400 chars	2	2000 chars/sec	.0222	225/hr	20	1
	Output (Reports)	200		2 lines= 160 chars	2	2000 chars/sec	.0089	225/hr	20	.40
	Subtotals						.0570 hours			$ 3.35
	TOTAL									$11.35
	COST/EFFECTIVENESS =									

Date _____   Analyst _____   Page _____

Study _____

Figure 14.31d   Large-scale batch computer.

470

Sub-System				File						
Administrative				Personnel Files						

Level of Analysis: Component
Personnel and Equipment

Level of Analysis: Function
Sub-System Schematic

Basic Unit of Work
Number of Staff

Comp.	Operation	Number	X	Size	X	Freq.	/	Rate	=	Time	X	Cost	X	%	=	Total
Cler. Pers.	Keyboarding of new hires	2		3200 chars		2		6000 chars/hr		2.1	$	3/hr		100	$	6
	Keyboarding of changes	10		80 chars		2		6000 chars/hr		.3		3/hr		100		1
	Keyboarding of exception time keeping	100		8 chars		2		6000 chars/hr		.3		3/hr		100		1
	Subtotals									2.7					$	8
Equip. & Oper. Pers.	Set-up Time					2		.01 hr/batch		.02		625/hr		4		.50
	Input	110		15 chars avg.		2		2000 chars/sec				625/hr		4		
	Sorting	110		15 chars avg.		2		3000 chars/sec				625/hr		4		
	File Access (Payroll)	200		2 access		2		100 /sec		.0022		625/hr		4		.06
	File Access (Changes)	12		4 access		2		100 /sec				625/hr		4		
	File Update (Payroll)	200		1 Stand. Proc.		2		25,000 /sec				625/hr		4		
	File Update (Changes)	12		2 Stand. Proc.		2		25,000 /sec				625/hr		4		
	Output (Checks)	200		5 lines= 400 chars		2		2000 chars/sec		.0222		625/hr		4		.56
	Output (Reports)	200		2 lines= 160 chars		2		2000 chars/sec		.0089		625/hr		4		.22
	Subtotals									.0533 hours					$	1.34
	TOTAL														$	9.34
	COST/EFFECTIVENESS =															

Date

Analyst

Page

Study

Figure 14.31e Large-scale on-line computer.

471

the general nature of library cost accounting as one of the primary sources of such data. The financial accounts, the "in-process" file, and the circulation records are other sources. From them, reports can be provided to the library management for control of operations.

General Nature of Management Data Processing

Cost Accounting. As discussed in Chapter 4, the objectives of cost accounting are to provide reports of the cost of each process and job order in the library. These would include comparisons of actual costs with standard costs and reports on the efficiency of each department.

Figure 14.32 presents a schematic of operations in a cost accounting system. The sources of data in a cost accounting system include employee payroll data, employee job tickets, and standard cost and time data. For each employee, production records must be maintained, usually daily. The files are usually historical and standard-cost data. The reporting function is the basic one.

Production Control. The objective of production control is to schedule work efficiently through technical processing. Figure 14.33 presents a schematic of the data processing required for production control. The sources of data include forecasts of services required (as derived from past statistics, management acquisition plans, and the like), standard times for technical processing steps,

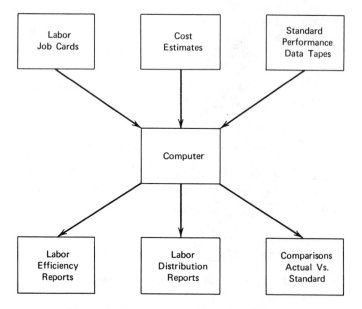

Figure 14.32   Cost accounting schematic.

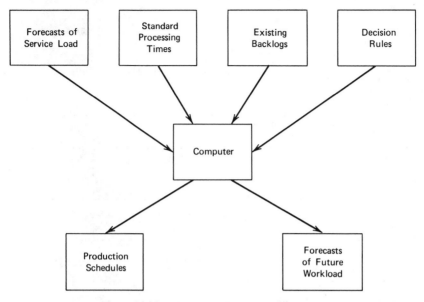

Figure 14.33   Schematic for production control.

statistics on existing backlogs and workloads, and decision rules for determining production schedules.

Forms and Files

In Chapter 4, we discussed some typical records for cost accounting data—both manual and punched card. These represent the basic source of data for both cost accounting and production control.

Estimates of Work load

The work load in management data processing is basically a function of the size of the library staff: the input for cost accounting requires the conversion of production and time data for each staff member; production control involves the printout of management data for each staff member (or at least, each departmental group). Figure 14.34 summarizes representative cost figures.

Estimates of Key-Punching and Input. Each day, each employee would record time data on cost-accounting sheets. Many employees are on tasks covered by "process-costing"; and, for them, the data can be obtained from pre-punched time cards; for those on tasks covered by "job-costing," it might mean five or ten lines of data each day. The bulk of employees are likely to be involved in process-costed work, and the key-punching task therefore is likely to average about 50 characters per employee per day.

Sub-System Administrative			File Management Files							
Level of Analysis: Component Personnel and Equipment										
Level of Analysis: Function Sub-System Schematic										
Basic Unit of Work										
Comp.	Operation	Number	X Size	X Freq. /	Rate	= Time	X Cost	X % =	Total
		The amount of work entailed makes the cost of manual processing prohibitive.							
	TOTAL								
	COST/EFFECTIVENESS =								

Date _____   Analyst _____   Page _____

Study _____

Figure 14.34a   Illustrative library. Manual system.

Sub-System			File							
Administrative			Management Files							

Level of Analysis: Component
Personnel and Equipment

Level of Analysis: Function
Sub-System Schematic

Basic Unit of Work

Comp.	Operation	Number	X	Size	X	Freq.	/	Rate	=	Time	X	Cost	X	%	=	Total
Cler. Pers.	Keyboarding of cost accounting data	200x20		50 chars		1		6000 chars/hr		33.3		$ 3/hr		100		$100
	Subtotals									33.3						$100
Equip & Oper. Pers.	Set-up Time					1		.05 hr/batch				6/hr		100		
	Sorting	7500x20		80 chars		1		100 rec/min		33.		6/hr		100		198
	File Access	1500x20		5 access		1		200 chars/sec		.2		6/hr		100		1
	File Update	1500x20		1 Stand. Proc.		1		1 /sec		8.3		6/hr		100		50
	Output (Reports)	1000		7 lines= 700 chars		1		200 chars/sec		1.0		6/hr		100		6
	Subtotals									42.5 hours						$255
	TOTAL															$355
	COST/EFFECTIVENESS =															

Date _____ Analyst _____ Page _____

Study _____

Figure 14.34b   Punched-card system.

Sub-System				File						
Administrative				Management Files						

Level of Analysis: Component
Personnel and Equipment

Level of Analysis: Function
Sub-System Schematic

Basic Unit of Work

Comp.	Operation	Number X	Size X	Freq. /	Rate =	Time X	Cost X	% =	Total
Cler. Pers.	Keyboarding of cost account- ing data	200	50 chars	20	6000 chars/hr	33.3	$ 3/hr	100	$100
	Subtotals					33.3			$100
Equip. & Oper. Pers.	Set up Time			1	.02 hr/batch		30/hr	100	$
	Input	1500x20	80 chars	1	600 chars/sec	1.1	30/hr	100	33
	Sorting	No Sorting Proposed							
	File Access	1500x20	5 access	1	5 /sec	8.3	30/hr	100	249
	File Update	1500x20	1 Stand. Proc.	1	250 /sec	.03	30/hr	100	1
	Output (Reports)	1000	7 lines= 700 chars	1	600 /sec	.3	30/hr	100	10
	Subtotals					9.7 hours			$293
	TOTAL								$393
	COST/EFFECTIVENESS =								

Date   Analyst   Page

Study

Figure 14.34c   Small-scale batch computer.

Sub-System Administrative				File Management Files						
Level of Analysis: Component Personnel and Equipment										
Level of Analysis: Function Sub-System Schematic										
Basic Unit of Work										

Comp.	Operation	Number	X	Size	X	Freq.	X	Rate	=	Time	X	Cost	X	%	=	Total
Cler. Pers.	Keyboarding of cost accounting data	200		50 chars		20		6000 chars/hr		33.3		$ 3/hr		100		$100
	Subtotals									33.3						$100
Equip. &	Set-up Time					20		.01 hr/batch		.01		225/hr		20		1
Oper. Pers.	Input	1500		80 chars		20		2000 chars/sec		.3		225/hr		20		14
	Sorting	1500		80 chars		20		2000 chars/sec		.3		225/hr		20		14
	File Access	1500		5 access		20		50 /sec		.8		225/hr		20		40
	File Update	1500		1 Stand. Proc.		20		2500 /sec				225/hr		20		
	Output	1000		7 lines= 700 chars		1		2000 chars/sec		.1		225/hr		20		5
	Subtotals									1.5 hours						$ 74
	TOTAL															$174
	COST/EFFECTIVENESS =															

Date _____   Analyst _____   Page _____

Study _____

Figure 14.34d   Large-scale batch computer.

477

Sub-System				File						
Administrative				Management Files						
Level of Analysis: Component										
Personnel and Equipment										
Level of Analysis: Function										
Sub-System Schematic										
Basic Unit of Work										

Comp.	Operation	Number	X	Size	X Freq.	Rate	= Time	X Cost	X %	= Total
Cler. Pers.	Keyboarding of cost account-ing data	200		50 chars	20	6000 chars/hr	33.3	$ 3/hr	100	$100
	Subtotals						33.3			$100
Equip. &	Input	1500		80 chars	20	2000 chars/sec	.3	625/hr	4	8
Oper. Pers.	Sorting	1500		80 chars	20	3000 chars/sec	.2	625/hr	4	5
	File Access	1500		5 access	20	100 /sec	.4	625/hr	4	10
	File Update	1500		1 Stand. Proc.	20	25,000 /sec		625/hr	4	
	Output	1000		7 lines= 700 chars	1	2000 chars/sec	.1	625/hr	4	3
	Subtotals						1.0 hours			$ 26
	TOTAL									$126
	COST/EFFECTIVENESS =									

Date _____   Analyst _____   Page _____

Study _____

Figure 14.34e   Large-scale on-line computer.

Estimates of Sorting. This represents the primary processing load in both cost accounting and production control. Each line entry of time data is likely to be sorted and allocated to as many as four or five different accounts (employee, department, function, job, work schedule, and so on).

Estimates of Computing.   Each line entry of time data will involve two or three totals for each of four or five kinds of accounts, representing perhaps one file update operation comparable to that shown in Figure 14.7.

Estimates of Output. The output will consist of summary reports and future schedules—by employee, department, and the like.

Estimates of Traffic Load. The resulting figures are then multiplied by the number of Employees, expressed as V_p. For example, with 200 employees, the management data processing system would involve costs like those shown in Figure 14.34.

Figure 14.35   Summary of monthly administrative data processing work load.

Hours, (Equipment and Operating Personnel)	Financial	Personnel	Management	Total	Percent of Capacity
Manual					
Punched-card	7.9	1.5	42.5	51.9	10
Small-scale	1.1	.2	9.7	11.0	2
Large-scale	.4	.1	1.5	2.0	.02
On-line	.2	.05	1.	1.25	.001
Hours (Clerical Personnel)	Financial	Personnel	Management	Total	Number of People
Manual	77.6	30.9		108.5	.6 persons
Punched-card	24.4	2.7	33.3	60.4	.3 persons
Small-scale	24.4	2.7	33.3	60.4	.3 persons
Large-scale	24.4	2.7	33.3	60.4	.3 persons
On-line	24.4	2.7	33.3	60.4	.3 persons
Total Costs	Financial	Personnel	Management	Total	
Manual	$233	$93	$	$326	
Punched-card	120	17	355	492	
Small-scale	106	14	393	413	
Large-scale	89	11	174	274	
On-line	77	9	126	212	

SUMMARY

As we indicated earlier in this chapter, administrative data processing for libraries represents a relatively small computing task. Figure 14.35 gives a summary of costs for a relatively large library.

Suggested Readings

The crucial readings on library administration are the classic texts:

Wheeler, Joseph L., and Herbert Goldhor, *Practical Administration of Public Libraries*. New York: Harper and Row, 1962.

Wilson, Louis Round, and Maurice F. Tauber, *The University Library*. New York: Columbia University Press, 1956.

Together, these two books summarize the administrative issues in libraries about as completely as is possible. They are essential to an understanding of the nature of library management at all levels. Furthermore, taken together, they complement each other and highlight some of the policy differences among types of libraries.

Chapter 15

CIRCULATION CONTROL SUB-SYSTEM

The basic purpose of circulation control is simple—to assure that the materials that the library holds are available to persons who need them, within a reasonable period of time, and for a reasonable period of time. To accomplish this aim, the library must maintain records indicating where material is located, who is responsible for it, and when it should be available for someone else. It usually will require that material be returned by a user within a defined period of time in order to have it available for other users. It frequently will establish reserve collections for which even more rapid availability is needed. It sometimes will schedule and control the distribution of material in order to assure that it is available when needed. It may establish priorities for users to guarantee availability to those who need it most. These, then, constitute the functions that a circulation control system must (to one extent or another) provide—all ultimately to serve the basic purpose of assuring availability of material.

Libraries, of course, differ greatly in the importance they attach to one or another of these functions, reflecting differences in the purposes of the libraries themselves. For example, public libraries usually have the least stringent requirements and expect a circulation control system merely to guarantee that material is returned within a defined time. Research libraries, on the other hand, have the requirement for very rapid accessibility and therefore must be able to tell immediately where a book is and must be able to recall it. Some special libraries have a very stringent requirement for this, in the control of military "classified" documents. School libraries, college libraries, and media centers have requirements that lead them to establish reserve collections of books in great demand, and to schedule and control the availability of audiovisual material.

As a result, libraries will correspondingly differ in the suitability of one or another system for data processing in circulation control. In particular, as the study by Fry Associates has very well demonstrated, the manual and photographic systems used in most public libraries are well suited to their needs and economic in operation.[1] Mechanized systems eventually may be competitive with them, but they are not now competitive nor are they likely to be for some time. In contrast, several university libraries have, over the past 10 to 20 years, installed one or another kind of mechanized system. It seems clear that the functions they require are well served by such systems which, while relatively expensive, will become increasingly economic. Large numbers of industrial libraries, especially those in the aerospace industry, have used such systems operationally for a long time. Finally, while it is only recently that libraries in public schools have begun to experiment with comparable control of their collections, there are clear indications that mechanized control and distribution of films and other audiovisual materials with high utility will have great value to them.

Examples

As we have indicated, a number of organizations have experimented with computer-based circulation control systems, ranging from essentially punched-card systems, to small-scale batch processing systems, to on-line systems.

Lehigh University installed a system using a combination of book card-borrower card, inserted in an IBM 357 point-of-action recorder to produce a transaction card.[2] These are input to the computer daily, sorted, stored in Call Number order on magnetic tape, and used to produce a variety of printed outputs. The most important is the daily circulation file, listing all books in circulation. Others include notices to borrowers, lists of problems, lists of holdings by borrower, statistics, and the like. The system handles a yearly circulation of 150,000 volumes, at a monthly cost for terminal equipment, key-punches, and computer use of about $1200.

Rice University uses a comparable system (Figure 15.1).[3]

Brooklyn College uses what, by now, has become the standard punched card system. It is shown in detail in Figure 15.2.[4]

---

[1] Fry, George, and Associates, *Study of Circulation Control Systems.* Chicago: Library Technology Project, American Library Association and Council for Library Resources, 1961.

[2] Flannery, Anne, and James D. Mack, *Mechanized Circulation System, Lehigh University Library.* Bethlehem, Pa.: Center for the Information Sciences, Lehigh University, 1966.

[3] Ruecking, Frederick, "Selecting a Circulation Control System: A Mathematical Approach," *College and Research Libraries,* **25** (5) (September, 1964), 385-390.

[4] Birnbaum, Henry, *IBM Circulation Control at Brooklyn College Library: General Information Manual.* White Plains, New York: IBM, 1960.

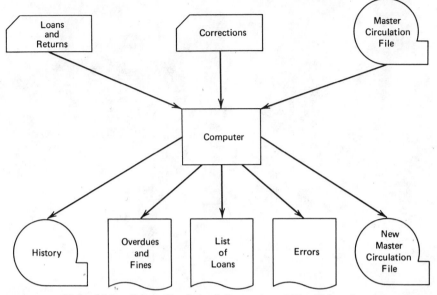

Figure 15.1   Schematic of circulation system at Rice University.

UCLA has installed a computer-based counterpart, in which IBM 1031 Data Collection Units are used to pick up book identification data from book cards, directly at the time of charging out the book.[5-7]. This avoids the necessity of key-punching this data.

Redstone Arsenal experimented with the use of IBM 1050 remote terminals for on-line maintenance of 7000 registration records and circulation records for 33,000 books.[8] The *Bell Telephone Laboratory* has installed a similar, operational system.[9-11] It also uses IBM 1050 terminals, on-line to an IBM 360/40 computer. The system requires 32 real-time programs and 23 batch programs, totaling about 10,000 instructions. It is expected to handle an average of 300,000 circulation per year.

[5] Black, Donald V., and James R. Cox, *IBM Circulation Control at the University of California Library, Los Angeles: A Preliminary Report.* Los Angeles: UCLA, March 1963.

[6] Cox, J. R., N. E. Jones, and A. F. Hall, *Computer-Based Circulation Control System, UCLA Library, Performance Requirements.* Los Angeles, October 1963.

[7] *Automated Circulation Control in the University Research Library: A Progress Report.* Los Angeles: UCLA, November 1965.

[8] Haznedari, I., and H. Voos, "Automated Circulation of a Government R & D Installation," *Special Libraries,* **55** (February 1964), 77-81.

[9] "Computerized Instant Library Loan System Designed at Bell Laboratories," *News, Bell Telephone Laboratories,* January 9, 1968.

[10] "Bellrel, a Computer-Aided Loan System," *American Library Association Bulletin,* **62** (4) (April 1968), 407-408.

[11] Kennedy, R. A., "Bell Laboratories' Library Real-Time Loan System," *Journal of Library Automation,* **1** (2) (June 1968), 128-46.

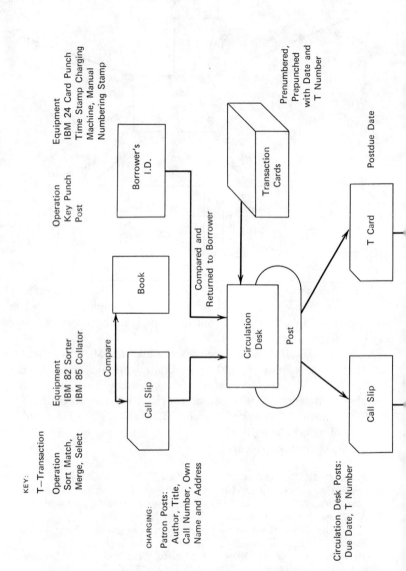

KEY:

T—Transaction

Operation
Sort Match,
Merge, Select

Equipment
IBM 82 Sorter
IBM 85 Collator

Operation
Key Punch
Post

Equipment
IBM 24 Card Punch
Time Stamp Charging
Machine, Manual
Numbering Stamp

CHARGING:

Patron Posts:
Author, Title,
Call Number, Own
Name and Address

Circulation Desk Posts:
Due Date, T Number

Compare

Book

Call Slip

Borrower's
I.D.

Compared and
Returned to Borrower

Transaction
Cards

Prenumbered,
Prepunched
with Date and
T Number

Circulation
Desk

Post

T Card

Postdue Date

Call Slip

484

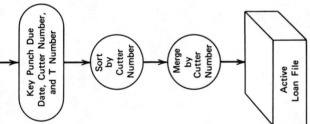

Figure 15.2 IBM transaction card system for circulation control. (Brooklyn College Library). Source: (1) Flow chart for charging was taken from a paper by Donald H. Kraft, written under the auspices of IBM Corporation, entitled "IBM Circulation Control System." (2) Flow charts for discharging and for description of the system found in IBM General Information Manual E20-0072. "IBM Circulation Control at Brooklyn College Library" by Henry Birnbaum.

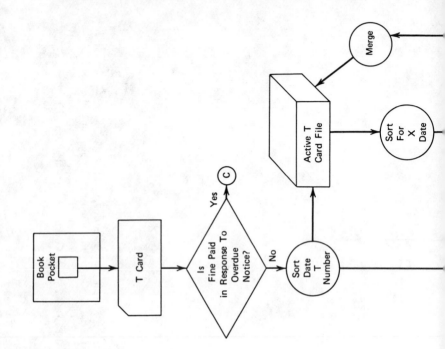

486

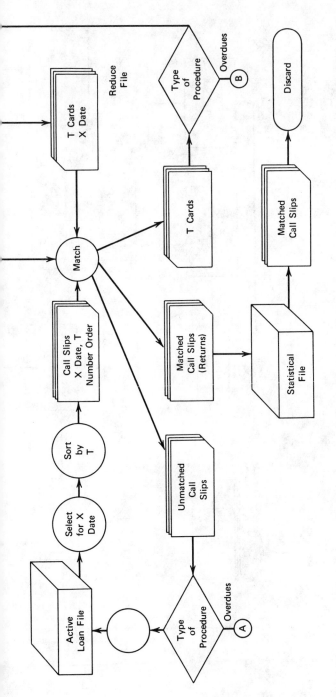

Figure 15.2 *(Continued)*

487

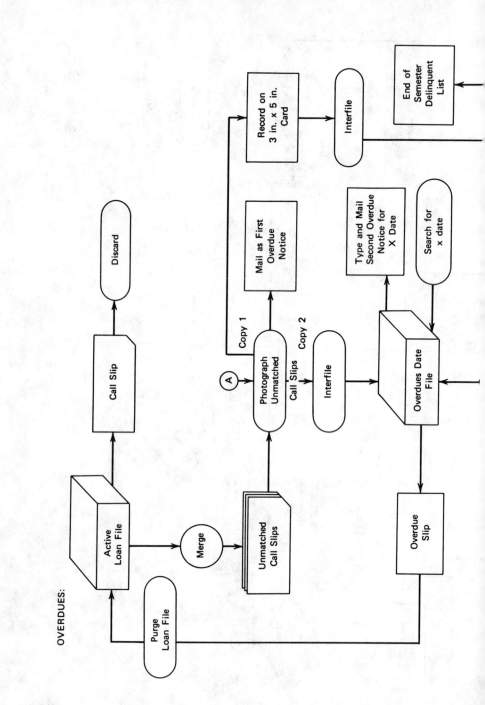

OVERDUES:

488

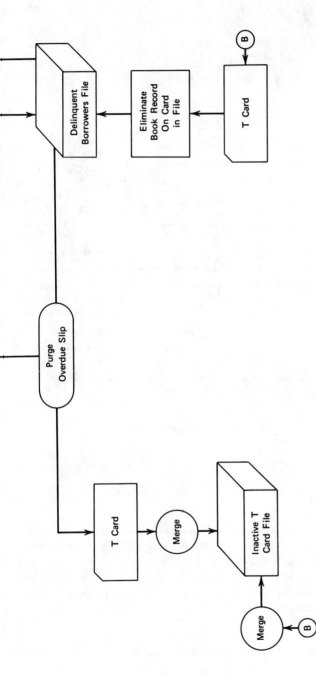

Figure 15.2 (Continued)

489

Illinois State Library installed an on-line circulation control system in December 1966, designed to handle about 1500 transactions per day (charge-outs, renewals, holds, and returns).

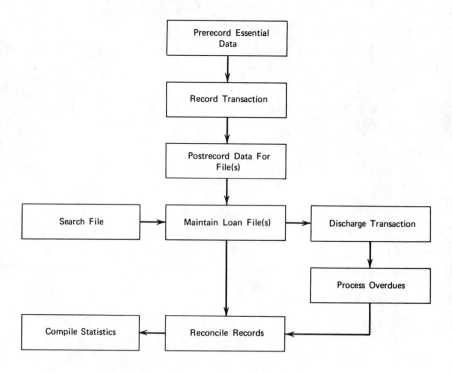

Figure 15.3   Circulation control system schematic.

Criteria for Evaluation

Figure 15.3 shows the major steps required in a circulation control system, and Figure 15.4 summarizes relevant criteria for evaluation of a system, keyed to the functional blocks affected. Basically, aside from the obvious criterion of cost, they relate to the speed with which operations take place, the ease of handling renewals and holds, the capacity for handling large amounts of activity, and the ability to provide statistical data.[12]

[12] Goldhor, Herbert, "Criteria for an Ideal Circulation System," *Wilson Library Bulletin,* **14** (April 1955).

Figure 15.4 Qualitative criteria for evaluation.

Qualitative Factors	Functional Blocks Affected	Explanation of Factors Related to Functional Blocks as Requisites in Selection of a Circulation System
Purposes of Circulation Control 1. Identify borrowers	Prerecord Data Record Transaction Process Overdues	In selecting a system, the library must decide to what degree it wants to identify its borrowers in its circulation records, degree of identification ranging from existing I.D., name on call slip, library card, registration file, delinquent borrowers file, to complete borrowers file.
2. Identify materials charged out	Prerecord Data Record Transaction Maintain Loan File Search File	Alternate systems offer different means of recording materials—photographic, punched cards, etc., and different types of identification—author, call number, etc. If a library circulates other types of materials as well as books (i.e., pamphlets, audiovisual materials), an important question in determining a system is whether these materials can be circulated within the book circulation system so an auxiliary system is not needed.
3. Secure return of materials	Record Transaction Postrecord Transaction Maintain Loan File Discharge Transaction Process Overdues Reconcile Records	Due date access to a loan file (containing book and borrower information) is a prerequisite for any circulation system with this qualitative factor. If accuracy is a goal, the availability of and types of error control devices in various systems must be analyzed.
4. Provide a total count of all materials charged out	Prerecord Data Record Transaction Discharge Transaction Reconcile Records Compile Statistics	A system with numbered transaction cards can sometimes provide this total count. Usage statistics require other prerecording and recording and a means of compiling them. An example is the UCLA Library which uses an IBM call slip requiring prerecording of type of borrower (i.e., grad. student, faculty member).

Figure 15-4 *(Continued)*

Qualitative Factors	Functional Blocks Affected	Explanation of Factors Related to Functional Blocks as Requisites in Selection of a Circulation System
Priorities of Service 1. System simple for patrons to use	Prerecord Data Record Transaction Discharge Transaction	If a library's policy is elimination of borrower participation in charging transactions, certain systems would not be considered. A public library might have this priority of service due to different levels of its clientele. Whereas a college library with a homogeneous knowledgeable clientele might desire a system with borrower participation.
2. Library staff understands	All Blocks	The smooth functioning of any circulation system depends on the staff's ability to operate in that system.
3. Return of books when library is closed	Discharge Transaction Process Overdues Maintain Loan File Reconcile Records	As an example, if an IBM 357 with a circulation recorder was used for recording and discharging (which requires a book card and library card), a bookdrop for returning books when the library was closed could not be used.
4. Renewal of books Recognize holds placed against books	Discharge Transaction Maintain Loan File Reconcile Records Prerecord Data Record Transaction Search File Postrecord Data	The treatment of renewals as either new charges or as extensions of old charges and their relative efficiency could be considered in selecting a system. If renewal of books by telephone or mail was a desired service, a system such as one employing a Recordak machine with transaction cards (where books must be brought to the library for renewal) would not be selected.
5. Make available requested materials	Prerecord Data Maintain Loan File Search File	A reserve book service requires a system with apparatus for searching the file and the shelves, and for a waiting list or file.
6. Books which can be charged out at various locations in the library	Record Transaction Discharge Transaction Search File	As a desired service, this requires that systems be analyzed in terms of equipment needed for recording and discharging, their mobility and cost, and in terms of personnel.

Figure 15-4   *(Continued)*

Qualitative Factors	Functional Blocks Affected	Explanation of Factors Related to Functional Blocks as Requisites in Selection of a Circulation System
Special Requirements 1. Library integral unit or part of a system	All Blocks	Centralized processing in a large system with branches allows the use of sophisticated equipment.
	Prerecord Data Process Overdues Discharge Transaction Maintain Loan File Reconcile Records	Returning books anywhere in the system requires uniform circulation procedures throughout the system, and requires a coding of the transaction cards for locations (i.e., branches) as well as for transaction number and date so the books can be returned to their own library.
2. Knowledge of location of every book at all times Knowledge of holds placed on books	Prerecord Data Maintain Loan File Search File	This factor necessitates a system providing a loan file by book identification (call number, Cutter number, etc.) rather than a due date file. This need in most college and university libraries has prevented the use of systems employing transaction cards alone, in favor of systems employing transaction cards and charge cards.
3. Permit library clearance at the time a borrower leaves the organization	Prerecord Data Maintain Loan File Search File	This factor calls for a system which includes a borrowers file of loaned books, as well as either a date due file or a location file, and is usually a need of special libraries.

FORMS AND FILES

Figure 15.5 lists the various forms and files involved in the operation of a circulation system. Some of them are essentially manual forms—book cards, badges, call cards, dummy cards, and discharge cards. Others are magnetic tape and disk files—Transaction File, Holds File, Borrower File, and the like. Of them, the Transaction File is the central one, to which all others relate.

Transaction File

This contains a record for every book that is not located where it is normally supposed to be—whether charged out to a borrower, to another library, to a

Figure 15.5   Forms and files

F_6	Transaction File	
	Book Card	Dummy Book Card
	Borrower Card	Dummy Borrower Card
	Hold Card	
F_7	Call Card File	
	Call Card	
F_8	Borrower Registration File	
F_9	Scheduling File	
	Distribution Lists	
F_{10}	Miscellaneous Files	
	Recall Form	
	Overdues Form	

branch or reserved book room, or to be bound or repaired. The record includes the unique identification of the book, the date it was charged out, and the place or person to which it is charged. Figure 15.6 shows the format of a Transaction File Record designed for a disk file system.

In most mechanized systems, this file will be sequenced by call number (or other unique identifier). In some systems, such as that at Brooklyn College, two separate files are needed, one being in order by call number and the other in order by a "transaction" number, providing an index to the former. In the system described later in this chapter, provision is made for both kinds of operation.

The basic sources of data for input to the Transaction File are Transaction Cards (Figure 15.7), produced usually from data on Book Cards and Borrower Cards (often called Badges).

Book Cards (Figure 15.8), or their equivalent in the form of machine-readable information on the book itself, are usually required for an automated circulation system. Such cards are produced as books are accessioned (as discussed in Chapter 16). The data on a book card normally will include a call number (or other unique identifier of the book), a short author-title, and perhaps a code for allowable type of loan. It can be recorded in a variety of forms—punched card, punched plastic or metallic card, machine readable data imprinted on the book, and the like. In conversion from a prior system, it is usually necessary to produce book cards for the existing collection. Several approaches can be taken:

1.   Prepare new cards for all books in the library.
2.   Prepare cards only when a book circulates, during the loan period.

Figure 15.6   Transaction File

FUNCTION: The transaction file contains three categories of entries—all with the same format.

(1)   Records of books currently in circulation to patrons on short-term loans. Short term loans will remain in the Circulation File until they are returned, at which time they will become books which have been returned but not purged from the disk (see category 3 below).

(2)   Records of books recently charged out to internal library functions, as well as books on quarter loan, are called long-term loans. Long-term loans will remain in the Circulation File until they are transferred, at regular time intervals, to the Long-Term Loan File. At that time they become books which have been returned but not purged from the disk (see category 3).

(3)   Records of books that have been returned but not purged from the disk are called Empty Loans. Books that are in circulation tend to remain in circulation (except those from category 2). Therefore, unless a shortage of space in disk storage occurs, records marked for purging will remain in the Circulation File.

FORMAT: All records in the circulation file contain 80 alphameric characters. A definition of the parameters stored in the 80 characters follows:

Character Position	Field Description
1-24	Call number
25-54	Short author and title
55-64	Social security number or Transaction number
65-66	Status code
67-69	Due date
70-72	Return date
73	Charge-out day
74	Transmitting station
75	Branch library
76	Type-of-book
77-80	Control characters

3.   Prepare cards for books which prior statistics imply are the most frequently circulated.

4.   Prepare cards for recent materials.

Borrower Cards ("Badges"), as illustrated in Figure 15.9, are also usually required in mechanized systems (although those, such as the Brooklyn College System, which separate the Transaction File from the Call Number File do so to avoid the need for Borrower Cards). The data in machine-readable form will usually be limited to a short identification number—for example, the Social Security Number.

Figure 15.7 Transaction Cards.

Type of Card	Columns	Field Description
Book Card and Badge	1–3	Current day
	4–6	Time of day
	7	Transmitting station
(Same format for	8	Transaction code (6)
Call Card, Discharge	9	Branch library code
Badge)	10	Type of book loan-Code
	11–34	Call number
Badge Number	35–64	Short author title
	65–75	Borrower badge number
	76	Transmission check Character
		(12 = correct, 11 = error)
Book Card, No Badge	1– 3	Current day
	4– 6	Time of day
	7	Transmitting station
	8	Transaction code (3)
	9–15	Transaction number
	16	First transmission (12-8-3)
	17	Transaction code (6)
	18	Branch library code
	19	Type of book loan-code
	20–43	Call number
	44–72	Short author-title
	73–79	Dummy badge
	80	Transmission check character
No Book Card, Badge	1– 3	Current day
	4– 6	Time of day
Call Card, Discharge	7	Transmitting station
Badge)	8	Transaction code (3)
Badge Number	9–15	Transaction number
	16	First transmission (12-8-3)
	17	Transaction code (9)
No Book Card, No Badge	18–28	Badge number
Badge Number	29	Transmission check character
Hold Call Card,	1– 3	Current day
Badge	4– 6	Time of day
	7	Transmitting station
(Hold Call Card,	8	Transaction code (8)
Discharge Badge)	9	Transaction code (3)
Badge Number	10–33	Call number
	34–40	Transaction number
	41	First transmission (12-8-3)
Hold Call Card	42	Transaction code (9)
No Badge	43-53	Badge number
Badge Number	54	Transmission check character

Figure 15.7 *(Continued)*

Type of Card	Columns	Field Description
Renewal, Book Card,	1– 3	Current day
Badge	4– 6	Time of day
	7	Transmitting station
Renewal, Book Card	8	Transaction code (7)
No Badge	9	First transmission (12-3-8)
Badge Number	10	
	11	Branch library code
	12	Type of book loan-code
	13–36	Call number
	37–66	Short-author title
	67-77	Badge number
	78	Transmission check character

Miscellaneous Forms. In addition, other forms may be needed to handle special situations—for instance, "Hold Cards" when a patron wishes to place a hold (or reservation) on a book, "Dummy Cards" for cases when Book Cards or Borrower Cards are missing, and "Discharge Cards" to provide control data indicating that a book has been returned.

The output from the Transaction File includes, among other things, recall notices, overdue notices, and various reports and lists. Principal among them is a Long-Term Circulation List, required in a system with limited storage capability

Figure 15.8 Book Card format.

Type of card	Columns	Field Description
Book Card	1	Transaction code (6)
	2	Branch library code
	3	Type of book loan-code
	4– 5	Class letters
	6–10	Class numbers
	11–19	Cutter number, date
	20	Series number
	21–23	Volume number
	24–25	Part number
	26–27	Copy number
	28–57	Short author-title
	58	End transmission (12-8-4)
	59–79	Continuation of author-title
	80	Blank
Dummy Book Card	1	Transaction code (9)
	14	End transmission (12-8-4)

Figure 15.9   Borrower Card (Badge)

Type of card	Columns	Field description
Badge	1— 9	Badge number
	10	Blank
	11—12	Borrower status
Dummy Badge	1— 9	000000000
	10	Blank
	11—12	00
Discharge Badge	1— 9	999999999
	10	Blank
	11—12	99

so that books that will have a longer circulation period will not use valuable direct access storage. A second list is a Hold List indicating which books have been placed on hold and are therefore not available for renewal.

Call Card File

There are several circumstances in which a complete transaction record cannot be created: there may be no Book Card or no Borrower Card; there may not even be a book, as in the case of a hold. Under these conditions, a Call Card must be created to identify the book or the patron or both. It must be stored in a manual Call Card File and, in cases where no Book Card was available, a new Book Card must be created and filed until the book is returned. Figure 15.10 is a representative Call Card.

The Call Card File is the repository of all Call Cards used in charge transactions. Call Cards used only to identify the patron (that is, containing a Call Number) are merged into the file without changes. Those used to identify the book are processed first: (1) the type-of-loan code is punched in column 8 and the Call Number is punched in columns 9-32; (2) the cards are processed to update the circulation record; (3) the cards are used as source documents for preparation of Book Cards, using the shelf list for obtaining added data.

The Call Card File is maintained in Transaction Number sequence. It is processed periodically (once a week, for example) for automatic merging of new cards and extraction of old ones.

In addition, a New Book-Card File serves as the repository of book cards created because ones were not available at charge-out. When books subsequently are returned without Book Cards, the new card should be found in this file.

Figure 15.10 Call Card.

FORM: Call Card (front view).

FUNCTION: The Call Card is filled out by the patron when either the Book Card or Badge or both will be missing from the charge-out process. The Call Card is always filled out completely; it is a record of the Call Number and author and title of the book and of the patron's name, address, and status. The Call Card is read into the input station of the Data Collection System at the time a book is charged out, before the Book Card, or Dummy Book Card, is read.

DESCRIPTION: This is an exact image of the front side of a Call Card. See FORM: Call Card (interpreted) for the details of the data punched on the card.

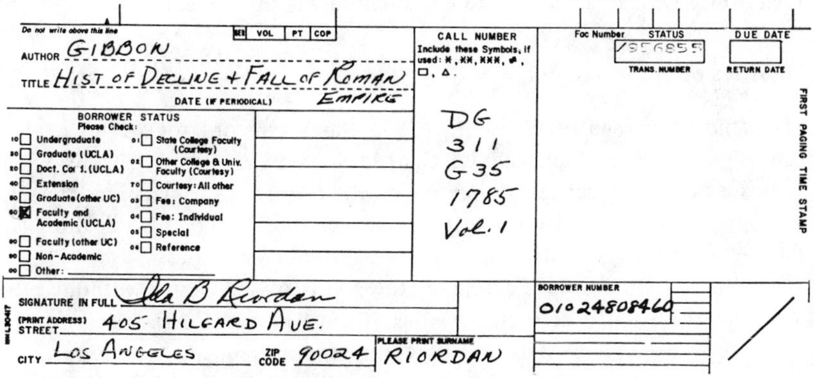
Do not write above this line
SER VOL PT COP
AUTHOR GIBBON
TITLE HIST OF DECLINE + FALL OF ROMAN EMPIRE
DATE (IF PERIODICAL)
BORROWER STATUS
Please Check:
10 Undergraduate
30 Graduate (UCLA)
20 Doct. Cd. 1. (UCLA)
40 Extension
50 Graduate (other UC)
60 ☒ Faculty and Academic (UCLA)
80 Faculty (other UC)
90 Non-Academic
00 Other:
01 State College Faculty (Courtesy)
02 Other College & Univ. Faculty (Courtesy)
70 Courtesy: All other
03 Fee: Company
04 Fee: Individual
05 Special
06 Reference
CALL NUMBER
Include these Symbols, if used: ✱, ✱✱, ✱✱✱, #, □, △.
DG
311
G35
1785
Vol. 1
Foc Number STATUS
/956855
TRANS. NUMBER
DUE DATE
RETURN DATE
FIRST PAGING TIME STAMP
SIGNATURE IN FULL Ila B Riordan
(PRINT ADDRESS) STREET 405 HILGARD AVE.
CITY LOS ANGELES
ZIP CODE 90024
PLEASE PRINT SURNAME RIORDAN
BORROWER NUMBER 010248084 60

Type of card	Columns	Field Description
Call Card	6	Transaction code (3)
	65–71	Transaction number
	74	First transmission code (12-3-8)
Hold Call Card	5	Transaction code (8)
	6	Transaction code (3)
	9–32	Call number
	65–71	Transaction number
	74	First transmission code (12-3-8)
Do-Not-Renew Call Card	5	Transaction code (6)
	6	Transaction code (3)
	9-32	Call number
	65-71	Transaction number
	74	First transmission code (12-3-8)

Hold Call Card File and List

When Call Cards are produced for the purpose of placing a hold on a book (and then become "Hold Call Cards"), they must be filed in a Hold Call Card File. When a book is returned, the Hold Call Card is used as the source document for sending a mailing notice. It is then placed in the pocket of the book, along with the book card, and used in the subsequent charge-out process. Figure 15.11 describes the Hold Call Card.

Hold Call Cards also serve as the source documents for recording the hold against the circulation record, sending out a recall notice if necessary, and causing an entry in a "Hold List."

The Hold List is produced daily, as a cumulative list of all books on hold. Its primary purpose is to assure that books on hold will not be renewed.

Borrower Registration File

This file (described in Figure 15.12) contains a record for every person or location to which a book can be charged. A typical record (Figure 15.13) contains a borrower identification number, the borrower's name, his address, his status, and his date of registration. It may also contain data on his affiliation (for instance, department), his frequency of use, and other statistics.

This file is used for verification of the status of individuals without other library identification. For such purposes, it must be available in visual form—a printed copy or on-line. It is also used for sending requests for the return of books, notices of overdues, fines, and the like. For those purposes, batch processing is adequate.

Scheduling File

Much of the material in the library has high immediacy of interest—recent issues of journals, audiovisual material, and so on. For such material, the circulation must be controlled. To do this, a schedule for distribution of each item must be established and maintained. Distribution lists must be prepared, and sometimes pick-up and delivery must be controlled by schedules.

The simplest form of Scheduling File is that used for distribution of issues of a journal as it is received. From it, distribution lists can be easily produced, as a by-product of "receiving" data from the Serial Records Subsystem (as discussed in Chapter 18). A more complex form is illustrated in Figure 15.14, which shows an illustrative record for scheduling of audiovisual material.[13]

---

[13] Lane, Nancy Diane, *Maximum Utilization of Audio-Visual Materials in the Public Schools through Computer Booking*, Master's Thesis, UCLA, 1969.

Figure 15.11 Hold Call Card.

FORM:	Hold Call Card (as processed by the Hold Service Program).
FUNCTION:	The Hold Call Card is filled out by the patron in the same manner as required for a call card when it is desired to place a hold on a book. The card is presented at the control checkout station at which time the librarian stamps it as a "HOLD AND NOTIFY." The current date is also stamped and the patron's telephone number is obtained if notification is not to be made by mail. The Hold Call Card, after being identified with an 8 punch in column 5 and having the call number punched in columns 9-32, is processed by the Hold Service Program. This service program records the hold in the circulation file, the hold file, and if a hold already exists on the book, in the additional hold file.
DESCRIPTION:	This is an image of a hold-call that was filled out by a patron after the punching of identification and call number.

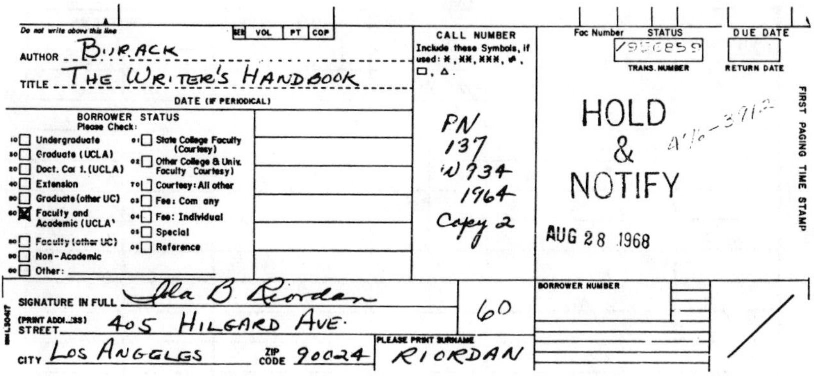
Do not write above this line
SER VOL PT COP
AUTHOR Burack
TITLE The Writer's Handbook
DATE (IF PERIODICAL)
CALL NUMBER
Include these Symbols, if used: *, **, ***, #, □, △.
PN 137 W934 1964 Copy 2
Fac Number STATUS DUE DATE
TRANS. NUMBER RETURN DATE
HOLD & NOTIFY
AUG 28 1968
FIRST PAGING TIME STAMP
BORROWER STATUS Please Check:
Undergraduate
Graduate (UCLA)
Doct. Cat. 1. (UCLA)
Extension
Graduate (other UC)
Faculty and Academic (UCLA)
Faculty (other UC)
Non-Academic
Other:
State College Faculty (Courtesy)
Other College & Univ. Faculty Courtesy)
Courtesy: All other
Fee: Com any
Fee: Individual
Special
Reference
SIGNATURE IN FULL Ida B Riordan
(PRINT ADDRESS) STREET 405 Hilgard Ave.
CITY Los Angeles ZIP CODE 90024
60
PLEASE PRINT SURNAME RIORDAN
BORROWER NUMBER

Type of Card	Columns	Field Description
Hold Call Card	5	Transaction code (8)
	6	Transaction code (3)
	9–32	Call number
	65–71	Transaction number
	74	First transmission Code (12-3-8)
Do Not Renew Call Card	5	Transaction code (6)
	6	Transaction code (3)
	9–32	Call number
	65–71	Transaction number
	74	First transmission code (12-3-8)

File Name BORROWER REGISTRATION FILE			File No. F8		
Location ↲		Storage Medium *			
Access Requirements LIBRARIAN, OVERDUES BILLINF, CALL-IN AND OVERDUE NOTICES					
Sequenced By BORROWER NUMBER					
Content Qualifications BADGE NO, BORROWER NAME AND ADDRESS, OUTSTANDING OVERDUE FEES, EXPIRATION DATE AND VALIDITY CHECK					
How Current MONTHLY					
Retention Characteristics RECORDS REMOVED UPON EXPIRATION OF LIBRARY PRIVILEGES AFTER ALL FEES ARE CLEARED					
Labels AS REQUIRED BY COMPUTER SYSTEM					
Remarks					

CONTENTS

Sequence No.	Form Name	Volume		Characters Per Record	Characters Per File	
		Avg.	Peak		Avg.	Peak
1	BORROWER RECORD	50,000		150	7.5 million	

1968	BR	Figure 15.12	1
Date	Analyst	Source	Page

Representative
Study

* Determined uniquely by each library

Figure 15.12   Borrower record.

Miscellaneous Files

There are many other files that may be necessary or useful for control of circulation—security files (for control of the circulation of military classified

Form Name BORROWER RECORD				Form No. R7	
Other Names Used				Layout No.	
				Related Form Nos.	
				No. of Copies	
Media MAGNETIC DISK		How Prepared KEYBOARDING			
Operations Involved In BORROWER REGISTRATION, PREPARATION					
OF NOTICES AND BILLS, POSTING OF BILL PAYMENTS					
Remarks FILE SEQUENCED BY ID NUMBER					

		CONTENTS				
			Characters			
No.	Data Name	Freq.	Min.	95%	Max.	A/N	Origin
	ID NUMBER				9	N	
	STATUS				2	N	
	NAME		7	20	25	A	
	ADDRESS		30	50	60	A/N	
	AFFILIATION		4	30	40	A/N	
	FREQUENCY OF USE				3	N	
	OUTSTANDING FEES						
	CALL NUMBER				24	A/N	
	FEE		2	3	4	N	

1968 _____ Date   JBR _____ Analyst   Figure 15.13 _____ Source   1 of 1 _____ Page

Representative _____ Study

Figure 15.13   Borrower registration file.

records), overdue files for books that are overdue, a history file for analysis of prior circulation records, and the like.

A SAMPLE COMPUTER SYSTEM

To provide a definitive basis for evaluation of the magnitude of the task of circulation control, a detailed analysis and design has been made of a system which combines some of the aspects of both batch processing and on-line

Figure 15.14   Audiovisual schedule record.

Film cataloging data (not detailed here)	80 characters
Schedule (for each planned showing)	
{ School identification	3 characters
{ Delivery date	3 characters
{ pick-up date	3 characters

processing. Figure 15.15, a schematic of this system, shows that it is designed around a small-scale batch processing computer.

An on-line computer facility, of course, would be the ideal for circulation control, since then verifications of borrower status, reports on incompatibility of data on renewals, and checks on the location of material can be made and reported to the input station while the patron and book are still in the library. However, no matter how ideal this situation may be, a back-up system is essential in order to allow the library to continue providing service during computer downtime. It should have as much of the flexibility of the on-line system as possible and should not require any evident change in operating procedure. Since a back-up system in the library must be inexpensive, it must be based on a small computer, with more stringent operational limits than the on-line system. The design outlined here provides as general a back-up system as possible with a small-scale batch system, and is able to handle the functions desired of the on-line system even though in a less convenient manner.

It is designed to handle charges and discharges, to place holds on books currently charged out either to library patrons or to library required functions, to control renewals for books with holds to discharge holds, to process overdues, to maintain statistics, and to serve other circulation functions. The system must also be able to handle some queries in real time, even though the handling of such queries with this back-up system is not as convenient as it would be with an on-line system.

The configuration is that of Figure 14.2. It includes a central processor, a multifunction card machine, a printer, at least one disk drive, two tape drives, and an on-line typewriter; it is suitable for punched-card operation, the first step away from manual practice, as well as magnetic tape and disk file processing. The *central processor*, with 16,000 bytes of core storage, has an excess of 4000 bytes over that required for the largest of the systems programs which it uses. This should provide ample storage for processing programs as well as for communicating with a large-scale, on-line processor. The multifunction card machine operates under control of the central processor and combines the functions of a card reader, card punch, collator, sorter, interpreter, and card-document printer. Thus, one piece of equipment combines the functions of

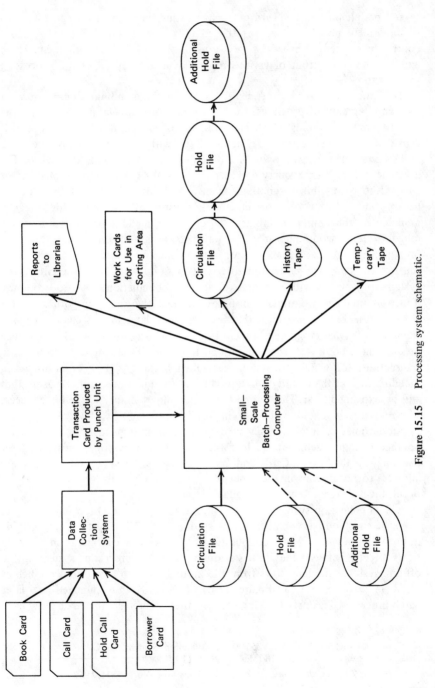

Figure 15.15 Processing system schematic.

505

several peripheral punched-card devices, reducing the number of separate pieces of equipment needed to support the computer operation. The *printer*, under control of the central processor, performs the function of a tabulating machine and handles the output of various reports generated by all of the processing programs.

The *disk drive* provides sufficient storage for the minimum required number of computer control programs, the file of currently circulating books, and the files pertaining to holds which are required to be on a direct-access device; it provides a storage capacity of 5.4 million bytes with an average access time of 75 milliseconds. The use of only one disk drive certainly limits the size of file available for real time querying; therefore, books out on long-term loans or charged to other library functions, such as a reserve book room or a branch library, must be recorded on tape with a listing of books in this category available at the computer inquiry station. Recent additions to this group of long-term loans would appear in the active circulation file on disk until the tape on which the long-term loans are recorded is updated. This would help to keep the size of the active circulation file to a minimum and allow the circulation system to function with one disk for an active circulation of 40,000 volumes. Tapes are used for two primary purposes, although there are many other uses for them in the service programs that are described later in this chapter (in the section on Service Programs): a record of each loan is stored on a History Tape at the time a book is discharged, and an In-Process Tape is used to store those transactions for which no action was taken because of lack of information, inability to find the record desired on disk, or for a myriad of other reasons that will be explained later. The on-line *typewriter* allows inquiry of the direct-access file; alternatively, batch mode querying can be used.

An automated circulation system requires that, in some manner, transactions be recorded in machine-readable form. The system described normally uses machine-readable Book Cards and Borrower Cards. However, transactions are allowed to occur even in the absence of a Book Card, Badge, or both. Such occurrences also lead to machine-readable input.

A data collection system (such as is listed in Figure 11.7) transmits the data from the check-out station or discharge station.[14,15] These systems are available in both on-line and off-line configurations. In the on-line configuration, the data flows directly between the input station and the data processing system. In the off-line system, the data flows from the input station to a card punch (such as listed in Figure 11.4 or Figure 11.6). The cards thus punched are later batch-processed against the circulation file. Although the data for each

[14] Harris, Michael H., "The 357 Data Collection System for Circulation Controls" *College and Research Libraries,* **26** (March 1965), 119 ff.

[15] *IBM 357 Data Collection System.* White Plains, New York: IBM, 1963.

transaction is edit-checked for proper length of transmission at both the input station and the card punch, errors of other types, caught readily by the on-line system, are now not detected until long after the book and patron have left the library. When these errors are later recognized during the computer processing of a batch of transactions, notification is prepared either for immediate action or for action when the book is returned to the library.

The following sections discuss the creation, processing, and maintenance of the forms and files used in each of the circulation functions: charge-outs, discharges, renewals, holds, and service programs.

Before discussing the processes in detail, however, let us comment generally about the effects of equipment limitations on the content and organization of files, in order to give an insight into the processes themselves.

1.   The primary storage medium for the Circulation File is a single disk. However, nothing precludes the use of additional disks if the computer system is so configured.

2.   No two keys in a file may be identical. Therefore, a new charge record may not be stored on the disk while an old one with the same call number exists on the disk. New charges in this case are stored in the Temporary File, and the existence of a duplicate record is entered into the record on the disk. This can lead to some awkwardness if an almost immediate discharge of the new charge occurs, but the system does handle this situation.

3.   The programming language used may impose a definite order of processing. For example, the Report Program Generator language requires that all data required for a transaction must first be read into memory, then it must be processed and, finally, the output to the various files and reports must be created, with overlap not allowed among these functions. In such a case, processing is a succession of input time, compute time, and output time. Frequently, therefore, limitations of the language necessitate performing some processes in two steps, when one step might have seemed sufficient.

Charge-Outs

For a book to be charged out, the borrower presents some combination of Book Card, Call Card, and Badge to the attendant at a checkout station. The attendant enters the required forms into the input station of the data collection system and the data is transmitted to the card punch where a transaction card is created. The set of accumulated transaction cards is read into the computer at scheduled time intervals for machine processing of the charge.

The charge process has five stages: (1) actions from the checkout station to the data collection system, (2) the handling of Call Cards, (3) the input to the computer maintained files, (4) processing, and (5) the communication between the computer and the librarian.

Figure 15.16 Charge-out operations.

Type of Transaction	Enters into Card Reader	Enters into Badge Reader
BOOK CARD, BADGE	Book Card	Badge
BOOK CARD, NO BADGE	Book Card	Dummy Badge
NO BOOK CARD, BADGE	Call Card, followed by Dummy Book Card	Badge
NO BOOK CARD, NO BADGE	Call Card, followed by Dummy Book Card	Dummy Badge
HOLD-CALL CARD, BADGE	Hold-Call Card, followed by Dummy Book Card	Badge
HOLD-CALL CARD, NO BADGE	Hold-Call Card, followed by Dummy Book Card	Dummy Badge

Actions from Checkout Station to the Data Collection System. There are six categories of charge transactions that can be handled at the checkout stations (see Figure 15.16).

In the first case, the two machine-readable reentry records serve as data sources for the transaction recording. In the next three cases, when either the Book Card or the Badge, or both are missing, the borrower must fill out a Call Card completely. The Call Card is used instead of the missing form(s) during the recording of the transaction and later serves as a record of borrower identification in the case of the missing Badge, or as a source document for the preparation of a new Book Card in the case of a missing Book Card. Finally, the last two cases arise because the requestor must have prepared a Call Card (called a "Hold-Call Card") at the time he placed the request.

When the book requested is returned to the library, this Hold-Call Card is placed in the pocket of the book and is used in the subsequent charge process.

In any of these cases, the checkout attendant compares the Book Card or Call Card with the book, stamps the return date on the date slip, enters the forms into the data collection system, and then performs the following operations, depending on the type of charge.

> BOOK CARD, BADGE. Returns Book Card to book and Badge to borrower.

> BOOK CARD, NO BADGE. Returns Book Card to book and places Call Card in a group, called the "Book Card" Group.

NO BOOK CARD, BADGE. Returns Badge to borrower and places Call Card in a second group—the "No Book Card" Group.

NO BOOK CARD, NO BADGE. places Call Card in "No Book Card" Group.

HOLD-CALL CARD, BADGE. Returns Book Card to book, Badge to borrower, and places the Hold-Call Card in the "Book Card" Group.

HOLD-CALL CARD, NO BADGE. Returns Book Card to book and places Hold-Call Card in "Book Card" Group.

Errors in character transmission, record length, or punching will cause an error indication at the input station and will require a retransmission of the transaction.

The entering of these forms causes a transaction card to be created by the card punch, as has been shown in Figure 15.15. A check character is included to indicate whether the record is correct or in error. If the record is in error, additional information is given in the check character to indicate the type of error. Error transaction cards will later be filtered out by the computer.

Figure 15.17 presents a schematic or subsequent processing of transaction data to the computer and of call cards to the Call Card File.

The Handling of Call Cards. On a regular basis the Book Card Group and the No Book Card Group of Call Cards are picked up from the checkout stations. The Book Card Group is sorted on Call Number and directly enters the Call Card File, since the Call Number of the book has already been entered into the computer system. The only missing piece of information may be the status of the borrower which affects overdue billing; the type of loan code is available from the Book Card data in the (BOOK CARD, NO BADGE) charge and from the previous charge record for the (HOLD-CALL CARD, BADGE) and (HOLD-CALL CARD, NO BADGE) charges. Figure 15.18 shows a schematic of the subsequent processing. The cards in the No Book Card Group go to key-punching, where call number and type of loan code are punched into them. They are then used to complete the data in the charge transaction that was recorded by the card punch and is being held on a Temporary Tape. These same cards are later used as source documents for the preparation of new book cards which will be held in the New Book Card File awaiting the return of the book; thus no book should ever be charged out twice without a book card.

Input to Computer Files. The transaction card created by the card punch of the data collection system is used to update the computer files. When a batch of transaction cards are taken to the computer for processing, they are in the order in which the transactions occurred, with various types of charges as well as discharges and renewals intermingled. A date card, containing the day of the year, is placed in front of each batch of transaction cards before processing.

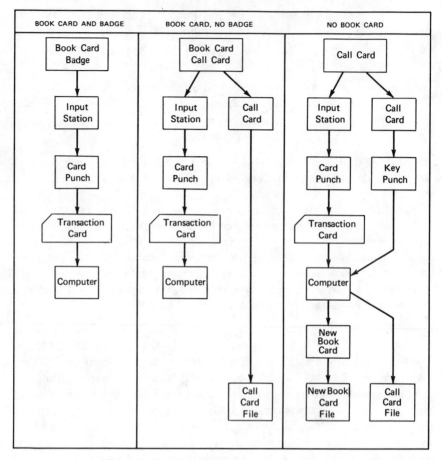

Figure 15.17   Schematic of transaction handling.

As each transaction card is read, it is checked for validity, for the existence of a call number, for the existence of a badge number, and for the type of transaction. Figure 15.19 is a decision table for the control of subsequent processing if there is a call number; Figure 15.20, one for the cases with no call number. The significant factors in the decision process are as follows.

Call Number.   The call number is the key by which all transactions are recognized. When it is missing from the Transaction Card, the incomplete charge is held on the Temporary Tape until the call number can "catch up" to the charge transaction.

Short Author and Title. The short author and title along with the call number uniquely determine an entry. However, it is *not* a part of the key, since this

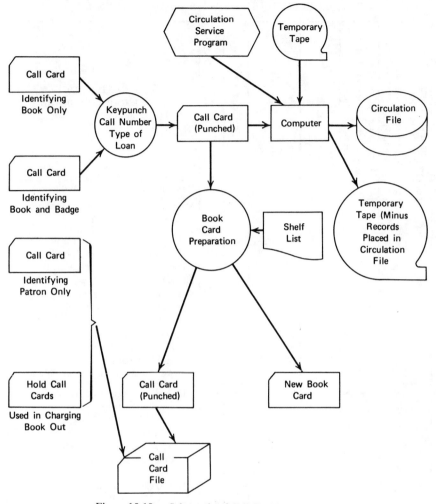

Figure 15.18   Schematic of Call Card handling.

would make the key too long for practicality. Nevertheless, it is examined when an apparent duplicate call number is found in the system.

Transaction Number. The transaction number is the tie between information that is eventually stored in the Call Card File and the Circulation File. It is used to replace all missing data in the circulation record at the time of placement on the Temporary Tape. Thus if the Book Card is missing in a transaction, the call number field and the short author and title field hold the transaction number when the charge record is written on the Temporary Tape. After the call number has been punched into the Call Card and the Call Card has been processed by the

Figure 15.19 Decision table of Book Card transactions.

Call number on transaction card is not on disk	Call number on transaction card is on disk	Short author and title on disk matches short author and title on transaction card	Short author and title field on disk is a transaction number	Return date is in disk record	Control Character 1 = H	Control Character 4 = P	Control Character 4 = D	(BOOK CARD, BADGE) (BOOK CARD, NO BADGE) Transactions
Yes								Write new charge record on disk.
	Yes					Yes		Overwrite old charge record with new charge record.
	Yes	Yes		Yes	Yes	No	No	This book was on hold but is not charged out with Hold-Call Card. Rewrite old record on disk with D in control character 4. Write new charge on Temporary Tape Print message to librarian with the following data: 1. Old Charge Record 2. New Charge Record 3. Holds Record 4. Additional Holds Record (if any)
	Yes	Yes			No		No	This book has been recharged without a discharge. Rewrite old record on disk with D in control character 4. Write new charge on Temporary Tape. Print message to librarian with the following data: 1. Old Charge Record 2. New Charge Record 3. Holds Record (if any) 4. Additional Holds Record (if any)
	Yes	No	No				No	Rewrite old record on disk with a D in control character 4. Write new charge on Temporary Tape. Print message to librarian with the following data (this is a duplicate call number, both charges active): 1. Old Charge Record 2. New Charge Record 3. Holds Record 4. Additional Holds Record (if any)

Figure 15.19   (*Continued*)

Call number on transaction card is not on disk	Call number on transaction card is on disk	Short author and title on disk matches short author and title on transaction card	Short author and title field on disk is a transaction number	Return date is in disk record	Control Character 1 = H	Control Character 4 = P	Control Character 4 = D	(BOOK CARD, BADGE) (BOOK CARD, NO BADGE) Transactions
Yes	No	Yes				No	Yes	Write new charge on Temporary Tape. (No message needed since one generated the first time duplicate appeared).
Yes	No	Yes	No			No	No	This is a *possible* recharge without a discharge or a *possible* duplicate call number. Rewrite old record on disk with D in control character 4. Write new record on Temporary Tape. Print message to librarian with all data available: 1. Old Charge Record 2. New Charge Record 3. Holds Record (if any) 4. Additional Holds Record (if any)
Yes	No	Yes		Yes	Yes	No		This is a charge of book which should have *possibly* been made with a Hold-Call Card or this is a *possible* duplicate call number. Rewrite old record with a D in control character 4. Write new record on Temporary Tape. Print message to librarian with all data available.

Circulation Service Program, the call number appears in the call number field but the short author and title field still holds the transaction number. In this way, if a Badge were present in the transaction, there still is a record of the transaction number in the circulation record that eventually reaches the disk.

Return Date. Normally when the return date is filled in, the record is marked for purging from the file.

Figure 15.20   Decision table for No Book Card transactions.

Call number on transaction is not on disk	Call number on transaction is on disk	Short author and title field on disk contains an author and title	Return date in disk record	Control Character 1 = H	Control Character 4 = P	Control Character 4 = D	(NO BOOK CARD, BADGE) (NO BOOK CARD, NO BADGE) Transactions
Yes							Write new charge record on disk.
	Yes				Yes		Overwrite old charge record with new charge record.
	Yes	Yes	Yes	Yes	No	No	This book is a *possible* hold that is not charged out with a Hold-Call Card or a *possible* duplicate call number and/or has a *possible* lost book card. Rewrite old record on disk with a D in control character 4. Write new charge on Temporary Tape. Print message to librarian with the following data: 1. Old Charge Record 2. New Charge Record 3. Holds Record 4. Additional Holds Record (if any)
	Yes	Yes	No	Yes	No		This is a *possible* duplicate call number or a *possible* charge of a book not discharged through the system or a *possible* lost book card. Rewrite old record on disk with D in control character 4. Write new charge on Temporary Tape. Print message to librarian with the following data: 1. Old Charge Record 2. New Charge Record 3. Holds Record 4. Additional Holds Record (if any)

Figure 15.20   (*Continued*)

Call number on transaction is not on disk	Call number on transaction is on disk	Short author and title field on disk contains an author and title	Return date in disk record	Control Character 1 = H	Control Character 4 = P	Control Character 4 = D	(NO BOOK CARD, BADGE) (NO BOOK CARD, NO BADGE) Transactions
	Yes	No	No	No	No		This is a *possible* duplicate call number or a *possible* charge of a book not discharged through the system. Rewrite old record with D in control character 4. Write new charge on Temporary Tape. Print message to librarian with the following data: 1. Old Charge Record 2. New Charge Record 3. Holds Record 4. Additional Holds Record (if any)

Control Characters. There are four control characters in a circulation record. As shown in Figure 15.21, they control and initiate a variety of functions.

All transactions for which there is no Book Card are first written on the Temporary Tape. The Circulation Service Program subsequently will append the call number to these records and then they will be ready for entry into the Circulation File. Although the charges made from these (NO BOOK CARD, BADGE) and (NO BOOK CARD, NO BADGE) transactions are now similar to the transactions for (BOOK CARD, BADGE) and (BOOK CARD, NO BADGE), the absence of the short author and title field causes the decision table for them to look somewhat different (Figure 15.20). The description of the processing of (HOLD-CALL CARD, BADGE) and (HOLD-CALL CARD, NO BADGE) is described later in this chapter in the section on Holds.

Communication between Computer and Librarian. The extent of this interface will be determined by library policy and practice. At the very least, it consists of the printouts describing unusual conditions that arise during processing. When the computer program doesn't know what to do and needs

Figure 15.21   Control characters.

Control Character	Symbol	Function
1	H	A hold has been requested on book in this record. Consult holds file and additional holds file.
2	R	This record is a renewal.
3	C 0 1	Multiple call-in notice prepared. Multiple overdue notice prepared. Librarian has requested call-in notice to be prepared.
4	P D R	Record may be purged or overwritten. A record with the same call number exists on Temporary Tape. (On History Tape) this record was discharged by a renewal.

human assistance, it records the troublesome transaction on the Temporary Tape and prints out as much information as it knows for the librarian. The decisions that the librarian makes may institute a call-in on a problem book, a "do-not-renew" for library use, a discharge of a charge erroneously left in the system, or a variety of other actions. To modify circulation records, the librarian has cards prepared which identify the record and the field(s) to be changed. These cards are processed by the Librarian Program, which executes the librarian's wishes.

Holds

When a patron or a library department would like to place a hold on a book not found on the shelf, a Call Card is filled out completely and turned in at a designated library location. At that time, it is possible to determine whether the book is charged out to a library function or is already marked to be held for another patron. This information is available in the Internal Systems Checkout Listing which is prepared at regular intervals and on the Holds Listing which is prepared once a day. Based on information obtained from these references, the hold is then accepted or not.

If accepted, the Call Card then goes to key-punching where an identifying 8 punch is entered in column 5 of the Call Card and the call number is punched. From this point, the Call Card is a Hold-Call Card (identified by the 8 punch in column 5). The Hold-Call Cards are then batch-processed by the Hold Service Program.

The call number in the Hold-Call Card is the key by which the circulation record is extracted from the Circulation File and the holds record, if any, is extracted from the Holds File. Then, depending on the number of holds posted against this call number, the Additional Holds File is accessed as many times as is required. A flow chart of the holds process is shown in Figure 15.22.

Printouts of unsatisfied holds will occur as a result of the charge process, and by using the Librarian Service Program, adjustments can be made to alter holds in the file. On occasion, certain holds will take precedence over all existing holds. Generally this will be the result of library-generated needs. When these holds will cause an extended delay in getting the book to the patron, all patron holds are cancelled and the Hold-Call Cards are sent back to the patron. It is expected that this mode will be used judiciously.

Discharges

When a book is returned to the library, it either has a Book Card or it does not. If it has no Book Card, the charge process presumably will have caused one to be created. Therefore, every returned book should have a Book Card available for the discharge process. In case Book Cards have been lost or are otherwise unavailable, new ones must be prepared for the discharge.

When the record on the disk is identified as corresponding to the discharge transaction, the return date is entered and a P (for purge) is placed into control character 4 of the circulation record. The space where this record was stored is now, in effect, empty and may be overwritten by a charge with the same call number or may be erased from the disk whenever the file is recopied. A copy of the record is stored on the History Tape for use in overdue billing and statistical studies.

Of course, if the circulation record on disk has a D in control character 4, it is possible that the charge to which the discharge corresponds is on the Temporary Tape. It may even be impossible for the computer program to ascertain to which charge this particular discharge belongs. If such is the case, then the discharge transaction is written on the Temporary Tape in the format of a charge transaction preserving all information known at the time of discharge. Each time the Temporary Tape is processed all discharges are reconciled in so far as possible.

There will be times when the librarian, after having examined the error printout from the charge process, will want to discharge a record. If a Call Card is available, in the Call Card File, it will be used with the discharge badge to create the discharge transaction. Otherwise the discharge will occur by entering the return date and the purge character via the Librarian Service Program (described below), which will then write the discharged record out onto the History Tape.

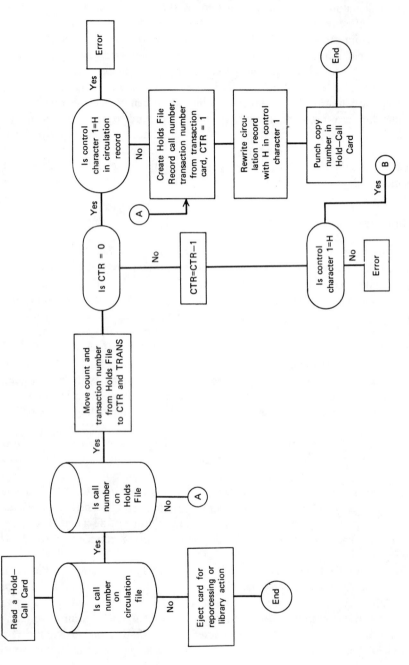

Figure 15.22 Flow chart holds service program process.

518

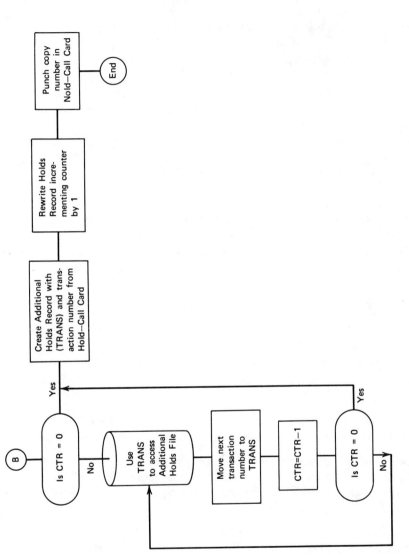

Figure 15.22 *(Continued)*

519

The discharge process also creates work cards for all books that have an H in control character 1. These work cards are sent to the book-sorting area where they are used as source documents for retrieving books before shelving and for routing them to the holding area. In the holding area, the Hold-Call Card File has a card for each book retrieved with routing information. If the hold is for a library function, such as route to reserve book room, route to librarian, and route to bindery, it is sent to its appropriate destination after having been charged out with a Hold-Call Card and the destination badge. If the hold is for a patron, the Hold-Call Card is photostated for the mailing notice and is then placed in the pocket of the book. The book is sent to the holds area to await pick-up.

Occasionally, books on hold are not picked up, and we must have a means of discharging the hold. This is done using the Hold-Call Card and the discharge badge. If there are any following holds in the Additional Holds File, a new work card is prepared and the process is repeated.

There are thus four ways in which a book can be discharged: (1) BOOK CARD, DISCHARGE BADGE, (2) CALL CARD, DISCHARGE BADGE, (3) HOLD-CALL CARD, DISCHARGE BADGE, and (4) by use of the Librarian Service Program. Remember that Call Cards and Hold-Call Cards must be followed by dummy book cards when entering the transactions into the input station because they contain no end-of-transmission code.

The decision table describing the discharge process is shown in Figure 15.23.

Renewals

Renewals are made at one location in the library so that the Holds Listing can be consulted. Once it has been determined that a renewal can be permitted, the following conditions can arise.

Book Card and Badge Are Both Present. The Renewal Card (transaction code = 7) followed by the Book Card and Badge are entered at the input station.

Book Card Is Not Present but Badge Is Present. If the borrower does not have the book card with him, the information for the renewal is filled in on a log sheet (Figure 15.24) and, after key-punching, the renewal is processed by the Renewal Service Program.

Book Card Is Present but Badge Is Not. The Renewal Card is read followed by the Book Card and dummy Badge.

Neither Book Card nor Badge Is Present. This is the situation that arises from telephone renewals. The information for the renewal is filled in on the log sheet (Figure 15.24) and, after key-punching, is processed by the Renewal Service Program.

Figure 15.23 Decision table for discharges.

Call number on transaction card is not on disk	Call number on transaction card is on disk	Short author and title field on transaction card matches short author and title field on disk	Short author and title field on disk is a transaction number	Return date is blank	Control Character 1 = H	Control Character 4 = { P, D, blank }	DISCHARGES
Yes							This is a discharge for which no charge has been recorded. Write discharge on Temporary Tape.
	Yes	Yes	a	Yes b		Blank	Enter return date and place a P in control character 4.
	Yes	Yes	a	Yes b		D	Enter return date and place a P in control character 4.
	Yes	No	Yes	Yes b		Blank	Enter return date and place a P in control character 4.
	Yes	No	No			D	This discharge is just for the entry on disk but probable for charge still on Temporary Tape. Write discharge on Temporary Tape.
	Yes	No	No			Blank	This is a discharge for which no charge has been recorded. Write discharge on Temporary Tape.
	Yes			No		P	This is a discharge for which no charge has been recorded. Write discharge on Temporary Tape.

a If control character 1 = H, create a work card with printed and punched call number. If not, no work card is created.

b If the discharge is made with the (HOLD-CALL CARD, DISCHARGE BADGE) or the (CALL CARD, DISCHARGE BADGE) then the short author and title fields can match on transaction number.

The renewal process causes the old charge to be discharged and creates a new charge. The discharged record is placed on the History Tape with the renewal date used as the return date and an R in control character 4 to indicate that it was discharged by renewal. The new charge is written over the old charge on the disk with a new due date and an R in control character 2 to indicate that this is a renewal charge. If the book renewed was overdue, the Overdue Billing Program

Date _____

Renewal Log Sheet

Call Number						Badge Number If Known	Taken By
Class Letters	Cutter Number	Series	Volume	Part	Copy		

Figure 15.24   Renewal log sheet.

will bill for the overdue based on the discharge record created by the renewal. At the library's discretion this book can be called in for a violation of library practices.

A book that is on renewal is subject to call-in if a hold is placed on it. The Hold Service Program prints out the data necessary for the librarian to initiate the call-in.

Service Programs

Clean-Up Program. The Clean-Up Program reads the entire Circulation File serially. If a record is charged out to a long-term library function (such as graduate reserve or a bindery), it is written on tape to go to Internal Systems Checkout. If a record is active in some way (that is, control character 4 is not a P), it is written on the new circulation file. The disk for the old circulation file is then temporarily saved for back-up and, using a tape-to-disk program, the new circulation file is written onto disk. A schematic of the Clean-Up Process is shown in Figure 15.25.

Internal Systems Checkout Update Program. This program will take the records that have been accumulated on tape by the Clean-Up Program along with unsatisfied discharges from the Temporary Tape, sort them, and then process

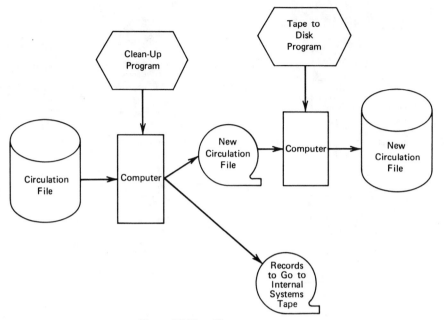

Figure 15.25   Clean-up process.

them against the Internal Systems Checkout Tape. When a discharge is successful, it is written out temporarily on disk so that it may later be removed from the Temporary Tape. A new printout of the Internal Systems Checkout Tape is prepared at the same time. A description of the process is illustrated in Figure 15.26.

Circulation Service Program. The Circulation Service Program processes the Call Cards into which call numbers have been key-punched because the book card was missing in the transaction. It appends the call number to the record that was written on the Temporary Tape and attempts to record the charge on the Circulation File just as the main Circulation Program does, checking for errors in the same manner.

The flow diagram for the Circulation Service Program is shown in Figure 15.27.

Hold Service Program. The Hold Service Program is used to place holds and to record discharges of holds. At the time a hold is placed, the copy number of the book that this hold is recorded against is punched into the call number in the Hold-Call Card. Thus, in all later processing, we know the precise call number of the book against which this hold has been placed. If a book on which a hold is placed is a renewal, a printout allows the librarian to generate a call-in notice. The flow chart of the processing of holds is shown in Figure 15.23.

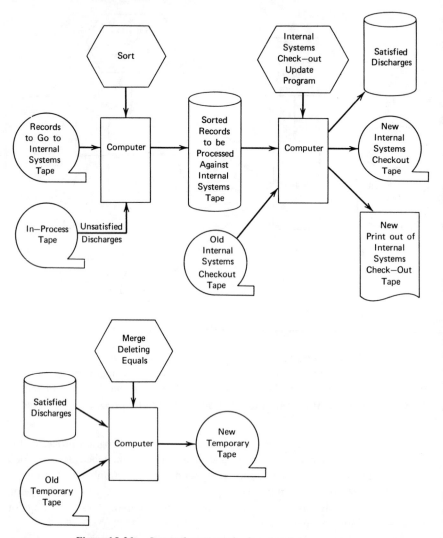

Figure 15.26   Internal systems check-out update process.

Renewal Service Program. The Renewal Service Program is used to recharge books when the Book Card is missing. In this situation, an exact call number is given by the patron (including copy number). The old record is discharged by entering the return date and writing a copy of it on the History Tape with an R in control character 4. The recharge appears as a new charge with a new due date but is distinguished by an R in control character 2. If the book is overdue when it is renewed, the Overdue Billing Program will generate a bill for the overdue

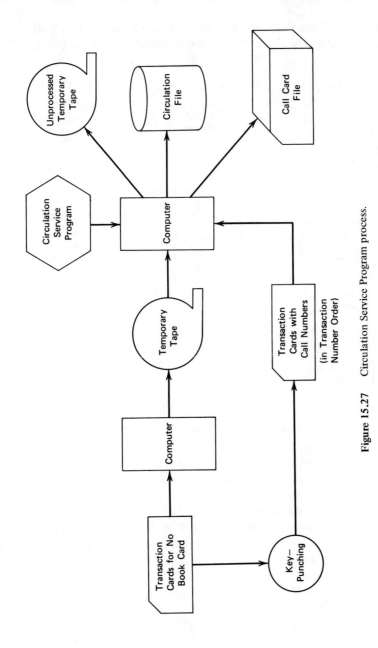

Figure 15.27 Circulation Service Program process.

525

period and the librarian can make the decision as to whether to call the book back in.

A schematic of the files used by the Renewal Service Program is shown in Figure 15.28 and a flow chart of the renewal process is shown in Figure 15.29.

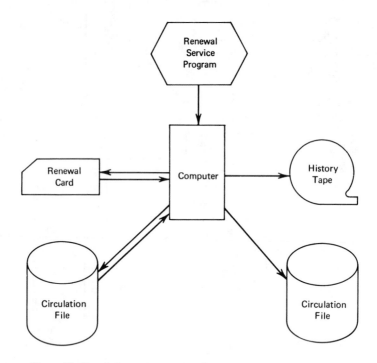

Figure 15.28   Schematic of files used by Renewal Process Program.

Overdues Billing Program. Overdues billing is performed by using the History Tape as the source document. Every discharged record is recorded on the History Tape in order by calendar day of discharge. Thus, by inputting the day on which the billing should start, the Overdues Billing Program processes the History Tape for that day and all succeeding days. If a Borrower File is available, then it would be accessed by badge number to allow the patron name and address to be printed automatically.

In cases where the borrower charged out a book without a Badge, the Call Card is the document used for obtaining the billing name and address. The Overdues Billing Program writes out onto tape not only those returns that were overdue but also all other returns for which a Call Card was part of the transaction. A code of 1 in control character 4 indicates that this is a normal return. If the return was generated by a renewal (that is, control character 4

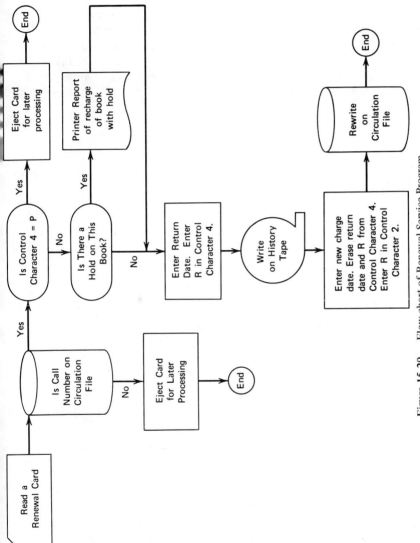

Figure 15.29 Flow chart of Renewal Service Program.

527

contained an R), the generated return is written onto tape only if an overdue charge is to be made. In this case, a code of 3 is entered in control character 4.

A schematic of the files involved in the Overdues Billing Program is shown in Figure 15.30.

Call Card Service Program. The Call Card Service Program is used to extract Call Cards from the Call Card File after the books to which they refer have been returned to the library. These Call Cards may represent books that have been returned overdue, books that have been returned on time, or books that have been renewed overdue. The Overdue Billing Program has recorded these transactions on tape with control character 4 set to 1, 2, or 3, respectively,

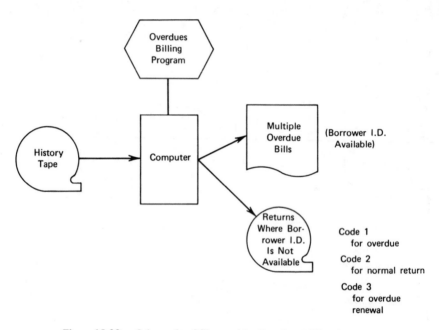

Figure 15.30   Schematic of files used by Overdues Billing Program.

depending on which of the above conditions holds true. The transactions recorded on tape by the Overdue Billing Program may be stacked from several executions of the program, but eventually all of these return transactions will be sorted by transaction number and the results held on temporary disk storage.

The Call Card Service Program then passes the Call Card File against the sorted entries on the disk and the call cards are run into four different hoppers of the multifunction card machine depending on whether control character 4 is a 1, 2, or 3, or no return transaction exists. Any entry on disk for which a Call

Card is not found is written out on the printer so that a later search may be performed.

The Call Cards for overdues go to the overdue billing clerk. The Call Cards for overdue renewals are kept in a separate group, since they will be returned to the Call Card File after overdue billing. The Call Cards for normal returns may now be discarded if the library so wishes.

A schematic of the files processed by the Call Card Service Program is shown in Figure 15.31.

Overdue and Call-In Notice Program. Overdue notices and call-in notices are generated by entirely passing the Circulation File. If a book is determined to be

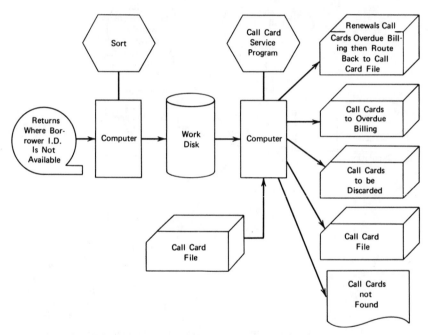

Figure 15.31   Schematic of files used by Call Card Service Program.

overdue and control character 3 is a 1 (the signal to generate a call-in notice), the call-in notice takes precedence over the overdue notice. If an overdue notice or call-in notice has already been sent, control character 3 will be either a C or an O. Second and final notices are sent from the multiple copies of these notices and are not generated again by the computer.

If a transaction has been determined to require a notice, and if the borrower is identified in the transaction, the appropriate notice is prepared on the printer in multiple copies. However, if the borrower identification is not available, the transaction is written out onto a work tape with control character 4 set to 4 for overdues and 5 for call-ins. Notice that a C or O, as appropriate, is recorded into the transaction on the circulation file.

This work tape is then sorted and the Call Card Service Program is used to pass the Call Card File to extract the call cards needed to prepare the notices. Transactions for which call cards are not found are printed out. After the notices have been prepared the Call Cards are returned to the Call Card File.

The schematic showing files processed by the Overdue and Call-In Notice Program is shown in Figures 15.32 and 15.33.

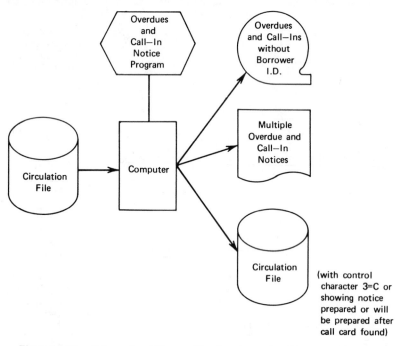

Figure 15.32   Schematic of files used by Overdue and Call-in Notice Program.

Librarian Service Program. The Librarian Service Program has two modes: a query mode and an alter mode. The query mode may be activated either by the console typewriter or batch processing. The alter mode may only be activated in the batch mode. Ideally the query mode should always be resident in the computer, available to be accessed at will. However, with the large number of servicing programs required as the result of limited peripheral equipment, it seems best at present to treat the Librarian Service Program as any other service program which has control of the computer only at specifically allotted times. The description that follows applies to batch processing of queries and "alters."

All batch queries are identified by a Q in column 1. The file to be queried is identified in column 3: C for circulation, H for holds, and A for additional holds. Starting in column 5, the key to be searched for is entered. The Circulation File and the Holds File are keyed by call number and the Additional Holds File is keyed by transaction number. Because of the organization of the files they may only be entered by these keys. At times the complete key will not be known; for example, the copy number may be missing from the call number. The query mode will either print out the record with the exact key requested or it will print out "NOT FOUND" followed by the record with the next highest key. In the case where the copy number is missing from the inquiry,

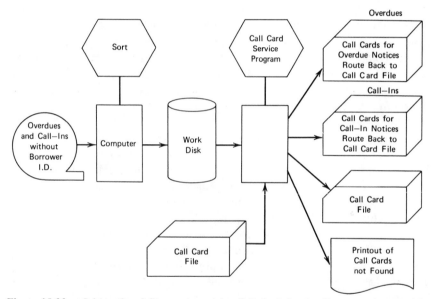

Figure 15.33   Schematic of files processed by Call Card Service Program when used in conjunction with the Overdue and Call-in Notice Program.

the printout following the "NOT FOUND" could have the same call-number with a copy-number entry. This should help to provide some of the information being sought.

The "alter" mode requires an exact key to function. If a match is not made, no alteration will occur. Keys may not be altered. All alters are identified by an A in column 1, the file to be altered is identified in column 3 by a C for Circulation File, and H for Holds File, or an A for Additional Holds File. The key to be searched for is entered starting in column 5. The starting character position in the record to be altered is entered in columns 30-31, the number of characters to be altered in column 33-34 and the characters to be placed in the record start in column 40. Control character 4 of the circulation record may not be set to P for purge unless the History Tape is available in the system for receiving the purged record. A similar situation holds true for renewals. In all cases a printout of the record before alteration and after alteration occurs.

Extending the Off-Line Circulation System

The off-line circulation system, just described, can be given some of the features of an on-line circulation system by connecting the small-scale batch computer to a larger time-shared computer via a high-speed communication line. The larger computer would have remote terminals, which could be used to query the Circulation File. The software that supports the terminals is resident in the larger computer, as would be the programs that would format the information entered to make it ready for transmission to the smaller computer. Thus the smaller computer would need only a minimum program to process interrupts from the larger computer, to receive the data request already formatted, and to extract the record requested from the computer files. The raw data would be transmitted to the larger computer where it would be formatted for output at the requesting terminal.

The reverse process is also possible. If the Borrower File, for example, is created and maintained by the large on-line computer, borrower information can be requested from the larger computer by programs resident in the small computer. Again, all formatting takes place in the larger computer so that the smaller, slower computer is not burdened with additional memory or time requirements.

Other files can be cross-examined in a similar manner as applications present themselves. Always the smaller computer will only transmit requested data to the larger computer for formatting and processing there. This technique greatly expands the computing power of the smaller computer while allowing the library functions to run autonomously on a small, less-costly computer.

ESTIMATION OF PROCESSING TIMES AND COSTS

Parameters for Estimation

Figure 15.34 lists parameters involved in estimation of processing times and costs. Where possible, "representative values" (which ought to be relatively similar from one library to another) and "illustrative values," based on the library of Figure 14.11, have been specified. These will be used in the estimates of processing times and costs. Of the various files described, the magnitudes of the

Figure 15.34   Parameters for estimation (Circulation Control).

			Representative Values	Illustration
1.	*Amounts of Activity (per Month)*			
	V_1	Number of charges and renewals		100,000
	V_2	Number of holds (or other interrogations)		10,000
	V_3	Number of changes to borrower Register		1,500
	V_4	Number of overdues		2,500
2.	*Size of Records with Files*			
	R_1	Borrower record	150	150
	R_2	Charge record	80	80
3.	*Number of Records*			
	N_1	Average number of outstanding charges		50,000
	N_2	Number of borrowers		50,000
4.	*Size of Output (Lines per Form)*			
	O_1	Overdue notices	4	4
	O_2	Request for return	4	4
	O_3	Notice of availability	4	4
	O_4	Borrower listing (alphabetic sequence)	2	2
	O_5	Borrower listing (budget number sequence)	2	2
	O_6	Holds listing		

Transaction File and the Borrower File dominate, by far, all other files. Therefore, estimates are based primarily on the handling of them.

Illustration

For illustrative purposes, the cost of processing the Borrower File is given in Figure 15.35(*a*) to (*e*) and the cost for the processing of the Circulation File is given in Figure 15.36(*a*) to (*e*). Some assumptions have been made, as already described and as listed below. We must emphasize that this is for illustration only; for accurate estimation, data must be examined in the context of the specific library.[16]

[16] For comparison with the estimates of Figures 35*a* and 36*a*, the reader should examine those given in George Fry and Associates, *Study of Circulation Control Systems*. Chicago: American Library Association and Council for Library Resources, 1961.

Sub-System					File				
Circulation					Borrower Registration				

Level of Analysis: Component
Personnel and Equipment

Level of Analysis: Function
Sub-System Schematic

Basic Unit of Work
Borrower

Comp.	Operation	Number	X Size	X Freq. /	Rate =	Time	X Cost	X % =	Total
Cler. Pers.	Keyboarding additions, changes, and payments	4000	50 chars avg.	1	10,000 chars/hr	20	$ 3/hr	100	$ 60
	File Access for changes and additions								
	for name and address for overdue bills	6800	1 access	1	.03 /sec	63	2/hr	100	126
	for payment of overdue bills for interrogation								
	File Update	Keyboarding and file access achieve updating in a manual system							
	Sorting overdue bills	2500	150	1	10 rec/min	4.1	2/hr	100	8
	borrower file	Not required since file maintained in alphabetic order by patron name							
	Output overdue bills	2500	Photo-copy charges	1	600 /hr	4.1	.025 each	100	63
	borrower listing	The file takes the place of borrower listing							
TOTAL						91.2 hours			$257
COST/EFFECTIVENESS =									

Date   Analyst   Page

Study

Figure 15.35a, b   Manual system and punched card system.

Sub-System Circulation				File Borrower Registration							
Level of Analysis: Component Personnel and Equipment											
Level of Analysis: Function Sub-System Schematic											
Basic Unit of Work Borrower											

Comp.	Operation	Number	X	Size	X	Freq.	/	Rate	=	Time	X	Cost	X	%	=	Total
Cler. Pers.	Keyboarding additions,	4000		50 chars avg.		1		6000 chars/hr		33.3		$ 3/hr		100		$100
	charges, and payments															
	Subtotals									33.3						100
Equip. &	Set-up Time			7 batches				.02 hr/batch		.14		30/hr		100		4
Oper. Pers.	Input file maintenance	1500		100 chars avg.		1		600								
	overdue payment	2500		15 chars				chars/sec		.08		30/hr		100		2
	overdue notices	2500		80 chars		1		15,000								
	overdue billing	2500						chars/sec								
	File Access for file maintenance	10,500		2 access		1		5 /sec		1.17		30/hr		100		35
	overdue payment and															
	billing and overdue notices															
	File Update for file maintenance	10,500		1 Stand. Proc.		1		250 /sec		.01		30/hr		100		
	overdue payment and															
	billing and overdue notices															
	Output Borrower File	100,000		150 chars												
	alphabetic badge number					1		600		7.20		30/hr		100		216
	Overdue and call-in notices	2500		80 chars				chars/sec								
	Overdue bills Subtotals	2500		150 chars						8.60						$257
	TOTAL									hours						$357
	COST/EFFECTIVENESS =															

Figure 15.35c   Small-scale batch computer.

Sub-System				File						
Circulation				Borrower Registration						

Level of Analysis: Component
Personnel and Equipment

Level of Analysis: Function
Sub-System Schematic

Basic Unit of Work
Borrower

Comp.	Operation	Number	X Size	X Freq.	/ Rate	= Time	X Cost	X %	= Total
Cler. Pers.	Keyboarding additions, changes, and payments	4000	50 chars avg.	1	6000 chars/hr	33.3	$ 3/hr	100	$100
	Subtotals					33.3			100
Equip. &	Set-up Time		7 batches		.01 hr/batch	.07	225/hr	20	3.2
Oper. Pers.	Input file maintenance	1500	100 chars avg.	1	2000 chars/sec				
	overdue payments	2500	15 chars			.02	225/hr	20	.9
	overdue notices	2500	80 chars	1	50,000 chars/sec				
	overdue billing	2500							
	File Access for file maintenance notices, billing and payments	10,500	1 Stand. Proc.	1	2500 /sec	.12	225/hr	20	
	Output Borrower File alphabetic	100,000	150 chars						
	Borrower File badge number			1	2000 chars/sec	2.16	225/hr	20	97.2
	Overdue and call-in notices	2500	80 chars						
	Overdue bills	2500	150 chars						
	Subtotals					2.37 hours			$106.7
	TOTAL								$206.7
	COST/EFFECTIVENESS =								

Date _____   Analyst _____   Page _____

Study _____

Figure 15.35d   Large-scale batch computer.

536

Sub-System Circulation		File Borrower Registration								

Level of Analysis: Component
Personnel and Equipment

Level of Analysis: Function
Sub-System Schematic

Basic Unit of Work
Borrower

Comp.	Operation	Number	X	Size	X	Freq.	/	Rate	=	Time	X	Cost	X	%	=	Total
Cler. Pers.	Keyboarding additions, changes, and payments	4000		50 chars avg.		1		6000 chars/hr		33.3	$	3/hr		100		$100
	Subtotals									33.3						100
Equip. &	Set-up Time			6 batches				.01 hr/batch		.06		625/hr		4		1.5
Oper Pers.	Input file maintenance	1500		100 chars avg.		1		2000 chars/sec								
	overdue payments	2500		15 chars						.02		625/hr		4		.5
	overdue notices	2500		80 chars		1		100,000 chars/sec								
	overdue billing	2500														
	File Access for file maintenance notices, billing and payments	10,500		2 access		1		100 /sec		.06		625/hr		4		1.5
	File Update for file maintenance notices, billing and payments	10,500		1 Stand. Proc.		1		25,000 /sec				625/hr		4		
	Output Borrower File	100,000		150 chars												
	alphabetic and badge number					1		2000 chars/sec		2.16		625/hr		4		54.0
	Overdue and call-in notices	2500		80 chars												
	Overdue bills	2500		150 chars												
	Subtotals									2.30 hours						$ 57.5
	TOTAL															$157.5
	COST/EFFECTIVENESS =															

Date

Analyst

Page

Study

Figure 15.35e   Large-scale on-line computer.

537

Sub-System					File							
Circulation					Circulation File							

Level of Analysis: **Component**
Personnel and Equipment

Level of Analysis: **Function**
Sub-System Schematic

Basic Unit of Work
Book Register

Comp.	Operation	Number	X	Size	X Freq. /	Rate	=	Time	X Cost	X	% =	Total
Cler. Pers.	Chargeout							1500	$ 2/hr	100		$3000
	Sort. Charges	3300		80	30	10 rec./hr		165	2/hr	100		330
	File Access to place charges in trans- action file	7000		1 access	30	.03 /sec		1944	2/hr	100		3888
	pull discharges											
	interrogate											
	for call-in and overdue notices	50,000		1 access	4	5 /sec		11	2/hr	100		22
	for refiling call-ins and overdue cards after notices sent	625		1 access	4	.03 /sec		23	2/hr	100		46
	Subtotals							3643 hours				7286
Equip.	Storage			10^6 chars								1
	Subtotal											$ 1
	TOTAL											$7287
	COST/EFFECTIVENESS =											

Date _____   Analyst _____   Page _____

Study _____

Figure 15.36a   Manual system.

538

Sub-System				File						
Circulation				Circulation File						

Level of Analysis: Component
Personnel and Equipment

Level of Analysis: Function
Sub-System Schematic

Basic Unit of Work
Book Register

Comp.	Operation	Number X	Size X	Freq. /	Rate =	Time X	Cost X	% =	Total
Cler. Pers.	Chargeout					1500	$ 2/hr	100	$3000
	Keyboarding call number	330	24 chars						
	for charges			30	6000 chars/hr	139	3/hr	100	417
	Keyboarding new book cards	330	60 chars						
	File Access for discharge	3700	1 access	30	.03 /sec	1028	2/hr	100	2056
	interrogation								
	Subtotals					2667			5473
Equip. & Oper. Pers.	Storage								1
	Set-up Time for all input		64 batches		.05 hr/batch	3	6/hr	100	18
	Sorting charges	3300	80 chars	30	100 rec./hr	17	6/hr	100	102
	Merge charges into trans-action file	53,300	80 chars	30	200 chars/sec	178	6/hr	100	1068
	Extraction of overdues from transaction file	50,000	80 chars	4	200 chars/sec	22	6/hr	100	132
	Subtotals					220 hours			$1221
	TOTAL								$6694
	COST/EFFECTIVENESS =								

Date _____   Analyst _____   Page _____

Study _____

Figure 15.36b   Punched-card system.

Sub-System				File							
Circulation				Circulation File							

Level of Analysis: Component
Personnel and Equipment

Level of Analysis: Function
Sub-System Schematic

Basic Unit of Work
Book Register

Comp.	Operation	Number	X	Size	X	Freq.	/	Rate	=	Time	X	Cost	X	%	=	Total
Cler. Pers.	Chargeout									1500		$ 2/hr		100		$3000
	Keyboarding call number for	730		24 chars												
	charges and queries					30		6000 chars/hr		187		3/hr		100		561
	Keyboarding new book cards	330		60 chars												
	Subtotals									1687						3561
Equip. &	Storage			10^6 chars												
Oper. Pers.	Chargeout (terminals)									3000		.30/hr		100		900
	Set-up Time for all batches			60 batches				.02 hr/batch		1.2		30/hr		100		36
	Input for charges and discharges, for queries	7000		80 chars		30		600 chars/sec		8		30/hr		100		240
	File Access for charges and discharges, for queries, for placing holds	7200		2 access		30		5 /sec		46		30/hr		100		1380
	for overdue and call-in notices	50,000		2 access		4										
	File Update for charges and discharges, for placing holds	6800		1 Stand. Proc.		30		250 /sec		.4		30/hr		100		12
	for notices	625		1 Stand. Proc.		4										
	TOTAL															
	COST/EFFECTIVENESS =															

Date _____   Analyst _____   Page _____

Study _____

Figure 15.36c   Small-scale batch computer.

Sub-System			File								
Circulation			Circulation File								

Level of Analysis: Component
Personnel and Equipment

Level of Analysis: Function
Sub-System Schematic

Basic Unit of Work
Book Register

Comp.	Operation	Number	X Size	X Freq.	Rate	= Time	X Cost	X %	= Total
Equip. &	Output Holds Listing	1775	36 chars avg.	30	600 chars/sec				
Oper. Pers.	History Tape (of discharges)	100,000	50 chars	1	15,000 chars/sec	.9	$ 30/hr	100	$ 27
	Tape for notice information	625	80 chars	4	15,000 chars/sec				
	Subtotals					56.5 hours			$2595
	TOTAL								$6156
	COST/EFFECTIVENESS =								

Date   Analyst   Page

Study

Figure 15.36c *(Continued)*

541

Sub-System						File							
Circulation						Circulation							

Level of Analysis: Component
Personnel and Equipment

Level of Analysis: Function
Sub-System Schematic

Basic Unit of Work
Book Register

Comp.	Operation	Number	X	Size	X	Freq.	Rate	=	Time	X	Cost	X	%	=	Total
Cler. Pers.	Chargeout								1500	$	2/hr	100			$3000
	Keyboarding call numbers	730		24 chars											
	for charges and queries					30	6000		187		3/hr	100			561
	New book cards	330		60 chars											
	Subtotals								1687						3561
Equip. &	Storage	50,000		80 chars											2
Oper. Pers.	Chargeout (Terminals)								(3000)		.30/hr	100			900
	Set-up Time for all batches			60 batches			.01 hr/batch		.60		225/hr	20			27
	Input for charges, discharges, and queries	7000		80 chars		30	2000 chars/sec		2.33		225/hr	20			105
	File Access for charges, discharges, for queries, and placing holds	7200		2 access		30	50 /sec		4.62		225/hr	20			208
	for overdue and call-in notices	50,000		2 access		4									
	File Update for charges, discharges and placing holds	6800		1 Stand. Proc.		30	2500 /sec		.02		225/hr	20			1
	for notices	625		1 Stand. Proc.		4									
	TOTAL														
	COST/EFFECTIVENESS =														

Date _____ Analyst _____ Page _____

Study _____

Figure 15.36d   Large-scale batch computer.

Sub-System				File						
Circulation				Circulation File						

Level of Analysis: Component
Personnel and Equipment

Level of Analysis: Function
Sub-System Schematic

Basic Unit of Work
Book Register

Comp.	Operation	Number	X	Size	X	Freq.	/	Rate	=	Time	X	Cost	X	%	=	Total
Equip. &	Output for action	1775		36 chars avg.		30		2000 chars/sec								$
Oper. Pers.	messages and Holds Listing									.27		$225/hr		20		12
	History Tape	100,000		80 chars		1		50,000								
	Tape for overdue notices	625		80 chars		4		chars/sec								
	Subtotals									7.84 hours						$1255
	TOTAL															$4816
	COST/EFFECTIVENESS =															

Date _____   Analyst _____   Page _____

Study _____

Figure 15.36d   *(Continued)*

543

Sub-System					File					
Circulation					Circulation File					

Level of Analysis: Component
Personnel and Equipment

Level of Analysis: Function
Sub-System Schematic

Basic Unit of Work
Book Register

Comp.	Operation	Number	X	Size	X Freq.	/ Rate	= Time	X Cost	X %	= Total
Cler. Pers.	Chargeout						1500	$ 2/hr	100	$3000
	Keyboarding call numbers	730		24 chars						
	for queries				30	6000 chars/hr	187	2/hr	100	561
	new book cards	330		60 chars			1687			3561
	Subtotals									
Equip. &	Storage	50,000		80			.021000 chars/mo		100	80
Oper. Pers.	Chargeout						(3000)	.30/hr	100	900
	Set-up Time for all batches			60 batches		.01 hr/batch	.60	625/hr	4	15
	Input for charges, discharges and queries	7000		80 chars	30	2000 chars/sec	2.33	625/hr	4	58
	File Access for charges, discharges and queries	7200		2 access	30	100 /sec	1.20	625/hr	4	30
	for overdue and call-in notices	50,000		2 access	4					
	File Update for charges. discharges and queries	6800		1 Stand. Proc.	30	25,000 /sec		625/hr	4	
	for notices	625		1 Stand. Proc.	4					
	TOTAL									
	COST/EFFECTIVENESS =									

Figure 15.36e   Large-scale on-line computer.

544

Sub-System Circulation			File Circulation File							
Level of Analysis: Component Personnel and Equipment										
Level of Analysis: Function Sub-System Schematic										
Basic Unit of Work Book Register										
Comp.	Operation	Number	X Size	X Freq.	/ Rate	= Time	X Cost	X %	= Total	
Equip. & Oper. Pers.	Output for action messages and Holds Listing	1775	36 chars avg.	30	2000	.27	625/hr	4	$ 7	
	History Tape	100,000	80 chars	1	100,000 chars/sec					
	Tape for Overdue Notices	625	80 chars	4						
	Subtotals					.27 hours			$1100	
	TOTAL								$4661	
	COST/EFFECTIVENESS =									

Date _____ **Analyst** _____ **Page** _____

Study _____

Figure 15.36e   *(Continued)*

Estimates of Key-Punching Time and Input. The Borrower Registration File is assumed to have been created as an adjunct to other processing (for example, from student records in the university administration); therefore, maintenance of this file must cover only changes and additions from creation of one such file to creation of a replacement, estimated at 3 percent per month or 1500 items. If the library must create the master file itself, additional costs (roughly estimated at 10c per borrower) will be incurred each time it must be done. For example, if the file involves 20,000 student records which must be recreated each semester, keyboarding and input costs will be incurred averaging about $500 per month. Overdue fee payments during the month must also be punched; these are estimated at about 2500, or 2 percent of the transactions. For the Transaction File, 10 percent of the charges are assumed to have been made without Book Cards and therefore require keypunching of the call number into the transaction cards as well as the preparation of new Book Cards.

About 400 queries per day are assumed; these may be requests for information only or may cause the placing of a hold on a book in circulation. On a daily basis, charges and queries are input into the system in a volume that represents 10 to 15 percent of the Transaction Files.

Estimates of Sorting Time. Except in the handling of the Borrower Registration File in the manual and punched-card methods, little sorting is performed. The amount of time used in sorting the files themselves would be far in excess of that used in direct access to the files.

Estimates of File Access. The estimates for file access (both direct and sequential) are computed from the amount and frequency of input to both the transaction file and the borrower file. However, it has been assumed that two borrower files must be maintained, one in badge number order (for processing with the Transaction File) and one in alphabetic order by name (for production of borrower name lists). Updating both files is less time consuming than updating only the first and then sorting it once a month to obtain a listing by name.

Both the transaction and borrower files must be sequentially accessed on a weekly basis in order to prepare overdue and call-in notices. In the manual system, it has been assumed that such sequential access is based on using edge-notched cards. Estimates have been made which imply rates up to 30,000 cards per hour; we have assumed a production rate of 5 per second (18,000 per hour).[17]

Estimates of Output. All discharges cause a record of the transaction to be stored on a History Tape. The History Tape is used on a monthly basis to

[17] Scheele, Martin, *Punched-Card Methods in Research and Documentation.* New York, Interscience, 1961, p. 73.

prepare overdue bills. All notices and bills are estimated at three lines of printed output. On a daily basis, items that are on hold, and therefore may not be renewed, are printed out, at one line per hold. Two Borrower Lists are printed out each month, one in alphabetic sequence and one in badge number sequence, with two lines of printout for each borrower record.

Estimates of Component Costs. It has been assumed that charge-out terminals are manned by student personnel (at a cost of $2 per hour). The number of terminals and the length of time that each must be manned are dependent on many factors. It is assumed that they total 100 man-hours a day.

If the library is responsible for the issuance of borrower badges, then an additional cost of about 25c per badge must be added to cost estimates.

Suggested Readings

The following provide coverage of a variety of circulation control systems:

Becker, Joseph, "Circulation and the Computer," *American Library Association Bulletin*, **58** (5) (December 1964), 1007-1010, in a series on Data Processing Equipment in Libraries.

Fry, George, and associates, *Study of Circulation Control Systems*. Chicago: Library Technology Project, American Library Association and Council for Library Resources, 1961.

This should be a model for anyone concerned with the analysis and evaluation of library clerical systems, in general, and circulation control systems, in particular. It provides detailed cost analyses for a large number of systems—manual, photographic, and mechanized.

Hunt, Donald H., ed., *Charging Systems, Drexel Library Quarterly*, **1** (3), July 1965.

This provides a description of a variety of circulation control systems.

Pizer, Irwin H., et al., "Mechanization of Library Procedures in the Medium-Sized Medical Library: II. Circulation Records," *Bulletin of the Medical Library Association*, **52** (2) (April 1964), also **53** (January 1965), pp 99-101.

This provides an excellent description of an operational, computer-based circulation control system.

Chapter 16

ORDERING SUB-SYSTEM

INTRODUCTION

This chapter discusses the part that the computer can play in the clerical processes involved in the acquisition and ordering of library materials, whether by purchase, gift, or exchange. The term "library materials" includes monographs, serials, and other printed materials as well as nonbook materials such as microforms, phonodiscs, and magnetic tapes.

Acquistion and ordering involves the steps illustrated in Figure 16.1:[1,2] receiving requests for material; verifying bibliographic descriptions; ordering, receiving, and paying; physical preparation of the material; and keeping track of its status from the beginning through cataloging, until it reaches its final destination and all documentation is complete. Input to the financial subsystem of the library's operation, for encumbrance of funds and control of expenditures, and for statistical data in support of library management, must be provided. Although gifts, blanket orders, and exchanges enter the processing later than orders originating from within the library or from individual requestors, these types of orders must also be included in subsequent operations.

This is quite a broad array of requirements, and there are several areas in which the computer can provide significant assistance in handling the work load. For example, for items appearing on a Library of Congress MARC tape, much of

[1] Brutcher, S. J., "The Acquisition of Books," *Library Association Record,* **54** (8) (August 1952), pp 259–262.
[2] Goldhor, Herbert, ed., *Selection and Acquisition Procedures in Medium Size and Large Libraries,* University of Illinois, November, 1962.

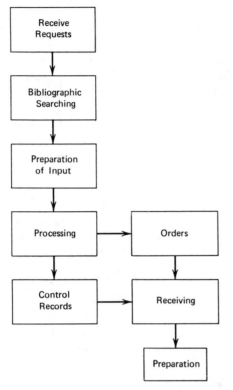

Figure 16.1   Overall schematic: ordering subsystem.

the burden of bibliographic verification (as well as subsequent cataloging) can be assumed by the computer. Information concerning which titles are on order and what their progress is can be readily provided from "in process files" maintained by the computer system.[3,4]

The computer can be particularly valuable in fund accounting. The appropriate fund can be encumbered immediately, as soon as the material is ordered. Reports on the status of all the funds can be produced periodically, showing the encumbered and expended totals for each fund and providing up-to-the-minute information of free balances available on funds. Such a system has been operational since December 1966 at the Brown University Library. It is

[3] Randall, G. E., and Roger P. Bristol, "PIL (Processing Information List), or a Computer-Controlled Processing Record," *Special Libraries,* **55** (2) (February 1964), 82–86.

[4] Schultheiss, Louis A., "Data Processing Aids in Acquisitions Work," *Library Resources and Technical Services,* **9** (1) (Winter 1965), 66–72.

reported to have reduced clerical time by about 20 hours per month and also to have given tighter control of fund accounting.[5]

An automated acquisitions system can produce order forms automatically. As long ago as 1957 the University of Missouri printed their purchase orders by using punched-card equipment.[6] Today there are many other libraries that produce their purchase-order documents by using computer-based systems. Some, such as the University of Michigan, Cornell, and Texas A & M, key-punch the order data and then feed the order information to the computer, which prints the purchase order form.[7] In others, such as Yale, Harvard, and Brown, the order form is typed on a typewriter; a decklet of cards is simultaneously key-punched for subsequent input to the computer, which then updates files.[8]

Claiming is an area where the automated system can also be helpful. The University of Michigan has a system whereby claims notices on overdue orders are printed at monthly intervals.[9] It provides facility for stating, as part of the input information, the period after which any particular order becomes overdue. For example, this period will be longer for orders sent overseas than for orders delivered at home. It also prints a list of exceptional orders for detailed investigation, such as those for which three claims notices have been sent.

Other useful end products can be the automatic production of spine labels and book pocket labels for use in preparation of the book for shelving and of prepunched book cards for use in circulation control, as illustrated by the library system at IBM's Advanced Systems Development Division in Los Gatos, California.[10] Bibliographic data developed during ordering can also be used for input to the production of catalogs (as discussed in Chapter 17). Machine processing also can provide information for library management. For instance, if a user's request lags in preorder searching longer than the maximum period set by management, the machine monitor will inform the supervisor that the particular request must be processed and moved on, and the monitor will continue to notify the supervisor until a purchase order is issued. Similarly, the monitor will put out claim notices to dealers when material has not arrived on time, and

[5] Wedgeworth, Robert, "Brown University Library Fund Accounting System," *Journal of Library Automation,* 1 (1) (March 1965), 51–65.

[6] Parker Ralph H., "Automatic Records System at the University of Missouri Library," *College and Research Libraries,* 23 (3) (May 1962), 231–232, 264–265.

[7] Thomas, Ellen, *Automated Acquisitions System: Draft of Manual of Procedures,* Cornell University Library, January 1968.

[8] Wedgeworth, Robert, *op. cit.*

[9] Dunlap, Connie R., "Automated Acquisitions Procedures at the University of Michigan Library," *Library Resources and Technical Services,* 11 (Spring 1967), 192–202.

[10] Hayes, R. M., *The Concept of an On-Line, Total Library System,* Chicago: Library Technology Project, American Library Association, May 1965.

following a predetermined number of claim notices, the monitor will issue a cancellation of the order.

In addition, the monitor also regularly supplies library managers with information about the amount of material in each subsection of manual processing, the amount of material entering and leaving manual processing, and the amount moving from one subsection to the next. These graphs can be produced weekly to show activity for past weeks plus the most recent week so that management can detect trends in processing activities.

In summary, the functions of the computer in an ordering system can be thought of on three levels: (1) machine processing of specific clerical functions, such as preparation of orders, posting to fund accounts, preparation of reports; (2) machine monitoring of the flow of materials through the system, based primarily on the maintenance of an "in-process file"; and (3) machine assistance to management, in the scheduling of work loads, pinpointing of danger areas, and reporting of performance.

Manual operations will usually still be necessary in preorder and postorder searching, selection of dealers, cataloging of material for which no catalog data is available, and physical preparation. The machine, however, will produce supporting tools: a list of all items being processed, arranged by author; another list arranged by order number; and a fund commitment register.

FILES AND FORMS

Figure 16.2 lists the various files required in an automated ordering system.[11] One file is central- the 'In-Process File.' It is the primary means by which the library controls the progress of an item, from request to order to processing to cataloging.

Figure 16.2
Forms and files in ordering module.

F_9:	In process File
	Request Form
	Input Form
	Change Form
F_{10}:	Order File
	Order Form
	Fiscal Change Cards
F_{11}:	Vendor File
F_{12}:	Fund File
F_{13}:	Invoice File

[11] Sweet, A. P., "Forms in Acquisition Work," *College and Research Libraries,* **14** (October 1953) 398–401, 452.

File Name _In-Process File_		File No. _F9_	
Location *		Storage Medium *	
Access Requirements _Library Administration, Acquisitions, Accounting, Cataloging Depts._			
Sequenced By _Author/Title_			
Content Qualifications _Contains Bibliographic Data As well as Accounting Data Related to Purchase_			
How Current _Daily_			
Retention Characteristics _Records are not cleared until book is shelved and catalog card has been filed_			
Labels _(Subject to Processing System)_			
Remarks			

		CONTENTS				
Sequence No.	Form Name	Volume		Characters Per Record	Characters Per File	
		Avg.	Peak		Avg.	Peak
1	_In-Process Record_	30,000		300	9,000,000	

_1968_   _BR_   _Figure 16.2a_   _1_
Date   Analyst   Source   Page
Representative
Study

* _determined uniquely by each library_

Figure 16.2a   Forms and files in ordering module. In-Process File.

File Name *ORDER FILE*				File No. *F10*	
Location			Storage Medium *MAGNETIC TAPE OR DISK*		
Access Requirements *LIBRARY ADMINISTRATION, PURCHASING,*					
ACQUISITIONS					
Sequenced By *ORDER NUMBER*					
Content Qualifications					
How Current *DAILY*					
Retention Characteristics *UNTIL ORDER CLEARED*					
Labels *(AS REQUIRED BY PROCESSING SYSTEM)*					
Remarks					

		CONTENTS			

Sequence No.	Form Name	Volume Avg.	Peak	Characters Per Record	Characters Per File Avg.	Peak
1	*ORDER FILE*	*30,000*		*84*	*2,520,000*	
	RECORD					

1968   *JBR*   *Figure 16.2b*   *1 of 1*

Date   Analyst   Source   Page

Representative

Study

Figure 16.2b   Order File.

File Name VENDOR FILE		File No. F 11		
Location ✱		Storage Medium ✱		

Access Requirements LIBRARY ADMINISTRATION, ACCOUNTING,
ACQUISITIONS

Sequenced By VENDOR NUMBER

Content Qualifications VENDOR NAME AND ADDRESS FILE,
PURCHASE ORDER AND RECEIVING DATA

How Current DAILY

Retention Characteristics UNTIL USAGE REQUIRES TRANSFER
TO "OCCASSIONAL VENDOR" FILE.

Labels

Remarks

CONTENTS						
Sequence No.	Form Name	Volume		Characters Per Record	Characters Per File	
		Avg.	Peak		Avg.	Peak
1	VENDOR RECORD	100		1000	100,000	

1968	JBC	Figure 16.2c	1
Date	Analyst	Source	Page

Representative
Study

Figure 16.2c   Vendor File.

File Name FUND FILE				File No. F12		
Location *			Storage Medium MAGNETIC TAPE OR DISK			
Access Requirements LIBRARY ADMINISTRATION, ACCOUNTING,						
ACQUISITIONS						
Sequenced By FUND CODE NUMBER						
Content Qualifications						
How Current DAILY						
Retention Characteristics FISCAL YEAR						
Labels (AS REQUIRED BY COMPUTER SYSTEM						
Remarks						

CONTENTS

Sequence No.	Form Name	Volume Avg.	Volume Peak	Characters Per Record	Characters Per File Avg.	Characters Per File Peak
1	FUND ACCOUNT RECORD	300		100	30,000	

1968	RKR	Figure 16.2d	1
Date	Analyst	Source	Page

Representative
Study

Figure 16.2d   Fund File.

File Name INVOICE FILE				File No. F13		
Location *			Storage Medium MAGNETIC TAPE OR DISK			
Access Requirements LIBRARY ADMINISTRATION, ACQUISITIONS, ACCOUNTING						
Sequenced By INVOICE NUMBER WITHIN VENDOR NUMBER						
Content Qualifications						
How Current WEEKLY						
Retention Characteristics RECORDS CLEARED WHEN PAYMENT AUTHORIZED						
Labels (SUBJECT TO PROCESSING SYSTEM)						
Remarks						

		CONTENTS				
Sequence No.	Form Name	Volume		Characters Per Record	Characters Per File	
		Avg.	Peak		Avg.	Peak
1	INVOICE RECORD	250	1000	155	38,750	155,000

1968	JBK	Figure 16.2a	1
Date	Analyst	Source	Page

Representative
Study

* determined uniquely by each library

Figure 16.2e   Invoice File.

In-Process File

This file provides the machine record describing the progress of each order through the system. As shown in Figure 16.3, each record includes a purchase

Form Name _IN-PROCESS RECORD_						Form No. _R8_	
Other Names Used						Layout No.	
						Related Form Nos.	
						No. of Copies	

Media _MAGNETIC TAPE OR DISK_ | How Prepared _KEYBOARDING_

Operations Involved In _CREATED AND MODIFIED BY INFORMATION FROM REQUEST FORMS, CHANGE FORMS._

Remarks _RECORDS STORED IN IN-PROCESS FILE. THE AUTHOR, TITLE FIELDS COULD BE RUN INTO A SINGLE FIELD OR PLACED IN VARIABLE FIELD TERMINATED BY A_ (see next page)

CONTENTS

No.	Data Name	Freq.	Characters Min.	95%	Max.	A/N	Origin
20	ORDER NO				6	A/N	
	AUTHOR				50	A	
	TITLE				100	A	
29	NO OF COPIES				2	N	
	DEST OR DEPT				3	N	
	VOLUME				3	N	
	EDITION				2	N	
	SERIES				1	N	
	PLACE PUBLISHED				4	N	
	YEAR PUBLISHED				4	N	
31	ENC AMT / LIST PRICE				8	N	
	LC CARD NO				12	N	
	PUBLISHER				16	A	
32	VENDOR NO				3	N	
	RUSH ITEM				1	N	

_1968_   _BR_   _Figure 16.3_   _1 of 2_
Date   Analyst   Source   Page

Representative
Study

Figure 16.3   In-process file record.

order number and bibliographic information giving the author's name and title in full as well as the LC card number, if known. It includes indications of the present status of each item—"order received," "waiting to be cataloged," and others such as those shown in Figure 16.4. Other information, which may or may not be included, are the dealer's code number, estimated price, invoice number and price, and requestor's name or identification number. The file is in author/title order.

Since, at the time of conversion, there will be a considerable number of items

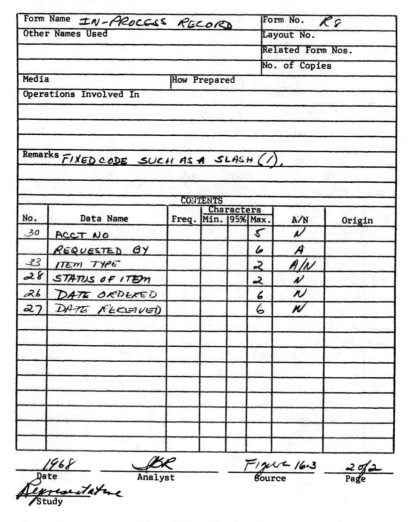

Form Name IN-PROCESS RECORD						Form No. R 8	
Other Names Used						Layout No.	
						Related Form Nos.	
						No. of Copies	
Media			How Prepared				
Operations Involved In							
Remarks FIXED CODE SUCH AS A SLASH (/),							

		CONTENTS					
				Characters			
No.	Data Name	Freq.	Min.	95%	Max.	A/N	Origin
30	ACCT NO				5	N	
	REQUESTED BY				6	A	
33	ITEM TYPE				2	A/N	
28	STATUS OF ITEM				2	N	
26	DATE ORDERED				6	N	
27	DATE RECEIVED				6	N	

1968	BKR	Figure 16.3	2 of 2
Date	Analyst	Source	Page

Representative
Study

Figure 16.3   *(Continued)*

in process in an existing manual acquisitions system, it would seem reasonable initially to enter only new orders to the automated system. Cards must be punched giving the information shown in Figure 16.3, except for those fields, such as invoice number and price, not known at the time. After a period of five or six months, the number of items in the manual system should have decreased to a size where entering them into the automated system can be contemplated.

Status Change Cards giving the change of status of items—"order received," "canceled," and so on—are entered to update the In-Process File. These change

Figure 16.4   Status indicators for In-Process File records.

Edited	Back ordered
Purchase order written	Partial order received
I.D. Card written	Wrong material
Encumbered	Defective material
Order received	Canceled
Invoice received	Waiting to be cataloged
Order paid	Clear from In-Process File
Overdue	Copied to Standing Order File

cards are produced by output from the computer when an order is initiated, and can be prepunched as shown in Figure 16.5. Blanket orders, gifts, and other such items for which there are no prior ordering operations might also be initially entered in this way. Once items have been fully cataloged and shelved, the records are removed from the file (after a suitable length of time to ensure that catalog cards have been filed for these items). Canceled and out-of-print items are listed, transferred to a historical record, and then erased from the file.

The primary output from this file is an In-Process List providing a visual record showing the status of each item. In a batch system, such a list is essential. Although an on-line system seems to eliminate the necessity for such a visual record, it still has importance, as back-up and as a means of satisfying request needs that do not require up-to-date information. Such a list involves a considerable amount of printing and would be printed relatively infrequently. In a batch system, it must therefore be supported by a cumulative supplement. In an on-line system, direct interrogation of the file would be used instead. Other reports produced are notices to requestors, estimates of cataloging work loads, lists of fully cataloged new acquisitions, and lists of canceled and out-of-print items. Provided that the bibliographic information is up-to-date, book labels, circulation cards, and spine labels can also be printed as illustrated in Figure 16.6.

In an on-line system, the In-Process File will be available for direct access in response to any need for information or for addition and change of information, limited only by the capacity of the system to handle the volume of interrogation activity. In this way, the status of items being processed will be up to date and can be known immediately without the delays and inaccuracies inherent in the In-Process List and its Supplement, required in a batch system.

In summary, the In-Process File gives information on those items that are on order, indicating what their status is. The updating and printing of the corresponding printed list may take several hours for a medium-size library and, hence, is a costly operation. Therefore, it should be printed relatively infrequently—perhaps weekly, biweekly, or even monthly—and supplemented by a daily cumulative change list. Where an on-line system is feasible, the printed

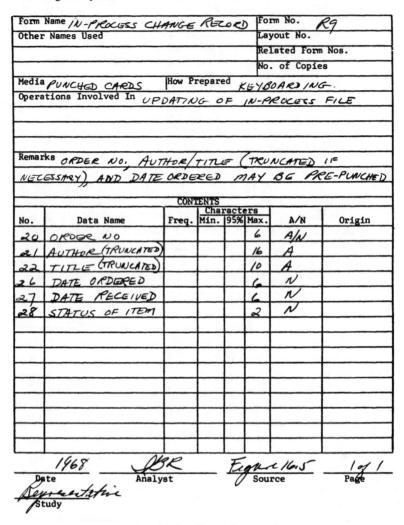

Form Name *IN-PROCESS CHANGE RECORD*					Form No. *R9*	
Other Names Used					Layout No.	
					Related Form Nos.	
					No. of Copies	
Media *PUNCHED CARDS*			How Prepared *KEYBOARDING.*			
Operations Involved In *UPDATING OF IN-PROCESS FILE*						
Remarks *ORDER NO., AUTHOR/TITLE (TRUNCATED) IF NECESSARY), AND DATE ORDERED MAY BE PRE-PUNCHED*						

		CONTENTS				
No.	Data Name	Freq.	Characters Min.	95%	Max.	A/N	Origin
20	*ORDER NO*				*6*	*A/N*	
21	*AUTHOR (TRUNCATED)*				*16*	*A*	
22	*TITLE (TRUNCATED)*				*10*	*A*	
26	*DATE ORDERED*				*6*	*N*	
27	*DATE RECEIVED*				*6*	*N*	
28	*STATUS OF ITEM*				*2*	*N*	

1968   *JBR*   *Figure 16.5*   *1 of 1*
Date   Analyst   Source   Page
Representative
Study

Figure 16.5   Status charge cards.

list provides a back-up record and serves those functions that do not require up-to-the-minute accuracy.

Order File

This file, together with the Vendor, Fund, and Invoice files, provides the information necessary for input to the accounting subsystem. The typical Order File record is considerably shorter than the corresponding In-Process File record as can be seen from Figure 16.7. It contains all the accounting information, but

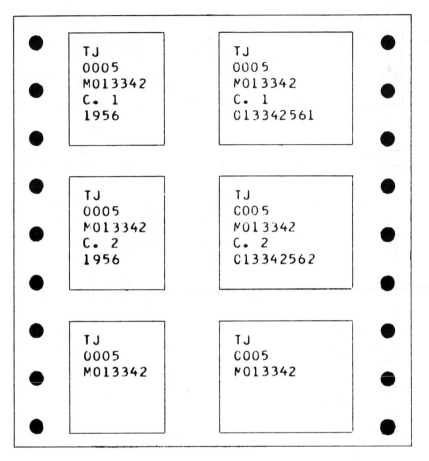

Figure 16.6   Spine and book labels printed by computer.

omits the bulk of the bibliographic information. Truncated forms of the author
and title fields are used.

This file is sequenced by order number, a unique number given to each item
on entry to the system. Normally, orders can be grouped according to the date
ordered and within that according to assigned dealer. At the time of ordering,
the items are sorted by dealer to produce consolidated printed orders.

The creation of the Order File follows the same pattern as the creation of the
In-Process File, and actually the same input can be used to create both files. In a
batch system, new items are entered daily to the Order File. In an on-line
system, they would be entered directly.

Order Change Cards, indicating that a book has been received (Figure 16.8)
or canceled, and Invoice Information Change cards (Figure 16.9) are entered

Form Name ORDER FILE RECORD	Form No. R10
Other Names Used	Layout No.
	Related Form Nos.
	No. of Copies

Media MAGNETIC TAPE OR DISK | How Prepared FROM SAME KEYBOARDED DATA AS IN-PROCESS FILE.

Operations Involved In CREATING ORDERS ALONG WITH VENDOR FILE

Remarks

CONTENTS

No.	Data Name	Freq.	Min.	95%	Max.	A/N	Origin
20	ORDER NUMBER				6	A/N	
26	ORDER DATE				6	N	
21	AUTHOR (TRUNCATED)				16	A	
22	TITLE (TRUNCATED)				10	A	
29	NO. OF COPIES				2	N	
30	ACCOUNT NO.				5	N	
31	ENCUM AMT/LIST PRICE				8	N	
32	VENDOR NO.				3	N	
33	ITEM TYPE				2	A/N	
23	INVOICE NUMBER				6	A/N	
24	INVOICE DATE				6	N	
25	INVOICE AMOUNT				8	N	
27	DATE RECEIVED				6	N	
28	STATUS OF ITEM				2	N	

1968	BR	Figure 16.7	1
Date	Analyst	Source	Page

Representative Study

Figure 16.7   Order file record.

to update the file. As mentioned previously, part of these change cards can be prepunched. Output from the Order File therefore includes order forms, vouchers or authorizations for payment, checks, and claims notices to dealers.

When authorization of payment of an account has been made and (if desired) a check issued, the items on that account can be transferred from the file to an historical file, along with any canceled items.

Form Name *ORDER CHANGE RECORDS*			Form No. *R11*
Other Names Used			Layout No.
			Related Form Nos.
			No. of Copies
Media	How Prepared *KEYBOARDING*		
Operations Involved In			

Remarks *ORDER NO., AUTHOR, TITLE, DATE ORDERED, AND NUMBER OF COPIES MAY BE PREPUNCHED*

CONTENTS

No.	Data Name	Freq.	Min.	95%	Max.	A/N	Origin
20	ORDER NO.				6	A/N	
21	AUTHOR (TRUNCATED)				16	A	
22	TITLE (TRUNCATED)				10	A	
26	DATE ORDERED				6	N	
29	NUMBER OF COPIES				2	N	
28	STATUS (REC'D OR CANCELLED)				2	N	
27	DATE RECEIVED				6	N	

1968	*JBR*	*Figure 16.8*	*1*
Date	Analyst	Source	Page

Representative
Study

Figure 16.8   Order change cards.

In summary, the Order File is the main record for all internal library accounting procedures. Although it duplicates some of the information in the In-Process File, it has deliberately been kept separate because accounting procedures in the library are quite independent of the bibliographical procedures. This therefore allows the timing of the production of accounting information and bibliographic information to be determined independently.

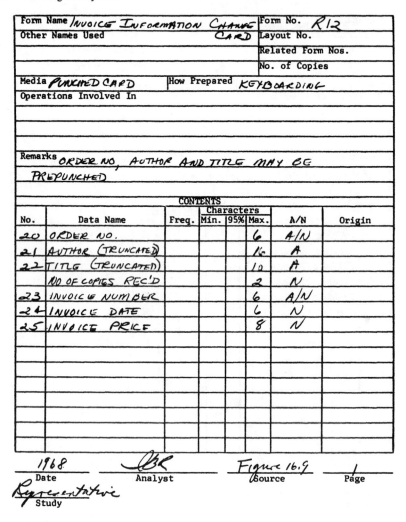

No.	Data Name	Freq.	Min.	95%	Max.	A/N	Origin
20	ORDER NO.				6	A/N	
21	AUTHOR (TRUNCATED)				16	A	
22	TITLE (TRUNCATED)				10	A	
	NO OF COPIES REC'D				2	N	
23	INVOICE NUMBER				6	A/N	
24	INVOICE DATE				6	N	
25	INVOICE PRICE				8	N	

Form Name *INVOICE INFORMATION CHANGE CARD*   Form No. *R12*
Other Names Used
Layout No.
Related Form Nos.
No. of Copies
Media *PUNCHED CARD*   How Prepared *KEYBOARDING*
Operations Involved In
Remarks *ORDER NO, AUTHOR AND TITLE MAY BE PREPUNCHED*

CONTENTS
Characters

Date *1968*   Analyst   Source *Figure 16.9*   Page *1*
Study

Figure 16.9   Invoice change cards.

Vendor File

The Vendor File correlates the vendor code number with the vendor's name and address for the printing of orders and claims notices. It also keeps statistics of the vendor's activities. The format of the records is shown in Figure 16.10. The file is in vendor code number order.

The vendor name and address is punched from the manual file. A code

Form Name VENDOR RECORD					Form No. R13	
Other Names Used					Layout No.	
					Related Form Nos.	
					No. of Copies	
Media MAGNETIC TAPE OR DISK			How Prepared KEYBOARDING *			
Operations Involved In RECORDS STORED IN VENDOR FILE						
Remarks						

CONTENTS

No.	Data Name	Freq.	Min.	95%	Max.	A/N	Origin
				Characters			
32	VENDOR NO				3	N	
	VENDOR NAME		4	30	40	A	
	VENDOR ADDRESS		30	50	60	A/N	
	TERMS (STD CODE)				3	N	
20	ORDER NO EACH ORDER	10			6	A/N	
26	ORDER DATE	10			6	N	
31	ORDER AMT	10			8	N	
23	INVOICE NO	20			6	A/N	
24	INVOICE DATE	20			6	N	
20	PURCHASE ORDER CHGD	20			6	A/N	
25	INVOICE AMT	20			8	N	
	VOUCHER NO	5			6	A/N	
	VOUCHER DATE	5			6	N	
	VOUCHER AMOUNT	5			8	N	
	VARIOUS STATISTICS				100	N	

1968	BK	Figure 16.10	1 of 1
Date	Analyst	Source	Page

Representative
Study

* VENDOR DATA IS KEYBOARDED. PURCHASE ORDER AND INVOICE
DATA ARE POSTED DURING PROCESSING.

Figure 16.10 Vendor file record.

number must be provided for each vendor. Since the number of vendors is reasonably limited, these codes can be assigned to the list in alphabetic order by vendor name, with intervals sufficient to allow for interleaving of new dealers. The file will then be in alphabetical order as well as code number order. New dealers are manually assigned an appropriate number to retain the alphabetic order of the file and this information together with their name and address entered into the system.

The statistical information kept in the dealer record will indicate that some dealers, although in the permanent file, are used only occasionally. The information on these dealers can, if necessary, be transcribed to an "Occasional Dealer file" on magnetic tape and the record erased from the direct access file. They would then be added to the file only when an item is ordered from them. When the item has been processed through the accounting procedures, the dealer record is retranscribed.

Periodically a statistical report is generated giving the number of items handled by each dealer, the average delivery time, and the number of items canceled because of inefficiency on the part of the dealer. This report will also flag those dealers who have handled very few items so that records on these dealers can be transferred to the Occasional Dealers File.

Fund File

This file contains complete information on the status of each fund. The format of the records is shown in Figure 16.11. The file is in fund code number order.

As in the case of the Vendor File this file is created from data in existing manual files. Fund code numbers must be assigned. The number of them is relatively small and therefore, as with the Vendor File, the codes can provide a specified order, alphabetically (by name) or any other desired.

New orders initiate encumbrances on the appropriate fund. Entry of the Invoice Information Change Card causes this amount to be disembursed, by reference to the appropriate item in the In-Process Fiscal File, and causes the total spent to be updated. At the beginning of a new fiscal year, the total allotted to each fund must be entered and the previous years' balance must be adjusted. New funds may be entered as they are established.

Fund reports consist of a full statement giving the present state of all funds and a "danger" list of funds nearing depletion. The first of these two reports will be printed weekly. The "danger" list will be printed daily, or as needed. The decision to place a fund on it is based on rate of expenditure and expiration date.

Invoice File

This file contains invoice information. The format of the records is shown in Figure 16.12. The file is in invoice number order. This file will be created as invoices arrive from the dealers for items ordered under the automated system. When an invoice is received, the invoice number, the corresponding order

Form Name FUND ACCOUNT RECORD	Form No. R14
Other Names Used	Layout No.
	Related Form Nos.
	No. of Copies

Media MAGNETIC TAPE OR DISC	How Prepared KEYBOARDING

Operations Involved In

Remarks

CONTENTS

No.	Data Name	Freq.	Characters Min.	95%	Max.	A/N	Origin
	FUND ACCOUNT NO.				5	N	
	FUND NAME				+5	A/N	
	CARRYOVER FRM						
	PREVIOUS YEAR				8	N	
	FUNDS ALLOCATED						
	THIS YEAR				8	N	
	TOTAL FUNDS AVAILABLE				8	N	
	TOTAL ENCUMBERED				7	N	
	TOTAL PAID				7	N	
	FREE TOTAL				8	N	
	EXPIRATION DATE				6	N	

1968	JBR	Figure 16.11	1
Date	Analyst	Source	Page

Representative
Study

Figure 16.11   Fund file record.

numbers, and the prices of the items on the invoices are added to the Invoice File.

The Invoice Information Change Cards indicate when a book has been received or canceled, and this information is transmitted to the Invoice File. When all the items on an invoice have either been received or canceled, a voucher or an authorization of payment can be issued for the invoice and its record erased from the file. Output from this file is the authorization of payment of invoices report as described above.

Form Name *INVOICE RECORD*					Form No. *R 15*	
Other Names Used					Layout No.	
					Related Form Nos.	
					No. of Copies	
Media *MAGNETIC TAPE OR DISK*			How Prepared *FROM INVOICE CHANGE RECORD*			
Operations Involved In						

Remarks

CONTENTS

No.	Data Name	Freq.	Characters			A/N	Origin
			Min.	95%	Max.		
	VENDOR NUMBER				*3*	*N*	
	INVOICE NUMBER				*6*	*A/N*	
	INVOICE DATE				*6*	*N*	
	ORDER NUMBER	*10*			*6*	*A/N*	
	AMT PER LINE ITEM	*10*			*8*	*N*	
	REC'D / NOT REC'D	*10*			*1*	*N*	

1968   *JBR*   *Figure 16.12*   *1*
___Date___   ___Analyst___   ___Source___   ___Page___
Representative
___Study___

Figure 16.12   Invoice file record.

A SAMPLE COMPUTER SYSTEM

A schematic of a processing system is shown in Figure 16.13. Viewed as a batch-processing system, machine configurations such as the ones shown in Figures 14.2 and 14.3 would be used; for an on-line system, a machine configuration like that in Figure 14.4 would be used. Even in an on-line system, however, much of the processing will still be handled best in batch mode.[12]

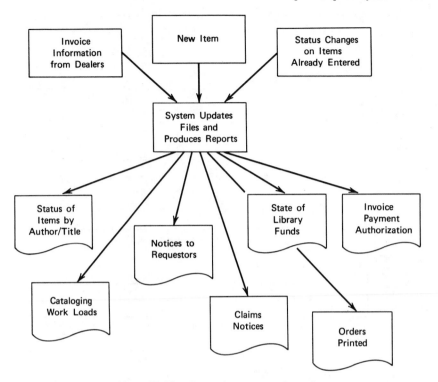

Figure 16.13   Processing system schematic.

In operation, on-line disk packs maintain the active file of information on all items being processed by the library. Within this file are records for each item containing all the various data—bibliographic, processing status, and fiscal—relating to it. Normally, the record is created at the time an order decision is made, and the data entered is then in as complete and accurate a form as possible. If, for example, an LC proofsheet is available, all of the bibliographic data elements (through "series note") are entered, properly tagged. Procedures are included for making corrections, changes, additions, or deletions to any record at any time.

Request and Search

The requestor of an item, either a librarian or library user, fills in a request notice (like that in Figure 16.14) giving as much information as he knows on the

---

[12] Burgess, T., and L. Ames, *LOLA—Library On-Line Acquisitions Subsystem,* Washington State Univeristy, July 1968.

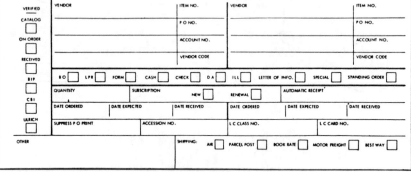

Figure 16.14   Request form.

item.[13] An entry is made in the In-Process File, listing only the barest of identification data. Then, the librarian receives the request slip and searches the library holdings to see if the item is there. She checks the In-Process File, or the corresponding list and its supplement, to see if the item is already on order. If it is, then she still may decide whether more copies are justified.

The librarian selects a suitable fund, checking its status in the Fund File, or the corresponding report supplement, and "danger list" to see that the fund is not depleted. The vendor is then selected, and an estimate of the price is made. Then the librarian types this information onto a process sheet (shown in Figure 16.15) which becomes the permanent, hard-copy record of this order.

In a batch system, a decklet of cards (shown in Figure 16.16) is then produced to enter each new order into the system. In an on-line system the

[13] Hayes, R. M., *op. cit.*

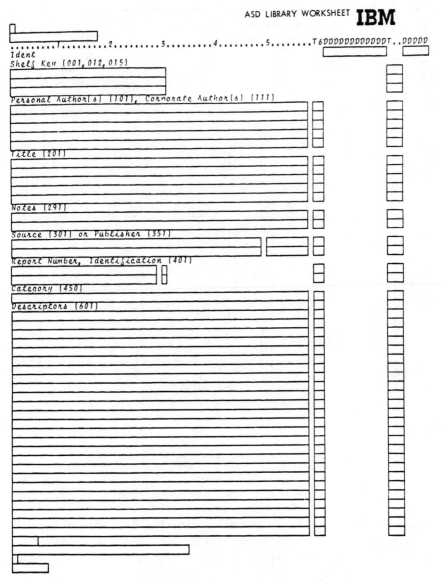

ASD LIBRARY WORKSHEET **IBM**

Figure 16.15   Process sheet.

purchase request information, when completed and verified, is entered directly at a terminal in communication with the computer.

Each field of data is tagged at the time of input, and the computer then checks and edits the data. This includes checking for valid fund code numbers,

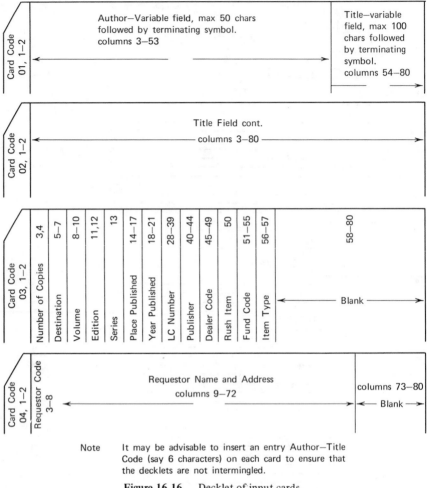

Note   It may be advisable to insert an entry Author–Title
        Code (say 6 characters) on each card to ensure that
        the decklets are not intermingled.

Figure 16.16   Decklet of input cards.

budget information, order type, amounts, and the like. The computer then adds
the resulting records to the In-Process File, and outputs prepunched book
control cards. These cards will subsequently be used to input data when books
are received and as they move from one process to the next.

Order Writing

This program (Figure 16.17) prints orders, updates files, and produces prepunched change cards. It is run daily. As Figure 16.18 shows, all of the files are
accessed by the Order Writing Program, the In-Process Fiscal, Vendor, and Fund
Files—and all are on a disk file unit.

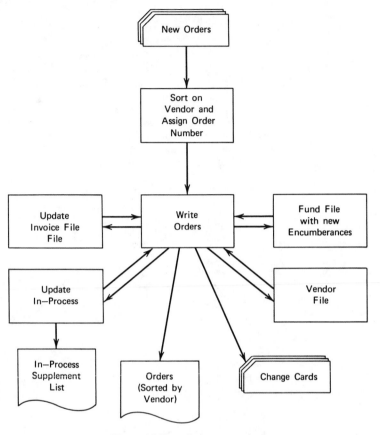

Figure 16.17   Order processing.

   The new orders are sorted by vendor, and an order number is assigned. The Fund File is checked by the computer to ensure that the funds are available and then is encumbered by the stated amount. A "danger list" of funds depleted to within 5 percent (or similar percentage) of total available is printed. The Vendor File is updated with the required Occasional Vendor records, adding the relevant order numbers of items ordered from these vendors. The orders can now be printed. Three different change cards are produced to control subsequent operations. These are prepunched with the order number, short author and title, number of copies, and date ordered, as shown in Figures 16.5, 16.8, and 16.9.[14] Then the new orders are sorted by author/title and merged into the In-Process File. At the same time, the In-Process Supplement Program can be run.

[14] *Ibid.*

Figure 16.18   Contents of Disk File.

Order File	2,520,000 characters
Vendor File	100,000 characters
Fund File	30,000 characters
Invoice File	40,000 characters

The total capacity required is 2,700,000 characters. The file sizes are based on a representative library, with 30,000 orders in process, 2,500 new orders and 2,500 blanket orders per month, 300 different fund records, and 100 vendors.

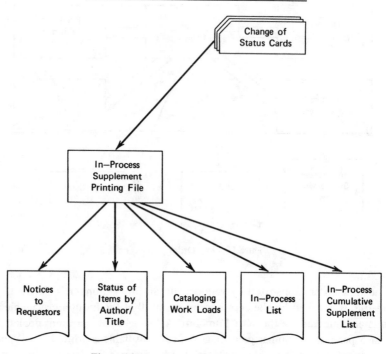

Figure 16.19   In-process printing operation.

In-Process List Printing

From the new orders and other changes to the In-Process File, the weekly "In-Process List" and, in a batch system, a daily cumulative supplement are produced. For the latter, the In-Process File will result in a one line output of relevant data (Figure 16.19).

The input consists of In-Process Status Changes cards (Figure 16.5). These cards were prepunched by the Daily Order Writing Program, and it only remains to enter the appropriate code each time the item changes status—for example, when the book is received or sent for binding or cataloged, and the like.

The status of items in the In-Process File is updated by using the change cards described above. After items have been cataloged they are retained on the In-Process file for perhaps another three or four weeks to ensure that the catalog data has been filed in the library holdings. During this time they carry a special marker to show that the complete record is to be transferred to an archives file (this can take the form of magnetic tape, punched cards, or printed list) and then erased. When items are received for requests not originating in the library, records must be added.

The output includes the In-Process List and its Cumulative Supplement giving full bibliographic information on each item and its present status. Requestor notices, cataloging work loads, newly cataloged items list, and the Archive File are also produced.

Fiscal Processing

This program (Figure 16.20) is run weekly and is the main accounting program. It updates and lists the fund records, prints claims, and produces invoice payment authorization. The In-Process Fiscal, Vendor, Fund, and Invoice Files are all used by this program.

When an item is received, the prepunched Order Fiscal Change Card is pulled from a manual file, and the "book received" code is punched. Similarly, for canceled items, the "book canceled" code is punched. As the invoices arrive the information shown in Figure 16.9 is punched in the prepunched Invoice Information Change Card. An invoice record must also be prepared. This must contain the information shown in Figure 16.12 except for the "Received/Not Received" code. Blanket orders can be included in this program. Prepunched cards do not, of course, exist for blanket orders. Therefore, the change cards have to be punched in entirety.

The Fiscal Change Card provides information to update the status of items in the Order Fiscal File while the Invoice Information Change Card provides the price and invoice number. Encumbrances can now be removed and expenditures made on these items. This program looks for overdue items and prints claims notices; it also produces a list of potential cancellations in cases where several claims notices have already been dispatched. The last major process is the preparation of the Receiving Report, best handled as a batch processing operation, as shown in Figure 16.21.

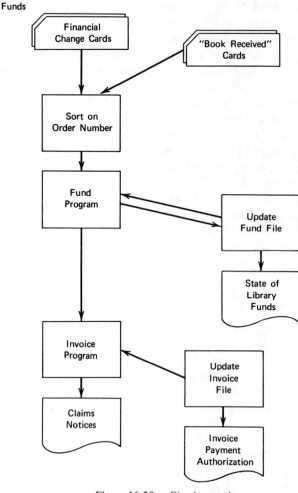

Figure 16.20   Fiscal operations.

ESTIMATION OF PROCESSING TIMES AND COSTS

Figure 16.22 lists the parameters relevant to estimation of processing times and costs, and Figure 16.23 illustrates their use in various contexts.

Estimates of Key-Boarding

The estimates for key-boarding are based primarily on the assumption that full bibliographic data is input for each title at the time or ordering. Of course, if machine-readable cataloging data is already available—from Library of Congress

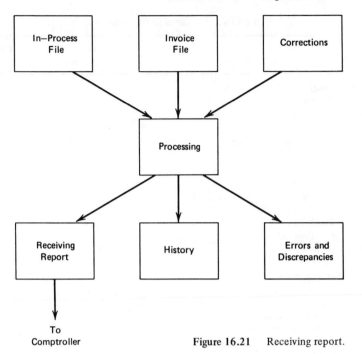

Figure 16.21   Receiving report.

MARC tapes, for example—the amount of key-boarding required will be significantly less. In particular, all that would be needed is the identifier of the stored catalog record, such as the LC Card Number. On the other hand, determining that a machine-readable record was available would involve other costs—in looking at LC proof slips or in key-boarding short author-title data for search of on-line catalog files.

Aside from the initial entry of descriptive cataloging data, other key-boarding may be needed to correct that data and to introduce changes when the book itself arrives. However, these key-boarding estimates are included as part of the cataloging subsystem (discussed in Chapter 17).

Estimates of Input

Data is input at the time of requesting a title and then at the time of ordering, both as a result of key-boarding. Later, data is also input by using reentry cards (the "Change Cards" shown in Figures 16.5, 16.8, and 16.9).

Estimates of File Access

Each change in the status of a request results in a comparable change in the files, and therefore requires access by the computer to stored records. Most of

Figure 16.22   Parameters for estimation.

		Representative Values	Illustration
1.	*Amounts of Activity (per Month)*		
	V_1 Orders		2,500
	V_2 Blanket orders		2,500
	V_3 Invoices		5,000
	V_4 Changes per title order	5	5
2.	*Size of Records*		
	R_8 In-Process record	300	300
	R_9 Change record (also R_{11}, R_{12})	46	46
	R_{10} Order record	86	86
	R_{13} Vendor record	1,000	1,000
	R_{14} Fund record	100	100
	R_{15} Invoice record	155	155
3.	*Number of Records*		
	N_1 Number of vendors	100	100
	N_2 Number of outstanding orders		30,000
	N_3 Number of book funds	300	300
	N_6 Number of outstanding invoices	250	250
4.	*Size of Output (Lines per Form)*		
	O_1 In-Process List (per outstanding order)	4	4
	O_2 Supplement (per change)	1	1
	O_3 Fund List (per fund)	2	2
	O_4 Requester Notices	5	5
	O_5 Orders (per title)	2	2
	O_6 Change Cards (per title)	5	5
	O_7 Labels, etc. (per book)	10	10

these changes are described by the Change Cards. In the estimates of Figure 16.23 it has been assumed that an average of five changes are required involving several file accesses to update the affected files.

In addition, in an on-line ordering system, file access will be required to handle interrogations of the files—particularly of the In-Process File.

Estimates of Processing

As in most library clerical data processing, the amount of actual computing or internal processing is negligible. Each transaction might generate five to ten record update operations, like that shown in Figure 14.7. However, generally, the timing is determined primarily by input-output and file access.

Sub-System				File						
Ordering				Ordering Files						

Level of Analysis: Component
Personnel and Equipment

Level of Analysis: Function
Sub-System Schematic

Basic Unit of Work
Title Order

Comp.	Operation	Number	X	Size	X	Freq.	/	Rate	=	Time	X	Cost	X	%	=	Total
Cler. Pers.	Keyboarding Book data on multiple-copy forms (10 copies)	250		300 chars		20		10,000 chars/hr		150		$ 3/hr		100	$	450
	Orders	25		25 lines= 2500 chars		20		10,000		125		3/hr		100		375
	Labels	5000		100 chars		1		10,000		50		3/hr		100		150
	File Access Before Ordering	250		2 access		20		.03 /sec								
	To In-Process File	250		6 access		20		.03 /sec								
	To Author/Title File in Order Department	250		2 access		20		.03 /sec		509		3/hr		100		1527
	To Order File (order number sequence)	250		1 access		20		.03 /sec								
	File Processing Posting of location of book and proces- sing orders, payments fund records	250		10 Stand. Proc.		20		.01 /sec		1389		3/hr		100		4167
	TOTAL									1389 hours						$6669
	COST/EFFECTIVENESS =															

Date _____   Analyst _____   Page _____

Study _____

Figure 16.23a   Manual system.

Sub-System					File					
Circulation					Circulation File					

Level of Analysis: Component
Personnel and Equipment

Level of Analysis: Function
Sub-System Schematic

Basic Unit of Work
Title Order

Comp.	Operation	Number X	Size X	Freq. /	Rate =	Time X	Cost X	% =	Total
Cler. Pers.	Keyboarding Orders	250	300	20	6000 chars/hr	250	$ 3/hr	100	$ 750
	Changes	250	24	20	6000 chars/hr	20	3/hr	100	60
	Labels	5000	24	1	10,000 chars/hr	12	3/hr	100	36
	Requestor Notices (Addressing)	500 (multi-copy)	200 chars	1	10,000 chars/hr	10	3/hr	100	30
	Purchase Orders (Addressing)		By Addressograph						
	File Access In-Process, Cum., Catalog	250	3	20	.03 /sec	140	3/hr	100	420
	Charge Cards	250	5	20	.03 /sec	232	3/hr	100	696
	Author/Title Code List	250	1	20	.03 /sec	46	3/hr	100	138
	Requestor File	500	2	1	.03 /sec	9	3/hr	100	27
	Vendor File	250	1	20	.03 /sec	46	3/hr	100	138
	Order File	500	1	20	.03 /sec	93	3/hr	100	279
	File Update Author/Title Code List	250	32 chars	20	10 chars/sec	4	3/hr	100	12
	Order File	250	100 chars	20	10 chars/sec	14	3/hr	100	42
	Subtotals					876			$2628
	TOTAL								
	COST/EFFECTIVENESS =								

Date _____ Analyst _____ Page _____

Study _____

Figure 16.23b   Punched-card system.

Sub-System			File						
Ordering			Ordering File						

Level of Analysis: Component
Personnel and Equipment

Level of Analysis: Function
Sub-System Schematic

Basic Unit of Work
Title Order

Comp.	Operation	Number	X Size	X Freq.	Rate	= Time	X Cost	X %=	Total
Equip. &	Set-up Time			125	.05 hr/batch	6.3	$ 6/hr	100	$ 38
Oper. Pers.	Input Orders	250	300	20	200 chars/sec	2.1	6/hr	100	13
	Charges	250	400	20	200 chars/sec	2.8	6/hr	100	17
	Invoices	250	80	20	200 chars/sec	.6	6/hr	100	4
	Sorting Orders (by vendor)	250	300	20	30 rec./min	3.	6/hr	100	18
	Orders and Charges (by Author/ Title Code)	500	190 chars avg	20	60 rec./min	3.	6/hr	100	18
	Merging Cumulative File	3000	190 chars avg	20	200 chars/sec	15.8	6/hr	100	95
	In-Process File	30,000	300 chars avg	4	200 chars/sec	50.0	6/hr	100	300
	File Processing	250	50 Standl. Proc.	20	1 /sec	69.4	6/hr	100	416
	Output Charge Cards	250	5 cards= 400 chars	20	200 chars/sec	2.8	6/hr	100	17
	Orders*	25	2 lines= 2000 chars	20	200 chars/sec	1.4	6/hr	100	8
	Requestor Notices	500	300 chars	1	200 chars/sec	.2	6/hr	100	1
	Subtotals					157.6 hours			$ 945
	TOTAL								$3573
	COST/EFFECTIVENESS =								

Date

Study

Analyst

Page

*Orders are printed in duplicate and a file in order number sequence is maintained.

Figure 16.23b   *(Continued)*

Sub-System				File					
Ordering				Ordering File					

Level of Analysis: Component
Personnel and Equipment

Level of Analysis: Function
Sub-System Schematic

Basic Unit of Work
Title Order

Comp.	Operation	Number	X	Size	X	Freq.	/ Rate	= Time	X Cost	X % =	Total
Cler. Pers.	Keyboarding Orders	250		300		20	6000 chars/hr	250	$ 3/hr	100	$ 750
	Charges	250		24		20	6000 chars/hr	20	3/hr	100	60
	File Access Lists	250		3		20	.03 /sec	140	3/hr	100	420
	Charge Cards	250		5		20	.03 /sec	232	3/hr	100	696
	Subtotals							642			1926
Equip. & Oper. Pers.	Set-Up Time					84 batches	.02 hr/batch	1.7	30/hr	100	51
	Input Orders	250		300		20	600 chars/sec	.7	30/hr	100	21
	Charges	250		400		20	600 chars/sec	.9	30/hr	100	27
	Invoices	250		80		20	600 chars/sec	.2	30/hr	100	6
	File Access	250		50 access		20	5 /sec	13.9	30/hr	100	417
	File Processing	250		50 Stand. Proc.		20	250 /sec	.3	30/hr	100	9
	Output In-Process List.	30,000		4 lines= 400 chars		4	600 chars/sec	22.2	30/hr	100	67
	Cumulative Supplement	3000		1 line = 100 chars		20	600 chars/sec	2.7	30/hr	100	81
	Charge Cards	250		5 cards= 400 chars		20	600 chars/sec	.9	30/hr	100	27
	Orders	25		25 lines= 2500 chars		20	600 chars/sec	.6	30/hr	100	17
	Labels	5000		10 lines= 1000 chars		1	600 chars/sec	2.3	30/hr	100	69
	Requestor Notices	2x500		5 lines= 500 chars		1	600 chars/sec	.2	30/hr	100	6
	Subtotals							46.2 hours			$ 798
	TOTAL										$2724
	COST/EFFECTIVENESS =										

Figure 16.23c   Small-scale batch computer.

Sub-System		File								
Ordering		Ordering File								

Level of Analysis: Component
Personnel and Equipment

Level of Analysis: Function
Sub-System Schematic

Basic Unit of Work
Title Order

Comp.	Operation	Number	X Size	X Freq.	Rate	= Time	X Cost	X %	= Total
Cler. Pers.	Keyboarding Orders	250	300	20	6000 chars/hr	250	$ 3/hr	100	$ 750
	Charges	250	24	20	6000 chars/hr	20	3/hr	100	60
	File Access Lists	250	3	20	.03 /sec	140	3/hr	100	420
	Charge Cards	250	5	20	.03 /sec	232	3/hr	100	696
	Subtotals					642			1926
Equip. &	Set-Up Time			84 batches	.01 hr/batch	.84	225/hr	20	37.8
Oper. Pers.	Input Orders	250	300	20	2000 chars/sec	.21	225/hr	20	9.4
	Charges	250	400	20	2000 chars/sec	.28	225/hr	20	12.6
	Invoices	250	80	20	2000 chars/sec	.06	225/hr	20	2.7
	File Access	250	50 access	20	50 /sec	1.39	225/hr	20	62.6
	File Processing	250	50 Stand. Proc.	20	2500 /sec	.03	225/hr	20	1.4
	Output In-Process List.	30,000	4 lines= 400 chars	4	2000 chars/sec	6.67	225/hr	20	300.2
	Cumulative Supplement	3000	1 line = 100 chars	20	2000 chars/sec	.83	225/hr	20	37.4
	Charge Cards	250	5 cards= 400 chars	20	2000 chars/sec	.28	225/hr	20	12.6
	Orders	25	25 lines= 2500 chars	20	2000 chars/sec	.17	225/hr	20	7.8
	Labels	5000	10 lines= 1000 chars	1	2000 chars/sec	.69	225/hr	20	31.1
	Requestor Notices	2x500	5 lines 500 chars	1	2000 chars/sec	.07	225/hr	20	3.2
	Subtotals					11.52 hours			$ 518.8
	TOTAL								$2445
	COST/EFFECTIVENESS =								

Date   Analyst   Page

Study

Figure 16.23d   Large-scale batch computer.

Sub-System				File					
Ordering				Ordering File					

Level of Analysis: Component
Personnel and Equipment

Level of Analysis: Function
Sub-System Schematic

Basic Unit of Work
Title Order

Comp.	Operation	Number X	Size X	Freq. /	Rate =	Time X	Cost X	% =	Total
Cler. Pers.	Keyboarding Orders	250	300	20	6000 chars/hr	250	$ 3/hr	100	$ 750
	Charges	250	24	20	6000 chars/hr	20	3/hr	100	60
	File Access Lists	250	3	20	.03 /sec	140	3/hr	100	420
	Charge Cards	250	5	20	.03	232	3/hr	100	696
	Subtotals					642			1926
Equip. &	Set-Up Time			84	.01 hr/batch	.84	625/hr	4	21.0
Oper. Pers.	Input Orders	250	300	20	2000 chars/sec	.21	625/hr	4	5.3
	Charges	250	400	20	2000 chars/sec	.28	625/hr	4	7.0
	Invoices	250	80	20	2000 chars/sec	.06	625/hr	4	1.5
	File Access	250	50 access	20	100 /sec	.69	625/hr	4	17.3
	File Processing	250	50 Stand. Proc.	20	25,000 /sec		625/hr	4	
	Output In-Process List.	30,000	4 lines= 400 chars	4	2000 chars/sec	6.67	625/hr	4	166.8
	Cumulative Supplement	3000	1 line = 100 chars	20	2000 chars/sec	.83	625/hr	4	20.8
	Charge Cards	250	5 cards 400 chars	20	2000 chars/sec	.28	625/hr	4	7.0
	Orders	25	25 lines= 2500 chars	20	2000 chars/sec	.17	625/hr	4	4.4
	Labels	5000	10 lines 1000 chars	1	2000 chars/sec	.69	625/hr	4	17.3
	Requestor Notices	2x500	5 lines	1	2000	.07	625/hr	4	1.8
	Subtotals					10.79 hours			$ 270.2
	TOTAL								$2196
	COST/EFFECTIVENESS =								

Date _____   Analyst _____   Page _____

Study _____

Figure 16.23e   Large-scale on-line computer.

Estimates of Output

Three primary forms of output must be considered: the printing of orders; the punching of reentry Change Cards; and the printing of In-Process Lists and Supplements. The largest work load is caused by the In-Process List, because a given title will appear in it each time it is printed, from the time the title is requested until the title is completely processed.

Suggested Readings

For this and subsequent chapters, one reference is crucial:

Tauber, Maurice F., *Technical Services in Libraries,* New York: Columbia University Press, 1954.

More specifically concerned with mechanized systems are the following descriptions of installations in addition to those footnoted in the chapter:

Cox, Carl C., "Mechanized Acquisitions Procedures at the University of Maryland," College and Research Libraries (May 1965), 232–236.
Juhlin, Alton P., "The Use of IBM Equipment in Order Procedures at Southern Illinois Library," *Illinois Libraries,* **44** (9) (November 1962), 587–592.
Minder, Thomas L., and Gerald Lazorick, "Automation of the Pennsylvania State University Acquisitions Department," *IBM Mechanization Symposium,* 1964, pp. 157–165.

Chapter 17

CATALOG AND INDEX PRODUCTION SUB-SYSTEM

INTRODUCTION

Ultimately, the degree to which the computer has any real meaning to the library will depend on how catalogs and indexes are handled. They are the central records of the library and the intellectual heart of its operations. What does the automation of a catalog or an index mean?

In the boldest view, mechanization of catalogs or indexes implies storage of them in on-line, direct access stores, with "man-machine dialogue" as the means of communication with them. This is the view presented by the report, *Automation and the Library of Congress,*[1] by the book, *Libraries of the Future,*[2] by the experiments in Project Intrex,[3] and by much of the research on "information storage and retrieval." However, although very rapid progress is being made—as these reports and projects obviously demonstrate—there are still a large number of basic problems that must be solved before this bold and challenging view becomes a reality for most libraries. In Chapter 20, we shall examine these problems and discuss the present state of the art in their solution.

A more limited view, admittedly more mundane but now well-proven and practical, is the use of computers for the preparation and distribution of catalogs

---

[1] King, Gilbert, *Automation and the Library of Congress.* Washington, D.C.: Library of Congress, 1963.

[2] Licklider, J. C. R., *Libraries of the Future.* Cambridge, Mass.: MIT Press, 1963.

[3] Overhage, Carl F. J., and R. Joyce Harmon, (eds.), *INTREX.* Cambridge, Mass.: MIT Press, 1965.

586

and indexes—in card form, book form, microform, or magnetic tape form. In Chapter 2, we reviewed a large number of projects that have provided the major thrust for mechanization in libraries. The bulk of them were focused on problems in the mechanized production of printed catalogs and indexes such as: the efforts by federal agencies—DDC, NASA, AEC—to produce indexes for their report literature; those by the national libraries—NLM, LC, NAL—to provide machine produced catalogs and indexes in their domains of interest; and those by the large university and public libraries to produce catalogs of their holdings. As a result, there now exists a broad foundation of experience and of machine readable data bases on which virtually any library can reasonably consider comparable use of computers.

In doing this, however, the library must carefully examine a number of vital issues: What are the purposes that such catalogs or indexes are to serve? What content, organization, form, and format should they have to provide the necessary functions? How should the data for them be acquired in machine readable form? How can the library evaluate the relative costs of using computers to produce them? These issues are the concern of this chapter.

FUNCTIONS OF CATALOGS AND INDEXES

A catalog is usually regarded as being a very different thing from an index. Historically, library catalogs have been viewed as dealing with "full bibliographical units" (that is, books rather than parts of books); indexes have been viewed as telling where data relating to specific topics can be found within bibliographical units, whether books or journals. As we will see later, this difference in view led to differences in content and organization, catalogs providing very full and complete data and indexes providing only very brief data.

However, despite these evident historical differences, there are very good reasons for considering all forms of catalogs and indexes together. First, from the standpoint of production of them by data processing equipment, the similarities are far more significant than the differences. Second, the semantic distinction is not really clear. There are, in fact, all kinds of catalogs and indexes—vendor catalogs as well as library catalogs, indexes to single books as well as to subject fields covered by many books. Finally, the apparent need to distinguish between catalogs and indexes merely emphasizes that each can be at any point in a broad spectrum of bibliographic description. By considering the entire spectrum, without regard to semantic distinctions, emphasis can be placed where it belongs: on the real functional differences.

Many different functions, indeed, are served by catalogs and indexes: they provide *bibliographic descriptions* of material, frequently specific collections; they provide means of *intellectual access* to material, an aid to searching for

SHAKESPEARE (WILLIAM) [OTHELLO.]

—— Shakspear's Othello. . . . Aus dem Englischen, von L. Schubart. [In prose.] pp. xii. 156.
Leipzig, 1802. 12°. **11766. b. 16.**

—— Shakspeare's Othello und König Lear übersetzt von J. H. Voss. 2 pt. *Jena*, 1806. 8°. **11762. b. 2.**

—— Othello. Trauerspiel in fünf Aufzügen, von Shakspeare. Für die Darstellung eingerichtet von C. A. West. pp. 132. *Wien*, 1841. 8°. **11766. bbb. 41.**

—— Othello; der Mohr von Venedig. Tragödie nach Shakspeare von O. Marbach. pp. x. 244.
Leipzig, 1864. 12°. **11764. aa. 9.**

Hebrew.

—— איתיאל הכושי מוינציא (Othello, the Moor of Venice. Translated by J. E. S. [i.e. Isaac Eliezer Salkinson.] Edited by P. Smolensky.) pp. xxxv. 298. *Vienna*, 1874. 8°. **1979. a. 49.**

Hindi.

—— उथेलो [Translated by Gadādhara Siṃha.] pp. 60.
काशी 1894. 12°. **14158. a. 8. (2.)**

—— ओथेलो या वेनिसका मूर . . . Shakespeare's Othello in Hindi. Translated by Pandit Gobind Prasad Ghildial. pp. 2, 3. 168. vii. *Moradabad*, १९०२ [1916.] 12°.
14158. a. 28.

—— Othello. ओथेलो [Translated by Lālā Sītā-rama.] pp. 3. 2. 136. इलाहावाः 1926. 12°. **14158. aaa. 7. (5.)**
Part of " Sitaram's Hindi Shakespeare."

Hindustani.

—— جعفر [Translated by Munshī Aḥmad Ḥusain Khān.] pp. 91. لاهور 1895. 8°. **14112. bb. 5. (2.)**
Lithographed.

—— تبيلو [Translated by Gopāl Go'il.] pp. 80. ميرٿ 1911. 8°. **14112. bb. 18.**
Lithographed.

Icelandic.

—— Óthélló; eða, Márinn frá Feneyjum . . . M. Jochumsson hefur íslenzkað. pp. 130. *Reykjavík*, 1882. 8°.
11766. f. 9. (8.)

Italian.

—— Ottello. [A single part of " Opere drammatiche di Shakspeare volgarizzate di una Cittadina Veneta."] 1797. 8°. *See supra* : WORKS.—*Italian.* **840. c. 2.**

—— Otello o il Moro di Venezia. Tragedia . . . recata in versi italiani di M. Leoni, *etc.* pp. xv. 262.
Firenze, 1814. 8°. **642. e. 22. (2.)**

—— Otello o il Moro di Venezia. Tragedia . . . ridotta per la scena italiana da M. Leoni. pp. 78.
Torino, 1823. 8°. **11761. f. 1. (2.)**

—— Otello . . . ridotta per la scena italiana da Michele Leoni. pp. 76. *Napoli*, 1825. 12°. [*L'Ape teatrale.* fasc. 9.] **11716. a. 6/9.**

—— Otello, tragedia . . . recata in Italiano da I. Valletta. [In prose.] pp. 206. *Firenze*, 1830. 8°
11762. bb. 23.

SHAKESPEARE (WILLIAM) [OTHELLO.]

—— Il Moro di Venezia, *etc.* [Translated from the French version of Alfred de Vigny into Italian prose, by G. Barbieri.] pp. 223. *Milano*, 1838. 12°. **11763. de. 3.**
Tom. 3 of the " Teatro completo di A. di Vigny."

—— Otello e la Tempesta di Guglielmo Shakspeare. Arminio e Dorotea di Wolfango Goethe. Traduzioni di A. Maffei. pp. vii. 504. *Firenze*, 1869. 8°.
11765. aaa. 27.
The half-title and the title on the cover read : " Shakspeare e Goethe."

—— Otello, o il Moro di Venezia . . . ridotto per le scene italiane [in prose] da L. E. Tettoni. pp. 67.
Milano, 1874. 8°. **11715. c. 50.**
Fasc. 300 of the " Florilegio Drammatico."

—— Otello, il Moro di Venezia...Traduzione di G. Carcano. pp. 291. *Milano*, 1852. 8°. **11764. i. 13.**

—— Otello...Traduzione di L. E. Tettoni. pp. 70.
Firenze, 1896. 12°. **011765.de.5.(2.)**

—— Otello . . . Traduzione di L. E. Tettoni. pp. 70.
Firenze, 1901. 12°. **11763. de. 6.**

—— Otello...Ballo tragico...di S. Viganò, *etc.* [Founded upon Shakspeare.] [1818.] 8°. *See* VIGANÒ (S.)
11764.aaa.19.(3.)

—— Otello, ovvero l' Africano di Venezia, dramma tragico per musica, *etc.* [Founded upon Shakspeare.]
[1819.] 8°. *See* OTHELLO. **11715. g. 13. (4.)**

—— Otello ; ossia il Moro di Venezia ; dramma tragico in tre atti. [Founded upon Shakespeare.] pp. 48.
Genova, [1828 ?] 12°. **11763. aa. 7. (1.)**

—— Otello. Dramma lirico [founded upon Shakespeare]...
Versi di A. Boito, *etc.* [1887.] 8°. *See* BOITO (A.)
11715. cc. 11. (2.)

Judæo-German.

—— [Otelō. Translated by J. Goldberg.] pp. 150.
[*Minsk*,] 1935. 8°. **11766. i. 87.**

Marathi.

—— Othello . . . Translated . . . by Ráv Sáheb Mahádev Govind Shástri Kolhatkar. pp. iii. 220. iv. *Bombay*, 1867. 12°. **14140. e. 10.**

—— इुंगाररावु नाटक [An adaptation of " Othello." By Govinda Ballāḷa Deval.] pp. ii. 131. मुंबई 1890. 12°.
14140. e. 22.

Panjabi.

—— ਉਥੇਲੋ [Translated by Bhāī Jīvan Singh.] pp. 50.
ਅੰਮ੍ਰਿਤਸਰ 1911. 8°. **14162. gg. 29.**

Polish.

—— Otello...Tłumaczył Sz. Kluczycki. pp. 217.
Lwów, [1889 ?] 16°. **11764. aa. 19.**

Portuguese.

—— Othello ; ou, O Mouro de Veneza. Tragedia...imitação [from Shakespeare] por L. A. Rebello da Silva. 1856. 8°. *See* OTHELLO. **11765. f. 29. (2.)**

—— Othello . . . Tradução do Dr. Domingos Ramos. Terceira edição, *etc.* pp. xvi. 232. *Porto*, 1925. 8°.
11768. de. 5.
Obras de Shakespeare. vol. 3.

Figure 17.1   Catalog of the British Museum.

SHAKESPEARE (William) [Othello.]

Roumanian.

—— Otello . . . Tra/Ꮳсъ слобод [in prose] An лимба Романеаскъ de T. Багдат. *See* Le Tourneur (p.ᴀᴘ) Biografia лзꙋ Вꙑлꙗм Г. Шекспір, *etc.* 1848, 8°.
         11763. d. 4.

—— Othello . . . Trad. in forma originală de M. Dragomirescu. pp. 185. *Bucureşti,* 1923. 8°.   **11767. e. 8.**
The cover bears the date 1924.

—— Tragedia lui Othello . . . Din şi în forma originală de Dragoş Protopopescu. pp. 205. *Bucureşti,* 1943. 8°.
         11768. aaa. 1.
Part of the series "Scriitorii streini."

Russian.

—— Отелло, венеціянскій мавръ : драма въ пяти дѣйствіяхъ [and in prose]. . . Переводъ съ англійскаго Ив. II——ва [i.e. I. I. Panaev]. pp. vi. 213.
Санктпетербург, 1836. 8°.   **11765. cc. 3.**

—— Отелло, трагедія. . . Переводъ П. И. Вейнберга. pp. 160. *С.-Петербург,* 1864. 8°.   **11764. g. 7.**

—— Изданіе четвертое. . . исправленное. pp. 64.
Санктпетербург, 1877. 8°.   **11763. g. 1. (6.)**

—— Отелло, Венеціанскій Мавръ. Трагедія. . . Переводъ П. Кускова. pp. 194. [*Saint Petersburg,* 1870.] 8°.
         11764. g. 8.

—— Отелло . . . Перевод П. И. Вейнберга. Подготовлено к печати проф. В. К. Мюллером. *See* Stanislavsky (K. S.) Режиссерский план " Отелло." 1945. 8°.
         11767. h. 4.

—— Отелло, венецианский мавр, *etc.* (Перевод Б. Пастернака.) pp. 227. *Москва, Ленинград,* 1951. 16°.
         011768. a. 1.

Serbocroatian.

—— Отело. . . . Пр вели: Г. Гершић и А. Хаџић. За српску позорницу удесио: А. Хаџић. pp. 123.
у Новоме Саду, 1886. 8°.   **11764. p. 1.**

—— Отело, Црнац млетачки . . . Превео с енглеског Др. Св. Стефановић. pp. 118. 1908. *See* Novi Sad.
~~Novost.~~—*Моዸница Српска.* Књиге. Број 24.
1901, *etc.* 8°   Ac. **8984/2.**

Spanish.

—— Otelo, el Moro de Venecia, drama trágico en cuatro actos, en verso, escrito con presencia de la obra de W. Shakspeare, por. . .F. L. de Retes. . .Segunda edicion. pp. 98. *Madrid,* 1879. 8°.   **11762. bb. 3.**

—— [Another copy.]   **11762. df. 4. (6.)**

—— Otelo, el Moro de Venecia . . . Version al Castellano de Guillermo Macpherson. pp. x. 124.
Madrid, 1881. 8°.   **11762. bbb. 3. (2.)**

—— [Another edition.] pp. 199. 1886. *See* Biblioteca. Biblioteca Universal. Coleccion de los mejores autores, *etc.* tom. cxii. 1876, *etc.* 16°.   **739. b. 33.**

—— Otelo . . . Versión castellana de Antonio de Vilasalba. pp. 120. *Barcelona,* 1904. 8°.   **11768. de. 13.**
Teatro antiguo y moderno. vol. 13.

—— Otelo, el Moro de Venecia. Tragedia . . . traducida y arreglada par la escena española por F. Navarro y Ledesma y J. de Cubas. pp. 78. *Madrid,* 1905. 8°.
         11764. l. 12.

SHAKESPEARE (William) [Othello.]

—— Otelo . . . Traducción y refundición en verso adaptada a la escena española por Ambrosio Carrión y José M.ᵃ Jordá. pp. 79. *Barcelona,* 1912. 8°. **11768. de. 9.**

—— Otelo, el moro de Venecia. La traducción . . . ha sido hecha por uis Astrana Marín. pp. 247. *Madrid,* 1934. 16°.   **11761. ee. 7/39.**

Swedish.

—— Othello, Mohren i Venedig. Sorgspel. . .Öfversätt och lämpadt för Svenska Skådeplatsen af K. A. Nicander. pp. 144. *Stockholm,* 1826. 8°.   **11764. c. 9.**

—— [Another edition.] 1841. *See* Nicander (c. a.) Samlade Dikter. del. 4. 1839, *etc.* 8°. **1339. m. 5.**

—— Othellos rolę uti Mohren i Venedig af S. Återgifsen på Engelska språket af I. Aldrige. [Translated in Swedish by C. A. Hagberg.] pp. 26.
Stockholm, 1857. 12°.   **11765. aa. 42. (3.)**

Tamil.

—— ஒடெல்லோ நாடகம். ச. ஜடெல்லோ என்ற தெனிசு ஒருவன். (Shakespeare for Tamil Homes. 1. Othello. [A translation, with a life of the poet and notes.] By A. Madhaviah.) [With a portrait.] pp. xii. 192. *Madras,* 1902. 12°.   **14171. i. 1. (1.)**

—— புத்தோடவன் யூ. (An adaptation of Othello by P. S. Duraiswami Aiyangar.) pp. 199. *Madras,* 1910. 12°.
         14171. i. 3. (4.)

—— உதயவன் என்ற கொற்றவன் சிங்களவன். [Translated by A. Mādhav'-aiyā.] pp. 156. *Madras,* 1918. 12°.
         14171. i. 17. (5.)

Turkish.

—— Othello . . . Orhan Burian tarafından tercüme edilmiştir. pp. 166. *Ankara,* 1943. 8°. **14479. c. 13.**
Dünya edebiyatından tercümeler. İngiliz klâsikleri : 3.

TRAVESTIES.

English.

—— Othello-travestie : in three acts. With burlesque notes in the manner of the most celebrated commentators ; and other curious appendices. [By "Ibef."] pp. 88.
J. J. Stockdale : London, 1813. 12°. **1344. f. 19.**

—— Othello-Travestie . . . Second edition. [The author's preface signed : Ibef. With a frontispiece.] pp. 84.
John Kempston ; Dublin, 1813. 12°. **2300. b. 11. (1.)**

French.

—— *See* Arlequin Cruello. Arlequin Cruello, parodie d'Othello, en deux actes, et en prose, mêlée de vaudevilles, *etc.* [With musical notes.] [1795.] 8°.
         11738. b. 37. (3.)

German.

—— Othello. Parodie . . . Von Caprice. [1885?] 8°.
See Caprice, *pseud.*   **11762. b. 21. (3.)**

Italian.

—— Otello, parodia tragica . . . del Cav. A. Codebò.
See Codebo (a.) Un Avventuriere, *etc.* 1858. 8°.
         11715. c. 4.

Figure 17.1   (*Continued*)

sources of data; they can embody a pattern of *intellectual organization* of material, usually as a guide to the structure of the subject matter covered; they provide an aid to *physical access* to material, a "finding tool"; they can *alert* people to the existence and availability of relevant material; and they can provide an *administrative tool* for the library. A given catalog or index may be used to serve one or more of these functions, but its form, its content, and its organization will almost certainly be dictated by the needs of one primary purpose. It is therefore most important to understand these purposes and their differences.

Bibliographic Description

Historically, a library catalog has been a record of the contents of a given collection, with the function of showing exactly what books (or other material) the library has. As such, it must provide as precise and complete a description of each book as is possible. The purpose of much of analytical and historical bibliography is really to assure that the description of a book is precise, complete and, above all, accurate. Much of what superficially might appear to be "niceties" are necessary if this function is to be served. The classic example is undoubtedly the Catalog of the British Museum (illustrated in Figure 17.1).[4] It is a masterpiece of bibliographic description, containing data that, in itself, is frequently the product of profound scholarship.

The primary purpose in the use of a catalog for this function is to determine whether the library has a specific book and in what ways a book it has may differ from another one. For example, in the selection of material to be acquired, the librarian must know whether a potential acquisition duplicates what the library may already have. Or, as another example, a scholar may want to know whether a book the library does have is different from others he knows of. In each case, the catalog provides at least part of the answer.

Since, in this kind of usage, much of the data about the book is already known by the user, catalogs serving this function are organized around the bibliographic description. As a result, the author's name and the title of the book are the means for access to the records in such catalogs, and they are commonly referred to as "author and title catalogs."

Intellectual Access

But books are ultimately of value because of the ideas contained in them. Library catalogs, subject bibliographies, and indexes are also a means of access to

---

[4] Harrison, John, and Peter Laslett (eds.), *The Brasenose Conference on the Automation of Libraries.* London: Mansell, 1966.

published material that may be sources of data on various subjects. This function is quite distinct from that of bibliographic description, and the issue of which is the more essential to the user of the library has repeatedly been debated—from the hearings of a Royal Commission in London, in 1847-1849 (on the catalog designed by Panizzi for the library of the British Museum)[5] to the present discussions of the proper roles of libraries and information centers.[6,7] The facts are that both functions are necessary, but each dictates a different mode of access, a different criterion for organization, and even a different content to the stored record.

Access by subject requires that the catalog record of the book be augmented to include subject content description as well as bibliographic. The difficulties in doing this are, of course, immensely greater, from both an intellectual standpoint and an economic one. Subject authorities must be created and maintained; materials must be read and evaluated for their content; and the catalog or index must be organized by the resulting subject entries. In all of this, the needs of the user must be kept in mind because, unlike the person who knows the book he wants and can describe it, the person who wants information on a subject usually can describe either the subject or the data desired only in the most general terms.

This function is of special importance in the areas where no single library can afford the investment involved. As a result, in contrast to the "subject catalog" maintained by a library for its collection of books, bibliographies and indexes for journals and reports are usually nationally produced. *Biological Abstracts, Chemical Abstracts, Index Medicus, STAR, TAB*—each of these and many others provides libraries with the means of intellectual access to their collections far beyond that which their own resources could provide. Figure 17.2 shows a typical page from one such specialized index.[8]

Intellectual Organization

Each of the above-listed functions implies an organization of the catalog—by main entry or by subject, respectively. But other criteria for organization are possible. In particular, a catalog may embody a conceptual framework of relationships among the books beyond those explicit in the mere description of

---

[5] Great Britain, Commissioners Appointed to Inquire into the Constitution and Government of the British Museum, *Report*, London, HMSO, 1850 ("The Panizzi Report").

[6] Weinberg, Alvin, *Science, Government, and Information*, President's Science Advisory Committee, January 10, 1963.

[7] Carlson, Walter, "Statement by the Director of Technical Information, Department of Defense," in Luther Evans et al., *Federal Departmental Libraries*. Washington, D.C.: The Brookings Institution, November 1963, p. 148.

[8] *Index Medicus*, a monthly publication of the National Library of Medicine, U.S. Department of Health, Education, and Welfare.

Index Medicus

(Mosk) 36:81-5, Mar 60 (Rus)
WEAVER EJ, BALME RH: Carcinoma of the bronchus presenting with gastro-intestinal symptoms. Brit Med J 5185:1543-5, 21 May 60

etiology

DAVIES DF: A review of the evidence on the relationship between smoking and lung cancer. J Chron Dis 11:579-614, June 60
KOTIN P, FALK HL: The role and action of environmental agents in the pathogenesis of lung cancer. II. Cigarette smoke. Cancer 13:250-62, Mar-Apr 60
LONG PH: Smoking and lung cancer. Med Times 88:512-4, Apr 60
PUCCINI C: [The problem of cancer-silicosis] Med Lavoro 51:18-36, Jan 60 (It)
RIGDON RH: The smoking controversy. JAMA 173:293-5, 21 May 60

experimental

ISHIBASHI Y, OKADA K: Experimental studies of inhibitory factors to lung cancer: inhibitory effect of homologous lung tissue-adjuvant on metastatic lung tumors of mice. Jap J Exp Med 29:665-9, Dec 59
MOGILA MT, DOBRYNIN IaV: [On the changes in the morphology of explants of connective tissue in rats under the influence of methylcholanthrene and extract of human lung tumor] Biull Eksp Biol Med 49:95-8, Feb 60 (Rus)
MAZUREK C, DUPLAN JF: [Favorable action of irradiated Ehrlich ascites cells on the development of pulmonary embolic tumors induced by the intravenous injection of normal Ehrlich ascites cells] C R Soc Biol (Par) 153:1954-6, 1959 (Fr)
MORI K, YASUNO A, MATSUMOTO K: Induction of pulmonary tumors in mice with isonicotinic acid hydrazid. Gann 51:83-90, Mar 60

pathology

BATSAKIS JG, JOHNSON HA: Generalized scleroderma involving lungs and liver with pulmonary adenocarcinoma. AMA Arch Path 69:633-8, June 60
INGLIS K: The nature and origin of smooth-muscle-like neoplastic tissue in the lungs and corresponding lymph nodes in a case of so-called "honeycomb lungs." Arch De Vecchi Anat Pat 31:179-209, 1960

radiography

BRIUM BI, KRYMOVA KB, SAVCHENKO ED: [On the x-ray diagnosis of lung cancer] Klin Med (Mosk) 41:61-6, Jan 60 (Rus)

RABINOVICH RM, NIKONOVA ON: [The course of metastatic sarcoma of the lung during gamma-ray and sarcolysin therapy] Vestn Rentgenol Radiol 35:66, Jan-Feb 60 (Rus)
STOLL BA: Nitromin and corticosteroids in the treatment of advanced cancer. Acta Un Int Cancr 16:919-26, 1960
WURNIG P, SCHEUBA G, KARRER K: [Preliminary results of chemotherapeutic prevention of recurrences with mitomen in patients with bronchial carcinoma after surgery] Acta Un Int Cancr 16:935-6, 1960 (Ger)

LUPUS ERYTHEMATOSUS

HOLMAN HR: The L.E. cell phenomenon. Ann Rev Med 11:231-42. 1960
KOURILSKY R: [Disseminated lupus erythematosus] Algerie Med 64:97-143, Feb 60 (Fr)
LENOCH F, VOJTISEK O, MARSIKOVA L: [Studies on the L.E. phenomenon in active progressive polyarthritis] Lijecn Vjesn 82:187-93, Mar 60 (Ser)
RADOSEVIC Z: [L.E. phenomenon] Lijecn Vjesn 82:221-2, Mar 60 (Ser)

case reports

LOSADA M, JIMENEZ E, SILVA L: [Association of acute disseminated lupus erythematosus and periarteritis nodosa] Rev Med Chile 88:129-32, Feb 60 (Sp)
PAILHERET P, ROUSSEL, SIMON: [Acute lupus erythematosus with fatal course] Bull Soc Franc Derm Syph 5:769-71, Nov-Dec 59 (Fr)
VIAL S, SILVA L: [Lupus erythematosus and periarteritis nodosa] Rev Med Chile 88:125-8, Feb 60 (Sp)

complications

CASANEGRA A, MANCINI D, FRANCHELLA JL, BUZZI A: [Cardiac changes in generalized lupus erythematosus] Dia Med 32:594-8, 14 Apr 60 (Sp)
HOLMAN H, TOMASI T: "Lupoid" hepatitis. Med Clin N Amer 44:633-8, May 60

diagnosis

KAYHOE DE, NASOU JP, BOZICEVICH J: Clinical evaluation of the DNA bentonite flocculation test for systemic lupus erythematosus. New Engl J Med 263:5-10, 7 July 60
RAPPAPORT F, EICHHORN F: Sulfosalicylic acid as a substitute for paratoluene sulfonic acid. A. In the estimation of cholesterol. B. In the diagnostic test for systemic lupus erythematosus. Clin Chim Acta 5:161-3, May 60
SOGAARD-ANDERSEN J: [Analysis of precipitation tests in disseminated lupus erythematosus] Ugeskr Laeg 122:517-8, 14 Apr 60 (Dan)

Figure 17.2   Index Medicus.

them. The purpose in doing so is to bring together, in the catalog, entries that are likely to be related and that are potentially of interest when considered together. The most evident example is the so-called "classed catalog" in which entries in the catalog are organized according to an overall classification schedule covering the subject matter of the collection.

However, another (possibly even more important) basis for organization arises from the growing realization that the book, as a material record, is not coterminous with either the work, as the intellectual product embodied in it, or with the information content.[9] Thus, a given book is actually only one representation of the work, which may be found in a given library or system of

GUISS LW, KUENSTLER P: A retrospective view of survey photofluorograms of persons with lung cancer. Cancer 13:91-5, Jan-Feb 60

GUISS LW: A 5-year follow-up of roentgenographically detected lung cancer suspects. Cancer 13:82-90, Jan-Feb 60

LI TY, LI SN: [Soviet medicine: a review of the Soviet literature on roentgen diagnosis of carcinoma of the lung] Zhong Fang Z 8:62-4, Feb 60 (Ch)

MOREL L, DAMBRIN P, LAYSSOL M, ESCHAPASSE H, MATHE J, GIRARD M, DIRAT J: [Massive intrathoracic "tumor" (diagnostic problems)] J Radiol Electrol 41:165-6, Mar-Apr 60 (Fr)

radiotherapy

HILTON G: The present position relating to cancer of the lung. Results with radiotherapy alone. Thorax 15:17-8, Mar 60

statistics

PETERSEN GF: Cancer of the lung in Iceland. A study on cases diagnosed during the period 1931-1957. Acta Radiol (Stockh) Suppl 188:20-9, 1959

surgery

BROCK R: The present position relating to cancer of the lung. Radical pneumonectomy. Thorax 15:7-8, Mar 60

CAHAN WG: Radical lobectomy. J Thor Cardiov Surg 39:555-72, May 60

FEINMANN I: The present position relating to cancer of the lung. Long-term functional results after pneumonectomy. Thorax 15:19-21, Mar 60

JATENE AD, ZERBINI E J: [Lobectomy in the surgical treatment of bronchial carcinoma] Rev Ass Med Bras 5:434-40, Dec 59 (Por)

MASON GA: The present position relating to cancer of the lung. Introduction. Thorax 15:1-2, Mar 60

NOHL HC: The present position relating to cancer of the lung. A three-year follow-up of classified cases of bronchogenic carcinoma after resection. Thorax 15:11-6, Mar 60

PAULSON DL, SHAW RR: Results of bronchoplastic procedures for bronchogenic carcinoma. Ann Surg 151:729-40, May 60

TAYLOR AB: The present position relating to cancer of the lung. Results of surgical resection. Thorax 15:3-4, Mar 60

THOMPSON VC: The present position relating to cancer of the lung. Results of resection. Thorax 15:5-6, Mar 60

THOMAS CP: The present position relating to cancer of the lung. Lobectomy with sleeve resection. Thorax 15:9-11, Mar 60

therapy

experimental

BENCZE G, LAKATOS L, LUDANYI M: Two types of lupus erythematosus cell factor, shown by induced L.E. cell phenomenon in dogs. Brit Med J 5187:1707-9, 4 June 60

BENCZE G, LUDANYI M: Production of lupus erythematosus (L.E.) cells in the dog by the transfusion of systemic lupus erythematosus plasma. Ann Rheum Dis 19:48-51, Mar 60

immunology

BOZICEVICH J, NASOU JP, KAYHOE DE: Desoxyribonucleic acid (DNA)-bentonite flocculation test for lupus erythematosus. Proc Soc Exp Biol Med 103:636-40, Mar 60

in infancy & childhood

BARTA K, SOWINA D: [A case of Libman-Sacks syndrome in a 13-year-old girl] Pediat Pol 34:1554-7, Dec 59 (Pol)

pathology

VITERBO F, ALBANO O, CAVALLO A: [Radiological aspects of the small intestine in collagen diseases. b) The small intestine in periarteritis nodosa and in disseminated lupus erythematosus] Arch Ital Mal Appar Dig 26:642-54, 1960 (It)

therapy

GRUPPER C: [Pyridoxine in the treatment of lupus erythematosus] Bull Soc Franc Derm Syph 5:672-3, Nov-Dec 59 (Fr)

LAUGIER P, LENYS R, BULTE C: [Chronic recurring pigmentogenic figured erythema in a patient with chronic lupus erythematosus, treated by nivaquine] Bull Soc Franc Derm Syph 5:813-5, Nov-Dec 59 (Fr)

Lutembacher's Syndrome see HEART DEFECTS, CONGENITAL

Lye see CAUSTICS

LYMPH

JOHNSTON ID, CODE CF: Factors affecting gastric secretion in thoracic-duct lymph of dogs. Amer J Physiol 198:721-4, Apr 60

LYMPH NODES

DIFFERENTIAL diagnosis; the significance of the cervical node. Cancer Bull [Tex] 12:34-5, Mar-Apr 60

VOS O, GOODMAN JW, CONGDON CC: Donor-type lymphatic tissue cells in lethally irradiated mice treated with homologous fetal liver. Plast Reconstr Surg 25:408-11, Apr 60

S-2269

Figure 17.2   *(continued)*

libraries in different media (books, manuscripts, films, and magnetic tapes, for instance), different forms (editions, translation, and versions), and even under different titles or different authors. This view implies the need to identify not only the book itself but the work and the author represented by it—bibliographic dimensions only sporadically provided by the rules of descriptive cataloging.

This need is partly reflected in the new Anglo-American Cataloging Rules and has great implications for the organization of the library catalog. When the

---

[9] Lubetzky, Seymour, *Principles of Cataloging*. Los Angeles: Institute of Library Research, University of California, July 1969.

To find citations to a specific paper:

1. locate cited author
2. locate reference year
3. locate reference publication, volume and page
4. note that source citations follow reference lines

The data shown here simulate the type of material which appears in the Science Citation Index - 1964.
The data in these entries are fictitious.

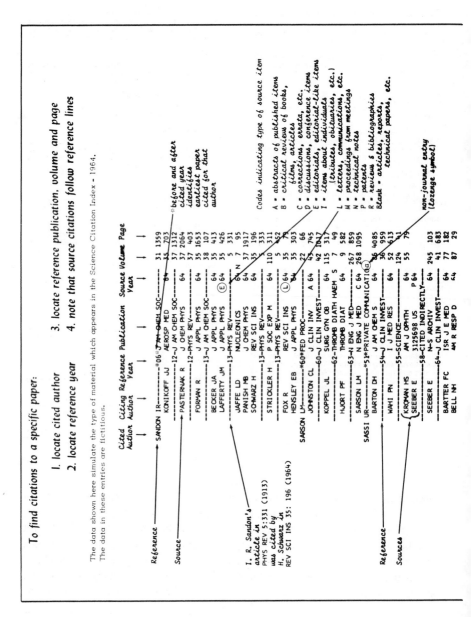

To locate sources which cite a particular paper, first look for the cited or reference author or patent number, located on the left.

For each cited paper by that author there is a dashed line which continues to the column reserved for the year of reference publication, followed by journal, volume and page. To the right of each cited patent is the year and country. When a given reference has been cited more than once, the sources are arranged alphabetically by author. Each type of source item is further identified by a code. Note: only the first author is listed in the *Science Citation Index* proper. See the *Source Index* for all citing co-authors and full article titles.

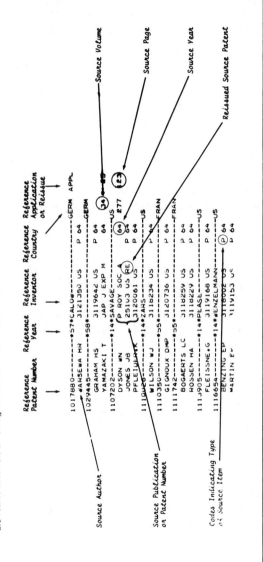

Figure 17.3 Page from Science Citation Index.

"main entry" is designed to represent a specific publication as a representation of a particular work by a particular author, the result is that, other, added entries will be similarly related. It also has implications for other kinds of indexes. For example, the *Science Citation Index*,[10] (Figure 17.3), in effect, uses authors and works as symbolic "subject headings" to designate the subject fields and ideas represented in them and to bring together other, subsequent, sources in which the authors and works are cited.

Physical Access

Since the users of the library do not always know where a desired book may be found, catalogs and indexes also serve a directory function; they are a "finding tool." The call number assigned to each book and recorded in the catalog provides the means of locating a book within the individual library; comparable location codes in a union catalog, illustrated in Figure 17.4 (a directory of the holdings of a group of libraries), serve to locate material among them.[11] In this function, a catalog facilitates interlibrary loan.

Alerting

Recently, the value of catalogs and especially of indexes as alerting tools has been recognized. This function is perhaps best represented by the machine-generated Key-Word-In-Context (KWIC) index, which provides current listings of reports.[12] KWIC has been exploited by technical-scientific library users and has been well received by science-engineering personnel. It can be prepared as corollary to production of other forms of catalog, without added input. As the program is generally written, nonselective permuting of key words would result in entries for perhaps seven to ten significant words in the title of each report. Permutation to this extent makes a voluminous index and is usually not suitable for large collections, but it does provide many points of access for alerting. An example is shown in Figure 17.5.[13]

Administration

Finally, although this function is not generally emphasized, a catalog can provide a tool to aid administrative control of the library. If it included consolidated statistical data on the frequency of use of material, the catalog

---

[10] *Science Citation Index*, Institute for Scientific Information, Philadelphia, Pa.

[11] *National Union Catalog*

[12] Luhn, Hans P., *Keyword-in-context Index for Technical Literature*, (ASDD Report RC-127). Yorktown Heights, NY: IBM, August 31, 1959.

[13] *Permuted Index to Computing Reviews*, Association for Computing Machinery.

could aid in decisions on allocation of material to reserve collections, to branch libraries, or to compact storage. The frequency of assignment of subject terms and their frequency of co-occurrance can be used to analyze the structure of the fields covered.

CONTENT OF CATALOGS AND INDEXES

The different uses of catalogs and indexes have a profound effect on the content of entries in them. These range from brief "author-title" entries, to full bibliographic records, to entries with expanded descriptions.

Full Bibliographic Entries

The traditional library catalog provides full bibliographic and subject description for all types of entries—main entries, title added entries, author added entries of all types, analytic entries, subject added entries, and series added entries. This is chiefly a result of the ready availability of standard sets of catalog cards from the Library of Congress and the H. W. Wilson Company, as illustrated in Figure 17.6. There are three specific circumstances in which a full description of the item in question is useful or even necessary:

1.   When the user wishes to compare the various editions of a given work that the library has.

2.   When the user wishes to know whether the library has a certain edition of a work which he is able to specify in some detail.

3.   When the user wishes to choose from among the works on a given subject the one that will best suit his purposes, insofar as this can be determined on the basis of the information listed in the catalog entry.

Brief Entries

Because of this, it might be considered to be desirable that a catalog contain a "full" description of each item under each entry; in fact, such "full" entries are often a hindrance rather than a help to the casual or hurried user of the catalog, since the catalog size and search time are increased without providing additional desired information. Many times, therefore, it is sufficient and even desirable to provide very brief entries—sometimes merely an author and title.

If this form of entry is used, main entries or a "register" entry may still contain the full information now contained on the catalog card. Other entries will then contain at least three elements: (a) the "access point" (title, series, or joint author, for instance) under which the entry is filed; (b) a reference to the main entry or register entry in exactly the form in which it is entered in the catalog; and (c) the call numbers and location codes.

Becker, Jacob.
סודו של "מורה נבוכים"; הערכה חדשה על תפיסת עולמו של הרמב"ם. מאת יעקב בקר. תל־אביב, י. שמעוני, תשט"ז ‏[1955]
130 p. 22 cm.
"שתי הרצאות בחברה הפילוסופית בירושלים."
1. Moses ben Maimon, 1135–1204. Dalālat al-ḥā'irīn. I. Title.
Title transliterated: Sodo shel Moreh nevukhim.
BM545.D35B4 HE 67–229

Becker, Jacob, *ed.*
התודעה היהודית; אוסף מאמרים מתקופת בית שני עד ימינו. לקט וערך: יעקב בקר. תל־אביב, י. צ'צ'יק ‏[1966]
2 v. in 1 (399 p.) 24 cm.
"לוח המקורות": p. 397–399.
1. Judaism—Collections. I. Title.
Title transliterated: ha-Toda'ah ha-yehudit.
BM42.B36 HE 66–1685
PL 480: Is–3087

Becker, Jacques.
Jacques Becker. Présentation par Jean Queval. Textes et propos de Jacques Becker. Extraits de découpages de films. Panorama critique. Témoignages. Filmographie. Bibliographie. Documents iconographiques. [Paris] Seghers [1962]
223 p. illus. (Cinéma d'aujourd'hui. 3)
Bibliography: p. 219–[221]
1. Becker, Jacques, 1906– I. Quéval, Jean, joint author. (Series)
NNC CLU WU CU MH NUC64–1551
CoU MiU DSI C NB CLSU

Becker, Jakob.
Bessarabien und sein Deutschtum. Bietigheim/Württ., Krug (1966)
227 p. 2 maps. 21 cm. DM 17.80
(GDB 66–A37–224)
Bibliography: p. 219–226.
1. Bessarabin—Hist. 2. Germans in Bessarabia. I. Title.
DK511.B4B4 947.7 67–75884

Becker, James L
Autotext; programed instruction in basic symbolic logic. 2d ed. Camden, N. J., Radio Corporation of America, 1963.
v, 22 p.
1. Logic, Symbolic and mathematical. 2. Programmed text. I. Radio Corporation of America. II. Title. III. Title: Basic symbolic logic.
NYhI CLSU NUC64–3924

Becker, Joan, tr.
They lived to see it; a collection of short stories, tr. from the German, by Alexander Abusch [and others] Berlin, Seven Seas publishers [1963]
167 p. 19 cm. (Seven seas books)
1. Short stories, German—Translations into English. 2. Short stories—Translations from German. I. Abusch, Alexander. II. Title.
LNHT NUC65–86591

Becker, Johann Philipp, 1809–1886
see Engelberg, Ernst. Johann Philipp Becker in der I. Internationale ... Berlin, Dietz, 1964.

Becker, John Angus, 1936–
Associated particle spectrometer study of CR^{51}. [Tallahassee] 1962.
v, 60 l. illus.
Thesis (Ph. D.)—Florida State University.
Bibliography: leaves 58–60.
1. Spectrum analysis. 2. Chromium. I. Title.
FTaSU NUC63–24321

Becker, John H.
Sociale und politische zustände in den Vereinigten Staaten Nordamerika's. Von John H. Becker. Mit einleitung von Friedrich von Hellwald. 2. ausg. von Becker, Die hundertjährige republik. Augsburg, Lampart & comp., 1879.
2 p. l., iv, 384 p. 22½ cm.
L. C. copy replaced by microfilm.
Microfilm 7969 E
1. U. S.—Pol. & govt. 2. U. S.—Soc. life and cust. I. Hellwald, Friedrich Anton Heller von, 1842–1892.
[E168.B39 1879] G–478 rev

Becker, John Leonard, 1901–
Near-tragedy at the waterfall. Illustrated by Virginia Campbell. [New York] Pantheon Books [1964]
40 p. col. illus. 25 cm.
I. Title.
PZ10.3.B388Ne 64–13079

Becker, Josef, ed.
see Köhler, Heinrich. Lebenserinnerungen des Politikers und Staatsmannes... Stuttgart, W. Kohlhammer, 1964.

Becker, Joseph M
Programs to aid the unemployed in the 1960's, by Joseph M. Becker, William Haber and Sar A. Levitan. Kalamazoo, Mich., W. E. Upjohn Institute for Employment Research, 1965.
v, 42 p. illus. 23 cm. (W. E. Upjohn Institute for Employment Research. Studies in employment and unemployment)
1. Unemployed—U. S. 2. Economic assistance, Domestic—U. S. 3. Insurance, Unemployment—U. S. I. Haber, William, 1899– joint author. II. Levitan, Sar A., joint author. III. Title. (Series: Upjohn Institute for Employment Research. Studies in employment and unemployment)
HD5724.B37 65–8417
GU ICarbS MoKU NNC NjP DHHF NIC MiU N MoU IU CoU ICU

Becker, Jürgen.
Das Heil Gottes; Heils- und Sündenbegriffe in den Qumrantexten und im Neuen Testament. Göttingen, Vandenhoeck & Ruprecht [1964]
288 p. 24 cm. (Studien zur Umwelt des Neuen Testaments, Bd. 3)
Based on the author's thesis, Heidelberg, 1961, with title: Ṣᵉdaka: Heils- und Sündenbegriffe in den Qumrantexten und im Neuen Testament.
Bibliography: p. [283]–288.
1. God—Righteousness. 2. Justification. 3. Tsdk (Hebrew root) I. Title. (Series)
BT145.B4 67–100473
WU NhD MiDW OSW TNJ-R TxFTC OCH ICU KyLxCB CBPac NNG NjNbS CtHC NjPT MH-AH GEU PPULC

Becker, Jürgen, 1932–
Felder. [Frankfurt am Main] Suhrkamp [1964]
145 p. 18 cm. (Edition Suhrkamp, 61)
I. Title.
CoU NB NIC MoU CtY NUC65–11674
NcD MNS

Becker, Jürgen, 1932– *ed.*
Happenings. Fluxus. Pop art. Nouveau réalisme. Eine Dokumentation. Hrsg. von Jürgen Becker und Wolf Vostell. (Reinbek b. Hamburg) Rowohlt (1965)
470 p. with illus. 21 cm. (Rowohlt-Paperback, 45) DM 19.80
(GDB 66–A23–275)
1. Happening (Art) I. Vostell, Wolf, 1932– joint ed. II. Title.
PN3203.B38 66–76408 rev
NIC FTaSU MH CSt

Becker, Julio E
Tratado práctico de horticultura y floricultura [por] Julio E. Becker. Santiago, Chile, Editorial Nascimento, 1964.
319 p. 19 cm.
1. Gardening—Chile. I. Title.
SB453.3.C5B4 67–36487

Becker, James L
A programed guide to writing auto-instructional programs. Camden, N. J., RCA Educational Programs, RCA Service Co. [1963]
[8] p. illus. 28 cm.
Three folded answer sheets inserted.
1. Programmed instruction. I. Title.
LB1028.5.B4   63-25334
NYhI

Becker, Jean Jacques, joint author
see Kriegel, Annie, 1914 [i. e. Dix neuf cent quatorze; la guerre et le mouvement ouvrier français. Paris, A. Colin [1964]

Becker, Joachim.
Gottesfurcht im Alten Testament. Rom, Päpstliches Bibelinstitut, 1965.
xix, 303 p. 24 cm. (Analecta Biblica, 25)
1. Fear of God–Biblical teaching. I. Title. (Series)
MBS NjPT MH–AH   NUC66-19719

Becker, Joachim.
Israel deutet seine Psalmen; Urform und Neuinterpretation in den Psalmen. Stuttgart, Verlag Katholisches Bibelwerk [1966]
98 p. 21 cm. (Stuttgarter Bibelstudien, 18)
Bibliographical footnotes.
1. Bible. O. T. Psalms–Criticism, interpretation, etc. I. Title. (Series)
NNG   NUC67-77896

Becker, Joan, ed. and tr.
A pair of mittens and other stories [by] Werner Bräunig [and others. Selected and tr. from the German] Berlin, Seven Seas Publishers [1961]
145 p. 20 cm. (Seven seas books)
1. Short stories, German–Translations into English. 2. Short stories, English–Translations from German. I. Bräunig, Werner. II. Title.
WU LNHT NcD   NUC64-62554

Becker, Josef, 1905–
Akute Porphyrie und Periarteriitis nodosa in der Neurologie. Berlin, Springer, 1961.
2 p.l., 56 p. 26 cm. (Monographien aus dem Gesamtgebiete der Neurologie und Psychiatrie, 92)
Bibliography: p. 47–56.
1. Porphyrinuria. 2. Neurology. I. Title: Periarteriitis nodosa in neurology. (Series)
CtY-M WU IaU   NUC63-5787

Becker, Josef, 1905–   ed.
Betatron und Telekobalttherapie; Internationales Symposion am Czerny-Krankenhaus für Strahlenbehandlung der Universität Heidelberg vom 1. bis 3. Juli 1957. Hrsg. von J. Becker und K. E. Scheer. Berlin, Springer, 1958.
296 p. illus. diagrs. 26 cm.
In German, English, or French.
Includes bibliographies.
1. Radiotherapy. I. Scheer, Kurt Ernst, joint ed. II. Heidelberg. Universität. Czerny-Krankenhaus für Strahlenbehandlung. III. Title.
RM845.B4 1957   615.842   59-3376 rev
WU ICU TONS CtY-M ICJ DNLM NNC-M

Becker, Josef, 1905–   ed.
see Strahlenforschung und Strahlenbehandlung. München, Urban & Schwarzenberg, 1956–

Becker, Joseph.
Information storage and retrieval: tools, elements, theories [by] Joseph Becker [and] Robert M. Hayes. New York, Wiley [1963]
448 p. illus. 24 cm. (Information sciences series)
1. Information storage and retrieval systems. I. Hayes, Robert M., joint author.
Z699.B37   010.78   63-19279 ‡
MH-M CtY-M DNLM MH-L DNAL IU MoSW
MH-BA NjR KU OrU CLU NIC

Becker, Joseph M   ed.
In aid of the unemployed, edited by Joseph M. Becker. Baltimore, Johns Hopkins Press [1965]
xiii, 317 p. illus. 25 cm.
Bibliographical footnotes.
1. Unemployed–U. S. 2. Insurance, Unemployment–U. S. 3. Economic assistance, Domestic–U. S. I. Title.
HD5724.B36   362.8   64-25066
MIU CoU CSt NIC NjR MoSW TNJ NjR MoU

Becker, Karl, 1907–   ed.
Freigeistige Anthologie. Stuttgart, Koerperschaft des oeffentlichen Rechts [n. d.,] v. 19 cm. (Freireligioese Landesgemeinde Wuerttemberg, Schriften)
Contents–L Altertum.-
MH–AH   NUC630-5788

Becker, Karl, 1907–
Die katholischen caritativan Ausbildungsstätten in Deutschland nach dem Stand vom 1. Januar 1961. 3. Aufl. Freiburg im Breisgau, Lambertus-Verlag, 1961.
54 p. 19 cm.
1. Social service–Direct.–Germany.
2. Education–Direct.–Germany.   NUC64-8652
NN

Becker, Karl, 1907–   ed.
Sag nein zum Krieg. Stuttgart, Verlag der Freireligiösen Landesgemeinde Württemberg [1962,]
140 p. illus.
1. War in art. 2. War poetry–Coll.–German.
3. War and religion. I. Title.
MH   NUC64-1552

Becker, Karl, 1907–   ed.
see Katholische Rundfunk- und Fernseharbeit in Deutschland. Wem gehört der Rundfunk? Frankfurt am Main, J. Knecht [1959]

Becker, Karl, 1909–
15 [i. e. Fünfzehn] Jahre ländliche Siedlung und Eingliederung und 10 Jahre landwirtschaftliche Strukturverbesserung; Erfahrungen und Folgerungen. Hannover, M. & H. Schaper, 1965.
188 p. [p. 164–168 advertisements] illus. 21 cm. (Schriftenreihe für ländliche Sozialfragen, Heft 45)
Bibliography: p. 161–162.
1. Agriculture–Economic aspects–Germany (Federal Republic) 2. Germany (Federal Republic, 1949–)–Population, Rural. I. Title.
HD1955.B36   67-34187

Figure 17.4   National Union Catalog (NUC).

```
ON THE DEVELOPMENT OF A  LESSON IN FIRE BEHAVIOR FOR THE LOS-      6233 1958
INTED ENGLISH (ARTINT)=  LETTER CONSTRAINTS WITHIN WORDS IN P      6125 0980
SYSTEM FOR CODESORTING   LETTER MAIL (INTRSRVY)= MAGNETIC DRU      6123 0765
CAN (ARTINT)=            LETTER RECOGNITION USING A CAPTIVE S      6123 4696
USSIAN TEXTS INTO LATIN  LETTERS (HMNITIES)= TRANSLITERATION       6123 0792
CHANNELS WHICH TRANSMIT  LETTERS OF UNEQUAL DURATION (INFTHRY      6236 3255
GNTDP, FOREIGN-GERMAN)=  LETTERS THAT CAN BE READ BY MACHINE       6233 1819
UTILPROG)=               LETTERS, SYMBOLS, PUNCTUATION READ (      6125 1051
COMBINATIONAL FREQUENCY  LETTERS, SYMBCLS, PUNCTUATION READ F      6236 2967
TER (ANLGAPPL)= 2        LEVEL CORRELATION ON AN ANALOG-COMPU      6236 2981
R, A NEW CONCEPT IN LOW  LEVEL DATA ACQUISITION (ANLGAPPL)= T      6235 1842
SIS OF VARIANCE FOR A 2  LEVEL FACTORIAL DESIGN (STATIST)=         6236 2933
AND OF THE PERMISSIBLE   LEVEL FLUCTUATION OF CODENNING SYSTE      6341 3811
MS (MGNTDP)=        LOW  LEVEL HIGH-SPEED DATA SCANNING SYSTE      6234 2144
CKOUT SYSTEM FOR HIGHER  LEVEL LANGUAGE PROGRAMS (PROGLANG)=       6234 2144
FORTRAN (PROGLANG)= LOW  LEVEL LANGUAGE SUBROUTINES FOR USE W      6234 1679
SIGN MODEL FOR A FOURTH  LEVEL MODEL IN THE BOULDING SENSE= A      6234 1141
OCESSING (DSGNGENL= LOW  LEVEL MULTIPLEXING FOR DIGITAL-DATA-      6126 1141
FECT OF QUANTIZATION BY  LEVEL ON PROCESSES IN DIGITAL AUTCMA      6016 0321
S INTERPRETER, A HIGHER  LEVEL PROGRAMMING LANGUAGE AND AN IN      6236 2969
STIMATING THE EFFECT OF  LEVEL QUANTIZATION ON PROCESS IN DIG      6012 0031
EALTIME)= THE EFFECT OF  LEVEL QUANTIZATION ON THE DYNAMIC PR      6122 0624
DATA SYSTEM SOLVES GNE   LEVEL SIGNAL PROBLEMS (REALTIME)= HI      6232 1696
                         LEVEL STORAGE SYSTEM (LITILPROG)=        6343 4176
ANSISTOR AT HIGH STRESS  LEVELS= RELIABILITY OF TYPE USAF-2N4      6233 1913
TAL COMPUTER (SOCLSCI)=  LEVIATHAN, A SIMULATION OF BEHAVIORA      6344 4348
OF COMPUTERS (SOCLSCI)=  LEXICAL CODING OF MESSAGES=              6126 1141
RITER, A SYSTEMATIC      LEXICAL PROCESSING OF STENOTYPE (ART      6232 1603
) THE JOVIAL GRAMMAR AND LEXICON (PROGLANG)= THE JOVIAL MANUA      6232 1664
  PROGRAMMING FOR THE    LGP-30 (DSGNGEN, FOREIGN-GERMAN)=        6012 0031
ACHINE PROGRAMMING THE   LGP-30 TO SOLVE PROBLEMS IN SYMBOLIC      6122 0624
ACHINE PROGRAMMING THE   LGP-30 TO SOLVE PROBLEMS IN SYMBOLIC      6234 2103
REMETHOD FOR GENERATING  LIAPUNOV (NUMRANAL)= A                   6233 1996
T (REALTIME)= STABILITY  LIAPUNOV FUNCTIONS (NUMRANAL)= THE V      6341 3455
REALTIME)= (PART 1)      LIAPUNOV'S DIRECT METHOD WITH APPLIC      6233 1892
RY (REALTIME)= (PART 2)  LIAPUNOV'S METHODS IN AUTOMATIC CONT      6344 4309
Y (PROGLANG)= THE CCBOL  LIAPUNOV'S METHODS IN AUTOMATIC CCNT      6344 3146
VAL AND THE PROBLEMS OF  LIBRARIAN, A KEY TO OBJECT PRGGRAM (      6232 1717
CKS IN THE YALE MEDICAL  LIBRARIES (INFRETR)= INFORMATION STO      6235 2601
ON AND USE CF A PRGGRAM  LIBRARY (PROCESSRS, FOREIGN-RUSSIAN)      6235 2351
                         LIBRARY FOR 2CCO A-D=                    6235 2351
AND OF UTILIZATION OF A  LIBRARY OF AUTOMATA (REALTIME)=          6341 3561
DUCE COSTS OF TECHNICAL  LIBRARY OF PROGRAMS (PROGGENL, FOREI      6345 4568
ICATIONS OF MACHINES TO  LIBRARY OPERATIONS IN THE DEPARTMENT      6235 2468
THE COMPUTER IN THE      LIBRARY TECHNIQUES, PERIODICALS (INF      6342 3816
ABLE IN THE STATISTICAL  LIBRARY=                                 6013 0122
ETRIEVAL (INFRETR)=      LIBRARY= INCEX OF STATISTICAL PRCGRA      6236 3239
        (PROGGENL)       LIBRARY-OF-CONGRESS CONTROL SYSTEM        6344 4309
ES (SCIENTIF)= PERIODIC  LIBRASCOPE OPERATIONS CONTROL SYSTEM      6345 4497
R THE UNITED-KINGDOM OF  LIBRATIONS ABOUT THE TRIANGULAR SOLU      6345 4519
ORIGIN AND SCOPE OF THE  LIBYA BY ELECTRONIC COMPUTERS (SOCLS      6234 2278
ARY BUSINESS AND SOCIAL  LIBYAN PILOT PROJECT (STATIST)=          6234 4285
        NAL)= THE        LIFE (STATIST, FOREIGN-GERMAN)= STAT      6345 4621
                         LIFE AND WORKS OF A.K. ERLANG (NLMRA      6345 4600
HE SOUTH AFRICAN MUTUAL  LIFE ASSURANCE SOCIETY'S PERSEUS COM      6345 1068
      AIRCRAFT ENGINE    LIFE CYCLE SIMULATION (MATHPROG)=         6345 1913
BILITY PREDICTIONS FROM  LIFE DISTRIBUTION DATA= SEMICNDCLCTG      6345 1913
N (COMPSYS)= TRANSISTOR  LIFE IN THE TX-O COMPUTER AFTER 10,       6235 2650

LEA


CMPUTATIONAL METHODS OF  LINEAR ALGEBRA (NUMRANAL)= C              6016 0374
RANAL FOREIGN-GERMAN)=   LINEAR ALGEBRA AND LINEAR ANALYSIS (      6126 1285
CTRIC MODEL FOR SOLVING  LINEAR ALGEBRAIC EQUATIONS (ANLGAPPL      6231 1320
FOR SOLVING SYSTEMS OF   LINEAR ALGEBRAIC EQUATIONS (ANLGDSGN      6236 2895
RECT METHOD FOR SOLVING  LINEAR ALGEBRAIC EQUATIONS (NUMRANAL      6232 1785
SOLUTION OF A SYSTEM OF  LINEAR ALGEBRAIC EQUATIONS (NUMRANAL      6342 4026
PLI= ON THE SOLUTION OF  LINEAR ALGEBRAIC EQUATIONS BY THE MO      6123 0831
AN)= LINEAR ALGEBRA AND  LINEAR ALGEBRAIC SYSTEMS WITH ANALOG      6121 0412
ANALYSIS (NUMRANAL, FOREIGN-G  LINEAR ANALYSIS (NUMRANAL, FOREIGN-G      6126 1285
RO OR UNITY (MATHPROG)=  LINEAR AND QUADRATIC PROGRAMMING WIT      6346 4855
A BOUNDARY PROBLEM FOR   LINEAR AND QUASI-LINEAR EQUATIONS AN      6345 4644
E)= ON THE SYNTHESIS OF  LINEAR AUTOMATIC CONTROL SYSTEMS (RE      6236 2933
E)= ON THE SYNTHESIS OF  LINEAR AUTOMATIC CONTROL SYSTEMS FOR      6342 3806
ABLE FUNCTIONS WITH THE  LINEAR AVERAGES OF THEIR FOURIER SER      6345 4631
RIODICALLY TIME VARYING  LINEAR BINARY SEQUENCE TRANSDUCERS=      6016 0312
METHODS OF SOLUTION OF   LINEAR BOUNDARY PROBLEMS (NUMRANAL=       6235 2840
CODE INTO AN ANGULAR OR  LINEAR CHANGE (ANLGHYBD, FOREIGN-RUS      6121 0502
AL PROCESSES (INFTHRY)=  LINEAR CODES FCR SINGLE ERROR-CORREC      6236 3139
                         LINEAR CODES OF MESSAGES (INFTHRY)=      6341 3664
FFERENCE EQUATIONS WITH  LINEAR COEFFICIENTS (NUMRANAL)= SOLU      6125 1101
R PROGRAMMING (PART 1),  LINEAR CONSTRAINTS (MATHPROG)= THE G      6123 0846
N RECOGNITION (ARTINT)=  LINEAR DECISION FUNCTIONS, WITH APPL      6342 3766
            REIGN-GERMAN)=  LINEAR DECISION MODELS (MATHPROG, FO      6344 4422
GN-FRENCH)= SOLUTION OF  LINEAR DIFFERENCE EQUATIONS (NUMRANA      6235 2836
E NUMERICAL SOLUTION OF  LINEAR DIFFERENTIAL BOUNDARY VALUE P      6234 2261
FOR SOLVING SYSTEMS OF   LINEAR DIFFERENTIAL EQUATIONS (NUMRA      6234 0867
PSYS, FOREIGN-RUSSIAN)=  LINEAR DIFFERENTIAL EQUATIONS (NUMRA      6344 4440
ING A CERTAIN PIECEWISE  LINEAR DISTORTIONS IN DISCRETIZATION      6232 1693
SYSTEM OF INCONSISTENT   LINEAR DYNAMIC SYSTEM WITH THREE PAR      6342 4025
SCALED ITERATIONS AND    LINEAR EQUATIONS (MATHPROG, FOREIGN-      6011 0007
A NOTE ON SYSTEMS OF     LINEAR EQUATIONS (NUMRANAL)=             6123 0864
SYSTEMS OF SIMULTANEOUS  LINEAR EQUATIONS (NUMRANAL)=             6125 1103
ST SQUARES SOLUTIONS OF  LINEAR EQUATIONS (NUMRANAL)= AN ITER      6123 0861
SOLUTIONS OF SYSTEMS OF  LINEAR EQUATIONS (NUMRANAL)= CN LEA      6232 0552
A PROGRAM FOR SOLVING    LINEAR EQUATIONS (NUMRANAL)= FOREIGN-     6232 1786
                         LINEAR EQUATIONS AFTER THE METHOD OF      6232 0546
RANAL)= THE SOLUTION CF  LINEAR EQUATIONS AND MATRICES (NUM       6234 2261
RANAL)= THE SOLUTION OF  LINEAR EQUATIONS BY THE CONJUGATE GR      6121 0548
SOLUTION OF SYSTEMS THE  LINEAR EQUATIONS BY THE METHOD OF DEX      6121 0547
OLUTION CF SIMULTANEOUS  LINEAR EQUATIONS PROBLEM (NUMRANAL)=      6342 3342
SOLUTION OF SYSTEMS OF   LINEAR EQUATIONS WITH DEFINITE MATRI      6014 0179
D NUMERICAL METHODS FOR  LINEAR EQUATIONS USING A MAGNETIC TA      6015 0278
                         LINEAR EQUATIONS, POLYNOMIAL EQUATIO      6346 4890
                         LINEAR ESTIMATION AND RELATED TOPICS      6236 3368
IGNS USING THE RATIO OF  LINEAR FORMS (NUMRANAL)= ALGORITHMS       6123 0857
IONS USING THE RATIO OF  LINEAR FORMS- ALGORITHMS FOR CHEBYSH      6234 2221
AL NOMENCLATURE (ENGRING)= AN  LINEAR FORMULA (ENGRING)= AN ALGORIT      6235 2431
O COMPUTER'S (NUMRANAL)= LINEAR FUNCTIONS RELATED TO AUTOMATI      6123 0739
GRAPHS AND ELECTRICAL NETWORK  LINEAR GRAPHS AND ELECTRICAL NETWORK      6341 3707
NUMRANAL)= THE USE OF    LINEAR GRAPHS IN GAUSS ELIMINATION (      6232 1792
TCTIC POWER OF TESTS OF  LINEAR HYPOTHESES USING THE PROBIT A      6345 2812
LES OF MATRICES INCIPLE  LINEAR INDEPENDENCE OF THEIR MINORS       6235 2812
INEQUALITIES AND THE PAULI PRI  LINEAR INEQUALITIES AND THE PAULI PRI      6125 1096
ATIONS OF THE THEORY OF  LINEAR INEQUALITIES TO EXTREMAL COMB      6125 1096
                         LINEAR INPUT LOGIC (LOGLDSGN)=           6231 1434
                         LINEAR INPUT LOGIC (LOGLDSGN)=           6232 1740
A NEW METHOD OF SOLVING  LINEAR INTEGRAL EQUATIONS OF THE FIR      6125 1098
IME)= ON THE ERROR OF A  LINEAR INTERPOLATOR FOR A PROGRAM CO      6121 0432
CONCERNING ERRORS OF THE LINEAR INTERPOLATOR FOR THE DIGITAL      6231 1335

LIN
```

Figure 17.5   KWIC Index.

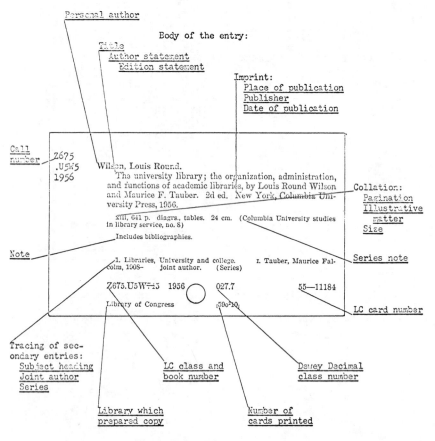

Figure 17.6   LC catalog card data.

Figures 17.7 and 17.8 give a number of examples of entries.[14] (Figure 17.7 presents the entries created from the LC card shown in Figure 17.6, and Figure 17.8 contains illustrations of some of the special situations that arise). Each of these kinds of entries is designed to be consonant with one or more of the functions that the catalog must perform.

Admittedly, with such abbreviated entries, the only place that the user can consult in order to fulfill the complete range of requirements is the main entry

[14] Cartright, Kelley L., and Ralph M. Shoffner, *Catalogs in Book Form.* Berkeley, California: Institute of Library Research, University of California, January 1967.

Figure 17.7   Form and content of catalog entries: standard entries.

1. *Main entry:*
WILSON, LOUIS ROUND.
————The university library; the organization, administration, and functions of academic libraries, by Louis Round Wilson and Maurice F. Tauber. 2d ed. New York, Columbia University Press, 1956. xiii, 641 p. diagrs., tables. 24 cm. (Columbia University studies in library service, no. 8) Includes bibliographies.
Z675.U5W5 1956

2. *Title reference entry:*
The university library. *See in Name Catalog under* Wilson, Louis Round.
Z675.U5W5 1956

3. *Joint author reference entry:*
TAUBER, MAURICE FALCOLM, 1908–
————The university library. See under Wilson, Louis Round.   Z675.U5W5 1956

4. *Subject added entry:*
LIBRARIES, UNIVERSITY AND COLLEGE.
—Wilson, Louis Round. The university library; the organization, administration, and functions of academic libraries, by Louis Round Wilson and Maurice F. Tauber. 2d ed. New York, Columbia University Press, 1956. xiii, 641 p. diagrs., tables. 24 cm. (Columbia University studies in library service, no. 8) Includes bibliographies.
Z675.U5W5 1956

5. *Series reference entry:*
Columbia University studies in library service.
The Library has the following titles in this series:
No. 2. Haines, Helen Elizabeth, 1872– Living with books.   028 H17
No. 7. Tauber, Maurice Falcolm, 1908– Technical services in libraries.   025 T191
No. 8. Wilson, Louis Round. The university library.   Z675.U5W5 1956
No. 12. Danton, J. Periam. Book selection and collections.   Z675.U5D3

or register entry. Anyone who does not first approach an item through the main entry but who wishes a full description of the item will be required to pursue a cross-reference to it. Thus the user who seeks an enumeration of all the editions of *Origin of Species* that the library has will find, under Origin of Species, a reference to "Darwin, Charles Robert, 1809-1882." In the latter location, he will find all the editions of this work. It should be pointed out, however, that such uses of the catalog are likely to be made by persons already quite familiar with the catalog structure, and who are therefore likely to look first under the main entry anyway. Such uses of catalogs are, in fact, most often made by librarians for reference and acquisitions.

Expanded Entry

Persons concerned with the use of catalogs for "information retrieval" have long felt that the contents of a typical library catalog record, although adequate for purposes of bibliographic description, are inadequate for their purposes.

Figure 17.8   Form and content of catalog entries: special situations.

1. *Author with multiple entries (including subject entries):*
    FIELDING, HENRY, *1707-1754.*
    ———An apology for the life of Mrs. Shamela Andrews. Ed. with an introd. and notes, by Sherman W. Baker, Jr. Berkeley, University of California Press, 1953. xxi, 86 p. 18 cm.   Gen. Coll.: PR3453.A7 1953
                                                                                                                 Sutro: PR5672.B23
    ———The history of the adventures of Joseph Andrews and of his friend Mr. Abraham Adams. New York, Modern Library [1950] x, 422 p. 21 cm.
                                                                                                                 PZ3.F46A3125
    ———Jonathan Wild; the voyage to Lisbon. London, Dent; New York, Dutton [1932] 286 p. 23 cm.   AC1.E8 No. 877

    FIELDING, HENRY, 1707-1754 (SUBJECT)
    ———Baker, Sheridan Warner, 1918– Setting, character, and situation in the plays and novels of Henry Fielding. Berkeley, 1950. vi, 400 p. Thesis (Ph.D.), University of California, June, 1950. Bibliography: p. 386-400. PN943.F459B168
    ———Byrd, Jane Carroll. Fielding: a force in the breaking down of the drama into the novel: a study of the merging of two types. 1914.   PN3084.B995
    ———Cross, Wilbur Lucius, 1862-1948. The history of Henry Fielding, New York, Russell and Russell, 1963 [c1945] 3 v., illus., ports., facsims. 23 cm. Bibliography: v. 3, p. 289-366.   PN943.F459C9 1963

2. *Title main entry:*
    Who's who in library service; a biographical directory of professional librarians of the United States and Canada. 3d ed. Dorothy Ethlyn Cole, editor. Prepared under the direction of the Council on Who's Who in Library Service for the School of Library Service, Columbia University. New York, Grolier Society, 1955. xxiii, 546 p. 26 cm.   Ref. Dept.: 020.92 W62 1955

3. *Author analytic*:
    HEARNSHAW, F. J. C.
    ———Chivalry and its place in history. (*In* Prestage, Edgar, 1869–. Chivalry.)
                                                                                                                 394.7 P93

4. *Main entry, followed by an entry for a related work and an entry for the work as subject:*
    AMERICAN LIBRARY ASSOCIATION. DIVISION OF CATALOGING AND CLASSIFICATION.
    ———A. L. A. cataloging rules for author and title entries. 2d ed., edited by Clara Beetle. Chicago, American Library Association, 1949. xxi, 265 p. 27 cm. "The preliminary American second edition of A.L.A. catalog rules, on Part I of which the present volume is based, was prepared by: American Library Association, Catalog Code Revision Committee." The 1st ed., published in 1908, has title: Catalog rules, author and title entries.   Ref. Dept. (2 copies): Z695.A52 1949
    ———A.L.A. cataloging rules for author and title entries.
        See also the following:
    Cataloging rules of the American Library Association and the Library of Congress. Additions and changes, 1949-1958. Washington, Library of Congress, 1959. 76 p. 26 cm. Includes all changes in the A.L.A. cataloging rules for author and title entries and the rules for descriptive cataloging in the Library of Congress.   Ref. Dept. (2 copies): Z695.C32
    ———A.L.A. cataloging rules for author and title entries.
        Works about this work:

Figure 17.8   *(Continued)*

Lubetzky, Seymour. Cataloging rules and principles; a critique of the A.L.A. rules for entry and a design for their revision. Prepared for the Board on Cataloging Policy and Research of the A.L.A. Division of Cataloging and Classification. Washington, Processing Dept., Library of Congress, 1953. ix, 65 p. 24 cm. Bibliographical footnotes.   Z695.L87

5. *Title added entry/reference to work with main entry under title:*
   The family Rosary edition of the Holy Bible. *See under* Bible. English. 1953. Douai.

   BS180 1953a

6. *Author added entry/reference to work with main entry under title:*
   COLUMBIA UNIVERSITY. SCHOOL OF LIBRARY SERVICE.
   ——Who's who in library service. *See under title in green catalog.*

   Ref. Dept.: 020.92 W62

7. *Multiple author entries, including "joint author" entry and entry for the author as editor of works of others:*
   FULLER, EDMUND, 1914–
   ——Books with men behind them. New York, Random House, 1962. 240 p. 21 cm.

   PS379.F78
   ——The Christian idea of education; papers and discussions by William G. Pollard and others. A seminar at Kent School. New Haven, Yale University Press, 1957-62. 2 v. 23 cm. Vol. 2 has also special title: Schools & scholarship. Includes bibliographical references.   LB7.F8
   ——Contemporary writers and their books. *See under* Pimentel, Walter William, 1902–   PS381.P4
   ——Man in modern fiction; some minority opinions on contemporary American writing. New York, Random House, 1958. 171 p. 21 cm.   PN3425.F8
   FULLER, EDMUND, 1914–
     See also the following:
   Fielding, Henry, 1707-1754. The history of the adventures of Joseph Andrews, and of his friend Mr. Abraham Adams; a student's edition, with introduction and notes by Edmund Fuller. New York, Putnam, 1958. xxxi, 386 p. Bibliography, p. 377-384.   PZ3.F46A32

There has, therefore, been a great deal of effort directed at defining an "augmented catalog record" which would provide additional data about the subject content of a book, about the physical characteristics of it, and about the intellectual context for it. For example, Figure 17.9 lists some of the data added in Project Intrex (the fields not listed are roughly counterparts of established cataloging practice).[15]

In another study of the need for additional data in the catalog record, Swanson (of Chicago) suggested criteria such as those shown in Figure 17.10.[16]

[15] *Project Intrex. Semi-Annual Activity Reports,* (March 15, and September 15) 1966–.
[16] Swanson, Don R., *Requirements Study for Future Catalogs.* Chicago: University of Chicago Graduate Library School, 1968.

Figure 17.9   Added descriptive information.

Field Number and Name	Data Elements
22. Personal Name Affiliations	Title of Position
	Corporate Name
	Place Qualification
	New or Former Affiliation
30. Medium (physical nature of the document)	Medium Code (1 = conventionally printed) (6 = microfiche) (18 = constructional model)
31. Format (arrangement of information within a document)	Format Code (f = directory) (r = professional journal) (bb = article like that found in a professional journal (ii = editorial)
36. Language of Document	Language Code (e = English) (f = French) (r = Russian)
37. Language of Accompanying Abstract	Language Code (see field 36)
39. Report Numbers and Patent Numbers	Report Number
	Paper Number
	Patent Number
	Patent Country of Origin
	Based-upon Relator Code (BR = based on a report bearing the accompanying number)
40. Contract Statement	Contracting Agency Name or Contract Monitor Name
	Contract Number
41. Supplement Referral	Type of Supplement Code (st = supplement to) (ib = indexed by)
	Number or Date of Supplement
	Record Number of Supplement

Figure 17.9 *(Continued)*

Field Number and Name	Data Elements
42. Errata	Location of Incorrect Data
	Corrected Data
	Corrector's Name
	Citation to Published Errata

65. Author's Purpose	Author's Purpose Code
	(t = report on original
	   research–theoretical)
	(e = report on original
	   research–experimental)
	(n = review–noncritical)

66. Level of Approach	Level of Approach Code (1 = professional (including graduate level) (4 = undergraduate level)
67. Table of Contents	Heading
	Beginning Page Number
68. Special Features	Special Features Statement
69. Bibliography	Type of Reference (1 = references) (2 = suggested readings)
	Location of References (e = end of complete text) (f = footnotes)
	Number of references
70. Excerpts	Excerpts
	Location of the Excerpt
71. Abstracts	Abstract
	Abstractor
	Citation to the Abstract
72. Reviews	Review
	Reviewer
	Citation to the Review

Figure 17.9   *(Continued)*

Field Number and Name	Data Elements
73. Subject Indexing	Subject Term
	Weight (1 = term representing most of document content) (2 = term representing section of document content) (3 = term representing small segment of document content) (4 = term representing materials, tools, techniques not appearing in another index term) (0 = term generic to document content)

Added Citation Information

80. Article Reference Citations	References Cited
	Citing References

Added User Feedback Information

85. User Comments	User Comments

The study tested a number of considerations about the comparative effectiveness of these "nonstandard" descriptive features. Two are shown in Figure 17.10:

1.   "Expected Search Length Reduction Factor," which indicates the extent to which knowledge of the feature reduced the time required to search a file.

2.   "Memorability Level," which indicates the extent to which the study showed the feature would be remembered correctly.

Maron, of the Institute of Library Research, University of California, Berkeley has suggested that data, such as that listed in Figure 17.11, concerning the "context" of the document would be relevant to searching and selection.[17]

---

[17] Maron, M. E., and R. M. Shoffner, *The Study of Context: An Overview*. Berkeley, California: Institute of Library Research, University of California, January 1969.

Nonstandard Feature (1)	Expected Search Length Reduction Factor (Percent) (2)	Memorability Level (Percent) (3)
Date	57	15
Type of work	49	15
Number of pages	43	19
Binding	32	9
Color	29	11
Level	27	17
Height	27	12
Quotes	26	10
Condition	26	9
Index	23	4
Figures	21	16
Tables	21	13
Chapter titles	20	3
Graphs	18	7
Footnotes	18	8
Case Studies	16	18
Translation	15	7
Preface	14	2
Bibliography	8	4
Single volume	7	3
Reprint or revision	7	5
Dedication	5	4
Glossary	3	1
Problems	3	0.4
Average	21.4	9

Figure 17.11   Context Information.

Review (of the article) author, journal, and classification
(descriptors)
Author (of the article) affiliation(s), degrees (field, level,
year, institution, societies, and research interests
Publication (of the article) sponsor, publisher, editors, and
scope
Citations (by the article itself) bibliographic, footnotes,
content, and comment

ORGANIZATION OF CATALOGS AND INDEXES

The rules for sequencing or ordering the entries in the catalog or index are greatly affected by its intended primary function.

The computer, when it is given a set of rules to follow, is a very fast and very accurate tool for the filing of data. It will execute the rules given it with a speed and an accuracy that human filers cannot begin to match. But the translation of library filing rules into a set of rules that the computer can apply is not a simple task.

There appear to be four major ways to approach a solution to the filing rules problem. Each represents an extreme and probably none of them would be acceptable by itself. These are:

1.   Retain a system in which filing is essentially done by people. Such a system would involve the assignment of a sorting code to each entry heading to be used in the catalog. In such a system, a person would determine the desired sequence of entries, and would then assign the sorting code to each entry. The computer would then file these entries by number, rather than filing by the headings themselves.

2.   Have the computer file entries exactly as they occur by using simple "alpha-numeric" sorting, with very little machine application of what are called "conversion rules."

3.   Systematically change the format of headings so that the text itself, when filed by the machine in accordance with simple sorting rules, would achieve the sequence desired. Thus, if we wanted to file historic subdivisions chronologically, we would systematically rewrite these subdivisions in forms such as "U.S.–Hist.–1861-1865 (Civil War)."

4.   Program library filing rules, or modifications of them, and have the computer file on the text as it stands.

Each of these methods has its attractions and its drawbacks, of course. The straightforward alpha-numeric sorting of the text as it stands would be the most economical solution; but it would probably not constitute a solution acceptable to the library. On the other hand, the process of systematically revising headings is probably the most expensive, although it would probably result in a filing system that is more intelligible to the user than any other, since the relationships between the filing order and the sequence of entries on the printed page would be readily apparent. The essentially manual system of filing by the assignment of sort codes is a very expensive method. Finally, it is by no means certain that library filing rules can be programmed. All the methods open, then, would seem to present either unacceptable results, difficulties of achievement, or uneconomic operation.

For these reasons, it is likely that a solution will not employ exclusively any of the four techniques mentioned above, but will require the use of all of them to some degree. That is, certain types of headings will be identified which will be filed as desired if the computer uses a very simple set of conversion rules. Other types of entries will require special handling by a combination of the following techniques.

1.   Some categories of headings will be systematically revised so that the form in which they are input will result in the desired filing sequence. A computer edit can provide assistance in converting such headings.

2.   A "file as" device can be employed for more unusual categories. (This is a device by which the editor indicates the text—different from the actual text—upon which the computer is to file. For example, the editor could indicate that the title "34 ans de lutte" is to be filed as though it were "trente quatre ans de lutte.") Associated with this technique should be a monitoring system, which will help to identify the most frequently recurring categories of filing problems which require this kind of solution. The information thus gained could be used to decide what additional computer routines may be needed.

Let us now examine the four basic alternatives in detail.

Library Filing Rules.

The standard ALA or LC filing rules are similar in character, and various "simplifications" of these rules have been adopted by many libraries. Recently, the Anglo-American Filing Code Revision has tried to introduce greater rationality in these rules.[18]

They are all designed to give the catalog a structural pattern that would reveal more meaningfully the contents of the library and guide the catalog user more helpfully to the appropriate sources. The need for rules arose from the fact that the catalog is not only a list of individual entries that might be arranged in one alphabetical order, but can be an organized record bringing together groups and subgroups of related entries. There was, in addition, the fact that some words (articles, for example) are not useful in filing and other words are variously spelled or represented in different forms (for instance, as words, abbreviations, symbols, Arabic numbers, or Roman numbers). The various library filing rules are thus designed to provide arrangements which facilitate the location of an entry that could appear in different forms and display related entries together. Unfortunately, the underlying pattern of arrangement of the entries may not be readily apparent to many of the library's staff and users. Those unfamiliar with

[18]*Anglo-American Cataloging Rules*, North American Text. Chicago: American Library Association, 1967.

the system, therefore, often find it unnecessarily complicated and demand a "simple alphabetical" order, unaware of the fact that what may be a simplification to one person, in search of a specific citation, may be perplexing to another.

Filing Codes

Several early systems for mechanized production of book catalogs—the sequential camera systems used by LA County[19] and NLM,[20] for example—depended on the assignment by a cataloger of numerical "filing codes." These are designed to sequence catalog entries in filing order if the computer simply sorts them into numerical order on the filing code.

Generally, this approach has been abandoned as being unsatisfactory whenever it has been used on a catalog production task of any real size. There are a number of reasons. (1) Files of already assigned sorting codes must be maintained, so that when the cataloger considers the addition of a new entry he can assign a number in proper sequence with those already assigned; the costs of maintaining such files—for authors, titles, and subjects—are great enough to make such an approach uneconomic. (2) The time required for the cataloger to

Figure 17.12   Limits on additions to filing codes.

Process. Normally, when an entry is to be filed between two existing entries, it is given a filing code approximately halfway between. Consider the effects of this rule under the following seven-digit code system (which appears to allow up to one hundred insertions between entries):

Starting Entries

The History of America	1234500
History of Europe	1234600

Entries in Order of Receipt (with associated codes as they would be assigned)

Addition	Entry	Code
1	The History of Asia	1234550
2	History of American Life	1234525
3	History of American Foreign Policy	1234512
4	History of American Industry	1234518
5	History of American Idealism	1234515
6	History of American Ideals	1234517
7	History of American Ideas	(?)

[19] Mac Quarrie, Catherine, and Beryl L. Martin, "Book Catalog of the LA County Public Library: How It Is Being made," *Library Resources and Technical Services*, 4 (3) (Summer 1960), pp. 208-227.

[20] The National Library of Medicine Index Mechanization Project," *Bulletin of the Medical Library Association*, 49 (No. 1, Part 2), January 1961.

determine the proper filing positions, to look them up in the files of filing codes, and to assign them to entries is also expensive enough, in itself, to make such approach uneconomic. (3) Any system of filing codes will provide facility for limited insertion of new entries among old ones; typically a code might be 7 decimal digits and would appear to allow the insertion of 100 entries between any two entries in a file of 100,000. Unfortunately, however, in such a case, the insertion of even 7 successive new entries could destroy the code—as Figure 17.12 illustrates.[21]

Alpha-Numeric Sorting

The most economical and straightforward solution to the filing problem is simply to disregard it almost entirely and program the computer to file by simple alpha-numeric sorting of the text exactly as it appears. Such a method was proposed by Hines, and the description of the arrangement method given by him shows the basic ordering concept.[22]

Filing is from left to right, with the single exception of numerals as noted below, in the following order:

1. *By entry unit.* An entry unit is a single complete index, bibliographic, or catalog entry, with the exception of those elements deliberately excluded by designating a section or sections of the entry as non-filing elements. This exclusion may be achieved by use of a special symbol. It should be noted that page or other references to location in index entries would usually be included as part of the entry unit to be filed on, since they are arranging elements.

2. *By field or filing unit within entry unit.* The fields in the usual catalog entry would be: filing element if other than author (subject heading, added entry, title, added or variant title, etc.), author (except in added entries), and title statement and imprint. Fields may be separated by any convenient device. Where one form of the entry unit is to be used as input for multiple entries under different fields, fields would usually be designated as to type by their order; but other means may be used if desired.

3. *By sub-field or sub-filing unit within field or filing unit.* A sub-field is defined as being separated from other sub-fields by two spaces in the procedures presented by this code.

4. *By word within field or sub-field.* In the procedures presented by the code, a word is defined as an element set aside from other words in the field by a single space.

[21] Ranganathan, S. R., *Prolegomena to Library Classification*. Madras: 1937.

[22] Hines, Theodore C., and Jessica L. Harris, *Computer Filing of Index, Bibliographic, and Catalog Entries.* New York: Columbia University, School of Library Service, 1965.

5.   *By the following order of sorts.*
   (a)   Blank (i.e., space).
   (b)   The order of the English alphabet, A-Z. A capital letter is considered to be identical to the same lower-case letter, the same letter from a different font, etc. Modified letters (a, ü, φ, etc.) are to be considered identical to their unmodified equivalents. In the case of umlauts, cross-references should be made from the form written with an *e* (from Mueller to Müller, for example) when the umlaut occurs in the first syllable of a field.
   (c)   The order of the Arabic numerals. Note that numbers are to be considered as numbers, not as isolated numerals. (E.g., 19 comes before 195, and 19.5 precedes 20, etc.) The computer must file outward from the decimal point. It must distinguish the end of number sequences. In program composition, care should be taken with the hyphen in inclusive dates, and with decimal points, fractions, and other mathematical symbols used as part of number sequences when these appear in the entry.
   (d)   Signs, symbols, punctuation, and letters not given as part of the sort sequence are otherwise to be disregarded. It should be emphasized that they are to be disregarded completely, not treated as if their removal created a space which was to be considered in the order of sorts. If it is desirable that a sign be filed by (an ampersand in a title, for example), it must be written out as a word or words in the entry.

With such a method, the result will be a filing order to some extent unlike what we now know. Abbreviations would be filed exactly as spelled; numbers would file as numbers, never as if spelled out, and they would often not file in what we regard as correct numerical order; articles would be filed as part of the text; titles of honor that occur between last names and first names would be regarded as filing elements; Roman numerals would be filed alphabetically rather than numerically; different spellings of the same word (for example color and colour) would be filed in different places; historic subdivisions would sometimes file chronologically and sometimes alphabetically; the surname Paris and the city name Paris would probably interfile in most cases. The list of such departures from standard practice which would result from straightforward, uncomplicated filing by the computer is very long. However, the frequency of occurrence of these exceptions from purely alpha-numerical sorting may not be very great. Experiments with a fairly typical catalog show that alpha-numeric sorting would misfile less than 2 percent of the entries; furthermore, several of these misfilings could even be eliminated by relatively simple additions to the filing program (for example, the detection and elimination of initial articles).[23] If the resulting

[23] Unpublished data from a study at the Washington State Library of the Timberland Library Demonstration Project Catalog.

extent of departure from ALA filing rules were acceptable, pure alpha-numeric sorting would be an ideal, economic answer. Unfortunately, for most large libraries, even so limited a departure is not regarded as acceptable, and other approaches must be considered.

Sort Fields

Another alternative is to include in the catalog entry record an additional "sort field" in cases where the text would not produce the proper filing sequence under pure alpha-numeric sorting. Figure 17.13 shows some examples.

Figure 17.13   Use of sort fields

Entry	Sort As
365 Party Ideas	Three Hundred and Sixty Five Party Ideas
The History of Asia	History of Asia
McDonald, James	MacDonald, James
Louis XVI, King of France	Louis, King of France 16

Programmed Rules

Programming of a set of library filing rules, such as those of the ALA, is best seen as a two-step process involving the application of what we may call "conversion rules" and "sort rules."[24] For example, ALA Rule 13(b) requires that names beginning M, Mac, and Mc be filed together as if spelled "Mac." Therefore, when a name such as "McDonald" is encountered, it must first be translated into the word "Mac Donald." Then one is able to apply the basic alpha-numeric filing rule—the order of the English alphabet. The difficulty lies, of course, in the formidable task of creating the conversion rules.[25,26] There are two major reasons for this.

1.   In converting natural text to a text that can be used for sorting, the human filer makes use of much information that is either only implicit in the data presented, or cannot be derived from the data at all. For example, it is only implicit in the word "McDonald" that it is, in fact, a *name*—a condition required

[24] Cartwright, Kelley, and R. M. Shoffner, *op. cit.*

[25] Culbertson, Don S., Louis A. Schultheiss, et al., *An Investigation into the Application of Data Processing to Library Filing Rules.* Chicago: University of Chicago, December 5, 1962.

[26] Perreault, Jean M., "The Computer and Catalog Filing Rules," *Library Resources and Technical Services,* 9 (3) (Summer 1965), 325-331.

if the rule for names is to be applied. As another example, consider the subject heading "U.S.–Hist.–Civil War." Filing rules might require that we file this entry chronologically, rather than alphabetically; we therefore need to know that the Civil War occurred after the Revolutionary War.

2.   The order of elements in a heading does not always correspond to the order in which we file them. For example, ALA rules require us to file the heading "Louis XVI, King of France" as if it were "Louis, King of France, XVI."

Machine Filing Standards

In the long run, we shall need a national code of rules for filing catalog entries by computer. The possibilities of achieving national standardization will be greater than have heretofore existed. First, the advent of nationally distributed catalog copy in machine-readable form will make standardization in cataloging even more attractive than it has been in the past, and the costs of applying nonstandard methods will be much greater than they have been in the past. Second, there is a very close relationship between the form of heading adopted and the filing rules that will apply to it. Therefore, the national agency that adopts a new set of filing rules should be in a position to influence cataloging rules as they apply to the form of heading it uses. Finally, it may develop that the amount of care that must be expended in creating headings will be far greater than is now employed. The process of creating these headings and of converting them to machine-readable form, therefore, will be considerably more expensive than if such care were not required.

FORM OF THE CATALOG OR INDEX

Catalogs and indexes can be produced in a variety of forms—card form, book form, microform, or magnetic tape form. The choice among them is determined partly by the function the catalog or index is to serve and partly by the relative difficulties in producing and maintaining each of them. It is important to bear in mind the major differences among them:

1.   Catalog cards are separate physical entities; book catalog entries are always part of a large physical entity, the printed page; microforms may be either. This fact has numerous implications for catalog design. For example, it is usually readily apparent in a card catalog when one entry ends and another begins, since the new entry will almost always begin on a new card and a new card is almost always a new entry. In a book catalog, on the other hand, it is

important that the layout of the page and of the individual entries make it apparent to the user where one entry begins and another ends, so that they can easily be scanned, rather than examined one at a time by the reader. This fact has implications for arrangement and for filing sequence. Yet another implication of the basic physical differences is that the control of individual entries will differ. One of the reasons for typing the applicable heading on every catalog card or microfiche is that if the card is out of sequence, it can easily be restored to its proper place in the file. This consideration does not apply to book catalog entries or to continuous microforms.

2.   The content and organization of book, card, and microform catalogs may be quite different. The amount of information on a catalog card is not directly related to the cost of maintaining that card in a file. This is not the case with book catalog entries or microforms. The question of the format of entry, the content of the entry, and its layout on the page, are therefore very important considerations for the latter two.

3.   The production and maintenance of each form of catalog involves quite different problems. Card catalogs can, in principle, be up-dated and maintained more rapidly and less expensively than the other forms, because the interfiling of new entries does not require rewriting the entire catalog. Book form and microform catalogs therefore usually require supplements. On the other hand, multiple copies of book form and microform catalogs are economical to produce and can therefore be made available at widely distributed points.

4.   For the same information content, the physical size of a book catalog is considerably smaller than that of a card catalog. Even the largest book catalogs we have (those of the Library of Congress and the British Museum) do not require the amount of space that a card catalog of even a moderate sized library requires. One implication is that when a user of a book catalog is referred from one point in the catalog to another by a cross reference, he need not travel the length of a large room; instead, he can reach for another volume near the one he has. The converse of this, of course, is that because one volume of a book catalog replaces many drawers of a card catalog, the likelihood that a person seeking a certain part of the alphabet will find the applicable volume in use is much higher than the likelihood that he will find the desired drawer of a card catalog in use. For this reason it will no doubt prove desirable to provide several copies of the catalog in various parts of the library for the patron's use.

Card Form Catalogs and Indexes

The preparation of catalog cards is a function that the computer can perform very efficiently, once the catalog data is available in machine-readable form.[27,28] The processing results in the generation of library catalog cards on catalog card stock (Figure 17.14). For each title a number of separate cards are produced, to provide for multiple entry points and for catalogs at multiple libraries. In addition, the catalog cards can be output in a "prefiled" order, thus reducing manual filing time, even by as much as 60 percent.

Book Form Catalogs and Indexes

The printed book form catalog reached the height of its popularity in the last half of the nineteenth century.[29] The advantages of a printed book catalog were numerous and obvious: it is portable, compact, and can be distributed to remote locations; a number of entries can be seen at once, making comparisons easy.[30,31]

On the other hand, the printed book catalog had serious defects that finally led to its abandonment. It was enormously expensive to typeset, proofread, correct, print, and bind. Since it could never be up to date because of the time needed to produce the work, supplements of one kind or another were required, and it was always necessary to search more than one record to be certain of completeness. (Medical librarians who have spent years searching the pages of the Index-Catalogue of the Library of the Surgeon General's Office understand this problem well.) Because printed catalogs were so costly, condensed lists, finding guides, and catalogs limited by time span, by subject matter, or by form of publication were introduced until, finally, the problems of the cyclically published, costly, always retrospective book catalog led to the acceptance of the card catalog.

Recently, however, problems of libraries, resulting from the increased volume of publication and the widened interest in world literature on the part of scholarly communities, have again made the book form catalog important and even necessary. The need to solve the problems is urgent, as library systems expand rapidly and as collections increasingly are counted in hundreds of thousands or millions of volumes. Just as size, economics, and demands for better service are forcing libraries into branch systems, these issues are also

[27] Fry, George, and associates, *Catalog Card Reproduction.* Chicago: Library Technology Project, American Library Association, 1964.

[28] Treyz, Joseph H., "Equipment and Methods in Catalog Card Reproduction," *Library Resources and Technical Services,* 8 (3) (Summer 1964) 267-278.

[29] Shera, Jesse H., "The Book Catalog and the Scholar: A Reexamination of an Old Partnership," *Library Resources and Technical Services,* 6 (Summer 1962) pp. 210-216.

[30] Kingery, Robert E., and Maurice F. Tauber, *Book Catalogs.* New York: Scarecrow, 1963.

[31] Parker, Ralph, et al., "The Book Catalog" (as a series of articles), *Library Resources and Technical Services,* 8 (4) (Fall 1964), 349-398.

```
***********************************************************
*                                                         *
*                                                         *
*                                                         *
*   GOLDMAN, ERIC FREDERICK,  1915 -                      *
*     THE CRUCIAL DECADE: AMERICA,                        *
*     1945-1955.                                          *
*     THE CRUCIAL DECADE--AND AFTER;                      *
*     AMERICA, 1945-1960. NEW YORK,  KNOPF,               *
*     1966 _C1960'                                        *
*     VIII, 349 P. 22 CM.                                 *
*     FIRST PUBLISHED IN 1956 UNDER TITLE:                *
*   THE CRUCIAL DECADE: AMERICA, 1945-1955.               *
*     U.S.--HIST.--1945-                                  *
*                                                         *
*                                                         *
*                                         6400791         *
*     F813.G6 1966                        973.918         *
*                                                         *
***********************************************************

***********************************************************
*                                                         *
*   U.S.--HIST.--1945-                                    *
*                                                         *
*   GOLDMAN, ERIC FREDERICK,  1915 -                      *
*     THE CRUCIAL DECADE: AMERICA,                        *
*     1945-1955.                                          *
*     THE CRUCIAL DECADE--AND AFTER;                      *
*     AMERICA, 1945-1960. NEW YORK,  KNOPF,               *
*     1966 _C1960'                                        *
*     VIII, 349 P. 22 CM.                                 *
*     FIRST PUBLISHED IN 1956 UNDER TITLE:                *
*   THE CRUCIAL DECADE: AMERICA, 1945-1955.               *
*     U.S.--HIST.--1945-                                  *
*                                                         *
*                                                         *
*                                         6400791         *
*     F813.G6 1966                        973.918         *
*                                                         *
***********************************************************
```

Figure 17.14   Computer printed catalog cards.

forcing library catalogs into various combinations of card and book form listings and away from the ideal of a single master file.[32-35] The reasons are clear.

1. *The need to have catalogs at affiliated libraries.* The growth of the

---

[32] Heinritz, Fred, "Book versus Card Catalog Costs," *Library Resources and Technical Services,* 7 (3) (Summer 1963), 229-236.

[33] MacDonald, M. Ruth, "Book Catalogs and Card Catalogs," *Library Resources and Technical Services,* 6 (3) (Summer 1962), 217-222.

[34] Pizer, Irwin H., "Book Catalogs versus Card Catalogs," *Bulletin of the Medical Library Association,* 53 (April 1965), 225-238.

[35] Richmond, Phyllis A., "Book Catalogs as Supplements to Card Catalogs," *Library Resources and Technical Services,* 8 (4) (Fall 1964), 359-365.

"multi-versity," as well as public and county library systems, has led to the provision of duplicate catalogs, and the production of duplicate catalogs is most feasible in book form.[36]

2.   *The size and complexity of any single library catalog itself.* The larger libraries are literally outgrowing their space for card files, and catalogs are getting too large to be used easily and meaningfully. This has led libraries to turn toward the book form to ease the physical pressure—and the book form of catalog seems particularly suited to materials selected for secondary access or auxiliary collections.

3.   *The heavy turnover of book titles within one collection.* With the large effort required to interfile new cards and withdraw older records, libraries dealing largely with current publications have been prompted to turn to the mechanically-produced catalog, and again the book form is most convenient for automated output.

4.   *The need for consolidated catalogs of holdings, even for a single library.* Since interdisciplinary growth complicates the formerly rather clear division among major departmental libraries, union lists of currently received journals and joint catalogs of science holdings are increasingly useful when there is a dispersion of resources—and these lists and catalogs are most practicable in book form.[37]

Microform Catalogs and Indexes

Another answer to these same problems is in the use of microforms. There are significant hurdles in the degree to which microforms have found acceptance by the users of libraries. However, the economic advantages they have for catalog production, distribution, and storage are so great that they are becoming increasingly prevalent. For example, Chemical Abstracts Service has begun distribution of *Chemical Abstracts* on microfilm.[38] Commercial catalogs and indexes (like those of Information Handling Services, Inc.[39] and Sears Roebuck) have been distributed in this form for many years. Several large industrial special libraries have produced their library catalogs on microfilm.[40,41]

[36] Geller, William Spence, "Duplicate Catalogs in Regional and Public Library Systems," *Library Quarterly,* **34** (January 1964), 57-67.

[37] Blackburn, Robert H., "On Producing Catalogues in Book Form for Five Libraries at Once " *A Collection of Papers by Canadian Librarians,* June 1965, pp. 20-22.

[38] *Chemical Abstracts on Microfilm,* A Service of Chemical Abstracts Services, Columbus, Ohio.

[39] *VSMF,* A Service of Information Handling Services, Inc., Denver, Colorado.

[40] Kozumplik, W. A., and R. T. Lange, "Computer Produced Microfilm Library Catalog", *American Documentation,* **18** (2) (April 1967), 67-80.

[41] Matsumiya, H., and M. Bloomfield, "A Working Microfilm Card Catalog," *Special Libraries,* **55** (March 1964), 157-159.

Magnetic Tape Catalogs and Indexes

In Chapter 19, we shall discuss the variety of catalogs and indexes that are becoming available in magnetic tape form. As data bases from which printed forms can be produced and from which information services can be provided, such catalogs and indexes are certain to become an essential part of library services.[42]

TYPOGRAPHIC QUALITY

The quality of the typography and the number of fonts required for use in the production of a catalog or index have an effect on both the quality and the cost.[43,44] In general, the greater the typographical quality, the more expensive the production process. Admittedly, the better the typography the higher the density of recording that can be provided, thereby potentially reducing the total number of page masters required in a book catalog. However, the effect is probably not great enough to overcome the higher costs involved in producing the page masters. The major justification for the higher quality typography, therefore, must be greater user satisfaction or easier utilization.

Figures 17.15 to 17.17 and Figure 17.2 provide, in order of quality, sample pages of book catalogs produced by various methods—from computer printer output to photocomposition.

Upper-Case Computer Print-Out

Figure 17.15 shows a typical "upper-case only" computer printer output. The first thing likely to be noticed by the user of a catalog with this typography is the lack of variety: all of the letters are capitals; there is no difference in lightness or darkness of the letters, the letters are not spaced proportionally, and so on. As long as the entries under any one author are few in number the sameness of the print seems to pose little problem, but anyone attempting to find his way about the section of the author catalog beginning with "U.S." will almost certainly quickly give up with aching eyes. One can try to attain variety by means of spacing and indentions but it is obvious that more differentiation is

---

[42] Rogers, Frank B., "Relation of Library Catalogs to Abstracting and Indexing Services," *Library Quarterly*, **34** (January 1964), 106-112.

[43] Cornos, D. Y., and F. C. Rose, *Legibility of Alphanumeric Characters and Other Symbols*, National Bureau of Standards, February 10, 1967.

[44] Sparks, David E., et al., "Output Printing for Library Mechanization," in Barbara E. Markuson (ed.), *Libraries and Automation*, Washington, D.C. Library of Congress, 1964, pp 155-200.

*A 41

MCHENRY, EARLE WILLARD, 1899-1961. SEE BEATCN, GEORGE H....
                                                QU 145 B369V 1964

MCKAY, DONALD G. DISSEMINATED INTRAVASCULAR COAGULATION, AN INTERMEDIARY
MECHANISM OF DISEASE. N. Y., HOEBER, 1965. 493 P.
                                                WH 310 M153D 1965

MCKUSICK, VICTOR A. HUMAN GENETICS. N. Y., PRENTICE-HALL, 1964. 148 P.
                                        RES   QH 431 M159H 1964

MCNEILL, DONALD BURGESS SEE JERRARD, H. G....
                                        REF   QC 82 J 56D 1963

MCNERNEY, WALTER J. REGIONALIZATION AND RURAL HEALTH CARE, AN EXPERIMENT IN
THREE COMMUNITIES. BY WALTER J. MCNERNEY AND DONALD C. RIEDEL. WITH THE
ASSISTANCE OF DARWIN O. FINKBEINER AND EDWARD M. DOLINSKY. ANN ARBOR,
UNIVERSITY OF MICHIGAN PRESS, 1962. (MICHIGAN. UNIV. BUREAU OF HOSPITAL
ADMINISTRATION. RESEARCH SERIES, NO. 2.).
                                                WA 390 M169R 1962

MEAD, MARGARET. FOOD HABITS RESEARCH, PROBLEMS CF THE 1960-S. WASHINGTON,
NATIONAL ACADEMY OF SCIENCES-NATIONAL RESEARCH COUNCIL, 1964. 39 P.
(NATIONAL RESEARCH COUNCIL PUBLICATION. NO. 1225.).
                                        PAM   P 92 1964

MEAKER, SAMUEL R. PREPARING FOR MOTHERHOOD, A MANUAL FOR EXPECTANT PARENTS.
2D ED. CHICAGO, YEAR BOOK, 1965. 197 P.
                                        CL SH WQ 150 M482 1965

MEDICAL DIRECTORY. LONDON, CHURCHILL. 1 V. IN 2.

    LIBRARY HAS, 1965, PT. 1 A-L, PT. 2 M-Z- LATEST ISSUE ONLY ON REFERENCE.
    FOR PREVIOUS DIRECTORIES IN THIS LIBRARY, SEE PRE-1965 CATALOG.
                                        REF   W 22FAI M489 1965

MEDICAL ECONOMICS. SURVEY OF INTERNAL MEDICINE. ORADELL, N. J., 1964. 229
P.   W 74 M489S 1964

MEDICAL ECONOMICS. SURVEY OF PEDIATRICS. ORADELL, NEW JERSEY, 1965. 223 P.
                                                W 74 M489S 1965

MEDICAL EXAMINATION REVIEW BOOK. FLUSHING, N. Y., MEDICAL EXAMINATION PUB.
CO., 1965. 1 V.

    CONTENTS.- V. 15, OPHTHALMOLOGY. FOR PREVIOUS REVIEW BOOKS IN THIS
    LIBRARY, SEE PRE-1965 DICTIONARY CATALOG.
                                                W 18 M489 1965

MEISTER, ALTON. BIOCHEMISTRY OF THE AMINO ACIDS. 2D ED. N. Y., ACADEMIC
PRESS, 1965. 2 V.   QU 60 M515B 1965

MELIN, HANS. AN ATROPHIC CIRCUMSCRIBED SKIN LESION IN THE LOWER EXTREMITIES
OF DIABETICS. UMEA, 1964. 75 P. (ACTA MEDICA SCANDINAVICA. SUPPLEMENTUM
423.).   JNLS   ACTA MED SCAND 1964

MELLON INSTUTUTE, PITTSBURGH, PA. A LIST OF THE BOOKS, BULLETINS,
PERIODICALS, JOURNAL CONTRIBUTIONS, AND PATENTS BY MEMBERS OF THE MELLON
INSTITUTE, 1964- PITTSBURGH. 1 V.

    FOR PREVIOUS LISTS IN THIS LIBRARY, SEE DICTIONARY CATALOG.
                                                Z 5055.U5 M527 1964

MENEELY, GEORGE R. SEE SYMPOSIUM CN RADICACTIVITY IN MAN, 2C, NORTHWESTERN
UNIVERSITY, 1963....   WN 415 S989R 1963

MERSHON, MILLARD M. SEE CONFERENCE CF CCNTRACTCRS FOR SKIN RESEARCH,
EDGEWOOD ARSENAL, MD., 1962....   PAM   P 118 1964

METCALF, DONALD. SEE DEFENDI, VITTORI....
                                                QP 187 D313T 1964

Figure 17.15   Upper-case book catalog page.

desirable if not absolutely necessary. On the other hand, it should also be pointed out that upper case printing is highly economic, and futhermore the product of such a printing process can be quite attractive, as Figure 17.16 shows.

Even if a library should decide to use a straight upper case print chain, we would strongly advise that the catalog data be coded at the time of input for upper and lower case. Programs can be written easily so that material coded for upper and lower case printing would be printed in upper case only, but it would be very difficult to write a program to translate material coded only for upper case into information that would yield a satisfactory upper and lower case output.

Upper-Case, Lower-Case Computer Printout

Computer printers are available with upper and lower case letters and the punctuation symbols necessary to the production of this catalog (Figure 17.17 gives an example of this typography). In general, they are slower in operation than upper-case only and are more expensive.

Multiple Fonts

As Figure 17.1 clearly demonstrates, the catalogs of large research libraries require a variety of characters far greater than computer printers can provide. Chinese, Cyrillic, Greek, Hebrew, Hindi, Japanese—the symbols of the non-Roman alphabets are beyond count. Even Roman alphabets pose problems in the use of diacriticals, as shown in Figure 17.18.

Fortunately, within the past ten years, equipment has become available that can produce a large variety of type fonts and special characters. Figure 11.26 lists some presently marketed devices. As it shows, the price even for the cheapest of these devices is high. However, service bureaus are making them available and they are remarkably efficient printing devices. Figure 17.2 shows an example of an index page (from *Index Medicus*) produced by means of such computer controlled photocomposition equipment.

FORMAT

The format of entries and their placement on the printed page are very important factors in determining the ease with which the catalog can be used, its readability, and the costs of producing it. The reduction ratio in size of characters, the number of columns to a page, the placement of column headings, the size of margins, the indentation of lines—all have their effect on the appearance of the page. Figure 17.19 provides a list of some typical format specifications.[45]

[45] West, William, and John Welt, *Sample Book Index Formats*, State University of New York at Buffalo, July 1968.

BUSINESS—DICTIONARIES (Cont'd)

R016.65 SPECIAL LIBRARIES ASSOCIATION. BUSINESS AND TRADE DICTIONARIES. COMPILED BY SPECIAL COMMITTEE, 1934. A. C. MITCHELL, CHAIRMAN. CLASSIFIED GUIDE TO THE SOURCES OF BUSINESS TERMINOLOGY AND DEFINITIONS.

BUSINESS—DIRECTORIES

R650.5 CELEBRITY INFORMATION AND RESEARCH SERVICE, INC. CONTACT BOOK.

R016.65 DAVIS, MARJORIE VEITH. GUIDE TO AMERICAN BUSINESS DIRECTORIES. PUBLIC AFFAIRS PR., 1948. 242 P. EARLIER EDITION HAS TITLE "AMERICAN BUSINESS DIRECTORIES".

G317.3 DEUBEL, STEFAN. DEUTSCH-AMERIKANER VON HEUTE. DEUTSCH-AMERIKANISCHES ADRESSBUCH FUER DIE USA UND WESTDEUTSCHLAND. DER MASSGEBENDE FUEHRER DURCH DIE BEDEUTENDSTEN WIRTSCHAFT-LICHEN UNTERNEHMUNGEN FUER IMPORT UND EX-PORT—EINE EINZIGARTIGE STUETZE FUER DEUTSCH-AMERIKANISCHE VEREINE UND ORGANISATIONEN. WÄCHTER UN ANZEIGER. 468 P. ILLUS., PORTS. HISTORY OF AMERICANS OF GERMAN DESCENT IN THE UNITED STATES, THEIR CONTRIBUTIONS TO AMERICAN CIVILIZATION, CULTURE, AND ENTERPRISE. INCLUDES A DIRECTORY OF GERMAN-AMERICAN SOCIETIES IN THE UNITED STATES AND A DIRECTORY OF GERMAN-SPEAKING BUSINESSMEN IN THE UNITED STATES.

R382 DIRECTORY OF AMERICAN FIRMS OPERATING IN FOR-EIGN COUNTRIES. WORLD TRADE ACADEMY PR.. OVERSIZE. LIBRARY HAS 1955/56, 1961/62.

R016.65 GUIDE TO AMERICAN DIRECTORIES; A GUIDE TO THE MAJOR BUSINESS DIRECTORIES OF THE UNITED STATES COVERING ALL INDUSTRIAL, PROFESSIONAL AND MERCANTILE CATEGORIES. A SECTION ON SELECTED FOREIGN DIRECTORIES IS INCLUDED. 4TH ED. KLEIN, 1960. 424 P. OVERSIZE.

R650.58 INTERNATIONAL YELLOW PAGES. LAS PAGINAS AMARILLAS INTERNACIONALES. DIE INTERNA-TIONALEN GELBEN SEITEN. INTERNATIONAL YELLOW PAGES INC. ANNUAL. CONSOLIDATED YELLOW PAGES OF TELEPHONE DIRECTORIES FROM 125 COUNTRIES.

R650.58 LOS ANGELES BUSINESS DIRECTORY. CHAMBER OF COMMERCE. OVERSIZE. COVER TITLE: LOS ANGELES AREA BUSINESS DIRECTORY.

BUSINESS—HANDBOOKS, MANUALS, ETC.

R650.3 BRADDY, NELLA. NEW BUSINESS ENCYCLOPEDIA. EDITED BY H. MARSHALL, PSEUD. REV., UP-TO-DATE ED. DOUBLEDAY, 1963. 526 P. ILLUS., MAPS, TABLES. FIRST PUBLISHED IN 1930 UNDER TITLE "THE BUSINESS ENCYCLOPEDIA". PRACTICAL INFORMATION FOR BUSINESSMEN, HOUSEWIVES AND STUDENTS.

658 FINANCIAL HANDBOOK. 3D ED. RONALD, 1948. ILLUS.

658 LASSER, JACOB KAY. BUSINESS EXECUTIVE'S GUIDE. MCGRAW, 1945. 252 P. A CHECK LIST ON PROBLEMS OF ORGANIZATION, FINANCE, TAXES, AND MANAGEMENT.

BUSINESS—INFORMATION SERVICES

010 INSTITUTE OF PETROLEUM, LONDON. INFORMATION AND ITS DISSEMINATION. REPORT OF THE SUMMER MEETING OF THE INSTITUTE HELD AT HARROGATE, 7-10 JUNE 1961. ED. BY M. J. WELLS. 1961. 109 P. SIX PAPERS BY LEADERS IN BRITISH INDUS-TRIAL MANAGEMENT INTENDED TO AID THOSE WHO WISH TO ESTABLISH TECHNICAL INFORMATION CENTERS.

R016.65 NEWARK, N. J. FREE PUBLIC LIBRARY. BUSINESS INFORMATION AND ITS SOURCES. COMPILED BY M. C. MANLEY, 1931. 32 P. WITH 1939 SUPPLE-MENT, 37 P.

R016.65 SPECIAL LIBRARIES ASSOCIATION. GUIDES TO BUSINESS FACTS AND FIGURES. COMP. WITH THE COOPERATION OF THE STAFF OF THE BUSINESS BRANCH OF THE NEWARK PUBLIC LIBRARY, BRANCH LIBRARIAN, M. C. MANLEY. 1937. INDEXED AND DESCRIPTIVE LIST EMPHASIZING THE LESS KNOWN BUSINESS REFERENCE SOURCES. FOR OTHER EDITIONS, SEE AUTHOR CATALOG.

026.6 SPECIAL LIBRARIES ASSOCIATION. PUBLIC BUSI-NESS LIBRARIANS GROUP. BUSINESS AND THE PUBLIC LIBRARY; STEPS IN SUCCESSFUL COOPER-ATION. ED. BY M. C. MANLEY, 1940.

R016.65 WINSER, MARIAN CATHERINE MANLEY. BUSINESS INFORMATION. HARPER, 1955. 265 P. HOW TO FIND AND USE IT. A BIBLIOGRAPHY COVERING BUSINESS PERIODICALS, BOOKS, PAMPHLETS, AND DIRECTORIES. CROSS REFER-ENCE INDEX.

BUSINESS—PERIODICALS
      SEE ALSO
         HOUSE ORGANS.

R016.6   MEIXELL, GRANVILLE. TRADE. CATALOG COLLECTION. 1934.

R016.65 NEWARK, N. J. FREE PUBLIC LIBRARY. BUSINESS MAGAZINES. COMPILED BY M. C. MANLEY. THE PUBLIC LIB., 1933. 31 P.

070   WOOLF, DOUGLAS GORDON. BUSINESS PAPER EDITOR AT WORK. MCGRAW, 1936. 54 P.

BUSINESS—PERIODICALS—INDEXES
R016.6   BUSINESS PERIODICALS INDEX. WILSON. EDITOR. 1968- V. CRAUMER. 3V. LIBRARY HAS JAN. 1958-JUNE 1962. CONTINUES IN PART ''THE INDUSTRIAL ARTS INDEX''.

BUSINESS—RECORDS
      SEE
         BUSINESS RECORDS.

BUSINESS, SMALL
      SEE
         SMALL BUSINESS.

BUSINESS—STATISTICS
R016.338 DAVENPORT, DONALD HILLS. INDEX TO BUSINESS INDICES. BUSINESS PUBLICATIONS, INC., 1937. 187 P.

311.2   FREUND, JOHN ERNST. ELEMENTARY BUSINESS STATISTICS, THE MODERN APPROACH. PRENTICE, 1964. 478 P. ILLUS., TABLES. BIBLIOGRAPHY.

311   HAUSER, PHILIP MORRIS. GOVERNMENT STATISTICS FOR BUSINESS USE. 2D ED., 1956. 440 P. ILLUS., MAP.

BUSINESS—TERMS AND PHRASES
650.3   DE LEVIE, DAGOBERT. BUSINESS PHRASES IN SIX LANGUAGES. 1946. FOR WRITING LETTERS IN ENGLISH, SPANISH, FRENCH, DUTCH, GERMAN AND RUSSIAN.

R650.58 LOS ANGELES METROPOLITAN AREA BUSINESS DIRECTORY. CHAMBER OF COMMERCE. OVERSIZE. COMPILED BY THE RESEARCH DEPT., LOS ANGELES CHAMBER OF COMMERCE.

R016.65 NEWARK, N. J. FREE PUBLIC LIBRARY. BUSINESS DIRECTORIES- A KEY TO THEIR USE. COMPILED BY M. C. MANLEY. 1934. 63 P.

R016.65 U. S. BUREAU OF FOREIGN COMMERCE. GUIDE TO FOREIGN BUSINESS DIRECTORIES. GOVT. PRINT. OFF., 1955. 132 P.

BUSINESS—DIRECTORIES—CALIFORNIA
      SEE
         CALIFORNIA - DIRECTORIES.

BUSINESS—FORMS, BLANKS, ETC.
651.05   KNOX, FRANK M. DESIGN AND CONTROL OF BUSINESS FORMS. MCGRAW, 1952. 219 P. ILLUS. OVERSIZE.

651.5   MARIEN, RAY. MARIEN ON FORMS CONTROL. PRENTICE, 1962.
         HOW TO CUT COSTS AND INCREASE PROFITS THROUGH CONTROLLED BUSINESS FORMS. ADDRESSED TO SMALL COMPANIES AS WELL AS LARGE ORGANIZATIONS.

R347.4   PRENTICE-HALL, INC. SALES CONTRACTS AND FORMS. 1928. 455 P. FORMS.

651.5   REMINGTON RAND, INC. VISIBLE RECORDS- THEIR PLACE IN MODERN BUSINESS. 1930. 91 P. ILLUS.

651.5   SADAUSKAS, WALLACE B. MANUAL OF BUSINESS FORMS. OFFICE PUBLICATIONS, 1961. 235 P. ILLUS.
         HOW TO DESIGN AND CONTROL THEM. ILLUS.

BUSINESS—GRAPHIC METHODS
311.26   FRANCIS, FLY. USING CHARTS TO IMPROVE PROFITS. PRENTICE, 1962.
         HOW A COMPANY CAN UTILIZE A SIMPLE CHART PROGRAM FOR CONTROLLING ITS SALES AND COST TRENDS, AND MAXIMIZING ITS PROFITS.

658.01   ROSE, THOMAS GERALD. HIGHER MANAGEMENT CONTROL. MCGRAW, 1957. 290 P. ILLUS.
         'THIS BOOK WAS DEVELOPED FROM THREE BOOKS- 'HIGHER CONTROL IN MANAGEMENT', 'THE INTERNAL FINANCE OF INDUSTRIAL UNDERTAKINGS', AND 'BUSINESS CHARTS'.'

Figure 17.16   Photographically reduced upper case.

ALPHABETICAL NAME CATALOG
THE. ALEXANDER LECTURES, 1934-35.
PN   SEDGEWICK, Garnett Gladwin.
1680 Of irony, especially in drama. 2d ed.
.S45 Toronto, U. of T. Pr. 1948. 127 p.

THE ART OF DRAMA.
PN   PEACOCK, Ronald.
1631 The art of drama. London, Routledge
.P36 (1957) 263 p.

THE ART OF THE PLAY.
PN   DOWNER, Alan .S., ed.
1657 The art of the play. N.Y., Holt
.D75 (1955) 451 p.

BRO, MARGUERITTE (HARMON) 1894-
PN   O hara Frank Hurburt, and M.H. Bro.
1655 Invitation to the theater. N.Y.,
.O36 Harper (1951) 211 p.

PN   BROOKS, Cleanth, and R.B. Heilman, eds.
1657 Understanding drama. N.Y., Holt
.B87 (1948) 674,64 p.

THE DRAMA AND THE STAGE.
PN   LEWISOHN, Ludwig.
1655 The drama and the stage. N.Y., Harcourt
.L68 (c1922) 245 p.

THE DRAMA OF TRANSITION.
PN   GOLDBERG Isaac.
The drama of transition. Cincinnati,
.G62 Stewart + Kidd (c1922) 487 p.

THE ELEMENTS OF DRAMA.
PN   STYAN, J L
1655 The elements of drama. Cambridge (Eng.)
.S94 U.P., 1960. 306 p.

PN   ELLIS-FERMOR, Una Mary.
1623 The frontiers of drama. 3d ed. London,
.E47 Methuen (1948) 154 p.

THE ENJOYMENT OF DRAMA.
PN   MARX, Milton.
1655 The enjoyment of drama. N.Y., Crofts,
.M39 1940. 242 p.

EURIPIDES
PN   NORWOOD, Gilbert.
1721 Euripides and Shaw with other essays.
.N88 London, Methuen (1921)

EURIPIDES AND SHAW.
PN   NORWOOD, Gilbert.
.N88 London, Methuen (1921) 226 p.

EUROPEAN THEORIES OF THE DRAMA.
PN   CLARK, Barrett Harper, ed.
1661 European theories of the drama. 2d rev.
.C59c ed. N.Y., Crown (1947) 576 p.

PN   FERGUSSON, Francis.
1661 The idea of a theater. Garden City,
.F35b Doubleday, 1953 (c1949) 255 p.

PN   FERGUSSON, Francis.
1661 The idea of of a theater. Princeton,
.F35 Princeton U.P., 1949. 258 p.

THE FRONTIERS OF DRAMA.
PN   ELLIS-FERMOR, Una Mary.
1623 The frontiers of drama. 3d ed. London,
.E47 Methuen (1948) 154 p.

PN   BROWN, Ivor John Carnegie.
1655 Parties of the play. London, Benn,
.B88 1928. 192 p.

PN   CLARK, Barrett Harper, ed.
1661 European theories of the drama. 2d rev.
.C59c ed. N.Y., Crown (1947) 576 p.

PN   CLARK, Barrett Harper, ed.
1661 European theories of the drama. Cincinnati,
.059 Stewart + Kidd, 1918. 503 p.

THE ARTISTIC AND ThE DRAMA.
PN   NATHAN, George Jean.
1655 The critic and the drama. N.Y.,
.N25 Knopf, 1922. 152 p.

THE DEVELOPMENT OF DRAMATIC ART.
PN   STUART, Donald Clive.
1721 The development of dramatic art. N.Y.,
.S93 Dover (1960) 679 p.

PN   DOWNER, Alan S., ed.
1661 The art of the play. N.Y., Holt
.D75 (1955) 451 p.

Figure 17.17   Upper case-lower case.

Figure 17.18   Diacritical marks and special characters

Part A: Diacritical Marks

Diacritical	Name	Use	Languages
´	Acute	á é ś í ó ú ć ý ń ź ḿ ṕ ŕ ẃ	Afrikaans, Albanian, Assamese, Bengali, Catalan, Croatian, Czech, Dutch, French, Gujarati, Hawaiian, Hindi, Hungarian, Icelandic, Kannada, Malayalam, Marathi, Oriya, Polish, Portugese, Prakrit, Sanskrit, Serbian, Slovak, Slovene, Spanish, Tagalog, Tamil, Telegu, Vietnamese, Wendic
`	Grave	à è ì ò ù	Catalan, Dutch, French, Italian, Portugese, Vietnamese
¨	Umlaut or dieresis	ä ë ï ö ü	Albanian, Catalan, Chinese, Dutch, Estonian, Finnish, French, German, Hungarian, Icelandic, Lithuanian, Norwegian, Russian, Spanish, Swedish, Turkish, Ukrainian
˘	Breve	ă ğ ĭ ŏ ŭ m̆ ĕ	Bulgarian, Chinese, Hindi, Korean, Panjabi, Russian, Turkish, Ukrainian Vietnamese, White Russian
^	Circumflex	â ê î ô û	Albanian, Chinese, Dutch, French, Gujarati, Hindi, Marathi, Portugese, Rumanian, Slovene, Telegu, Turkish, Vietnamese
¯	Macron	ā ē ī ō ū r̄ œ̄ ǣ	Anglo-Saxon, Arabic, Armenian, Assamese, Bengali, Burmese, Greek (Modern), Gujarati, Hindi, Japanese, Kannada, Korean, Latvian, Lithuanian, Malayalam, Marathi, Oriya, Persian, Prakrit, Punjabi, Pushto, Russian, Sanskrit, Tamil, Telegu, Thai, Urdu
°	Circle	å ů	Czech, Danish, Finnish, Lithuanian, Norwegian, Slovak, Swedish
·	Superior dot	ė ṅ ś ẏ ż ḟ ṫ	Assamese, Bengali, Gujurati, Hebrew, Hindi, Kannada, Lithuanian, Malayalam, Marathi, Oriya, Polish, Prakrit, Punjabi, Pushto, Russian, Sanskrit, Tamil, Telegu, White Russian
¸	Cedilla	ç ş ļ	Albanian, Catalan, French, Latvian, Portugese, Turkish

Figure 17-18 *(Continued)*

Diacritical	Name	Use	Languages
,	Left hook	ḑ ķ ņ ş ţ ŗ Ģ	Rumanian, Latvian
؛	Right hook	a̦ e̦ i̦ ș ț o̦ u̦	Anglo-Saxon, Lithuanian, Polish
؛	Inverted cedilla	ǫ	Thai
ˇ	Hacek	č ě ň ǒ ř š ž ǐ ť ď ǔ	Armenian, Croatian, Czech, Latvian, Lithuanian, Serbian, Slovak, Slovene, Thai, Wendic
~	Tilde	ã ñ õ ĩ ũ ẽ	Assamese, Bengali, Estonian, Gujarati, Hindi, Kannada, Malayalam, Marathi, Oriya, Portugese, Prakrit, Punjabi, Sanskrit, Spanish, Tamil, Telugu, Vietnamese
″	Double acute	ő ű	Hungarian
⌒	Ligature	i͡e i͡u i͡a t͡s z͡h	Bulgarian, Russian, Ukrainian, White Russian
..	Two dots under letter	s̤ t̤ z̤ l̤	Hindi, Kannada, Pershian, Pushto, Urdu
.	Dot below letter	u̇ ȧ ḋ ė ḣ i̇ k̇ l̇ ṁ ṅ ȯ ṙ ṡ ṫ ż	Arabic, Assamese, Bengali, Burmese, Gujarati, Hebrew, Hindi, Kannada, Malayalam, Marati, Oriya, Persian, Prakrit, Sanskrit, Tamil, Telugu, Urdu, Vietnamese
°	Circle under letter	l̥ n̥ r̥	Assamese, Bengali, Gujurati, Hindi, Kannada, Malayalam, Marathi, Oriya, Prakrit, Sanskrit, Telugu
⏝	Candra-bindu	ñ̆ m̆ ŭ	Assamese, Bengali, Bulgarian, Hindi, Oriya, Prakrit, Sanskrit, Telugu

Figure 17.18   *(Continued)*

Diacritical	Name	Use	Languages
’	High comma	g̊	Latvian
’	High comma (off-center)	t’ l’ d’ g’ k’	Czech, Macedonian, Slovak, Wendic
◡	upadhmān-iya	ḫ	Sanskrit
_	Underscore	h̲ l̲ n̲ r̲ z̲ t̲ s̲ g̲	Assemese, Bengali, Hindi, Kannada, Malayalam, Persian, Punjabi, Pushto, Sanskrit, Prakrit, Tamil, Telugu, Urdu
=	Double underscore	gh̳	Hindi
~	Double tilde	n͠g	Tagalog
᾿	Pseudo question mark	å̉	Vietnamese

Part B: Special Characters

Character (Lower Case)	Character (Upper Case)	Name	Languages
ø	Ø		Danish, Norwegian
ł	Ł		Lithuanian, Polish, Wendic
’		miagkiĭ znak	Bulgarian, Russian, Ukrainian, White Russian
”		tvĕrdyĭ znak	Russian
’		alif	Arabic, Assamese, Bengali, Gujarati, Hebrew, Hindi, Japanese, Malayalam, Marathi, Oriya, Persian, Prakrit, Turkish, Urdu
		ayn	Arabic, Armenian, Chinese, Hebrew, Korean, Persian, Pushto, Thai, Urdu
æ	Æ		Anglo-Saxon, Danish, Icelandic, Norwegian, Thai
œ	Œ		Anglo-Saxon, Icelandic, Thai

Figure 17-18   *(Continued)*

Character (Lower Case)	Character (Upper Case)	Name	Languages
2		Super-script 2	Indonesian
đ	D		Croatian, Serbian, Vietnamese
ð	Đ	eth	Anglo-Saxon, Icelandic
þ	Þ	thorn	Anglo-Saxon, Icelandic
ı	I	Turkish i without dot	Turkish
ư	Ư		Thai, Vietnamese
ơ	Ơ		Vietnamese
·		Dot in center of line	Catalan

Figure 17.19   Specifications of formats.

Figure Number	Number of Columns	Original Size (Inches)	Character Reduction (Percent)	Column Width in Characters	Interior Margin in Characters	Height in Lines
17.20	1	8½ x 11	0	60	None	56
17.21	1	8½ x 14	20	83	None	75
17.22	2	8½ x 11	0	30	5	56
17.28	2	8½ x 14	20	39	4	75
17.24	3	11 x 14	35	32	4	82

ACQUISITION OF DATA BASES

In order even to consider the use of computers for the production of catalogs and indexes, the data from which entries would be produced must be available in machine readable form. In every respect, this represents the most formidable hurdle to the use of computers in libraries.

First, the size of catalogs and indexes makes their conversion into machine readable form a truly immense task. The catalog of even a moderate sized library will contain between 10^8 and 10^9 characters; that of a typical research library, between 10^9 and 10^{10} characters; that of the Library of Congress, between 10^{10} and 10^{11} characters. Any reasonable estimate just of key-boarding catalog data (not even counting the costs of editing for input) implies a cost of at least 30c to 40c per title. Second, the complexity of format for catalog data is so great that a high level of editing is required just to provide a record suitable for key-boarding. Third, the data in catalog records frequently requires the use of a very large character set, sometimes even in non-Roman alphabets. Aside from the problems we have discussed with respect to output, this implies comparable problems at input.[46,47]

MARC II Tapes

Probably the most important single step in the solution of this problem is the program of the Library of Congress for distribution of catalog data in magnetic tape form.[48] From these tapes, any library in the world can economically acquire machine-readable catalog data, just as it has been able to acquire catalog cards.

With the Library of Congress now beginning to distribute its cataloging data in magnetic tape form, the content and format of MARC II tapes becomes especially important.[49]

The basic machine-readable catalog record on a MARC tape, as summarized in Figure 9.14, consists of five different sections: the Leader, the Record Directory, the Variable Control Number, the Variable Fixed Fields, and the Variable Fields:

The Leader is a set of fields describing the general structure of the individual entry. It consists of the following fields.

1. *Record Length.* This five-character field contains the logical record length. A logical record is the basic unit of information in a processing system. It contains all fields necessary to describe an item. The maximum logical record length is 99,999 characters since this is the largest number that can be expressed by five digits. This is longer than the average record, however, and was included to allow for records containing abstracts.

---

[46] Buckland, Lawrence F., *The Recording of Library of Congress Bibliographical Data in Machine Form,* Inforonics, February 1965.

[47] Buckland, Lawrence F., *Problems of Recording Text Information in Machine Form for Use in a Scientific Information Communication Network*, Inforonics, May 24, 1966.

[48] Avram, Henriette D., and Barbara Evans Markuson, "Library Automation and Project MARC: An experiment in the Distribution of Machine Readable Cataloging Data," in John Harrison and Peter Laslett (eds.), *The Brasenose Conference on the Automation of Libraries.* London: Mansell, 1967, pp 97-126.

[49] Avram, Henriette, et al., *The MARC II Format.* Washington, D.C.: Library of Congress, January 1968.

2. *Record Status.* This one-character field is used to indicate the following:

        N   Record is new this week
        L   Record was new last week
        R   Record is revised this week
        O   Record is at least two weeks old

3. *Legend Control.* If this one-character field contains a ϕ there is no extension of the legend information. If it contains a number, it indicates that additional information can be found in one of the variable fields.

4. *Type of Record.* This is a one character field which indicates what type of material is being cataloged in this record; for example, printed language materials, language materials in manuscript form, motion pictures and filmstrips, and the like.

5. *Bibliographical Level.* This three character field describes the hierarchical bibliographic level of the work being cataloged; that is, its relationship to any other work of which it may be a part, as a book which is part of a series.

6. *Indicator Count.* This contains a number describing the length of the indicator codes used to identify variable fields.

The Record Directory is an index to the location of the variable fields in the record. It consists of a series of fields of fixed length, one for each variable field in the record. However, since the number of variable fields in a record can vary, the total length of the Record Directory section of the record is also variable.

1. *Tag.* Each variable field is assigned a number called a tag, which identifies the field as containing a particular type of cataloging information. This tag is carried as a three-character field as the first element of a record directory entry.

2. *Length.* This is a four-character field, which tells the length in characters of the variable field being described by the record directory entry.

3. *Starting Character Position.* This field indicates the starting character position of the variable field relative to the first character of the record.

Variable Control Number is a unique number assigned to a MARC record.

1. *Indicators.* Indicators are codes associated with a field which supply additional information about the field. They were formerly carried in the directory but now are placed at the beginning of the fields with which they are associated.

2. *Prefix and LC Card Number.* This is an eleven-character field which contains the LC stock number which uniquely identifies this cataloging information as pertaining to this particular work.

3. *Check Digit.* This is a number that is derived by performing a set of

mathematical operations on the digits in the LC card number and is used as a check on the accuracy of the LC card number.

4.   *Supplement Number.* Supplements are treated as separate entities. The field is blank if the work is not a supplement. If it is a supplement, this field contains the supplement number.

Variable Fixed Fields. Such units of information are always expressed in the same number of characters. The fixed fields are those for which there are no equivalents on the LC catalog card, but the information supplied in them is implied in most cases by information on the card.

1.   *Indicators. (see above)*
2.   *Number of Directory Entries.* This field gives the number of entries in the Record Directory or, in other words, the number of variable fields in the record.
3.   *Date entered in file.* The date is given in six digits; two for the day, two for the month, and two for the year.
4.   *Date Code.* The date code refers to the date of publication. It tells whether the date is a known date (S), an unknown date (N), a multiple date (M), whether one of the digits is missing (Q), or whether the work is a reproduction (R).
5.   *Date 1.* This field contains the date of publication unless the date is not known.
6.   *Date 2.* This field contains the copyright date if it appears in the imprint statement, the date of the original publication if the work is a reproduction, and the terminal date if the date of publication consists of a multiple date.
7.   *Country Code.* This field contains a three-character mnemonic code for the place of publication.
8.   *Illustration Codes.* This field contains alphabetic codes for the types of illustrations in the work; for example, A—illustration, B—maps.
9.   *Intellectual Level.* This field indicates whether the work is a juvenile work.
10.   *Form of Reproduction.* This field indicates whether the work is a microfilm, microfiche, or micro-opaque.
11.   *Form of Contents.* This is a code to identify types of material used frequently for reference purposes; for example A—bibliography, B—catalog. The following fields are self-explanatory. If they apply to the work, this is indicated by the presence of a character in the field. If not, the field is blank.
12.   *Government Publication.*
13.   *Conference or Meeting.*
14.   *Festschrift.*
15.   *Index Present.*
16.   *Main Entry in Body.*

17. *Biography*.

18. *Fiction*.

19. *Language Code*. This is a three-character mnemonic code indicating the language of the text.

Variable Fields are ones not of fixed length. The variable fields correspond to the elements on the LC catalog card; for example, main entry, title, imprint, and so on. Each field is assigned a tag which identifies it; for instance, 100–main entry, personal name. These tags are listed in Figure 9.14.

Retrospective Conversion

Even when MARC II tapes become available, they will be limited, for some time, to current acquisitions. Each library considering the use of computers for production of catalogs therefore is faced with a problem. How is the file of catalog entries for the existing collection to be converted? Ultimately, the answer must be a national program of retrospective conversion of past catalog data, centered at the Library of Congress but involving the cooperative effort of a large number of major libraries throughout the United States. An initial project, called RECON, is now underway under sponsorship of the Library of Congress. Its immediate goal is to convert catalog data for English language monographs issued from 1967 to 1969. However, in the meantime, individual libraries will still need to convert catalog data. To do so involves two major steps: editing and key-boarding. The most difficult is the editing step, especially if the full detail of the MARC II format is desired. Few libraries can afford the investment it requires, and they have therefore adopted simplified formats, more or less compatible with MARC II, but with very limited identification of data elements.

Editing. The editing of source catalog records (for instance, catalog cards) to be converted to machine-readable form is the first major step in the input process. The Input Editor is provided with coding sheets, which contain preprinted spaces, check lists, and codes, together with a copy of the catalog card or facsimile of the record to be converted. The Input Editor has the job of writing predetermined field codes, identifying marks, separation symbols, and other instructional signals on the coding sheet. These marks and symbols, together with the catalog data itself, will then be key-punched by the operator of an input device for subsequent "reading in" to the computer.

The coding sheet is a preprinted form on which the input editor enters codes, catalog information, and other instructions necessary to generate a single record in the master tape of the inputting organization. The form shown in Figure 17.20 is an example of the coding sheet developed for implementation of the

Figure 17.20 University of California common input coding sheet—monographs.

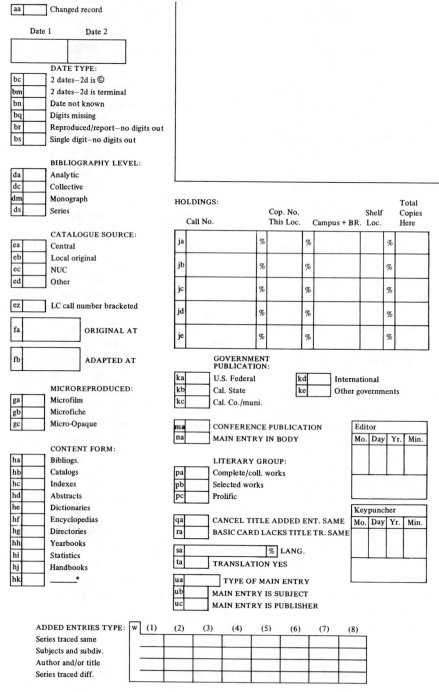

aa ☐ Changed record

Date 1   Date 2
☐   ☐

DATE TYPE:
bc ☐ 2 dates—2d is ©
bm ☐ 2 dates—2d is terminal
bn ☐ Date not known
bq ☐ Digits missing
br ☐ Reproduced/report—no digits out
bs ☐ Single digit—no digits out

BIBLIOGRAPHY LEVEL:
da ☐ Analytic
dc ☐ Collective
dm ☐ Monograph
ds ☐ Series

CATALOGUE SOURCE:
ea ☐ Central
eb ☐ Local original
ec ☐ NUC
ed ☐ Other

ez ☐ LC call number bracketed

fa ☐ ORIGINAL AT

fb ☐ ADAPTED AT

MICROREPRODUCED:
ga ☐ Microfilm
gb ☐ Microfiche
gc ☐ Micro-Opaque

CONTENT FORM:
ha ☐ Bibliogs.
hb ☐ Catalogs
hc ☐ Indexes
hd ☐ Abstracts
he ☐ Dictionaries
hf ☐ Encyclopedias
hg ☐ Directories
hh ☐ Yearbooks
hi ☐ Statistics
hj ☐ Handbooks
hk ☐ _____*

HOLDINGS:

	Call No.	Cop. No. This Loc.	Campus + BR. Loc.	Shelf Loc.	Total Copies Here
ja		%	%		%
jb		%	%		%
jc		%	%		%
jd		%	%		%
je		%	%		%

GOVERNMENT PUBLICATION:
ka ☐ U.S. Federal   kd ☐ International
kb ☐ Cal. State   ke ☐ Other governments
kc ☐ Cal. Co./muni.

ma ☐ CONFERENCE PUBLICATION
na ☐ MAIN ENTRY IN BODY

LITERARY GROUP:
pa ☐ Complete/coll. works
pb ☐ Selected works
pc ☐ Prolific

qa ☐ CANCEL TITLE ADDED ENT. SAME
ra ☐ BASIC CARD LACKS TITLE TR. SAME

sa ☐ ___ % LANG.
ta ☐ TRANSLATION YES

ua ☐ TYPE OF MAIN ENTRY
ub ☐ MAIN ENTRY IS SUBJECT
uc ☐ MAIN ENTRY IS PUBLISHER

Editor			
Mo.	Day	Yr.	Min.

Keypuncher			
Mo.	Day	Yr.	Min.

ADDED ENTRIES TYPE: w ☐

	(1)	(2)	(3)	(4)	(5)	(6)	(7)	(8)
Series traced same								
Subjects and subdiv.								
Author and/or title								
Series traced diff.								

University of California Common Input Format for monograph catalog records.[50] A copy of the source catalog card would be attached.

It is hard to estimate the time required for such editing, and no firm data has yet been published. Approximately, however, production rates of 10 to 20 catalog entries per hour are to be expected, for an editing cost of about 50c to 75c per entry. Unfortunately, this estimate not only is approximate but is likely to be increased by any of a number of circumstances.

Keyboarding. In Chapter 11 we discussed the major methods of key-boarding. In general, conversion rates of 20 to 30 catalog records per hour can be expected, depending on the quality of the editing and the equipment available for key-boarding and input. This implies a cost, for direct labor and equipment, of about 30c to 40c per title. Of all the costs in conversion, this is the most well measured and the most likely to be reduced.

Continuing Maintenance

Aside from the use of MARC II tapes as a source of both retrospective data and continuing data, the ordering subsystem can also be the source of data for continuing maintenance of the catalog.

COMPUTER PROCESSING SYSTEMS

The decision of whether to use the computer requires careful, detailed, comparative analysis of the various methods for producing a book catalog. As in the other chapters, we approach this task by defining the quantitative variables that are significant in evaluating the cost of producing a book form of library catalog and the quality of the resulting product. Each method will be analyzed into its component productive operations, and equations will be developed that relate their costs to the significant variables.

General Schematic

Regardless of the particular method chosen, the production of the book catalog requires the following component steps.

(a)   Provision of the bibliographical entry citation.

(b)   Input of the citation and duplication for the required number of catalog entries.

---

[50] *Instruction Manual for Editorial Preparation of Catalog Source Data.* Berkely, California: Institute of Library Research, University of California, 12 April 1968.

(c)   Editing of the input to correct errors.

(d)   Sequencing or sorting of the new entries so as to put them into the appropriate order with respect to the existing catalog information.

(e)   Merging the new material with the existing catalog information.

(f)   Creation of the new page masters from which the catalogs will be produced.

(g)   Reproduction, collating, and binding to produce the requisite number of catalogs.

Figure 17.21 is a block flow diagram illustrating the sequence of these operations with respect to the various catalog production methods.[51] It can be seen from this figure that there are a large number of alternative procedures that can be utilized in producing a book catalog within most of the major methods. For example, virtually any card catalog can be utilized to produce a book catalog through the use of the first four methods for page master creation: typing pages, photographing of a shingled layout, photographing of a side-by-side layout, and photographing by use of a sequential camera. Although special arrangements are needed to use the other methods for page master creation, there are a similar number of choices that can be made.

The operations required to produce a book catalog (listed above) can be grouped into three categories: maintenance of the information file to be made into the catalog; creation of the catalog page masters; and reproduction of copies of the book catalog. The maintenance activities include introducing and duplicating new citations, merging them into the master file, changing records to correct errors, and deleting records for obsolete citations. The requirements for maintaining the catalog information file are virtually the same, regardless of the final form of the catalog—card or book. The costs of the operations in this category will be incurred simply to have available the information about the collection and, therefore, one may question whether they should be considered as a cost of book catalog production. They can be included to ensure a uniform treatment of all sources of cost. However, in establishing a true picture of the cost of the book catalog, particularly in arriving at a selling price for it, these catalog maintenance costs should probably be handled separately.

Furthermore, certain costs (such as those involved in keypunching) may become absorbed by other major functions. For example, an automated acquisition process within an integrated system would also take advantage of the keypunching and could therefore be assigned some proportion of those costs.

Creation of the catalog page master is, of course, a function whose costs are wholly assignable to the production of a book catalog. These costs depend on

[51] Hayes, Robert M., Ralph M. Shoffner, and David C. Weber, "The Economics of Book Catalog Production," *Library Resources and Technical Services*, **10** (Winter 1966), 57–90.

the number of pages created and, thus, on the total size of the collection and the catalog page layout chosen. Similarly, the reproduction operations are concerned solely with the production of a book catalog. Reproduction costs consist of a fixed set-up charge plus a "per-page copied" charge and, thus, are a function of the number of pages in the catalog and the total number of copies produced.

Because these variable costs are directly attributable to the publication of the catalog and are almost solely a function of the number of copies, it would probably be advisable to print only that number of copies for which there is a guaranteed market. This obviously includes those used in the library itself; it may also include those distributed to other departments. The ones that are anticipated for sale to students and others outside the library should be estimated very conservatively—the additional spread of fixed costs over a large printing does not compensate for the gamble with large variable costs.

The computer approach is of additional value if consideration is given to the possibilities of special bibliographies, easy catalog revision, integration with acquisitions, and similar fringe benefits. However, costs should not be allocated to these "intangible" benefits unless they are actually included in the design from the beginning. In other words, a system must be completely justified on the basis of all economic considerations involved in its own operation and *not* on some larger system considerations, "possible" extensions, intangible benefits, and similar arguments. On the other hand, if a system is judged to be economically competitive on its own merits, then the fringe benefits are of great significance. The results of this study indicate that the use of a computer for the production of a book catalog is competitive, and therefore the extended possibilities that it provides should be given consideration. In Chapters 19 and 20, we shall discuss some of the benefits from use of magnetic tape data for information retrieval, special bibliographies, and other information services.

ESTIMATION OF PROCESSING TIMES AND COSTS

Parameters for Estimation

The cost of producing a book form of library catalog and the quality of the resulting product are functions of three classes of variables or constraints that must be related to each other: (1) the characteristics of the collection to be cataloged, (2) the characteristics of the published catalog, and (3) the characteristics of the production method. The important variables in each of these classes have been defined and are listed in Figure 17.22. Where possible, normal or typical values are presented for each, but only for the sake of illustration and particular application to the illustrative library presented in Figure 14.11.

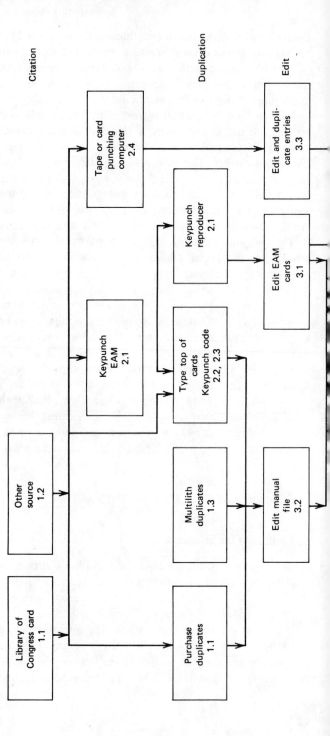

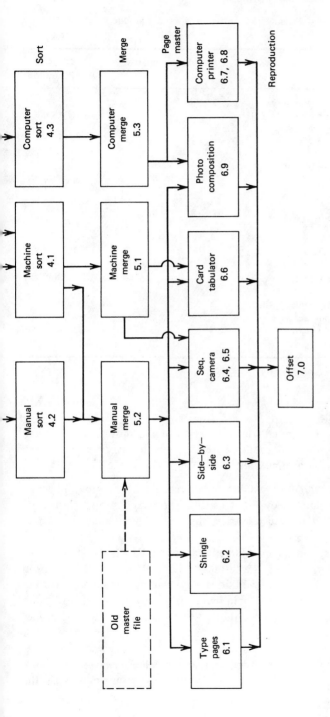

Figure 17.21 Flow-chart summary of book catalog production methods.

Figure 17.22   Parameters for estimation, catalog production.

		Representative Values	Illustration
1.	*Amounts of Activity (per Month)*		
	V_1 New titles (see also Figure 16.20)		5,000
	V_2 Supplements	1	1
2.	*Size of Records*		
	R_1 Full catalog record (average)	500	500
	R_2 Main entry record	300	300
	R_3 Added entry	180	180
	R_4 Shelf list entry	300	300
	R_5 Printed catalog entry (average)	200	200
3.	*Number of Records*		
	N_1 Size of collection (titles)		1,500,000
	N_2 Number of entries per title	5	5
	N_3 Size of supplement (titles)		30,000
4.	*Size of Output*		
	O_1 Number of catalog copies produced		100
	O_2 Number of columns per page	2	2
	O_3 Number of lines per entry	5	5
	O_4 Number of lines per page	60	60

Illustration

Figure 17.23(*a*) to (*e*) presents an estimation of the processing times and costs for production of a book catalog by each of the primary methods. They are based on the following assumptions.

Key-Boarding and Input. In a manual system, cards must be provided for all entries. These can be purchased, but it usually is less expensive to photocopy and multilith them. Then, for added entries, filing data and call numbers must be key-boarded.

For the computer systems, it is assumed that catalog data is already available in machine-readable form, either as a result of the ordering subsystem or from MARC II tapes. In the former case, additional keyboarding is required to correct and update original bibliographic data; in the latter, to provide the identification (such as LC card number or short author title) necessary to select the proper catalog data from tapes; even in an on-line system, the key-boarding of identification data is necessary. It has been assumed that, in any case, about 30 percent of the data must be key-boarded (that is, about 150 characters per title). Since retrospective conversion is such a major task and occurs only once, the

Sub-System									
Catalog Production			File	Card Catalog (Master and Branch)					
Level of Analysis: Component									
Personnel and Equipment									
Level of Analysis: Function									
Sub-System Schematic									
Basic Unit of Work									
Catalog Entry									

Comp.	Operation	Number	X	Size	X	Freq. /	Rate	=	Time	X	Cost	X	%=	Total
Cler. Pers.	Purchase Cards	5000									$ .10 each			$ 500
	Photocopying*	25,000				2**	600 /hr		83		6/hr		100	498
	Keyboarding	20,000		30 chars		2**	10,000 chars/hr		120		3/hr		100	360
	Sorting	25,000				2**	10 /min		83		3/hr		100	249
	Filing (Master File)	25,000		into 7.5 million		1	.04 ent/sec		174		3/hr		100	522
	Filing (Branch File)	25,000		into .3 million		1	.12 ent/sec		58		3/hr		100	174
	Total	5000 titles							518 hours					$2303
				*Less expensive than purchase of cards										
				**Entries for two catalogs, a master and a branch.										
	TOTAL													
	COST/EFFECTIVENESS =													

Date _____   Analyst _____   Page _____

Study _____

Figure 17.23a Estimation of processing times and cost. Manual system (filing directly into master file each month).

Sub-System				File					
Catalog Production				Master Catalog					

Level of Analysis: Component
Personnel and Equipment

Level of Analysis: Function
Sub-System Schematic

Basic Unit of Work
Catalog Entry

Comp.	Operation	Number X	Size X	Freq. /	Rate =	Time X	Cost X	% =	Total
Cler. Pers.	Keyboarding	5000	500 chars	1	6000 chars/hr	420	$ 3/hr	100	$1260
	Sorting	25,000		1	30 /min	14	3/hr	100	42
	Filing into Cumulative	250,000	into avg 150,000	1	.12 /sec	60	3/hr	100	180
	Yearly filing into master--	300,000	into 7.5	1 /12	.08 /sec	87	3/hr	100	261
	prorated over 12 months		million						
	Subtotals					581			1743
Equip. &	Set-Up Time			6 batches	.05 /hr	.3	6/hr	100	2
Oper. Pers.	Duplicating	5000	10 cards	4	100 /min	33	6/hr	100	198
	Output of Supplement	150,000 avg.	200 chars	1	200 chars/sec	42	6/hr	100	252
	Output of Master	7,500,000	200 chars	1 /12	200 chars/sec	168	6/hr	100	1008
	Subtotals					243 hours			$1460
	TOTAL								$3203
	COST/EFFECTIVENESS =								

Date

Analyst

Page

Study

Figure 17.23b Punched-card system (monthly cumulative supplement and yearly master).

Sub-System					File					
Catalog Production					Master Catalog					

Level of Analysis: Component
Personnel and Equipment

Level of Analysis: Function
Sub-System Schematic

Basic Unit of Work
Catalog Entry

Comp.	Operation	Number	X Size	X Freq.	/ Rate	= Time	X Cost	X %	= Total
Cler. Pers.	Keyboarding	5000	150	1	6000 chars/hr	125	$ 3/hr	100	$ 375
	Subtotals					125			375
Equip. &	Set-Up Time			3 batches	.02 chars/hr	.1	30/hr	100	3
Oper. Pers.	Input	5000	150	1	600 chars/sec	.3	30/hr	100	9
	Search of Yearly File and order MARC Files	5000 vs 100,000	500 chars	1	7500 chars/sec	2	30/hr	100	60
	Duplication	5000	1 Stand. Oper.	4	250 /sec		30/hr	100	
	Sorting	25,000	500 chars	1	1000 chars/sec	4	30/hr	100	120
	Filing into Cumulative File	25,000 into 125,000	500 chars	1	7500 chars/sec	3	30/hr	100	90
	Output of Cumulative File	150,000	200 chars	1	600 chars/sec	14	30/hr	100	420
	Filing into Master File (prorated each month)	300,000 into 7.5 million	500 chars	1 /12	7500 chars/sec	12	30/hr	100	360
	Output of Yearly File (prorated each month)	7.5 million	200 chars	1 /12	600 chars/sec	60	30/hr	100	1800
	Subtotals					95 hours			$2862
TOTAL		5000 titles							$3237
COST/EFFECTIVENESS =									

Date _____   Analyst _____   Page _____

Study _____

Figure 17.23c   Small-scale batch computer (monthly cumulative supplements and yearly master file).

Sub-System			File							
Catalog Production			Master Catalog							

Level of Analysis: Component
Personnel and Equipment

Level of Analysis: Function
Sub-System Schematic

Basic Unit of Work
Catalog Entry

Comp.	Operation	Number	X	Size	X	Freq.	/	Rate	=	Time	X	Cost	X	%	=	Total
Cler. Pers.	Keyboarding	5000		150		1		6000 chars/hr		125		$ 3/hr		100		$ 375
	Subtotals									125						375
Equip. & Oper. Pers.	Set-Up Time					3 batches										
	Input	5000		150		1		2000 chars/sec		.1		225/hr		20		5
	Search of MARC and Order Files	5000 vs 100,000		500 chars		1		25,000 chars/sec		.5		225/hr		20		25
	Sorting	25,000		500 chars		1		2000 chars/sec		2		225/hr		20		90
	Filing into avg. Cumulative File	150,000		500 chars		1		25,000 chars/sec		1		225.hr		20		46
	Output of Cumulative File	150,000		200 chars		1		2000 chars/sec		4		225/hr		20		180
	Filing into Master Catalog	300,000 into 7.5 million		500 chars		1 /12		25,000 chars/sec		3		225/hr		20		135
	(prorated over 12 months)															
	Output of Yearly File	7.5 million		200 chars		1 /12		2000 chars/sec		17		225/hr		20		765
	Subtotals									59 hours						$1246
TOTAL		5000 titles														$1621
COST/EFFECTIVENESS =																

Date _____   Analyst _____   Page _____

Study _____

Figure 17.23d   Large-scale batch computer (monthly cumulative supplements and yearly interfile).

Sub-System Catalog Production					File Master Catalog					
Level of Analysis: Component Personnel and Equipment										
Level of Analysis: Function Sub-System Schematic										
Basic Unit of Work Catalog Entry										
Comp.	Operation	Number X	Size X	Freq. /	Rate =	Time X	Cost X	% =	Total
Cler. Pers.	Keyboarding	5000	150	1	6000 chars/hr	125	$ 3/hr	100	$ 375
	Subtotals					125			375
Equip. & Oper. Pers.	Set-Up Time								
	Input	5000	150	1	2000 chars/sec	.4	625 hr	4	10
	Search of MARC and Order Files	5000 vs 100,000	500 chars	1	50,000 chars/sec	.3	625/hr	4	7
	Sorting	25,000	500 chars	1	3000 chars/sec	1.2	625/hr	4	30
	Filing into avg. Cumulative File	150,000	500 chars	1	50,000 chars/sec	.5	625/hr	4	11
	Output of avg. Cumulative File	150,000	200 chars	1	2000 chars/sec	4	625/hr	4	100
	Filing into Master Catalog	300,000 into 7.5 million	500 chars	1	50,000 chars/sec	1.5	625/hr	4	43
	Output of Yearly Catalog	7.5 million	200 chars	1	2000 chars/sec	17	625/hr	4	425
	Subtotals					25 hours			$ 626
	TOTAL								$1001
	COST/EFFECTIVENESS =								

Date _____   Analyst _____   Page _____

Study _____

Figure 17.23e   Large-scale batch computer (monthly cumulative supplements and yearly master).

costs of it are not included. However a rough estimate of $1 per entry (60c for editing and 40c for key-boarding) should be both reasonable and conservative (although not for MARC II format).

Sorting. Each input record must be "exploded" into the number of entries that will appear in the printed catalog—main entry, title entry, subject entries, and the like. Then, the entire set must be sorted into filing order. It has been assumed that each title will generate a total of five entries. For a manual system, this must also be multiplied by the number of card catalogs to be maintained. Usually, entries will be filed into both a main catalog and a branch catalog, for example. It has therefore been assumed, for the manual system only, that two card catalogs must be maintained.

In a punched card system, it frequently is the case that manual sorting and filing is less expensive than mechanized; the estimates are therefore based on such manual operation; the times are based on Figure 12.5.

File Access. Catalog access is required both for the purpose of merging new entries into the master file (usually by sequential access) and for obtaining catalog data from it. Access for on-line interrogation is discussed in Chapter 20.

Output. For purposes of these estimates, it has been assumed that entries will average 200 characters (considering both full main entries and shorter added entries) and will require five lines of printing, including a blank line between entries. The volume of output is a function of three things: (1) the number of different listings to be produced (catalogs, shelf lists, supplements, and special bibliographies), (2) the frequency of printing supplements,and (3) the schedule for reprinting the master catalog. Below, we will discuss the scheduling of supplements and will use that schedule in the estimates for machine produced book catalog output.

Printing and Distribution. Estimates have been included for printing and distribution as a separate set of figures in Figure 17.24.[52]

Processing of Supplements

The size of catalogs and indexes is usually so large that they cannot economically be maintained on a completely current basis. At the very least, new entries must be batched and sorted into filing order for merging into the master file. Usually, supplementary files must be created in order to produce a size of batch large enough to warrant the costs of reprocessing and reprinting the entire master file. Sometimes, a number of such supplementary files are produced and maintained.

[52] *Ibid.*

Figure 17.24   Costs of offset printing.
(The prices shown are for black ink on 20 or 16 white bond.)

Paper size	Number of copies	Price per copy	Price per run	Number of passes per copy side	Number of pages per sheet side	Price per Multilith master	Price per offset master	Price per Multilith copy page	Price per offset copy page
8½ x 11in.	100	$.001	$.003	1	1	$2.00	$5.50	$.024	$.059
8½ x 11in.	500	.001	.003	1	1	2.00	5.50	.008	.015
8½ x 11in.	1000	.001	.003	1	1	2.00	5.50	.006	.010
11 x 17in.	100	.025	.005	1	2	–	8.00	–	.044
11 x 17in.	500	.0025	.005	1	2	–	8.00	–	.012
11 x 17in.	1000	.0025	.005	1	2	–	8.00	–	.008

The need for supplements is most clearly evident with printed book catalogs and indexes, because the cost of a complete reprinting of a master catalog is prohibitive. As a result, supplements and cumulative supplements are commonplace. It must be emphasized, however, that anyone maintaining a card catalog of any size faces an equivalent problem and must utilize supplementary catalogs because of the almost equally prohibitive costs of merging small sets of entries into very large files of cards.

The two kinds of catalogs thus reflect the different effects of two problems in maintenance of a catalog: the costs of merging and the costs of printing. For a manually maintained card catalog, printing is of negligible cost, since it is done once and only once for each entry; merging can be very expensive because of the time required to find entry positions in a large catalog. For a computer-produced book catalog, merging is of negligible cost because of the data-handling rates of the computer; printing can be almost prohibitively expensive.

Figure 17.25(*a*) presents a tabulation of the costs to be expected in the maintenance of the master card catalog of the illustrative library (of Figure 14.11) under various alternative strategies for maintaining supplements. The estimated rates for merging are based on Figure 12.5. The first strategy is to merge each month's new entries directly into the master catalog (if the same thing were done on a weekly basis the costs would go up even another 20%). The second strategy is to maintain a yearly cumulative supplement; at the end of the year, it is then merged into the master file. The third alternative is to maintain a cumulative supplement one year, a second the next; at the end of the second year, the two are merged together and then the pair into the master file.

Figure 17.25(*b*) presents another set of three alternative strategies as they would apply to production of printed book catalogs. The estimated costs are taken as those of the large-scale batch system of Figure 14.9.

Sub-System				File						
Processing Card Catalog Supplement				Catalog Supplement						

Level of Analysis: Component
Personnel and Equipment

Level of Analysis: Function
Sub-System Schematic

Basic Unit of Work
Card Entry

Comp.	Operation	Number	X	Size	X	Freq.	/	Rate	=	Time	X	Cost	X	%	=	Total
Cler. Pers.		Monthly Merging Directly into Master File														
	Merging	25,000		into 7,500,000		12 /yr		.04 ent/sec		2080		$ 3/hr		100		$6240
Cler. Pers.		Monthly Merging into an Annual Cumulative Supplement														
	Merging	25,000		into avg 150,000		12 /yr		.12 ent/sec		695		3/hr		100		$2085
		Yearly Merging Annual Cumulative into Master File														
	Merging	300,000		into 7,500,000		1 /yr		.1 ent/sec		830		3/hr		100		2490
	Total									1260 hours						$4575
Cler. Pers.		Maintaining Annual Cumulatives for Two Years														
	Merging	25,000		into avg 150,000		24 /2yrs		.2 ent/sec		830		3/hr		100		$2490
		Merging Year 1 into Year 2														
	Merging	300,000		into 300,000		1 /2yrs		.25 ent/sec		335		3/hr		100		1005
		Merging Combined Cumulative into Master File														
	Merging	600,000		into 7,500,000		1 /2yrs		.15		1110		3/hr		100		3330
						Two year Total				2275 hours						$6825
						Average per Year				1140 hours						$3410
	TOTAL															
	COST/EFFECTIVENESS =															

Date _____ Analyst _____ Page _____

Study _____

Figure 17.25a   Processing of supplements. Manual system.

Sub-System Processing Book Catalog Supplement				File Catalog Supplement						
Level of Analysis: Component Personnel and Equipment										
Level of Analysis: Function Sub-System Schematic										
Basic Unit of Work Book Entry										
Comp.	Operation	Number X	Size X	Freq. /	Rate =	Time X	Cost X	% =	Total
Equip. & Oper. Pers.	Printing Base Catalog	7,500,000	500 chars	1 /yr	2000 chars/sec	500	$225/hr	20	$22,500
Equip. & Oper. Pers.	Printing Monthly Cumulative Supplements	avg. 150,000	500 chars	12 /yr	2000 chars/sec	125	$225/hr	20	$ 5625
Equip. & Oper. Pers.	Printing Monthly Supplements	25,000	500 chars	12 /yr	2000 chars/sec	21	$225/hr	20	945
	Printing Qrtly. Cumulative Supplements	75,000	500 chars	4 /yr	2000 chars/sec	21	$225/hr	20	945
	Printing Yearly Cumulative Supplement	300,000	500 chars	1 /yr	2000 chars/sec	21	$225/hr	20	945
	Totals								$2835
	TOTAL								
	COST/EFFECTIVENESS =								

Date _____   Analyst _____   Page _____

Study _____

Figure 17.25b   Large-scale batch system.

651

Of course, the difficulty with supplements is that they increase the number of files in which users of the catalog must search for data. If finding data in one catalog takes 30 seconds, having a look for it in three more supplements could make finding the data take four times as long. Clearly, in arriving at a strategy of use of supplements, the costs of producing catalogs must be weighed against the costs of using them.

Suggested Readings

The following provide especially valuable coverage of the issues in production of catalogs and indexes:

Avram, Henriette D., et al., *The MARC II Format.* Washington, D.C.: Library of Congress, Jan 1968.

This presents details of the organization of bibliographic records, "the MARC II Format," as established for communication among libraries. It is essential to any library contemplating a mechanization effort.

"The Book Catalog," *Library Resources and Technical Services*, 8 (Fall 1964), 349-398

This is a series of articles by Ralph Parker, Margaret C. Brown, Phyllis A. Richmond, Robert Jones, Catherine MacQuarrie, George Moreland, Ida Harris, and Wesley Simonton.

Harrison, John, and Peter Laslett (eds.), *The Brasenose Conference on the Automation of Libraries.* London: Mansell, 1966.

This is the report of a conference, held at Oxford in 1966. It initiated from a concern at Oxford, Cambridge, and the British Museum about how best to produce catalogs of their respective holdings.

Hayes, Robert M., Ralph M. Shoffner, and David Weber, "The Economics of Book Catalog Production," *Library Resources and Technical Services,* **10** (1) 1966, pp 57-89.

This is the report of a study to determine the aspects of importance in evaluating the costs of producing book catalogs by various methods.

Chapter 18

SERIALS RECORDS SUB-SYSTEM

INTRODUCTION

The "Glossary of Library Terms" of the American Library Association defines a serial as " . . . a publication issued in successive parts, usually at regular intervals, and as a rule intended to be continued indefinitely. Serials include periodicals, annuals (reports and yearbooks), and memoirs, proceedings, and transactions of societies." The continuing nature of serials gives rise to the need for repeated updating of the records and requires the creation of a special subsystem of the library for serials processing.[1]

In general, the initial ordering, the cataloging, and the circulation of a serial parallels that for a monograph, as discussed in the preceding three chapters. There are, however, several features that are unique to the handling of these functions for serials. In particular, the continued receipt of the successive issues of a serial and the recurring necessity for renewing subscriptions are points of departure from monographic acquisition. Another point of departure arises in the cases where serial publications are a benefit of membership in an association or society, since the serial record must contain membership data in addition. Even the data recorded in a catalog will be more extensive than it is for a monograph, since it must describe not only the serial but also the library's holdings. Furthermore, since journals frequently have changes in name, the catalog entries must provide tracings from prior names and variant names to the present one. Finally, libraries usually will bind sets of successive issues into bound volumes, so that a serials systems must satisfy the added requirement of

[1] Whelstone, G., "Serials Practices in Selected Colleges and University Libraries", *Library Resources and Technical Services,* 4 (Fall 1961), 284-290.

controlling when such binding should be done—a function without any parallel in monographic control.

These functions require relatively large amounts of data for each serial record and frequent repetitive record keeping. Taken together, this has implied that processing of serial records would be an especially attractive application for computers.

Functions

Figure 18.1 presents an overall schematic of the functions required in a serials record subsystem. There are six principal functions: ordering and accounting, cataloging and identification, receiving and claiming, binding, reader services, and management.

Ordering and Accounting. The processes for initial ordering of a serial, in principle, are comparable to those for monographs; however, there are sufficient

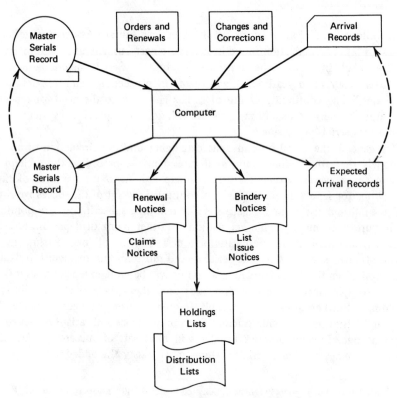

Figure 18.1   Serials record subsystem schematic.

differences (such as multiple subscriptions due to membership in an association or society) to require that the entire ordering process be included as part of the serials subsystem. This means that the functions outlined in Chapter 16 must be considered again in the design of the serials subsystem, including procedures for requesting, approving, searching and checking, ordering, and accounting. But we shall not review these here.

It is in the area of continuing subscriptions and membership that the significant additional functions occur. Periodically, renewals must be generated. This requires that the master serials record contain data on renewal dates and amounts. The identification of vendors or societies from whom to order must be included as well. And procedures to scan the serial records for renewal dates and to output renewal orders must be an integral part of the processing programs.

Cataloging. The processes for cataloging of serials and for production of printed catalogs of them are the same as those for monographs. The only real complication represented in cataloging is the need for added entries for variant names or older names of a given serial. For example, variant names will arise from transliterated and translated titles (of foreign journals); a given journal may become two journals, sometimes with the same basic name but two different series, sometimes with different names; two journals may merge into one; and so on. Furthermore, unlike monographic titles, which are likely to be cited correctly, serial titles tend to be cited in widely variant ways: "Proceedings of the American Mathematical Society," "American Mathematical Society Proceedings", and the like.[2]

This means that the cataloger must be aware of the variants and of the older names when originally cataloging a serial. But it also means that subsequent changes in title may lead to revision of catalog entries.

The problem of uniquely identifying serials has led some to suggest a standard system of serial numbering.[3] The best established is the CODEN system (Figure 18.2).[4] Maintained under the cognizance of the American Society for Testing and Materials it consists of a 5-character alpha-numeric code assigned to serials on a worldwide basis. It has been adopted by several indexing and abstracting services (such as Chemical Abstracts Service) as the basis for controlling union lists and computer operations. Other efforts include those by the ALA Joint Committee on Universal Numbering Systems,[5] the British Standard Book

---

[2] Tompkins, Mary L., *MAST: Minimum Abbreviations of Serial Titles—Mathematics.* Los Angeles: Western Periodicals Company, 1969.

[3] Harrer, G. A., and Alex Ladenson, "A Proposal for a National Code Number System for Current Publications," *Library Resources and Technical Services*, 6 (2) (Winter 1962), 4-12.

[4] Saxl, Lea, "Some Thoughts on CODEN," *Special Libraries*, 59 (April 1968), 279-280.

[5] ALA Joint Committee on Universal Numbering Systems.

Figure 18.2   Illustrative CODEN codes

The following is a list of journal names, primarily from the field of Physics, and their associated CODEN abbreviations.

Acta Phys. Austria.	APASA
Acta Phys. Austria. Suppl.	APAUA
Acta Phys. Polon.	APPOA
American J. Phys.	AJPIA
Ann. Inst. Henri Poincare	AIHPA
Annalen Phys. (Germany)	ANPYA
Annales Phys. (France)	ANPHA
Annals Phys. (New York)	APNYA
Ann. Math.	ANMAA
Ark. Fys.	AFYSA
Astron J.	ANJOA
Astrophys. J.	ASJOA
Aust. J. Phys.	AUJPA
Bull. Amer. Phys. Soc.	BAPSA
Can. J. Phys.	CJPHA
Commun. Math. Phys.	CMPHA
Dokl. Akad. Nauk USSR	DANKA
Fortschr. Phys.	FPYKA
Helv. Phys. Acta	HPACA
Indian J. Phys.	IJUPA
Ind. Acad. Sci. Proc.	PIASA
Jap. J. Phys.	JAJPA
JETP, see Soviet Phys. JETP	
J. De Physique	JAJPA
J. De Physique et de Radium	JPRAA
J. De Physique et de Radium Suppl.	JPRUA
J. Appl. Phys.	JAPIA
J. Chem. Phys.	JCPSA
J. Geophys. Res.	JGREA
J. Math. Phys.	JMAPA
J. Phys. Chem.	JPCHA
J. Phys. Soc. Jap.	JUPSA
J. Phys. Soc. Jap. Suppl.	JPJSA
J. Sci. Instrum.	JSINA
Kong, Dan Mat.-Fys. Med.	KDVSA
K. Dan. Mat.-Fys. Shrifter	KVMFA
Nature	NATUA
Naturwiss.	NATWA
Nucl. Instrum. Methods	NUIMA
Nucl. Instrum. Methods Suppl.	NIMSA
Nucl. Phys.	NUPHA
Nuovo Cim.	NUCIA
Nuovo Cim. Suppl.	NUCUA
Phil. Mag.	PHMAA

Figure 18.2   (Continued)

Physica	PHYSA
Phys. Rev.	PHRVA
Phys. Rev. Lett.	PRLTA
Phys. Lett.	PHLTA
Physics	PYCSA
Proc. Natl. Acad. Sci.	PNASA
Proc. Cambridge Phil. Soc. Proc.	PCPSA
Proc. Cambridge Phil. Soc. Trans.	TCPSA
Proc. Phys. Math. Soc. Japan	PPMJA
Proc. Phys. Soc.	PPSOA
Proc. Roy. Soc.	PRSLA
Prog. Theor. Phys.	PTPKA
Prog. Theor. Phys. Suppl.	PTPSA
Rev. Sci. Intrum.	RSINA
Rev. Mod. Phys.	RMPHA
Soviet J. Nucl. Phys.	SJNCA
Sov. Physics Jetp	SPHJA
Sov. Phys. Usp. (Eng. Transl.)	SOPUA
Sov. Physics, Jetp Letters	JTPLA
Yadernaya Fiz.	YAFIA
Z. Naturforsch.	ZNTFA
Z. Phys.	ZEPYA
ZH. Eksp. Teor. Fiz.	ZETFA

Numbering System,[6] and the Z–39 Committee (of USASI) on Periodical Title Abbreviations.[7] The latter has specifically proposed that the cover of every periodical issue include a coded identification of the issue, consisting of the CODEN for the title, the volume and issue number, the pagination, and the date of issue.[8]

Receiving and Claiming. The receiving function, including all of the necessarily related operations in maintaining records and claiming, is the major component of any serial records subsystem. For even a moderately large library, it creates a truly enormous work load. For example, a typical university library with 25,000 active serials might receive as many as 100,000 different individual issues each year—an average of 300 to 500 per day. Each issue must be checked for validity, and the master records must be updated; if items are not received when due, appropriate action must be taken to claim them from the supplier—which may be the publisher, or the agent, or the society, or someone else; and if items are defective, they must be returned.

[6] British Standard Book Numbering System.
[7] Pratt, Alan D., "Standardizing Periodical Title Abbreviations," *Special Libraries* (February 1964), 109-111.
[8] Standards for Periodicals, *Format and Arrangements*, USASI (Z-39 Committee), 1967.

Receiving adds up to a staggering data processing work load. It is therefore the crucial function in evaluating the cost and processing time of the serial subsystem. As we shall see, a variety of approaches have been taken to the problem of providing input to a computer system without the back-breaking cost of key-boarding massive amounts of data each day—tub files of reentry punched cards, one for each expected issue; lists of expected receipts; machine-readable data printed on the journal; and the like.

Claiming is a derivative function, of much smaller magnitude but with its own complications. Specifically, at what point in time does a delay in receipt imply that the issue has been lost? The answer is not simple. Journals can be irregular; issues may be published out of order; foreign materials may be delayed in the mail. Furthermore, there may be cases, such as a supplement to an issue, for which there are no immediate clues that an issue should have been received. In general, therefore, it is to be expected that claiming will require a combination of machine reporting and professional judgment.

Binding. The decision that the library has received (or should have received) all of the issues of a serial to be bound together is also a complex decision process, dependent on a number of aspects of the bound journal.[9] Is an index to be included, and has it been received? How many issues are to be bound together in a single volume? When are a set of issues to be bound to go to the bindery? The purpose of the binding function is to apply these decision rules to each of the master serial records and produce the output records needed to have the specified issues brought together, sent to the bindery, bound appropriately, returned, and the results reflected in the serials holding records.

Closely related to the binding function is that of missing issue control—both as it relates to issues that the master record shows are missing and those that are discovered to be missing.

Reader Services. This function includes the control of distribution of material, as it is received, as well as the publication of holding lists readily available for the public to use. The problems in producing holdings lists are not much different from those in producing any catalog or index (as covered in Chapter 17) except for the frequency with which they must be produced to be up to date.

Management. Because of the magnitude of the work load, management data is especially important in serials control. Unit cost data, production rates in receiving, financial status—all are a necessary part of the serials record subsystem.

[9] Bishop, David, et al., "Publication Patterns of Scientific Serials," *American Documentation,* **16** (2) (April 1965), 113-121.

Existing Serials Mechanization Programs

Although the functions outlined above seem to suggest that serials data processing is a "natural" for mechanization, it has proved to be one of the most difficult tasks undertaken in the application of computers to libraries. Uniformly, libraries have had to take an evolutionary approach, implementing no more than one or two functions at a time. Some have started with holdings lists; some, with ordering; some, with check-in.

University of California at San Diego. Probably the earliest use of the computer for serial record maintenance was started in 1961 at the University of California at San Diego.[10],[11] Two factors helped to influence their decision. (1) the availability of a computer facility on campus; and (2) the fact that the UCSD library was just starting and would be expanding its serial holdings at a prodigious rate. Pilot operation was completed in July 1962, and full operation has been underway since 1965.

As shown in Figure 18.3, the system calls for monthly output of punched cards for issues which are expected, for manual interfiling of them in a tub file of existing cards, for manual pulling of the cards at the time of receipt, and for entry of the cards to the computer for update of records. Holdings printouts are relatively sketchy and difficulties in control of numbering—with many variations from one journal to another—cause many irregular journals to be treated as regular. However, as a pioneer, this system has served as a model for most subsequent systems.

University of Illinois and Florida Atlantic University. In particular, the designers of these two systems regarded them as expansions of the San Diego one rather than radical departures from it. They are similar to each other, since Mssrs. Heiliger, Culbertson, Schultheiss, and Kozlow influenced both. The Chicago Campus of the University of Illinois started its developments in 1962 and had an operational system in 1965.[12],[13] The Florida Atlantic system was started in 1964.[14]

[10] *Report on Serials Computer Project.* San Diego, California: University Library and Computer Center, University of California, San Diego, July 1962.

[11] Vdovin, George, and Melvin J. Voigt et al., "Computer Processing of Serial Records," *Library Resources and Technical Services*, 7 (1) (Winter 1963), 71-80.

[12] Heiliger, Edward, "Application of Advanced Data Processing Techniques to University Library Procedures," *Special Libraries*, 53 (9) (October 1962), 472-475.

[13] Schultheiss, Louis A., "Two Serial Control Card Files Developed at the University of Illinois, Chicago," *Library Resources and Technical Services*, 9 (3) (Summer 1965), 271-287.

[14] Srygley, Ted F., "Serials Record Instructions for a Computerized Serial System," *Library Resources and Technical Services*, 8 (3) (Summer 1964), 248-256.

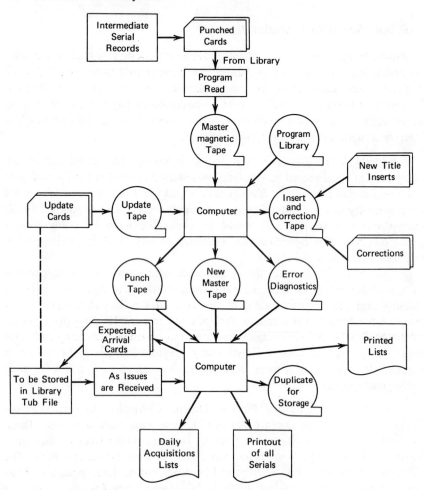

Figure 18.3   UC San Diego serials holding records system.

Washington University School of Medicine. Since 1963, the Washington University School of Medicine has maintained a holdings list with the aid of the computer.[15] The list of holdings for each of some 2500 titles is kept on magnetic tape, updated once a month, and printed out in its entirety. The monthly list is supplemented by daily lists which are cumulated weekly. When needed, other lists are also produced. Figure 18.4 is a schematic for this progression of holdings lists.

[15] Brodman, Estelle, Irwin H. Pizer, and Donald R. Franz, "Mechanization of Library Procedures in the Medium-Sized Medical Library: I. The Serial Record," *Bulletin of the Medical Library Association,* **51** (3) (July 1963), 313-338.

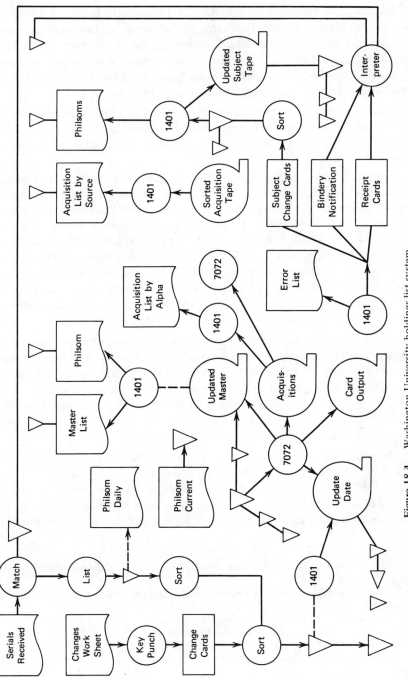

Figure 18.4 Washington University holdings list system.

661

University of California at Los Angeles Biomedical Library. In 1964, the Biomedical Library of the University of California at Los Angeles started development of a computer based system for serial check-in. It has been operational since 1966. It differs from other systems in its use of a complete system for counting, or numbering issues based on publication patterns, from which it could predict the identification of issues to be received.[16]

Texas A & M. This system has been proposed as a logical successor to the UCSD-UI-FAU systems.[17] It would include reentry cards (as do the other systems) for control of receiving, but proposed that vastly more data be recorded on them.

New York State Library. In June 1966, the New York State Library began an "Automated Serials Acquisition Project" as its first step in computerization of library functions.[18] Its aim was to provide more positive control over acquisition and maintenance of their serials holdings while at the same time making current information more readily available to both staff and public. It presently is implemented on a GE 235, batch mode processing. Plans are to implement an on-line mode system in 1970. The present system differs from those like UCSD in its use of printed lists for receiving rather than punched cards. This means that manual filing and pulling of cards are eliminated, but data must be keyboarded, using the printed list as a control record, instead.

University of California at Davis and Riverside. As part of a larger project for cooperative development of computer-based library systems, these two campuses of the University of California have been working together since 1966 on the development of a complete serials record system.[19] It combines the use of printed lists, as in the NYSL system, with the use of prenumbered punched cards—the listing for a given journal issue indicating the card number to be used for entry, the card number being otherwise meaningless.

Chemical Abstract Service. A somewhat different, yet vitally important aspect of the serial record problem is represented by the production and use of union lists of serials. One effort in this direction was that started in 1967 by Chemical Abstracts Services.[20] Through cooperative arrangement with all the major research libraries of the country, complete verifications were made of the

---

[16] Bishop, David, et al., *op. cit.*

[17] Stewart, B. W., *Data Processing in the Texas A & M University Library*, 1966 (mimeographed) (thesis).

[18] *New York State Library Automated Serials Acquisition Project: Summary Description*, SUNY, Albany, May 1968.

[19] Newton, Gerald D., *Design Specifications for . . . a Computer Based Serials Control System.* Davis, California: General Library, University of California, Davis and Institute of Library Research, N.D. (1967).

[20] "Chemical Abstracts Introduces ACCESS," *Chemical and Engineering News,* 47 (March 31, 1969), 46.

holdings each had of a set of some 5000 journal titles of importance to chemistry. CAS prepared a consolidated Union List, called ACCESS, of the reports from the participating libraries, using the computer.

National Serials Data Program. In this respect, the joint program of the Library of Congress, the National Library of Medicine, and the National Agricultural Library for the development of a National Serials Data Program occupies a crucial position.[21] Started early in 1968, the program is aimed at the use of the computer for control of serials literature in every subject field. As the first step in doing so, a survey was taken, at major libraries throughout the United States to determine what data elements should be recorded in centralized national records of serial holdings.[22] Subsequent stages were contracted to the Association of Research libraries, starting in 1969.

The Problems in Conversion to a Serials System Conversion to a new serials system is complicated by the desire to ensure that the data is accurate, up to date, and consolidated. This frequently means that in addition to the usual problems of editing and key-boarding, one must consider making a physical inventory and bringing together a diversity of existing records. Furthermore, since the existing records are already an integral part of on-going day to day operations, great care must be taken in conversion to ensure that it does not interfere with operations and that incoming data after conversion is included in both the existing records and the new ones.

FORMS AND FILES

A serials record system is relatively limited in terms of the number of files which it involves. One is crucial—the Master Serial Records File. All data comes to it and all output is generated from it. A second file, from which machine-readable data can be obtained for input, or at least a listing which can be used to control key-punching, is usually required as part of the receiving function. Other files—of vendor data and of funds—are required as part of the accounting functions, but these are simply counterparts of those discussed in Chapter 16.

A large variety of output lists are produced—holdings lists, bindery orders, routing lists, claiming letters, shelf lists, membership lists, receiving lists, expected arrival lists or cards, and the like.

---

[21] Woods, Elaine W., *National Serials Data Program (Phase 1): A Working Paper.* Washington, D.C.: Library of Congress Information Systems Office, August 1967.

[22] Curran, Ann T., and Henriette D. Avram, "The Identification of Data Elements in Bibliographical Records," *Final Report of the Special Project on Data Elements* (USASI), May 1967.

In this section, we shall discuss the nature and content of the Master Serial Records File the Receiving File (or List), and the various output lists.

Master Serials Data Record

Figure 18.5 presents the general description and Figure 18.6 presents a representative input record format for the Master Serial Records file, and Figure 18.7 presents details about the file itself. The record format can be divided into

Form Name _MASTER SERIALS DATA RECORD_						Form No. _R16_	
Other Names Used						Layout No.	
						Related Form Nos.	
						No. of Copies	
Media _MAGNETIC TAPE OR DISK_			How Prepared _KEYBOARDING_				
Operations Involved In _CATALOGING, ORDERING, RECEIVING,_							
BINDING HOLDINGS, AND DISTRIBUTION							
Remarks							

CONTENTS

No.	Data Name	Freq.	Characters			A/N	Origin
			Min.	95%	Max.		
40	ID OR CODED NO.				5	A/N	
41	MAIN ENTRY				67	A/N	
	HOLDINGS				100	A/N	
	LANGUAGE				1	A	
	PUBLISHING STATUS				1	N	
42	FREQUENCY				2	N	
	MEDIA				1	N	
	STATUS INDICATORS				5	N	
	CALL NUMBER				50	A/N	
	RECEIVING LOCATION				2	N	
	GENERIC LOCATION				2	N	
43	HOUSING LOCATION				2	N	
	DOMESTIC OR FOREIGN				1	N	
	CLAIMS CODES				3	N	
	BINDING DATA				180	A/N	

1968	JbR	Figure 18.5	1 of 2
Date	Analyst	Source	Page

Representative
/Study

Figure 18.5   Master serials data record description.

Form Name MASTER SERIALS DATA RECORD					Form No. R 16	
Other Names Used					Layout No.	
					Related Form Nos.	
					No. of Copies	
Media			How Prepared			
Operations Involved In						
Remarks						

CONTENTS

No.	Data Name	Freq.	Min.	95%	Max.	A/N	Origin
	ACCOUNTING DATA				200	A/N	
	DISTRIBUTION DATA						
	NAME	5	7	20	25	A	
	ADDRESS	5	30	50	60	A/N	

1968   LBR   Figure 18.5   2 of 2
Date   Analyst   Source   Page
Reorientation
Study

Figure 18.5   (*Continued*)

six main parts: cataloging data, ordering data, receiving data, binding data, holdings data, and distribution data.

Cataloging Data. This includes the standard cataloging data, as in any catalog record. It includes, for instance, name changes, alternative titles, and analytic entries for separately titled issues. It includes a unique serial identifier, which might be the CODEN. It may include a limited set of subject headings.

In addition to these more or less standardized and self-evident items of

SERIALS BASIC INPUT FORM — U.C. DAVIS		1. I.D. No.:		

			COL.	TYPE
2. FULL MAIN ENTRY:			1-67 Var. #	1

3. HOLDINGS:	COL.	**4. INCLUDE IN WANT LIST?**		
	1-37	(C) ___ Yes (I) ___ No	67	2

5. CALL NUMBER:	1-67 Var. #	3

6. DOCUMENT STATUS:		
(BL) ___ Not a Document (1) ___ Is a Document	1	4

7. PUBLIC HOLDINGS LIST SUPPRESSION:

(1) ___ Suppress From *Annual List* Only (3) ___ Total Suppress	4	4
(0) ___ Do Not Suppress (2) ___ Suppress From *Monthly List* Only		

8. MATERIAL IS CHECKED IN AT:

		(5) ___ Ag Econ	(8) ___ P.S.-Physics	
(1) ___ Gen Lib, Ser Rec	(3) ___ H.S. Lib	(6) ___ Docs Dept	(9) ___ Department	7-8
(2) ___ Law Library	(4) ___ Pri Ctr	(7) ___ P.S.-Chem	(10) ___ I.G.A.	4

9. GENERIC HOUSING OF MATERIAL IS:

(1) ___ Gen Lib, Other Than Docs	(6) ___ Documents Department	NUM: 10-11
(2) ___ Law Library	(7) ___ Chemistry Library	
(3) ___ Health Sciences Library	(8) ___ Physics - Geol Lib	ALPHA 12-25
(4) ___ Primate Center Library	(9) ___	
(5) ___ Ag Econ Library	(10) ___ IGA Library (Dept Name)	4

10. SPECIFIC POINT OF HOUSING IN GENERAL LIBRARY:

(1)___ Periodicals Room	(7)___ Libn Off	(13)___Reserve Coll	(18)___Microfilm Coll	
(2)___ Stacks	(8)___ Acq. Dept	(14)___Newspaper Coll	(19)___Coll. Dev.	
(3)___ Ag Exp Collection	(9)___ Cat. Dept	(15)___Bindery Prep	(20)___Staff Rm 1	28-29
(4)___ Ref Dept Coll	(10)___Ser. Dept	(16)___Asian Coll	(21)___Staff Rm 2	4
(5)___ Spec Collection	(11)___Loan Dept	(17)___Map Collection	(22)___Systems & Automation	
(6)___ Browsing Coll	(12)___Bib Ctr.			

11. MEDIA:

(Blank) ___ Original Paper Form	(4) ___ Phonodisc	
(1) ___ Microfilm	(5) ___ Score	33
(2) ___ Microfiche	(6) ___ Tape	4
(3) ___ Microcard		

12. CATALOGING STATUS PRINT CONTROL:

(BL) ___ Uncat., but you want a blank	(2) ___ Separate, individual call numbers	36
(1) ___ One Call No.	(0) ___ If you want word 'UNCATALOGED' printed	4

13. ACTIVITY STATUS:

(1) ___ Active subscription	(0) ___ Inactive (Dead; subscr. not active)	39
		4

14. BINDING TITLE, AREA 1:	1-67 Var. #	5

15. BINDING TITLE, AREA 2:	''	6

16. WORK MARK, AREA 3:	1-35	7

17. WORK MARK, AREA 4:	37-67	7

Figure 18.6   Representative input record format.

18. IS BINDING TITLE SAME AS FULL MAIN ENTRY, AND ONE WHICH DOES NOT REQUIRE AREA 1-2 SEGMENTATION? (1) ___ Yes (2) ___ No (If answer is yes, do not fill in 14-15)	1	8

19. STYLE OF BINDING MATERIAL:
  (1) ___ Buckram   (3) ___ Half Morocco   (5) ___ Quarter Bind
  (2) ___ Full Cloth   (4) ___ Portfolio
	3	8

20. COLOR OF BINDING MATERIAL:
  (1) ___ Black   (6) ___ Red
  (2) ___ Green   (7) ___ Purple
  (3) ___ Tan   (8) ___ Brown
  (4) ___ Gray   (9) ___ Maroon
  (5) ___ Blue   (10) ___ Orange
	5-6	8

21. NUMBER OF ISSUES PER BINDING VOLUME:	8-10	8

22. BINDING FREQUENCY (GENERAL):
  (0) ___ Monthly   (3) ___ Odd years only
  (1) ___ Annually or more often, but not monthly   (4) ___ Inactive binding status (Dead, comes bound, etc.)
  (2) ___ Even years only   (5) ___ Irregular, no pattern of frequency
	12	8

23. BINDING FREQUENCY (SPECIFIC) IF NUMBERS 1-3 CHECKED ABOVE:

BINDING SHOULD OCCUR IN THESE MONTHS:

	JAN	FEB	MAR	APR	MAY	JUN	JUL	AUG	SEP	OCT	NOV	DEC	14-48	8
NUMBER OF BINDING VOLS. ANTICIPATED:														
	14-15	17-18	20-21	23-24	26-27	29-30	32-33	35-36	38-39	41-42	44-45	47-48		

24. SPECIAL INSTRUCTIONS TO U.C. PRESS: 1. _____ (*) 3. _____ (*) 2. _____ (*) 4. _____ (*)	1-67	9

25. SPECIAL INSTRUCTIONS TO BINDERY PREP STAFF: 1. _____ * 2. _____ * 3. _____ *	1-67	10

26. ON ORDER ACCOUNTING DATA:

ACCT STATUS	PROV	PO#	AGENT CODE	DIRECT AGENT NAME	FUND NAME	F.R.#	MULT PMNT?		
[1] ACT [2] INACT [3] SEC	[1] PAID [2] GIFT [3] EXCH [4] PD EXCH						BL=NO [1]=YES	1-67	11
1	3	5-12	14-16	17-44	46-61	63-66	67		

DIRECT CHARGE FUND CODE	DATE ORDERED			NEW ORDER CLAIM DATE		FOR:	REG OR CONF.	COST		
	MO / DAY / YR			MO / YEAR			[1] REG [2] CONF [3] ADV PAY		1-54	12
1-16	18/9	21/2	24/5	27/8	30/1	33-44	46	48-54		

ACCOUNTING COMMENTS		
	1-67	13

D-1071

File Name SERIALS FILE | File No. F 14

Location * | Storage Medium *

Access Requirements LIBRARY ADMINISTRATION, RECEIVING, CATALOGING, ACQUISITIONS, BINDERY, CIRCULATION, ACCOUNTING

Sequenced By ID NUMBER

Content Qualifications RECORDS FOR ACTIVE AND INACTIVE

How Current DAILY

Retention Characteristics PERMANENT

Labels (SUBJECT TO PROCESSING SYSTEM)

Remarks

CONTENTS

Sequence No.	Form Name	Volume Avg.	Volume Peak	Characters Per Record	Characters Per File Avg.	Characters Per File Peak
1	MASTER SERIALS DATA RECORD		25,000	1000		25,000,000
2	RECEIVING RECORD					

1968 — Date | JBK — Analyst | Figure 18.7 — Source | 1 — Page

Representative — Study

* Determined uniquely by each library

Figure 18.7 Master serials record file.

cataloging data, it might also be reasonable to include references to abstracting and indexing journals by which the serial is being covered, or is likely to be covered.

Ordering Data. These data include renewal dates; names and addresses of publisher, society or association; code for vendor; code for funds from which subscriptions are to be paid; costs; and references to associated publications.

Receiving Data. These include data on frequency of publication, on volume and issue numbering practice, on irregularities to be expected (such as delays, supplements, and multiple issues), check-in points, and claiming criteria. They are used to control the issuance of reentry cards or listings for control of the receiving operation and for initiating claiming.

Binding Data. These data include style and color of binding, number of issues per binding volume, binding frequency, binding dates, and other special instructions for binding.

Holdings Data. These include all of the standard data on holdings, both bound volumes and separate issues, lacunae and missing issues, wants, locations at which holdings are kept.

Distribution Data. These data are used to produce distribution lists or SDI lists at the time of receipt of an issue. They include the name and address of individuals, organizations, and locations to which issues are to be circulated.

Receiving File

The Receiving File is the set of records or printed lists used to control the receiving operation itself and to provide for subsequent input to the computer concerning issues which have been received.

Contents. Figure 18.8 lists data that might be included in a receiving record. The amount of data actually included in a typical situation will depend primarily on the form in which the record is produced.

Use. The receiving record, as we have indicated, is used to update the master serials file record when a single, specific issue has been received. It can, however, be used for much more than this. For example, if an issue other than an expected one, if more than one, or if a defective issue has been received, the receiving record can be used to indicate what has happened. If the need for claiming becomes evident before the computer would ordinarily recognize it, the receiving record can be used to initiate a claiming letter.

Form. The choice of form for the receiving record is probably the most

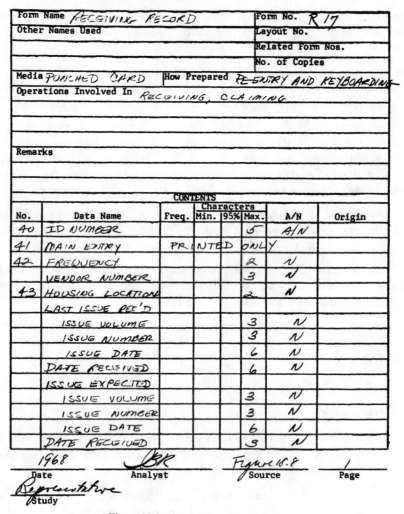

No.	Data Name	Freq.	Min.	95%	Max.	A/N	Origin
40	ID NUMBER				5	A/N	
41	MAIN ENTRY	PRINTED		ONLY			
42	FREQUENCY				2	N	
	VENDOR NUMBER				3	N	
43	HOUSING LOCATION				2	N	
	LAST ISSUE REC'D						
	ISSUE VOLUME				3	N	
	ISSUE NUMBER				3	N	
	ISSUE DATE				6	N	
	DATE RECEIVED				6	N	
	ISSUE EXPECTED						
	ISSUE VOLUME				3	N	
	ISSUE NUMBER				3	N	
	ISSUE DATE				6	N	
	DATE RECEIVED				3	N	

Form Name RECEIVING RECORD   Form No. R 17
Other Names Used   Layout No.
                                 Related Form Nos.
                                 No. of Copies
Media PUNCHED CARD How Prepared RE-ENTRY AND KEYBOARDING
Operations Involved In RECEIVING, CLAIMING

Remarks

CONTENTS
Characters

1968   BR   Figure 18.8   1
Date   Analyst   Source   Page
Representative
Study

Figure 18.8   Receiving record card.

crucial consideration in design of the serial subsystem. It will determine, for example, how effective and expensive the receiving operation itself will be, how much data the computer needs to output, and how frequently it must be output.

The UCSD system uses punched card (Figure 18.8a) processing records. These are output monthly, based on expectation of receipt, and must be manually inter-filed into the Receiving File. As punched cards, they contain a limited amount of data. When an issue is received, the relevant card is manually found and pulled. If the relevant card is not in the file, the data must be key-punched to create an entry record.

The UCLA-Biomedical system also uses a punched card receiving record. However, instead of attempting to predict each month what issues will be received, a receiving record is produced each time an issue is received, which then serves as the receiving record for the next issue, whenever it may arrive. Again, the amount of data is quite limited.

The Texas A & M system also uses a punched card receiving record. However, instead of limiting the data on it to that which can be punched and interpreted, it includes a very complete set of additional data printed on its face. As a result, the receiving clerks have a much more accurate picture of the nature of expected issues.

The problems of interfiling and manually pulling cards in a tub file have led some systems to use printed receiving lists instead. For example, the New York State Library does so, and then uses it as a source record from which to key-punch data. In particular, each expected issue is listed with an associated control number. When they are received, the receiving clerks need only check off the relevant entry. All that need be key-boarded are the control numbers of issues received (or alternatively of issues *not* received if this results in less volume of keying). The UC Davis system carries this a step further, by replacing the key-boarding with the pulling of pre-punched, pre-numbered cards from a tub file. Manual filing of cards, however, is eliminated, since the numbers are completely non-significant. In either case, the entry for an expected issue can be quite complete, giving the receiving clerks an accurate picture of its nature.

Output Lists

Figure 18.9 is a set of typical output lists and records: receiving records, information lists, invoices, and bindery lists.[23] (It is based on the plans of the New York State Library.) Their functions are each self-evident.

ESTIMATION OF PROCESSING TIMES AND COSTS

Figure 18.10 gives a list of parameters relevant to estimation of processing times and costs.[24] Figure 18.11(a) to (e) gives estimates for our illustrative library of Figure 14.11. In making these estimates, no provision was made for handling *new* orders nor for the production of distribution lists.

[23] *New York State Library Serials Project, op. cit.*
[24] Voigt, Melvin J., "The Costs of Data Processing in University Libraries—in Serials Handling," *College and Research Libraries*, **24** (6) (November 1963), 489-491.

02882MEDIZINISCHE KLINIK   AC U63N51,20DEC1968   909642   021969   03MA

IBM 5081

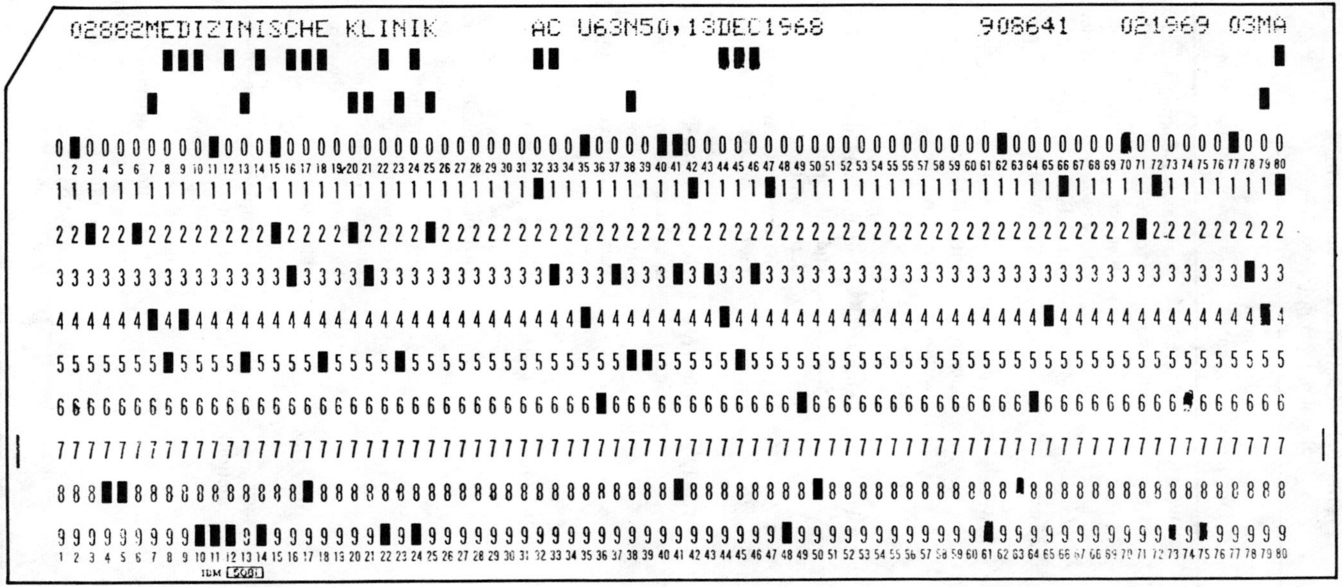

Figure 18.8a   Receiving cards.

673

Figure 18.9   Computer generated reports from
the library periodicals system.

Report Title	Frequency	To Whom Sent	Function
Receiving Records	Weekly	Check-in clerks	To match incoming issues against those expected and to record any others received. The information recorded is processed by the flexowriter and entered into the computer resulting in an updated Work List.
Serials Information List	Weekly	Subject Library Section Heads	Provides the library reader service staff with current information on all titles in the active file.
Invoice Control	Weekly	Order Section	Contains all invoice charges approved and disapproved for payment. Further action on these invoices is transcribed by the flexowriter into data to be processed by the computer to update the file.
Bindery Control List	Weekly	Bindery Unit	Used as a check-off list for the issues that must be collected for binding. Missing and on-hand issues are identified. Any discrepancies found will be re-entered in the system via the flexowriter.
Claims/Renewal Requests	Weekly	Supplier or Vendor	Forms printed by a high speed printer ready to be stuffed into window envelopes for mailing. Claim notices will be sent for each issue anticipated, but not received within a certain time span. To prevent the collapse of a subscription thru non-payment, renewal requests will be generated when the expiration date is approached.
Inquiry/Proof	(See Function)	Staff/ Requestor	A complete printing of the Master file for any one title for staff-used in examining questionable transactions. The report is automatically generated when a title is originally converted or a revision is entered for a title on the Master File. Other than that, the report may only be generated via an inquiry transaction.

Figure 18.9   *(Continued)*

Report Title	Frequency	To Whom Sent	Function
Error List	Weekly	Library	Contains a list of information entered into the system which is incomplete or contains errors. The correct information is reentered in the form of revisions.
New Acquisitions List	Monthly	Library Staff	Contains new additions to the NYSL Serials collection. It will be published as part of *The Bookmark* and used for reporting new acquisitions to the New Serials Titles Project of L.C.
Holdings List	Monthly	Library Staff	An interim report to the Annual Master List. A list of all new additions to retrospective holdings of titles on the Master File.
Control List	Quarterly	Periodical Section Head	A list of serials, categorized as unpredictable, for which no addition to holdings has been recorded within the past quarter. Periodical section staff will initiate a transaction to generate a claim notice from the computer system.
Statistical Summaries	Annual	Library Staff	Contains information concerning certain characteristics of the serials acquisitions program. Designed to provide management with facts on current expenditures to guide them in making decisions about the NYS Library Serials Collection.
Classified List	Annual	Library Staff	A list of all titles in the file. Unclassified titles will be omitted.
Subject Heading List	Annual	Library Staff	Designed to provide the library staff and general public with a new tool.
Master List	Annual	Library Staff	A comprehensive listing of all titles in the Master File, with the full cataloging and detailed holdings statement.

Estimates of Physical Handling Times

No data is readily available of the average time required for receiving personnel to unwrap, check, stamp, and sort the estimated numbers of received issues. The values shown are therefore not based on even the experimental data for other manual handling rates, but are purely nominal. The workload is based on data from several libraries (including the University of California at San Diego) on the distribution of frequency of publication among serials. These data imply an average of 4 to 5 issues per year per serial.

Estimates of Manual File Access

The estimates for manual file access in the computer systems are based on the use of prepunched re-entry receiving cards, which must be interfiled and then pulled when issues are received. If a receiving list is used instead, the time for interfiling would be replaced by increased key-boarding costs, and the time for pulling cards would be replaced by that for looking up in a list.

Estimates of Key-Boarding

Using prepunched receiving cards, key-boarding is required for entry of issues for which no card is available and for introducing changes in machine records. These have been estimated, nominally, at 10 percent of the daily activity.

Estimates of Computer Time

These are all quite straightforward and self-explanatory.

Figure 18.10   Parameters for estimation.

	Representative Values	Illustrative Values
1. Work Load		
V_1 Monthly receipts of Issues		5,000
V_2 Monthly Renewals		1,500
V_3 Monthly Claims		150
V_4 Number of Monthly Holding Lists		1
2. Record Sizes		
R_{16} Master Serial Record		1,000
R_{17} Receiving Record		45
3. File Sizes		
F_{14} Master Serial Record File		25,000
Receiving File		20,000
4. Output		
Yearly Master Serial Record File (Full Master Serial Record = 1000 characters)		25,000
Monthly Cumulative Holdings List (240 characters/serial)		15,000

Sub-System				File						
Serial Records				Serial Master Records and Receiving						

Level of Analysis: Component
Personnel and Equipment

Level of Analysis: Function
Sub-System Schematic

Basic Unit of Work
Serial Title

Comp.	Operation	Number	X	Size	X	Freq. /	Rate	= Time	X Cost	X %	= Total
Cler. Pers.	Physical Receiving	250*				20	1 /3 min	250	$ 3/hr	100	$ 750
	Physical Sorting	250				20	1 /2 min	167	3/hr	100	501
	File Access	250				20	2 /min	42	3/hr	100	126
	Posting	250				20	1 /2 min	167	3/hr	100	501
	File Scanning	15,000**				1	3 / /min	83	3/hr	100	249
	Claims Writing	150		240 chars		1	10,000 chars/hr	4	3/hr	100	12
	Renewals	1500		240 chars		1	10,000 chars/hr	36	3/hr	100	108
	Binding Orders	1500		240		1	10,000	36	3/hr	100	108
	Totals							785 hours			$2355

Monthly cost per Active Serial, $0.16
for (Clerical Personnel)***

*Based on average of 4 issues per year for
15,000 active serials (10,000 inactive
serials)

**Based on month by search of active file,
for claims, renewals, binding orders.

***The CLR study shows about $2.50 per year
for clerical (non-professional) personnel.

TOTAL

COST/EFFECTIVENESS =

Date   Analyst   Page

Study

Figure 18.11a, b   Manual and punched-card system.

Sub-System						File					
Serial Records						Serial Master Records and Receiving					

Level of Analysis: Component
Personnel and Equipment

Level of Analysis: Function
Sub-System Schematic

Basic Unit of Work
Serial Title

Comp.	Operation	Number	X Size	X Freq.	/ Rate	= Time	X Cost	X %	= Total
Cler.	Physical Receiving	250		20	1 /3 min	250	$ 3/hr	100	$ 750
	File Access for pre-punched receiving card*	250		20	2 /min	42	3/hr	100	126
	Keyboarding of receiving cards not found	25	20 chars	20	6000 chars/hr	2	3/hr	100	6
	Interfiling of new receiving cards	250		20	15 /min	6	3/hr	100	18
	Subtotals					300			900
Equip. &	Set-Up Time			30 batches	.02 hr/batch	.6	30/hr	100	18
Oper. Pers.	Input	250	80 chars	20	200 chars/sec	.6	30/hr	100	18
	File Access	250	10 access		5 /sec	2.8	30/hr	100	84
	File Update for receiving	250	5 Stand. Proc.	20	250 /sec		30/hr	100	
	File Processing others	1500	20 Stand. Proc.	1	250 /sec		30/hr	100	
	Output Holdings List	15,000	240 chars	1	200 chars/sec	5.	30/hr	100	150
	Receiving Cards	250	80	20	200 chars/sec	.6	30/hr	100	18
	Claims Output	150	240 chars	1	200 chars/sec	.1	30/hr	100	3
	Renewal Orders	1500	240 chars	1	200 chars/sec	.5	30/hr	100	15
	Binding Orders	1500	240 chars	1	200 chars/sec	.5	30/hr	100	15
	TOTAL								
	COST/EFFECTIVENESS =								

Date _____

Analyst _____

Page _____

Study _____

Figure 18.11c Small-scale batch computer.

678

Sub-System			File								
Serial Records			Serial Master Records and Receiving								

Level of Analysis: Component
Personnel and Equipment

Level of Analysis: Function
Sub-System Schematic

Basic Unit of Work
Serial Title

Comp.	Operation	Number	X Size	X Freq.	/ Rate	= Time	X Cost	X %	= Total
Equip. & Oper. Pers.	Yearly Holdings List (prorated over 12 months)	25,000	1000 chars	1	200 chars/sec	2.9	$30/hr	100	$ 87
	Subtotals					11.4 hours			$ 408
	*Monthly Cost per Active Serial, $0.087								
	TOTAL								$1308
	COST/EFFECTIVENESS =								

Date _____   Analyst _____   Page _____

Study _____

Figure 18.11c   (*Continued*)

Sub-System					File					
Serial Records					Serial Master Records and Receiving					

Level of Analysis: Component
Personnel and Equipment

Level of Analysis: Function
Sub-System Schematic

Basic Unit of Work
Serial Title

Comp.	Operation	Number	X	Size	X	Freq.	/	Rate	=	Time	X	Cost	X	%	=	Total
Cler. Pers.	Physical Receiving	250				20		1 /3 min		250	$	3/hr	100		$	750
	File Access for Pre-Punched receiving card	250				20		2 /min		42		3/hr	100			126
	Keyboarding of receiving cards not found	25		20 chars		20		6000 chars/hr		2		3/hr	100			6
	Interfiling of new receiving cards	250		20		20		15 /min		6		3/hr	100			18
	Subtotals									300						900
Equip. & Oper. Pers.	Set-Up Time					30 batches		.01 hr/batch		.30		225/hr	20			14.0
	Input	250		80 chars		20		2000 chars/sec		.20		225/hr	20			.9
	File Access	250		10 access		20		50 /sec		.26		225/hr	20			18.7
	File Update -receiving	250	5	Stand. Proc.		20		2500 /sec				225/hr	20			
	File Processing -other	1500	20	Stand. Proc.		1		2500 /sec				225/hr	20			
	Output Holdings List	15,000		240 chars		1		2000 chars/sec		.50		225/hr	20			22.5
	Receiving Cards	250		80 chars		20		2000 chars/sec		.06		225/hr	20			2.7
	Claims Output	150		240 chars		1		2000 chars/sec		.01		225/hr	20			.5
	Renewal Orders	1500		240 chars		1		2000 chars/sec		.05		225/hr	20			2.3
	TOTAL															
	COST/EFFECTIVENESS =															

Date _____   Analyst _____   Page _____

Study _____

Figure 18.11d Large-scale batch computer.

Sub-System Serial Records				File Serial Master Records and Receiving							
Level of Analysis: Component Personnel and Equipment											
Level of Analysis: Function Sub-System Schematic											
Basic Unit of Work Serial Title											
Comp.	Operation	Number	X	Size	X Freq. /	Rate	= Time	X Cost	X % =	Total		
Equip. &	Binding Orders	1500		240	1	2000	.05	$225/hr	20	$ 2.3		
Oper. Pers.	Yearly Holdings List (prorated over 12 months)	25,000		1000	1 /12	2000	.29	$225/hr	20	13.1		
	Subtotals						1.54 hours			$ 77.0		
	Monthly cost per Active Serial, $0.065											
	TOTAL									$ 977		
	COST/EFFECTIVENESS =											

Date _____ Analyst _____ Page _____

Study _____

Figure 18.11d *(Continued)*

Sub-System	Serial Records				**File** Serial Master Records and Receiving						
Level of Analysis: Component Personnel and Equipment											
Level of Analysis: Function Sub-System Schematic											
Basic Unit of Work Serial Title											

Comp.	Operation	Number	X	Size	X Freq.	/ Rate	= Time	X Cost	X	% =	Total
Cler. Pers.	Physical Receiving	250			20	1 /3 min	250	$ /hr	100		$750
	File Access for pre-punched receiving card	250			20	2 /min	42	3/hr	100		126
	Keyboarding of receiving card not found	25		20 chars	20	6000 chars/hr	2	3/hr	100		6
	Interfiling of new receiving cards	250			20	15 /min	6	3/hr	100		18
	Subtotals						300				900
Equip. & Oper. Pers.	Set-Up Time				30 batches	.01 hr/batch	.30	625/hr	4		7.5
	Input	250		80 chars	20	2000 chars/sec	.026	25/hr	4		.5
	File Access	250		10 access	20	100 /sec	.13	625/hr	4		3.3
	File Update -receiving	250	5	Stand. Proc.	20	25,000 /sec		625/hr	4		
	File Processing -other	1500	20	Stand. Proc.	1	25,000 /sec		625/hr	4		
	Output Holdings List	15,000		240 chars	1	2000 chars/sec	.50	625/hr	4		12.5
	Receiving Cards	250		80 chars	20	2000 chars/sec	.06	625/hr	4		1.5
	Claims Output	150		240 chars	1	2000 chars/sec	.01	625/hr	4		.3
	Renewal Orders	1500		240 chars	1	2000 chars/sec	.05	625/hr	4		1.3
	TOTAL										
	COST/EFFECTIVENESS =										

Date _____   Analyst _____   Page _____

Study _____

Figure 18.11e   Large-scale on-line computer.

Sub-System					File						
Serial Records					Serial Master Records and Receiving						

Level of Analysis: Component
Personnel and Equipment

Level of Analysis: Function
Sub-System Schematic

Basic Unit of Work
Serial Title

Comp.	Operation	Number	X	Size	X	Freq.	/	Rate	=	Time	X	Cost	X	%	=	Total
Equip. &	Binding Orders	1500		240 chars		1		2000 chars/sec		.05		$625/hr		4		$ 1.3
Oper. Pers.	Yearly Holdings List (prorated over 12 months)	25,000		1000		1		2000		.29		625/hr		4		7.3
	Subtotals									1.41 hours						$ 35.5
		Monthly cost per Active Serial, $0.062														
	TOTAL															$936
	COST/EFFECTIVENESS =															

Date _____ Analyst _____ Page _____

Study _____

Figure 18.11e (*Continued*)

683

Suggested Readings

The literature concerning serials record processing tends to be specific to the system of one or another library, rather than covering more general considerations. However, the following seems especially useful:

Brodman, Estelle, Irwin H. Pizer, and Donald R. Franz, "Mechanization of Library Procedures in the Medium-Sized Library: I. The Serial Record," *Bulletin of the Medical Library Association,* **51** (3) (July 1963) 313-338.

This reports on the system developed in the medical library at Washington University in St Louis.

Vdovin, George, Melvin J. Voigt, et al., "Computer Processing of Serial Records," *Library Resources and Technical Services,* **7** (1), (Winter 1963), 71-80.

This reports on the system developed at the University of California, San Diego. It represented the starting point for many subsequent systems.

Woods, Elaine W., *National Serials Data Program (Phase I): A Working Paper.* Washington, D.C.: Library of Congress, August 1967.

Eventually the National Serials Data Program will be as significant in the development of mechanized serials systems as the MARC project has been for catalog systems. This was the report which initiated the project.

Chapter 19

MECHANIZED INFORMATION SERVICES

BACKGROUND

In the previous five chapters, we considered the use of computers in the internal clerical processes of the library, representing the counterparts of business data processing. Although these uses are most important, they seem relatively mundane in comparison with the potential uses of computers in support of information services.

Information services include, in addition to normal library reference service: (1) information retrieval; (2) information analysis; and (3) information publication, announcement, and distribution. Libraries of all kinds are beginning to assume more responsibility in these areas, and eventually should serve as agencies for acquisition of data to support information services not previously considered within their scope—including, in particular, the use of machine-readable computer data. They will also serve as points for access to state, national, and even international resources through networks of various kinds. Perhaps most important the library can provide a point of assistance in the use of new forms of data for "mechanized information services."

The interest in mechanized information services in the library arises from the so-called "information explosion," the consequent need felt to exploit new tools in coping with the increasing amounts of research literature, the development of data bases in machine processible form, and the production of generalized computer programs that can process a variety of machine stored data. It is best represented by the general trends in developing information services to science and engineering. Increasingly, the research interests of scientific specialties are being served by critical analyses and syntheses of the results of existing work—as reported in the published literature and at conferences, but also as it is becoming available in less formal means of communication. Whether this effort is embodied in "information analysis centers" (such as the "material properties centers" listed in Figure 19.1,[1] the ERIC Clearinghouses listed in Figure 19.2,[2] and the NINDS centers listed in Figure 19.3[3]) or is simply an extension of the established practices in good research, it requires a more sophisticated means of acquisition, control, dissemination, and retrieval of the relevant results. This has led many different groups of researchers to turn to computer-based systems of data management, and the number of proposals for mechanized information services in one discipline or another steadily multiplies. Unfortunately the emphasis on mechanization has tended to result in duplication of effort,

Figure 19.1   Materials information centers.

Ceramics and Graphite Information Center
Air Force Materials Laboratory
Wright-Patterson Air Force Base
Dayton, Ohio   45433

Chemical Thermodynamic Properties Center
Texas A & M University
College Station Texas

Defense Metals Information Center
Battelle Memorial Institute
Columbus, Ohio   43201

Electronic Properties Information Center
Hughes Aircraft Company
Culver City, California   90230

Mechanical Properties Data Center
Belfour-Stulen, Inc.
Traverse City, Michigan   49684

Thermophysical Properties Research Center
Purdue University, Research Park
Lafayette, Indiana   47906

[1] *Materials Properties Information Centers,* Wright-Patterson Air Force Base, Dayton, Ohio.
[2] *Current ERIC Clearinghouses and Their Scopes,* Office of Education, March 1969.
[3] National Institute of Neurological Diseases and Stroke, *The Neurological Information Network,* U.S. Department of Health, Education, and Welfare, Public Health Service Publication No. 1691.

Figure 19.2   ERIC Clearinghouses.

Adult Education
Syracuse University
107 Roney Lane
Syracuse, New York   13210

Counseling and Personnel Services
611 Church Street
Ann Arbor, Michigan   48104

The Urban Disadvantaged
Teachers College
Box 40
Columbia University
New York, New York   10027

Early Childhood Education
University of Illinois
805 West Pennsylvania Avenue
Urbana, Illinois   61801

Educational Administration
Hendricks Hall
University of Oregon
Eugene, Oregon   97403

Educational Facilities
University of Wisconsin
606 State Street, Room 314
Madison, Wisconsin   53703

Educational Media and Technology
Institute for Communication Research
Stanford University
Stanford, California   94305

Exceptional Children
Council for Exceptional Children
1499 Jefferson Davis Highway
Arlington, Virginia   22202

Higher Education
George Washington University
Washington D.C.   20006

Junior Colleges
University of California at Los Angeles
405 Hilgard Avenue
Los Angeles, California   90024

Library and Information Sciences
American Society for Information Science
1140 Connecticut Ave., N.W.
Washington, D.C.   20036

Linguistics
Center for Applied Linguistics
1717 Massachusetts Avenue, N.W.
Washington, D.C.   20036

Reading
200 Pine Hall
School of Education
Indiana University
Bloomington, Indiana   47401

Rural Education and Small Schools
New Mexico State University
Box 3AP, University Park Branch
Las Cruces, New Mexico   88001

Science Education
Ohio State University
1460 West Lane Avenue
Columbus, Ohio   43221

Social Science Education
Social Science Building
University of Colorado
970 Aurora Avenue,
Boulder, Colorado   80302

Teacher Education
1156 Fifteenth Street, N.W.
Washington, D.C.   20005

Teaching of English
National Council of Teachers of English
508 South Sixth Street
Champaign, Illinois   61820

Teaching of Foreign Languages
Modern Language Association of America
62 Fifth Avenue
New York, New York   10011

Tests, Measurement and Evaluation
Educational Testing Service
Princeton, N.J.   08540

Vocational and Technical Education
Ohio State University
1900 Kenney Road
Columbus, Ohio   43210

Figure 19.3   Information centers of the
National Institute of Neurological Diseases and Stroke.

Brain Information Service
    Bio-Medical Library
    University of California
    Los Angeles, California   90024

Parkinson's Disease Research and Information Center
    Columbia University
    New York City, New York   10032

Vision Information Center
    Countway Library of Medicine
    Harvard University
    Boston, Massachusetts   02115

*Specialized Information Center for Hearing, Speech, and
Disorders of Communication*
    The Johns Hopkins
    Baltimore, Maryland   21205

dissipation of talents better directed toward substantive research, and proliferation of incompatible systems.

In parallel with these specialized interests, national organizations—federal agencies, professional societies, and commercial companies—have been developing mechanized systems for publication and for information services to support their own defined missions. (There are, for example, more than 400 installations of computer controlled typesetting equipment in the United States.[4,5]) Most of these national organizations view the resulting mechanized data bases as useful for providing information services to other interested parties.

Of immediate significance to libraries, in this respect, are the large number of national programs that are now generating cataloging and indexing data in mechanized form. For example, the Library of Congress, the National Library of Medicine, and the National Agricultural Library plan to distribute catalog data in magnetic tape form, and the National Library of Medicine has already distributed Medlars tapes to several centers (see Figure 19.4).[6] The Defense Documentation Center, NASA (see Figure 19.5),[7] and the AEC are

---

[4] Kuney, Joseph, "Publication and Distribution of Information," in Carlos Cuadra, *Annual Review of Information Science and Technology*, Vol. 3. Chicago: Encyclopedia Britannica, 1968, pp. 31-60.

[5] *Newsletter*, Composition Information Services, 15 October 1968.

[6] Reported in various issues of the *Bulletin of the Medical Library Association*.

[7] *NASA Regional Dissemination Centers*, NASA Technology Utilization Division, December 1969.

Figure 19.4   Regional Medlars centers.

University of Colorado
    Denison Memorial Library
    Denver Colorado   80220

University of California
    Bio-Medical Library
    Los Angeles, California   90024

Harvard University
    Countway Library of Medicine
    Boston, Massachusetts   02115

University of Michigan
    Medical Center Library
    Ann Abror, Michigan   48104

Ohio State University
    College of Medicine
    Columbus, Ohio   43210

Karolinska Institut
    Biomedical Documentation Center
    Stockholm, Sweden

University of Alabama
    Medical Center Library
    Birmingham, Alabama   35233

Texas Medical Center
    Jesse H. Jones Library Building
    Houston, Texas   77025

National Lending Library for Science and Technology
    Boston Spa, Yorkshire LS23 7BQ
    England

University of Sydney
    Basser Computing Department
    Sydney N.S.W.   2006
    Australia

Figure 19.5   NASA regional dissemination centers.

Aerospace Research Applications Center
    Indiana University Foundation
    Bloomington, Indiana   47405

Knowledge Availability Systems Center
    University of Pittsburgh
    Pittsburgh, Pennsylvania

Technology Application Center
    University of New Mexico
    Albuquerque, New Mexico   87106

New England Research Application Center
    University of Connecticut
    Storrs, Connecticut   06268

North Carolina Science and Technology Research Center
    Research Triangle Park
    North Carolina

Western Research Applications Center
    University of Southern California
    Los Angeles, California   90007

already distributing index data in this way. *Chemical Abstracts* (see Figure 19.6),[8] *Biological Abstracts, Engineering Index, Historical Abstracts*, and other abstracting services are experimenting with similar mechanization. There are a number of commercial organizations in book distribution—such as Bowker,

[8] *Information Services 1970,* Chemical Abstracts Service, the Ohio State University, Columbus, Ohio.

Figure 19.6   CAS experimental centers.

Alberta Information Retrieval Association
c/o Research Council of Alberta
Edmonton 7, Alberta
Canada

Danish Technical Library
Dokumentationsafdelingen
Copenhagen K, Denmark

Greater Louisville Technical Referral Center
University of Louisville, Speed Scientific School
Louisville, Kentucky   40208

IIT Research Institute
Computer Search Center
Chicago, Illinois   60616

National Science Library
National Research Council of Canada
Ottawa 2, Ontario
Canada

United Kingdom Chemical Information Service
University Park
Nottingham NG7 2RD, England

University of Iowa
University Computer Center
Iowa City, Iowa   52240

University of Pittsburgh
Knowledge Availability Systems Center
Pittsburgh, Pennsylvania   15312

Gesellschaft Deutscher Chemiker
Abteilung Chemisches Zentralblatt
Chefedakteur
Geisbergstrasse 39, Germany

Bro-Dart, and Abel—that are installing mechanized catalog services. In summary, mechanized data from which reference services can be provided are becoming readily available to every large library throughout the United States. The extent to which this kind of distribution is becoming an operational reality is so great now that an organization has been formed among the centers receiving tapes—The Association of Scientific Information Dissemination Centers (ASIDIC).[9]

Of perhaps even greater potential importance are the large number of socioeconomic data banks being established in magnetic tape form. The most prominent example are census tapes. The Bureau of the Census has decided to distribute them to university centers as well as governmental agencies and commercial information service centers.[10] In addition, however, there are a number of university centers that have formed a Council of Social Science Data Archives to deal with the sharing of more specialized data bases of this kind.[11] Perhaps the most important examples, in the long run, are the metropolitan data banks being created by a number of cities, counties, regions, and states.[12] These will provide a continuing flow of data of fundamental importance to research, to planning, and to economic development.

A third category of data are text tapes, a by-product of the process of publication as well as a result of conversion of data for research on the properties of text. With the large number of computer controlled type-setting installations, these text data bases are also becoming available for acquisition.[13]

Appendix 3 presents a detailed inventory of a representative set of data bases of all kinds, and Figure 19.7 is a summary listing of them. A most significant aspect of this listing is the number of commercial organizations in it, since they reflect the recognition of the potential market for magnetic tape data base. The extent of private investment in this kind of product has now reached the point that an "Information Industry Association" has been formed.[14] It includes publishers, subsidiaries of equipment manufacturers, and companies primarily concerned with the newer media of publication.

These existing national projects amply demonstrate the extent to which mechanized information retrieval is a reality today, and the number of national programs generating data in magnetic tape form is continually increasing. Although most of them have been oriented toward meeting the special requirements of the agencies involved, as a whole they now constitute a national resource of great magnitude and importance. In Chapter 1, we reviewed the

[9] *ASIDIC Newsletter*, Illinois Institute of Technology, Chicago, Illinois.

[10] See *Census Summary Tape User Memoranda*, (1–present, October 17, 1968–present), U.S. Department of Commerce, Bureau of the Census. See also *Small-Area Data Activities*, issued occasionally by the Bureau of the Census until 1969, subsequently called *Small-Area Data Notes*.

[11] *Social Science Data Archives in the United States,* 1967 Council of Social Science Data Archives, Columbia University, New York, 1967.

[12] Hayes, Robert M., "Metropolitan Data Banks," in *Papers Presented at the Census Tract Conference*, September 10, 1965, Bureau of the Census, 1966.

[13] Carlson, Gary, *Literary Works in Machine Readable Form.* Provo, Utah: Brigham Young University, July 1965. Subsequently updated in the January 1967 issue of *Computers and the Humanities.*

[14] *Inforum*, Newsletter of the Information Industry Association, Suite 700, 1025 15th Street, N.W., Washington, D.C.

Figure 19.7   List of representative data bases.

American Bibliographical Center
800 Micheltorena Avenue
Santa Barbara, California   93108
    Dr. Eric Boehm, Director (805) 962-6582
    Mechanized production of the five year index for Historical Abstracts, containing all
    bibliographic elements exclusive of the abstracts themselves.

American Chemical Society
1155 16th Street, N W
Washington, D.C.
    Joseph Kuney, Director of Publications Research (202) RE 7-3337
    Steve Walcavich, Programmer in Charge
    Began in 1966 to produce *Journal of Chemical Documentation* by computer-driven
    Photon 200. About 100 articles for 1966; 500-600 expected by end of 1968. Also
    putting some of the articles in the *Journal of Chemical Engineering Data* for 1966 in
    machineable form. Goal is to produce all of ACS journals in this way.

American Institute of Physics
335 East 45th Street
New York, New York   100717
    (212) MU 5-1940
    They are working on a thesaurus in magnetic tape format as the first step toward
    mechanization; a bibliographic tape service was scheduled for mid-1970.

American Petroleum Institute–Division of Refining
Central Abstracting and Indexing Service
555 Madison Avenue
New York, New York   10022
    Mr. Everette H. Brenner, Manager
    Currently abstracting 1,000 documents and journal articles and 1,000 patents per month
    and storing in magnetic tape form.

American Society for Metals
ASM Documentation Service
Metals Park, Ohio   44073
    Mrs. Marjorie Hyslop, Associate Director (216) 338-5151
    Literature in the field of Metallurgy, stored in magnetic tape form.

Applied Mechanics Review
Southwest Research Institute
8500 Culebra Road
San Antonio, Texas
    Mr. Stephen Juhasz (572) 684-2000
    Complete data in magnetic tape form for the WADEX (word and author index)
    system–actually a series of programs and data to create the index to AMR.

Atomic Energy Commission
Division of Technical Information
    Extension, PO Box 62, Oakridge, Tenn.   37830
    Fred E. Marsh, Jr., Chief, Computer Operations.
    Two sets of magnetic tapes currently produced: (1) Used in production of Nuclear
    Sciences Abstracts (2) A general type used in SDI programs.

Figure 19.7 *(continued)*

BioScience Information Service
3815 Walnut Street
Philadelphia, Pennsylvania   19104
   Phyllis V. Parkins, Director (215) 386-0414
   Miss Louise Shultz, Assistant Director for Systems Development
   Mechanized system is used for producing *Biological Abstracts* and its four indexes:
       1. Author
       2. Permuted fragments from an augmented title listing
       3. Coordinate Posted Index–a precoordinate index, using only the terms which are used as headings and subheadings of BA sections. These then are large terms rather than detailed specific uniterms.
       4. Biosystematic index (Taxonomic)

R. R. Bowker Company
1180 Avenue of the Americas
New York, New York   10036
   Mr. John Berry III (212) LT 1-8800
   Has automated the production of Pub Weekly, BPR, etc., and wishes to encourage general use of tapes (wish to market own tape eventually). They have more than one data bank available to any interested subscriber.

Bureau of the Census
Washington, D.C.
Marshall L. Turner, Jr., Chief, Central Users' Service
   The 1970 Census Summary will be the first to be available in its entirety in magnetic tape form (approximately 1500 reels).

Chemical Abstracts Service
2540 Olentangy River Road
Columbus, Ohio
   Mr. Elden G. Johnson, Manager: Subscriber Information Service (614) 293-7423 293-5022
       1. Chem Abstracts [CA] is available on tape in condensed form.
       2. Chem Titles [CT] began in 1962. This is a KWIC-type index with about 500,000 titles.
       3. Chemical Biological Activities [CBAC] began in 1964 and now has about 21,000 titles with abstracts.
   CAS has a registry system which takes two-dimensional drawings representing compounds and searches for those containing the same structure, no matter how displayed. Now have 500,000 compounds, with a capacity of 5 million.

Clearinghouse for Federal Scientific and Technical Information
5825 Port Royal Road
Springfield, Virginia   22151
   Peter F. Urbach; Assistant Director, Systems
   Embarked on the production of consolidated indexes to Federal STI (NASA, AWC and DOD) using computers. A tape version of USERDR was announced in early 1970

Figure 19.7   (*continued*)

Institute for Scientific Information
325 Chestnut Street
Philadelphia, Pennsylvania
   Dr. Eugene Garfield, Director (215) WA 3-3300
   Tapes available on lease or buy arrangement. File of Science Citation Index, ASCA, and
   ISI Search Service.

Library of Congress
First and Capital Streets
Washington, D.C.
   MARC is continuing an effort to provide primary cataloging data in magnetic tape form.

NASA (by contract with Documentation, Inc.)
Scientific and Technical Information Division, Office of Technology Utilization
Washington, D.C.   20546
   John F. Stearns, Director, STI Division.
   NASA-STAR is produced using magnetic tape. Now developing an on-line service.
   Establishing subcenters at several universities.

National Library of Medicine
8600 Rockville Pike
Bethesda, Maryland   20014
   (202) 656-4084 Bethesda Office (301) 654-9190
   Has been producing Index Medicus for several years using mechanized methods and is
   servicing requests for searching of the existing files. Establishing subcenters throughout
   the world.

National Standard Reference Data Systems
Gaithersburg, Maryland
   Dr. Steven Brady, Director (202) 921-1000
   Indexed bibliographies and data in magnetic tape form. Bibliographies run to 30K
   references with notes on data content.

Office of Education
400 Maryland Avenue S.W.
Washington, D.C.
   Project ERIC (Educational Research Information Center) distributes citations and
   abstracts on magnetic tape.

Science Information Exchange
Smithsonian Institution
Madison National Bank Building,
1730 M Street, N.W.
Washington, D.C. 20035
   Dr. Vincent Maturi, Chief, Physical Sciences Division
   Monroe E. Freeman, Director
   Magnetic tape files include descriptions of grant supported research projects and an
   inverted subject index to them.

many efforts to create information networks that would make the stored data readily available to users everywhere: the Stafford Warren proposal, the studies by COSATI, the program of the National Library of Medicine, and the efforts of EDUCOM for instance. The planning for them has focused on administrative issues in such networks, on the physical problems of creating communication systems that will link computers together, and on the kinds of usage that such networks might satisfy. But in all of this planning, there has been the explicit view that the nation's major university research libraries are necessary components in an adequately functioning system. An important issue, therefore, is the role that library automation can play in these developments of mechanized information retrieval services and national information networks.

It seems clear that each major research library, and especially the university library, potentially has a threefold responsibility:

1. As the agency for acquisition of data of high utility.
2. As the point of entry into the national networks.
3. As the point for assistance in the use of this form of data.

First, small but growing numbers of libraries are already acquiring and using magnetic tape data from a variety of sources. For example, university libraries are receiving, on a continuing basis, magnetic tape data from the Bureau of the Census, the National Library of Medicine, the Library of Congress, Chemical Abstracts Services, and numerous other sources. Many information tapes are immediate candidates for acquisition, covering academic fields from the sciences and humanities to education and business administration. The fact is that magnetic tape is becoming as important a form for support of research as the book and the journal—for certain purposes, an even more useful one. And the library is a useful administrative organization for acquiring it.

Second, whether or not the individual library itself acquires a given data base, availability of it from wherever it may be stored will require points of access—consoles, procedures, and programs, methods of communication and control. Although one can visualize the individual investigator sitting in his own office and using his own console for communication to remote data bases (at other libraries and at national information centers), the realities—of economics, of the operating schedules and available services at the remote points, of the sheer volume of data processing and data transmission involved—all suggest that the vision will apply only to a limited number of investigators and a limited set of data bases. And yet, the library can provide a convenient administrative mechanism for access to national networks by other investigators. It already serves this function for the traditional printed material; it can maintain the union catalogs and directories by which to locate the mechanized data as well; it has the procedural mechanisms to ask for it; it has its own needs to obtain such access; and it is now experimenting with the operational reality of rapid communication so necessary for use of it.

Finally, even though one can also visualize the "machine-aided search" (as we shall discuss in the next chapter), the fact remains that the use of mechanized data bases is extremely complex, requiring training not only in the methods of using machinery but in the ways of formulating requests and of interpreting results. There may be a limited number of investigators sufficiently informed and willing to work with new data bases, but for the bulk of researchers, technical assistance will be a necessity. Fortunately, libraries and library schools are now in the process of creating a new generation of librarians who will have the combination of capabilities required to provide such service, and practicing librarians can learn these techniques through the variety of workshops and symposia being given throughout the country.[15]

The point, of course, is that the combination of requirements—for acquisition of data on a continuing basis, for cataloging of it, for providing economic access to it, and for aiding in the use of it—all serve to make the library a key agent in providing mechanized information retrieval services. Furthermore, a crucial issue is whether mechanized information retrieval services are called for in a specific situation (their value, in general, seems self-evident and demonstrated by the ever-growing number of mechanized data bases). There are always alternative resources, most of which are a traditional part of library service, and the librarian is in an ideal position to evaluate their relative utility.

In this connection, it must also be recognized that mechanized information services require support from a great variety of printed publications. Reference data bases involve the use of thesauri which must be made available to the user, and they provide references to the primary literature that the user wants. The library is still the best agency to ensure the availability of that literature. Even the numerical data bases require supporting services from the library. Maps and directories are essential to proper use of data retrieved from mechanized files.

THE "CENTER FOR INFORMATION SERVICES"

But we are faced with some enormous pragmatic problems—economic, administrative, technical. To provide a framework within which to discuss them, consider a "Center for Information Services" in the library providing the mechanized services involved in using such data bases. Figure 19.8 presents a schematic of relationships among the sources of data, the Center, and the researchers that it serves.

Such a Center, as an extension to normal library activities, would supplement both the media handled and the methods of operation. The usual library

[15] Note especially the "MARC Institutes," jointly sponsored by the Library of Congress and the Information Science and Automation Division of the American Library Association.

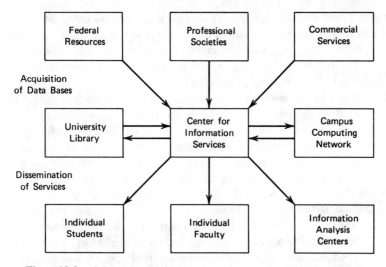

Figure 19.8   Schematic of information services from national data bases.

functions are those of acquisition, storage, cataloging, and circulation. The media presently include books, serials, microforms, and such special collections as manuscripts, incunabula, and archives. The Center for Information Services would emphasize the acquisition, storage, indexing, and dissemination of computer processible media, such as magnetic tapes. The emphasis on indexing rather than cataloging, dissemination rather than circulation, brings out the special attributes of a computer based system. Thus, while circulation suggests a reader taking a book out of a library, dissemination includes both this and active transmission of the contents to a reader at a remote console. Cataloging suggests the standard author, title, and subject guides. Indexing includes not only these, but greater depth of detail as well, through the ability of computer programs quickly to process vast amounts of data according to detailed and complex instructions. In this respect, the Center must be able to process a great variety of machine processible records. Many of these are already in existence but others are not and therefore the emphasis must be placed not just on the utilization of existing information retrieval programs. Instead, the need is for a software capacity for processing a variety of material.

A Center of this kind therefore must have the following characteristics. (1) It should be operational, designed to meet the daily needs of the community, and not simply a research system or an experiment. (2) It should be a general purpose system able to satisfy a variety of requests. (3) It should be adaptable in order to meet needs not initially anticipated, incorporating a capability for monitoring the history of its own operation and for continually studying that history to introduce improvements. (4) The system should encourage increased receptivity and use, with stress on education of prospective users, design for easy use, and responsiveness to changes in use. (5) The Center, as an administrative part of the library, should be designed so that library personnel can operate and provide the ongoing services of acquisition, cataloging and indexing, storage, and dissemination of the material peculiar to it.

Physically the Center can be envisioned as a storage facility with a library-based computer, linked to a larger network computer which would provide connection to on-line consoles. Requests to the Center would be handled by library personnel who could decide whether to use traditional resources, to use the library-based computer, to use it in conjunction with the more powerful network computer, or to allow the user to conduct searches himself at his console connected to the large-scale computer.

Because data bases stored elsewhere will also be important, the Center must be designed as a potential node in a computer-based information network. Before the end of the next ten-year period, computer networks and time sharing will have to become a normal educational tool and an operational aid to research. Since networks connecting various universities, research centers, and government agencies will require well-defined points of access, suitable for those not familiar with them as well as for those sophisticated with their use, the Center will occupy a particularly important role. The library has been the traditional operational informational resource, and it should be natural to turn to it for the service we are considering here.

In summary, the concept of a Center for Information Services is engendered by the imperatives of modern information technology. Its development will provide a supplement to the media and method of operation of the usual library and will include creation of new policies and procedures, new relations to other organizations, and new forms of cooperation with other centers. Emphasis must be placed on integrating a variety of data bases and programs. The system must be operational, general purpose, adaptable, and designed to encourage easy use. Organizationally the Center is viewed as an administrative part of the library. Physically it is viewed as a storage and processing facility embedded in a large complex network of computers.

THE PROBLEMS

Since machine-readable data bases have been developed for a variety of purposes outside those normally considered within the scope of the library, several problems are faced by the library in extending its scope to include acquiring such media, cataloging them, and providing "information services" based on them.

Some of the issues relate to the content: What kinds of material should the library acquire? Some of the issues concern library processes: How do we catalog magnetic tape materials? Some of the problems are technological: How do we provide man-machine communication? Some of them are administrative: How do we finance information services? How do we fit them within the traditional library structure? In 1965, the Institute of Library Research of the University of California, under funding from the National Science Foundation, started a program to study these problems, with emphasis on the following five questions.

1.   Are mechanized information services viable in themselves?

2.   Should the single university concern itself with acquisition of mechanized data bases?

3.   What types of data bases are of particular importance for consideration in acquisition?

4.   Is the library the appropriate agency in the university to acquire nationally produced data bases and provide mechanized information services from them?

5.   What are the technical problems involved in handling such data bases?

Viability

The first question to be considered in developing mechanized information services is whether such a Center will be viable. Will it offer information services not otherwise available, and will there be sufficient exploitation of the system to justify it? Will it justify the costs of acquiring and maintaining machine equipment and mechanized data bases?

These are not idle questions. Although most of the words of enthusiasts imply that these systems are indispensable it is not entirely clear that they are. When considered by the library (which, presently, has clear limits on the funds it can allocate to the various functions in its domain), it is a very serious question whether the use of such a system will justify its installation.

The costs of acquiring magnetic tape data bases vary from about $10,000 per tape (if the library must key-punch the data itself) to $70 per tape (if it is acquired from a national source). It seems clear that the upper range of costs, involved in preparing large information files, is great enough to preclude the library from incurring them solely for limited, local interest. However, the many large stores of information becoming available through national sources at the lower range of costs make it feasible to consider such services.

It is uncertain whether individuals will use a mechanized system. As is true with any revolutionary concept, there is little or no existing experience on which to predict future utilization. As a result, no concrete data can be produced on which to project more than a minimal demand for mechanized retrieval services, beyond those needs met just as well by printed indexes; on the other hand, availability of usable services may well create demand beyond the wildest present expectation. In discussing the issue of demand, the enthusiasts will emphasize the presumed effects of a new technology and present arguments on what can, in principle, be done. Those concerned with operation will emphasize the utility and quality of their present services. The users, by and large, are either apathetic or tend to emphasize the deficiencies in the present library system and speculate wildly about potential capabilities of mechanization. However, the general feeling seems to be that this kind of service is necessary and will be used more and more as the users are educated to its existence and potential.

The need for computerized information stores seems greater among those who need reference to factual data-engineers, social scientists, and doctors—than among those whose research depends more on ideas expressed in the literature. Where the compilation of data is as large as it is in the social sciences, for instance, computerization is the only means of tapping the store.

Some research is so closely associated with current directions that frequently identical work is done simultaneously. Here delay is intolerable—if the experimenter cannot find his answer immediately, it will be easier and more satisfactory to duplicate the research itself. Breakthroughs in the forefront of knowledge cannot wait for the information to make its way into the information system (nor does this kind of creativity depend on material that is easily retrievable). Until such time as results are filed directly in the system, by-passing the lag of conventional publication and review, the researcher "in the forefront of discovery" will continue as he always has. On the other hand, a great amount of research is concerned with history, description, and exposition. What might be called background research, whether it relates to a narrow or to a more general field systematic, exhaustive, historical, bibliographical research—lends itself to machine searching. Research that leans on analyzing, synthesizing, cataloging, and organizing data may benefit and even come to depend on the rapid scan, search, and retrieval from the large machine-readable files which computers make possible. It is this last kind of activity that has provided the pressure for creation of information analysis centers and that probably represents the primary service of a Center for Information Services.

Acquisition versus Use of National Networks

The local acquisition of data bases is, of course, not the only alternative available. In fact, the implication of all of the present planning for information networks is that remote access to data bases will eliminate the need for local acquisition. Will the university attempt to acquire machine-readable tapes that could contribute to academic research, or will it depend on outside agencies for service? Will it participate in some form of mechanized "information network?"

It seems, however, that university research libraries must consider the acquisition and manipulation of many mechanized information stores, as well as the use of outside agencies and participation in networks of information centers: First, although a central storehouse is promoted by some, it seems clear that at some level of activity the single point will become saturated and decentralization must be effected. As a result, the prospect for the future indicates that a national network system incorporating many separate, mechanized information stores will exist within ten years. University libraries with reputations as "centers of excellence" should be expected to continue their leadership in the transfer of information even as that transfer becomes more and more mechanized. It seems reasonable that network centers will gravitate to already recognized centers of excellence. Therefore, it is logical to assume that established campus "nodes" will acquire magnetic tape data bases and will serve as regional centers in the nationwide system.

Second, even before a national mechanized network becomes an actuality, single, mission-oriented systems are being developed at universities. There is economy in basing computer retrieval systems on mission-oriented tasks of critical size, matching current needs. It will be more significant to convert, combine, and extend currently operational systems than to create, *de novo*, the ultimate complete nationwide network. The resulting system would then be reliable enough to convince the user that this new tool would help him. It seems likely that an initial service of a university Center for Information Services would then be a directory of machine manipulable information— where it is, and what programs are available to tap it. This extension of a traditional library function (of union lists and interlibrary loan) will be necessary no matter how complete and complex the campus holdings in themselves may grow, since mechanized services should exploit national sources in networks and other large centers.

Third, it is realistic to consider that even when a network is in operation, data bases of high utility and high frequency of use will be acquired and stored at individual university campuses. Admittedly, many of the largest files cannot be used outside their own systems. For example, the Science Information Exchange and the Biological Abstracts Science Information Center (BASIC) feel that searching at present must be done by their own staffs. On the other hand, the *Citation Index* files of the Institute for Scientific Information have been formatted with the expectation of their being purchased and used by others. Chemical Abstracts Service is marketing its tapes, as well as the printed versions of *Chemical Abstracts*. Other data files, in rather rigid formats, are readily usable, and research progresses—exemplified by the Library of Congress MARC project—to develop formatted information files for wide-scale use.

This illustrates one of the primary difficulties in planning a Center for Information Services—the variety of the materials that it must handle. What can and must be done is to anticipate the problems they represent and experiment with solutions for them. Eventually, of course, networks will have great impact on standardization of data structures, representing a crystallization phenomenon like the dropping of a crystal into a supersaturated solution. Once something exists, people will tend to think about developing the system they are dreaming about in terms of compatibility with the operational system. Already the effects of such crystallization can be seen in the increasing acceptance of LC's MARC II format as a standard.

Content

The content of the tapes to be acquired by the library demands careful analysis. As we have indicated, in general, the following three kinds of information are being recorded in machine readable form.

Numerical Data. This kind of data can be very tightly formatted, so that searching can be done on fixed fields. Examples of such files are those containing records of the Census Bureau (Figure 19.9),[16] of hospitals, of engineering properties. The social scientists are strong in their feelings of the desirability—even necessity—for available numerical data banks. There already exists a National Council of Social Sciences Data Archives to represent their needs. These are collections of data from academic, commercial, and governmental sources, which include sociological, historical, political, and geographical information, primarily gathered by survey and poll. The ability to manipulate this sort of information is giving a forward thrust to social science research.

Reference. Reference data bases constitute a relatively new growing body of information. They exist primarily to tell where information can be found; they are the tools of the bibliographic trade.

They might, therefore, be labeled descriptive files, since they attempt to characterize a primary text in some way—by title, by descriptor, by abstract, or by all three. The descriptors and abstracts may be contributed manually or by machine techniques. But, in any case, there is an attempt not only to describe the content of the text but also to recognize future uses of it. Examples of this sort of computerized information are the Medlars tapes (Figure 9.15), the Library of Congress MARC tapes (Figure 9.14), *Chemical Abstracts* tapes, and *Biological Abstracts* tapes. Most of these tapes are part of large information systems which include other kinds of data bases as well. For example, CAS maintains a registry of chemical compounds, illustrated in Figure 19.10. As a class of data bases, they share many features in common beyond just the

---

[16] *1970 Census Summary Tape User Memorandum No. 20*, Bureau of the Census, October 6, 1969.

Figure 19.9   1970 Census Test Tapes.

TAPE DESCRIPTION

One 7-channel IBM compatible tape containing complete-count first count tallies of data for Dane County, Wisconsin based on the 1968 Madison, Wisconsin SMSA dress rehearsal for the 1970 Census. This tape has some data distributions suppressed to insure conformance with the confidentiality provisions of Title 13 of the U.S. Code. For further details concerning suppression conventions refer to the User Guide appendix section on confidentiality and data suppression in Complete-Count Technical Document No. 2, dated December 1968 (will be sent on receipt of order).

In 1970 the First-Count Tape Will Consist of Two Data Files as follows:

FILE A   The file is composed of ED, and block group summary records. The sequence of the file is ED and/or block group, within county, within State. Block groups split by MCD boundaries are shown separately for each part. (Block groups can be summed to tract totals by the user.)

FILE B   The file consists of summary records for the State, each county, each MCD, each MCD place total, and each Congressional District. The records are presented in four segments:

1. State Total Summary – Note: Because Dane County is the largest geographic unit for which data are tabulated, summary totals for Dane County are substituted for all Wisconsin State summaries.

2. County Component Summary Records – County by MCD by MCD place within State (Note: Only Dane County components are tabulated for Wisconsin. State totals agree with Dane County totals.)

3. Place Total Summary Records

4. Congressional District Summary Records – (Only one CD in Dane County.)

NOTE: For the test tape only, the two files are merged onto a single reel.

Special Technical Conditions Affecting Use of Tape:

Tape Width . . . .½ inch.

Reel Size . . . . . .10½ inch diameter: maximum 2400 feet.

Recording Density (CPI) . . . 556

Logical Record Size . . . 3,840 characters (Four 960 character blocks) per record for each block group, ED, or other summary area.

Block Size . . . . .960 character blocks subdivided into 8 sub-blocks of 120 characters each.

Size of Data Field . . . Generally 8 characters. Some 16 character fields exist and are identified.

File Size . . . . . .(For the test reel these files are contained on a single reel.);

File A – Approximately 400 to 600 logical records per tape.

File B – Approximately 80 logical records per tape.

Language . . . . . .BCD characters in 8 character groups. A limited set is used. See User Guide appendix "1107 Programming, Section 10-B-2, Character Set for Information Exchange."

Block Spacing . .¾ inch inter-block spacing. Tape label conventions – See User Guide Appendix "1107 Programming Section 10-B-3, Conventions for 1970 Summary Tapes."

TAPE COST: The cost of one reel of tape is $70.00. This fee includes the cost of physical tape reel itself plus the cost of copying, handling, postage, and technical documentation printing costs.

If you wish to purchase this test reel and documentation, please fill out the reverse side of this form.

purpose for which they are created. The fact that printed materials often have more than one author, that each document is described by a varying number of subject headings, and so on, have led to characteristic variable length records, individual fields themselves being repeated and variable in length.

Figure 19.10   Compound register data sheet.

MF	*	$C_4H_5N_5S$
PINH	*	*s*-Triazolo[3,4-*b*][1,3,4]thiadiazole, 6-amino-3-methyl-
PINTM	*	preparation and spectrum of
ID	*	66:2516c-2
T/R	*	591556N

Text. Files that have major portions of text in them can be used to provide automatic retrieval from the textual material. Such files run the gamut from short abstracts with a single small body of text, through report forms with several fixed fields and multiple short bodies of text, to full-blown large quantity complete text.

The abstract, illustrated in Figure 19.11, is the simplest kind of textual file. An abstract in a "reference" data base offers advantages that mere subject heading indexing cannot offer, as an aid in choosing the desired document. On the other hand, an abstract will usually occupy as much as ten times the space required for the citation and its associated index terms. Its "cost/effectiveness" is therefore open to question.

Recently, as the storage capacity in computer files has been increased, it has become feasible to record complete text. Texts hitherto available have been painstakingly and expensively key-punched, but as input devices are improved and as more and more journals employ computer-aided composition, increasing supplies of full text materials will be available. For example, the *Journal of Chemical Documentation* (JCD) (Figures 19.12 and 19.13), published by the American Chemical Society (ACS), is devoted to information retrieval problems in chemistry and related sciences. In 1966 the ACS undertook production of JCD by a computer-driven Photon 200. By the end of 1966, almost 100 articles were printed in this fashion. The number is expected to rise considerably in the future and, by the end of 1968, 500 to 600 articles will have been published. Eventually the ACS will publish other journals with the same technique.

With this wealth of material for the future, how is the library to choose? It will be an expensive even if imperative addition to the acquisition program. In the cases where the computerized material duplicates published material, what should be the criterion for selection—or is there a case for duplication? Will a source of information that is little used in book form perhaps justify the roughly comparable cost of being acquired on tapes because they may be more usefully and productively searched by machine than by hand?

oe 6000 (REV. 9-66)

DEPARTMENT OF HEALTH, EDUCATION, AND WELFARE
OFFICE OF EDUCATION

(TOP)	ERIC ACCESSION NO. ED 010 162	ERIC REPORT RESUME

| 001 | CLEARINGHOUSE
ACCESSION NUMBER | RESUME DATE
01-24-67 | P.A. | T.A. | IS DOCUMENT COPYRIGHTED?   YES ☐   NO ☐
ERIC REPRODUCTION RELEASE?   YES ☐   NO ☐ |

| 100
101
102
103 | TITLE
EFFECTS OF REDUCED LOADS UPON INTENSIVE INSERVICE TRAINING UPON THE CLASSROOM BEHAVIOR OF BEGINNING ELEMENTARY TEACHERS. |

| 200 | PERSONAL AUTHOR(S)
HITE, F. HERBERT * AND OTHERS |

300 310	INSTITUTION (SOURCE) OFFICE OF SUPT. OF PUBLIC INSTRUC., OLYMPIA, WASH.	SOURCE CODE XL079510
	REPORT/SERIES NO. CRP-2973	
320 330	OTHER SOURCE WASHINGTON STATE UNIV., PULLMAN	SOURCE CODE XL079700
	OTHER REPORT NO. BR-5-0360	
340	OTHER SOURCE	SOURCE CODE
350 400	OTHER REPORT NO.	
	PUB'L. DATE — — 66	CONTRACT/GRANT NUMBER

| 500
501 | PAGINATION, ETC.
EDRS PRICE   MF-$0.27   HC-$5.64   141p. |

| 600
601
602
603
604
605
606 | RETRIEVAL TERMS
INSERVICE TEACHING, *INSERVICE TEACHER EDUCATION, *TEACHER EVALUATION, ELEMENTARY SCHOOL TEACHERS, *WORK EXPERIENCE PROGRAMS, *BEGINNING TEACHERS, TEACHER ATTITUDES, EXPERIMENTAL PROGRAMS, *EFFECTIVE TEACHING, BEHAVIOR DEVELOPMENT, |

| 607 | IDENTIFIERS
PULLMAN, WASHINGTON |

| 800
801
802
803
804
805
806
807
808
809
810
811
812
813
814
815
816
817
818
819
820
821
822 | ABSTRACT
A STUDY WAS MADE TO SEE WHETHER EXPERIMENTAL TREATMENTS INVOLVING REDUCED WORK LOADS AND INTENSIVE INSERVICE INSTRUCTION WOULD AFFECT THE PERFORMANCES AND ATTITUDES OF BEGINNING TEACHERS. IT WAS HOPED THAT THE STUDY DATA WOULD SHOW TO WHAT EXTENT AN INTERNSHIP PROGRAM FOR CAREER TEACHERS WOULD BE JUSTIFIED. THE EXPERIENCE IN THIS STUDY WITH THE APPRAISAL TECHNIQUES USED TO EVALUATE BEGINNING TEACHERS PERFORMANCES SUGGESTS THAT EXPERIENCED TEACHERS CAN BE TRAINED TO USE AN OBSERVATION CHECKLIST AND ARRIVE AT A FAIR DEGREE OF AGREEMENT WITH OTHER SUCH TRAINED OBSERVERS. (LP) |

Figure 19.11   ERIC Abstract.

Location of a Center for Information Services

The library has long served the informational needs of the community. The usual library functions of acquisition, storage, cataloging, and circulation of books, serials, microforms and special collections are equally applicable to the

Computer-Aided Typesetting for the *Journal of Chemical Documentation*

J. H. KUNEY, B. G. LAZORCHAK, and S. W. WALCAVICH
American Chemical Society Publications, Washington, D. C.

Received January 21, 1966

A computer program designed to handle the variety of formats encountered in the typesetting of scientific manuscripts for journal publication is now in the production stage. The process starts with the preparation of a punched tape as input to the computer and results in a punched tape keyed to operate a photocomposition device

This issue of the *Journal of Chemical Documentation* marks the beginning of regular production of this journal using computer-aided typesetting methods and an important first step in evaluating the encoding of scientific manuscripts in machine-readable form at the time of primary publication. More than two years of ACS staff effort has gone into the development of computer programs suited to the handling of the variety of type formats and special characters required in the publication of scientific manuscripts. Further, work is in progress to improve procedures of typesetting—*via* computer—of chemical structures, mathematics, editing and correction routines, and page formatting.

The significance of computer-aided composition in the handling of chemical information will be developed in two papers to be presented before the Division of Chemical Literature at the ACS national meeting in Pittsburgh, March 23-25, 1966: "Encoding Manuscripts as Primary Input to Chemical Information Handling Systems," by J. H. Kuney, B. G. Lazorchak, and S. W. Walcavich, and "Computer-Based Composition at Chemical Abstracts Service," by W. C. Davenport and J. T. Dickman. The procedure used in producing this journal (Figure 1) begins in the traditional manner with the edited manuscript prepared in the same way as for other composition systems. The manuscript is then keyboarded on a Friden Flexowriter (Programmatic) to produce an eight-channel, punched paper tape in Flexowriter code (a binary-coded decimal system of odd parity).

In addition to the text, the operator of the Flexowriter inserts instructions to the computer for format control or typesetting instructions. There are 45 keys on the standard keyboard; three keys are used to originate instructions to the computer while the remaining 42 keys are used for text. To achieve the 90-character positions required for a font of type on the matrix disc, three ligatures are moved from text keys into one of the two control modes.

Two control keys are used to tell the computer that the character or characters which follow are instructions to be controlled by the computer program. For example, *Control 1* is used basically to control size and spacing of characters, and *Control 2* is used for type face, space between lines, line width, and end-of-line functions. The use of two control keys minimizes case shifts, results in a more readable copy, and gains more flexibility in placement of items on the keyboard. Through the use of the

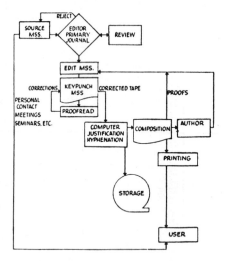

Figure 1. Simplified flow diagram of information transfer from source to user, including flow of manuscript for primary publication using computer-aided typesetting.

two control keys, access is provided to 1440 characters available on the matrix disc of the Photon 200, in different sizes and in a variety of line lengths and leading, limited only by the width of the film and the dictates of good typography. A sample of hard copy is shown in Figure 2.

A third control, *Control 3,* is obtained by punching the color shift of the Flexowriter which permits the operator to originate or to use a MACRO which is, in effect, a series of instructions stored within the computer. To set the title for this article, the operator performed the following keystrokes: (1) Color Shift, (2) a, (3) Color Unshift, (4) Text of title. When these codes were read by the computer, instructions were issued as follows: center the title, 14-point Century Bold type, 18 points lead between and after each line, 500-unit line length,

Figure 19.12 *Journal of Chemical Documentation* text.

SAMPLE PAGE FROM THE JOURNAL OF CHEMICAL DOCUMENTATION

0316010060A1624868444244206844412412T96080292420424172248420564418077208029224817265256444417224856
8S76080172664444244446524424T64720280444418444242/24544412454440005000T7296087620Y44612/24Y44884/56T72S80/
36/56Y44576420564Y4429288WT76/36/56T64/36T64Y44884/56T72S80/36/24Y44S00S76/36
S88N56960T72/24/56S76T12T6454441235444000I60I00004A1681624857641266068WT608076660402084866088080028
0412660248424444412T640804206848660652684180444466096000805884206841726525644444172248568576544412154
4000E005444

032926125644S200802926005884444256568248172172684S200000802928017266068465242496008041256465268444496
6606 00T640804205646526844446609S76080666006001720806444420480588420684172660660S0808084125644204424 68
4172564/32080172248004100004080292660444125617256444446601726840/24080412564452684496660600T640806664444
24080420424684248684180684S8808066600172080660444444246464606580805766601724206602486604444S20R40816
F5254413254440006I0100004A1610410412440040802004400408041268444444S08576080576660180684660652660/5654
44124544000

02484424444445082424080576660412412564652080420660172664442400080292224857641266 60B4808057666040420B4
86605760802802412660248424441265208042068480802486606526841804444466024808058842068417265256444441722248
56854408026868424808066444240805884206846600246864402048480224042068408066605040206660684444
46605582866008044448660650017208049642444466480248420420426842482564412652420424652080184564444457
608024044444246001722565408066600884544412554440016010000W4A1661210410410412440040802901500808060006
524444564S08080

FIGURE I-18: A portion of a tape dump of the Journal of Chemical Documentation (machinable) data base. Decoding occurs by reading from right to left with "normal" ending of the paragraph being the starting point. An illustration of the coding at the individual character level is the following:

080280565808057666060024868444125685650808 0

0802805658080576660600248684441256856508080	
Space	
p	
u	
b	
l	
i	
s	
h	
e	
d	
Space	
b	
y	
Space	

Figure 19.13 Journal of Chemical Documentation sample data.

acquisition, storage, indexing, and dissemination of computer processible media, such as magnetic tapes. A Center for Information Services is therefore a natural extension to normal library activities. However, because large-scale mechanized information services imply sophisticated computer systems, the question has been raised as to whether the library can provide adequately trained personnel. Although librarians are being educated (both in schools and on the job) to be more knowledgeable about modern machine handling, some people feel that computing-facility personnel could absorb information-handling techniques more easily than librarians could learn computer techniques. Others have pointed out that the issue is not merely one of machine operation but rather of man-machine communication. They feel that formulating requests to a computer for a search program requires an expertise in serving informational needs which is outside the usual interest of programmers and operators in the computing center. Figure 19.14 lists some of the pros and cons concerning the desireability of providing mechanized information services as extensions of library service.

Financial Issues

In financial planning, consideration must be given to three areas of cost (equipment, personnel, and acquisitions) and three sources of funding (regular library budget, special project budgets, and a "community service" budget). Figure 19.15 presents a hypothetical, but representative budget.

Library Budget. First, funding for personnel and library equipment in a Center for Information Services, since it is an operational part of the library, might be built into the regular library budget (although funding for the library's computer and at least some of its remote terminals may be handled as part of the capital costs of a library building program). The equipment specifications outlined later in this chapter are designed to produce an operation that will be economically viable and not represent a burden on the library's budget. They therefore assume that the CIS computer is predominantly a service computer to the library. As such, its costs should be completely covered by the library's budget, with the CIS being simply one of the functions served. Many of the personnel, particularly those in the acquisitions, cataloging, and reference staff, will already be in regularly budgeted positions and the CIS will merely be a service added to those they now provide. Library systems staff ought to be part of the regularly budgeted staff of any large library, regardless of whether or not a CIS is involved. Operating staff for the library's computing facility must already be considered as part of the operating budget if the library is to mechanize any of its clerical processes.

Special Projects Budgets. Second, funding for personnel and equipment needed to serve the needs of special projects should be funded by them. In particular, the existence of the CIS is likely to stimulate the establishment of a variety of information centers which will depend upon it for services. Their budgets should cover their own costs for information specialists, remote terminals, large-scale direct access stores, and the use of the campus computer. The services of the CIS would still be covered by the library's budget, provide 1 the degree of utilization—including such special projects—falls within the capacity of the CIS. If the degree of utilization exceeds the planned capacity of the CIS, consideration might then be given to establishment of a direct cost for utilization of CIS beyond a defined maximum level. In this way, a facility larger than needed for library processes, but required by a greater CIS load, could be funded by special project charges.

Community Service Budget. Third, the methods of financing which basically regard the CIS as a university funded extension of the library will only be adequate to provide services to the single campus—its faculty, its students, and its own specially funded projects. The costs of serving larger communities, including participation in computer-based information networks, are an entirely different matter. Such networks may place a burden upon the individual institution completely beyond its financial capacity. The present pattern of inter-library loans provides an analogy. Although there is a presumption of reciprocity in the existing interlibrary loan systems, it is well known that larger university libraries lend significantly more than they borrow. The resulting inequities are generally ignored, since the total traffic, and thus the cost to any individual library, is of a size that can be absorbed in the interest of the general welfare. The effects of a national network may not change the general pattern of such services, but they will substantially increase the traffic. Thus the university with a wealth of resources may find its costs skyrocketing to the point where they cannot be absorbed. For this reason it is imperative that mechanisms for resolving these inequities be defined. Payments based on the number of requests processed would recognize that the well-endowed universities are providing more than simply content—whether books or data bases; they are providing services to check the validity of the request and to determine its availability as well as processing services. On the other hand, payment based on the number of requests satisfied would recognize actual value received.

In some cases, contractual arrangements with federal agencies may be used to cover the costs of services provided by the centers of excellence and make it possible to avoid pricing of individual services (the Regional Medical Libraries, funded by the National Library of Medicine, representing a case in point). In other cases, reimbursement of costs may be treated as a burden on the general network. Finally, biparty (or multiparty) contracts may provide for a mutually acceptable basis for equalization.

Figure 19.14   Should the library acquire magnetic tape data bases—PROS and CONS.

PRO	CON

ISSUE: THE PURPOSE OF THE LIBRARY AS AN INSTITUTION

As a general principle, the library is the permanent agency of the university commissioned to collect, systematize and disseminate recorded knowledge to the academic community. This it does, exclusively and on a continuing basis.

Magnetic tape, although a new medium of information, is certainly well within this general scope, just as microforms, slides, and phonorecords are.

Furthermore, if the library is regarded not merely as the repository of the *record*, but as the agency chiefly involved in the transfer of *information* from the producer to the user, the case for adding information on magnetic tapes is strengthened, because of the ease with which it can be processed.

The modern library developed as the historical concomitant to the ascendancy of the book, from which it even derives its name. It stores anything else with difficulty, and only by treating it like books (Serials and pamphlets are bound like books, and microforms are miniaturized printed documents.)

There is no inherent reason why, as a general principle, the library should be responsible for all forms of recorded knowledge; for example, an Academic Communications Facility is the agency on some campuses designated to acquire and disseminate instructional films, which it may do at least as well as the library could.

ISSUE: THE NATURE OF THIS PARTICULAR MEDIUM

Information in a machine–readable format does not exist *in vacuo*, but bears an organic relationship to the traditional forms of recorded knowledge:

(a) Some tapes contain the full text of printed documents already to be found in the library.

(b) Other tapes provide reference and bibliographic information to assist the patron in using the traditional materials.

(c) Libraries, information centers and publishing houses are foremost among the organizations creating data bases or supplying services from them.

(d) In view of these factors, it appears that most large special libraries will develop this side of their activities, if only because they see themselves among the primary users.

Essential to the use of magnetic tapes are the computer and a staff of people trained in programming and machine use. If some central computing facility on the campus is used, the library will be dependent upon the efficiency and cooperative spirit of that facility. The library might be in the position of telling its patrons that this or that range of services is available, only for the patron to find that they are not.

A second feature of magnetic tape data bases which is not found in any of the library's 'traditional' records is the dynamic nature of the medium. Additions to the file come, not only as a fresh issue in a series of issues, but as changes in the file itself as well. Apart from the programming tasks foreseen in the updating of files, the library will become responsible for the security, the

Figure 19.14 *(continued)*

PRO	CON
(e) Placing the tapes under the supervision of the librarian will enable him to deploy the printed collection with the tapes, to evaluate better the relative merits of tapes, and to direct the borrower to the best source for his information needs—tapes or printed documents.	currency, the manipulation, and perhaps also for the formatting and reformatting of the information on these very complex files.

ISSUE: THE QUALIFICATIONS AND EXPERTISE REQUIRED TO PERFORM THIS SERVICE

The library is a specialist organization wholly dedicated to the problems of recorded information. The 3 essential processes—(1) obtaining the records, (2) systematizing them, and (3) making them available—form the very lines of its organizational structure (Acquisitions, Cataloging, and Circulation or Reference). These will be as necessary if the university acquires magnetic tapes (whoever may be made responsible for them) as they are for books, serials, etc. The *basic* expertise, however, is the same, and the library already possesses it.

Naturally some special training will be necessary, but libraries generally are now beginning to benefit from the introduction, some years ago, of data processing and information retrieval classes into the library school curriculum.

The dynamic nature of magnetic tape files has been adduced as a debit for the library—it may equally be seen as a credit, since the library alone has had many years of experience in the technical and administrative aspects of serials control.

Far from the library being structured to handled "recorded information," its acquisition procedures are built around the print-publishing industry, its cataloging techniques around the single-subject monograph and its public services around the attributes of portability and legibility.

The processing of machine readable data bases requires totally new skills not presently to be found within the library. For the operation of the hardware itself, people with a detailed knowledge of both hardware and software are indispensable. Even if this aspect is controlled by the campus computing facility, there are still many specialized tasks requiring computer programmers, system analysts, and staff trained in logic, statistics or structural linguistics, and of course information science as a separate discipline. Suddenly to expect librarians to be familiar with terms like "Boolean operations, codes, search strategies, compilers"—to take only the software side—is unrealistic, especially in view of the content of library education in the past and the composition of its personnel. To overcome such difficulties will take more than a "quickie" course of instruction for existing library staff—it will take perhaps a decade more of intensive training in library schools.

Figure 19.14 *(continued)*

PRO	CON
ISSUE: REQUIREMENTS OF SPACE AND PHYSICAL FACILITIES	
The library is a permanent campus body, having its own physical facilities and procedures for the maintenance of the collections. It is likely that the library's computer can be utilized for C.I.S. processing tasks, thus helping to justify costs.	To locate tapes in the library would require temperature control, humidity control, separate tape cabinets and other devices. There would be no point in having any tapes stored in the library if the computer on which they are to be processed is elsewhere. Even if all these special facilities were to be set up in the library, they would only add to the existing problems of overcrowding.
ISSUE: ADMINISTRATION	
The library usually is a well-administered organization, with a history of performance and dependability. It possesses the administrative mechanisms, the personnel, and the proven fiscal stability. In contrast to many computing facilities and "audiovisual media centers" which often do not know from year to year the precise extent or sources of their funding, the library is not a grant-supported, or a temporary, or an experimental operation—it is permanent, stable and efficient.	Administratively, libraries are already overly large bureaucracies. Adding to them another major activity would simply burden them further. Also, the library has always been a conservative organization, relatively slow to change. It is not reasonable to expect it to handle such a radical shift in administration needs.
ISSUE: COST	
Since the library already has the organization, the personnel and the expertise to provide information services on a whole-campus basis, it will be cheaper to handle magnetic tapes using these existing facilities than either (a) Using any other campus body (which?), or	It is by no means clear that a systematic acquisition program which operates in advance of any stated demand is the best way to approach the costly business of acquiring data bases. *Ad hoc* acquisition might make individual items more expensive, but it could be vastly cheaper in total. In those cases where the tapes are not

Figure 19.14 (*continued*)

PRO	CON
(b) Adapting any other campus body to this function, or (c) Creating a complete new agency. —it is obvious that the last alternative would simply add enormously to the developmental and operational costs without any guarantee of a competent and continuing service afterwards. The librarian has developed working relations with departments (e.g. via the faculty library committees) by which to resolve the problems of allocation of financial resources among various campus needs for library materials.	available for purchase, but for rent or remote consultation only, complicated service agreements are called for, often entailing issues of copyright: the fewer of these that the library has to become involved in, the better. The library's budget is already seriously strained, and there are grounds to wonder whether it could bear the huge increases needed for the acquisition of data bases. A separate agency with its own funding might prove more efficient, even including the immediate capital outlay for its creation. Furthermore, the allocation of funds among the many competing subject interests is already a difficult enough problem without adding these data bases, which customarily cost hundreds or even thousands of dollars each.

ISSUE: OFF-CAMPUS SERVICE

PRO	CON
The library long ago accepted that it had a responsibility to off-campus users, and has developed a set of reasonable guidelines as to the extent of that responsibility. One thing is certain: whatever problems the library would have to face arising from the possession of data bases, no other campus agency has a fraction of its administrative and professional capacity to deal with off-campus use, and any other agency would therefore confront an extra problem over and above the considerable task of serving the whole campus.	There are many very serious problems: (a) The library is finding its existing rate of off-campus service something of a burden. With data bases, their scarcity and sophistication will ensure that the off-campus demand will rise. (b) Paid outside user demand is usually satisfied at the expense of ongoing campus services and campus users. If industrial and business firms have paid for a service they are in a position to demand priority, and this creates a strain on the regular ongoing library services. (c) The general public may well consider that they have the absolute right to free access to the census (and other government products) and a tax-supported institution might find it hard to charge for costly service.

Figure 19.14   (*continued*)

PRO	CON
ISSUE: TIMING	

PRO	CON
Although certain questions of the extent of library involvement may stand unresolved, it is plain that if the library does not take the initiative at this point, then all this new mechanized activity will inevitably flow round the library and it will be reduced to the role of a kind of housing facility for humanities literature, while the sciences and the social sciences will come to depend basically on another type of facility located elsewhere, completely outside of and unrelated to the traditional library.	Before the library becomes involved in a computerized information scheme it should give top priority to mechanizing its ongoing daily bread-and-butter operations such as Acquisitions, Circulation and Serials. This is a major effort which will require complete attention of all existing library staff, departments and the Library Systems staff, and the library can ill afford to have their attention diverted into the information aspect which would be possible and profitable only as a subsequent development.
By 1969 there were about 100 major data bases available, many of them reference and bibliographic in nature, and the U.S. Census of 1970 will itself demand a response from the library—so the timing is already very close-run. Tactical problems can be attacked as they develop, but there is no doubt of the larger issue of whether or not data bases will be used—the library itself will be among the heaviest users, with MARC tapes already becoming essential tools in the library.	It has been pointed out that the rapidly changing computer technology may leave the library with a heavy investment in a lot of obsolescent data bases. For example, in the last four years the density of the magnetic structures on these tapes has changed three times. Each change requires a large reprogramming effort and reinvestment in equipment.

Acquisitions Budget. The costs of acquisitions represent a particularly difficult and touchy issue. A rough estimate of the cost of magnetic tape data bases, considering the data bases studied, seems to be about $500 per tape (each containing up to 20 million characters). A single campus CIS might reasonably acquire, over its first five years of operation, about 2000 tapes (an average of 400 each year at an estimated annual cost of $200,000). As a percentage of the book budget of a large university library, this does not seem to be excessive, and in fact viewed in terms of "characters per dollar" it is comparable with books and serials (about 40,000 characters per dollar in each case). However, such a quantitative picture fails to recognize the difficulties that the "book budget" represents, and it would require an especially courageous and far-seeing university librarian to commit 10 to 20 percent of his book budget to this form of acquisition (at least, without a clear demand for it on the part of his faculty). Therefore, although eventually the costs of magnetic tape data bases should be a part of the library's budget for acquisition, initially some other special sources of funds should be a necessity. In many cases, the budgets of special projects might

Figure 19.15   Representative CIS annual budget, (dollars).

	Regular Library Budget	CIS Library Budget	Special Projects Budgets
Equipment costs			
Library computer	30,000	70,000	
Remote terminals	12,000	6,000	12,000
Direct access stores	2,000		10,000
Campus network computer	10,000	20,000	150,000
Operating Staff			
Library staff		2,200,000	
Information specialists	30,000		200,000
Computer Staff			
Systems staff		30,000	
Programmers	10,000	20,000	
Machine operators	30,000	70,000	
Key-punchers	5,000	10,000	25,000
Acquisition costs	150,000	1,500,000	
	3,926,000	279,000	397,000
Activity per year	2,000,000 volumes circulated	1000 files searched	

include funds to cover acquisition of magnetic tape data bases; in other cases, a separate commitment of university funds may be necessary.

Technical Issues

Several technical issues must be considered. How should the great variety of formats and operating programs implicit in the acquisition of a number of data bases be handled? Should the data be stored in direct access stores or on tapes? What functions should be served by the library and what by the computing facility?

1. *The issue of the variety of materials.* As discussed earlier, it constitutes one of the primary difficulties in planning future networks. But it exists even at the level of the single-campus information service. If a library acquires 20 different data bases, should it also acquire and use the 500 or more operating programs associated with them? Studies indicate that the answer is no. The

logistic problem is too great in handling and controlling this many programs; the problems of system compatibility are almost unresolvable. A second alternative is the conversion of acquired data bases to a standard, common format. Again, studies indicate that the answer is that too much data cannot be so reduced and would be lost. A third alternative is the definition of a single set of "task-oriented," generalized programs capable of performing a defined set of tasks on a wide range of data bases. It is this alternative that we shall explore in more detail.

2.   *The issue of direct access storage versus tape storage.* Studies indicate that library use of these mechanized information stores must be based on tape storage, with scheduled batch processing. The retrieved data resulting from such batch operation may then be stored in direct access files for utilization by the requester himself. However, there has been a strong belief that only on-line, direct access was worthy of consideration, that only imaginative, creative uses of data bases would provide a valid rationale for acquisition of them, and that such uses will not develop in a pedestrian environment of batch access to the data.

3.   *The issue of appropriate division of function between the library and the computing facility.* This issue is particularly germane. The library has functions analogous to the traditional ones of acquisition, cataloging, storage, and service. As such, their role becomes one of assuring the ready availability of the desired data. The use of that data, once it is made available, can best be made directly through the computing facility. Under these conditions, the access to the stored data bases must be accompanied by technical advice from the library staff. It is expected that the librarian will help to determine for each inquiry how the answer is best found. This may be by reference to traditional printed sources or by searching library held tapes. The tape search itself might be best conducted on the library's own computer or it might require the larger facilities of the computing network. If necessary, the librarian must be able to direct the investigator to remote systems that can be entered through telecommunication links.

Now let us examine these technical problems in detail, considering both library issues and computer issues.

CATALOGING MAGNETIC TAPE DATA BASES[17]

The cataloging of magnetic tapes offers some unique problems to libraries. These tapes differ from printed materials and microforms in that the information on a given physical reel can be erased, copied onto another reel, or

[17] Troutman, Joan, "Standards for Cataloging of Magnetic Tape Material," Part 4 of the Final Report on *Mechanized Information Services in the University Library*. Los Angeles: Institute of Library Research, December 15, 1967.

stored in other machineable forms (for example, on disk or drum). Magnetic tapes for information interchange do not contain the equivalent of a title page, and the visible tape label is often scant identification. Therefore, most of the information used for cataloging must be taken from associated documentation, from sample printouts, and from programmers or others working with the files.

There are three requirements for the records that must be kept of magnetic tapes. (1) There is the catalog record which will be used in the library. This must identify the tapes, indicate what type of information is on them and what is retrievable under a given programming system, and refer to other materials which must be utilized in order to formulate a search strategy. This record should also indicate associated data and programs, refer to other system files (for example, vocabulary and cross-references tapes), and provide reference to detailed documentation of format. (2) There are the operational records to be kept by the data processing facility. These are concerned with physical handling, updating, and keeping track of the current status of each physical reel, and include all tapes utilized by the facility. (3) There is the complete and detailed documentation as to the format (length of each field, field identification codes, and the like), which would be supplied by the issuing agency and be utilized by programmers.

Although these records are in many ways interrelated, the one of most importance to the library is the first type indicated: the catalog to be used in the library A possible standard catalog form is shown in Figure 19.16. Its use is discussed in detail in the Appendix to this chapter, including several illustrative examples.

It is anticipated that at a Center for Information Services a reference librarian will serve as the primary point of contact between the patron and the computer. That is, on receiving a reference request, the librarian will decide whether that question could best be answered through conventional reference services or through a machine search of one of the magnetic tape files. The catalog record of those files, then, must serve certain functions.

Conventional Requirements

First, it must be a conventional and approachable record of holdings. This would include entry, title, date, a brief description, a serials holding record where applicable, and subject analysis.

Entry and Title. The Anglo-American Cataloging Rules (American Library Association, Chicago, 1967) would be appropriate for both choice and form of entry, and the use of those rules, although not always insuring consistency from place to place in the handling of magnetic tape, would go a long way toward doing so. In the title statement (or entry under title as in the case of certain

Figure 19.16   Standard catalog form for magnetic tapes.

ENTRY   CALL No.

BRIEF DESCRIPTION

MAJOR SUBJECT AREAS

FIELDS OF DATA

Computer   _____   Recording mode _____
Bit Density   _____   Record format   _____
Tracks, Parity _____   Record length   _____
File name   _____   Block length   _____
Tape label   _____

File size: Tape reels   _____   Logical records _____
Increment/yr: Tape reels _____   Logical records _____
File organization   _____
Copying restrictions _____
Holdings   _____

RELATED FILES	MATERIALS RELATING TO SEARCH FORMULATION
PROGRAMS FOR UTILIZATION OF DATA	FOR MORE INFORMATION, DOCUMENTATION

serials and the like), a distinction must be made between two "types" of tape files: those that represent original records, and those that represent transcription of printed sources. The latter will have a title corresponding to the printed material (for example, *Journal of Chemical Documentation*) and can be listed accordingly. However, a problem arises with "original" tape files in that many of them are issued without a clear-cut title designation. For example, documentation from the American Petroleum Institute refers to its "master document tape file"; the Bonneville Power Authority refers to the "Abstract file"; National Library of Medicine (MEDLARS) refers to the CCF (Compressed Citation File); General Electric Flight Propulsion Division refers to its "uniterm Master Tape," and project URBANDOC refers to its "master file." Such tapes, though issued serially, would be entered under the corporate body (Rule 6B), since that name is required for adequate identification of them. In addition, a title that might better identify or describe the contents of such tapes should probably be assigned. For example, the NLM tapes are commonly referred to by the project name "MEDLARS." Similarly, files issued by projects MARC and URBANDOC have become best known by those names. Assigned titles would be enclosed in brackets.

Date. The date of issuance of a file should be given. Many tapes will be issued serially. Thus the date would be that of the first reel or portion of a reel.

Brief Description. A field has been allotted for a brief description of each tape file, roughly corresponding to the types of statements that would be included in informal notes. For example, the description might include an extended subtitle, or deal with such items as clarification of title, contents, or date (if the date of issuance varies significantly from the period covered by the contents), or correlation of the tape file with published (printed) material, for example MEDLARS Condensed Citation File and *Index Medicus*. For serials, a statement as to the basis of issuance should be included. Some confusion might arise here because some tapes will be "serials" in that they will be issued periodically, while others will actually be transcriptions of published periodicals. Care must be taken not to confuse the basis of issuance of the published serial with that of the tape itself. Two more items included in this field, where applicable, are: (1) the name of the agency that actually created (that is, programmed) the file, if it is not under its title; and (2) the beginning date of the printed form of a serial that is being issued in machineable form.

Holdings. For tapes that are transcriptions of published periodicals, volume numbers and date designations can be given. For files original to tape form, holdings can be indicated by date. Detailed (that is, weekly or monthly) records will not be included here, but will be kept elsewhere.

Subject Cataloging. Another requirement would be subject cataloging of the tapes. For bibliographic and index files, this presents certain problems. For example, NASA index tapes cover hundreds of subjects ranging from "management planning" to "information retrieval" to "infrared astronomy." Obviously, a visible, nonautomated catalog cannot economically list all of these approaches. Here the librarian has an added help, however, in that bibliographic tape files usually have a corresponding printed thesaurus of terms (subjects) that are covered. These thesauri could be shelved near the reference desk and be used (by librarian and patron) as an aid in determining which files would yield the most appropriate answer to a given request. There is, however, still the need for a general characterization of subject—"Medical Bibliography" for MEDLARS, or "Educational Research" for ERIC, etc. Since a wide range of subject matter will be available on magnetic tapes, much of it corresponding to printed material, and since the CIS will be in a university library, use of the *Library of Congress List of Subject Headings* seems feasible at this time.

Classification and Numbering. The last "conventional" aspect to the cataloging of magnetic tape files is the assignment of a "call number": that is, a number that will uniquely identify each file. If there is more than one *file* on a physical tape reel, then each file will have its own call number. Conversely, one file can span several reels and, in this case, each reel will be further identified by the portion of the file it contains. This division will usually be by date, although other divisions (for example, alphabetically by subject) are possible.

As a means of categorizing the files and relating them to other library materials, as well as identifying them, it seems logical to assign a Library of Congress call number. However, this number will not be indicative of the actual shelving location of the tapes, but will serve as a "key" to the data processing facility's record of the tape reels. This is necessary because a given physical reel can hold different data at different times as files grow, are merged, erased, transferred, or reorganized in various ways. (Many data processing facilities print a daily record of the status of each reel.) Thus, for example, if the librarian sends a request to data processing for Z6660 U58m 1963-1967 (part of the Medlars Condensed Citation File), a look-up will be done, and perhaps reels 407, 411-417 and 423 will be pulled for processing. Or, if a request is sent for PR 3560 M39t (*Milton's Paradise Lost*) the look-up may reveal that this is file number 2 on reel 117.

Additional Requirements

Up to this point we have discussed cataloging of tapes in much the same manner as one might discuss cataloging a book, that is, as an identification and record of holdings. Now we shall consider the added aspects to the record that must be kept because of specific properties of magnetic tapes.

Physical and Logical Characteristics. There are certain physical and logical characteristics of a tape which are indications of possible computer compatibility, and which can be important factors in programming and in the processing of a search or a tape copy request. They are: the equipment on which the tape was created (manufacturer, computer number and model), density (bits per inch), parity, number of tracks (channels), recording mode (that is, binary, bcd, ebcdic), record format (fixed, variable, blocked, unblocked), record length, file name, and tape label information (since knowledge of labels can be essential in order to work with certain tapes on certain computers). Given these characteristics, then, it should be possible for a librarian or patron to specify to a data processing facility all that is needed in order, at least, to have a tape copied successfully. (Also included here is a statement as to copying restrictions on the data involved. If the material is restricted, tape label information will not be given.)

Related Files. A special aspect of magnetic tapes is that they are often involved in multifile systems. For example, the Library of Congress MARC project issued four files: the MARC catalog record, the MARC author title record, the MARC descriptive cross reference tracing record, and the MARC subject cross reference tracing record. It is possible for these files to be utilized independently, but some or all of them could be involved at one time in a sophisticated information retrieval system. Therefore, although each file is described in a separate catalog record, it is obvious that cross-references should be made in each case to the related files. A file that is necessary to the searching of another (as the MeSH file is to the MEDLARS Compressed Citation file for a subject search) could be indicated by an asterisk. Then, the catalog record for that file would be consulted also, as an aid to the formulation of an appropriate search strategy.

Programs and Documentation. There is information relating to a tape file that would be useful to a patron in certain circumstances; for example, if he wished to create a program for special manipulation of the data. Therefore, references should be given to existing programs (whether those created by the issuing agency or those written elsewhere) and to complete documentation as to file format. Much of this data would probably be on file at the CIS and copies might be made available on request.

Format and Field Information. We have stated that the reference librarian will serve as the primary point of contact between the patron and the computer. She will receive a request and, let us suppose, decide that this could best be answered by a machine search. She (or the patron) will either have a file in mind or will look under the desired subject to find an appropriate entry. The information previously discussed will be found, but more must be known about the file before a search request can be formulated.

The catalog record of a file must reflect the type of information that it contains. For "reference" and "source data" tapes, this will mean a listing of the fields of data that are in each logical record (for example, a bibliographic entry). For most files, this information can be given in the space allotted on the catalog form. However, some records (such as those on the Census tapes) are so extensive that several pages are required to describe them. In such a case, a summary paragraph will be given and also, if applicable, a list of major retrieval points. A reference will be made to other printed sources for the complete field information

For "natural language text" files, since no specific fields can be named, any special manipulative features or retrieval possibilities will be listed, and references will be given to further documentation.

Retrieval Possibilities. Librarian and patron together must understand the file in terms of possible search parameters, which depend partly on the format of the tapes and partly on a specification of what various programs (or levels of programming) will handle. This part of the catalog record becomes specialized, then, in that it was meant to be consulted in the context of a given programming situation with a given tape format. This record will change as programs and formats and computer technology change.

Union Catalogs and Directories

Up to the present time, most magnetic tapes have been retained and used solely by the agency that originated them. Now, directories are being compiled which will serve to make known the wide range of information and data available on tape.[18]

The function of Centers for Information Services (or similar agencies) will be to acquire tapes of more general interest from a variety of sources, and provide the capabilities to process them. Inherent here are possibilities for coordination of acquisitions, and the creation of a Union Catalog. This catalog would represent the holdings of Centers with a broad spectrum of data bases, and the ability and resources to process them for an individual or another agency.

Union Catalogs have traditionally served as a basis for interlibrary loan of printed materials. However, magnetic tapes would not be loaned as such, but rather they would be copied (if they were compatible with the requesting agency's system), or else searched, and the results sent to the requester. The evaluation of compatibility could be based on information found in the catalog record, assuming that a full listing of physical characteristics is included. The Union Catalog, then, would serve as an indicator of system compatibility, as well

---

[18] *Directory of Computerized Information in Science and Technology.* New York: Science Associates International, 1968.

as a locating device. (Hopefully, directories would also indicate compatibility data and would be utilized in the CIS in deciding which tapes to acquire as well as in ascertaining available data bases.)

If we assume the Union Catalog to be a major form of communication between Centers for Information Services, then standardization of cataloging practice becomes extremely important. The ideal would, of course, be for each participant to use the same cataloging format. A duplicate of each record could then be sent to a central location, which would be responsible for coordination and assignment of logograms.

The size of the catalog, the number of agencies interested in acquiring its information, and available funding would determine what would then be feasible. Ideally, the catalog would be indexed or cross-referenced, printed, and frequently supplemented.

SOFTWARE FOR THE CIS SYSTEM

The dominating technical constraint on the computer programs needed in a Center for Information Services is the requirement for the ability to handle data from a variety of existing files—to maintain, read, select, and extract data from files prepared by other organizations. As it now is, each data base has its own format, its own thesaurus, and its own package of "file management" programs which provide capability for maintenance and search. Each data base now requires a separate set of forms and procedures for utilization. With 20 data bases, each representing 3 or 4 files, the installation would be faced with the spectre of perhaps 500 different operating programs and procedures, few of which would be compatible with the library's operating system.

Therefore, how do we add data bases without proliferating programs to the point of virtual strangulation? The answer might lie in standardization, but that seems hardly likely, in view of the enormous variety of purposes served by the data bases to those who originate them. Custom programming for each data base is too lengthy, too costly, and too unresponsive to the needs of the Center and its users. It might lie in conversion of the data bases to some standard format and structure for storage and processing by the library using them, but this also seems unlikely, in view of the sheer bulk of data involved. Translation or transliteration of files for use in some standard system is impractical because of the possible loss of meaningful information, the costs, the continual changing of formats, and the difficulty in processing. It might lie in the use of generalized file management programs, like those listed in Figure 10.13, which can handle the variety of data bases and provide standardized services based on them.

The design of such a generalized system would be special purpose insofar as it reflects the special requirements of the Center for Information Services. Many recently developed generalized file management techniques, however, can form the basis for system design.

To use such generalized programs requires a careful description of each data base so that the generalized programs can operate on it and so that the user can know what level of service he can call on. Usually, these programs provide a clearly distinguishable set of stages of processing, from fixed field, fixed format processing (the simplest and most efficient), to variable format processing, to text processing. Their relative efficiencies differ so radically that the prospective user must be well aware of precisely what data from a given data base can be effectively processed by a given level of program.

In the Center for Information Services, certain general purpose programs will be applied to all files. Possible "levels" of program might be: retrieval from fixed fields (program "A"), from repeated fixed fields (program "B"), from variable fields (program "C"), from repeated variable fields (program "D"), and from text (program "E"). The catalog record must give a clear indication of possible retrieval points for a file under each of the operational levels. The librarian would consult the catalog and state: "If we search this file under program 'A', we can retrieve on the following points: journal, language, date, etc.; under program 'B' we can search by subject, and under program 'C', by author, title, etc." Indications must also be given of file organization and size (number of reels) for this will determine, to some extent, how accessible desired information may be. For example, if a file consists of several tape reels and is organized by date the librarian might state: "We can search the most recent portion of the file today, but a complete run, which requires several hours of computer time, must be scheduled in advance." (File size should also be indicated in terms of number of records or number of bibliographic entries where applicable, for this information would be more meaningful to a patron than number of reels.)

Specifications for CIS File Management Software

With a general purpose file management system, a great variety of file structures may be defined independently of the processing functions performed. Actually, any computer programming language is general purpose in the sense that it is not limited to particular files and functions. In order to relieve the programmer of some detail, the notion of higher level languages was developed. The best known of these languages are COBOL, PL/1, FORTRAN, and ALGOL. The use of these languages is said to result in an average reduction of about 5 to 1 in the number of instructions that must be written by the programmer to perform a given application.

A general purpose file management system introduces a still higher level of communication between the user and the computer. By relieving the user of many more requirements to communicate his needs to the computer, it may be used by library personnel, system analysts, or computer programming specialists—at the appropriate level of detail. Thus, instead of employing assembly language or a higher level language, the user employs a small set of structured forms to describe his problem solution in the amount of detail required.

Such a system can be used for producing computer programs for normal day-to-day operations, as well as for specialized requirements. The functions that may be involved in such operations include the creation and maintenance of files from original input (for example, punched card and magnetic tape data), the selection of records from files according to either defined or computed criteria, computations involving data from selected records, extraction and sequencing of results dependent on these data, and the formation of new files for other, subsequent use. As we have stated, the file(s) and the functions are independent of each other, thus providing great flexibility in use. In execution, however, they are tied together in order to minimize the information that must be provided by the user.

File Definition. The operation of such a programming system is centered around the concept of master files. In order to extract or retrieve data from files, the problem statement must refer to file definition tables.

The file definition specifies certain overall file parameters (such as record format and block size). More important, the record structure is described also, thus providing the capability of reading record structures that are fixed or variable in length and that can contain:

1. Variable length fields and segments.
2. Repeated fields and segments of the same type.
3. More than one type of format of field or segment at any hierarchical (nested) level.
4. An adequate number of hierarchical (nested) levels of segments within a record.
5. Various techniques to identify the format types and sizes of records, segments, and fields in a file.

File Organization Concepts. The organization of a file is generally independent of its specific content. Thus, files can be organized sequentially, in terms of some field in the data items in the file; randomly, so that records must be located by reference to an index or an algorithm; or in other ways.

File Search Concepts. The processing of CIS files must begin with the search of a particular file to select records for subsequent use by a requester. The file management program therefore must at least provide capabilities for the simplest forms of such a selection. An obvious extreme is to provide the requestor with a copy of all records in a file. Normally, of course, more selective search criteria are specified. One may request, for example, records identified by particular data values in specified fields (for instance, specified document numbers or subjects). Still more complex search criteria may seek to relate a set of data values in each record to one another for the purpose of selecting those records in which specified relationships exist.

These retrieval capabilities enable the users to select and extract data from the files. The key to effective retrieval is the logical selectivity of the system, including an appropriate set of comparators, Boolean connectors, and types of comparands. Conditional expressions may need to be combined and a number of nesting levels may need to be provided.

System Monitoring. Monitoring capabilities should include provisions for:

1. Preparing utilization statistics by user, file, type of request, and the like.
2. Cost accounting and charging of accounts.
3. Protection of proprietary files.

System Functions. Many file management functions must be included:

1. *Read existing files* from punched cards, magnetic tapes, and other machine-readable input
2. *Maintain files* by making additions and deletions.
3. *Reformat files* to reflect changing specifications and requirements.
4. *Select,* from files, records that contain data of interest in a problem.
5. *Extract* data items from the selected records, or use whole records.
6. *Arrange* output by sorting, sequencing, and grouping.
7. *Format* printed reports that contain such elements as Preface, Page, Title, Page Number, Column Headings, Column Footings, Line Numbers, Detail Entries, Summaries, Statistics, Line Count, and other details that make a printed report or document informative and attractive.
8. *Summarize* data to as many levels of total and subtotals as required, with wide flexibility in format and content of printed output.
9. *Compute* new values based on values in the file, for use in selection, further computation, printed output, subfiles, or the updated file.
10. *Produce* printed reports or other printed documents such as 3 x 5 cards, labels, or output on preprinted forms.
11. *Produce* subfiles on cards, magnetic tape, disk, or other media for further processing by other systems.

System Operation. The system could provide for the storage of source programs in a "library" for subsequent compilation. By storing the source program, rather than the object program, the system could enable the user to conserve space in his system library for other purposes. In operation the user would have the option of rerunning such programs by recalling them either in source or object language form and operating under the system. This capability supplements the ability to define new data base requirements.

The capability to maintain and query master files, once the user has defined the master file and the query specifications, should be essentially automatic. This type of implicit specification is a basic design concept of the system. For example, a "standard" mode of operation will automatically be invoked unless the user specifically requests an alternative mode. These standard cases are applicable in many situations.

The most important advantage of a generalized file management system should be its simplicity of use. Use of "programming by questionnaire," in which the user merely answers a series of questions describing the results he requires, means that an ordinary search request can be described directly by the research or library-oriented user in a few minutes.

In summary, the Center for Information Services Software should allow the library to use computers in the handling of many separate files with a minimum of lapsed time between acquisition of a data base and operational use of it. It reduces the demands for skilled programmers and analysts, and minimizes communications problems between the academic community and data processing people.

Specifications for CIS Reference Retrieval Software

Since the basic CIS File Management Software would provide capability only for the simplest, field structured search logic, the CIS system of software must also include a module for the processing of more complex requests. Reference Retrieval Software is of primary value in searching of reference data bases that involve the use of "subject" descriptions.

File Definition. The file definition can be identical with that for file management. The fields of particular concern, however, are the "repeated fields," which are characteristic in reference retrieval situations.

File Organization Concepts. The need for methods of organization beyond those of the sequential and indexed sequential is evident. A variety of indexing aids must be included:

1. "Inverted" files (such as key-word indexes).
2. Dictionaries, hierarchically structured subject headings, and thesauri.
3. Word frequency lists and tables of statistical association.

The maintenance of these indexing aids, as well as the use of them in the formulation and processing of search requests, must be included in the system.

File Search Concepts. Search of reference files differs from that in simple file management in at least two respects:

1.   It involves simultaneous, interactive processing of at least two files (the master file containing the data of interest and index files).

2.   It provides more sophisticated processing of repeated field data.

In particular, search requests can be formulated as Boolean combinations of terms as well as of specified field values. The terms will be searched for in the indexing aids, and provision must be made for automatic explosion of them based on the set of inter-term references found. Capability must be included for correlating index records, based on defined request logic, to derive master file entry references for subsequent processing.

A portion of the search request form might resemble the example shown in Figure 19.17. On the form as shown, a desired search element has been indicated by specifying a field and a value (or values) for that field, and its relationship to other search elements. Guidelines for formulating a search can be described briefly as follows:

1.   Specifying a desired value for a field:

   (A)   A required value is indicated by listing it on the relevant line of the request form, with an appropriate operator. Possible operators

Figure 19.17   Search request form.[a]

Phrase No.	Field Name	OP.	Value or Constant
1	AUTHOR	EQ	SHAKESPEARE, WILLIAM
1	PUB-DATE	GE	1900
1	PUB-DATE	LT	1968
11	TITLE	EQ	HAMLET)JULIUS CAESAR)OTHELLO
11	LANG	EQ	ENG.)GER.
12	TITLE	EQ	KING LEAR)MACBETH
12	LANG	NE	ENG.
2	AUTHOR	EQ	MARLOWE, CHRISTOPHER
2	TITLE	EQ	DOCTOR FAUSTUS

[a]This search can be described as follows: (A) Retrieve all records in which the author is William Shakespeare, the publication date is greater than or equal to 1900 and less than 1968, the title is Hamlet, Julius Caesar or Othello, and the language is English or German. (B) Retrieve all records in which the author is Shakespeare, the publication date is 1900–1967, the title is King Lear or Macbeth, and the language is not English. (C) Retrieve all records in which the author is Christopher Marlowe and the title is Doctor Faustus.

are: EQ (equal to), NE (not equal to), GT (greater than), LT (less than), GE (greater than or equal to), and LE (less than or equal to).

(B)   Alternative values for a field are shown by listing them, in order, on the same line. If these values cannot be listed on one line they are treated as alternative values involving more than one field (see 2-B below).

2.   Specifying relationships between fields:

(A)   Various search values that are required to appear in the same record are indicated by relating them through a common phrase number (or portion of a number). Items having identical phrase numbers, or which agree over all of the digits of one of the numbers are regarded as belonging to the same phrase.

(B)   Alternative values (involving more than one field) that may appear in a record are indicated by assigning them phrase numbers which differ in one or more digits. In the example, we have the numbers 1,1,1,11,11,12,12. The phrases which can be formed are 1,1,1,11,11, and 1,1,1,12,12. (Since the numbers 11 and 12 do not agree over all of the digits of one of them, they cannot be part of the same phrase.)

3.   Specifying multiple requests in one search formulation:

In our example, there are actually two searches shown: one related to Shakespeare, and the other related to Marlowe. Since they are unrelated (except that they involve the same file), they are given completely different phrase numbers. If the search on Marlowe were to be made more elaborate, then other phrase numbers using 2 as a "base," would be added.

In order to phrase a search request correctly, it may be necessary to refer to certain materials in addition to the catalog record. These would consist of such things as thesauri and lists of codes, abbreviations or symbols to be used for language or geographic designations, and the like (if these are not handled by the computer). The catalog should contain a record of and references to these materials, which would be shelved or filed in the reference area.

Specifications for CIS Text Processing Software

Although in principle, text data can be processed by treating each word as a separate entry in a repeating field, such processing is relatively inefficient. To provide specific functional capabilities, the CIS system should include a module, the CIS Text Processing Software, designed around the particular needs in generalized text data processing.

File Definition. The file definition for such a module must be identical with that for the other modules. The fields of particular concern however are the "text fields." Particular attention must be given to provide for "character coding" of multiple font text.

File Organization Concepts. The same kinds of indexing aids involved in reference retrieval can be used. However, their scope of coverage is likely to be much broader, since all terms appearing in text must be considered (as terms either to be processed or not to be processed).

File Search Concepts. Although search logic considerably more complex than that provided in reference retrieval appears to be desirable (including, for example, automatic parsing), it is not possible to specify at this time an adequate operational definition of it.

System Functions. For text processing, file management and search functions must be supplemented by an ability to:

1. Produce concordances and other word lists.
2. Collate texts for the detection of differences and similarities.
3. Accumulate statistics on frequency of occurrence of words and word strings.
4. Derive indexing terms based on a variety of clues, including frequency of occurrence, format, context, and the like.

Appendix

OUTLINE OF INSTRUCTIONS FOR FILLING IN CATALOG FORM

I. *ENTRY*

Use Anglo-American Cataloging Rules for Choice and form of entry. Items to be included are:

A. Name of Agency and Division, if applicable (or entry under title).
B. Title of file (in brackets if supplied by cataloger).
C. Date.

II. *BRIEF DESCRIPTION*

Give short indication of general content of the file, any special features, correlation to published materials (i.e., MEDLARS, CCF, and Index Medicus), clarification of title or date if necessary, and, if applicable, statement as to how often file is issued or updated. Name the agency which actually (physically) created the file if it is not the same as the agency named in the entry, or if the tape is entered under its title. If the tape file is a serial which exists in printed form, give the beginning date of the published serial.

III. *MAJOR SUBJECT AREAS*

List of broad areas covered. *Use Library of Congress List of Subject Headings.*

IV. *FIELDS OF DATA*

List the types of field on the tape, and the data each contains. Possible field categories are:

Fixed Fields
Repeated Fixed Fields
Variable Fields
Repeated Variable Fields
Text

List field names as they are defined to the generalized program. If a name is not clear, follow it with a fuller name or short clarifying statement in parenthesis.

V. *PHYSICAL CHARACTERISTICS*

A. Computer: Give manufacturer and full model description (ex. IBM 360/40).
B. Bit Density: Bits per inch.
C. Number of Tracks (channels); Parity: Odd or even.
D. File name.
E. Tape label.
F. Recording mode: (binary, bdc, ebcdic, other).
G. Record format: Fixes or variable, blocked or unblocked. If the records are blocked, give the blocking factor in parenthesis if it is not clearly implied under block length.
H. Record length: If variable, give maximum.
I. Block length: If variable, give maximum.
J. File size: Tape reels, logical records.
K. Increment/yr: Tape reels, logical records.
L. File organization: The sequence of records in the file. For example: alphabetic by author or subject, numeric by citation number, by date, etc.
M. Copying restrictions: Give brief statement as to policy.
N. Holdings: Apply to tapes issued serially.

VI. *RELATED FILES*

List other files involved in the system. For example: dictionary tapes, cross-reference tapes, etc.

VII. *MATERIALS RELATING TO SEARCH FORMULATION*
For example: thesaurus or dictionary, language or other codes, manual or publication containing complete field information, etc.

VIII. *PROGRAMS FOR UTILIZATION OF DATA*
Give brief listing of, or reference to existing programs for file manipulation. Indicate agency which created the program, and language used.

IX. *FOR MORE INFORMATION, DOCUMENTATION*
If possible, list persons to contact at the systems and/or programming level, and refer to documentation on tape formats.

ENTRY	CALL NO.	Z
U.S. Library of Congress. Technical Processing Division		881
MARC catalog record. 1966–		U58c

BRIEF DESCRIPTION

Contains current LC cataloging information (augmented). English language works, monographs only. Upper and lower case coding.

Updated tapes issued weekly.

MAJOR SUBJECT AREAS

1. Library Catalogs
2. American Literature – Bibliography
3. U.S. – Imprints

FIELDS OF DATA

FIXED FIELDS:

LC catalog number, supplement number, type of main entry, form of work, bib. indicator, illus. indicator, map indicator, juvenile indicator, series indicator, lang. indicator, lang. 1 & 2, type of pub. date, date, place of pub., publisher, height of vol., types of secondary entries (and various fields related to internal processing).

VARIABLE FIELDS:

Main entry, conventional or filing title, title statement, ed. statement, imprint statement, collation statement, LC call number, Dewey decimal class number, nat'l bib. number.

REPREATED VARIABLE FIELDS:

Notes, series notes, subject tracings, personal author tracings, corporate author tracing, uniform tracing, title tracing, series tracing.

Computer	IBM 360/30	Recording mode	EBCDIC	
Bit Density	800 bpi	Record format	Variable blocked	
Tracks, Parity	9, Odd	Record length	2004 Chars. Max	
File name	MARC - CAT	Block length	2008 Chars. Max	
Tape label				

File size: Tape reels	1	Logical records	10,000 (May,1967)
Increment/yr: Tape reels		Logical records	26,000
File organization	By LC Card Number		
Copying restrictions			
Holdings	1966–		

RELATED FILES	MATERIALS RELATING TO SEARCH FORMULATION

MARC author/title record
MARC subject cross reference
    tracing record
MARC descriptive cross reference
    tracing record
	(possible) MARC codes: Publisher,
	    Country, City, Language

PROGRAMS FOR UTILIZATION OF DATA	FOR MORE INFORMATION, DOCUMENTATION

From LC: Production of catalog
    card set
Bibliographic listing (listing of
    entire MARC record)
	Library of Congress
	Information Systems Office
	Director MARC Pilot Project:
	    Mrs. Henriette Avram

U.S. Library of Congress Technical Processing Division   881

     MARC Author/Title Record. 1966–   U58a

BRIEF DESCRIPTION

Contains an author and title listing for each MARC catalog record. Issued weekly.

Update tapes issued weekly.

MAJOR SUBJECT AREAS

1. Library Catalogs
2. American Literature – Bibliography
3. U.S. – Imprints

FIELDS OF DATA

FIXED FIELDS:

LC card number, supplement number, type of main entry, status of record (new or revised), author/title (for a title main entry, only title information is present in the field).

(Total author/title field is fixed, but author and title entries are variable.)

Computer	IBM 360/30	Recording mode	EBCDIC
Bit Density	800 bpi	Record format	Fixed, unblocked
Tracks, Parity	9, Odd	Record length	134 Chars
File name	MARC-Author	Block length	
Tape label			

File size: Tape reels	1	Logical records	10,000 (May 1967)
Increment/yr: Tape reels		Logical records	26,000
File organization	Alphabetic by Author		
Copying restrictions			
Holdings			

RELATED FILES	MATERIALS RELATING TO SEARCH FORMULATION
MARC catalog record MARC subject cross reference tracing record MARC descriptive cross reference tracing record	

PROGRAMS FOR UTILIZATION OF DATA	FOR MORE INFORMATION, DOCUMENTATION
From LC: Abbreviated author/title listing	Library of Congress Information Systems Office Director MARC Pilot Project: Mrs. Henriette Avram

ENTRY | CALL NO.   Z

    U.S. Library of Congress. Technical Processing Division   695

    MARC subject cross reference tracing record. 1966-   U58s

---

BRIEF DESCRIPTION

Contains the subject cross reference tracing information which is generated in the cataloging of monographs which are incorporated into the MARC catalog record.

Update tapes issued weekly.

MAJOR SUBJECT AREAS

1.   Subject headings

FIELDS OF DATA

FIXED FIELDS:

Information related to internal processing, status of record (new or carried over).

VARIABLE FIELDS:

Subject heading, subject references ("see" references, "see also" references, and "refer from" references).

Computer	IBM 360/30	Recording mode	EBCDIC
Bit Density	800 bpi	Record format	Variable, unblocked
Tracks, Parity	9, Odd	Record length	
File name	MARC-Subject	Block length	
Tape label			

File size: Tape reels	1	Logical records	
Increment/yr: Tape reels		Logical records	
File organization	Alphabetic by Subject Heading		
Copying restrictions			
Holdings	1966-		

RELATED FILES	MATERIALS RELATING TO SEARCH FORMULATION
MARC catalog record MARC author/title listing MARC descriptive cross reference tracing record	

PROGRAMS FOR UTILIZATION OF DATA	FOR MORE INFORMATION, DOCUMENTATION

From LC: Printing of 3 x 5 subject
          cross reference cards
	Library of Congress
	Information Systems Office
	Director MARC Pilot Project:
	   Mrs. Henriette Avram

ENTRY   CALL NO.   Z

U.S. Library of Congress. Technical Processing Division   695

   MARC descriptive cross reference tracing record. 1966–   U58d

---

BRIEF DESCRIPTION

Contains the descriptive cross reference tracing information which is generated in the cataloging of monographs which are incorporated into the MARC catalog record.

Update tapes issued weekly.

MAJOR SUBJECT AREAS

1.   Authority Lists

FIELDS OF DATA

FIXED FIELDS:

  Information related to internal processing, status of record (new or carried over).

VARIABLE FIELDS:

  Descriptive heading, descriptive references ("see" references, "see also" references).

Computer	IBM 360	Recording mode	EBCDIC
Bit Density	800 bpi	Record format	Variable, unblocked
Tracks, Parity	9, Odd	Record length	
File name	MARC-Descr.	Block length	
Tape label			

File size: Tape reels	1	Logical records	
Increment/yr: Tape reels		Logical records	
File organization	Alphabetic by Descriptive Heading		
Copying restrictions			
Holdings	1960–		

RELATED FILES	MATERIALS RELATING TO SEARCH FORMULATION
MARC catalog record MARC author/title record MARC subject cross reference tracing record	

PROGRAMS FOR UTILIZATION OF DATA	FOR MORE INFORMATION, DOCUMENTATION
From LC: Printing of 3 x 5 descriptive cross reference cards	Library of Congress Information Systems Office Director MARC Pilot Project: Mrs. Henriette Avram

ENTRY   CALL NO.   Z

National Library of Medicine, U.S.   6660

    MEDLARS condensed citation file (CCF) 1964–   M42

BRIEF DESCRIPTION

Index of current medical literature of the world. Contains citations appearing in *Index Medicus*, plus added subject terms (coordinate indexing for machine retrieval). (Published *Index Medicus* "new ser." dates from January 1960.)

Update tapes issued monthly.

MAJOR SUBJECT AREAS

1.   Medicine – Bibliography
2.   Medicine – Periodicals – Indexes

FIELDS OF DATA

FIXED FIELDS:

Place of publication, year of publication, citation number, journal title code, language code, form and subform of entry, date of entry, type of author, number of tag words (and fields related to internal processing).

REPEATED FIXED FIELDS:

Tag words: main heading code, subheading code, *Index Medicus* indicator, tag group indicator, classification number.

VARIABLE FIELDS:

Author or authors, title, journal title abbreviation, volume, page, publication date, vernacular of title if in foreign language, references (number of references made to other material if the citation is a review article).

Computer	H. 800/200	Recording mode	Binary, BCD
Bit Density	556 bpi	Record format	Variable
Tracks, Parity	7, Odd	Record length	254 Words Max.
File name	MEDLARS-CCF	Block length	
Tape label			

File size: Tape reels	20	Logical records	500,000 (1967)
Increment/yr: Tape reels		Logical records	170,000
File organization	By Computer Entry Date		
Copying restrictions			
Holdings	1964–		

RELATED FILES	MATERIALS RELATING TO SEARCH FORMULATION
*MEDLARS Medical subject heading file (MeSH) MEDLARS language and subheading file (LANDS) MEDLARS journal record file (JRF) *Needed for subject search of CCF	MeSH (published) MeSH ("internal") Scope note file MEDLARS dictionary

PROGRAMS FOR UTILIZATION OF DATA	FOR MORE INFORMATION, DOCUMENTATION
See: *MEDLARS Maintenance Guide*, Planning Research Corporation June, 1966.	National Library of Medicine Associate Director for Intra-Mural Programs: Joseph Leiter, Ph.D.

CALL NO. Z

National Library of Medicine, U.S.

MEDLARS medical subject heading file (MeSH) 1964—

695.1

M48m

BRIEF DESCRIPTION

Contains the 6-digit main heading codes used in the MEDLARS CCF, their English equivalents, allowable subheadings, and their tree words. (classification numbers)

Update files issued monthly.

MAJOR SUBJECT AREAS

1.   Subject headings — Medicine
2.   Medicine — Terminology

FIELDS OF DATA

FIXED FIELDS:

Tally (number of times a medical subject heading has been tagged). Main heading code (octal), code for type of article, bibliog. of medical reviews indicator, *Cumulated Index Medicus* indicator, *Index Medicus* indicator, main heading in English, allowable subheadings, main heading code (six-bit format), type of *Index Medicus* main heading; plus fields related to internal processing, output formatting and printing.

VARIABLE FIELDS:

Classification numbers (tree words), bibliography and sub-bibliography numbers, and fields related to output formatting and printing.

Computer	H. 800/200	Recording mode	Binary, BCD
Bit Density	556 bpi	Record format	Variable
Tracks, Parity	7, Odd	Record length	254 Words Max.
File name	MEDLARS–MeSH	Block length	
Tape label			

File size: Tape reels	1	Logical records	
Increment/yr: Tape reels		Logical records	
File organization			
Copying restrictions			
Holdings			

RELATED FILES	MATERIALS RELATING TO SEARCH FORMULATION
MEDLARS condensed citation file (CCF) MEDLARS language and subheading file (LANDS) MEDLARS journal record file (JRF)	

PROGRAMS FOR UTILIZATION OF DATA	FOR MORE INFORMATION, DOCUMENTATION
	National Library of Medicine Associate Director for Intra-Mural Programs: Joseph Leiter, Ph.D.

ENTRY   CALL NO.   HA
                                                              268
    California. University. Los Angeles.   L8Al
        Department of Political Science.
        POLCEN: Political Census for Los Angeles County

BRIEF DESCRIPTION

    Contains electoral and demographic records of the 1,305 census tracts in Los Angeles
    County including registration and voting figures from 1958, 1960, 1962, and 1964
    general elections as well as the 1964 primary elections.

MAJOR SUBJECT AREAS

    Los Angeles County, California − Population − Statistics
    Elections − Los Angeles County, California
    Los Angeles County, California − Census

FIELDS OF DATA: All Fields are Fixed Length

    There are 1,185 fields of information for each Census Tract. For complete documenta-
    tion, see "Materials Relating to Search Formulation," below.

    MAJOR DEMOGRAPHIC CATEGORIES ARE:
        Tract ID, Land Use, Population Characteristics, *Income, *Education, *Housing,
        *Employment, *Age-Sex Characteristics, *Employment.**

    ELECTORAL INFORMATION INCLUDES:
        Turnout Figures, outcome Figures, Democratic and Republican Efficiency, Ballot
        Propositions, 1966 Democratic Party Canvassing, Political Units, Voter Registration
        (1958, 1960), Voting Returns (1958, 1960, 1962, 1964).

        *Subdivided by White, Non-White, Spanish Surname.
        **Further Subdivided by Male, Female.

Computer	IBM 7094-7040 DCS	Recording mode	Binary
Bit Density	800 bpi	Record format	Fixed, unblocked
Tracks, Parity	7, Odd	Record length	1185 words
File name	POLCEN	Block length	1185 words
Tape label			

File size: Tape reels	1	Logical records	1305
Increment/yr: Tape reels		Logical records	
File organization	By Census Tract Number		
Copying restrictions			
Holdings			

RELATED FILES   MATERIALS RELATING TO SEARCH
    UCLA Political Behavior Archives   FORMULATION
        (Special Emphasis on Southern   Marvick, Dwaine
        California).   Los Angeles Political Statistics:
                                                 A Tape Record Dictionary
                                                 November 1964

PROGRAMS FOR UTILIZATION   FOR MORE INFORMATION,
    OF DATA   DOCUMENTATION

                                         Department of Political Science
                                         Statistical Laboratory
                                         4343 Social Science Building − UCLA
                                         Director: Dwaine Marvick

Science Citation Index. Citation Index Tapes. 1964–   1

                                                                       S43c
---

BRIEF DESCRIPTION

Contains references cited by current literature of science and technology, including the
social sciences. In 1967, coverage included items from more than 1600 scientific
journals, and all current U.S. patents issued including primary and reissued patents.
(Printed *Science Citation Index* was first published in 1961.) Update tapes issued weekly
by the Institute for Scientific Information.

MAJOR SUBJECT AREAS

1. Science – Bibliography
2. Social Science – Bibliography
3. Citation Indexes

FIELDS OF DATA

ALL FIELDS ARE FIXED:

Source* journal abbreviation, volume number, page, code indicating type of source
item (i.e., article, review, patent, etc.), year. First source author, first reference**
author, reference journal (or non-journal title), volume, page, year, and number
identifying the source item.

When work cited is a patent, reference patent number, first inventor, and reference
patent class are given instead of reference author and journal.

When record is for the organization where the work was performed for the source
item, the abbreviated name and location are given instead of reference author and
journal.

* "Source" indicates "citing."
** "Reference" indicates "cited."

Computer	IBM 1401/7074	Recording mode	BCD
Bit Density	556 bpi	Record format	Fixed, blocked (10)
Tracks, Parity	7,	Record length	900 Chars.
File name	SCI-CIT	Block length	900 Chars.
Tape label			

File size: Tape reels		Logical records	9,000,000 (1966)
Increment/yr: Tape reels		Logical records	3,000,000
File organization	In Sequence Per a Unique Number for Each		
Copying restrictions			Source Item
Holdings			

RELATED FILES	MATERIALS RELATING TO SEARCH FORMULATION
Science Citation Index. Source Index Tapes.	(see) ISI Magnetic Tapes Institute for Scientific Information, 1967.
PROGRAMS FOR UTILIZATION OF DATA	**FOR MORE INFORMATION, DOCUMENTATION**
From ISI: General utility citation index list program (IBM 1401, 4k,). Can list complete citation data, or portions appropriate to a specified group of reference authors.	Institute for Scientific Information Philadelphia, Pennsylvania Director of Research: Irving H. Sher

ENTRY

Science Citation Index. Source Index Tapes. 1964–

BRIEF DESCRIPTION

Indexes current literature of science and technology, including the social sciences. In 1967, coverage included items from more than 1600 scientific journals, and all current U.S. patents issued including primary and reissued patents. (*Science Citation Index* was first issued in published form in 1961.)

Update tapes issued weekly by the Institute for Scientific Information.

MAJOR SUBJECT AREAS

1. Science – Bibliography
2. Social Science – Bibliography
3. Citation Indexes

FIELDS OF DATA

FIXED FIELDS:

Source* article number, primary source author, source journal, volume, page, year; code indicating type of source (i.e., article, review, patent, etc.), number of references and fields related to internal processing.

VARIABLE FIELDS:

Secondary authors and article title data.

* "Source" indicates "citing."

Computer	IBM 1401/7074	Recording mode	BCD
Bit Density	556 bpi	Record format	Variable, blocked
Tracks, Parity	7,	Record length	246 Chars. Max.
File name	SCI-Source	Block length	1200 Chars. Max.
Tape label			

File size: Tape reels	Logical records	775,000 (1966)
Increment/yr: Tape reels	Logical records	285,000
File organization	In Sequence Per a Unique Number for Each	
Copying restrictions		Source Item
Holdings		

RELATED FILES

Science Citation Index. Citation
   Index Tapes.

MATERIALS RELATING TO SEARCH
FORMULATION

(see) Institute for Scientific
   Information
   ISI Magnetic Tapes, 1967

PROGRAMS FOR UTILIZATION
OF DATA

Available from ISI:
1. Source index listing (IBM 1401, 4k, 2 tapes)
2. SDI programs, (written for IBM 7074, 12 tapes, 10k, card reader and console, uses 1401 as ancillary output device)

FOR MORE INFORMATION,
DOCUMENTATION

Institute for Scientific Information
Philadelphia, Pennsylvania
Director of Research: Irving H. Sher

Science Information Exchange   7405.R4
Grant Master File [of current research projects]

BRIEF DESCRIPTION

Contains information (not classified for national security) on current research projects in the life, phsyical, engineering, and social sciences. Coverage includes research tasks performed by or supported by agencies of the Federal Government, and (increasingly), universities, and industry. Subject index codes are assigned to each project included.

MAJOR SUBJECT AREAS

1. Research – Directories
2. Research Grants
3. Science – Information Services

FIELDS OF DATA

ALL FIELDS ARE FIXED:

Accession number (includes supporting agency).
Sub group code (further breakdown of supporting agency).
Principal Investigator.
Location code for principal investigator.
Beginning date of project.
End date of project.
Dollar amount (annual funding level).
Other investigators.
Location codes for other investigators.
Multiple location code for principal investigator.
Subject index codes.

Computer	IBM 360/30	Recording mode	EBCDIC	
Bit Density	800 bpi	Record format	Fixed, blocked (4)	
Tracks, Parity	9,	Record length	450 Chars	
File name	SIE-Grant	Block length	1800 Chars	
Tape label				

File size: Tape reels	20	Logical records	500,000 (1967)
Increment/yr: Tape reels	4	Logical records	75,000
File organization	By accession number		
Copying restrictions			
Holdings			

RELATED FILES

Index File
Contract No. – SIE No. Cross Ref. File
Title File
Investigator File
Pending Projects File

MATERIALS RELATING TO SEARCH FORMULATION

(possible) Indexes to codes for
supporting agencies,
location, and index terms

PROGRAMS FOR UTILIZATION OF DATA

FOR MORE INFORMATION, DOCUMENTATION

Science Information Exchange
Smithsonian Institution
Washington, D.C.
Director: Monroe E. Freeman, Ph.D.

Suggested Readings

Bisco, Ralph, (ed), *Data Bases, Computers, and the Social Sciences.* New York: Wiley, 1970.

This is a product of the Fourth Annual Conference of the Council of Social Science Data Archives, held at UCLA in June, 1967. It demonstrates the extent to which quantitative methods are becoming a significant part of social science research and the extent to which they depend upon the basic socioeconomic data becoming available in magnetic tape data bases.

Committee on Scientific and Technical Communication (SATCOM), *Scientific and Technical Communication: A Pressing National Problem and Recommendations for Its Solution.* Washington, D.C.: National Academy of Sciences, 1969.

The SATCOM committee was established in February 1966 to investigate scientific and technical communication. "Information analysis centers," national networks, and the use of magnetic tape data bases occupy prominent roles in this report.

Mechanized Information Services in the University Library, Phase I: Planning. Los Angeles: Institute of Library Research, University of California, December 1967.

This report summarizes work done, under a grant from the National Science Foundation, to establish a "campus-based system," in contrast to the more standard "discipline-oriented system" which had been the primary focus of mechanized information service. The concern was with how a university should handle the problems in acquisition and use of a multiplicity of magnetic tape data bases.

Gipe, George A., *Nearer to the Dust; Copyright and the Machine*, Baltimore, Williams and Wilkins, 1967.

One of the crucial, still unresolved problems in the distribution and use of magnetic tapes is that of copyright. This book examines the issues with an admitted bias.

Chapter 20

INFORMATION SCIENCE IN LIBRARIANSHIP

As the complexity of our society has increased, the need for informed decisions has correspondingly increased. The result has been an ever greater demand for information services adequate to the decision-making process. At the same time, mechanical tools have become available which can be used to aid the processes of obtaining, analyzing, storing, and retrieving ever greater volumes of data. The confluence of these two developments—the growing needs for information with the increasing capability for handling it—has led to the implementation of a variety of informations systems, both manual and mechanized. In technical fields, these have been called "information centers"; in social and political fields, "data banks"; in business, "management information systems"; in the military, "command and control systems." To date, these have all been chiefly experimental, since there are still many unresolved problems in their design, in their operation, and in their integration with the decision processes they serve. However, it is clear that these problems will be solved and that more and more information systems, of all kinds, will be established on an operational basis.

These information systems create a real challenge for librarianship, since on the surface it would seem that librarians can have a central role in their development, their operation, and their management. But to do this, librarians must recognize the contribution that they can make and be willing to accept the challenges.

Librarianship has repeatedly been faced with such a "crisis of identity." Are libraries simple "storehouses" or are they "centers for information?" Which do librarians regard as important, the "medium" or the "message?" These are not idle questions, nor are the answers obvious. They were explicit in the arguments

744

that reverberated loudly at the hearings of the Royal Commission on the Library of the British Museum in 1847-1849 concerning the relative importance of the author-title catalog and the subject catalog.[1] At that time, the answer was clear: the role of the library was to preserve the records of the past and to assure that they were available for the needs of the future; although both catalogs were needed, the author-title catalog was the more urgent in order to tell whether the library held a particular book. The results of that decision have set the tone for libraries ever since.

But the ever increasing demand for "information" has forced librarianship into a reexamination of the answer made over 100 years ago. Clearly, the historical role of the library as preserver of the records of the past is still an important one. "Information" does not exist in abstract form but only as data recorded in some record and, therefore, even for those whose interest is only in the information, the record in which it is recorded must be preserved and made available. But should libraries continue to regard this as their *primary* function?

Whatever the answer may be, it will have a profound effect on the nature of libraries and their relationship to their users. It is therefore imperative that librarians make a conscious effort to understand the nature of "information," the processes by which it is generated, the extent to which they can be provided by libraries, and the extent to which they have been formalized and can be provided by computers.

Of course, this has been well recognized by librarians. As a result, library education is undergoing a minor revolution and is experiencing the addition of curricula requiring new and radically different backgrounds, concepts, and approaches. Information science is becoming an integral part of library education, an increasingly important part of the librarian's professional and operational responsibility, and a part of the theoretical foundations of librarianship.

What, then, is "information science?" The purpose of this chapter is to define it, with emphasis on its relevancy to librarianship. In doing so, the attempt will be made to crystallize the great number of theoretical concepts and practical methods that have been developed in this rapidly growing field. The result should serve as an introduction to its literature and help librarians to visualize the proper relationship between information science and librarianship.

Definitions

From the outset, we are faced with the fundamental problem of definition: What is "information?" What is an "information system?" In a real sense, the difficulty in defining these terms epitomizes the field. They are slippery

[1] Great Britain, Commissioners Appointed to Inquire into the Constitution and Government of the British Museum, *Report.* London: HMDS, 1850 ("The Panizzi Report").

concepts, amorphous, loaded with connotations and implications. They deal with a crucial aspect of human endeavor and thus are always viewed in terms of the specifics of each individual situation. Any definition is bound to be either too general or too specific.

Compounding the difficulty in definition is the prevailing tendency to identify information science with the computer. In fact, as we shall see, in some circles the term "computer sciences" is considered synonymous with information science.[2] However, the view of this chapter is that such an identification is invalid. Although mechanization has provided the catalyst and has made information science of immediate value and importance, the problems are present in *any* system, whether mechanized or not. And it is the problems with which information science is concerned, not the specific use of machinery as the method for solving them.

Definition of Information. It is clear that "information" has had a variety of meanings. At the one extreme, engineers will identify it with transmission over communication lines and will measure it by the statistical properties of signals.[3] At the other extreme, philosophers may well claim that it is a something with which they have struggled for years; don't presume to have an answer. Some have identified information with recorded facts; others, with the content of text, others, with the experience stored in the human mind. Therefore, it is almost presumptuous to consider answering as nettlesome a question as "What is information?" Yet, the facts remain that information science deals with "information," and that we must have a suitable definition, even if it is at the most elementary level.

As a first step, let us consider some related terms—data, information, knowledge, and wisdom—and in doing so adopt a specific view of their relationship:

Data is the raw material from which the others derive. Data is that which is recorded as symbols from which other symbols may be produced. The data may be intended to represent "facts," as statements of truth, but more generally it is anything recorded in a form that can be processed.

Information (as we shall define it) is the result of processing of data, usually formalized processing. Typical processes include transmission, selection, and analysis.

Knowledge is accumulated data, which has been systematized, formulated, and evaluated with reference to the discovery of general truths.

Wisdom is subjective, ethical, judgmental. If knowledge is usually considered

[2] Tou, Julius T., and Richard H. Wilcox, (eds.), *Computer and Information Sciences.* Washington, D.C.: Spartan, 1964.

[3] Cherry, Colin, *On Human Communication.* New York: Wiley, 1957. Especially Chapter 4 and 5.

as the province of science, wisdom may be considered as the province of the humanities. "Wisdom", says Agnes Repplier, "is said to be the fund of experience which man has gathered by living. But for so many harvests the crop is still a light one. Knowledge he has gained and power, but not goodness and understanding."[4]

The following is therefore the precise and operational definition of "information" that we shall adapt in all subsequent uses of the word:

> *Information* is the data produced as a result of a process upon data. That process may be one simply of *data transmission* (in which case, the definition and measure used in communication theory are applicable); it may be one of *data selection*; it may be one of *data organization*; it may be one of *data analysis.*

Since information is itself recorded as data, it can be subjected to subsequent processing. The issue is therefore really one of the degree to which data constitutes information, as a function of the complexity of the process to which it has been subjected. Therefore, measures of information must recognize not only "amount" but "complexity."[5]

An important point about this definition is that, given it, information like life cannot exist independent of the processes which produce it. Although some of its properties may be subject to investigation independent of the means of performing those processes, the important and interesting ones cannot be. That means that "information" can be studied only in the context of specific "information systems."

Definition of Information Systems. Consider any complex phenomenon (that is, "system") of interest. If one wishes to study it, one may be concerned with a variety of things about it—its physical structure, its cybernetic response to environment,[6] its chemical and metabolic balance, and its information processing. Thus, a person can be viewed as a complex of bones and muscles, capable of performing mechanical tasks; as a chemical factory processing ingested food, water, and air and converting it to energy; or as a thinking human being, taking in sensory data, making decisions, and controlling its physical and chemical structure. A library can be viewed as a physical structure, with physical records and a mechanical flow of materials; as an administrative organization, with the assignment of people to a variety of tasks; or as an information processing institution, taking in data and providing it out again in response to requests.

[4] Repplier, Agnes
[5] Goodman, Nelson, *The Structure of Appearance.* Cambridge, Massachusetts: Harvard, 1961.
[6] Wiener, Norbert, *Cybernetics, or Control and Communication in the Animal and the Machine.* New York: Wiley, 1961.

We study such systems by using methods of research appropriate to each—biology for living organisms, organization theory for administrative systems and so on. The results of study are a variety of models, or scientific theories, which we then use to explain behavior and predict future behavior.

But among the aspects of interest in a system are the ones that we may want to identify as information processing. If those are the ones on which we focus the system then becomes an Information System. Hence,

> An *Information Sytem* is that set of aspects of a general system (a natural phenomenon, a physical construct, or a logical construct) which are identified as information producing.

The usual abstract description of a system is given in Figure 20.1.[7] As it shows, information producing processes are grouped into the standard categories: communication for input and for output, storage, processing, and feedback.

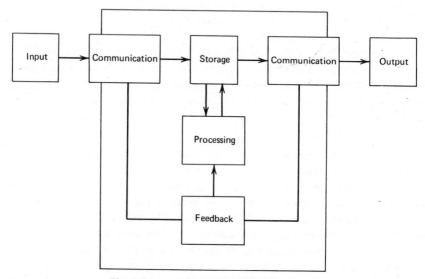

Figure 20.1　Information system schematic.

The purpose of complex information processing is to help a system respond properly and effectively to the data which it receives. Processes more complex that simple transmission of data are apparently built into all information processing systems, including biological as well as mechanical. The need is particularly evident in a condition of "data overload," when the transmission into a system exceeds its capacity to respond properly to the data. Under such

---

[7] Borko, Harold, *The Analysis and Design of Information Systems.* Los Angeles: System Development Corporation, November 1966.

conditions, the system may make what are unacceptable responses: it may eliminate data by accident, or accept all the data but with inaccuracy, or try to escape and avoid response to the data. It is therefore necessary for the system to process the data in order to accommodate the load. For example, it may store the data, delaying response until later; it may select and thus eliminate some data, but by choice; it may abstract the data, which reduces the detail in the data, again by choice; and it may classify and thus reduce the amount of data by coding.

Definition of Information Science. This leads to a very natural definition of Information Science:

> *Information Science* is the study of information producing processes
> in any information system in which they may occur.

However, although this indeed is the definition that we shall use, it implies something that may not be true: that information science can exist as a separate discipline.

In fact, any real system can be studied only by use of the scientific methodologies appropriate to it. And that includes the study of the information producing processes embodied in it. For example, RNA and DNA can be studied for the information processes which they embody and, as such, are information systems of vital interest to information science. But it would be impossible to study, in any real sense, the means by which they transmit, select, and even analyze "data" (represented by various configurations of amino acids) without the use of microbiology.

This means that while "information science" may, in principle, be concerned with pure analysis of processes, in reality it cannot be separated from the methodology of specific disciplines. It is therefore more appropriate to talk in terms of "information science in genetics," or "information science in social theory" or "information science in documentation" than to talk of "information science" in isolation from specific systems.

Specific Contexts

What then are the "systems" with which information science is concerned? What are the methodologies for scientific study with which it must work? Figure 20.2 summarizes some relevant examples, a few of which will be discussed in detail.

The Computer. The computer has been an especially important context for information science, for very clear reasons. The *raison d'etre* for the computer is its data processing capabilities. Furthermore, those capabilities are very well defined and can be measured in very precise ways. The computer is therefore a relatively predictable system to study.

Figure 20.2 Representative information systems.

	The Science	Specific Examples	Related Sciences	Data Form	Representative Processes
Formal Systems	Mathematics	Mathematics	Mathematics	Symbolic	
		Logic	Logic	Symbolic	
		Language	Linguistics	Sounds Printed	Branching
		Computer Software	Computer Science	Symbolic	
Engineering Systems	Engineering	Computer Hardware	Computer Science	Pulses States	Switching
		Communication	Info. Theory	Pulses States Codes	
Computer-Based Information Systems	Systems Methodology	Mgt. Info. Syst.	OR, Mgt. Sci.	Numerical	PERT
		Urban Data Banks	Urban Planning	Numerical	
		Command & Control	Military Sci.	Numerical	
		Config. Mgt.	Engineering	Numerical	
		Mech. Lit. Retr.	Documentation	Textual	
Recorded Data Systems	Systems Methodology	Libraries	Library Sci.	Print. Microform	Cataloging, Reference
		Info. Centers	Documentation	Print. Microform	Indexing, Analysis
		Sci. Info. Network	Documentation	Print. Microform	Meetings
Education Systems	Psychology	Education	Psychology		
Social Systems	Social Science	Economy	Economics		
		Politics	Political Sci.		
		Organization	Organ. Theory		
Biological System	Biology	Human Brain	Neurology	Neurons	
		Human Response	Psychology, Psychiatry	Responses	
		Genetics	Microbiology	Amino Acids	

There now exist a large number of Departments of Computer Science which bring to bear the combined methodologies of engineering (for study of the characteristics of computer hardware) and of mathematics and logic (for study of the characteristics of computer software). In general, if any one focus can be defined for computer science, it is that of "realizeability."[8,9] Thus, it should be expected to answer questions of "formal realizeability" (representing recursive function theory), "program realizeability" (representing the ability to produce an operating program for a specified task), and "pragmatic realizeability" (representing the ability of hardware to execute the program within specified time limits).

Because computer science has become formalized at the same time as information science, and because the computer is the most clear-cut example of an information system, it has been natural to identify information science with computer science. However, to do so limits information science unnecessarily.

Computer-Based Information Systems. As the computer has been used in an increasing variety of applications, the resulting computer-based information systems have become a fruitful spawning ground for information science activities. They embody information producing processes considerably more complex than those of the computer itself. The result has been the growth of "systems work" or "application work"—the body of techniques by which an organization is studied, and alternative systems for information processing are designed and evaluated. However, the use of those techniques requires an informed substantive knowledge of the area of application, whether it be a business company, an urban community, a military command and control system, a scientific information center, or a library.

Since the primary focus of systems work is on the information processes in these areas of application of computers, it has been natural to identify information science with systems work on computer applications. Again, to do so unnecessarily limits the scope of information science.

Libraries and Information Centers. Libraries and information centers, as institutions, exist solely for the information functions they serve. Furthermore, the information processes they use—cataloging and indexing, for example—are relatively well formalized, although there are still large areas of their work that are not well understood. As a result, they provide ideal subjects for study by information science, and there has been a corresponding interest in libraries and information centers to utilize the insights that information science could provide. The extent of interest, on both sides, has been so great that some have identified information science with library science. But is seems clear that to do so unnecessarily restricts the scope of information science.

[8] Davis, Martin, *Computability and Unsolvability*. New York: McGraw-Hill 1958.
[9] Nagel, Ernest, and J. R. Newman, *Gödel's Proof,* New York University, 1958.

Social Systems and Biological Systems. That a social system or biological system can be regarded as an "information system" may seem somewhat unnatural, at least in the sense used here. But it is clear that each performs processes upon what we can regard as data (symbolic representations). For example, an elected official can be treated as a symbol of his constituency; there are clearly defined mechanisms for selection of such symbols and these constitute "information generating processes." Similarly, the "genetic code" is simply arrays of amino acids, but these can be regarded as data (symbolic representations).[10] Economics is concerned with processes upon symbols of capital; psychology, with processes upon symbols of response, and so on.

Each of these is therefore a proper domain for information science to study. However, the ones of interest to us are, of course, libraries and information centers and the information processes in them.

LIBRARIES AND INFORMATION CENTERS AS INFORMATION SYSTEMS

Figure 20.3 describes a number of points on a spectrum of information processing, in the context of a typical science information system.[11] They cover at least four steps in a process of communication:

1.   Generation of data—usually the province of a scientific investigator.
2.   Dissemination of data—tasks performed by a series of individuals ranging from the data generator himself, to the journal referee, to the book editor.
3.   Selection, acquisition, indexing, and cataloging of data—tasks performed by librarians, documentalists, indexers and abstractors, and the like.
4.   Substantive analysis of data—tasks usually handled by the scientific investigator, but increasingly the province of "science information specialists."

In this spectrum of information activities, the library plays an especially important role as the institution for selection and acquisition of materials that processes of review have demonstrated to be of lasting importance, for the cataloging and indexing of them, for the storage and maintenance of files of them, and for providing access to them. Thus, as a preserver of the records of the past, the library acts first as a means of data selection, when it determines what books to preserve. Then, when it produces an author-title catalog as a means of locating a specific book wanted, it acts as a vehicle for data transmission. (The historical role thus represents the simplest level of information processing on the

---

[10] Beadle, George, and Muriel, *The Language of Life.* Garden City, New York: Doubleday, 1966.

[11] Stokes, Joseph, and Robert M. Hayes, "A Commentary on the Biomedical Information System," *Journal of Medical Education,* 45 (April 1970), 243-249.

data in the collection of the library.) When it produces subject catalogs, on the other hand, it acts as a means of selection from the data in the collection of the library.

Unfortunately, however, catalogs are not designed to provide more than a rough-cut approach to content. For the clientele served by general libraries this may be all that is needed, but when the same subject classification techniques are applied to highly specialized collections of nonbook, technically detailed data, the imprecision of such methods of content retrieval becomes apparent. Even indexes only lead one to potentially relevant documents and not to their content as such. Emphasis has thus been placed on finding new ways and means of codifying or indexing data so that they will lend themselves to the selection and manipulation of fragments of data, rather than of entire documents.

The distinction between systems that select and locate documents and systems that provide a higher level of information processing was emphasized by Y. Bar-Hillel, who pointed out that the problems of storing and retrieving documents should be considered apart from problems concerning analysis of the data contained in them.[12] Literature searching, he contends, involves only determining which documents or books are relevant to a chosen topic. He defines "information retrieval" as the act of obtaining answers to questions about a selected subject.

Therefore, as the complexity of information processing required increases, it becomes more and more important to bring to bear substantive knowledge in the research field itself. It is for this reason that the "information specialist" has been defined as a person with competence in a field of research sufficient for him to analyze results reported in published literature, to synthesize new results as evaluative "state-of-the-art" reports, and to provide control over the less formalized means of data communication. It is for this reason also that "information analysis centers" and other specialized information systems have become increasingly important. By bringing to bear a degree of subject matter expertise, they provide levels of processing beyond those normally associated with the library itself.

The Information Processes in the Library and Information Center

To put these issues in a specific context, consider a typical system for storage and retrieval of references to documents. The processes are illustrated in Figure 20.4. The documents themselves are considered to be of potential interest because of the ideas, concepts, and data recorded—more or less well—in them. Needs for them are also more or less well expressed, in the form of requests. In

[12] Bar-Hillel, Yehoshua, *Language and Information: Selected Essays on their Theory and Application,* Reading, Massachusetts: Addison-Wesley, 1964.

Figure 20.3 Information processing in libraries and information centers.

	Point One ("Raw" Data)	Point Two ("Closed" Data)	Point Three ("Intermediate" Data)	Point Four ("Open" Data)	Point Five ("Open" Data)	Point Six ("Open" Data)
Purpose of Communication	Real time monitoring and control	Internal, within an organization, a project, or for a single individual	Personal, point-to-point among professional colleagues	Broadcast to prefessional colleagues	Broadcast to professional colleagues	Broadcast to world
Nature of Audience	Machinery	Closely working team	"Invisible College"	Peer group	Professional group	General Professional audience
Size of Audience	—	1-10	10-100	100-1000	1000 10,000	10,000 100,000
Response Time from generation to availability	$10^{-2} - 10^2$ seconds	$10^2 - 3 \times 10^3$ seconds (2 min.-1 hr.)	$3 \times 10^3 - 10^6$ seconds (1 hr.-2 wks.)	$10^6 - 3 \times 10^7$ seconds (2 wks.-1 yr)	$3 \times 10^7 - 10^8$ seconds (1 yr.-3 yrs.)	$10^8 - 3 \times 10^8$ seconds (3 yrs.-9 yrs.)
Quality of Review		None	None	Low	Reasonably High	High
Volume/year (within group)	—	3×10^3?	3×10^3?	3×10^3?	3×10^3?	3×10^3?
Form of Communication	Signals	Personal files internal memos. etc.	Telephone, letters	Reports (issued by individual). conference papers	Journals. conference proceedings	Books

Figure 20.3 (continued)

	Point One ("Raw" Data)	Point Two ("Closed" Data)	Point Three ("Intermediate" data)	Point Four ("Open" Data)	Point Five ("Open" data)	Point Six ("open" data)
Communication Functions	?	Manage files	Facilitate Communication	Professional Writing / Mission oriented indexes and abstracts / Analysis and Evaluation	Review, publication, distribution / Discipline oriented indexes and abstracts / Selection cataloging, storage, and access	Editing, publication, distribution / National Catalogs / Selection cataloging storage, and access
Professional Roles (in Communication Process)	?	Information Specialists?	Information Specialists	Librarians and Documentalists / Information Specialists?	Editors and referees / Librarians	Editors / Librarians
Institutionalization	?		Information Exchange Groups. Special Interest Groups, etc.	Libraries / Information (Analysis) Centers	Professional Societies / Libraries	Publishers / Libraries
Role of Mechanization	Sensing, processing, transmitting, recording, control	Data Analysis File Management	Conference calls, "On-line" intellectual community	Reference retrieval, Data analysis	Publication of abstracts and indexes, Reference retrieval	Publication of Catalogs

755

each case, the precision with which ideas are expressed is usually uncertain because of the almost inherent difficulties that people have in expressing themselves. Language, both written and spoken, is at best an imprecise method of communication. Nevertheless, this is the nature of the input source for the information system.

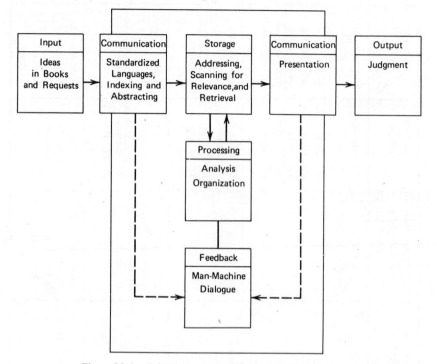

Figure 20.4   Schematic of document retrieval processes.

The first component of the system—the communication component—must now attempt to handle this usually diffuse input of documents and requests, and to represent them in the language of the system itself—by descriptive cataloging, by subject cataloging, by indexing and abstracting, and the like. Any imprecision in the original form of the input is now compounded by the almost inevitable mismatch between its language and that of the system itself. The communication process—by selection of data, by evaluation of its usefulness in description of content, and by translation into standardized form—must overcome these deficiencies. It is this need that makes the "dialogue" between input and system such a crucial area of study. To the extent that the dialogue is effective, the system will be effective, since the records that result from it are the elements of which all subsequent operations are constructed.

Locations must now be determined, within the store of references, to which new references are to be added or in which old references are to be looked for. The process of finding the proper address, while a formalized one—in fact, perhaps because it is a formalized one—is the point at which the system's *efficiency* (as contrasted with simply effectiveness) is most determined. The sequencing and organization of the files, the allocation of addresses, the structuring of indexes—all are essentially mechanical methods by which to provide rapid access to potentially relevant references at reasonable cost. And since "rapid," "relevant," and "reasonable" are all qualitative terms, the problems in this aspect of system design are precisely those of quantifying them, combining them into a single measure of efficiency, and optimizing the addressing process in terms of that measure.

The translation from identifier to address, however, merely defines the locations of sets of potentially relevant references. These must be found and scanned. The combination of mechanical problems in high speed positioning to desired addresses and high speed scanning of their contents has made this aspect of system operation the one of most intense attention by the manufacturers of computing equipment. As we have shown in Chapter 12, there have been innumerable developments of large capacity direct access memories, of specialized searchers of coded microforms, and of computer components such as "associative memories" which provide capability for extremely fast scanning of data.

As it is scanned, each reference must be evaluated for its relevency to the incoming request (or document to be stored). The logical problems in interpretation of "relevancy" and the practical problems of providing usable criteria by which to evaluate it have been the subject of especially intense study.

These processes—description, location, and evaluation of documents—are all typical of library operations. However, the next step in operation of an information system—analysis and reduction of the data—is rarely implemented in a document reference system to any degree of real significance, perhaps because the level of detail stored in the mechanical system is usually so minimal, but more importantly because the process of analysis is just too complex. Of course, some degree of organization for presentation of the references is relatively easy and has been implemented in libraries. These include, for example, various forms of permuted title indexes. Listings in order of relevancy are equally straightforward but have not been as frequently used. If more content of the documents themselves were included in the mechanized storage, it would be possible to extend the degree of analysis provided. This is standard in information systems such as inventory control and data reduction systems, where the mechanically stored data includes all of the content. To the extent that such analysis can be mechanically executed on the content of documents, the communication of the results to the user and interpretation of them by him (the final steps in operation of the system) would be facilitated. Therefore, a principal focus of the work of researchers in information science has been the development of algorithms and heuristics by which natural language text could be processed and results automatically generated which would answer questions. This is certainly the most challenging and intellectually exciting work in information science. In fact, Bar-Hillel and others have claimed that it is impossible to accomplish, because of the inherent illogicalities of natural language.[13] Despite that, however, it continues to be the real interest of many information scientists.

All of these processes constitute the things of interest to information science in the field of librarianship. In the following sections, we shall summarize some of the theoretical and practical problems with which researchers involved with information science in librarianship have been concerned. In doing this, our aim is not to be either deep or comprehensive, but rather to provide a framework within which further reading can be started. Furthermore, even the suggested readings at the end of the chapter are themselves not intended to be exhaustive, but have been limited to those that will best lead the reader to the more basic research papers. Among them, one set of references is crucial—the *Annual Reviews of Information Science and Technology,* edited by Dr. Carlos Cuadra for the American Society of Information Science.[14] Together, they constitute the best and most comprehensive continuing coverage of this field. At most, this chapter should be regarded as an introduction to those annual reviews and an overview of the issues that they cover.

Problems in Communication for Data Input.

The first set of problems that we shall discuss arises in the communication for data input. One of them, the "standardization of vocabulary," is a counterpart of the problems in maintenance of a subject authority; it includes the establishment of dictionaries, thesauri, and classification schedules. Another, "man-machine communication," has no formal counterpart in librarianship, but it is analogous to any dialogue between two people without an accepted pattern of communication. The third, "indexing, abstracting, and coding," is a counterpart of cataloging—in fact, more than a counterpart, differing only in the level of detail which is considered.

The Standardization of Vocabulary. An information system, whether mechanized or not, is based on the representation of its basic store of data in terms of a vocabulary which is, to some extent, standardized. In general, the problem of creating or discovering such a vocabulary has been a fundamental

[13] Kasher, Asa, *Data Retrieval by Computer: A Critical Survey,* The Hebrew University, Jerusalem, Israel, 1966.

[14] Cuadra, Carlos, *Annual Review of Information Science and Technology,* Vols. I and II, New York: Wiley, 1966 and 1967; Vols. III, IV, and V, Chicago: Encyclopedia Britannica, 1968, 1969, and 1970.

one, with which linguists, philosophers, and psychologists have long been concerned. The linguists have tended to approach it as an observational problem: What is the language used in the particular "information system" of people?[15] The tools of linguistics are designed to uncover the syntactic and semantic structure underlying the actual usages. They must be capable of defining the terms themselves, as they may be represented in phonic utterances or visual images.

The philosophers, on the other hand, have tended to view language and its standardization as a logical problem: What are the underlying structures that could be the basis of language? Their approach has been by way of various levels of formalized languages, from the simplest logical languages exemplified by the calculus of propositions, to finite state languages, to languages approaching natural language in their complexity.[16]

The psychologists have adopted a somewhat different approach: What is the effect that language has on the user of it and on the person to whom it is directed? The field of "psycholinguistics," while a new one, is well rooted in the tradition of "general semantics."[17]

The data-processing specialists have also been concerned with standardization of language, and in two different ways: (1) at the level of the language for communicating processes to a computer,[18] and (2) at the level of the terms for representing information in the computer.[19]

The aim, no matter what approach has been adopted, is to transfer relations implicit in the language into an explicit form. Since whatever is handled by a mechanical operation must have been formalized, the issue is basically how much of language processing can be handled by mechanical processes. In a real sense, the distinction between syntactics and semantics is simply a distinction between the parts of the language that have been formalized, and thus made explicit, and the parts that are still implicit.

Since we are concerned precisely with the problem of developing a more or less formalized vocabulary, we must examine the extremely complex problem of semantic analysis.[20] The first step in semantic analysis is the creation of a dictionary which contains the definition, in a form appropriate to the operation

[15] See the introduction to: Fodor, Jerry A., and Jerrold J. Katz, *The Structure of Language, Readings in the Philosophy of Language,* Englewood Cliffs, N. J.: Prentice-Hall, 1964.

[16] See especially, Chomsky, Noam, "A Transformational Approach to Syntax," In Fodor and Katz, op. cit.

[17] Korzybski, Alfred, *Science and Sanity,* 2nd ed., The International Non-Aristotelian Library Publishing Company, 1941.

[18] Higman, Bryan, *A Comparative Study of Programming Languages,* New York: American Elsevier, 1967.

[19] See below, in the discussion of thesauri.

[20] Minsky, Marvin (ed.), *Semantic Information Processing,* Cambridge, Massachusetts: MIT Press, 1968.

of the information system, of each term to be used in the system.[21] Such definitions must reduce to a specification of the relationships between a given word (the one being defined at the moment) and other words in the system. Ultimately, the definitions are expressible in terms of a relatively limited number of "undefined terms," whose meaning is known only in an operational sense, and which are accepted as such.

Typically, provision is made for specification of other terms that are more specific than the given one, or more general, or that are preferred to the given one.[22] The dictionary will include provision for specification of classes into which the term falls or to which the term is related. It will allow specification of the differences between the given term and other terms of similar "meaning" and application. For example, Roget's "thesaurus" is an arrangement of terms first into classes and then into groups under the terms more generic to them.

In data base systems, vocabulary control is not usually difficult and the terms are either implicit in the records themselves or, at most, are represented by a word list or code book. In reference retrieval systems, vocabulary control is much more complex, and thesauri play an especially important role. For example, the description of the content of documents requires the use of subject words chosen from the vocabulary. Since words can be interpreted in many different ways, exactly the meanings that are used in the system must be specified. To do this, subject authorities and thesauri show *a priori* relationships among the allowable terms (Figure 20.5).[23] In this same context, a classification schedule is a vocabulary that shows relationships by arranging terms in a hierarchical order.[24]

In text processing systems, the complications are even greater, since the meanings of words in natural language depend not only on *a priori* definitions but on the syntactic structure of the sentence in which they are used and the context of other words in the sentence. Dictionaries stored in the computer must therefore describe the kinds of sentences in which a word will take on each of its alternative meanings. For even a narrow field of discourse, the size of such a dictionary exceeds the capacity of rapid access memory in the largest present-day computers. This is one reason that sophisticated text processing is still speculative or, at most, experimental.

The problems in vocabulary development are the ones that have been central to librarianship and documentation: How do we derive appropriate words for

[21] Salton, Gerard, *Automatic Information Organization and Retrieval*, New York: McGraw-Hill, 1968. Chapters 2 and 3.

[22] Holm, Bart E., and L. E. Rasmussen, "Development of a Technical Thesaurus," *American Documentation*, 12, July 1961, pp. 184-190.

[23] *Thesaurus of ERIC Descriptors*, Office of Education, June 1969.

[24] de Grolier, Eric, *A Study of General Categories Applicable to Classification and Coding in Documentation*, UNESCO, 1962.

FIGURE 20.5   Representative subject authority.

Information Processing

More Specific Terms: Information Dissemination, Information Retrieval, Information Storage, Information Utilization

Related Term: Computers

Information Retrieval

Broader Term: Information Processing

Related Term: Data Processing

---

document description? How do we define them, particularly in terms of their relationship to one another? How do we impose a structure on the set of them?

1.   We can call on some existing authority, such as the indexes to journals of the field or existing glossaries. This approach is, of course, of particular value in establishing an initial vocabulary. However, some workers have questioned this, and even if we recognize its value, it merely begs the question.

2.   We can call on the documents themselves to generate their own terms. In discussing the methods— statistical and conceptual—for deriving information bearing words from text, we are not concerned here with their use in indexing the source documents themselves. Instead, we are concerned with their use as the first step in constructing a subject authority. The aim is to determine what words are used in the field of interest, as exemplified in a particular document. They may or may not adequately describe the information content of any given document itself. The permuted title index is the most obvious example, but the statistical extract and some approaches to coordinate indexing are others. Unfortunately, the inadequacy of the resulting vocabulary is immediately evident to anyone using a permuted title—or permuted key-word—index. The lack of organization, or even of cross references, forces the user either to scan through the index or to generate term associations himself.

3.   We can introduce the elements that convert a simple word list into a true subject authority: definitions and scope notes, references and cross-references, class relationships and analytic ones. What methodologies do we have here? There are many mechanical aids that can be drawn on to assist the subject specialist. The permuted index and the concordance, by bringing together the different contexts in which a word or phrase appears, can aid the subject specialist in recognizing relationships. The "semantic map," by picturing the extent to which words have been associated in common, uses statistical strength of association to show an underlying semantic one.[25] There are many specific

---

[25] Doyle, L. B., "Semantic Road Maps for Literature Searchers," *Journal of the Association for Computing Machinery,* 8 (October 1961), 553-578.

notations developed for representing the associations involved in a subject authority—those of Western Reserve System,[26] of the Engineer's Joint Council,[27] and of the colon classifications.[28]

Many systems stop at this point and assume that the subject authority or thesaurus is sufficient. However, usually some attempt is made to impose a further structure on it—a classification.

First, simply to set the one end of the spectrum, we have the purely intuitive approach to classification, the organization of a field of knowledge—including its vocabulary—based solely on a view of what is "rational." The methodologies are the classical ones of taxonomy.[29]

Second, there is a methodology, called "facet analysis," by which each term in a thesaurus can be represented by its position relative to each of a set of fundamental facets, as an ordered array.[30] In this way, the inherent structure of the vocabulary is displayed in a simple form, easy to grasp.

Third, there is the structure exemplified by the *filing rules* of the subject catalog.[31-33] To the extent that such rules are formalized, they impose a sequence on the vocabulary (that is, subject authority) designed to bring together these terms that are related, although the result is a structure only in a local sense.

Fourth, there are the several approaches which start from the premise that semantic structure is derivable from statistical associations among terms as they are used together.[34,35] These seek to decompose—again in the mathematical sense—the matrices which describe the degree of association among terms. Whether the technique is factor analysis, eigenvalue analysis, clumping, or

---

[26] Perry, James W., Allen Kent, and M. M. Berry, Machine *Literature Searching.* New York: Interscience, 1956.

[27] *Thesaurus of Engineering Terms,* Engineers Joint Council May 1, 1964.

[28] Tyaganatarajan, T., "A Study in the Development of Colon Classification", *American Documentation,* 12 (4) (October 1961) 270-278.

[29] Richardson, E. C., *Classification: Theoretical and Practical.* New York: Wilson, 1930.

[30] Hayes, Robert M., "The Decomposition of Vocabulary Hierarchies " in Kjell Samuelson, *Mechanized Information Storage, Retrieval, and Dissemination.* Amsterdam: North-Holland, 1968, pp. 160-191.

[31] Cutter, Charles A., *Rules for a Printed Dictionary Catalog,* Government Printing Office, 1875.

[32] Coates, E. J., *Subject Catalogs, Headings and Structure.* London: The Library Association, 1960.

[33] Allen, Thelma E., and Daryl Ann Dickman, *New Rules for an Old Game.* Vancouver: University of British Columbia, 1967.

[34] Sokal, Robert P., and Peter H. A. Sneath, *Principles of Numerical Taxonomy.* San Francisco: Freeman, 1963.

[35] Stevens, Mary E., et. al. (eds.), *Statistical Association Methods for Mechanized Documentation,* Government Printing Office, December 15, 1965.

latent-class analysis, the approach is almost the same. The only real differences lie in the particular choice for the measure of association.

Fifth, there is an approach that has masqueraded under a variety of names—"Scan-Column Index" of Claire Schultz,[36] "Multi-List" of Prywes at the University of Pennsylvania.[37] More or less the methodology simply develops groups of terms by assigning each term to a group whose existing members have never been used with it. In this way, a single field of the record can be assigned to all terms in a group without fear of overlap. The result may be a weird sort of structure, but perhaps not. In fact, this methodology is implicit in all fixed field format item records, although of course one would not normally consider deriving them in so mechanical a fashion.

Man-Machine Communication. Man-machine dialogue involves four things: (1) a set of allowable input symbols by which the man can communicate, (2) a data base available to the machine, (3) a set of message forms or "stereotypes" by which the machine can combine the input symbols with symbols from its data base and effectively communicate, and (4) a strategy or pattern of choices, by which either the man or the machine or both can determine the sequence. Figure 20.6 presents a schematic of the decision processes in such a dialogue (as exhibited in a program for computer-aided instruction).[38]

These issues are especially significant in systems that try to handle natural language. In particular, the communication problem is almost insurmountable because of the size of the vocabulary that must be stored in the machine (in the dictionary), the degree of semantic ambiguity arising from the number of different meanings that a word can have, and the limited number of syntactic patterns that the machine can recognize.

Indexing, Abstracting, and Coding Since an information system deals with descriptions of things essentially external to it, some means must be provided for selecting pertinent characteristics for description of particular things and for properly combining them into records. This results in the assignment of terms from the vocabulary which then become the content of corresponding records. A useful way of visualizing the result of the assignment of terms to records is the "record-term" matrix shown in Figure 20.7.[39] Methods for selecting terms to be assigned to a given document include statistical clues, "syntactic" clues, and "semantic" clues, based on the form of the input data.

[36] Schultz, Claire, "Generalized Computer Method for Information Retrieval", *American Documentation,* **14** (January 1963), 39-48.

[37] Lefkovitz, David, and N. S. Prywes, "Automatic Stratification of Information" *Conference Proceedings,* American Federation of Information Processing Societies, 1963.

[38] Suppes, Patrick, *Computer Aided Instructional System for Mathematics,* Stanford University, 1966.

[39] Becker, Joseph, and R. M. Hayes, *Information Storage and Retrieval.* New York: Wiley, 1963, Chapter 14.

GRADE _4_
CONCEPT BLOCK _02_

DESCRIPTION – *SUBTRACTION*

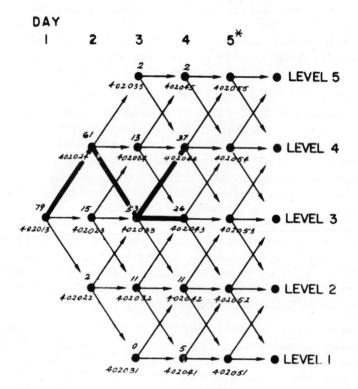

DAY

| 1 | 2 | 3 | 4 | 5* |

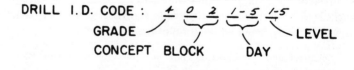

DRILL I.D. CODE :   _4_ _0_ _2_ _1-5_ _1-5_

GRADE — CONCEPT BLOCK — DAY — LEVEL

* NO DATA AS OF DATE OF REPORT

Figure 20.6 Typical dialogue decision progression.

The storage of these descriptions involves the definition of a set of "formats" or data structures, as discussed in Chapter 6, which provide not only the facility for the assignment of allowable terms to a description but the facility for showing their interrelationships in that description as well, by the use of roles, links, and standard syntactic patterns.

Figure 20.7   Record-term matrix

Terms

$$
\begin{array}{c c c c c}
 & T_1\ T_2 & \cdots & T_j & \cdots & T_n \\
R_1 & a_{11}\ a_{11} & & a_{1j} & & a_{in} \\
R_2 & a_{21}\ a_{22} & & a_{2j} & & \\
\vdots & & \ddots & & & \\
R_i & a_{i1}\ a_{i2} & & a_{ij}{}^a & & a_{in} \\
\vdots & & & & \ddots & \\
R_m & a_{m1}\ a_{m2} & & & & a_{mn}
\end{array}
$$

[a] The element a_{ij} is taken as 1 if term T_j is used in record R_i and is taken as 0 if not.

Problems in Storage and Retrieval

The second set of problems that we shall discuss arises in the storage and retrieval of data. One problem, "file organization," includes counterparts of filing rules for sequencing of a catalog; in addition, however, indexes and cross indexes must be constructed to aid the processes in direct access to data. The second problem, "evaluation of relevancy," and the third, "strategy of search," are counterparts of reference work and relate to the problems of locating and evaluating references.

File Organization.

Strangely, the area of file organization has been remarkably neglected as one for study by the documentalists. In fact, only the data processing specialists, concerned with the effective utilization of mass storage media, have devoted analytical attention to it.[40] Yet, this area is as central to librarianship as that of vocabulary development and control.

Perhaps the comparative neglect results from the tendency to identify file organization with vocabulary organization, to consider that physical organization necessarily reflects the intellectual one. This view is such a superficial one that some basic problems in file organization have been obscured and neglected.

[40] Meadow, Charles, *The Analysis of Information Systems*. New York: Wiley, 1967.

Underlying the need for file organization is the fact that in large files it is impossible to consider scanning the entire file, looking for desired items or information. We must therefore select, on the basis of some simple criteria, a relatively small set of items that can then be examined more deeply. Evidently, the problem is the development of a suitable structure by which to provide a mechanism for successive screening. Figure 20.8 is a schematic representation of a file system.

Figure 20.8   File organization and structure

Master File
(Rows of Document/Term Matrix)

Address	Record		Index to Master File
1	D_1: $T_{11}, T_{11}, \ldots, T_{1k_1}$		$D_1 - D_b$: Address 1
2	D_2: $T_{21}, T_{22}, \ldots, T_{2k_2}$		$D_{b+2} - D_{2b}$: Address $b + 1$
3	D_3: $T_{31}, T_{32}, \ldots, T_{3k_3}$		$D_{2b+1} - D_{3b}$: Address $2\,b + 1$
⋮	·..		⋮
i	D_i: $T_{i1}, T_{i2}, \ldots, T_{ik_i}$		$D_{n-b} - D_n$: Address $n - b$
⋮	·..		
n	D_n: $T_{n1}, T_{n2}, \ldots, T_{nk_n}$		

Cross Indexes
(Columns of Document/Term Matrix)

Address	Record		Index to Cross Indexes
a	T_1: $D_{11}, D_{12}, \ldots, D_{1p_1}$		$T_1 - T_c$: Address a
$a + 1$	T_2: $D_{21}, D_{22}, \ldots, D_{2p_2}$		$T_{c+1} - T_{2c}$: Address
⋮	·..		⋮
$a + j + 1$	T_j: $D_{j1}, D_{j2}, \ldots, D_{jp_j}$		$T_{m-c} - T_m$: Address $a + m - 1 - c$
⋮	·..		
$a + m - 1$	T_m: $D_{m1}, D_{m2}, \ldots, D_{mp_m}$		

In all of the methods of file organization, file *sequences* must be established, because the records must each be stored in some location. The choice of sequence, however, becomes important, since the location of a record is the place to which the computer must later go to retrieve it. In most systems, file sequence is usually determined by one field of the record format, called the "record identifier" (document number, for example), the set of records being stored in numerical or alphabetical order according to the values in that field.

The obvious file structure is that which, in fact, has obscured the difference between vocabulary structure and file structure: use the structure of the vocabulary—the subject headings, the class numbers, and the key-words. The advantage of this method is its relative ease and simplicity; it is a familiar approach, and therefore one that anyone can understand. Superficially, it appears that this *is* the criterion for organization in virtually all libraries.

But there is another method for file organization that has been used, almost unconsciously, to an equal extent. This is the method of "activity" organization, based on the concept of making readily available the items in the file that are *likely* to be used. Of course, this begs the question of what is meant by "likely to be used" and of how it might be measured. Recognizing the difficulties, however, we must also recognize that there are many criteria, virtually any of which may have deficiencies but will be pragmatically adequate. The real question is how to derive a file organization from the one chosen. The result of this approach might be to make a single well-used book as available—both physically and intellectually—as large categories containing many books.

A third approach is a much more speculative one. It bases the organization on the similarity of items, and groups together items that are similar. Again, this begs the question of how similarity is to be determined. It is this question that makes the method so speculative; however, it should be recognized that organization by subject or class number really represents the use of a simple measure of similarity—concern with a common subject—so as we extend our knowledge of the intellectual concepts of relevancy, we should correspondingly extend our concepts of file organization.

Whatever method of sequencing is used, the computer can find a desired record in the master file only by knowing where it is located (that is, by "direct access") or by looking at every record until it is found (that is, by "sequential access"). Since sequential access in large files can be very time consuming, indexes must be established which tell the computer the locations of records with desired characteristics. An example of this is the "inverted file" or "term oriented file," in which an "index record" is stored for each term of the vocabulary. It lists all master file records to which that term has been applied (that is, it stores the columns of the "record-term" matrix, whereas the master file stores the rows).

Another kind of indexing structure is designed around the concept of "lists." A list is a succession of records in which each record contains the address of the next record in the list (except the last one, which may reference the first record in the list so as to produce a closed list). A list may be established to correspond to a given term, with the records in the list being those to which the term has been assigned. The "term file" would then need to contain only the address of first record in the list, subsequent ones being addressed from one record to the next.

Relevancy. An information system functions by analyzing data "relevant" to a need for processing of it.[41] The problem of determining the relevancy of data to a need relates partly to the requirements of the user, partly to the manner by which a request is described, and partly to the efficiency of operation which requires the use of a succession of "screens," each with its own measure of relevancy or degree of match. The final screen is the user himself, using his sophisticated criteria and applying them to the most complicated form of the stored data. But, since he cannot afford to do this to the entire file of descriptions, preliminary screens are used to reduce the file to a size that he can handle.

Requests come in a variety of forms. They differ in detail, in accuracy of description, in area of subject interest, and in the form of information desired. Some of them are standardized and can be answered by preprinted reports.[42] Others are "standing requests," used for "selective dissemination of information" (SDI) to the requestor as data is acquired.[43] Others represent needs that require a personalized search of the file. In all cases, the request must be expressed in a form that can be matched against the stored records, by identifying terms that should appear in specified fields in the desired records. (In data base systems, many of the "terms" are numerical values recorded in a field, and both single values and ranges of values may be requested, using the relationships "equal to," "greater than," and "less than"). The terms are then combined in *Boolean* expressions, using logical AND, OR, and NOT. For example, a request might specify that field 1 is to contain terms A_1 or A_2 or A_3, that field 2 is to contain values greater than B, and that field 3 is not to contain term C. The request would be expressed as

$$\text{Field 1 } (A_1 \text{ OR } A_2 \text{ OR } A_3) \text{ AND Field 2 } (>B) \text{ AND Field 3 (NOT } C).$$

In reference retrieval systems, identifying the terms that best express a request usually requires a "dialogue" between the requestor and the stored thesaurus, in which words the requestor uses lead him to equivalent words in the vocabulary. Sometimes a requested term must be "exploded," because the thesaurus indicates that it is related to a number of other terms with similar or more specific meanings by which documents may also be described. These terms must be connected by logical "OR" in the request description. For example, the requestor may ask for subject A, and the thesaurus may indicate that subjects A_1 and A_2 are more specific and that subject B is similar. The request term A

[41] Cuadra, Carlos, *On the Utility of the Relevance Concept*, System Development Corporation, March 18, 1964.

[42] See, for example, the standardized lists produced by NASA.

[43] Luhn, H. P., "Selective Dissemination of New Scientific Information with the Aid of Electronic Processing Equipment," *American Documentation,* 12 (April 1961), 131-138.

would then be exploded and the request would become

$$\text{Subject } (A \text{ OR } A_1 \text{ OR } A_2 \text{ OR } B).$$

In text processing systems, a request can be formulated in the same manner as in a data base or reference retrieval system, with roughly comparable problems. On the other hand, part of the rationale for text processing is that requests can be phrased as ordinary English sentences, with negligible effort on the part of the requestor (but, of course, with complexity in the programs required to translate them and process them comparable to that in handling the stored text).

Once a request has been formulated, records must be examined to determine whether they are *relevant* to it. Since relevancy is an ill-defined concept, the computer program will use a simple measure of "degree of match," such as the number of terms in the request which appear in the stored record. The records that match most closely are then treated as relevant, insofar as the computer is concerned. However, with large files, it becomes too time consuming to compare every record with the request, and index files are used to locate those records which will be matched. This process of comparing the request with index records constitutes the *search* of the file.

Strategy of Search. Searching of files thus involves a succession of scanning records and their surrogates, matching them with requests, and selecting relevant ones. However, since the matching is uncertain (both because of uncertainty and error in description and because the surrogates represent groups of items), there is a problem of strategy of search. Basically, in search through a file, a decision must be made between pursuing a direction of search or changing to another direction. In doing this, consideration must be given to the reponse time, the required reliability of the result, and the cost of the search process itself.

The result of the search process will be the retrieval of a set of records which the system presents to the user as the "relevant ones." At this point, the effectiveness of the entire operation becomes an issue.[44] The user usually wants some assurance that most of the relevant material has been found. Otherwise, he will feel great uncertainty as to whether the records he really wanted may not have been missed. Furthermore, he also wants assurance that the material given him is not largely irrelevant. Otherwise, he will spend a great deal of his own time in effectively wasted effort screening out the irrelevant material. These two issues have been characterized as "recall ratio" and "precision ratio." The former is extremely difficult to measure, because of the lack of knowledge of how much was "really" in the file. The latter is easy to measure and leads to quite straightforward measures of cost/effectiveness.

---

[44] Lancaster, F. W., *Information Retrieval Systems: Characteristics, Testing, and Evaluation.* New York: Wiley, 1968.

Problems in Data Analysis and Presentation   *are data organization question answering*

The third set of problems that we shall discuss arises in the analysis and presentation of data. One of the problems, "data organization," is quite simple, amounting to the arrangement of data in a prescribed order. Another problem, "question answering," is so complex that some researchers feel that it is impossible to mechanize.[45]

Data Organization. Usually, file management systems include capabilities for "report generation." These allow specification of output formats, sort sequences, and simple statistical summaries. For example, retrieved references may be arranged in "order of relevancy," in chronological order, in alphabetical order by author, in filing sequence, and so on. A typical format is the KWIC index, which sequences titles in order by key words contained in them.[46] The problems in producing desired arrangements are not difficult.

Question Answering. On the other hand, the problems involved in making logical inferences from stored data—in "answering questions"—are immense. Programs have been written that will carry through syllogisms, that will analyze implications according to the propositional calculus, and that will analyze record interrelationships according the the predicate calculus. Figure 20.9 gives a list of experimental question-answering systems.[47] All of them are highly speculative, and each is severely limited—by file size, by complexity of logical analysis, and by kind of language.

ROLE OF INFORMATION SCIENCE IN LIBRARY EDUCATION

In light of this picture of information science and its relationship to librarianship, what are its implications for library education? They amount to this: library education, as it now exists, is concerned with professional needs, with particulars, with "functional" education, and with techniques as they are used in existing library environments. If questions are raised in the educational process, they are answered in terms of the environments and the solutions that are already operational. The result, at worst, is the education of a set of well-trained clerks, familiar with all of the rules and all of their exceptions, able to fit into any existing library situation, but unable to adjust to a new one. At best, although creative minds will be able to remold the solutions developed in the past and will be able to adjust them better to meet a new environment, they will be constrained to the familiar paths in doing so.

[45] Kasher, Asa, *op. cit.*
[46] Luhn, H. P., *Keyword-in-Context for Technical Literature,* IBM, August 1959
[47] Hayes, Robert M., Review of Asa Kasher, *Data Retrieval by Computer,* in *American Documentation,* 18 (3) (July 1967), 187-189.

Unfortunately, this kind of education, while it may very well meet the needs of some libraries, completely fails to meet the needs of new information environments or the needs of growth in understanding of the library profession itself. Metcalfe said, "Librarians are not without blame in having degraded cataloging and classifying ... to fixed techniques or routines, in having allowed

Figure 20.9   Question-answering systems.

Person and System	Journal and Date	Language Data Processing	Searching	Data Reduction
Phillips "ORACLE"	1960	One syntactic pattern (SVO, time, place)	Simple matching on words in syntactic pattern	
Sable "IDL"	C-ACM, Jan. 1962	Generic relations		
Salton	C-ACM, Feb. 1962	Tree-structures		
Householder "Auto Lang Anal"	1962	Roget's codes	Correlation of terms	
Simmons "Synthex"	AD, Jan. 1963		Complete index	
Harrah	Communication: A logical model, 1963			Predicate calculus (definitions of questions and answers)
Green, Clonsky "BASEBALL"	1963		List structures	Simple counting
Simmons "Protosynthex"	1963			
Lindsay "SADSAM"	1963	Basic English words (1413) and syntactic classes. Predictive analysis. Specific syntactic class defined formats	List structures	Tree structure for defined relations
Doyle	Nov. 1963	Statistical properties		

Figure 20.9 (*continued*)

Person and System	Journal and Date	Language Data Processing	Searching	Data Reduction
Cooper Fact Retrieval	J-ACM, Apr. 1964	Sublanguage of English. Trans. by *grammatical classes* into "logical" equivalents. Specific algorithm for constituent structure languages which steps thru grammatical classes	All possible subsets of up to three stored data sentences, each of which contains at least one basic term from the question	Aristotelian logic
Salton "SMART"	June 1964	Specific syntactic structures including "semantic" classes)	Matching terms with weights in structure	Statistical tree-structure
Simmons "Synthex"	AD Jan. 1963		Complete index	
Bobrow "STUDENT"	AD 604730, Sept. 1964	Kernel sentences (20 different formats) Conversion routines	Simple table look-up	Arithmetic for simultaneous linear equations

so much to be identified with the popular library and its simple needs."[48] It is wider needs that education in information science hopes to meet. Through a critical examination of how solutions are developed, we can educate personnel in the general foundations on which any solution can be developed.

Does this imply that librarians cannot operate libraries without an education including information science? Certainly not. In fact, it is not even clear that such education will produce "better" librarians. However, it is clear that we are dealing with an increasingly complex world and that the problems that librarians face are correspondingly complex. If they are to cope with them, they must have sophisticated, objective, well-defined tools to do so.

To pursue this last point further, it is evident from history that each

[48] Metcalfe, John, *Information Indexing and Subject Cataloging*. New York: Scarecrow, 1957, p. 16.

Figure 20.9   (*continued*)

Person and System	Journal and Date	Language Data Processing	Searching	Data Reduction
Raphael "SIR"	1964	20 fixed formats		Set relationships Simple arithmetic
Cooper	1964			Syllogisms and propositional calculi
Darlington	1964			Predicate calculus
Thompson "DEACON"	1964	Word classes (functions, lists, attributes, modifiers)	List structures	
Kirsch, et al. "PLM"	1964	Descriptions of pictures Phrase structure		1st order predicate
Black "SQA"	1964	Fixed formats	Exact match on words and structure	Rules of inference

Abbreviations. C-ACM, Communications of the Association for Computing Machinery. J-ACM, Journal of the Association for Computing Machinery. AD, American Documentation.

generation, each person in fact, learns anew the lessons of the past. At a superficial level, it may appear that we learn nothing new, that the fundamental truths are always the same. But it must be recognized that in each era, although the truths may be the same, the context is different, the structure of it is more complex, and the problems in it are larger. This forces us to learn anew, because the fundamental truths are really abstractions and each generation must view these abstractions in totally new situations and, usually, in more complex ones.

Even at the very simplest of levels, consider the situation for a library school graduate, perhaps with two or three years of operating experience, who is in one way or another faced with the installation of a new library or information center. Recognize the problems that he is faced with:

He is working under a very limited budget, perhaps just himself and a clerk. Should he use the organization's data processing equipment to supplement the limited help? Perhaps he can use it without cost;

in fact, using it may even strengthen his own position. What should he have the equipment do?

He is working in a relatively undefined information environment—no acquisition policies, no source definition, no prescribed services, and little knowledge of the needs of his clients. How should he develop policies, sources, and services? How does he determine the needs of clients?

He is working in a highly specialized field for which no established glossary exists and for which standard classifications are not adequate. How should he develop a glossary and classification adequate to the specialized needs and yet well controlled and compatible with broader ones?

He has no well-defined criteria for indexing, for file organization, and for all the other technical processes he must install. How does he create them?

It is clear that what we have defined are the problems of librarianship, whether we view them in the context of information centers, special libraries, large research libraries, or the public library. Even for the librarian in an existing library, where his problem may be limited to the clerical aspects of library operation and whether to automate them or not, the librarian is faced with many questions for which he has few tools for assistance. If he is further faced with such problems as a change of classification system (from Dewey to LC) or addition of new fields of interest such as technical information for small business and industry, the lack of tools becomes almost embarrassing.

The purpose of information science is to develop the tools needed for these decisions, and its role in library education is to provide the student with the basic abilities to use those tools.

General Nature of Information Science Curricula

Unfortunately, however, programs for education in information science have been defined in such a variety of ways that it is almost impossible to extract a common curriculum from them. Let us list a few of the existing kinds of programs.

1.   Some schools (all of them library schools) have identified information science with the use of computers in libraries. Thus, such schools will imply that they have an "information science curriculum" if they have added one or two courses on "data processing in the library." The confusion created by this definition has been compounded by federal legislation in its references to "library and information science," which has frequently been interpreted in this sense.

2.   Some schools (all of them library schools) have identified information science with "science information" and usually regard it as synonymous with "documentation." Such schools will add courses on "Indexing and Abstracting," on "The Management of Information Centers," and on "Mechanized Information Retrieval" as their curriculum on information science.

3.   Some schools (usually, engineering schools) have identified information science with computer science, often with emphasis on the use of computers for processing natural language, on "question-answering," perhaps on heuristic programming and "artificial intelligence."

4.   Some schools (usually, engineering schools) have identified information science with communication theory and regard it purely as a subset of their existing curricula.

5.   Some schools (of a variety of kinds—medicine, urban planning, business administration, engineering, and librarianship) have identified information science with the design of information systems in their own specialized fields of interest (with patient monitoring systems, with urban data banks, with management information systems, with command and control systems, and with library systems). Usually, they will call their curricula "Information Systems" curricula and include courses on system design and on the application of computers to their specialized field.

6.   Some schools regard information science as a discipline in its own right which, although applicable in many fields, has its own problems of research interest and its own "discipline." Such schools will include both theoretical courses (drawn, usually, from the formal disciplines of mathematics, logic, and perhaps linguistics) and applied courses (from fields like psychology, engineering, or microbiology).

With such an array of differing views, it is natural to expect a comparable array of curricula. At the moment, four have been most clearly defined and identified with information science. Figure 20.10 presents a comparison of the different emphasis they will place on different courses. Of the four, the first and second are unlikely to be adopted by a library school. The third and fourth, however, are of great importance to library schools. We shall, therefore, provide more detailed description of possible course content for them in a library school.

Curriculum in Data Processing in the Library

There is an unprecedented demand for understanding by librarians of data processing technology and of its application in libraries. In part the needs have been met by data processing clinics, special short courses, and ad hoc training programs by which existing library personnel have been introduced to the technology.

Figure 20.10   Various course emphases.

Representative Courses	Curricula			
	Theory Oriented	Computer Oriented	Systems Oriented	Library Oriented
Formal Disciplines				
Calculus	Pre-req.	Pre-req.	Pre-req.	–
Programming	Pre-req.	Pre-req.	①	2
Symbolic Logic	①	①	3	–
Recursive Functions	①	①	3	–
Linguistics	①	2	2	–
Applied Disciplines				
Statistics	3	3	①	–
Operations Research	3	3	①	3
Psychology	2	3	–	–
Information Theory	①	①	3	–
Systems Analysis	–	3	①	2
Methods of Social Research	–	–	2	–
Computer Oriented Courses				
Computer Hardware	3	①	2	3
Compiler Construction	3	①	–	–
Data Base Management	3	①	①	2
Information Retrieval System	①	①	①	①
Management Information System	–	3	2	–
Management Oriented Courses				
Managerial Accounting	–	–	①	3
Organization Theory	3	–	2	–
Information Center Mgt.	–	–	①	①
Service Oriented Courses				
Sources of Information	–	–	2	①
Catal., Class., Index., Abst.	2	2	2	①
Documentation	–	–	2	①

Pre-req.   Pre-requisite
①   Required
2   Recommended
3   Elective

These measures are mere stopgaps, however. The needs are far greater than such measures can satisfy, and the only real solution is a continuing flow of graduates from professional library schools with this kind of knowledge already an integral part of their education. Of course, school after school has recognized the need, and each is struggling to find ways of including data processing in its curriculum without perverting the essential character of library education. The difficulties are great: Where do we get the faculty to teach such courses? How do we design them around the qualifications and interests of students, the majority of whom have had nontechnical academic backgrounds and are frequently alarmed by the "other culture?" How do we reconcile the deep-seated humanistic traditions of librarianship with the formalistic approaches of technology? In other words, how do we place systems analysis, data processing, and information science in proper perspective with the traditions and professional requirements of librarianship?

The particular approach, summarized in this section, is the one that was adopted as part of the MLS program at the University of California at Los Angeles. It consists of a succession of three courses. The first is a relatively elementary introduction to the principles of systems analysis and data processing, with emphasis on the judgmental issues in evaluation with which the librarian should be concerned; it is a required course for all MLS students. The second is a detailed examination of data processing applications to library operations, with emphasis on computer programming and on methods analysis; it is an elective for MLS students. The third is a detailed study of the methods and techniques of systems analysis as applied to information systems; it is also an elective for MLS students.

The next few sections summarize the content of each of these courses, the approach to a presentation of them, and the major pedagogical tools used in them. As such, they describe the particular approach used at UCLA; however, comparable courses, with different emphasis but with basically the same kind of content, are now in existence in a large number of schools.

Introduction to Library Data Processing Systems. The purpose of this course is to introduce the MLS student to the technology of computing in such a way that he will view it in the total context of library purposes and goals, not as either a panacea or a disaster. The emphasis is therefore on the systems approach, which starts from goals and purposes, which continually evaluates alternatives in terms of them, and which views data processing technology as simply one tool among a large variety that can be used.

The structure of the course can be seen in the sequence of topics shown in Figure 20.11. It is organized around an 11 to 12 week quarter. The weeks can be roughly divided into three parts: the first week, which is an introduction; the next five weeks, which present the general issues involved in systems analysis; and the last five weeks which present data processing technology. Normally, there will be a written examination after week six and a final examination (as shown) in week twelve. The course roughly covers the material of Sections 1 to 3 of this book.

During the first week (the introductory section), the intent is to familiarize the student with the general context of library data processing today, with emphasis on the growth of library networks, the various federal mechanization projects, and the like. These provide the rationale for the immediate interest in library systems analysis and thus represent an incentive and stimulus to student interest.

Figure 20.11
Course outline:
Introduction to library data processing systems.

Week 1. Current Trends in Library Data
Processing and Networks

2. The Approach of Systems Analysis

3. Definition of Library Goals and Objectives

4. Planning and Implementing Library Systems

5. Methods of System Description

6. System Evaluation and Cost Accounting

7. Coding of Data

8. Input, Output, and Display of Data

9. Punched Card Processing

10. Storage of Data

11. Computer Hardware and Software

12. Final Examination

The second section presents a somewhat traditional approach to systems analysis but with perhaps an unusual emphasis on criteria for evaluation. Among the traditional techniques covered are included flow charting, Gantt charting, time and motion study, forms design, procedural analysis, and the like. In this respect, the content is comparable to typical "methods analysis" courses. But during weeks two, three, and six, the importance of evaluation is heavily emphasized, particularly in terms of qualitative criteria of library effectiveness. The section then concludes with discussion of cost-effectiveness as the basis for modern system evaluation and, in this context, the possibility of a cost accounting system for library operations is presented as a tool for library administration as well as the basis for design and evaluation of new systems.

The third section is also a traditional approach to the teaching of data processing technology, except perhaps for the relatively greater emphasis placed on coding and storage of data, with the "computer" as such being presented only at the very end of the course. As a result, the student is given only enough knowledge about the role of programming for him to appreciate, on the one hand, the immense capabilities which the programmed general purpose computer provides, and, on the other hand, the even more immense problems which arise when the programs must be written to make them a reality. In this respect, the primary point of the entire course is brought to a final focus. The issue is never "Can the computer do it?" (which the students always start by asking) but rather "Should it?"

The sequence of presentation and the relative emphasis reflect the necessity of teaching students who, even though they may be mature graduates have little knowledge of even such simple topics as binary coding. The intent, therefore, is to bring the students step by step through the arithmetic of coding, the methods of communicating with machinery, and the various means of storing data in machine-processible form before discussing processing. The emphasis on "storage" is particularly important because it reflects the character of the library problem in contrast with other applications of computers.

Data Processing in the Library. This course covers the applications of data processing to various library operations, as a natural successor to the course on library systems analysis discussed above. Figure 20.12 presents the sequence of topics to be covered, based on an 11- to 12-week quarter. Again, the course can be roughly divided into three sections: the first, an introductory week presenting the concept of "total library systems"; the second, a seven-week coverage of essentially clerical areas of library operation; and the third, a three week coverage of those applications in support of the intellectual, service functions of library operation. As can be seen, the course roughly covers Section 4 of this book.

Figure 20.12
Course outline: Data Processing in the Library.

Week 1. Total Library Systems

  2. Library Administrative Systems

  3. Acquistions and Ordering Systems

  4. Catalog Production Systems

  5. Serial Record Systems

  6. Circulation Control Systems

  7. Interlibrary Loan Systems

  8. File Conversion and Input Systems

  9. Subject Authority Control Systems

  10. Mechanized Indexing Systems

  11. Information Retrieval Systems

  12. Final Examination

This course includes the use of a laboratory of computer programs, representative data bases, and peripheral devices so that the student can obtain actual experience in the operation of computer based systems. Each class is required to program—in some appropriate language—an expansion of the existing set of operating programs.

The succession of topics is not very startling, since the purpose is to cover specific parts of library operation within the context of the total library system. Therefore, the only real issue is the structure of the presentation of each topic. Briefly, it can be summarized as follows. Each area of operation is described in terms of its goals, and then analyzed into component functions. Then a number of alternative ways of executing those functions are presented and evaluated in terms of their relative effectiveness. Where the laboratory includes representative programs for specific functions, they will be included among the alternatives presented.

Methods of Information System Analysis and Design. The third course has a very different concern. Its emphasis is on the analysis and design of mechanized systems for information handling. To an extent, of course, there is an area of overlap with library operations, such as those involved in the control of subject authorities, in mechanized indexing, and in reference work. However, these are simply examples from the library of comparable functions that arise in the great number of other areas of computer application—management information systems, information centers, socioeconomic data banks, and the like. The purpose of this third course is to provide the student with the methods for analysis and design as they may be applicable in a broad variety of fields.

The structure of the course can be seen from the outline of topics in Figure 20.13. The course starts with a summary of the available methodology of system

Figure 20.13
Course outline:
Methods of Information Systems Analysis and Design.

Week 1.	Summary of Systems Analysis Methodology
2.	Study of User Requirements
3.	Standardization of Vocabulary
4.	Man-Machine Communication
5.	Formalized Abstracting, Indexing, and Description
6.	File Organization
7.	Request Formulation and File Searching
8.	Data Reduction and Analysis
9.	Data Presentation
10.	Equipment Evaluation
11.	Criteria for Total System Evaluation
12.	Final Examination

design—operations research, cost/effectiveness measures, information theory, and control systems theory. It then presents each of the primary problem areas, in turn, in the manner outlined below. It concludes with a summary of approaches to evaluating total system performance. The course represents a fairly typical coverage of the different issues involved in the design of specialized information systems. Therefore, again, the only real issue is the structure of presentation of each topic. Each area of interest (as outlined in Figure 20.13) is described. Then the set of available methods for handling the problems is presented, using illustrative examples from the variety of types of information systems. Finally, various criteria for measurement of performance are presented and, where possible, they are embodied in a theory appropriate to the problem area.

A term paper is used as a primary pedagogical tool. Each student chooses an information system of interest to him (the choice being made in the second week of the course). Because of the variety of backgrounds from which students come (from business administration, engineering, education, and the sciences, as well as from the library school), there is a comparable variety of term papers. Each week the student proceeds to apply the methodologies presented in class to the corresponding problem in the system he has chosen so that, by the end of the course, he has effectively designed and evaluated a possible system.

Summary. The three courses outlined above represent one approach to the introduction of data processing into the library school curriculum. Their organization and sequence of presentation have been designed to accommodate a variety of problems that must be recognized:

1.   Library school students generally lack the technical background necessary for data processing work as such, and yet, as library school graduates, they will find themselves in a world where that technology will play an increasingly important role. They must be given a sufficient orientation to be able to fit data processing into the context of library goals and purposes. The intent of the introductory course is to bridge the gap between their existing background and their future work.

2.   There is a great and ever-growing need for library systems analysts, educated as librarians but with the technical tools for competent work with data processing technology. Fortunately, there is an increasing flow of students into library schools with a technical background and capacity for systems work. But they require both a complete picture of the present capabilities for library use of computers and actual experience with them. The purpose of the second course is to fill this need, with the laboratory as the means for gaining experience.

3.   The development of computer-based information systems is a phenomenon of our times. Mechanization in libraries certainly represents one example, but perhaps even more important is the extent to which the experience in the

library field is applicable to the variety of other information systems. The purpose of the third course is to bring together the highly formalized methods developed in a number of fields of study—operations research, mathematics, linguistics, engineering, business administration, and sociology— and show how they are applicable to information system design. There is a great need for adding a new dimension to the character of library research, and it has been well recognized that "information science" represents one direction which should be taken.

Curriculum in Information Systems Analysis

A systems analysis curriculum must be designed to provide the student with the intellectual orientation and technical tools necessary for successful professional work and research in this field. It should provide a common core of technical knowledge, integrated by a framework of the total field; it should provide directions of specialization within the field; and it should bring the student to the point of successful, independent work.

Because of the nature of information systems work, the student must understand the problems in *utilization* of recorded information, the problems in *operation* of information systems, and the problems in their *technical implementation.* Therefore the common core of technical knowledge must give the student the tools for developing his understanding in these aspects. The direction for his specialization will normally be in one of these three aspects—the information *specialist* being concerned with utilization, the *manager* of an information system being concerned with operational techniques, and the system *designer* being concerned with technical problems in implementation.

After completing such a curriculum, the student should be prepared to work in one or more types of applications, including libraries and information centers. He should be able to evaluate the proper directions to take in creating new systems and manage the progress of systems development through each of the necessary phases, from feasibility study to implementation and operation. He should be prepared to work effectively with each of the groups necessary for a system to be successful—with the people whom it will serve, with the people who will be responsible for its operation, and with the suppliers of equipment.

Course Requirements and Recommended Sequence. The program adopted at UCLA comprises an integrated course of study in the theoretical and practical foundations of information handling. The program is an interdisciplinary one with emphasis on research and basic principles of information system design. Within this general scope, there are four areas of course work: (1) system design and integration, (2) organization of information records, (3) management of information activities, and (4) use of equipment.

Each student is required to complete his background in a common core of knowledge in each area so as to be able to understand how all of the parts fit together. Specifically, the student must complete at least three quarter courses in each of the four areas. Figure 20.14 summarizes the recommended courses.

Figure 20.14   Curriculum in information systems.

Area	Course Description	Department	Comments
I	Integrating Course in Systems Analysis	Library School	Must be taken in Third Quarter
	Statistics	Business Administration Mathematics, Economics etc.	
II	Cataloging and Classification	Library School	
	Comprehensive Bibliography	Library School	
	Specialized Bibliography	Library School	
III	Managerial Accounting	Business Administration	Covers Cost Accounting. Management use of data
	Type of Library	Library School	Usually Research Library or Special Library
	Management of Libraries	Library School	
IV	Computer Programming	Business Administration Library School, or Engineering School	Basic Course in Computer Program
	Data Base Systems	Library School	Covers On-Line Data Base Management
	Information Retrieval Systems	Library School	Covers Reference Retrieval and Text Processing
Thesis	Seminar	Library School	Covers Research Methodology
	Thesis Study	Library School	
	Specialty Courses	Various Departments	

Such a program, with the thesis requirement, requires one and one-half to two years of work.

Because of the interdisciplinary nature of information problems, the course work of the curriculum is drawn from a number of departments and schools. Specifically:

1.   The core courses of the information science curriculum ("Information System Analysis and Design" and "Seminar in Information Science"), those which integrate the diverse tools into a single focus, have been placed in the School of Library Service because librarianship is the profession most completely concerned with the handling of information as such.

2.   Other courses providing the students with knowledge of the technical tools of system design—statistics, operations research, optimization techniques, and the like—are taken in the Mathematics Department, Engineering, or Business Administration. The specialized course in this area offered by the School of Library Service—Methods of Information System Analysis and Design—is required of all students in the program.

3.   Courses providing the students with knowledge of the technical tools of information service—bibliography, cataloging and classification, and reference— are taken in the School of Library Service.

4.   Courses providing the students with knowledge of the tools of management are taken in the School of Business Administration (managerial accounting, for example) and in the School of Library Service (Library Administration and the Management of special types of libraries).

5.   Finally, courses providing the students with knowlege of the computer are taken in a number of schools and departments, including the Schools of Business Administration, Engineering, and Public Health and the Departments of Linguistics and Mathematics. Four specialized courses in this area are offered by the School of Library Service—Data Base Systems, Information Retrieval Systems, Management Information Systems, and Library Data Processing—and the student is required to take at least two of those.

Normally, the student is expected to spend his first year (three academic quarters) in course work covering all four areas, the integrating course—Methods of Information System Analysis and Design—being taken in the third quarter. The second year is then spent in developing and writing the thesis, with course work chosen to support the thesis topic.

Thesis Requirements and Advisory Committee. The thesis occupies a central role in the degree program. It provides the means for the students to develop and explore a research problem in the design of modern information systems. It also provides an instructive experience in preparing a proposal for a definite project, scheduling the work which needs to be done, and carrying out the work itself.

As a result, the student is better able to evaluate his own capacity and that of others to execute projects.

To provide a formal basis for development of his thesis proposal, the student is required to take a course in research methodology—a Seminar in Information Science—during the fourth quarter. The course is organized to provide a forum for each student participating to explore a problem area in information science (presumably one arising out of the discussions in the prior course on Methods of Information System Analysis and Design). The student is expected to present the problem area to the class, to develop an annotated bibliography of prior work in it, to define a specific issue within the problem area which will be the topic of his thesis, to propose an approach to resolution of the issue, and to schedule his work over the succeeding two quarters (or longer time as required) for completion of his thesis.

This thesis proposal becomes the basis of the student's subsequent work An advisory "Thesis Committee" is established, consisting of two members of the faculty of the School of Library Service (one of them the student's thesis advisor) and one from another department with specific interest in the area of the thesis. The Committee reviews the thesis proposal, makes recommendations concerning related studies, the validity of the proposed approach, and the conduct of the study itself. The Committee also conducts the final examination and approves the thesis.

Suggested Readings

The literature of "information science" is as diverse as the set of definitions. The following references, however, will provide the reader with introductions to it.

Becker, Joseph, and Robert M. Hayes, *Information Storage and Retrieval: Tools, Elements, Theories.* New York: Wiley, 1963.

Although written nearly 10 years ago, this still provides a useful coverage of the systems view of information retrieval systems. It emphasizes the need for consideration of all aspects in the design of information systems, including their usage, operation, technical design, and equipment.

Cuadra, Carlos A. (ed.), Annual Review of Information Science and Technology, *Vols. I and II, New York: Wiley, 1966 and 1967; Vols. III and IV, Chicago: Encyclopedia Britannica, 1968 and 1969.*

This is an annual publication which provides complete and exceptionally well written reviews of various aspects of information science, taken in its broadest sense.

Fodor, Jerry A. and Jerrold J. Katz, *The Structure of Language.* Englewood Cliffs, New Jersey: Prentice-Hall, 1964.

This set of "readings in the philosophy of language" provides an excellent overview of the problems with which modern structural linguistics is concerned. It covers linguistic theory, theories of syntax and semantics, and some psychological implications of linguistic theory.

Heilprin, Laurence B., et al (eds.), *Education for Information Science.* Washington, D.C.: Spartan, 1965.

There has been a whole series of conferences and symposia held on "education for information science" at which the most prominent feature was the diversity of meanings attributed to the subject. This one occupies a kind of landmark position, since out of it came a clear picture of the differences. It therefore serves as both a summary of prior conferences and a prelude to subsequent ones.

Lancaster, F. Wilfred, *Information Retrieval Systems: Characteristics, Testing, and Evaluation.* New York: Wiley, 1968.

This is one of the best and clearest descriptions of information retrieval systems. It provides historical background; it presents the conceptual and mathematical basis for evaluation; it illustrates procedures in terms of the most currently viable systems; and it describes the issues in evaluations as they were developed in the Cranfield project and at the National Library of Medicine (MEDLARS).

Meadow, Charles T., *The Analysis of Information Systems.* New York: Wiley, 1967.

This emphasizes the systems aspects of information science, especially in the context of the organization and search of files.

Salton, Gerard, *Automatic Information Organization and Retrieval.* New York: McGraw-Hill, 1968.

This book is based on experience with an experimental system (called SMART), developed by the author for study of various aspects of text processing. It presents details about various techniques for construction and use of dictionaries, for statistical processing of term associations, for analysis of the syntax of sentences, and for evaluation of retrieval effectiveness.

Wiener, Norbert, *Cybernetics, or Control and Communication in the Animal and the Machine.* New York: Wiley, 1961.

This book both coined a new word and created a new field of research—cybernetics. Its thesis was that both animals and machines (especially computers) are continually adjusting to their environment. By studying the analogies between them, in this respect, much could be learned about both animals and machines.

GLOSSARY – REFERENCES

The definitions in this glossary are those of the authors, reflecting the usage in this book, and not necessarily those of any other glossary. The reader may want to turn to one of the following for more standardized definitions.

A Brief Glossary of Data Processing Terms, by G. D. Roth, 1959, IBM Data Processing Div., White Plains, N.Y.

ACM Committee on Nomenclature, 1957, Association for Computing Machinery, New York, N.Y.

A Dictionary of Documentation Terms, by Frank S. Wagner, Jr., 1960, American Documentation.

ADP Glossary, 1961, Interagency Automatic Data Processing Committee, Washington, D.C.

AIEE Subcommittee on Logic and Switching Circuit Theory, 1960, American Institute of Electrical Engineers, New York, N.Y.

Basic IBM Applied Programming Teaching Glossary, by L. Ellsworth, 1960, IBM Data Systems Div., Applied Programming, New York, N.Y.

Bell Telephone Laboratories, Murray Hill, N.J.

Bendix Computer Div., The Bendix Corp., Los Angeles, Calif.

Business Equipment Manufacturers Association, New York, N.Y.

Communications Dictionary, by James F. Holmes, 1962, John F. Rider Publisher, Inc., New York, N.Y.

Computer Applications in the Behavioral Sciences, Harold Borko, editor, 1962, Prentice-Hall, Inc., Englewood Cliffs, N.J.

Computer Programming Handbook, by Robert Nathan and Elizabeth Hanes, 1962, Prentice-Hall, Inc., Englewood Cliffs, N.J.

Dictionary of Automatic Control, by Robert J. Bibbero, 1960, Reinhold Publishing Co., New York, N.Y.

Electronic Computers: Fundamentals, by Paul von Handel, editor, 1962, Prentice-Hall, Inc., Englewood Cliffs, N.J.

Fundamentals of Digital Computers, by Matthew Mandl, 1958, Prentice-Hall, Inc., Englewood Cliffs, N.J.

Glossary for Data Processing Machines, 1959, IBM Washington Education Center, Washington, D.C.

Glossary for Data Transmission Study Group, by D. E. Hannum, Northrup Aviation, Downey, Calif.

Glossary for Information Processing, IBM Corp., 1962, White Plains, N.Y.

Glossary of Computer and Programming Terminology, by Mandalay Grems, 1960, IBM Corp., Corporate Div., White Plains, N.Y.

Glossary of Computer and Programming Terms, by O. W. Perry, 1959, IBM Corp., Poughkeepsie, N.Y.

Glossary of Computer Engineering and Programming Terminology, by Martin H. Weik, 1957, Ballistic Research Labs, Aberdeen Proving Ground, Md.

Glossary of Computer Terminology, Computer Department, General Electric Co., Phoenix, Arizona.

Glossary of Programming and Computer Technology, by D. L. Mordy, 1960, IBM Data Systems Div., Applied Programming, New York, N.Y.

Glossary of Programming Terms, by M. Bolsky, 1961, System Development Corp., Santa Monica, Calif.

Glossary of Terms, By R. M. Herron, 1960, IBM ASD Div., White Plains, N.Y.

Glossary of Terms in Computers and Data Processing, by Edmund C. Berkeley and Linda L. Lovett, 1960, Berkeley Enterprises, Inc, Newtonville, Mass.

Glossary-Terms Used in Computer Programming and Engineering, by W. O. Bormann, 1960, IBM Data Systems Div., Poughkeepsie, N.Y.

Guide to IBM 1401 Programming, by Daniel D. McCracken, 1962, John Wiley & Sons, Inc., New York, N.Y.

Handbook of Automation, Computation, and Control, Vol. 2, 1959, John Wiley & Sons, Inc., New York, N.Y.

Installing Electronic Data Processing Systems, by Richard G. Canning, 1957, John Wiley & Sons, Inc., New York, N.Y.

IRE Standards on Electronic Computers—Definitions of Terms, 1956, Institute of Radio Engineers, New York, N.Y.

The Language and Symbology of Digital Computer Systems, 1959, RCA Service Co., Camden, N.J.

NOMA Glossary of Automation Terms, 1961, National Office Management Association, Willow Grove, Pa.

Operating System Description Standard Definitions, by Doris Rhine and D. Brandon, 1961, System Development Corp., Santa Monica, Calif.

Pocket Dictionary of Computer Terms, 1962, Howard W. Sams & Co., Indianapolis, Ind.

Programming Business Computers, by
D. D. McCracken, H. Weiss, and T.
Lee, 1961, John Wiley & Sons,
Inc., New York, N.Y.

Programming for Digital Computers,
by J. Jeenel, 1959, McGraw-Hill
Book Co., New York, N.Y.

Programming for Digital Computers,
by M. H. Wrubel, 1959, McGraw-
Hill Book Co., New York, N.Y.

Sandia Corporation Albuquerque, New
Mexico.

Share Glossary of Terms, by D. E.
Eastwood, 1960, Bell Telephone
Laboratories, Murray Hill, N.J.

Systems Design and Programming
Terminology, 1960, UNIVAC
Div., Sperry Rand Corp., Phila-
delphia, Pa.

Understanding Digital Computers, by
Paul Siegel, 1961, John Wiley &
Sons, Inc., New York, N.Y.

GLOSSARY—DEFINITIONS

Abstracting. The process of representing the contents of a book, journal article, or document by a short, more or less informative amount of text.

Acceleration Time (*see also* **Deceleration Time**). The time between acceptance of a read or write instruction by a tape unit and the start of reading or writing (that is, the time taken for the tape to accelerate to full speed).

Access. Related to the availability of data from internal memory or files. Several dichotomies can be defined for methods of access, each generally representing a difference between an on-line system and a batch system. Specifically:

On-line	Batch
Immediate Access	Delayed Access
Random Access	Sequential Access
Direct Access	Scan Access

(See the individual entries for each.)

Access, Delayed. Delayed access arises because of batch processing and the inherently slow speeds of a storage device.

Access, Direct. The process of obtaining data from a memory by going directly to its location, usually as specified by an address, without reading any other data.

Access, Immediate. The ability to obtain data from files within short periods of time, relative to other operations. Contrasted with delayed access.

Access, Random. The process of obtaining data from a memory in which the next location from which it is obtained is in no way dependent upon the previous one (in contrast to "Sequential access"). It usually requires direct access capabilities to be efficient.

Access, Scan. The process of obtaining data from files by looking at each item of data until that one of interest is found (contrasted with **Direct Access**).

Access, Sequential. The process of obtaining data from files, in which the next location follows the previous one, (contrasted with **Random Access**).

Access Time. The time between acceptance of a read or write instruction by a file device and the start of reading or writing of the data of interest. With magnetic tapes, it depends upon both "acceleration time" and the time to get to the data of interest; with magnetic disks, drums, and strips, it depends upon the speed of rotation of the file device.

Accessions List. A list of recent additions to a collection.

Accumulator. A register and associated logical circuitry in the arithmetic and control unit of a computer in which arithmetical and logical operations are performed including, in particular, addition (that is, accumulation).

Accuracy. Freedom from error. Usually contrasted with precision. For example, a call number might be recorded as QA 109.2357 and would be very precise; however, if it should be QA 109.2375 it would be inaccurate.

Acquisitions. The books acquired by a library, through purchase, gift, or exchange.

Activity Ratio. The proportion of records in a file which are active during a given time period.

Adder. *See* **Accumulator.**

Address. The identification (by name, label, or number) of the location of data in internal memory or in direct access files. Included as part of an instruction, it specifies either the location of data (for example, "operand address") or the location of the next instruction.

Address, Absolute. An identification of location by an exact address (contrasted with "relative address" and "symbolic address").

Address, Relative. An identification of a given location by reference to another one (for example, "the address one beyond address x").

Address, Symbolic. An identification of location by name, without reference to an absolute or even relative address.

Addressed Access. *See* **Access, Direct.**

ADP (*see also* **EDP**). An acronym for "Automated Data Processing," the use of mechanical equipment to carry out data processing operations.

ALGOL (*see also* **FORTRAN**). A special language by which numerical (computational) procedures can be precisely described in a standard form.

Algorithm. A numerical computing process. More generally, a step-by-step procedure which, when followed exactly, will produce precise results.

Alphabetic. Related to the specific set of symbols, called the "alphabetic characters," which is most frequently used in printed text in English (that is, the Roman alphabet and some punctuation marks).

Alphanumeric. Related to the specific set of symbols which includes the decimal digits as well as the Roman alphabet, punctuation marks, and a variety of other symbols.

Analog. Related to the representation of data by variable states (for example, voltage levels). Contrasted with **Digital**.

Analog Computer. A computer which represents data by variable states rather than discrete symbols. It solves equations represented by analogous relationships among the variable states.

Analysis. The process of breaking a complex thing (such as an organization or a process) into smaller, component parts. (*See also* **Subject Analysis**.)

AND. The logical operator (in Boolean algebra) used to represent the following relationship among statements: R is true if and only if both P is true AND Q is true. Symbolically $R = P$ AND $Q = P \cdot Q$.

AND-Gate. An electronic circuit which represents the AND operator by providing output current if and only if all input currents are present.

Aperture Card. A card, usually of punched card stock, with one or more rectangular holes designed to hold a frame of microfilm.

Application. The use of the computer for carrying out a specific task (for example "library application").

Application Program. A program designed to perform a specific task (as distinguished from "operating system," for example).

Arithmetic Operations. Those computer operations upon numerical quantities equivalent to addition, subtraction, multiplication, division, and similar basic arithmetic functions.

Arithmetic Register. A part of the **Arithmetic Unit** in which operations take place (see, for example, **Accumulator**).

Arithmetic Unit. The portion of the computer in which operations are executed upon data, including not only arithmetic operations but others as well.

ASCII. An acronym for "American Standard Code for Information Interchange," the only code system that is an American standard. (**See also** EBCDIC).

Assembler. A computer program which converts symbolic instructions into their equivalents in machine codes and assigns locations in the memory to instructions and data.

Auxiliary Memory *see* **External Storage.**

Backup. The means for providing service when the principal means for doing so is not operating.

Badge. A means of identification in the form of a card, the relevant data (borrower number, social security number, book number, etc.) being recorded on it in embossed, punched, or magnetic form.

Band. In computer usage, a group of recording tracks (or channels) on a magnetic drum, disk, or strip; in communication usage, a range of transmission frequencies between two defined limits.

Band Width. The difference (expressed in "cycles per second") between the highest and lowest frequencies of transmission in a communication band.

Base. The number of symbols in a system for representing any number by the convention of "positional notation." It is most familiar to us in base 10 notation, which uses the ten decimal digits and the decimal point in the conventional way. Base 2, involving two binary digits, is the one used in early digital computers.

Batch Processing. A procedure in which a number of transactions to be processed are accumulated and processed together. Usually they are sorted into order and matched sequentially against affected files.

Baudot Code. The code used with most teletypewriter systems today.

BCD. An acronym for **Binary Coded Decimal**.

Binary. Characterized by the use of the base 2 notation for representation of numbers; extended to the representation of any symbol set by any specified code of binary digits.

Binary Coded Decimal. The particular system of binary codes which uses base 2 notation for the decimal digits.

Binary Digit. One of a set of two symbols, usually represented by zero (0) and one (1).

Binary Number. The representation of any number by base 2 notation.

Biquinary. A representation of decimal digits, by binary codes, in two groups of five each, as follows: $0 = 0000$, $1 = 0001$, $2 = 0010$, $3 = 0011$, $4 = 0100$, $5 = 1000$, $6 = 1001$, $7 = 1010$, $8 = 1011$, $9 = 1100$.

Bit (a contraction of binary digit).

Bit Position. A location in space or time at which a binary digit can occur.

Bit Rate. In data transfer, the rate, usually in "bits per second," at which binary digits can be transmitted.

Blank. A character in the alphabetic and alphanumeric character sets used to indicate a space (between words, for example).

Block. A set of data, in internal memory or in files, which is treated as a unit in data transfer (as in reading or writing).

Block Diagram. A form of flow chart or schematic.

Book Form Catalog. A printed catalog in which several entries occur on a page and pages are bound together.

Boolean Algebra. A system for symbolizing logical statements by operators, usually AND, OR, and NOT, from which relationships among statements can be derived mechanically.

Bootstrap. A small set of instructions which will cause a much larger set to be brought into the internal memory (as in "pulling itself in by the bootstraps").

Branch. A choice among alternative sequences of instructions.

Break-Point. A point in a computer program at which it can be interrupted for special action to be taken. Especially useful in debugging and in monitoring complex programs.

Buffer Storage. Intermediary storage between two data handling components. Used to compensate for differences in data rates, in codes, or in formats.

Byte. Loosely, a specified number of binary digits. Generally used to refer to the eight-bit code-system used in many third generation equipment (that is, the EBCDIC character set).

Calling Sequence. The data provided by a major program in order for it to utilize a general subroutine. It includes data necessary for the subroutine to perform its operations and to know where to reenter the main routine.

Card. (*See* **Punched Card**).

Card Catalog. The form of library catalog familiar to most users of libraries.

Card Field. A set of columns in a punched card format dedicated to the storage of a specific kind of data. Usually these will be fixed in their location from one card to another within a given format.

Card Image. Storage of data in internal memory or magnetic files exactly as it would be stored on a punched card (usually as it was input from punched cards or will be output to them).

Card Reader. A device capable of feeding punched cards, sensing the presence of holes in the columns of them, interpreting them as codes, and transmitting the data to a computer.

Carry. A condition occurring during addition or multiplication, when digits being added result in a sum equal to or greater than the base. Also the digit (called the carry digit) which results.

Cataloging. The standard process by which books, journals, and other materials are described and recorded.

Cathode Ray Tube. A vacuum tube capable of generating an image on one surface by the effect of a stream of electrons upon phosphors on the surface. The television tube in a TV set is an example.

Cell. A location in a memory unit, usually with an assigned address.

Central Processor (also called "Main frame"). That portion of a computer which includes the arithmetic and control unit as well as the internal memory.

Change Record. *See* **Transaction**.

Channel. A track on tapes, drums, disks, and the like, in which data is recorded by a single recording head.

Character. One of a set of symbols used to record data. The usual character sets include: alphabetic characters, alphanumeric characters, decimal digits, binary digits, etc. In libraries, "multi-font" character sets and even non-Roman alphabetic character sets are also important.

Character Reader. See **Optical Character Reader**.

Check. A means of testing and verifying the correctness of data or of processing operations.

Check, Built-In or Automatic. A programmed means of testing the correctness of data (*see* **Validity Check**, for example) and of processing operations.

Check Digit(s). One or more digits generated from data and carried along with it as a means of checking the accuracy of the data during subsequent operations. (The check digit is periodically regenerated and compared with the original.)

Check, Forbidden-Combination. A set of codes usually includes some which are not assigned to any of the things being represented. If they occur in data, they are regarded as forbidden and are rejected.

Check, Marginal. To check the reliability of a computer, it is checked for its operability under marginal conditions of voltage and signal level.

Check, Modulo N. *See* **Check, Parity.**

Check, Odd-Even. *See* **Check, Parity.**

Check, Parity. Binary codes normally consist of either an odd or even number of 1's (for example, 1011, 0110). If another binary digit is added to such codes to make them always have an *odd* number of 1's (for example, 10110, 01101) it is called a parity bit. Subsequently, if a code ever has an even number of 1's, an error must have occurred.

Check Point. A point in a program at which the results of processing can be examined if desired.

Check, Redundancy. *See* **Check, Forbidden Character** and **Check, Parity.**

Check, Validity. Frequently limits can be established for the range of values which a given piece of data can have. A "validity check" can then be programmed which will check whether data indeed is within the specified range.

Circuit. *See* **Logical Circuit.**

Citation Index. A form of index to literature which lists for a given article all subsequent articles which refer to it.

Clear. To erase the contents of a register or memory location by replacing them with blanks or zeros.

Closed Shop. A policy for management of a computer facility in which all programming and operation are done by the facility itself and not by its users.

Closed Subroutine. A subroutine outside the main path of a major routine, to which the major routine must therefore transfer control (*see* **Calling Sequence**).

Coaxial Cable. A means of transmitting signals from one place to another. Because it is heavily insulated, it is capable of transmitting extremely high data rate.

COBOL. An acronym for Common Business Oriented Language, designed for describing data processing procedures (in contrast to computational algorithms) in a precise, standardized manner.

Code. A system of symbols for use in representing data (or, in the case of computer programs, machine language instructions).

Code, Computer. The code used to represent operations built into the hardware of a computer.

Code, Excess-Three. A binary code for representation of decimal digits, with the property that a decimal carry is generated directly from the binary carry.

Coden. A five-character identification for periodical titles which has been maintained by the American Society for Testing and Materials.

Coding. The process of converting programs into computer code.

Coding, Alphabetic. A system of codes using alphabetic characters as symbols (for example, LC class numbers).

Coding, Automatic. Any technique in which the computer is programmed to produce codes, but especially to produce codes for computer programs.

Coding, Numeric. A system of codes using decimal digits as symbols (for example, Dewey Class numbers).

Collate. The process of merging two or more similarly sequenced files of data (*see also* **Match-Merge**).

Collator. A punched card handling device that will collate or match-merge two sequences of cards.

Column. A position on a punched card in which a character may be recorded.

Command. *See* **Operation.**

Common Language. A representation of data which can be read by a number of different machines.

Comparator. A means of comparing two pieces of data for equality or relative size.

Compare. An operation built into all computers as a means of choosing among alternative sequences of instructions. (*See* **Decision.**)

Compatibility. The extent to which one device is capable of accepting and processing data prepared by another. This must be at the level of both hardware compatibility and software compatibility.

Compiler. A program which accepts programs written in a higher level language (called the "source language") and converts them into (usually) a lower level language (called the "object language") for subsequent execution.

Complement. A means of representing negative numbers, by subtracting each digit of the number from $n - 1$, where n is the base.

Compute Limited. Characterizing data processing tasks in which the time is determined primarily by the internal computing speeds. (*See also* **Input/ Output Limited.**)

Computer. A machine that manipulates symbols, in accordance with given rules, in a predetermined and self-directed manner.

Computer-Based. Dependent to a significant extent upon computer processing. A computer-based operation could be executed wholly by computer or be a combination of manual and computer processes.

Conditional Jump. *See* **Branch.**

Configuration. The specific set of hardware which are put together to form a computer system.

Conjunction. *See* **AND.**

Console. A device for direct communication between a person and a computer.

Contents. The data stored in any storage medium. A common convention is to use parentheses to refer to the contents of a location: (m) referring to the content of memory address m.

Control. That portion of the computer which controls the operation of all other parts, including peripheral devices.

Control Counter. That part of the control which stores the address of the next instruction.

Control Total. A check on the reliability of processing.

Control Unit. (*See* **Control**).

Conversion. Changing from one form of data representation to another.

Converter. A piece of equipment for conversion.

Core Storage. The form of high speed internal memory used in most present-day computers, based on magnetic cores for storage of individual bits.

Cost Accounting. The allocation of costs to individual tasks or processes, for the purpose of comparing them with standard costs, or with the cost of alternative methods.

Cost/Effectiveness. The standard measure of performance for evaluation of systems. It is expressed as a ratio of some measure of cost to some measure of performance (such as, "more bang for the buck.").

Counter. A set of circuitry which can store data and increase or decrease it by unity or by other arbitrary amounts.

CPU. Acronym for "central processing unit" *see* **Central Processor.**

CRT. *See* **Cathode Ray Tube.**

Cybernetics. The comparative study of machines and living organisms, with special emphasis on the methods for control and communication.

Cycle. *See* **Loop.**

Data. A general term used to denote any specific recording of symbols that are regarded as referring to or representing something else. As a term, it is properly plural, with "datum" as the singular. However, common usage in the computer field is to take it as either singular or plural depending upon its intended scope: "The data is correct." "The various data are correct." Data is the basic element which is processed and stored by a computer and from which other things are derived.

Data Bank. A data base, usually of very large size, intended for many users. (*see also* **Data Base**).

Data Base. A file of data in machine language, available for use.

Data Cell. A large capacity (for example, 400 million characters) data storage device. Specifically, one manufactured by IBM which utilized short strips of magnetic tape.

Data Link. Any means of communication of digital data from one location to another.

Data Management. *See* **File Management**.

Data-Phone. A device produced by the AT & T for data communication.

Data Processing. The generic term for all operations upon data with precise rules of procedure, especially in the context of business situations as contrasted with scientific computation.

Data-Reduction. The process of transforming masses of data into useful condensations. Typically, this involves producing approximations and representations as mathematical functions.

Data Set. A data base, usually of relatively small size, intended for only a few users. (*see also* **Data Base**).

Debug. To locate errors in a program and to correct them.

Deceleration Time. The time required for a tape unit, after reading or writing is completed, to slow the tape to a stop ready to initiate a new read or write (*see also* **Acceleration Time**).

Decimal Digit. One of the symbols 0, 1, 2, 3, 4, 5, 6, 7, 8, 9.

Decision. A choice between two or more alternative paths of processing, usually made by means of a comparison (*see* **Compare**).

Decode. To convert from one symbolic representation of data to another one, usually to reverse a prior step.

Delay Line. A type of memory in which data is recorded and then becomes available again after a fixed time interval.

Density. The number of units of data which can be recorded within a given linear distance (for example, bits per inch) along a recording medium.

Descriptor. A generic word for terms which can be chosen from a defined vocabulary for the purpose of describing the subject content of a document.

Design. *See* **Logical Design**.

Diagnostic Routine. A program used to aid debugging.

Diagram. *See* **Flow Chart**.

Diazo. A relatively slow photographic process, using dyes which are sensitive to blue or ultraviolet light and can be developed by ammonia (or, in the case of Kalvar, by heat).

Digit. One of any set of symbols, but usually numerical symbols (decimal or binary).

Digital. Related to the representation of data by means of discrete symbols, initially numerical (for example, decimal digits), but now extended to other sets of symbols. Contrasted with **Analog.**

Digital Computer. *See* **Computer.**

Digits, Check. *See* **Check Digits.**

Diode. A device, usually made from germanium or silicone crystals, which permits electrical current to flow easily in one direction but inhibits the flow in the reverse direction. Used as an element in logical circuits.

Direct Access. *See* **Access, Direct**

Disjunction. *See* **OR.**

Disk, Magnetic. A device which stores data on the magnetizable surfaces of one or more rotating disks (like phonograph records). Usually, the data is stored and retrieved by **Direct Access.**

Disk Pack. A set of magnetic disks which can be physically removed from the handling unit, for storage, and replaced by other similar sets.

Display. A device for visually presenting data from the computer to a user. Usually it incorporates a **Cathode Ray Tube.**

Documentation. In the computer field, the records which describe the purpose, structure, operation, and use of computer programs. In the context of information systems for science and technology, the process of acquiring reports and journals, indexing them, and making them available.

Down-Time. A period during which a computer is malfunctioning or not operating correctly due to machine failures and is therefore unavailable for use.

Drum, Magnetic. A device which stores data on the magnetizable surface of a cylinder. Usually the data are stored and retrieved using **Direct Access.**

Dump. To transfer the entire contents of internal memory or a file to some other storage medium (*see also* **Tape Dump**).

Dynamic Relocation. The process by which an assembler or compiler keeps track of the location of subroutines and data in the internal memory, especially when their locations must be changed.

EAM. An acronym for "Electrical Accounting Machinery," jargon for punched card handling equipment.

EBCDIC. An acronym for "Extended Binary Coded Decimal Information Code," the system of codes used by IBM model 360 computers and others.

Edit. To rearrange data, especially for the purpose of preparing it for input to a computer.

EDP. An acronym for "Electronic Data Processing," jargon for the use of computers, especially for applications in business.

Electronic. Using techniques which involve the flow of electrons in gas, in a vacuum, or in solid devices called semiconductors. Contrasted with "electric" which involves the flow of electrons only through conductors (such as wires).

Element, Logical. In computers and related devices, the smallest building block from which **Logical Circuits** are constructed. Typical logical elements are AND-GATES, OR-GATES., and the like.

Emulsion. A light-sensitive coating or photographic film.

Erase. See **Clear.**

Error. The generic term for any deviation of data from its correct form. In mathematics, it has a very precise meaning and is not synonymous with "mistake." Generally, however, it is synonymous with "mistake."

Excess-Three Code. *See* **Code, Excess-Three.**

Execution (of an instruction). The step through which the computer proceeds to produce the results specified by the instruction.

External Storage. Equipment used to store files (usually large files). *See also* **File.**

Extract. An operation built into most computers by which specified portions of data can be removed from other, surrounding portions so as to be operated upon independently. Also, a kind of **Abstract** produced by taking sentences from the text of an article.

Facsimile. The process for transmission of static images (pictures, maps, and printed pages). The image is scanned at a transmitter and reconstructed at a receiving station.

Factor, Scale. A means of indicating the magnitude of a number relative to a fixed standard. Usually expressed as a power of ten, it indicates where the decimal point should be located. *See* **Floating Point.**

Feedback. The means by which a **Servomechanism** learns the effect which its action has and adjusts its action to meet the desired objectives better.

Ferromagnetism. The phenomenon by which certain materials can retain one or another magnetic state.

Field. A set of characters treated as a whole and used to store a defined kind of data.

File. (Noun). An organized collection of data.

File Maintenance. *See* **File Management.**

File Management. The set of processes by which files are created, maintained (that is, added to, changed, corrected, and so on), and used.

File Organization. The arrangement of records in a file, including the sequence in which they are stored and the indexes by which they can be found. Also, the process of producing such an arrangement.

Fixed-Point. A notation for numerical data, equivalent to the familiar decimal notation.

Fixed Word Length. A property of some computers, in which data is stored in locations, called words, each of the same number of characters.

Flip-Flop. A circuit element designed to store a single bit and control other circuit elements.

Floating Point. A notation for numerical data which expresses a number in two parts: a **Scale Factor** which indicates where the decimal point is and a number between -1 and $+1$.

Flow Chart. A graphical representation of a sequence of operations.

Font. A set of characters comprising an alphabet.

Form. A printed record in a defined format, used for recording data of a defined kind.

Forms Control. The procedure for defining forms and assuring that they are needed and are consistent with each other.

Forms Design. The process of defining the formats and especially the physical arrangement of forms.

Format. The predetermined arrangement of fields and other structures for data in a record of any kind.

FORTRAN. An acronym for FORmula TRANslator, a language designed for the description of algorithmic processes.

Four Address Instruction. A form of instruction used in some computers, in which an operation is specified and usually the addresses of two operands, the address in which the result is to be put, and the address of the next instruction.

Function-Table. *See* **Table.**

Gangpunch. The use of a key punch or reproducing punch to copy the same data into a succession of punched cards.

Gantt Chart. A graphical means of showing the flow in time of processes from one component piece of equipment (or person) to another.

Gap. *See* **Interrecord Gap** and **Recording Head, Reading Head.**

Garbage. Data which is so filled with mistakes as to be worthless.

Gate. *See* **Circuit Element, AND-Gate, OR-Gate.**

Gray Code. A code system in which successive things are represented by binary codes differing in only a single bit position.

Half Adder. A logical circuit which performs addition without consideration of the carry, although it generates the carry.

Hamming Code. A code used for error detection in transmission.

Hard Copy. A printed copy of computer output.

Hardware. The physical equipment in a data processing system (contrasted with **Software**).

Hash. *See* **Garbage.**

Hash Total. A set of check characters generated by adding together portions of the data of interest and therefore usually meaningless in itself.

Head. *See* **Recording Head, Reading Head.**

Heuristic. Characterized by trial and error, in contrast to **Algorithmic.**

Hexadecimal. A code system using base 16, usually represented by sets of 4 bits each (that is, $2^4 = 16$).

Hollerith Code. The code system used on most punched cards (that is, the standard IBM punched card code).

Housekeeping. The operations in a program required for the program to maintain control of itself.

Identifier. *See* **Key.**

IDP. *See* **EDP.**

Immediate Access. *See* **Access, Immediate.**

Index. In computer operation, a means for determining the address of data in a **Direct Access** mode of operation.

Indexing (of documents). The process of assigning words or terms, from a vocabulary of allowable terms, to documents in order to describe their subject content for purposes of subsequent retrieval.

Indexing, Coordinate. A specific method of document indexing in which, in subsequent retrieval, combinations (that is, coordinations) of previously assigned terms are looked for.

Index Register. A register used by a program to hold a quantity used to modify addresses.

Index Sequential. A means of **Direct Access** to files sequenced by the criterion for access.

Indirect Addressing. A means of addressing data by telling where the address of the data will be found (that is, specifying the address of the address).

Information. A very ambiguous term, sometimes used as though synonymous with data; sometimes, with a collection of data; sometimes, with alphabetic data (distinguished then from "data" which would be numeric data); sometimes, with useful data; sometimes, as "facts"; sometimes, as a rather mystical meaning or content of data. In this book, "information" is defined as "the data which results from a process upon data." Information generating processes include: transmission of data, selection of data, reduction of data, and the like.

Information Retrieval. The process of finding desired data in a file.

Information Theory. The analytical and theoretical study of communication, especially in electronic systems. The emphasis is on coding of data for accurate transmission at high speeds.

Initialize. To establish the data required for a program to start processing.

Input. The process of transferring data into a computer system and especially into its internal memory. Also the data which is input (that is, "the input").

Input/Output. The combined set of equipment used for input and output.

Input/Output Limited. Characterizing data processing tasks in which the time is determined primarily by the rate of data transfer in the input/output equipment.

Instruction. A set of data stored in the memory of the computer and interpreted by it as specifying an operation to be performed, the location of the set of data to be processed, and the location of the next instruction.

Instrumentation. Equipment used to acquire data automatically.

Integrated Data Processing. *See* **EDP.**

Interactive System. Use of a computer in which direct communication between man and machine is so rapid that the thought processes of the man are not slowed down or interrupted by delays in the machine, but instead are stimulated by the speed of response.

Interface. The boundary between two things which react with each other. Usually the point of communication between them.

Internal Memory. That portion of a computer system in which instructions and data are stored and are immediately accessible to the control unit for processing.

Internal Storage. *See* **Internal Memory.**

Interpretive Routine. A program which decodes and interprets instructions written in a higher level language and executes them. It is like a compiler, but does not separate the two steps of conversion and execution.

Interrecord Gap. The space between blocks of data recorded on tape or disk. It is created by the **Acceleration Time** and **Deceleration Time**, during which no data is recorded.

I/O. The equipment used for **Input** and **Output**. Also, the process of **Input** and **Output**.

Item. A set of data treated as a logical unit. Usually synonymous with **Record**.

Iterative. Describing a process which repeatedly executes a series of operations until some desired result is obtained. Caused by a **Loop** in a program.

Job. A request for services (of a library, a computing facility, or any other organization), usually requiring a number of processes.

Jump. The process of moving from one instruction in a program to another one usually quite removed.

Jump, Conditional. See **Branch**.

Key. A group of characters used to identify a **Record**, usually the basis of file sequencing. Also a marked lever on a typewriter, key punch, and the like.

Key-Boarding. The process of operating a key board to produce typed copy and machine readable data.

Key-Driven. Describing any device for **Key Boarding** data.

Key-Punching. The production of punched cards by key-boarding.

KWIC. An acronym for Key-Word-in-Context, a form of document index obtained by producing an entry in the index for each word of interest but including the context in which it occurs, like a concordance. Sometimes, but not necessarily, restricted to title words. A variety of formats are available for presentation of the entries and their contexts.

KWOC. *See also* **KWIC.** A form of concordance in which the term, under which an entry is listed, is shown at the left of the entry itself.

Label. A set of data used to identify a record or a file. Frequently includes descriptive data as needed for processing.

Lag. A delay between two events.

Language, Higher Level. A means of describing a process close to that a person would naturally use.

Language, Machine. A means of description which a machine can recognize directly.

Language, Natural. The means by which a person would normally communicate with another person.

Language, Object. *See* **Compiler**.

Latency. *See* **Access Time**.

Level of Addressing. *See* **Indirect Addressing**.

Line-Printing. The means of printing used by most computer output printers, in which an entire line is printed at once. In contrast to character by character printing, as with a typewriter.

Linkage. The process of returning to a main program from a sub-routine.

Linked Subroutine. *See* **Closed Subroutine**.

Load. *See* **Input**.

Location. *See* **Address**.

Location Counter. That portion of the **Control** of a computer in which the address of data to be operated upon is stored.

Logic. In computer context, the basis of design and interconnection of circuitry.

Logic, Symbolic. *See* **Boolean Algebra**.

Logical Circuit. A set of logical elements inter-connected so as to carry out a defined processing task as part of a computer **Logical Design**.

Logical Design. The process of planning a computer and tying logical elements together to perform the specified functions. Also the result of such a process.

Logical Diagram. A means of graphically showing a **Logical Circuit**.

Logical Element. *See* **AND-Gate, OR-Gate, NOT-Gate**.

Logical Operations. These operations built into a computer which allow it to make decisions and carry out nonnumeric processes. *See* **Compare**.

Logical Record. A record treated as a unit from the standpoint of its content. Contrasted with the physical record, on which it may be stored.

Loop. A programming technique in which a group of instructions is repeatedly executed, with modifications each time, until some desired result is obtained. The use of a loop involves four stages: (1) initialization, in which necessary starting data are established, (2) computing during each pass through the loop, (3) modification of instructions in the loop, and (4) testing to see whether the desired results have been obtained.

Machine Language Coding. *See* **Language, Machine**.

Machine Readable. *See* **Language, Machine**.

Machine-Sensible. *See* **Language, Machine.**

Macroinstruction. An instruction which is used to represent a sub-routine.

Magnetic Core. The basic unit of a **Core Storage** memory, in which a bit is represented by the magnetization of a small toroid ("doughnut").

Magnetic Disk. *See* **Disk, Magnetic.**

Magnetic Drum. *See* **Drum, Magnetic.**

Magnetic Tape. *See* **Tape, Magnetic.**

Main Frame. *See* **Central Processor.**

Main Memory. *See* **Internal Memory.**

Malfunction. A failure in computer hardware operation.

Marc. Acronym for MAchine Readable Cataloging, the Library of Congress project for distribution of catalog data in magnetic tape form.

Master File. The set of basic records in a file system from which other records, such as indexes, are derived.

Match-Merge. The process of comparing successive records in two sets of records for any of a variety of purposes: to find records which have the same **Key**, to extract records from one set which match ones in the other, etc.

Mathematical Model. A description of something in symbolic form in such a way that it can be formally manipulated and results derived without direct reference to the thing being modelled. Any scientific theory expressed as a set of equations is a mathematical model, for example.

Matrix. A rectangular array of numbers which can then be manipulated according to defined rules, called matrix algebra. A matrix is an especially useful model, very widely used.

Medium. The material on which data is recorded.

Mega-. A prefix meaning "one million."

Memory. *See* **Internal Memory.**

Memory Register. That portion of the **Control** through which data passes in going to and from the **Internal Memory.**

Merge. *See* **Collate.**

Microfiche. A micro photographic storage medium in card form, usually 4 x 6in. and usually containing 60 images of 8½ x 11in. pages.

Microsecond. One millionth of a second (that is, 10^{-6} seconds).

Microwave. A means of communication using superhigh frequency radio and "point-to-point" transmission.

Millisecond. One thousandth of a second (that is, 10^{-3} seconds).

Mnemonic. Intended to assist the memory of a person.

Mode. A defined manner of operation.

Modify. To alter an instruction (as in a loop).

Module. A defined portion of a system, discrete and identifiable.

Monitor. A program which supervises the operation of other programs, usually to assist in debugging.

Multiple Address Instruction. An instruction having more than one address (see for example, **Four Address Instruction**).

Multiplexing. The division of a system into two or more parallel subsystems which operate relatively independently.

Multiprocessing. Executing several programs at the same time within a computer system.

Multiprogramming. Executing several programs at the same time by interleaving successive operations from each of them.

Nanosecond. One thousandth of a millionth of a second (that is, 10^{-9} seconds).

Network. A set of interconnected points.

Node. A point in a network.

Noise. Erroneous data caused by natural phenomena beyond direct control.

Not. The logical operator (in Boolean algebra) used to represent the following statement: R is true if *and* only if P is not true. Symbolically, $R = \text{NOT } P = \overline{P}$.

Object Language. See **Compiler**.

OCR. *See* **Optical Character Recognition**.

Octal. A code system using base 8, usually represented by sets of 3 bits each (that is, $2^3 = 8$).

Off the Shelf. Of hardware, meaning available from the manufacturer without any need for development.

Off-Line System. A system in which peripheral devices can operate independent of the **Central Processor**.

On-Line System. A system in which peripheral devices are in direct and continuing communication with the **Central Processor** (in some uses, this is in contrast to **Off-Line**, but other uses connote different meanings).

One Address Instruction. An instruction including only one address for the location of data or of the next instruction.

Open Subroutine. A subroutine inserted directly into a larger routine where it is needed.

Operand. Data which is to be operated upon.

Operating System. A program by which the computer controls its management of other programs, assigning storage and input/output devices to them, controlling compilation of them, sequencing them, and the like.

Operation. A built-in capability of a computer.

Operation Code. That part of an instruction which defines the operation to be performed.

Operation, Logical. *See* **Logical Operations**.

Operation, Parallel. A flow of steps in which independent sequences are executed at the same time.

Operation, Serial. A flow of steps in which one step must follow another.

Operation, Transfer. A computer operation which moves data from one location to another.

Operations Research. The use of mathematical models for solving operational problems.

Operator. A symbolic representation of a process or relationship.

Optical Character Recognition. The use of mechanical equipment for conversion of printed data to machine-readable form.

Optical Scanning. The method of converting printed characters (or, more generally, any image) into data which can be processed by a computer. Variations in tone (from black to white) result in comparable variations in electrical signal which can then be analyzed.

OR. The logical operator (in Boolean algebra) used to represent the following relationship among statements: R is true if and only if either P is true or Q is true. Symbolically, $R = P$ OR $Q = P + Q$.

OR-Gate. An electronic circuit which represents the **OR** operator by providing output current if any input current is present.

Output. The process of transferring data from a computer system to the outside world.

Output-Block. A portion of the **Internal Memory** reserved primarily for storing data which is to be output.

Overflow. In an arithmetic operation, the generation of a number larger than the capacity of the register or location into which it must be stored.

Overhead (accounting). Those costs which while necessary cannot easily be attributed directly to productive work and which must be allocated to the cost of production in order to get a true picture of costs.

Overhead (operating system). The use of an operating system to manage other programs consumes operating time which, while necessary, does not contribute directly to their results. The costs of this time must be allocated to the users.

Overlay. *See* **Paging.**

Pack. To include several short items of data in a single location.

Packing Density. *See* **Density.**

Paging. A technique of bringing routines and data into memory in large blocks (called pages). Several pages will then occupy the same storage locations, but at different times.

Parallel. Handled simultaneously.

Parallel Transfer. Data transfer in which elements are transferred simultaneously.

Parameter. A quantitative characteristic which, while it may change from one situation to another, is fixed for any given situation.

Parity Bit. *See* **Check, Parity.**

Parity Check. *See* **Check, Parity.**

Partition. A portion of **Internal Memory** assigned to a given program by the operating system.

Peripheral Equipment. Auxiliary machines which can be placed under the control of the Central Computer.

Permuted Index. *See* **KWIC.**

PERT. An acronym for Program Evaluation and Review Technique, a method for monitoring the progress of a development project which focusses special attention on those efforts which will cause the longest delay in progress.

Photocomposition. A method of "typesetting" through use of a film recording system which photographs the face of a cathode ray tube display. The characters to be set are produced by the computer on the face of the tube, usually in the full page format.

Physical Record. A record treated as a unit because of its physical form (for example, a **Block**).

PL/1. An acronym for Programming Language 1, a higher level language designed to incorporate the best features of COBOL, FORTRAN, and the like.

Plug-Board. A removable panel containing terminals which can be interconnected by short wires in order to create **Logical Circuits** at will.

Posting. The process of adding data to an existing record.

Post-Mortem. A routine, used to aid **Debugging**, which points out the contents of all **Arithmetic Registers** and memory locations at the time a program being debugged fails.

Precision. The degree of exactness with which data is represented. *See also* **Accuracy.**

Program. A sequence of instructions by which a computer will execute a desired task.

Programmer. A person who analyzes a task to determine how the computer can execute it and defines the sequences of instructions which it will follow.

Programming, Automatic. Any technique by which the computer is used to aid the programmer.

Pseudoinstruction. An instruction which calls for a subroutine, and which therefore must be interpreted.

Punched Card. A heavy, stiff paper into which holes can be punched and subsequently sensed electrically, mechanically, or optically.

Punched Paper Tape. A narrow paper strip into which holes can be punched and subsequently sensed electrically, mechanically, or optically.

Queue. A line up of transactions waiting in succession to be served.

Random Access Storage. Any of several devices which provide capabilities of **Direct Access**. (See, for example, **Disk, Magnetic** or **Drum, Magnetic.**)

Rapid Access Loop. In drum computers, a small section of memory with shorter access time than the remainder.

Raw Data. Data which has not been processed.

Read. To copy data from one representation to another.

Reader. A device which reads.

Reading Head. A means of reading recorded data (usually magnetically recorded) from a storage medium. (*See* **Recording Head**).

Reading Rate. The rate at which data is read, usually in "characters per second."

Real-Time. Processing within the actual time that the related external process takes place. Necessary if the results of processing are to affect the external process directly.

Real-Time System. A processing system fast enough to operate in real-time, at least as far as the phenomenon of interest is concerned.

Record (noun). A group of related data, treated as a unit in most processing. *See also* **Item**.

Recording Head. A means of recording data on a storage medium. (*See* **Reading Head**).

Redundancy. More data than is necessary, usually for the purpose of checks on its accuracy.

Redundancy Check. *See* **Check**.

Register *See* **Arithmetic Register**.

Relative Coding. *See* **Address, Relative**.

Remote Terminal. A device for communication with a computer but located at a site physically separated from the computer, usually far enough so that it is connected to the computer only through communications facilities and not through a direct cable.

Report Generator. A program which will compile other programs as needed to produce reports in specified formats and sequences.

Resolution. A measure of the density with which data can be recorded, especially in photographic form, in terms of the distance at which two lines can be distinguished from each other.

Rewind (verb). Most magnetic tapes, after being read or written, must be rewound in order to be read or written again.

Round-Off. Deletion of the least significant digits of a number.

Routine. *See* **Program**.

Routine, Compiling. *See* **Compiler**.

Routine, Diagnostic. *See* **Diagnostic Routine**.

Routine, Executive. *See* **Operating System**.

Routine, Interpretive. *See* **Interpretive Routine**.

Routine, Sequence Checking. A program which will check a set of records to see whether they are in order.

Routine, Service. A part of an **Operating System** to provide capability for a specific kind of operation—such as sorting or input-output.

Routine, Test. A program designed to test whether the computer is functioning properly.

Run. The execution of a program by a computer.

Run Book. *See* **Documentation.**

Scan. To examine every record in a file.

SDI. An acronym for Selective Dissemination of Information, a method of alerting people to reports or articles of potential interest.

Search. The process of finding records in a file. A search program uses some systematic technique to do so (*see also* **Access**).

Segment (program). A portion of a program (*see also* **Paging**).

Segment (record). A group of fields in a record which, for some purposes, must be treated together.

Self-Checking Number. *See* **Check Digit.**

Semiconductor. A solid (usually crystalline) with electrical properties between the high conductivity of metals and the low conductivity of insulators (*see also* **Diode, Solid-State, Transistor**).

Sense Switch. A switch which the computer will periodically examine and then choose one sequence of instructions or another, depending upon the position of the switch.

Sequential Access Storage. Any device which is best used in a **Scan Access** or **Sequential Access** node (*see also* **Tape, Magnetic**).

Serial Numbering. The assignment of numbers in numerical order.

Serial Transfer. A method of communication in which elements of data are transferred in succession.

Service Program. Any of a set of standard processing programs (*see* **Subroutine**).

Servomechanism. A device capable of monitoring the effects of its own operation (through **Feedback**) and making adjustments in its operation to meet desired objectives.

Set. Any group of things of interest.

Sign. The symbol which distinguishes positive and negative numbers.

Signal. A representation of data for purposes of transmission.

Signal-to-Noise Ratio. The ratio of the amount of energy in a signal (conveying data of interest) to the amount of energy in noise (producing erroneous data).

Significance. A measure of the amount of information produced by a system, as a function of its value or relevance.

Simulation. The use of a computer program to represent a physical process or system, usually as a dynamic phenomenon.

Single Address Instruction. See **One-Address Instruction.**

Skew. A problem with magnetic tape in which bits are read from different characters.

Software. In computer contexts, the programs required in order for the computer to produce desired results. Sometimes extended to include external operating procedures. (In education, Software has been used to refer to the *Content* of instructional films, filmstrips, etc.—a totally different meaning).

Solid-State. Characterizing electronic components which are solid (or crystalline), including semiconductors and magnetic cores.

Sort. Arrangement of records into order according to the contents of a field, called the Sort field.

Sorter. A device which will sort punched cards.

Source Language. *See* **Compiler.**

Speed of Transmission. The number of data elements sent per unit of time, usually in bits or characters per second.

Storage (memory). *See* **Internal Memory.**

Storage, Buffer. *See* **Buffer Storage.**

Storage, Erasable. A device in which stored data can be altered and replaced by other data. Most magnetic recording is erasable.

Storage, External. *See* **External Storage.**

Storage, Internal. *See* **Internal Memory.**

Storage, Magnetic. *See* **Disk, Magnetic; Drum, Magnetic; Magnetic Core;** and **Tape, Magnetic.**

Storage, Nonerasable. A storage device in which stored data cannot be changed easily (punched cards, microfilm, etc., are examples).

Storage, Nonvolatile. A storage device which retains the stored data even when power is turned off.

Storage, Parallel. The storage of data so that all bits, or characters, or words are read at the same time.

Storage, Secondary. *See* **External Storage.**

Storage, Serial. The storage of data so that bits or characters or words are all read sequentially.

Storage, Volatile. A storage device which loses any stored data when power is turned off.

Storage, Working. The portion of the INTERNAL MEMORY reserved for data upon which operations are being performed (in contrast to "Program storage").

Store. To record data in a location.

Stored Program Computer. *See* **Computer.**

Subject Analysis. The process of determining the substantive content of a document and assigning appropriate descriptive terms.

Subroutine. A program designed to perform a well-defined, usually limited task and capable of being used as part of other programs when that task is required.

Summary Punch. A piece of punched card equipment operating under the control of other equipment (for example, a tabulator or a computer) to produce punched cards containing data transmitted from the other equipment.

Switching. The process of transferring a signal from an input line to a selected one of several output lines.

Switching Center. A place at which several input and output lines converge for switching.

Symbolic Coding. The representation of programs in a source language (*see* **Compiler**).

Symbol, Logical. Any of the operators used in Boolean Algebra, including AND, OR, NOT, IMPLIES, and the like.

System. A set of component devices and people, carrying out operations and procedures in a clearly defined manner for the accomplishment of established objectives.

Systems Analysis. The process of determining the objectives of the system and of defining the components, operations, and procedures by which it either achieves those objectives or could achieve them more efficiently. It thus involves four steps: (1) definition of objectives, (2) analysis of processes, (3) design of alternatives, and (4) evaluation.

Table. An array of data which associates value for one or more elements of data with each in a set of values of another element of data. The latter is called the "table argument" the former, the "table values." Frequently, a table provides values for a mathematical function, and the values are called "function values." Usually, a table is sequenced by the table argument.

Table Look-up The process of finding in a table the table values associated with a given table argument.

Tabulator. A punched card handling device which reads data from cards, adds it into one or more totals, and prints out the data and the related totals.

Tape Dump. *See* **Dump.**

Tape Limited. Characterizing data processing tasks, with relatively limited computations on large amounts of data, for which the time required is determined by the rate of transfer of data to and from magnetic tape.

Tape, Magnetic. A device which stores data on the magnetizable surface of a long strip (typically 1 in. wide by 2400 ft long). Usually data is stored and retrieved using sequential, scan access.

Teletypewriter. Generic term referring to equipment providing input and output to Teletype communication lines.

Terminal. Equipment attached to a communication channel which may be used for either input or output.

Time-Sharing. The use of a device, especially a computer, for two or more tasks during the same time interval by interspersing processes, allocating small divisions of the total time to each task in turn.

Track. *See* **Channel.**

Transaction. Data representing an event which will affect records in a file—changing them, posting to them, adding them, deleting them, and the like.

Transistor. A device used, for its properties as a semi-conductor, to control the flow of electrons (*see also* **Diode, Semiconductor**).

USASCII. *See* **ASCII.**

Verifier. A punched card device which detects errors by comparing data punched into a card with comparable data as it is keyed.

Verify. To check data.

Word. A set of characters, usually a fixed number of them, stored in a location in internal memory and treated as a unit in computer operations.

Write. To transfer data to a storage medium or location.

Zone. The portion of a Hollerith punched card code used to designate the section of the alphabet.

Appendix 2

SOURCES OF INFORMATION ON DATA PROCESSING IN THE LIBRARY

INTRODUCTION

The application of data processing technology to libraries is accelerating so rapidly that the control of its related literature is virtually nonexistent. In her review of it, Barbara Markuson commented that,[2] "The problems in assessing library automation literature are considerable. Some . . . are substantive and due to the complexity of the techniques being described. Some . . . are due to the manner in which the library automation literature is being produced and published." She comments on the use of the preprint, the report, and similar uncontrolled forms of publication, on the use of informal communication channels—the "invisible colleges"—and on the poor quality of editorial work even for the journal literature.

She did not comment on—but might well have done so—the diffuse character of the subject fields that must be considered. Automation in libraries has been of concern not only to librarians but to a broad spectrum of technologists as well. As a result, the literature on computers, on their programming, on communications, on operations research, even on linguistics and symbolic logic and mathematics—all must be considered, as well as the more familiar library related

---

[1] Presented at a talk given at Drexel on November 3, 1967; subsequently expanded, revised, and updated: Hayes, R. M., "Keeping up with Library Automation."

[2] Markuson, Barbara, "Automation in Libraries and Information Centers," in Carlos Cuadra, *Annual Review of Information Science and Technology*, Vol. 2. New York: Wiley, 1967, pp. 255-284.

literature. The difficulties are doubly compounded if we regard "library automation" as encompassing not only clerical activities in the library—circulation control, serial records, and ordering—but information processing ones as well (of which "information retrieval" is only one example). Much of the literature, in fact, is not really "literature" in any sense—it is flow charts, forms, cost analyses, computer programs, representative printouts, and operating instructions—paraphernalia that, in the computer business, we call "documentation." Not only does this appear in a miserable form and a great variety of sizes and shapes but it is usually so written as to be unintelligible to anyone but the person who created it. In certain respects, this material constitutes the most important source of the data necessary to "keeping up with library automation," since it is the most directly usable—if only people would use it and if only it were in a form to be used.

Another equally important but just as messy a form of literature is that put out by the manufacturers—the brochures, the operating descriptions, the sales literature on "applications," and the like. Such literature is easy to accumulate and is almost useless. It usually serves solely as a means of establishing contact with a "company representative" and is, almost by design, uninformative and sometimes even misleading. Yet it constitutes a primary resource for anyone planning the design of a mechanized system for a library.

Finally, the available literature—in nearly all of its forms—is of such generally poor quality that one begins to question its utility at all. Authors continually fail to disclose what is actually operational, as contrasted with purely speculative or developmental. It does not seem to be so much an attempt to delude the reader as a reflection of the writer's own uncertainties and his need to prove that something useful is, indeed, being accomplished. The whole effort to apply automation in libraries has been such a struggle and has produced so many abortive experiments that each person must feel a terrible need to prove that it can be done. As a result, wishes get translated into reality because, since we have wished for so long, it must be true. And each apparent success is seized upon as a demonstration of real success from which we can now move forward.

KEEPING UP WITH LIBRARY AUTOMATION

In summary, if we interpret "keeping up with library automation" as meaning keeping up with the relevant literature, we are faced with a difficult, time-consuming, and really not very rewarding job.

In other words, if you have, at most, a casual interest in automation in the library, then "keeping up with library automation" will be a relatively simple job. Read the articles in library literature and heap large tablespoons of salt on any that say "plan to" anywhere in the article. And that's enough. But if your interest is serious, it will require a major commitment of manpower, intellectual energy, and involvement in library automation itself. This means that you, in your own library, should have an active program of library systems analysis and development. In business, it is estimated that an organization must spend at least 10 percent of its operating budget on a continuing effort at analyzing and improving those operations in order to maintain efficiency. The library, as an operational organization, particularly requires this kind of self-analysis. And we're not talking about a "once-in-a-while" examination by the librarian or the head of techncal services. We're talking about a person, on the staff of the librarian, whose assigned and primary responsibility is the analysis of the library's operations

We're also talking about an active program of data acquisition and communication with other libraries. Barbara Markuson said,[3] "We have reached the point where further achievements will depend on the ability of a lot of us—librarians, computer specialists, systems analysts, and information entrepreneurs of various ilk—to march—at least occasionally, in step." And this can only be done by active communication and exchange of resources—costs, operating characteristics of equipment, programs, operating instructions, and system designs—directly among libraries (or, at least, groups of libraries).

Finally, we're talking about an active program of education. Symposia and "data processing clinics" can play a vital role; perhaps your local library school has a program of continuing education, which can include consideration of automation.[4] But most important is a program within your own library—a program of self-education, involving the entire professional staff, a program that makes the analysis of library operations—"keeping up with library automation"—an interest of all members of the library.

PRIMARY SOURCES

However, despite its difficulties and deficiencies, the literature of library automation is still the most readily accessible resource. Figure A2.1, therefore, is a listing of the journals and periodic publications that seem to provide the most central, primary sources for "keeping up with library automation."

SECONDARY SOURCES

However, the field is so diffuse and draws on so many sources of information that limiting consideration to just these primary ones would be entirely inadequate. The secondary sources—the abstracting and indexing services, the journals with reviews or bibliographic sections, the directories and state of the art reviews—provide the best means of access to the broader scope. These cover, the some extent, most of the primary resources—the journals, the projects, the

[3] Markuson, Barbara, *op. cit.*

[4] Goldhor, Herbert (ed.), *Proceedings of the 1963 Clinic on Library Applications of Data Processing.* Urbana, Illinois: University of Illinois, 1963.

Figure A2.1   Primary sources.

American Documentation, Washington, D.C. American Society for Information Science, quarterly $18.50. (now *Journal of the American Society for Information Science*).

American Society for Information Science. Annual Meetings, Proceedings. Washington, D.C. Thompson Book Company, various prices.

Annual Review of Information Science and Technology. Sponsored by the American Society for Information Science. Edited by C. A. Cuadra. New York, New York. John Wiley & Sons, Inc., Vol. 1, 1966; Vol. 2, 1967; Encyclopaedia Britannica Vol. 3, 1968; Vol. 4, 1969; Vol. 5, 1970;–

Aslib Proceedings. London, England. Aslib, monthly, 90s.

College and Research Libraries. Chicago, Ill. Association of College and Research Libraries, monthly, $10.

Current Research & Development in Scientific Documentation. Washington, D.C. National Science Foundation, irregular, price varies.

Information Retrieval & Library Automation Newsletter. Lomond Systems, Inc., Mt. Airy, Maryland 21771, monthly, $24.

Information Retrieval Letter. Detroit, Michigan. American Data Processing, Inc., quarterly, $24.

Journal of Chemical Documentation. Washington, D.C. American Chemical Society, quarterly, $7 to ACS members, $14 to nonmembers.

Journal of Documentation. London, England. Aslib, quarterly, 30s to Aslib members, 70s to nonmembers.

Journal of Library Automation, Chicago, Ill. American Library Association, Information Science and Automation Division, quarterly, membership or $10/year.

Journal of the American Society for Information Science, Washington, D.C., bimonthly, free to members; $27.50 to non-members.

Library Journal. New York, New York. R. R. Bowker Company, semi-monthly $10.

Library of Congress Information Bulletin. Washington, D.C. Card Division, Library of Congress, weekly, $2 (free to publicly supported libraries).

Library Resources and Technical Services. Richmond, Virginia. Resources and Technical Services Division, American Library Association, quarterly, free to members, $5 to non-members.

Nonconventional Scientific and Technical Information Systems in Current Use. Washington, D.C. National Science Foundation, for sale by the Superintendent of Documents U.S.G.P.O. $1.75

Program: News of Computers in British University Libraries. Aslib, monthly. Free to members, 40s to non-members.

Research in Education. Washington, D.C. U.S. Department of Health, Education and Welfare (Subscription through The Superintendent of Documents) monthly, $11.

Scientific Information Notes. New York, Science Associates International, bimonthly, $10.

Scientific Information Activities of Federal Agencies. Washington, D.C. National Science Foundation, irregular, No. 32, 1966, 10c.

Special Libraries. New York, New York. Special Libraries Association, 10 issues per year, $20.

University of Illinois. Clinic on Library Applications of Data Processing. *Proceedings.* Champaign, Illini Bookstore 1963-67; $2 for paper $3 for cloth.

---

reports, the manufacturers' literature. Figure A2.2 provides a listing of the secondary sources that one should consider in order to get a full coverage of the field of information processing (even though it will have full value only if one's interests were far broader than "library automation" today). AFIPS (The American Federation of Information Processing Societies)—encompassing IEEE, ACM, ASIS (née ADI), Simulation Council, and MT societies—has recently become very concerned about access to this breadth of literature and the list represents an overall picture of the scope and coverage that must be considered by them as well as libraries.

In the list, the 115 secondary sources have been roughly grouped into ten areas of subject specialization.

0.   General (coverage of the field so broadly as not to be classifiable in any one area as such).

1.   Theory (coverage of symbolic logic and its application to switching functions, information theory or communication theory, combinatorics, recursive functions, automata, artificial intelligence, cybernetics and control theory, linguistic theory).

2.   Hardware (coverage of circuitry; storage devices; peripheral equipment; digital, analog, "hybrid," and control computers).

3.   Programming (coverage of programming principles, program organization, formal syntax of programming languages, file organizations, graphics, and analog programming).

4.0   General applications (coverage of applications so broadly as not to be classifiable in any one application area as such).

4.1   Numerical applications (coverage of numerical analysis, statistics, and operations research).

4.2   Control applications (coverage of sampled data systems for control, cybernetic systems, and analog systems).

4.3   Business applications (coverage of business data processing, management information systems, and the like).

4.4   Library applications (coverage of library automation, documentation, and science information).

4.5   Nonnumerical applications (coverage of information retrieval, language data processing, and graphics).

5.   Management of information processing.

The ones of special relevance to library automation are those under areas 4.4 (Applications: Libraries and Science Information) and 4.5 (Applications: Nonnumerical).

However, most of these secondary sources provide significant coverage in many of the ten subject areas. Therefore, in Figure A2.3 will be found a judgmental evaluation of the areas covered by each. Again, areas 4.4 and 4.5 are the ones of special relevance to library automation.

Figure A2.2   Secondary sources on information processing.

O. GENERAL

Automation Express; Comprehensive Digest of Current Russian Literature Dealing with Automation Topics. International Physical Index Inc., 1909 Park Ave., New York, New York. Monthly. $110.

Clearinghouse Announcements in Science and Technology (CAST). Clearinghouse for Federal Scientific and Technical Information, Springfield, Va. 22151, semimonthly, $5. for first category; $5. for each additional two categories.

    6. Automation and data processing
    7. Behavioral sciences
   17. Information sciences
   18. Management planning
   29. Operations research–Theoretical
   40. Reprography and recording devices

   See U.S. Government Research and Development Reports. CAST is a fast announcement service of U.S.G.R.D.R.

Computer Bibliographic Index. American Data Processing Inc., 4th Floor Book Bldg., Detroit, Mich. 48226. V. 1, 1956-64; V. 2, 1965-67, both volumes, $45.

Computer Yearbook and Directory. American Data Processing Inc. 19830 Mack Ave., Detroit, Mich. 48236. Annual. $25.

Federal Information Processing Standards Register (FIPS Register) National Bureau of Standards; Superintendent of Documents, Govt. Print. Off., Washington, D.C. 20402. Federal Information Processing Standards Publications Series (FIPS PUBS). The official source of information on standards for: hardware, software, applications and data.

Gros, E., ed. *Russian Books on Automation and Computers.* Scientific Information Consultants Ltd., 661 Finchley Road, London, N.W.2 England, 1966, 91 pp.

IAG–Literature on Automation. IFIP Administrative Data Processing Group, 6. Stadhouderskade, Amsterdam W.1. Monthly. Free to members; $30 to U.S. nonmembers.

Information Processing Journal. Cambridge Communications Corp., 238 Main Street, Cambridge, Mass. 02142. Monthly. $50. Also available as Computer Abstracts on cards.

Rickles, Robert. *Marketing Guide to U.S. Government Research and Development.* 1966. Noyes Development Corp., 118 Mill Road, Park Ridge, New Jersey 07656. 229 pp. $20.

Studiecentrum voor Administratieve Automatisering. International Computer Bibliography. National Computing Centre, Quay House, Quay St., Manchester 3, England. 1968. 400 pp. $50.

Technical Abstract Bulletin. Defense Documentation Center, Cameron Station, Alexandria, V. 22314. Semimonthly. Available to government contractors who are eligible to receive classified material.

Youden, W. W. *Computer Literature Bibliography 1946-1963.* 1964. National Bureau of Standards (NBS misc. publication 266). 463 pp. $3.75.

1. THEORY

Advances in Mathematics. Herbert Busemann, ed. Academic Press, 111 Fifth Ave., New York, New York 10003. Irregular. V. 1, 1964-1965, $18; V. 2, 1968, $20.

Figure A2.2   (*continued*)

Cybernetics Abstracts. English translation of Referativnyi Zhurnal. Mathematika. Scientific Information Consultants Ltd., 661 Finchly Road, London, N.W.2, England. Monthly. 900 x. $135.

IEEE Transactions on Information Theory. Institute of Electrical and Electronics Engineers, 345 East 47th St., New York, New York 10017. Quarterly. Free to members; $17 to nonmembers.

Machine Intelligence. N. L. Collins and D. Michie, eds. Oliver and Boyd, 49 Elm Row, Edinburgh, Scot. American Elsevier, 52 Vanderbilt Ave., New York, New York 10017. Annual. V. 1, 1967, $12.50.

Mathematical Reviews. American Mathematical Soc., P.O. Box 6248, Providence, R.I. 02904. Monthly. $40 to members; $180 to nonmembers.

Sammet, J. E. An annotated descriptor based bibliography on the use of computers for non-numerical mathematics. In *Computing Reviews,* 7(4), B1-B31, July 1966. Bibliography 11. *See Computing Reviews,* Sect. 3.

Sammet, J. E. Revised annotated descriptor based bibliography on the use of computers for non-numerical mathematics. In, Bobrow, Daniel G., ed., *Symbol manipulation languages and techniques.* Amsterdam, North-Holland Pub. Co., 1968. Pp. 358-484.

2. HARDWARE

Advances in Computers. Franz L. Alt, ed. Academic Press, 111 Fifth Ave., New York, New York 10003. Annual. V. 8, 1967, $14.50.

Computer Characteristics Quarterly. Charles W. Adams Associates, 128 the Great Road, Bedford, Massachusetts 01730. Quarterly, $25.

Computer Display Review Charles W. Adams Associates, 575 Technology Square, Cambridge, Massachusetts. Updated, 3/yr.

Computer Directory and Buyers' Guide. Computers and Automation, Berkeley Enterprises, 815 Washington Street, Newtonville, Massachusetts. June issue is the Directory. Computers and automation subscription, $12.

Control Abstracts: Science Abstracts, Series C. Institution of Electrical Engineers, Savoy Pl., London W.C.2, England. Monthly, 20 L.

Control Engineering. R. H. Donnelley Corp., 466 Lexington Ave., New York, New York 10017. Monthly. Free to qualified U.S. engineers and management. $10 to non-qualified.

Data Processing Systems Encyclopedia. American Data Processing Inc., 4th Floor Book Bldg., Detroit, Michigan 48226. Original updated with supplements. $95, original–$95/yr. for updating.

Electronics and Communications Abstracts, Multi-Science Pub. Co., 33 S. Drive, Brentwood, Essex, Eng. Monthly, $35.

Electronics Abstracts Journal. Cambridge Communications Corp., Cambridge Massachusetts 02142. Monthly, $110.

Electronics Buyers' Guide. Electronics (June issue), McGraw-Hill, 330 West 42nd Street, New York, New York 10036. Annual, $3.

Figure A2.2 *(continued)*

Human Factors Engineering Bibliographic Series. Tufts University, Institute of Psychological Research, Medford, Massachusetts V. 1, 1940-59 literature $19.40 HC, $6.25 MF. V. 2, 1960-64 literature $3. HC, $.65 MF. Available from Clearinghouse for Federal Scientific and Technical Information, Springfield, Va. 22151.

IEEE Transactions on Automatic Control. Institute of Electrical and Electronics Engineers, 345 E. 47th St., New York, New York 10017. Quarterly, $17, nonmembers. Free to members.

IEEE Transactions on Electronic Computers. Institute of Electrical and Electronics Engineers, 345 E. 47th St. New York, New York 10017. Bimonthly. Free to members; $17 to nonmembers.

IEEE Transactions on Human Factors in Electronics. Institute of Electrical and Electronics Engineers, 345 E. 47th St. New York, New York 10017.

International Bibliography of Automatic Control. Presses Academiques Europeennes, 98 Chaussee de Charleroi, Brussels 6, Belgium. Quarterly, $6, or free with Review A, Mournal of Automatic Control, $10.

Kiersky, Loretta J. Bibliography on Reproduction of Documentary Information. In, *Special Libraries.* Special Libraries Association, 73 Main Street, Brattleboro, Vt. 05301. Annual. Subscription to Special Libraries, $12.50.

Library Technology Reports. Library Technology Program, American Library Association, 50 E. Huron St., Chicago, Ill. 60611. Bimonthly, $100.

Monthly Information Service. American Data Processing Inc., 4th Floor Book Bldg., Detroit, Michigan 48226. Monthly, $24.

Niederberger, A. R. V. *Documentation of Electronic Computers.* R. V. Dicker's Verlag, G. Schenck, Hamburg-Berlin, Germany 1963/1968. 600 pp. DM68.50.

Patterson, E. F. Some current sources of information on microphotography and document reproduction. In *Microdoc.* 1966 (2-3):26-31; 48-53. Reprints available from Anbar Pubs. Ltd. 34 The Mall, Ealing, London W.5, England.

Warren, Donna M. *Milestones: A Directory of Human Engineering Laboratory Publications, 1953-1965.* Human Engineering Laboratories, Aberdeen Proving Ground, Md. 109 pp. AD 636 082. Available from Clearinghouse for Federal Scientific and Technical Information, Springfield, Virginia 22151. $4 HC, $.75 MF.

Weik, Martin H. *A third Survey of Domestic Electronic Digital Computing Systems.* 1961. Ballistic Research Laboratories, Aberdeen Proving Ground, Md. (BRL Report 1115) 1116 pp., $10. PB 17126.

A Fourth Survey of Domestic Electronic Digital Computing Systems. 1964. Ballistic Research Laboratories, Aberdeen Proving Ground, Md. (BRL Report 1227) PB 171265.

3. PROGRAMMING

Annual Review in Automatic Programming. R. E. Goodman, ed. Pergamon Press, 44-01 21st St., Long Island City, New York 11101. Irregular. V. 4, 1964, $12.

Computer Abstracts. Technical Information Co. Ltd., Chancery House, Chancery Lane, London W.C. 2, Eng. Monthly, $96.

Computing Reviews. Association for Computing Machinery, 211 E. 43rd St., New York, New York 10017. Bimonthly. $2.50, members; $15, nonmembers.

Figure A2.2   *(continued)*

Computer Software. Cambridge Communications Corp., 1612 K St., N.W. Washington, D.C. 20006. 1968. 500 pp. $9.95.

ICP Quarterly. International Computer Programs, Inc. 2511 E. 46th St., Suite R-4, Indianapolis, Indiana 46205. Quarterly. $60/yr.

International Directory of Computer Programs, an Index to Computerized Information in Science and Technology, 1968-   L. Cohan, ed. Science Associates/International Inc., 342 Madison Ave., New York, New York 10017. Annual, quarterly updating.

Stewart, J. Real-time processing. In *Computing Reviews,* **7(6),** 553-63, Nov. 1966. Bibliography 12. See *Computing Reviews,* Section 3.

Systems Development Corporation Research and Technology Div. Report. 2500 Colorado Avenue, Santa Monica, California 90406. Annual.

4. APPLICATIONS GENERAL

Barnes, Colin I. Hatfield College of Technology, Hatfield, Herts, England. 66 pp.

The Information Sciences Newsletter. Ansell Associates, P.O. Box 102, Papillion, Nebraska 68046. Monthly. $15. U.S. and Canada; $20. other countries. Includes Educational Opportunities in the Information Sciences.

4.1. APPLICATIONS, NUMERICAL AND OPERATIONS RESEARCH

Batchelor, James H. *Operations Research: An Annotated Bibliography.* 2d ed. 1959. St. Louis University, Press. 966 pp. $10. (Out-of-print.)

Case Institute of Technology. Operations Research Group. A comprehensive bibliography on operations research through 1956 with supplement for 1957. 1968. Wiley, 605 3d Ave., New York, New York 10016. 188 pp. $6.50. (Out-of-print.)

International Abstracts in Operations Research. Operations Research Soc. of America, Mt. Royal and Guilford Ave., Baltimore, Md. Bimonthly, $12.50.

International Journal of Abstracts on Statistical Methods in Industry. International Statistical Inst., The Hague, Netherlands. $3/yr. 1954-63. Ceased.

Operational Research Quarterly. Operational Research Soc., London. Published by Pergamon Press, 122 E. 55th St., New York, New York. Quarterly, $6.

Operations Research. Journal of the Operations Research Society of America. Mt. Royal and Guilford Ave., Baltimore, Md. 21202. Bimonthly, $10.

Operations Research/Management Science Abstracts Service. Interscience 440 Park Ave. S., New York, New York. Monthly, looseleaf, $75. Combined with Quality Control and Applied Statistics $140.

Operations Research Society of America. Bulletin. Supplement. Proceedings of National Meeting. Mt. Royal and Guilford Ave., Baltimore, Md. 21202. Monthly, $9, or free with Operations Research.

Progress in Operations Research. Wiley, 605 3d Ave., New York, New York 10016. Irregular. V. 2, 1964, $11.

Quality Control and Applied Statistics Abstracts Service. Interscience, 440 Park Ave. S., New York, New York. Monthly, looseleaf, $90. Combined with Operations Research/ Management Science $140.

Figure A2.2   (*continued*)

4.2. APPLICATIONS, CONTROL

Advances in Control Systems. C. T. Leondes, ed. Academic Press, 111 Fifth Avenue, New York, New York 10003. Irregular. V. 5, 1967, $18.50.

Automatic Control and Computer Engineering. V. V. Solodovnikov, ed. Pergamon Press, 44-01 21st Street, Long Island City, New York 11101. Irregular. V. 3, 1966, $15.

Progress in Control Engineering. R. H. Macmillan, T. V. Higgins, and P. Naslin, eds. Academic Press, 111 Fifth Avenue, New York, New York 10003. Irregular. V. 2, 1964, $13.50.

4.3. APPLICATIONS, BUSINESS

Auerbach Standard EDP Reports. Auerbach Corporation, 121 North Broad Street, Philadelphia, Pa. 19107. Looseleaf with monthly updating.

Automation Reporter (also Automation Reports). Commerce Clearing House Inc., 4025 W. Peterson Ave., Chicago, Ill. 60646. Biweekly, 1963-66, ceased.

Data Processing Yearbook. American Data Processing Inc., 4th Floor Book Bldg., Detroit, Mich. 48226. Annual, $5.

Forms and Systems Letter. American Data Processing Inc., 4th Floor Book Bldg., Detroit, Mich. 48226. Monthly, $24.

Information Systems Bibliographic Index. 1962. American Data Processing Inc., 4th Floor. Book Bldg., Detroit, Mich. 48226. 195 pp.

Journal of Data Management. Data Processing Management Assoc., 505 Busse Highway, Park Ridge, Ill. 60068. Monthly, $5.

Notebook for Accountants. Auerbach Corporation, 121 North Broad Street, Philadelphia, Pa. 19107. Looseleaf with updating.

Total Systems Letter. American Data Processing Inc., 4th Floor. Book Bldg., Detroit, Mich. 48226. Monthly, $24.

4.4. APPLICATIONS, LIBRARIES AND SCIENCE INFORMATION

Directory of Computerized Information in Science and Technology. Leonard Cohan, ed. Science Associates/International, Inc., 23 E. 26th St., New York, New York 10010. 1968 + Supplements through 1969, $175.

FID News Bulletin. General Secretariat, International Federation for Documentation, 7 Hofweg, The Hague, Netherlands. Monthly, f15. (FID 174)

Information Handling and Science Information: a Selected Bibliography 1957-1961. Paul C. Janaske, Ed. 1962. American Inst. of Biological Sciences. Biological Sciences Communication Project. George Washington University, 2000 P St., N.W. Suite 700, Washington, D.C. 20036.

Information Retrieval and Library Automation. American Data Processing Inc., 4th Floor. Book Bldg., Detroit, Mich. 48226. Monthly, $24.

Information Science Abstracts. P.O. Box 8570, Philadelphia, Pa. 19101. Published by the American Society for Information Science, the Division of Chemical Literature of the American Chemical Soc., and the Special Libraries Assoc. $15/yr. to members; $25/yr. to nonmembers. Formerly called *Documentation Abstracts*.

Figure A2.2   (continued)

Journal of Documentation. Aslib, 3 Belgrave Square, London, S.W. 1, Eng. Quarterly. 30s to members; 48s to nonmembers.

Kent, Allen and Harold Lancour. *Encyclopedia of Library and Information Science.* Dekker, Marcel, Inc., 95 Madison Ave., New York, New York 10016. To be 18 vols. Vol. 1, 1968. 676 pp, $45, or $35 by subscription. Articles include extensive bibliographies.

LARC Reports. Library Automation Research and Consulting Services, 4500 Campus Dr. Suite 432, Newport Beach, California 92660. Quarterly, $50.

McCormick, Edward Mack. *Bibliography on Mechanized Library Processes.* 1963. National Science Foundation, Office of Science Information, 1800 G St. N.W., Washington, D.C. 20550. 27 pp. Mimeographed.

Nonconventional Scientific and Technical Information Systems in Current Use. National Science Foundation. Available from the Superintendent of Documents, Washington, D.C. 20412. Irregular. No. 4. December, 1966, $1.75.

Program: News of Computers in British University Libraries. Queen's University School of Library Studies, 2 College Gardens, Belfast 9, North Ireland. Quarterly. Available on request.

Rutgers University. Graduate School of Library Service. Bureau of Information Sciences Research. *Bibliography of Research Relating to the Communication of Scientific and Technical Information.* Rutgers University Press, New Brunswick, N.J. 1967. 732 pp. $15.

Scientific Information Notes. Science Associates International, 23 E. 26th St., New York, N.Y. 10010, bimonthly. $10.

Scientific and Technical Information. Abstract Journal 59. Academy of Sciences of the USSR, Institute of Scientific Information (VINITI), Moscow, A-219, Baltijskaya ul., 14. Monthly, $10.

Speer, Jack A., comp. *Libraries and Automation.* A bibliography with index. Teachers College Press, Emporia, Kansas 66801. 1967. 106 pp.

The Use of Data Processing Equipment by Libraries and Information Centers. 1966. Creative Research Services Inc., 220 Fifth Ave., New York, New York 10001. Available from Library Technology Program, American Library Assoc., 50 E. Huron St., Chicago, Ill. 60611. 160 pp. $10.

4.5. APPLICATIONS, NONNUMERICAL

Annual Review of Information Science and Technology. Carlos A. Cuadra, Ed. Interscience, 440 Park Ave. S., New York, New York. Annual. V. 2, 1967, $15.

Balz, F., and R. H. Stanwood. *Literature on Information Retrieval and Machine Translation.* 2d ed. 1966. International Business Machines Corp., Federal Systems Div., Gaithersburg, Md. 20760. 168 pp. $2.64 (IBM 953-0300-1, or IBM 320-0927). 1st ed. 1962 (IBM 320-1710).

Computer Applications Service. American Data Processing Inc., 4th Floor Book Bldg., Detroit, Mich. 48226. 2 vols., looseleaf with monthly updating, $95.

Computers and the Humanities. Annual Bibliography for 1966. March 1967. Computers and the Humanities. Queens College of the City University of New York, Flushing, New York 11367. 5 issues/yr., $4.

Figure A2.2   (*continued*)

Current Research and Development in Scientific Documentation. National Science Foundation, Office of Science Information Service. Available from the Superintendent of Documents, Washington, D.C. 20402. Semiannual. No. 14, 1966, $2.

Data Processing for Education. American Data Processing Inc., 4th Floor, Book Bldg., Detroit, Mich. 48226. Monthly, $24.

Documentation Abstracts. American Society for Information Science (formerly American Documentation Institute) 2000 P St., N.W. Washington, D.C. 20036. Quarterly. $15 to members; $25 to nonmembers.

Hays, David G., Bozena Heniza-Dostert, and Marjorie L. Rapp. *Annotated Bibliography of Rand Publications in Computational Linguistics.* 3d ed. 1967. RAND Corp., Reports Dept., 1700 Main Street, Santa Monica, California 90406. 34 pp. (RM-3894-3) $1.

Information Retrieval Letter. American Data Processing Inc., 4th Floor Book Bldg., Detroit, Mich. 48226. Monthly, $24.

Neeland, Frances. *A Bibliography on Information Science and Technology.* American Society for Information Science (formerly American Documentation Inst.), 2000 P St. N.W., Washington, D.C. 20036. Annual, 1967, $10 (set of 4 parts).

Optical or Graphic Information Processing (Information Sciences Series) Volume I. Defense Documentation Center, Alexandria, Va. 229 pp. 1968. (DDC-TAS-68-32) AD 673 993. Available from Clearinghouse for Federal Scientific and Technical Information, Springfield, Va. 22151. An annotated bibliography.

Programmed Learning and Educational Technology Journal of the Association for Programmed Learning. Sweet and Maxwell Ltd., 11 New Fetter Ln., London, E.C. 4, Eng. $3/yr. 21s ($2.94)

Research in Education. 1967- Educational Resources Information Center, Washington, D.C. Monthly $11. Available from Superintendent of Documents, Washington, D.C. 20402.

Stevens, Mary E. *Automatic Indexing: A State-of-the-Art Report.* 1965. National Bureau of Standards. Available from the Superintendent of Documents, Washington, D.C. 20402. 220 pp. $1.50 (NBS monograph 91).

Swanson, Rowena W., *Information Systems Networks.* Air Force Office of Scientific Research, Directorate of Information Sciences, Arlington, Virginia 22209. 48 pp. (AFOSR 66-0873) presented at the 3d Annual National Colloquium on Information Retrieval, University of Pennsylvania, May 12-13, 1966.

Walkowicz, J. L. *A Bibliography of Foreign Developments in Machine Translation and Information Processing.* 1963. National Bureau of Standards. Available from the Superintendent of Documents, Washington, D.C. 20402. 191 pp. $1 (NBS technical note 193).

Zell, Hans M. *An International Bibliography of Non-periodical Literature on Documentation and Information.* Compiled and edited by Hans M. Zell and Robert J. Machensney. 1965. Robert Maxwell and Company, 1/8 St. Clements, Oxford, England. 294 pp. 30x.

Figure A2.3   Subject coverage of secondary sources on information processing.

	0	1	2	3	4.0	4.1	4.2	4.3	4.4	4.5	5.0
(-0- General)											
Auto Ex	x	x	x								
Clearinghouse Announcements	x	x	x	x	x	x	x	x	x	x	x
Comp Bibl Ind		x	x	x		x	x	x	x	x	x
Comp Year Dir	x		x	x			x	x	x	x	x
Eng Ind	x	x	x	x		x	x			x	
Inf Proc J	x	x	x	x		x	x	x	x	x	
OAR Ind Res		x	x	x		x	x			x	
Rickles	x										
Tech Abst Bull		x	x	x		x	x		x	x	x
Studiecentrum											
Wasserman and Greer	x										x
Youden		x	x	x		x	x	x		x	x
IAG Lit Auto		x	x	x		x	x	x	x	x	x
(-1- Theory)											
Adv Math		x									
Cyb Abst		x		x		x	x			x	
IEEE Trans Inf Theory		x									
Mach Intell		x									
Math Rev		x				x	x				
Sammett		x									
IEEE Trans Auto Cont		x				x	x				
(-2- Hardware											
Adv Comp	x	x	x	x		x	x	x		x	
Comp Char Q	x		x	x							
Comp Dis Rev		x									
Comp Auto Dir	x		x	x				x			x
Cont Abst		x	x								
Cont Eng			x				x				
Da Proc Sys Ency			x					x			x
Electro Buy Gu	x		x								x
Electro Abst J			x				x				
Electro Comm Abst		x	x		x	x	x				
Hum Fact Eng Bibl Ser			x								
IEEE Trans Electro Comp		x	x	x		x	x	x		x	
IEEE Trans Hum Fact		x	x							x	
Int Bibl Auto Con		x	x				x				
Kiersky		x						x	x	x	x
Lib Tech Reps		x							x		
Mon Inf Ser			x			x		x			x

	0	1	2	3	4.0	4.1	4.2	4.3	4.4	4.5	5.0
(-2- Hardware continued)											
Niederberger			x								
Patterson			x						x		
Warren			x								
Weik			x								
(-3- Programming)											
Ann Rev Auto Prog				x							
Comp Abst		x	x	x		x	x	x	x	x	x
Comp Rev	x	x	x	x	x	x	x	x		x	x
Computer Software				x							
ICP Quarterly				x							
Int Dir Comp Prog				x	x						x
Stewart		x		x		x	x				
SDC Res Rep	x	x		x	x	x				x	x
Bat Tech Rev		x	x	x		x	x			x	
(-4.0- Applications General)											
Barnes					x						
Info Sci Newsletter					x						
(-4.1- Applications Numerical and Operations Research)											
Batchelor						x					
Case OR						x					
Int Abst OR						x					
Int J Abstr Stat					x	x	x	x			x
OR/Man Sci Abstr		x				x		x			x
OR Q		x	x		x		x	x			
OR		x		x		x		x	x		
OR Soc Bull		x				x		x	x	x	
Prog OR						x					
Qual Cont App Stat		x	x	x		x	x	x			x
(-4.2- Applications Control)											
Adv Cont Sys							x				
Auto Cont Comp Eng		x	x				x				
Prog Cont Eng		x	x			x	x				
(-4.3- Applications Business)											
Auer EDP Reps			x	x		x		x		x	x
Auto Rep			x	x	x		x	x		x	x
Da Proc Dig			x	x		x		x		x	x
Da Proc Year			x	x	x	x	x	x		x	x
For Sys Let			x					x			x
Inf Sys Bibl Ind	x		x	x		x	x	x		x	x
J Da Man								x			x

	0	1	2	3	4.0	4.1	4.2	4.3	4.4	4.5	5.0
(-4.3- Applications Business)											
Note Acc								x			x
Tot Sys Let			x		x	x	x	x			x
(-4.4- Applications Libraries and Science Information)											
USSR Sci Tech Inf			x						x	x	x
BSCP Inf									x	x	
FID News									x	x	
Inf Ret Lib Auto			x			x			x	x	
Directory of Computer Info									x		
Gros			x	x					x		
Info Sci Abst									x		
Kent Lancour									x		
LARC									x		
Rutgers									x		
Speer									x		
J Doc									x	x	
McCormick			x						x	x	
Noncon Sci Tech Inf			x								
Prog Br Univ Libs				x	x				x		
Sci Inf Not							x		x	x	
Da Proc Lib Inf									x		
(-4.5- Applications Nonnumerical											
Ann Rev Inf Sci			x	x	x				x	x	
Balz		x	x						x	x	
Comp Appl			x			x	x	x		x	
Comp Hum										x	
Cur Res Sci Doc		x	x						x	x	x
Da Proc Ed			x						x	x	x
Doc Abst	x		x				x		x	x	x
Hays		x	x	x						x	
Info Ret Let			x		x	x				x	
Neeland			x	x	x				x	x	
Optical Info Proc			x								x
Prog Learn			x							x	
Res Ed		x							x	x	
Stevens									x	x	
Swanson			x	x	x	x	x	x	x	x	
Walkowicz		x	x	x		x				x	
Zell			x		x				x	x	

Appendix 3

INVENTORY OF AVAILABLE DATA BASES

INTRODUCTION

This survey is based, in part, on information compiled in Part 3 of the Final Report on *Mechanized Information Services in the University Library* (NSF Grant GN-503), December 15, 1967, supplemented by data on other data bases available since then. The listing here emphasizes reference data bases and does not claim to be exhaustive even in that coverage; however, it is indicative of the growing variety and number of magnetic tape files in existence, of a type which might be utilized in a Center for Information Services in the University Library. It reflects, for the most part, projects undertaken on a large national scale, or to serve the needs of particular organizations. A National Science Foundation publication, *Nonconventional Scientific and Technical Information Systems in Current Use*, No. 4, December 1966, contains an additional listing of more than one hundred computer-based information retrieval systems which utilize reference data bases. In almost all cases, the primary storage medium is magnetic tape.

There are also increasingly large numbers of machine-readable files, many of them available at nominal charge, being created by individuals or by small groups in industrial organizations, or within university departments. A number of these (emphasizing text data bases) are noted in compilations such as *Literary Works in Machine Readable Form,*[1] and *Computerized Research in the Humanities: A*

---

[1] Carlson, Gary, *Literary Works in Machine Readable Form,* by Dr. Gary Carlson, Director, Computer Research Center, Brigham Young University, Provo, Utah. July 1965. (This list is updated in the January 1967 issue of *Computer and the Humanities*.)

Survey.[2] The Council on Social Science Data Archives has published a brochure, *Social Science Data Archives in the United States, 1967,*[3] which lists and describes files covering a wide spectrum of subject matter (emphasizing numerical data bases), many of which are available from sponsoring institutions.

A commercial publication, *Directory of Computerized Information in Science and Technology,* 1967,[4] was published in Spring 1968. Other directories, covering computerized information in Medicine, the Humanities, and the Social Sciences are planned. These will be published as part of an "International Information Network Series" and will serve to bring the existence of many more machine readable files to current awareness.

In the following pages, the information assembled about each tape file, where possible, is:

1. Address and Director of the creating agency.
2. A brief description of its nature and contents.
3. File characteristics and size
4. Availability.
5. References to further documentation.

In some cases, it was impossible to obtain all of this data while for other files, detailed information was readily available.

Several overall observations about data bases can be made from an examination of this listing:

Many of the files were created for specific purposes and were tailored to meet the special needs of the parent organization. Therefore, they have been designed without regard to a capability for easy readability for other purposes. Documentation in such cases is frequently poor and incomplete, and cooperation is apt to be uncertain or unenthusiastic.

On the other hand, some organizations (both profit as well as nonprofit) are in the business of maintaining data bases and providing a variety of services—searching, preparing reports, copying files, and producing extracts or subfiles. These data bases are generally, but not always, easy to read and well documented, and are usually furnished with computer programs to read, search, and otherwise process the data involved.

The majority of organizations surveyed initially used IBM equipment, particularly 1401/1410 systems. Most, if not all of these, have converted to 360 systems. The use of tapes is still dominant, the trend to greater use of disks being, at the moment, quite small.

From a file-management point of view, most of the existing data bases have

[2] Bowles, Edmund A., "Computerized Research in the Humanities: A Survey." ACLS Newsletter Special Supplement (June 1968) 1-49.

[3] "Social Science Data Archives in the United States, 1967." Council of Social Science Data Archives, New York, New York.

[4] *Directory of Computerized Information in Science and Technology Part 1, 1968.* New York, Science Associates/International.

simple, hierarchically arranged, field structures. Many have variable length records. Record formats (fixed or variable), from one file to another, are virtually unrelated. It is evident that translation or transliteration to a common format is nearly impossible, and custom programming a complete system for each data base is far too expensive. The maintenance and use of programs written by sponsoring organizations appears to be cumbersome and impractical (for example, there are 15 programs involved in the American Petroleum Institute system), and the incompatibility of software systems adds to the difficulty.

DEPARTMENT OF THE AIR FORCE
Legal Information Through Electronics (LITE)

Office of the Judge Advocate General/LITE (HQ USAF)
4700 Holly Street
Denver, Colorado 80216

Col. William E. McCarthy
Chief, LITE

Data: LITE is a total-text information storage and retrieval system developed by the Air Force Accounting and Finance Center in Denver, Colorado. The data base is unique in that it contains the total text of documents such as the United States Code, (1964 Ed.), Court of Military Appeals Decisions (CMR), and Armed Services Procurement Regulation (ASPR), rather than abstracts, citations and/or condensed scope notes. Existing LITE files have been classified into four groups: Statutes, Decisions, Regulations, and Other. The LITE system has been designed to retrieve documents containing words or phrases specified by the user and to give 3 types of computer printout: total-text printout (PRINT); citation printout, in which a published abstract can be printed out as part of a citation printout if desired, (CITE); key-word-in-context printout (KWIC). LITE now only has the most current documents in its data bases but in the future will have an historical file of all source documents including those that have been amended, repealed, or eliminated. Search and retrieval operations of the system are based two files: (1) the text file, (2) the vocabulary file. The latter contains all of the words used in retrieval, and their locations in lines of text processed. Techniques for a sophisticated system of computer indexing and for profile referral (selective dissemination of information) have also been developed.

Computer: IBM 1410
        RCA Spectra 70/45

Availability: The Department of the Air Force has authorized leasing of *LITE*

Data Bases and *LITE* Computer Programs to parties outside the Federal Government, including any person, firm, educational institution or other organization in the United States. The lessee may make the number of copies of the leased material specified under the terms of the lease. The lessee must furnish to LITE technical data developed through use of leased LITE property such as magnetic tapes, new data bases, programs etc. Two types of leases are offered: a lease for any purpose, including commercial use; or a lease for research only in which the lessee will be limited to using the reproduced LITE property for experimental, developmental or research purposes.

(LITE Data Bases and Programs are subject to continuing revision and update but leases will not include any such changes to leased LITE materials made by the Government subsequent to the execution of any LITE lease.)

The following pricing schedule was established and published in April 1969:

	Basic Charge	
Major Data Bases	*Research*	*Unrestricted*
U.S. Code, 1964 Edition, through Supplement III.	$1,581.65	$ 6,326.61
Published Compt.-Gen. Decisions, Volumes 1–46.	$4,788.52	$19,154.11
Unpublished Compt.-Gen. Decisions, June 1955–June 1967.	$4,290.58	$16,962.27
Court of Military Appeals, Court Martial Reports Vol. 1–38.	$1,572.64	$ 6,290.56
Boards of Review, Court Martial Reports, Vol. 1–37.	$2,656.96	$10,627.85
International Law Agreements (published)	$ 691.00	$ 2,763.99
International Law Agreements (unpublished)	$ 681.44	$ 2,753.76

All prices are subject to change without notice.

References
1. Davis, Richard P., "The LITE System." *The United States Air Force JAG Law Review*, V. 8, No. 6 (November-December 1966).
2. Dietemann, Donald C., "Using LITE for Research Purposes." *The United States AIR Force JAG Law Review*, V. 8, No. 6 (November-December 1966).
3. *LITE Newsletter,* V. 2, No. 3, March 1969.
4. *LITE Newsletter*, V. 2, No. 4, April 1969.

AMERICAN BIBLIOGRAPHICAL CENTER
HISTORICAL ABSTRACTS

American Bibliographical Center
800, Micheltorena Avenue
Santa Barbara, California 93103

Director: Dr. Eric Boehm

Data: ABC has utilized a computer in the production of yearly indexes to the quarterly abstract journals *America: History and Life*, and *Historical Abstracts*, and to cumulate the entries from five separate annual indexes to produce a five-year index (1960-64) to *Historical Abstracts*. More than 500 periodicals are surveyed for *America: History and Life*, which covers U.S. and Canadian history from prehistoric times to the present. Approximately 1,000 periodicals are surveyed for *Historical Abstracts*, which includes articles related to the history and social sciences of the world during the period 1775-1945. Machine-readable index elements for each periodical are: personal names (author, biographic, autobiographic), multifaceted terms covering subject and geographic area, and chronology. Plans are in process for conversion of the abstracts themselves and the bibliographic references to machineable form (*America: History and Life*, in 1968, and *Historical Abstracts* in 1969).

File characteristics and size: Files are presently on punched cards; conversion to magnetic tape was planned for early 1968. Approximately 35,000 abstracts are indexed, with an average addition of 3,500 abstracts per year.

Computer: IBM 1410. Conversion to a 360/50 was planned for early 1968.

References:
1. *Historical Abstracts*, V. 13, No. 1 (March 1967).
2. *America: History and Life*, V. 2, No. 4 (July 1966), Annual Index.

AMERICAN CHEMICAL SOCIETY
JOURNAL OF CHEMICAL DOCUMENTATION

American Chemical Society
Publications Department
1155 Sixteenth : Street, N.W.
Washington, D.C. 20036

Director of Publications Research: Joseph H. Kuney

Data: Computer-aided typesetting methods (utilizing the Photon 200) are used in the production of the *Journal of Chemical Documentation*. The complete text of the journal is in machine-readable form, with special codes added to control size and spacing of characters, and article formatting. The first issue to be produced in this manner was that of February 1966.

Computer: IBM 360/30. First used IBM 1460.

Availability of tape files: The ACS is currently setting four journals in this manner. This is significant not only for publishing purposes, but also because a by product is the encoding of scientific literature in machine-readable form at the time of original publication.

References
1. Kuney, J. H., Lazorchak, B. G., and Walcavich, S. W., "Computer-Aided typesetting for the *Journal of Chemical Documentation.*" *Journal of Chemical Documentation*, V. 6, No. 1 (February 1966).
2. Information in a letter from Joseph H. Kuney, Director of Publications Research, American Chemical Society, December 26, 1968.

AMERICAN GEOLOGICAL INSTITUTE
GEOLOGICAL SOCIETY OF AMERICA
BIBLIOGRAPHY AND INDEX OF GEOLOGY

American Geological Institute   Geological Society of America
1444 N Street NW   231 East 46th Street
Washington, D.C. 20005   New York, N.Y. 10017

Manager, GSA Bibliography Project: Joel J. Lloyd

Data: The computer-based Bibliography and Index of Geology is published by the Geological Society of America, in cooperation with the American Geological Institute.

Beginning with the January 1967 issue, the entire content of the journal is contained on magnetic tape. The data items included for each entry are: accession number (a 3-part number indicating 1) field of interest or category, 2) volume and year, 3) unique number of announcement); title (if in vernacular, English title is given); authors; complete bibliographic information, the UDC number, and an abstract (average of approximately 100 words). Also on tape is the subject index, consisting of three-level indexing term sets following the system devised and used by the U.S. Geological Survey. Each set of terms is followed by the abstract numbers of the relevant items.

File characteristics: The computer processing of the material follows the system developed and programmed by the U.S. Geological Survey for its *Abstracts of North American Geology*, and the AGI-GSA and USGS systems are compatible.

Computer: The original programs were written for an IBM 1410, and are presently run on a 360 in emulated mode.

Availability of tape files: A tape service is planned in addition to the hard copy issues of the bibliography. However, the existing tapes contain the typographic codes and other symbols utilized in the printing process. A cleaned version of the tapes was planned for early in 1969. A price has not yet been established. In addition, it is possible that the unedited tapes will be released to a few users for research purposes.

References
1. Juhasz, S., Editor. MAMMAX (Machine Made and Machine Aided Index) NFSAIS (National Federation of Science Abstracting and Indexing Services) Annual Meeting, Philadelphia, March 1967. San Antonio, Texas, Applied Mechanics Reviews (AMR Report no. 45), pp. 9-15.
2. Annex to Bibliography, Documentation, Terminology, Vol. VIII no. 1 1968. "United States of America National Bibliographical Services and Related Activities in 1966" by Helen Dudenbostel Jones) p. 14.

AMERICAN INSTITUTE OF PHYSICS
AIP BIBLIOGRAPHIC SEARCH TAPES

American Institute of Physics
Information Division
335 East 45th Street
New York, NY 10017

Enquiries to: Dr. Rita G. Lerner.

Data: The tapes will consist of the input records to the AIP information store (each tape is expected to contain an average of 2000 journal article records). The tapes are used in the production of *Physics Abstracts*.

File Characteristics: See "Characteristics and Format of AIP Bibliographic Tapes" by Kenneth D. Carroll. Presented at the Association of Scientific Information Dissemination Centers (ASIDIC) meeting, October 22-23, 1969, Midland, Michigan.

Computers: IBM 360/40 and 360/65 (for compiling the tapes). An RCA Spectra-70 and Videocomp 820 photocomposer are being used for printing selected items from these tapes by computer-based photocomposition.

Availability of tape files: During the period January-June, 1970, the tapes will be supplied to selected organizations for field testing—national laboratories, university information centers, and industrial corporate information centers, in a variety of programs, and operating on several types of hardware. Close liaison with these pilot tape users will be maintained so that the bibliographic tapes offered the physics community as the first production output of the National Information System for Physics might be as complete and as close to optimum format as possible. The tapes are scheduled to be offered to the community on a production basis as of July 1970.

References
1. *A.I.P. Information Program Newsletter.* See especially issues of April 1969 and November 1969.
2. "Characteristics and Format of A.I.P. Bibliographic Tapes," Kenneth D. Carroll. Presented at the Association of Scientific Information Dissemination Centers (ASIDIC) meeting, October 22-23, 1969, Midland, Michigan.
3. *Plans for a National Physics Information System*, Franz L. Apt, and Arthur Herschmann. New York: American Institute of Physics, March 1968.

AMERICAN PETROLEUM INSTITUTE

American Petroleum Institute
Division of Refining
Central Abstracting and Indexing Service
555 Madison Avenue
New York, New York 10022

Manager: Mr. Everette H. Brenner

Data: The API Central Abstracting and Indexing service receives 150 technical journals, various government reports, technical meeting preprints, and patent publications of ten different countries. Articles and patents relevant to refining or petro-chemicals are selected to appear (in abstract form) in the weekly journal, *Petroleum Abstracts*. In addition, the citations plus index terms serve as input for the following computer-produced items:

1. Printed *Alphabetic Subject Index* to *Petroleum Abstracts*. Issued monthly, cumulative every six months.
2. *Dual Dictionary* (alphabetic listing of subject terms, with the abstract numbers of documents indexed under each term). Issued every four months, cumulative for each year.
3. Reels of magnetic tape containing information about all abstracted documents. Separate files are issued for "literature" and patents.

File characteristics and size: Tape records include complete bibliographic citations, plus descriptors (average 20-25 per document). Descriptors are in alphabetic form, in fixed fields of 36 characters. "Links" serve to unite sets of two or more descriptors, and "roles" are used to cover such functions as "agent," "catalyst," "product," "substance being analyzed," etc.

In 1967 files contained more than 50,000 literature citations (with some 1,300 additions per month), and approximately 40,000 patent references (1,000 additions per month).

Computer: IBM 1401, 7090. (There are 15 computer programs involved in the API system: 10 for the 1401, and 5 for the 7090.) Search programs for the Master file involve the 1401.

Availability of tape files: Tapes are available on a subscription basis, and are issued every four months, with eight-month and annual cumulations. In addition to the tape files, a subscription includes: (1) *Petroleum Abstracts* (weekly), (2) *Alphabetic Subject Index* (monthly), (3) *Dual Dictionary* (quarterly), and (4) sets of Abstract cards. Search programs are provided for the 1401 or the 7090. Basic subscription rate depends on the type of company or institution and its financial assets. For example, charges to a non-petroleum company with assets of less than $100 million would be $2,000 per year.

References
1. Humphrey, Allen J., *API Information Retrieval System, Computer Manual.* New York, American Petroleum Institute, 1966.
2. Mulvihill, J. G., and Brenner, E. H., "Faceted Organization of a Thesaurus Vocabulary." American Documentation Institute, Annual Meeting. Proceedings, V. 3. *Progress in Information Science and Technology.* Santa Monica, California, 1966.

AMERICAN PSYCHOLOGICAL ASSOCIATION
PSYCHOLOGICAL ABSTRACTS

American Psychological Association
1200 Seventeenth Street, N.W.
Washington, D.C. 20036

Associate Director, *Psychological Abstracts*, William S. Learmonth

Data: The contents of the printed volumes of *P.A.* are available on tape from Jan. 1967. *P.A.* now covers some 850 journals and is reviewing a further 600 with a view to inclusion.

File Characteristics and Size: The tapes were created on a PDP-1 computer. Programs are being written to make the tapes IBM 360 compatible. The file size is approximately 55,000 records, increasing at about 20,000 per year.

Availability of the tape files: The establishment of a pricing schedule is still under consideration, but it is estimated that it will be in the region of $3000 per year at the present rate of input.

References
1. Information accompanying a questionnaire from Robert M. Sasmor (Sept. 1969).
2. Information in a letter from William S. Learmonth, Feb. 19, 1970.

AMERICAN SOCIETY FOR METALS

American Society for Metals
ASM Documentation Service
Metals Park, Ohio 44073

Director: Norman E. Cottrell
Associate Director: Mrs. Marjorie Hyslop

Data: The ASM Documentation and Information Retrieval Service collects and indexes literature in the following areas: general metallurgy; production and fabrication; properties; internal structures, transformations, and reactions; products, parts, and equipment; materials; and allied fields in chemistry, physics, applied mechanics, atomic energy and nuclear reactor technology. Types of literature included are: journals and serials, books and symposia, reports, patents, preprints of technical articles, translations, and industrial publications.

Input to computer consists of complete bibliographic citations, plus descriptors. The index terms are taken from the "Thesaurus of Metallurgical Terms," which is compatible in terminology and format with the EJC Thesaurus. The magnetic tape files created are used in the production of subject and author indexes to the monthly abstract journal *Review of Metal Literature*, and for "current awareness" retrieval requests (citation print-outs).

File characteristics and size: Two files are involved in the system: one is organized sequentially, and the other is an inverted subject record. Files retrospective to 1962 (approximately 100,000 citations) are being converted to the Mark II system, which is currently in use. Approximately 30,000 citations are added per year.

Computer: IBM 1401 (12k). Transition was planned to a 360/30 in Fall of 1967.

Availability of tape files: At present, tapes containing the Index files are available to ASM "Research Associate" organizations. Rates are $4,000.00 to $8,000.00 per year. Subscription includes programs necessary for retrieval, consulting on retrieval problems, and sets of printed abstracts on cards. (In addition to providing financial support, the participating companies supply user feedback information.)

References
1. Hyslop, Marjorie R., "What is Metallurgy Today?" *Metals Review*, V. 36 (November 1963).
2. American Society for Metals, Documentation Service. *Mark II Information Retrieval System* (brochure). Metals Park, Ohio, 1966.
3. Hyslop, Marjorie R., "The ASM Information Retrieval System: After Cranfield." *Journal of Documentation*, V. 21, (March 1965).

APPLIED MECHANICS REVIEW

Applied Mechanics Review
Southwest Research Institute
8500 Culebra Road
San Antonio, Texas

Director: Mr. Stephen Juhasz

Data: The WADEX (Word and Author Index) system was used to produce indexes to two volumes of *Applied Mechanics Review*. (1962-1963). This is a KWOC (Key-Word-out-of-Context) type index, and lists designators (either a word in the title, or an author's name) in alphabetic order, followed by the citations in which each word appears. Citations include names of all authors, full title, and reference (year, month, and review number) to an AMR issue.

Computer: IBM 1401 (12k).

Programs: There are fourteen computer programs involved in the system: eleven special programs prepared specifically for the WADEX, plus one also used for the AMR 1963 Subject Index, plus two IBM "canned" programs.

Reference
1.   *WADEX Word and Author Index: Description and program documentation.* Modified. Applied Mechanics Review, 1966 (AMR Rep. No. 38).

ASPEN SYSTEMS CORPORATION

Aspen Systems Corporation
The Webster Hall
4415 Fifth Avenue
Pittsburgh, Pa. 15213.

Director: John F. Horty

Data: Aspen's *System 50* contains the laws (i.e. constitution and statutes) of all 50 states in full text form; the original file comprised over 200 million words of text, and will be updated "as state legislatures enact new laws."

File Characteristics: Tape is 9-channel, 800 b.p.i., with no leader or trailer labels; 85 byte logical records in 1615 byte blocks. The data is encoded in lower as well as upper case.

Computer: IBM 360/40.

Availability of tape files: Aspen emphasizes its wide range of services rather than the sale of tapes, though these are available for purchase (for example, the California constitution and statutes file costs approximately $212,000.)

References
1.   Aspen Systems Corp. *Searching Law by Computer* (brochure).
2.   *Aspen Systems Magazine*, V. 1 No. 2, 1969.
3.   Information in a letter from Mr. J. Sperling Martin, Assistant Director, Computer R. & D., Aspen Systems Corp., Dec 12, 1969.

ATOMIC ENERGY COMMISSION
ATOMIC AND MOLECULAR PROCESSES INFORMATION CENTER

Atomic Energy Commission
Atomic and Molecular Processes Information Center
Oak Ridge National Laboratory
Oak Ridge, Tennessee 37831

Director: C. F. Barrett

Data: Data on particle physics, atomic and molecular structure, and transport phenomena in gases are collected and evaluated by the Center. The original and the screened data are on magnetic tape, and programming for computer searching is in process. The Center is presently operating from punched cards.

Availability of service: The Center's services (custom literature searches, compilations of data, or reprints of articles or reports) are available without charge to universities and research institutes as well as to government agencies.

Note: AEC-related specialized information centers are in operation throughout the United States. Many of them are in the process of creating machine-readable files in their respective subject areas.

Reference
1.   U.S. Atomic Energy Commission, Division of Technical Information. *Specialized Information and Data Centers for Nuclear Science and Technology* (brochure). Washington, D.C., 1965.

ATOMIC ENERGY COMMISSION
NUCLEAR SCIENCE ABSTRACTS

Atomic Energy Commission
Division of Technical Information Extension
Post Office Box 62
Oak Ridge, Tennessee 37830

Chief, Computer Operations: Fred E. Marsh, Jr.

Data: The Division of Technical Information Extension (DTIE) inputs descriptive cataloging information for generation of magnetic tape files used in production of *Nuclear Science Abstracts*, and for SDI programs. Input consists of bibliographic citations, plus such items as security classification, price, availability, distribution, contract number, etc. Basis of subject indexing is the DTIE Authority List of Field/Group Terminology, adapted from the COSATI Subject Category List. Materials handled include: reports and conference papers, journal literature and books, patents, translations, non-AEC unnumbered theses, and EML's (Engineering Materials Lists). Two main files are computer produced:

1.   Entry file, generated twice per month. Each file contains entries in the corresponding issue of *Nuclear Science Abstracts*, plus additional information which is not published, e.g., COSATI Field/Group words and codes. Entries are in order by *NSA* abstract number.

2.   Selector file, a linear file containing the selectors (keywords and various "additional terms") assigned to items within an issue of *NSA*. The file is ordered by abstract number, then by "split." Split indicators serve as "links" in that they are assigned to selectors which logically relate to each other.

File characteristics and size: Files are written in BCD notation, on 7-channel tapes at 556 bits per inch density. Records are variable length, with a maximum of 2004 characters. Input is approximately 40,000,000 characters per year. DTIE is in process of defining formats for files using 120-character set.

Computer: IBM 360/20 for input conversion; IBM 7090 for processing

Availability of tape files: Tapes have been made available to other users, among them Argonne National Laboratories and Lawrence Radiation Laboratory. Subscription information may be obtained from

Mr. Edward J. Brunenkant, Director
Division of Technical Information
U.S. Atomic Energy Commission
Washington, D.C. 20545

Reference
1.   Atomic Energy Commission, Division of Technical Information. *Descriptive Cataloging Guide*. Oak Ridge, Tennessee, December 1968 (TID-4577, Rev. 3).

BIOSCIENCES INFORMATION SERVICE

Biosciences Information Service, of Biological Abstracts
3815 Walnut Street
Philadelphia, Pennsylvania 19104

Director: Phyllis V. Parkins
Assistant Director for Systems Development: Miss Louise Schultz

Data: BIOSIS creates four tape files, which are used in the production of indexes to Biological Abstracts. These indexes are:

1. AUTHOR index, begun in 1959, and containing authors names, and volume and issue numbers.

2. BASIC (Biological Abstracts Subjects in Context), begun in 1959, containing permuted title fragments and abstract numbers.

3. CROSS (Computerized Rearrangement of Special Subjects) begun in 1963, containing five-digit numeric CROSS index codes, and abstract, volume, and issue number.

4. BIOSYSTEMATIC, dating from 1964, containing abstract number, BIOSYSTEMATIC code number and its alpha equivalent, and CROSS code number and its alpha equivalent.

5. BA PREVIEWS, a new service in 1969, which makes available the 18,000 plus references published monthly in *Biological Abstracts* and *BioResearch Index*—approximately one month in advance of the printed versions. File contains *BA* and Bio-Research *Index* volume numbers; abstract or reference number, primary author, primary journal reference, code for subject headings in the CROSS and BIOSYSTEMATIC Indexes.

File characteristics and size: Records are on 7-channel tape, recorded at 556 bits per inch density. Approximately 700,000 items (abstracts) are covered, for each of which there are an average of seven BASIC records and one AUTHOR record. For over 200,000 of those items there is also an average of five CROSS records and a BIOSYSTEMATIC record.

Further characteristics are: (1) AUTHOR file: all records 60 characters, 6 tape reels as of 1967; (2) BASIC file: 90-character records, 50 reels; (3) CROSS file: 18-character records, 7 reels; (4) BIOSYSTEMATIC file: 60-character records, 3 tape reels; (5) BA PREVIEWS file: tapes are 9-channel, 800 b.p.i., variable length, variable block.

Computer: IBM 1440. Conversion is planned to 360/30.

References
1. Parkins, Phyllis V., *Bioscience Information Service of Biological Abstracts.* 1965 (unpublished typescript).

2. *Biological Abstracts, 49* (15) 1 Aug 1968

3. *Biological Abstracts, 50* (17) 1 Sept 1969

BONNEVILLE POWER ADMINISTRATION

U.S. Department of the Interior
Bonneville Power Administration
Portland 8, Oregon

System Engineer: Val Lava

Data: BPA scans a wide segment of the scientific literature for articles relating to electrical engineering. Abstracts are taken from the original articles, or from abstract services such as Electrical Engineering Abstracts, Engineering Index, Physics Abstracts etc. Input to computer consists of bibliographic information, security classification of the document, the abstracts, and descriptors. Auto-indexing is used: that is, descriptors are appended to the tape records directly from the abstracts themselves. For SDI programs, multiple keywords are extracted if they correspond to phrases appearing in current user profiles. This is accomplished by use of a dictionary tape generated from the profiles. For files used for retrospective searching, single keywording is done (automatically) of all words, except those listed on an exclusion tape, which appear in an abstract.

File characteristics and size: Tape is 7-channel, recorded at 556 bits per inch density. File consists of approximately 9000 abstracts, with an addition of some 125 per week.

Computer: IBM 1401 (8k).

Reference
1.   Peterson, Norman D., *Selective Dissemination of Information* (unpublished typescript), Portland, Oregon; Bonneville Power Administration.

R. R. BOWKER COMPANY

R. R. Bowker Company
1180 Avenue of the Americas
New York, New York 10036

Mr. John N. Berry, III, Book Editorial Department

Data: Bowker has begun automating production of several of its bibliographic publications, including the comprehensive *American Book Publishing Record*. Materials in machine readable form (either on punched cards, punched paper tape or magnetic tape) include *Forthcoming Books, Publisher's Weekly, Paperbound Books in Print, Subject Guide to Books in Print, Children's Books for Schools and Libraries*, etc. In addition, *Ulrich's International Periodicals Directory* and the *American Book Trade Directory* are in the process of being converted to machineable form.

Computer: IBM 1460, Honeywell 200.

Availability of tape files: Bowker's basic policy is to make their bibliographic information available in machine readable form, including magnetic tape, "at an attractive price."

BRITISH NATIONAL BIBLIOGRAPHY

The Council of the British National Bibliography
The British Museum
London, W.C.1

Head of Research and Development: R. E. Coward

Data: The British National Bibliography has undertaken a project similar to and compatible with the Library of Congress MARC (Machine Readable Catalog). The (British) Office of Scientific and Technical Information of the Department of Education and Science has made the project possible through a grant to BNB for producing full bibliographic records of the current output of British publishers. The system analysis and programming will be carried out under a sub-contractual arrangement with a British firm and close cooperation with the LC/MARC project is expected. The system will also be designed to print a BNB Index, in coded standard book number sequence, and a Title Index in alphabetical sequence of all BNB records added to the catalog each week.

File Characteristics. The BNB MARC record will follow the agreed U.S. MARC II file structure with appropriate additions for British usage.

Availability: Arrangements have been made for a number of British libraries to use BNB tapes on an experimental basis. Regular exchange of magnetic tape files between BNB and LC will mean that users in both countries will have access to catalog records. Local institutions could take these tapes, add local data and use them in their own systems.

References
1. "Development of Computer-based Central Cataloging," ASLIB Proceedings, V. 19, No. 11 (November 1967).
2. "Machine-Readable Catalog Record for BNB," *LC Information Bulletin.* V. 27, No. 17, April 24, 1968), p. 229.
3. Coward, R. E., "The United Kingdom MARC Record Service." In *Organization and Handling of Bibliographic Records by* Computer, Edited by N. S. M. Cox and M. W. Grose. Oriel Press, 1967.

BRO-DART, INC.

Bro-Dart, Inc.
Box 923
1609 Memorial Avenue
Williamsport, Pa. 17701
Phone: (717) 326-2461

Vice-President: Stacey Division: Brett Butler

Data: Computer files are used at Bro-Dart for all catalog services and the

Books-Coming-Into-Print Program, and all inventory control, book ordering, invoicing and related operations within the company.

File Characteristics and size:

(1) *Master title file*: Over 300,000 records of basic book acquisition data containing a unique Bro-Dart book number indicating publisher and binding as well as giving unique identification.

(2) *Books-Coming-Into-Print*: A computer-based selection and acquisition file containing approximately 16,000 titles with special classification and description required to fit customers profile.

(3) *Book Catalog Files*: Complete catalog information is contained in the specific format used for Bro-Dart Book Catalog production. The format was developed prior to the Library of Congress MARC II format but is expected to be compatible with MARC II tapes when they are made available. A Register type Book Catalog is used with full depth cataloging in the Register entries. Three indexes, arranged by author, title, and subject, contain author, title, year of publication, call number, and unique register code number for each book.

Availability: The major files in use are not made available directly to users as data bases:

Reference
1.   Information in a letter from Brett Butler, Vice-President, Stacey Division, Bro-Dart Inc, Feb. 1969

BUREAU OF THE CENSUS

U.S. Department of Commerce
Bureau of the Census
Washington, D.C. 20233

Director: George Hay Brown
Chief, Central Users' Services; Marshall L. Turner, Jr.

Data: The Bureau has available a wide variety of magnetic tape files, which are byproducts of the work of processing Census data for publication. These files are

> computer tapes containing summary statistical information, which do not reveal confidential information regarding individuals, establishments or firms. In addition, sample sets of individual records from which names and other identifying information have been removed may also be purchased. Examples of these are the One-in-a-Thousand and the One-in-Ten-Thousand samples of the Censuses of Population and Housing.

Tape files cover such subjects as population, housing, agriculture, business, foreign trade, etc. Examples are:

1. County Business Patterns, 1962, 1964, 1965, 1966. Includes data on first-quarter employment, taxable payroll, employment-size class of reporting unit by county and industry, etc. Cost for IBM tapes is from $270.00 to $690.00 per year, depending on SIC (Standard Industrial Classification) level.

2. County and City Data Book, 1967 Edition. Contains information on agriculture, population, housing, retail and service trades, manufacturing, bank deposits, births, deaths, marriages, local governments, etc.; by counties, standard metropolitan statistical areas, and cities over 25,000 population.

3. U.S. Exports of Domestic and Foreign Merchandise—Monthly, 1967. Approximately three tape reels are produced each month. Cost is $140.00 per month if blank tapes are provided by the subscriber, or $230.00 if the Bureau furnishes tapes.

4. U.S. Imports of Merchandise for Consumption and General Imports of Merchandise—Monthly, 1967. Approximately 1 reel per month. Cost is $150.00 if tapes are furnished by the subscriber.

5. 1964 Census of Agriculture County Summary Data. Contains data on farms by size, type, and economic class; value of farm products sold, by source; farm operators by tenure, color, age, residence and off-farm work; persons in farm-operator households by age, sex, and year of school completed, etc. Cost is $60.00 per State, plus $35.00 for each tape reel provided. The Census of 1970 is the first to be available in its entirety on magnetic tapes (as well as continuing to appear in book form).

Computer: Most tape files were prepared for use on the UNIVAC 1105 or 1107 computers, with a few prepared for the IBM 1401. The Bureau will convert tapes from one of these types to the other (at additional cost to the purchaser).

Availability of tape files: In addition to those listed above, several other files are available for purchase. The cost for the 1970 summary tapes, about 1500 reels, is estimated at $120,000– $140,000.

References
1. U.S. Department of Commerce. Bureau of the Census. *Catalog*, January-September 1967.
2. U.S. Dept. of Commerce. Bureau of the Census. *1970 Census Summary Tape User Memoranda*. 1– , 1968–   .
3. U.S. Dept of Commerce, Bureau of the Census. *Data Access Descriptions*. 1– , 1967–   .
4. U.S. Dept. of Commerce. Bureau of the Census. *Small Area Data notes*, 1– , 1966–   .
5. U.S. Dept. of Commerce. Bureau of the Census, *1970 Census User Guide*. 2nd Draft (April 1969)

CHEMICAL ABSTRACTS SERVICE

Chemical Abstracts Service
2540 Olentangy River Road
Columbus, Ohio

Director: Dale B. Baker
Manager, Subscriber Information Service: Mr. Elden G. Johnson

Data: Chemical Abstracts Service is shifting from an indexing-publishing operation to a computer-based information system, with output possible in the form of printed pages (publications), microfilm, or computer searchable magnetic tapes. The publication of *Chemical Abstracts* itself is not yet automated, but plans were in progress for it to be produced by computer-driven photon by 1969. The following tape files are involved in the production of indexes to *CA*:

1. Those generated in the production of *Chemical Titles*. These files, dating from 1962, are used to produce a KWIC type index containing, in 1967, over 500,000 titles. Retrieval is possible by (1) words appearing in the title, (2) author names, and (3) journal Coden.

2. CBAC (*Chemical and Biological Activities*) tapes. Dating from 1964, and containing over 21,000 titles plus abstracts, CBAC files supply information on: (1) Action of organic compounds on animal and plant systems, (2) Action of animal and plant systems on organic compounds, (3) *In-vitro* reactions of organic compounds of biochemical interest. Search questions for these tapes may include phrases, words (words appearing in article titles and digests), fragments of words, author's names, journal name, and chemical compound registry numbers. Answers to such questions may be journal references, titles of papers, KWIC indexes, author indexes, molecular formula indexes, or any combination of these forms.

3. POST (*Polymer Science and Technology*) tapes. These serve as an index to literature concerned with the chemistry, chemical engineering, and technology of polymers. Two files are involved: (1) POST-P, a guide to the patent literature, and (2) POST-J, a guide to the journal and report literature. Tapes include full bibliographic information, chemical compound registry number, and a brief digest of the literature involved.

4. Chemical Compound Registry: "That portion of the Chemical Abstracts Service computer based system which identifies and records chemical compounds and their associated data." This system registers two-dimensional drawings representing com-

pounds, and searches can be made for compounds containing the same structure, no matter how displayed. The system at present has over 500,000 compounds, with a capacity of five million. Each structure is given a registry number, which appears in other CAS files, as applicable, and serves to link the structural information with bibliographic data.

Computer: Tapes are compatible with IBM 1410 and 360 computer systems.

Availability of tape files: Tapes are available on a subscription basis from ACS, as follows:

1. CT tapes, issued every two weeks. Cost: $1,500 to $2,200 per year. This includes fully documented search programs, and the corresponding printed issues of *Chemical Titles*.

2. CBAC tapes, issued every two weeks. Cost: $1,500 to $2,200 per year. Includes search programs, plus the corresponding issues of *Chemical and Biological Activities.*

3. POST tapes, issued weekly, alternating weekly between POST-P and POST-J. Cost: POST-P, $1,500 per year. Cost: POST-J, $1,700 per year. Cost includes search programs plus the corresponding issues of *Polymer Science and Technology*.

References

1. Tate, Fred A., "Progress Toward a Computer-Based Chemical Information System." *Chemical and Engineering News*, V. 45, January 23, 1967.

2. Davenport, William C., and Dickman, John T., "Computer-Based Composition at Chemical Abstracts Service." *Journal of Chemical Documentation*, V. 6, No. 4, November 1966.

3. Zabriskie, Kenneth H., Jr., "5-Year plan for a Computer-Based Chemical Information System at the Chemical Abstracts Service *Percolator*, V. 40 (July 1965).

4. Tate, F. A., et al, "Installation and Operation of a Registry for Chemical Compounds." *Journal of Chemical Documentation*, V. 5, No. 4 (November 1965).

5. Morgan, H. L., "The Generation of a Unique Machine Description for Chemical Structures—A Technique Developed at Chemical Abstracts Service." *Journal of Chemical Documentation*, V. 5, No. 2 (May 1965).

CLEARINGHOUSE FOR FEDERAL SCIENTIFIC AND TECHNICAL INFORMATION

Clearinghouse for Federal Scientific and Technical Information
5825 Port Royal Road
Springfield, Virginia 22151

Director: Hubert E. Sauter
Assistant Director, Systems: Peter F. Urbach

Data: The Clearinghouse accessions unclassified Government-sponsored technical documents, including those produced by Department of Defense R and D Laboratories and contractors. Magnetic tape files are available of the monthly abstract journal, *U.S. Government Research and Development Reports.* Tape records include, in addition to complete bibliographic information, accession number, COSATI fields, price, acronyms and report numbers, contract numbers, project numbers, task numbers, notes, descriptors, identifiers, abstract, and annotated title.

File characteristics and size: Files are written in a variable record format, with maximum block size of 3,000 characters (average record length, 1,200-1,500 characters). Descriptors are in variable length fields, in English. Tape is 9-track, recorded at 800 bits per inch density. Approximately 25,000 abstracts are added yearly.

Computer: UNIVAC 1107 until 1968. : At that time, the Clearinghouse was to convert to an IBM System 360.

Availability of tape files: Reports in the form of magnetic computer tapes are being sold by CSFTI for $75.00 a reel unless otherwise specified. The *U.S. Government Research and Development Reports* announces the availability of these reports on magnetic tape. Clearinghouse is closely watching the work of standard-setting organizations such as COSATI, and will comply with standards generally adopted for coding of bibliographic information.

References
1. Fry, Bernard M., "The U.S. Clearinghouse for Federal Scientific and Technical Information." *Percolator*, V. 40 (July 1965).

2. Schon, D. A., "The Clearinghouse for Federal Scientific and Technical Information." *Toward a National Information System: Second Annual National Colloquium on Information Retrieval,* April 23-24, 1965, Philadelphia, Pennsylvania. Washington, D.C., Spartan Books, 1965.

3. "Clearinghouse Reports on Magnetic Tapes." *Scientific Information Notes*, Vol. 10, No. 1 (February-March 1968), p. 22.

4. U.S. Dept. of Commerce, National Bureau of Standards, *Specifications for Proposed Clearinghouse Magnetic Tape Distribution*, Nov. 1969.

COMPUTER SOFTWARE MANAGEMENT AND INFORMATION CENTER (COSMIC)

COSMIC
Computer Center (C-B)
University of Georgia
Athens, Georgia 30601

Operations Supervisor: Mrs. Shirley Parten

Data: COSMIC functions as a part of the NASA Technology Utilization Program in an effort to identify technological advances derived from the space program and make them available to business, industry, and education. As a by-product of aerospace research a wide range of well-documented, operational, computer programs have resulted and are now accessible to other sectors of the economy. The University of Georgia was awarded a contract from NASA in July of 1966 to operate COSMIC through the Marshall Space Flight Center Technology Utilization Office in conjunction with all other elements of NASA. Tapes, card decks, run instructions, program logic—complete software packages—can be supplied by COSMIC. Programs obtained from NASA supported activities are evaluated to determine their utility to other prospective users and available programs are announced periodically.

Computer: IBM 360/65 and IBM 7094 with two IBM 1401 systems serving as input/output peripheral units for the 7094. In addition, an IBM 1620 computer and EAI TR-20 analog computer are operated on an open-shop basis.

Availability: A membership fee for one fiscal year is $10.00 entitling the member to receive periodic catalogs containing abstracts of computer programs available to that date. Purchase of one or more programs during the year eliminates the membership fee for the following year. Requests may be made for computer program documentation on any program announced by NASA or COSMIC and source decks, provided in tape or deck form, may be requested. All requests for tape copy will be provided on tape reels furnished by COSMIC, however, program decks of over 2,000 cards will not be disseminated without special agreement with COSMIC.

Reference
1.   University of Georgia, Computer Software Management and Information Center. *COSMIC* (brochure). Athens, Georgia, July 1968.

EDUCATIONAL RESOURCES INFORMATION CENTER (ERIC)

U.S. Office of Education
Educational Research Information Center
400 Maryland Avenue, S. W.
Washington, D.C.

Director: Division of Information Technology and Dissemination:
        L. G. Burchinal

Data: ERIC is a nationwide project directed towards collecting, indexing, storing, and disseminating information on research in the field of education. In addition to a central coordinating agency, there are at present 21 ERIC "Clearinghouses," each one concerned with selection and processing of materials in a major subject area.

Each Clearinghouse is responsible for screening of materials, and for cataloging and indexing of documents selected. Bibliographic elements, abstracts, and index terms are uniformly recorded according to principles developed centrally. The Panel on Educational Terminology (PET) is responsible for development of the ERIC Thesaurus, which is used by all Clearinghouses as a subject authority list. Each Clearinghouse prepares punched paper tape copy of its cataloging for input to a contractor who is responsible for preparation of the monthly abstract and index journal, RIE (*Research in Education*). The paper tape is converted to magnetic tape form, to be used in the photo-composition of the journal, and for subject searching and the preparation of special indexes.

File characteristics and size: Tape records are variable length, blocked, with maximum block size of 7,000 characters. File size (1970) is approximately 35,000 entries, with an increase of 900 citations per month.

Computer: IBM 360

Availability of tape files: Magnetic tapes containing the full bibliographic record of ERIC documents will be made available to organizations wishing to develop applicable search and retrieval capabilities.

References
1. Marron, H., and Burchinal, L. G., "ERIC—A Novel Concept in Information Management." American Documentation Institute Annual Meeting, Proceedings, V. 4. *Levels of Interaction Between Man and Information*. New York, 1967. Washington, D.C., Thompson Book Company.
2. Burchinal, L. G., *ERIC . . . and the Need to Know*. Washington, D.C., Division of Research, Training and Dissemination, U.S. Office of Education. 1967?
3. Educational Resources Information Center. *Information Processing, Storage and Retrieval, System and Program Documentation, Part 1*, Aug. 1968.

ELECTRONIC PROPERTIES INFORMATION CENTER (EPIC)

Electronic Properties Information Center (EPIC)
Hughes Aircraft Company
Culver City, California

Data: EPIC has developed a data base on electronic properties of materials and has established methods for searching, acquiring, abstracting, and indexing literature pertinent to these files. Hughes Aircraft was awarded a contract in 1961 by the Air Force Materials Central, Aeronautical Systems Division, to build data bases on semiconductors and insulators. Systems procedures and facilities for storing, retrieving, compiling, and evaluating data have been prepared as well as procedures for publishing and disseminating bibliographies, property tables, data sheets, and summary reviews.

File Characteristics and size: The data is organized into two files containing: (1) selected bibliographic citations with abstracts from journals dating 1955 to the present; (2) semiconductors and insulators ordered by property within material. The Bibliographic Master Tape presently contains 32,000 citations and an additional 4,500 are acquired each year. Fixed length records in this file contain the following items: 1, blank; 2-6, accession number; 7, blank; 8, code to indicate whether bibliography (B) or abstract (A); 9-10, print line number; 11-125 bibliography and abstract information. The Material-Property Master Tape now has 500 different materials and 52 electronic properties. This tape is organized with the following items in each record: 1-67, material name (alphabetic); 68, transaction code (alphabetic); 69-73, material code (numeric); 74-75, property code; 76-80, accession number. There are nine 80 character records in a block.

Computer: Honeywell 200 Computer—Central Processor with 32,000 character core memory (6 bits per character, words defined with word-mark). Original program was designed for the IBM 1401 Autocoder and converted to Easycoder for the Honeywell 200 by Easytran.

Plans are now being formulated for use of a GE-635 system designed for general information retrieval at Hughes and not just for EPIC use. A time-sharing interface with 10 teletype terminals is also planned. (GE 635–2 Central processors with 128,000 word core memory (36 bits per word.)

Availability: The two magnetic tape files may be purchased for $3,500. Five programs, written in COBOL, are also available for $1,000 to: (1) update the bibliographic file (2) update the material-properties file (3) display citations (4) partial index (5) retrieve through requests specifying material and property, (up to 500 requests from 100 requestors). Charges per search request are between $70-$100. Present service is limited to Defense contractors.

Reference
1.   Booz, Allen Applied Research Inc., Bethesda, Md. *Mechanization Study of the Electronic Properties Information Center, Hughes Aircraft Company, Culver City, California.* Defense Documentation Center, Defense Supply Agency, September 1966, (AD 640 128).

ENGINEERING INDEX
COMPENDEX (COMPUTERIZED ENGINEERING INDEX)

Engineering Index, Inc.
345 East 47th Street
New York, New York 10017

Executive Director: Bill M. Woods

Data: Engineering Index utilizes machine methods in the production of monthly abstract bulletins and indexes. The annual data base used by Engineering Index has grown to 72,000 abstracts of articles from 3,500 journals and other publications in 25 languages. Two types of services have been offered since 1969 to make computer search tapes available, as follows.

CITE (Current Information Tapes for Engineers): The CITE program provides coverage of approximately 350 journals in the fields of plastics engineering and electrical engineering. Monthly tapes contain about 500 articles in plastics engineering and 1,000 articles in electrical engineering. Each reference includes deep indexing terms, subject headings, "notation of content" or title, and complete bibliographic citations. The package service includes: (1) Monthly master file tapes containing a Plastics or Electrical Engineering data base, (2) Engineering Index Thesaurus Tape, updated monthly, (3) Source deck program tape, (4) Abstracts on hard copy (microfiche) for Electrical Engineering subscribers or one year subscription to the Plastics Monthly for Plastics subscribers, (5) Conversion from 9 to 7 track tape, if required, and (6) One man-day of consulting time from Engineering Index engineers.

COMPENDEX: This service makes available in tape form more than 5,000 items published in the *Engineering Index Monthly* spanning all engineering disciplines. Each item on tape includes: subject heading, subheadings (if used), title, author, and citation, and the EI number. The tape will be in TEXT-PAC input format, 9 track, 800 BPI, written in EBCDIC.
Computer: The system was designed originally for the IBM 1401 computer but the programs can be operated in a compatibility mode on the IBM 360, Models 30 and 40, with at least four tape drives.
Availability: The subscription rate for the Plastics Master File complete package is $2,300 and for the Electrical/Electronics complete package, $2,800. Commercial organizations which sell information for profit will be charged $6,900 or $8,400 for the packages respectively. The cost of magnetic tapes is extra and additional consulting time will be billed at $125 a day plus expenses.

The January 1969 Engineering Index was the first COMPENDEX produced. The basic annual subscription rate for the monthly COMPENDEX tapes will be $6,000. They may be bought month to month for $500 per month. The costs of the tapes is extra. Tapes will be produced on or before printed version of the Engineering Index *Monthly*

References
1. *Engineering Index Information Services 1969.* (brochure). Marketing and Business Division Engineering Index, Inc., 345 East 47th Street, New York, N.Y. 10017.
2. "Engineering Index, Inc. to Market 'Compendex'." *Library Journal*, February 15, 1969, Vol. 94, No. 4, p. 706.
3. Honnecker, Walter and Newmark, Mark. "Automated Maintenance of Highly Structured Thesaurus at Engineering Index." American Documentation Institute, Annual Meeting, Proceedings, V. 4, *Levels of Interaction Between Man and Information.* New York, 1967. Washington, D.C., Thompson Book Company.
4. "News–Search Tapes Available." *Information Retrieval and Library Automation.* V. 3, No. 7, December 1967.

5.   Whaley, Fred R., and Waino, Elizabeth A. "Experimental SDI Products and Services at Engineering Index." American Documentation Institute, Annual Meeting, Proceedings, V. 4, *Levels of Interaction Between Man and Information.* New York, 1967. Washington, D.C., Thompson Book Company.

ENGINEERS JOINT COUNCIL

Engineers Joint Council
345 East 47th Street
New York, New York 10007

Mr. Frank Speight

Data: The *Thesaurus of Engineering Terms* is available in a magnetic tape edition. It contains over 80,000 entries (10,515 main terms, and their cross-reference relationships), and includes each entry's processing codes.

File characteristics: Tape is 7-channel, 556 bits per inch density, with records fixed at 60 characters, 10 records to a block. The file is contained on a single tape reel.

Computer: IBM 1401 (4k).

Availability of tape file: The tape is available at the price of $500. Cost includes a set of punched cards containing programs (1401) for printing or punching either the complete contents of the tape, or main terms only. Simple computer operating instructions are included.

Reference
1.   Speight, Frank Y., and Cottrel, Norman E., *The EJC Engineering Information Program.* New York 1965. Engineers Joint Council, 1965.

EXCERPTA MEDICA FOUNDATION

Information Interscience Incorporated
2204, Walnut Street
Philadelphia Pa. 19103

Data: The E. M. Foundation screens 20,000 journals annually for biomedical references, and publishes the results in its multi-part serial, *Excerpta Medica.* This yields approximately 200,000 citations and 80,000 abstracts annually. As of 1969, the contents of the journal are available on tape. For subject searching, a thesaurus of about 40,000 preferred medical terms (and 500,000 synonyms and related terms) is maintained.

File characteristics and size: Approximately 20,000 records are processed per year. The layout of the tapes depends upon whether they contain full data, or only a given portion (e.g. for S.D.I.) Tapes are 8 track, 200 or 556 b.p.i.

Computer: NCR 315 (Rod Memory) with NCR 321 as communications controller. Up to 16 CRAM devices can be used on-line, and RCA Video comp equipment is used for automatic photocomposition of the printed form of E.M.

Availability of tape files: Tapes can be purchased or accessed. A variety of services is available.

References
1. *EXCERPTA MEDICA Automated Storage and Retrieval Program of Biomedical Information*. Excerpta Medica Foundation, n.d.
2. FID News Bulletin, **18**(8), 1968.

FROST & SULLIVAN, INC.

Frost & Sullivan, Inc.
179 Broadway
New York, New York 10007

Mr. Daniel M. Sullivan

Data: For their DM (2) (Defense Market Measures) system, Frost and Sullivan creates magnetic tape files containing information on award actions by agencies of the Army, Navy, Air Force, FAA, AEC, NASA, plus other government agencies, and several prime contractors in the defense and space industries. DM (2) covers announced R and D contracts and all production and service contracts over $25,000. Tape records include:

1. Date of award.
2. Receiving state (location of the receiving contractors division).
3. Receiving contractor.
4. Receiving contractor's division.
5. Awarding state (location of the awarding procurement center).
6. Awarding agency.
7. Awarding procurement center.
8. System product category (200 categories, covering the breadth of the engineering system markets).
9. Capability (hardware).
10. Product category (200 categories).
11. Phase (each contract action is coded by type of work performed, from R and D source sought through study, research, development, and production).

12. Contract amount (in thousands of dollars).
13. Program (i.e., MOL, Titan, Atlas, etc. if applicable).
14. Other information (may include such items as work statement, contract type, contract number, schedules, quantities, etc.).

File characteristics and size: Master file records are fixed at 435 characters, three records to a block. The file dates from January 1965, with approximately 50,000 items added each year.

Computer: Files can be processed on an IBM 1401 (8k), or 1410, or 7011.

Availability of tape files: DM (2) files are available for sale. Update tapes are issued quarterly. Programs are provided for selecting, sorting and summarizing data into a variety of reports, with retrieval possible on twelve of the categories of information listed.

GENERAL ELECTRIC–FLIGHT PROPULSION DIVISION

General Electric Corporation
Flight Propulsion Division
Cincinnati, Ohio 45215

Manager, Information Systems: George Carr.

Data: Flight Propulsion Division has developed a mechanized information retrieval system for handling the technical reports and papers available in the Division's library. Material in machine readable form includes abstract as well as bibliographic information and uniterms. Two tape files are involved:

1. The keyword file (in sequence by keyword, then by accession numbers of documents containing that term) and
2. The citation-abstract file (ordered by accession number).

File size: As of 1967, the file contained more than 100,000 abstracts, (9 tape reels).

Computer: IBM 7094.

Note: This GE automated retrieval system is typical of many such systems in existence throughout the country. Other organizations which have magnetic tape records of their holdings include Aerojet General Corporation (Technical Library), Dow Chemical Company (Computation Research Lab), Eastman Kodak Company (Research Laboratories, Department of Information Services), National Bureau of Standards (Computer Sciences Division, Technical Information Exchange), IBM Corporation (Technical Information Retrieval Center), etc.

INSTITUTE FOR SCIENTIFIC INFORMATION
SCIENCE CITATION INDEX

Institute for Scientific Information
325 Chestnut Street
Pheladelphia, Pennsylvania 19106

Director: Eugene Garfield

Data: ISI issues two tape files involved in the preparation of *Science Citation Index*. They are: "Source Index" tapes, and "Citation Index" tapes. The "Source" tapes contain bibliographic information about source (citing) articles in the current literature of science and technology (including the social sciences). "Citation" tapes contain bibliographic information about the references cited in those articles. The files are in order by a number assigned to each source item. Coverage at present includes more than 2,000 scientific journals, proceedings, and transactions, as well as all current U.S. patents issued (including primary and reissued patents).

File characteristics and size: Tapes are originally produced in 556 bits per inch density. However, other standard densities are available (7- or 9-channel). "Source index" tapes contain variable length blocked records (66-246 characters), with maximum block size of 1,200 characters. File size (1969): 1,800,000 records (source items), with approximately 400,000 items added per year. "Citation index" tapes contain fixed-length records, with each record 90 characters, 10 to a block. File size (1969): 22,000,000 items (cited references), with approximately 5,000,000 added each year.

Computer: Tapes are compatible with IBM computer systems.

Availability of tape files: Tapes are available on a subscription basis and are delivered at weekly intervals. Prices range from $15,000 to $24,000 per year for the Citation File, and from $5,000 to $8,000 per year for the Source File. The following programs are available at no extra charge to subscribers:

1. Sort control cards for IBM 7044.
2. Source index listing (IBM 1401).
3. A complete series of SDI programs for Source index tapes, written for 7074, 10k, with 1401 used as an ancillary output device.
4. A complete series of SDI programs for use with System 360.
5. An SDI system for use with the IBM 1401.

Additional programs are in preparation.

References
1. Institute for Scientific Information. *ISI Magnetic Tapes* (brochure). Philadelphia, Pennsylvania, 1967.

2. Garfield, Eugene, "Science Citation Index—A New Dimension in Indexing." *Science*, V. 144, No. 3619 (May 8, 1964). (Contains an extensive bibliography on citation indexing.)

3. Garfield, Eugene, "Citation Indexing: A Natural Science Literature Retrieval System for the Social Sciences." *American Behavioral Scientist*, V. 7, No. 10 (June 1964).

4. Martyn, John, "An Examination of Citation Indexes." *Aslib Proceedings*, V. 17, No. 6, 1965.

LIBRARY OF CONGRESS
PROJECT MARC (Machine Readable Catalog)

Information Systems Office
Library of Congress
1st Street and Independence Avenue, S.E.
Washington, D.C.

Director, Project MARC: Mrs. Henriette Avram

Data: The MARC project is concerned with the production of LC cataloging data in machine-readable form. Originally, four magnetic tape files were involved in the system: (1) the Catalog Record, containing bibliographic entries, tracing information, and data related to processing and retrieval; (2) an Author/Title Record for each entry in the Catalog file; (3) a Subject Cross Reference Tracing Record, and (4) a Descriptive Cross Reference Tracing Record. (Files 3 and 4 contained the cross-reference tracing information generated in the cataloging of works incorporated into the primary file). Production of files 2, 3, and 4 has been suspended, and the format of file 1 has been extensively revised and redefined. The "MARC II" format, (file 1) was implemented in June 1968. At present, MARC cataloging data is limited to English language works, monographs only. Plans are in progress for expansion of coverage, with publications in French and German to be added.

File characteristics and size: The Catalog record consists (in 1969) of approximately 80,000 entries, with an increment of more than 25,000 per year. Logical records are variable length (containing fixed fields, variable fields, and repeated variable fields) and unblocked. Physical records have a maximum size of 2,048 characters. Tape is 9-channel, recorded at 800 bits per inch density. MARC II tapes will contain variable length records (containing fixed fields, a "directory" consisting of repeated fixed fields; variable fields, and repeated variable fields). Format specs were made available in early 1968.

Availability of tape files: Tapes were first disseminated, on a weekly basis, to sixteen libraries participating in the MARC Pilot Project. LC also distributed computer programs to produce the following: (1) Diagnostic listing of the entire

Catalog Record (file 1), (2) Production of catalog card set (file 1), (3) Abbreviated author/title listing (file 2).

MARC II tapes are now generally available on a subscription of $600 per year. The subscriber may select weekly, quarterly, semi-annual, or annual service.

References

1. *A Preliminary Report on the MARC (Machine Readable Cataloging) Pilot Project.* Information Systems Office, Library of Congress, 1967.

2. Avram, Henriette D., and Markuson, Barbara Evans, "Library Automation and Project MARC—An Experiment in the Distribution of Machine-Readable Catalog Data." In *The Brasenose Conference on the Automation of Libraries,* Edited by John Harrison and Peter Laslett. Chicago, Marsell Information 1967.

3. Buckland, Lawrence F., *The Recording of Library of Congress Bibliographical Data in Machine Form*: A Report prepared for the Council on Library Resources, Inc. Revised. Washington, Council of Library Resources, Inc., 1965.

4. Cunningham, Jay L., and Leach, Theodore E., "Bibliographic Dimensions of the MARC Pilot Project," in *Proceedings of the American Documentation Institute,* Annual Meeting, V. 4, 1967.

5. Markuson, Barbara Evans, "The Library of Congress Automation Program: A Progress Report to the Stockholders." *ALA Bulletin,* V. 61, No. 6 (July 1967).

6. Markuson, Barbara Evans, "A System Development Study for the Library of Congress Automation Survey," *Library Quarterly,* V. 36, July 1966.

7. Avram, Henriette D., et al., *The MARC II Format.* Washington, D.C., Library of Congress, Information Systems Office, 1968.

8. Library of Congress, Information Systems Office. *MARC Manuals Used by the Library of Congress* (*Contents*: Subscriber's Guide to the MARC Distribution Service; Data Preparation Manual; MARC Editors; Transcription Manual; and Computer and Magnetic Tape Unit Usability Study.) Chicago, American Library Association, Information Science and Automation Division, 1969.

LIBRARY OF CONGRESS
SUBJECT HEADINGS

Card Division, Library of Congress
Building 159, Navy Yard Annex
Washington, D.C. 20541

Chief, Card Division: Loran Karsner

Data: LC has acquired magnetic tapes used by the *Government Printing Office* in the preparation of the 7th edition of the Subject Headings Used in the

Dictionary Catalogs of the Library of Congress. In addition to the headings and cross-references, the tapes contain typographical codes and other symbols necessary for the printing process. The LC Information Systems Office is in the process of "cleaning up" and reformatting the tapes.

Computer: GPO (unedited) tapes were produced on the IBM 1401. The edited file will be produced on the IBM 360/30.

Availability of tape files: The unedited file (3 tape reels) are currently available in 7-track format. Price is $200.00 and includes 6 pages of documentation. The edited file will be available (in either 7- or 9-track format), in early 1968.

Reference
1.   Library of Congress Information Bulletin, V. 26, No. 38 (September 21, 1967).

LOS ANGELES COUNTY PUBLIC LIBRARY

Los Angeles County Public Library
Box 111 (mailing address)
320 W. Temple Street
Los Angeles, California 90053

Assistant County Librarian: Robert Goodwell

Data: Los Angeles County Public Library began compiling records for production of a book catalog in 1952. A punched card method was first used for input but conversion is now taking place for input by selectric typewriter and the CDC 915 optical scanner. The conversion and book catalog production is being handled by Compu Center, 6300 Hollister Avenue, Santa Barbara, California. Entries are being stored on magnetic tape and include: (0) classification number; (1) author; (2) short title; (3) subtitle and additional information; (4) imprint; (5) collation; (6) notes; (7) annotation (8) subject headings (non-fiction juvenile); (9) subject headings (adult fiction). Approximately four computer programs are used to produce the Los Angeles County Public Library book catalog.

File size and characteristics: Average record size for entries is 450 characters and entries are divided into the ten fields noted in the data description above. The file presently produces 15,000 computer reduced pages and contains approximately 250,000 titles.

Computer: CDC 6400.

Availability: Los Angeles County retains rights to the use of the magnetic tape files and attempts to market the magnetic tape files will be made by Compu Center.

References
1. "Computerized Techniques." *Library Resources and Technical Services*, V. 11 (Summer 1967), p. 382.
2. MacQuarrie, Catherine. "The Book Catalog of the Los Angeles County Public Library—How It Is Made." *Library Resources and Technical Services*, V. 4 (Summer 1960), p. 208.

MEDICAL LIBRARY CENTER OF NEW YORK
Union Catalog of Medical Periodicals

Medical Library Center of New York
5 East 102 Street
New York, N.Y. 10029

Director, Union Catalog project: Mrs. Jacqueline W. Felter

Data: This publication was derived from a computerized data base in magnetic tape form, which is being continually updated with retroactive as well as current serials data. The present publication, Phase I, covers serials in existence in 1950 or later. Phase II of the project will provide information on serials published during the period 1930-1950, and Phase III (not to be published in book form) will cover pre-1930 publications.

Material in machine-readable form includes title (in form in which it appears in the journal), place, dates and frequency of publication, explanatory notes, title history, codes for country and language, and subject codes (basically, those of Washington University School of Medicine's PHILSOM project). In addition, detailed holdings information is given for sixty-eight libraries in the New York metropolitan area, using library symbols supplied by the National Union Catalog.

File Size: Estimated total file content will be some 35,000 titles.

Computer: IBM 1401 (8k).

Availability of tape files: The programs and data tapes utilized in the system have been made available to institutions involved in developing regional union lists.

References
1. Felter, Jacqueline W., and Tjoeng, Djoeng S. "A Computer System for a Union Catalog: Theme and Variations." *Bulletin of the Medical Library Association*, V. 53, No. 2, April 1965, pp. 163-77.
2. "Book Reviews." *American Documentation*, V. 19, No. 2, (April 1968), p. 209-210.
3. "Book Reviews and Journal Notes." *Bulletin of the Medical Library Association*, V. 56, No. 2 (April 1968), pp. 219-220.

NATIONAL AGRICULTURAL LIBRARY
Cataloging and Indexing System (CAIN)

National Agricultural Library
Computer Applications Division
Beltsville, Maryland 20705

Data: The CAIN tapes contain bibliographic data encompassing the broad field of agriculture, including agricultural economics and rural sociology, agricultural products, animal industry, engineering, entomology, food and human nutrition, forestry pesticides, plant science, soils and fertilizers, and other related subjects, previously included in the *Bibliography of Agriculture*, the *National Agricultural Library Monthly Catalog* and the *Pesticides Documentation Bulletin*. All references cited in the *American Bibliography of Agricultural Economics*, a publication issued by the American Agricultural Economics Association beginning February 1970, are also included.

File Characteristics and Size: All tapes are 9-track, 800 b.p.i. and are designed for use with the IBM System 360.

Availability of tape files: Anyone may purchase the tapes, which are available at cost; $60.00 for the first tape reel plus $47.50 for each additional reel on the same order. Tapes are cumulative.

References
1.   U.S. Dept. of Agriculture. *National Agricultural Library implements a new mechanized cataloging and indexing system (CAIN)*, Washington, D.C., U.S. Dept. of Agriculture, 13 Jan 1970 (Mimeographed sheet, USDA 92-70).

NATIONAL AERONAUTICS AND SPACE ASSOCIATION

National Aeronautics and Space Association
Scientific and Technical Information Division
Office of Technology Utilization
Washington, D.C., 20546

Director, Scientific and Technical Information Division: John F. Stearns

Data: Since Jan. 1962, NASA has maintained a comprehensive, continuously updated data base in magnetic tape form. Basis of input is the bibliographic information which results from document processing activities of NASA (in the production of *Scientific and Technical Aerospace Reports* and other bibliographies) and the American Institute of Aeronautics and Astronautics (in the production of *International Aerospace Abstracts*). Tape records include accession number, security classification of document and title, announcement category, language of text, document type (distribution code), etc., as well as conventional descriptive cataloging details. Descriptors are on the record both as English terms and as their equivalent 5-character "coded-terms."

File characteristics and size: File is linear by accession number. Tape records contain fixed fields, a "relative image" area (pinpoints the location, if present, of the fields in the third or variable portion of the record), and variable fields. Maximum record size is 3,000 characters. (File as described was used with the IBM 1410 Linear File search system. Tape formats for the System/360 have since been developed). Approximately 460,000 records were on tape (as of 1969), increasing by about 60,000 per year.

Computer: An IBM-1410 was used through 1966. Present equipment is an IBM 360/40.

Availability of tape files: NASA has distributed tape files (and computer programs for searching and manipulating the data) to a number of agencies; among them the University of Pittsburgh, North American Rockwell, University of Southern California, and others.

Reference
1. Brandhorst, W. T., and Eckert, Philip F., *Guide to the Processing, Storage, and Retrieval of Bibliographic Information at the NASA Scientific and Technical Information Facility*. Documentation (June 1966. NASA CR-62033).

NATIONAL BUREAU OF STANDARDS
(National Standard Reference Data System)

Office of Standard Reference Data
National Bureau of Standards
Washington, D.C. 20234

Data: The National Standard Reference Data System (NSRDS) was established in 1963 by action of the President's Office of Science and Technology. The Office of Standard Reference Data (OSRD) was set up within the National Bureau of Standards to manage and coordinate the program. OSRD is composed of a network of data centers, which in 1967 included:

Atomic and Molecular Processes Information Center, Oak Ridge Laboratories, P.O. Oak Ridge, Tenn. 37831.
Atomic Transition Probabilities Data Center, NBS Institute for Basic Standards.
Crystal Data Center, NBS Institute for Basic Standards.

High Pressure Data Center, Brigham Young University, Provo, Utah 85601.

Joint Institute for Laboratory Astrophysics, Information Center, Joint Institute for Laboratory Astrophysics, University of Colorado, Boulder, Colorado 80302.

Radiation Chemistry Data Center, University of Notre Dame, Notre Dame, Ind. 46556.

Thermodynamics Research Center, Department of Chemistry, Texas A & M University, College Station, Texas 77840.

and several others located in government agencies and academic institutions. These data centers are the source of critically evaluated compilations, computations, and bibliographies published by NSRDS. Data compilation activities have been organized into seven program areas:

Nuclear Properties
Atomic and Molecular
Solid State Properties
Thermodynamic and Transport Properties
Chemical Kinetics
Colloid and Surface Properties
Mechanical Properties of Materials

Each program area is directed by a Program manager who consults with advisory panels sponsored by the National Academy of Sciences/National Research Council and Data Centers of NSRDS for technical guidance relating to the specialized knowledge of their fields. NSRDS publications are presently produced in the form considered most convenient by users; ranging from formal monographs, through magnetic or paper tapes, to loose-leaf data sheets. The Data System Design and Research Section of the Office of Standard Reference Data (OSRD) is developing mechanized means for data acquisition and handling in the NSRDS. Its present emphasis is on systems for computer-aided composition and printing of compilations.

Availability: A complete listing of the compilations and other publications of the NSRDS is available from the Office of Standard Reference Data.

References
1. "Information and Data Centers Associated With the National Bureau of Standards Office of Standard Office of Standard Reference Data." *NSRDS News, National Bureau of Standards, Technical News Bulletin*, August 1967, V. 51, No. 8.
2. *Questions and Answers about the National Standard Reference* Data System, U.S. Department of Commerce, National Bureau of Standards, Washington, D.C. (brochure).

NATIONAL LIBRARY OF MEDICINE—MEDLARS
MEDLARS (MEDICAL LITERATURE ANALYSIS AND RETRIEVAL SYSTEM)

National Library of Medicine
8600 Rockville Pike
Bethesda, Maryland 20014

Associate Director for Intra-Mural Programs: Joseph Leiter

Data: NLM exhaustively acquires and indexes (for *Index Medicus*) material in over forty biomedical subject areas, plus, to a lesser degree, material in related fields such as physics, zoology, chemistry, botany, and psychology.

The MEDLARS CCF (Condensed Citation File), on magnetic tape, contains the bibliographic information generated in the production of *Index Medicus*, plus added index terms, and data related to computer processing and searching. Index terms ("tag words") appear in this file in coded form only. An accompanying file, the MeSH (Medical Subject Heading) record, contains the English equivalents of the codes appearing in the CCF.

File characteristics and size: Both files contain fixed and variable-length fields, with maximum record size of 254 computer words (48 bits per word). Tapes are 7-channel, recorded at 556 bits per inch density. The CCF contains more than 500,000 entries, comprising twenty tape reels. Approximately 175,000 items are added per year. The CCF is linear: that is, in order by computer entry date, with each entry identified by a serially assigned citation number. The MeSH file contains some 7,500 descriptors, and is in order (numerically) by main heading code.

Computer: Honeywell 800/200 system. (Conversion to an IBM 360 system was scheduled for completion by mid-1970).

Availability of tape files: Complete files have been distributed on a monthly basis to five MEDLARS search stations throughout the United States, plus the Karolinska Institut of Stockholm, and the National Lending Library for Science and Technology, England. Plans are in process for further expansion of distribution.

References
1. *Medlars Maintenance Guide*, Rev. 1 June 1966. Los Angeles, Planning Research Corporation.

2. Taine, Seymour, "Bibliographic Aspects of MEDLARS." *Bulletin of the Medical Library Association* V. 52, No. 1, January 1964.

3. Adams, Scott, "MEDLARS Performance, Problems, Possibilities." *Bulletin of the Medical Library Association*, V. 53, April 1965.

4. Becker, Joseph, "The MEDLARS Project," *ALA Bulletin*, V. 58 (March 1964).

5.   Austin, Charles J., "The MEDLARS System," *Datamation*, December 1964.
6.   U.S. Department of Health, Education, and Welfare, National Library of Medicine, *Guide to Medlars Services*, Public Health Service Pub. No 1694 (Revised March 1969).

NATIONAL WEATHER RECORDS CENTER

National Weather Records Center
Federal Building
Asheville, North Carolina 28801

Acting Director: Mr. William Haggard
Chief, Applied Climatology Branch: William M. McMurray

Data: The National Weather Records Center functions as the principal data processor for the Environmental Data Service (EDS) of the Environmental Science Services Administration (ESSA), U.S. Dept. of Commerce. The Center also houses and provides support for ESSA's National Geophysical Data Center, and works closely with the Air Force, Army and Navy weather services, NWRC also cooperates internationally through the World Meteorological Organization and houses the records for the World Data Center A (WDC-A) for Meterology and Nuclear Radiation, which operates under the sponsorship of the National Science Foundation. The data contained on magnetic tape at NWRC is comprised of a variety of meteorological data, such as, hourly surface observations; summary of the day data; radar, wind, and radiosonde observations; marine data; and solar radiation data obtained from the TIROS series of meteorological satellites. In addition to magnetic tapes NWRC will provide reproductions of original records, microfilm, punched cards, Satellite films, special data tabulations, radar films, and climatological publications that are out of print. Job requests filled by NWRC fall into 3 categories: (1) those requiring copies of basic observational data in various forms (magnetic tape, punched cards, microfilm, original records, etc.); (2) those satisfied by one or several of the previously published works or unpublished tabulations and summaries in our repository of climatological information; (3) those satisfied by a non-routine analysis or through scientific exploration.

File size and characteristics: In May of 1966 NWRC held 17,000 reels of magnetic tape and this collection is expected to grow at a rate of 5,000 a year. Field structure, record length, and block length vary depending on source material and tape format. With the acquisition of the RCA Spectra 70/45 system, NWRC will have the capability to provide 7 or 9 channel tape at a density of 556 or 800 bpi and will add Random Access Storage in the form of discs (70/564) and Mass Storage Units (70/568) to their data systems technology.

Computer: RCA Spectra 70/45

Availability: NWRC data bases are available to Federal Agencies and private organizations, companies or individuals. Private customers must establish a non-refundable trust fund based on NWRC estimates of the cost of the job. The present rate of charge for tape copy is $75.00 per reel of magnetic tape including the cost of the blank reel of tape but does not include any selection or reformatting of the data. Separate requests may be made of the center for specific programming or reformatting.

References
1. U.S. Department of Commerce. *National Weather Records* Center. (Brochure.) Asheville, N.C., January 1967.
2. Information in a letter from Richard Y. Dow, World Data Center A, Coordination Office, August 1, 1968.
3. Information in a letter from William M. McMurray, Chief Applied Climatology Branch, National Weather Records Center, July 6, 1968.

NEW YORK TIMES

Editorial Index Department
New York Times
229 West 43rd Street
New York, New York 10036

Director, Information Services: John Rothman

Data: The New York Times Index is now being produced with the aid of a computer. As a result subscribers are to receive some 15% more information through references shown under thousands of alphabetically arranged topical headings. References include events summarized in chronological order, with original publication date, page and column number. The index is presently published twice a month in magazine form and all material for the year is re-edited and cumulated into an annual volume. Production of the Index by computer will allow for custom searches for charts and a more legible type face from computer composition. There is also a thesaurus of descriptors.

File characteristics: There is no limit on the length of abstracts and records may be composed of up to seven fields. Coding is in upper and lower case.

Availability: The New York Times is not marketing the magnetic tapes at present and does not plan to have the facility to do so in the immediate future. With more experience, the New York Times will determine whether demand for tapes justifies the additional cost of programming and tape production and the appropriate price for such services.

References
1.   "New York Times to Be Computerized." *Library Journal,* January 1, 1968, Part I, p. 26.
2.   Information in a letter from John Rothman, Director, Information Services, *The New York Times*, March 5, 1968.

ONTARIO NEW UNIVERSITIES LIBRARY PROJECT (ONULP)

ONULP (Technical Services)
New Universities Library Project
University of Toronto Libraries
Toronto, Ontario

ONULP (Technical Services): Mrs. Susan Merry

Data: The Ontario New Universities Library Project was organized in 1964 for the purpose of cataloging and acquiring 35,000 titles in 44,000 volumes for five new academic libraries by 1967. Computer produced and computer maintained book catalogs were first issued in 1964 and provide author-title and subject union catalogs for the five participating libraries. Magnetic tape records are assembled from punched cards to produce various types of output including shelflists and quarterly, semiannual and annual cumulatings of the author-title and subject catalog. ONULP is participating in the LC/MARC Project by coordinating MARC tape records with ONULP records. Entries include Library of Congress classification number, edition statement, size of work, etc.

File characteristics: The master tape has variable field and record lengths. Output requirements from the magnetic tape entries require long computer-produced sort fields (maximum of sixty characters) to insure more accurate filing in subject cataloging and consolidation of all titles by a single author.

Computer: The IBM 1401 system is used for the master tape compilation and the IBM 7090 is used for catalog generation.

References

1.   Bregzis, R., "Ontario New Universities Library Project: Computer Generated Book Form Catalog—A Progress Report." February 27, 1967.
2.   Bregzis, R., "University of Toronto/MARC Pilot Project." *In Organization and Handling of Bibliographic Records By Computer*, Edited by N. S. M. Cox and M. W. Grose. Oriel Press, 1967, pp. 118-226.
3.   Merry, Susan A., "The Ontario New Universities Library Project; A Centralized Processing Experiment Completed." *Library Resources and Technical Services.* V. 29, No. 2, March 1968, pp. 104-108.

PANDEX

Pandex, Inc.
American Management Association Building
135 West 50th Street
New York, New York 10020

Vice President, Sales: Robert F. Johnston

Data: Pandex provides a comprehensive data base from 2,100 periodicals, 6,000 books, 5,000 selected patents, and 30,000 U.S. technical Reports annually. All areas of pure and applied science are included with coverage beginning in 1967. The contents of the Pandex data base is divided into four different types of entries: (1) Book records—year, publisher, level, LC Card Number, pagination, price, subjects, authors, title (including subtitle and serial name); (2) Journal records—year, journal, volume, issue number, pagination, subjects, authors, title (titles may be enriched); (3) patent records; and (4) technical report records. Each entry record contains manually indexed or manually edited thesaurus-generated subjects. Pandex serves research requirements not satisfied by single disciplinary indexes but provides access to all literature of interest to a discipline as well. The index generated by Pandex from this data base is divided into two parts: (1) Subject—entries containing full title, primary author and periodical reference, arranged by all significant subject words and subarranged by all significant secondary words; (2) Author—entries containing all authors arranged alphabetically (primary author entries containing full title, all other authors, and the periodical reference) (secondary author entry containing name of primary author and periodical reference). The data base may be integrated into an existing magnetic tape system, searched by programs provided by PANDEX or serve as a basis for SDI service.

File Characteristics: Magnetic tape files of either 7 or 9 track format, BCDIC or EBCDIC configuration and 556 or 800 bpi are created. Entries are recorded in variable length records, 3-20 records per block, with a maximum of 3528 bytes per block.

Computer: IBM 360/40.

Availability: A weekly airmail magnetic tape service is offered for „6,500 a year including program and full documentation. Programs are designed for in-house bibliographic searching and SDI service. The index generated by Pandex from magnetic tape may also be received quarterly on microfiche or printed.

References
1. "Air Mail Weekly Tape Service Specifications," *Pandex* (brochure). March 1968.
2. Information in a letter from Robert F. Johnston, Vice-President, Sales, Pandex, March 18, 1968.

RAND CORPORATION

Linguistics Department
Rand Corporation
1700 Main Street
Santa Monica, California 90406

Data: The RAND Linguistics Research Project has compiled a Bibliography of Computational Linguistics, which is being stored on magnetic tape. Input contains up to 55 different classes of data, including complete citation, abstract, abstract source, abstractor's name, subject headings and sub-headings, etc. Emphasis is on flexibility of the catalog structure, so that the data may be sorted, merged, rearranged, formatted (for printing), and retrieved in a variety of ways.

File characteristics and size: The file is recorded on 7-track tape, at 800 bits per inch. Size is approximately 5,000 items, with an addition of 100 items per month.

Computer: IBM 7044

Reference
1. *The Catalog: A Flexible Data Structure for Magnetic Tape.* Los Angeles, Rand Corporation, 1965 (RM-4645-PR).
2. Kay, Martin, Valadex, Frederick, and Ziehe, Theodore, *The Catalog Input/Output System.* Los Angeles, Rand Corporation, 1966 (RM-4540-PR).

SCIENCE INFORMATION EXCHANGE

Science Information Exchange
Smithsonian Institution
209 Madison National Bank Building
1730 M Street, N.W.
Washington, D.C. 20036

Director: Monroe E. Freeman

Data: SIE registers, stores, and disseminates information on current research projects in the life, physical, engineering, and social sciences. Several magnetic tape files serve as indexes to the information collected, and are involved in a retrieval and report program. The "Grant Master" file contains: names of researchers, codes for their location, project dates, amount of funding, and subject index codes. Approximately 8-10 codes are assigned to each item. They are selected from a series of independent subject indexes which are continually altered and updated in order to represent current research topics. Other tape files involved in the system are an Index file (contains codes and corresponding English captions for subject index points and location of researchers), a Contract number—SIE accession number Cross Reference file, a Title file, Investigator file, and a Pending Projects file (not indexed as to subject matter).

File characteristics and size: Master file records are in fixed blocked format, with record length of 450 characters, and four records per block. Tapes are recorded in 9-track format, at 800 bpi density. Total master file (1949-67) contains 500,000 records (20 tape reels). Approximately 75,000 research records are added annually. The useful life of each record is usually no more than one year. "Current" master file is contained on 7 reels of tape.

Computer: IBM 360/40 (1401/1460 compatibility).

References
1. Marron, Harvey, and Snyderman, Martin, Jr., "Cost Distribution and Analysis in Computer Storage and Retrieval," *American Documentation*, V. 17, No. 2 (April 1966).
2. Marron, Harvey, and Foster, W. R., "Subject Searches on Current Research Information of Parallel Computer and Manual Files." American Documentation Institute Annual Meeting, Proceedings, V. 3, *Progress in Information Science and Technology*. Santa Monica, California, 1966.
3. *Science Information Exchange User Requirements Study. Phase I. Description of Existing SIE System*. Columbus, Ohio. Batelle Memorial Institute, 1965, (NSF-C431).

STANFORD UNIVERSITY
Meyer Undergraduate Library Catalog

The Stanford University Libraries
Stanford, California 94305

Assistant Director for Automation: Allen B. Veaner

Data: In order to provide copies of the library catalog at various points throughout the Undergraduate Library and at other locations on campus, a book form is being produced through use of magnetic tape records and computer printing. In addition, a shelflist is produced in book form that lists all copies and volumes of books in the library. The catalog is kept current through monthly cumulative supplements and is printed annually.

File characteristics and size: A fixed length, 570 character, record is used for each title cataloged with provision to use 2 records for long entries. Upper and lower case characters may be recorded with upper case characters requiring two positions. Records are grouped 2 to a block. Seven fields for each record include: (1) A fixed field of 71 characters for classification, volume, and copy number and other data; and six fields of variable length with a maximum of 400 characters in each (2) Main entry (3) Conventional title; (4) title statement; (5) Notes; (6) subjects headings; and (7) added authors and added titles. In June 1966 25,000 titles had been processed.

Computer: IBM 1401 computer (12K) with four tape drives, modified with an expanded (upper-lower case) print chain on the 1403 printer.
IBM 7090 computer is used for alphabetic sorting.
IBM 360/30 system is being installed.

Availability: Existing tape records for the Meyer Library collection may be made available for research and experimentation purposes under certain conditions. Estimated price for use of the tapes for research purposes would be cost plus overhead, in the order of $50.

References
1.   Johnson, Richard D., "A Book Catalog at Stanford" Journal of Library Automation. V. 1, No. 1, March 1968.
2.   Johnson, R. D., Stanford Undergraduate Library Book Catalog, A Fact Sheet, November 21, 1966.
3.   Information in a letter from Allen B. Veaner, Assistant Director for Automation, Stanford University Libraries, March 7, 1968.

SYSTEM DEVELOPMENT CORPORATION
Webster's 7th Collegiate Dictionary and *The New Merriam Webster Pocket Dictionary.*

SDC Lexicographic Project
System Development Corporation
2500 Colorado Avenue
Santa Monica, Calif. 90406.

Project Director, John C. Olney

Data: For both the *Webster's 7th Collegiate* (W7) and *The New Merriam Webster Pocket Dictionary* (MPD) parsed and unparsed transcripts are available, together with tapes containing concordance indexes, semantically reliable suffixes, and base and inflected forms. The programs used to generate data from the basic unparsed transcripts are also available.

File Characteristics and Size: On 7-channel tape (556 bpi) the W7 set comprises 22 reels and the MPD set 7 reels: on 9-channel tape (800 bpi) the W7 set comprises 16 reels and the MPD set 5 reels. All these files consist of 80-character BCDIC logical records blocked 30 to a physical record. (*Note*: The unparsed transcripts of both W7 and MPD are also available on 9-channel tape at a density of 1600 b.p.i.).

Computer: IBM 360/67.

Availability of tape files: Since it is not convenient for SDC to supply magnetic tapes, they prefer that tapes be sent to them for copying on to. The cost for this is $9 per output reel regardless of whether the density is 556, 800 or 1600 b.p.i. The requester should include return postage. Application forms, which are available from SDC, should first be sent to the G. and C. Merriam Company, Springfield, Mass. 01101, to obtain their approval.

The requester agrees to certain copyright provisions, and the Merriam Company is prepared to grant approval on a broad basis to bona fide researchers: the form is then forwarded by the requester to SDC.

References
1. Olney, J., et al. *Toward the Development of Computational Aids for Obtaining a Formal Semantic Description of English*. SP-2766/001/00. Santa Monica, Calif., System Development Corporation, 1 October 1968.
2. Reichert, R. et al. *Two Dictionary Transcripts and Programs for Processing Them. Volume 1: The Encoding Scheme, PARSENT and CONIX*. TM-3978/001/00. Santa Monica, Calif., System Development Corporation, 15 June 1969.
3. Olney, J. (Letter) To: All Interested in the Merriam-Webster Transcripts and Data Derived From Them. 1 October, 1968. SDC letter L-13579.

UNIVERSITY MICROFILMS LIBRARY SERVICES
(Datrix)

University Microfilms Library Services
Xerox Corporation
Ann Arbor, Michigan 48106

Manager, Sales Planning: David H. Jedele

Data: Datrix, (*D*irect *A*ccess *to* *R*eference *I*nformation: a *X*erox Service), uses a data base of approximately 130,000 dissertation references covered by Dissertation Abstracts, from 1938 to date. Another 130,000 references for theses written between 1861 and 1967 are to be added. Monthly additions to the data base are to cover 90% of doctoral theses currently being written. All major fields of inquiry covered by 160 participating Universities in the United States and Canada are included. Dissertation titles, subject headings, and additional word descriptors supply key words for indexing.

Availability: Services now include computer searching and listing of relevant references, complete microfilm or xerographically reproduced copies of requested dissertations. Computer tapes are not presently available for purchase or lease.

Reference
1. Information in a letter from David H. Jedele, Manager Sales Planning, Xerox Corporation, April 1, 1968.

UNIVERSITY OF CALIFORNIA AT LOS ANGELES
"POLCEN"

Department of Political Science
Statistical Laboratory
4343 Social Science Building
University of California
Los Angeles, California 90024

Director: Dwaine Marvick

Data: The "POLCEN" (Political Census) file, from the UCLA Political Behavior archives, contains electoral and demographic records of Los Angeles County, including registration and voting figures from the 1958, 1960, 1962, and 1964 general elections as well as the 1964 primary elections. The file is organized by Census tract number, and includes information on land use, population characteristics, income, education, housing, employment, etc., as well as electoral information.

File characteristics and size: Records are written in binary notation, are fixed length, unblocked, recorded on 7-channel magnetic tape (conversion is in process to 9-channel tape). The file contains 1,305 records (one for each of the County's Census Tracts), of 1,185 words each.

Computer: IBM 7094. Conversion to System 360 is in process.

Availability of tape files: Files have been made available for use to faculty and graduate students at UCLA and other West Coast institutions.

Note: This file is one of many included in the UCLA Political Behavior Archives. A brochure, *Social Science Data Archives in the United States, 1967,* published by the Council of Social Science Data Archives (New York, New York), lists 25 organizations throughout the country which hold archives of a similar nature, covering a broad range of subject matter. Many of these files are on magnetic tape, and are available to qualified users.

Reference
1. Bisco, Ralph L., "Social Science Data Archives: A Review of Developments." *American Political Science Review*, V. 60, No. 1, March 1966.

UNIVERSITY OF SOUTHERN CALIFORNIA—McGRAW-HILL
NATIONAL INFORMATION CENTER FOR
EDUCATIONAL MEDIA (NICEM)

NICEM, Division of Cinema
University of Southern California
Los Angeles, California

Director: Glenn McMurry

Data: The NICEM project is concerned with the gathering and dissemination of information on non-book instructional materials. The project was established in 1967, under a grant to USC from McGraw-Hill, which plans to publish a 20-volume Educational Media Index. Media to be covered are motion pictures (16 mm, 8 mm), filmstrips, transparencies, motion cartridges, video tape, recordings (disc, tape), maps, globes and charts, realia, prints and study prints, and PI and CAI materials. Cataloging data for these items is being stored on magnetic tape, and includes title, producer, distributer, date, running time or number of frames, stock or color code, subject area, and a summary of content. Retrieval is possible on all but the last of the above items, as well as by media. An additional element of information to be added will be the grade level of the material.

A NICEM thesaurus has been developed, which contains approximately 1,000 subject categories. However, work is in progress on a more detailed edition, which will list more than 3,000 terms. The terms appear on tape records in coded form (7 digit codes, containing 1 alpha and 6 numeric characters).

File characteristics and size: Files are organized by media, then alphabetically by title. Tape records are variable length, with a maximum physical record size of 614 characters. To allow for extended annotations, logical records may consist of more than one physical record. Tape is 7-track, recorded at 556 bits per inch density. There are approximately 40,000 cataloged items, divided as follows: 18,000 films, 17,000 filmstrips, 1,500 transparencies, 2,000 motion cartridges, 600 recordings, 2,000 other.

Computer: IBM 1401. Tape formats are currently being revised, and changeover to a System 360 will be accomplished in 1968.

Availability of tape files: There are no announced plans as to availability or distribution at this time.

INDEX